W9-AHR-673

PRACTICAL GUIDE TO

CLIENT|SERVER

COMPUTING

SECOND EDITION

Hugh W. Ryan

Scott R. Sargent

Timothy M. Boudreau

Yannis S. Arvanitis

Stanton J. Taylor

Craig Mindrum

ANDERSEN
CONSULTING

AUERBACH

Library of Congress Cataloging-in-Publication Data

Catalog record is available from the Library of Congress.

No claim to original U.S. Government works
International Standard Book Number 0-8493-9951-3
Printed in the United States of America 1 2 3 4 5 6 7 8 9 0
Printed on acid-free paper

Contents

Contents

Introduction

Business today is in the midst of a revolution that is driven by the new capabilities available to organizations and their workers. At the technological center of this revolution is client/server computing.

THE CLIENT/SERVER REVOLUTION

To use the word "revolution" is not an overstatement. Most often we think of revolutions only as brief and violent skirmishes. The fact is that revolutions may begin quietly and may, in fact, go unnoticed by all but a few people. The American and French Revolutions began as a series of ideas about government and human rights long before the movements exploded into violence. It is more accurate to think of a revolution as an event from which, once it comes into being, we cannot retreat. To say that client/server computing is a revolution means that there is no going back to older, more restrictive forms of computing.

To the avid follower of the technology press, calling client/server revolutionary may seem like an outdated remark. Hasn't the Internet rendered the client/server model obsolete? Isn't client/server dead? The answer is no, for two reasons.

First, to say that client/server is dead reveals a basic misunderstanding of the computing model. Not only is client/server alive and well, it has evolved into a new model known as netcentric computing, discussed in Chapter I-1. In the netcentric computing environment, the communications fabric extends the client/server computing model by placing intelligence into the physical network—acknowledging the network as a kind of standalone system that provides intelligent shared network services.

Organizations moving aggressively into this environment should consult a new book from Andersen Consulting and Auerbach entitled *Netcentric Computing: Computing, Communications, and Knowledge*. The book is a comprehensive treatment of architectures and implementation issues related to netcentric computing.

A second response to the "client/server is dead" position must be simply to point out the abundance of statistics that indicate otherwise. In 1995, only 25% of information systems managers surveyed by Datapro Information Services Group, Inc. reported having implemented client/server applications. By 1996, that number had increased to 46%.

Specific industry examples bear out these numbers. For example, the 1996 American Banker survey of technology in banking revealed that the most important transition for many companies today is still the move from a mainframe to a client/server environment. Consider the following survey results:

- Only 34% of the 300 largest commercial banks now use networks of personal computers for applications once handled by mainframe computers.
- Only 54% of those same banks chose distributed computing, even for new applications.
- Only 12% of the top 300 banks said they had physically displaced their mainframes.
- At the top 100 banks, half of the software developed in 1996 was written in COBOL, the programming language of mainframe computers.

In short, we are not seeing the demise of client/server computing models. Rather, we continue to see an inexorable move toward client/server, and an evolution into a netcentric environment. The next generation of computing solutions begin from the point of technological freedom that client/server provides.

CLIENT-CENTRIC COMPUTING

Companies that have been participants in the client/server revolution have discovered new and innovative ways to solve business problems. Client/server recognizes that business users—and not a mainframe—are the real center of the business. Thus, client/server computing is also client-centric computing.

The revolutionary aspects of client/server, not surprisingly, relate to personal freedoms. Once people taste freedom, they never willingly give it up again. Once computer users see the autonomy they achieve through client/server applications, they will never willingly return to the dumb terminals of traditional computing solutions.

Client/server has taken over business computing today because it fits into a unique and specific set of concerns within business and society. Client/server has become revolutionary not because the system builders and vendors were clever, but because the times in which we live and work have made it inevitable.

Client/server cannot fail. However, the individual or the particular organization can fail with the technology. Indeed, we can already see the wounded lying on the client/server battlefield. The fact remains, however, that the client/server revolution is evolving or "morphing" into other kinds of revolutions. The clearest indication of this fact is that we are now seeing types of solutions that were not anticipated even at the beginning of the decade.

HOW TO USE THIS BOOK

This book reflects a combined experience of more than 70 years in the application of client/server computing to business. Our intent is to distill from this experience the essentials of what it takes to get client/server right.

If we are correct that client/server computing has entered the stage of revolutionary inevitability, it is increasingly vital for all organizations to get it right. The IS specialist today must understand and work with client/server networks.

There are still pockets of resistance. Many IT professionals are not convinced that client/server systems will become the replacement mainstays. Although negative reactions will probably continue for some time, ironically, these reactions will be forced to embrace the very terms and presumptions of client/server against which they are fighting. This is another sure sign of inevitability. A revolution changes our worldview, the way we see things, and the way we talk about them. To survive and thrive, IS professionals must keep pace. The alternative is to become a ghost of an old regime, a remnant of the past maintaining an old legacy until retirement.

A wide variety of publications, books, and training materials about client/server is available. In our estimation, however, there has been no satisfactory, comprehensive, and yet practical guide to understanding and implementing client/server technology. This book was written to fill that void.

The book is not designed to be read from cover to cover—not just because of its length but because it was written so that different parts would support the work of different groups of people within contemporary organizations. The book is organized into four major sections so that readers may dip in to parts of the book most appropriate to their work and easily access helpful support for their development projects. Occasionally there is some overlap—material covered in one section may be briefly summarized in another so that each section can continue to stand alone.

Readers will glean specific information from this book and its four sections:

- *The big picture of what client/server is and why it is important.* Section I looks at the subject from the perspective of the CIO or the head of a business unit who wants to grasp the basic steps in moving to client/server computing.

- *An understanding of key architectural components and technologies of client/server computing.* Section II contains information for CIOs, chief technology officers, project leaders, or lead architects.

- *Implementation details.* Section III covers change management; design specifics for architectures, applications, and networks; rollout strategies; and ongoing management of distributed operations. Project leaders will find detailed suggestions on how to structure a project and complete critical tasks and steps.

- *Forward-looking perspectives.* Section IV answers questions CIOs, project leaders, and project team members may have about the future direction of client/server technologies, so they can plan their strategies accordingly.

UPDATES TO THE 1997 EDITION

This edition of the *Practical Guide to Client/Server Computing* has been updated in many areas to account for rapid technological developments. Two new chapters have also been added: a chapter on evaluating client/server architectures and one on managing the cost of distributed computing environments.

CAN ANYTHING ENSURE SUCCESS?

Can a single book guarantee you success? Certainly not. Individual success depends on many factors including insight, timing, hard work, and a commitment to quality. We try here to contribute to your understanding and insight. The timing, hard work, and commitment is up to you. A little luck can help, too.

We began by saying that the information systems community—indeed, the entire business community—is in the midst of a revolution, one that has now moved from the idea stage to the stage of inevitability. In her book *In the Age of the Smart Machine*, Shoshanna Zuboff noted that the word "revolution" has an ambiguous etymology. On the one hand, the word suggests a revolt; on the other hand, it suggests a movement around a fixed point, as a planet makes revolutions around the sun.

For businesses, the fixed point in any technological change is profitability—success. Client/server is, we believe, the technological foundation for all successful organizations of the next century.

This revolution, in short, must become your revolution as well. If you have not been a part of the initial stages, many of the demands of the client/server revolution stand before you. The intent of this book is to make your personal revolution a little easier, and then to position you for the revolutions that are still to come.

Hugh W. Ryan, Andersen Consulting
August 1997

Section I
Current Trends in Business Computing

Section I is an overview of what client/server is and why it is important. The intended audience is chief information officers (CIOs) or the heads of business units, whose company is moving into client/server computing and who want to get an idea of the basic steps necessary to proceed. Readers can skip over the technical parts of this section if they want to focus more on the importance of client/server.

Specifically, in this section readers will find discussions on the following subjects:

- The evolution of client/server computing.
- Working definition of client/server computing, as used in this book and contrasted with other definitions used in the industry, as well as discussions of workstations, workgroup servers, and enterprise servers.
- Data and processing allocation issues.
- Models of client/server computing.
- Overview of the client/server technical architecture.
- Client/server's relationship to today's leading management initiatives.
- Client/server and today's knowledge workers.
- Client/server and legacy systems.
- Success stories from business.

I-1
An Overview of Client/Server Computing

To understand client/server appropriately, it is important to look at it in the context of prior technologies and prior solutions based on those technologies. This perspective helps to locate the differences as well as what is important about them. It can also help business users recognize the impact of these differences on future solutions.

WHAT IS CLIENT/SERVER?

Client/server computing is "a style of computing involving multiple processors, one of which is typically a workstation, and across which a single business transaction is completed." The many variations and implications of this definition are explored and explained later, but this definition is adequate for the following discussion.

Consider the case of an insurance program used to validate and evaluate the risk of an application for coverage. A client/server implementation might have the validation and risk-evaluation logic run on the workstation. If the application process were interrupted, the incomplete policy might be stored on a server in the local office. Finally, when the policy is complete and accepted, the bound (agreed-to) policy could be stored on the central file server where it would be available to the company as a whole.

Consider this example now in the context of the business computing solutions that have evolved over the past 30 years (see Exhibit I-1-1).

THE EARLY YEARS: BATCH PROCESSING

The majority of business solutions delivered in the mid- to late 1960s focused on the use of batch technology. There are many variations in this style of computing.

In batch processing, the business user would present a file of transactions to the application. The system would then run through the trans-

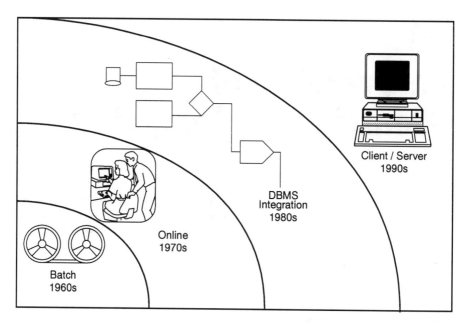

Exhibit I-1-1. Evolution of Computing Solutions

actions, processing each one, essentially without user intervention. The system would provide reporting at some point in the batch processing. Typically, the reports would be batch-printed. These in turn would be used by the business user to correct the input transactions that were resubmitted along with the next night's batch transactions.

THE 1970S: ONLINE TRANSACTIONS

In the 1970s, businesses began a transition to online, interactive transactions. Once again, there are many variations to online processing. However, at a conceptual level this processing opened up the file of transactions found in batch transactions and allowed the user to submit them one at a time, receiving either immediate confirmation of the success of the transaction or else feedback on the nature of the transaction error.

The conceptually simple change of having the user interact with the machine on a transaction-at-a-time basis caused huge changes in the nature of business computing. Those who were present at the beginning of this era can remember long discussions on such questions as what good screen design was and whether the concept of a dialogue was a good thing.

More important, users saw huge changes in what they could do on a day-to-day basis. A transaction was processed when it happened, and the impact of the transaction was known to all concerned. Customers were no longer forced to wait for a batch run to process the application. In essence, the machine had an impact on the entire flow of work for the business user. Technological impact became human impact and business impact.

With the advent of online interactive systems, it was equally significant that the systems provided a means for the business user to communicate with others in the business as the day-to-day business went along. This capability was provided on the backbone of a wide area network (WAN). The WAN was in itself a demanding technology; because of these demands, telecommunications groups emerged within organizations, charged with the responsibility to maintain, evolve, and manage the network over time.

THE 1980S: DATABASES

The theme of the 1980s was database and database management systems (DBMSs). Organizations used and applied database technology in the 1970s, but in the 1980s they grew more confident in the application of DBMS technology. They began to focus more on the sharing of data across organizational and application boundaries.

Curiously, database technology did not change the fundamental way in which business processing was done. DBMS made it more convenient to access the data and to ensure that it could be updated while maintaining the integrity of the data. In the long term it became apparent that DBMS was more about the business changing than about the technology changing. If the organization was willing to share information across organizational boundaries, DBMS could and did provide extraordinary benefits. If not, it was a rather machine-intensive way to achieve what could be done using more traditional access routines.

THE 1990S: THE COMING OF CLIENT/SERVER

In the 1990s, technology began to shift toward client/server computing. In this style of computing, once again, there were fundamental changes in technology.

First, there was another shift in the level of processing. Using the workstation, the transaction entered by the user could now be processed on a keystroke-by-keystroke basis. This was a change, again, in the level of interaction. This change led to a whole new set of discussions on how to do good window design, how to place widgets, and when and how to do processing driven off the keystrokes of the business.

Furthermore, there was a change in the communications. With client/server, users could communicate with others in the work group via a local area network (LAN). The LAN permitted workstation-to-workstation communications at speeds of 100 to 1,000 times what was typically available on a WAN area network. The LAN was a technology that could be grown and evolved in a local office with little need for direct interaction from the telecommunications group. This meant the local site could begin to evolve its own answer to the changing demands of the local business.

This brief bit of history suggests that there have been two fundamental shifts in technology over the years that have changed how the business user can do various business tasks.

1. The shift in the manner in which the business user interacted with the computer changed how business was transacted.
2. The shift or augmentation in the ability to communicate by increasing connectivity or the speed of connection made other fundamental business changes.

Both changes played a significant part in client/server computing and, as a result, laid the technological foundation for the revolution. (Chapter I-2 explores why business and society demanded that these technologies be applied—that is, why the success of the revolution was inevitable.)

CLIENT/SERVER: COMPETING DEFINITIONS

The term "client/server computing" has come to mean many things to many people. An *Information Week* poll asked readers to define the term. The responses varied widely.

Too much time is often spent trying to come up with a perfect definition of client/server computing. In many instances, this time could be more productively spent working toward solutions that are of value to the business user. Certainly there is some need to set some definitional limits, but the development of client/server solutions cannot wait for the perfect definition.

The picture is further complicated by the fact that the technology press and conventional usage have mixed terms and blurred definitions. As a result, words that were once useful (e.g., "cooperative processing") have lost currency and have been mixed with other terms.

Any book about client/server must revolve around a consistent sense of the term. Consistency is thus an internal concern here; if readers go to other sources, they may find definitions that are not perfectly consistent with the use of the term here. Readers should look beyond formal definitions to the section on "Working Definitions" to find definitions that are more useful for their particular work in designing a client/server application.

The insurance example offered earlier is one powerful application corresponding to the working definition used in this chapter: "Client/server computing is a style of computing in which multiple processors, one of which is typically a workstation, complete a business transaction."

As another example, consider the case of an order entry application for an organization that builds and delivers very complex electronic products. The application accepts the order from the sales engineer and validates that the proposed product configuration is one that actually can be built. Then the application checks central databases for availability of the product in inventory. The databases are found on servers at various places in the company. If the product is not available the application then goes through an allocation effort in real time, controlled from the workstation, to determine where and when the product can be assembled. This is returned to the sales engineer, who builds up the order initially as a confirmation of order acceptance.

This example illustrates most of the characteristics of our client/server definition.

- There are multiple processors: the workstation for the entry and then various servers to check availability of parts and assembly line for manufacturing.
- There is a complete business transaction processed across multiple servers: the entry of the order.
- Various databases are updated to reflect the existence of the order.

Comparison with Cooperative Processing

The definition of client/server used in this chapter competes with many other roughly equivalent terms. One term that has come in and out of favor over the years is "cooperative processing." Indeed, the definition used here was originally used to describe cooperative computing, though time and generally accepted usage have made "client/server" the accepted term for discussion purposes in this chapter.

Although the definition is straightforward, it contains some implicit subtleties that are worth elaborating on further.

Why Are Multiple Processors Important? Client/server processing, as defined here, means that developers are dealing with multiple processors in making decisions about where processing and data are located. The processors are distinct and connected through some form of a network.

Why Is One of the Processors "Typically" a Workstation? Workstations are not a requirement for client/server computing. Indeed, there are excellent examples of client/server computing solutions (one of which is discussed at some length later) where the business user input device has limited processing capability. Typically client/server applications using X-terminals have very limited processing capability in comparison to the typical workstation, but they can still provide excellent solutions in certain cases.

What Is a "Business Transaction"? A business transaction can cover a wide range of concerns. It can be no more than a simple update for a change of address, for example. It can also be a longer-running transaction such as the addition of an insurance policy that may occur in stages over several days.

Generically, a business transaction means a business event that is recorded as a part of the user interacting with the system. The recording typically is done in real time or near real time. It is also typically done by storing the information in data files that are used by the business.

The key factor within this concept of a business transaction is that it must have the integrity that is required by the business. Thus, if it is essential that the transaction have exclusive control of all related data when the update occurs, the impact often is that the update occurs in one data record under the exclusive control of a DBMS.

Conversely, if integrity constraints can be relaxed, the update may occur in a delayed fashion at other distributed sites where the data has been replicated. Most important here, the level of integrity required is a business decision and needs to be evaluated on a case-by-case basis. In a client/server solution, it is not a given that all updates must occur in real time.

Requester/Server Computing

Other conventions and approaches to achieve client/server computing also exist. "Requester/server computing," for example, is a style of computing where one processing unit requests a service and another processing unit provides the requested service. This definition, too, once referred to client/server computing, until client/server came to mean something related to the processing of business transactions.

Distributed Computing

Another related concept is "distributed computing." For our purposes, distributed computing is defined as "a style of computing that involves multiple distinct processors on which related data is kept."

The key in this definition is the concept of related data. The implication here is that if the data is related it must be kept synchronized in some way. Thus, when looking at distributed computing, the key design issue is deciding what data is to be placed where in the system. As this placement question is being resolved, the question of how to keep the data synchronized must be addressed.

These various definitions have been used successfully in recent years in a wide range of work with organizations implementing systems. The definitions have stood up well to queries and questions. One experience, however, serves as a good lesson about whether the pursuit of formal definitions has any value. One information systems (IS) group took example after example and put it up against the definition to see whether the definition would finally filter out a "real" client/server application. At the end of the session, the IS director concluded, "Well, you've proved to me that you would have made a good lawyer; now you need to prove that you can develop a system." To develop that real system, one has to go beyond formal definitions to arrive at working definitions.

WORKING DEFINITIONS OF CLIENT/SERVER

Working definitions not only define what a thing is; they also provide guidelines to developing the thing being defined. Following is an overview of some working definitions of client/server computing.

To understand client/server computing adequately, it is essential to view it in three dimensions:

- Hardware/network.
- Data allocation.
- Processing allocation.

Much of the difficulty in defining client/server computing results from confusion about which of these three dimensions is being talked about.

Hardware and Network

With regard to hardware, Exhibit I-1-2 suggests a typical three-level hierarchy of servers found in client/server computing.

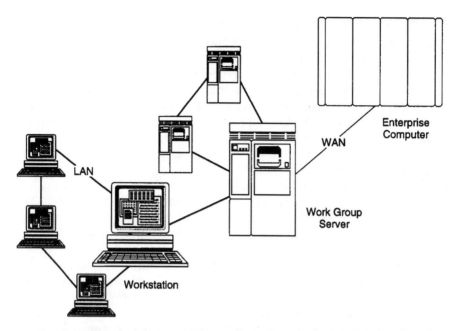

Exhibit I-1-2. Three-Level Client/Server Hardware and Network Configurations

The Workstation. The first level in the hierarchy is typically the workstation. The workstation is the device with which the business user interacts to record the business events. Such a machine may be anything from a personal computer (PC) to a high-speed, powerful workstation. Although some analysts have implied that client/server computing requires a very powerful workstation in terms of processing power, there seems to be little evidence that there is much value in such a differentiation. Further, given the power of PCs today, any differentiation that might once have existed is rapidly diminishing.

Work Group Server. The intermediate-level processor shown in Exhibit I-1-2 is the work group server, a server that is shared by a group of individuals. Typically, these individuals work in some way as a group performing common and shared business functions, although this is not a requirement of client/server computing.

The work group server also spans the range of processing capabilities, from a PC to a very large server including minicomputers (such as an AS/400) or even mainframes. The role of this server is to support the work of the group. This role is discussed more fully in the following sections. The other role of this server is to support the communications requirement of the work group by enabling the exchange of information with other work groups and with the enterprise as a whole. Although Exhibit I-1-2 implies a hierarchical view, the exchanges with the work group may in fact be on a peer-to-peer basis.

Enterprise Server. The highest level shown in Exhibit I-1-2 is the enterprise level. This level of server is used to share information and processing across the enterprise. Numerous computing analysts have conjectured that this level would cease to exist as client/server solutions evolved. Based on experience in actual implementations, however, this has not been the case. Experience suggests repeatedly that to share information across the enterprise, the most straightforward and simple solution is to have an enterprise server available to all processors in the enterprise.

For now, in the majority of implemented applications, the enterprise server tends to be a legacy machine such as a mainframe or a minicomputer. Several examples illustrate that the basic technology for the enterprise server is changing, and it is reasonable to expect this to continue. Indeed, a number of legacy vendors have statements of directions that suggest they will be supplying technology far different from the legacy mainframe and minicomputer technology. Examples include the Power PC chip as a basis for the IBM mainframe and the DEC Alpha chip as a basis for DEC's future machines.

In summary, experience to date suggests that the enterprise server will not go away as a result of client/server computing. In fact, as client/server computing provides new opportunities it is becoming apparent that the demands on the enterprise server may increase over time. The following sections on data and processing allocation suggest why this is the case.

Although Exhibit I-1-2 shows a three-level hierarchy, there may in fact be multiple servers with which the individual on the workstation interacts. In a client/server solution, the three- level hierarchy may in fact be many levels of servers. Conversely, many client/server applications have consisted of only two levels, where the workstation interacts directly with a server—often, an enterprise server. This type of solution is common in the IBM environment, where the workstation interacts directly with the mainframe.

The implication of all this is that the workstation and enterprise server tend to be fixed parts of the client/server solution. The middle level of Exhibit I-1-2 tends to be an optional level. Some client/server solutions need it, but others do not. The working advice, with regard to the number of levels, is to assume that one or more intermediary levels are present and then to use the following working definitions of data and application processing to decide what intermediate levels, if any, are required.

Networking in Client/Server. With regard to the networking aspect of Exhibit I-1-2, the following points can be made. Typically, the workstations are linked to each other and to the work group server on a LAN. The work group server may be linked with other work group servers on a LAN or through the use of a WAN and some forms of bridges and routers. The work group server may be linked to the enterprise server through the use of the WAN. (Networking is discussed in detail in both Sections II and III of this book.)

LANs. There are several key factors to keep in mind when designing a LAN for use in a client/server solution. One is that the LAN can perform at much higher bandwidths than is found in typical WAN technology. Typical speeds for the LAN are in the range of 10 to 16 megabits per second (MBPS). Also, the LANs differ from WANs in the ease with which they can be changed and evolved to meet the needs of the user in the work group. The prime limitation with regard to LANs is that, as their name implies, the distance over which they can communicate is limited to a relatively short distance—about one mile. Distances beyond this require the use of additional technology such as bridges and routers.

WANs. WAN technology is well-known and represents the type of technology present since the time of online systems. Although performance varies a great deal, today it is typically 100 to 1,000 times slower than is found with LAN technology. Also, arranging for WAN delivery typically involves numerous outside parties such as the enterprise telecommunications group, and telecommunications companies such as the regional Bell companies in the United States.

This brief overview of the underlying technology of the client/server solution has addressed only one of the dimensions of client/server—the hardware/network dimension. To understand better why these parts are required and how they are used, it is necessary to turn to the other dimensions.

Data Allocation in Client/Server Computing

The second dimension to consider in client/server computing is the allocation of data to the various processing levels. A key point to remember here is that decisions must be made on where to place data in a client/server environment.

The following guidelines for placing data on processors are based on work with numerous organizations over a period of years. We emphasize

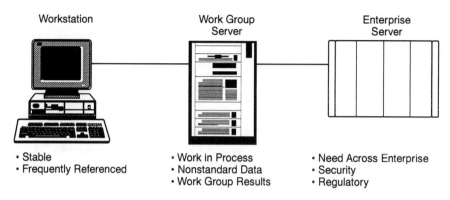

Workstation	Work Group Server	Enterprise Server
• Stable • Frequently Referenced	• Work in Process • Nonstandard Data • Work Group Results	• Need Across Enterprise • Security • Regulatory

Exhibit I-1-3. Allocation of Data in a Client/Server Environment

that the suggestions reflect an average over time and not an absolute. There are many variations in solutions based on the specifics of the business needs, hardware, network, and available software. It is best to view the following discussion not as a conclusion but as a point of departure for the design process. It represents a conceptual, not a physical, allocation of data in a client/server environment. (See Exhibit I-1-3.)

The Workstation. Data placed at the workstation is characteristically very stable. This data is referenced frequently in doing the application processing but tends not to be updated frequently.

As an example, consider once again the insurance system. Suppose that one of the applications is to create, validate, and underwrite new auto insurance policies. In this process, as a part of underwriting the policy, it is not uncommon to access and compute a total risk of the policy based on the coverages in the policy.

A common mechanism is a scoring approach where, for example, a high-performance automobile has a higher risk factor than a lower-performance automobile. These risk factors are accessed frequently in the process of underwriting the risk. The access should be rapid so as not to delay the underwriting process. The factors should be fairly stable—that is, they should not be subject to frequent change and they should never be subject to update by the insurance agent that enters the policy. In this case, allocating the risk data to the workstation may make good sense in terms of performance of the application.

Certainly the allocation of data to a local workstation is a point of controversy on occasion. The data allocated to a workstation will need to have support for updating it when the data needs to change. There is also a security risk that the workstation might be stolen along with any data on it. In a client/server solution, there tends to be many more clients than servers. As a result, there is a higher probability of data corruption because of the numbers of workstations involved. If the data is corrupted, systems management personnel are responsible for recovering it on a timely basis with integrity.

These are all reasons that might drive one away from placing data on the workstation. The trade-off, however, is that when frequently referenced data is available at the workstation, response time is consistently quick. Someone in the design process should be assigned to look for and designate data that is stable and frequently referenced and not sensitive from a security standpoint. In the first design pass, this data should be placed at the workstation. In subsequent design passes, one may choose to move this data to the work group server because of performance and management considerations.

In addition to the data just discussed, the workstation may be used to hold software executables and some personal data. Once again, the allocation of such data to the workstation leads to a set of questions. The questions to be addressed should include how and when the software executables will be updated and secured and, with regard to personal data, what types of data and how much of it are to be kept and what the responsibilities of the enterprise are in backing up and recovering such data.

Work Group Server. The data placed on the work group server can be divided into three major categories:

- Work flow data.
- Work group results.
- Nontraditional data.

Work Flow Data. A local work group tends to work on related business processes. In the local insurance office, for example, the work tends to revolve around the selling and administration of insurance policies and also around the initial collection and possibly resolution of claims against policies. Some of this work tends to be done in a single step by one person. For example, a change of address may be done by a single insurance agent in a single exchange. Other types of work may take several exchanges, extend over days, and involve many different people. To ensure that the work moves along as expected and gets done when needed, organizations require "business process management software." Within this broad set of software, a "work flow" component has evolved.

Work flow software essentially tracks business events and then, as the process proceeds through a series of events, assigns work tasks to the appropriate personnel. As a part of the assignment, the work flow software collects and dispatches to the business users the appropriate information they need to do their work. To perform this processing, the software must know who is involved in the work, the rules to be followed in assigning the work and detecting problems, and the routes by which the work may be delivered to the business user. Also, because such work tends to go into and out of queues as the work is moved along, the work queues must also be managed.

All this data is often stored and maintained in the local work group server. This allows business users to take advantage of the speed of the LAN to deliver the large volumes of information that tend to build up over time. The routes that are used to get to the business user can be maintained in part just by adding physically to the network. In this way a remote site, such as where the enterprise server is kept, does not need to be involved in the day-to-day changes in local office layout and work flow.

Also, the local office may decide to change local guidelines of how work is done and by whom. By placing such rules in the local office they tend to be easier to change. Obviously, such rule changes need to be carefully controlled. For example, a local office manager may be able to change the size of work queues so that more work is assigned to more skilled personnel. The manager would probably not be able to change the rules that decide who gets which cases in claims based on the criticality of the case.

Work Group Results. With regard to local work group results, many management strategies focus on how to motivate people by providing them with measures of how they are doing relative to plan. In an insurance setting this data could include numbers of customers to whom service has been provided, average wait times on phones, numbers of customers who have purchased policies, and amounts of coverage written by line of business such as auto or homeowners. This type of information should be of interest to the local office on a day-to-day basis. However, a central site might only care about this information on a periodic basis to use, for example, for trend analysis.

Furthermore, a loss of this information would not result in a loss of business to the company. Such information, then, might well be stored at the local office on the work group computer. Doing so provides immediate local access while not putting the business at risk, and it may contribute to at least some small reduction in network traffic. Having the data on the work group server may also reduce the vulnerability of the system as a whole to network failures.

Nontraditional Data. Nontraditional data refers to data formats that have not been typical of the systems that have been delivered over the years. Examples include image, video, and voice. The reasons for storing this type of data at the level of local work group server relate to the network discussion on the high performance of LANs.

Such data tends to be voluminous in comparison to traditional data. For example, a common estimate of the data space required to store an $8^1/_2$ " $\times 11^1/_2$ " sheet of paper is 50,000 bits. A common estimate of the storage required for one minute of video is 10 megabytes. Such large volumes of data require high-speed networks to deliver the data in acceptable time frames.

Typically, WANs do not have this performance capability. LANs, however, do have such a capacity. As a result, such nontraditional data is stored in local work group servers where the data can be immediately accessed with acceptable response times over the LAN. This data may be stored redundantly at some other site. For example, it could be stored at a central site so it can be made available to the user community as a whole. If it is accessed from such a central site over the WAN, however, there is typically some degradation in performance as a result.

Enterprise Server. The final server to consider for data allocation in client/server computing is the enterprise server. Although this level of server has usually been seen as a mainframe, it can actually take many forms. As argued earlier, the enterprise server continues to have a role in client/server computing solutions for businesses today. Its role is dictated primarily by the need to make information available across the enterprise as a whole.

Repeated experience suggests that if information is needed across the enterprise, the enterprise server is the most straightforward place to allocate the data. Distributing this data inevitably leads to the need to maintain indexes or some form of tracking facility so that users will always knows where data is allocated. These tracking strategies tend to become very complex. At the same time, having an enterprise server available to all requests provides a relatively simple answer with a track record of success and a history of known and understood problems. Basically, good engineering is simple engineering that meets business needs, and using an enterprise server for shared data meets this criterion very well. Thus, it seems likely that this solution will be available for the foreseeable future.

The proposed allocation of data in the previous discussion suggests that in client/server computing, data is allocated to all levels of the servers. However, within this proposed allocation, data that is critical to the ongoing operation of the business tends to be allocated to the more

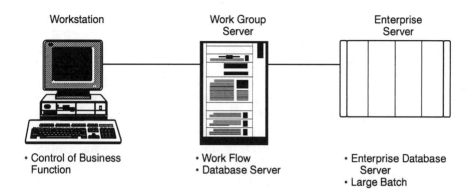

Workstation	Work Group Server	Enterprise Server
• Control of Business Function	• Work Flow • Database Server	• Enterprise Database Server • Large Batch

Exhibit I-1-4. Allocation of Processing in a Client/Server Environment

traditional processor in the hierarchy. This allocation, in turn, suggests that client/server computing will continue to require each of the three levels of servers identified here.

Processing Allocation in Client/Server Computing

The final dimension to consider in the working definition of client/server computing is the allocation of processing to the computers found within the client/server environment. As in the case of data allocation, one of the benefits of client/server computing is that it gives the designer many options on how best to allocate such processing. Exhibit I-1-4 represents a conceptual, not a physical, allocation of processing in a client/server environment.

The Workstation. The workstation is the new processing dimension in the client/server picture. Because it is new, organizations often have many questions about what processing should and can be allocated to it. The key difference between a workstation environment and previous computing environments is that the workstation is driven by, and can respond to, events as they occur. These events are as simple as keystrokes on a keyboard, a mouse movement, a pen stroke, or a message from the network.

The ability to respond to such events is an important consideration when deciding how to allocate processing to the workstation. The ability to respond to events means that we can build applications on the workstation that are far more responsive to the user. The application can respond to each action by the user at the instant the action is made. The application is able to present information or initiate processing immediately—as the event occurs or as the circumstances develop that need processing—without the users breaking from their normal work to request it from the server.

In essence, the event-driven architecture allows the designer to embed computing processing much more deeply in the business process and to make it much more a part of the business user's day-to-day work flow, as it happens, when and where it happens.

To achieve this level of processing, designers must allocate control of the business function to the workstation. This may seem obvious, but one of the difficult transitions today for systems designers trained in a traditional manner is to learn how to allocate processing to the workstation in order to take advantage of client/server computing capabilities. Another difficult transition for designers is learning to take advantage of the communications capability inherent within client/server solutions.

The difficulty in allocating control of the business function to the workstation arises from several causes. One is that the behavior of event-driven processing, like that found in graphical user interfaces (GUIs), is different from traditional online and batch interactions. Designers face a significant learning curve here.

A second cause of difficulty is learning to understand the computing power that is available to the business user on a workstation. Machines with 60 to 100 MIPS are now commonly being placed in front of business users. The amount of computing power dedicated to the end user in this situation exceeds that available through the traditional mainframe solution by a factor of 10 to 100, if not more. It is difficult to learn how to think in terms of this radically enhanced computing power.

Trusting that the computing power is there when one begins to design for client/server is even more difficult. Complicating the trust issue is the fact that learning how to test to determine whether the limits are exceeded takes experience, and not many people have that experience yet. It is easy to overuse such new technologies as GUIs, multimedia, and expert systems. At one time or another, even experienced designers in client/server have probably overused their technologies. (That is how they became experienced.)

Assuming that the user overcomes the learning curve of event-based processing and grows to trust the new computing power of workstations, the most effective solution is to begin by placing control of the business function on the workstation. Thus, when business users want to change the customer address or need to have a coverage code validated, the control of this effort is found in the workstation. Where the logic is actually executed tends to be driven by concerns about network performance, or about where to put the associated data needed to perform the process. As a going-in position, however, the decision to do the work, and the control that ensures that the work is done correctly, is often based on the workstation.

Work Group Server. Data allocation to the work group server is the foundation for issues related to the allocation of processing. As noted, the work group server often is allocated the work flow data and the work-in-process data. Associated with this data is work flow processing. This processing ensures that when work is ready to be done, it is delivered to the right person on a timely basis. It collects and moves to the right people the information they need to get their work done. When these people are finished with the work, the work flow software sees that the data is stored where appropriate and then records the status information that indicates when the case will next be ready for work.

The other role of the work group server is to keep track of events in the local office that contribute to the evaluation of the office's effectiveness. In the insurance example, as people are interviewed at the reception desk or as phone calls are received by the local office, these events can be tracked and stored on the local office server for needed reporting. The work group server can also serve as the processor for nontraditional data. In this role the processor is primarily filling the role of getting and storing data such as image and voice.

Enterprise Server. In the picture of client/server computing being drawn here, the enterprise server plays the role of database server to the enterprise. Associated with this role is accessing and storing large volumes of data and placing data onto the WAN so that the data arrives where it is needed. This server role tends to have relatively little application capability associated with it when the server is interacting with a business user through a workstation. This is not to say that there is no application capability on the enterprise server. Rather, in this model of client/server computing users should prove the need to put the function that directly interacts with the application on the enterprise server. The process for deciding what to allocate and why is discussed in subsequent chapters.

By taking a "minimalist" view to the use of application capability on the enterprise server, the enterprise server can be tuned and optimized for the database server role when it comes to interactive functions. This also tends to ensure that, whenever feasible, organizations take advantage of the processing capability available elsewhere in the client/server solution.

With regard to such noninteractive processing as batch, the enterprise server often continues to provide dedicated processing capability to the enterprise to do the large batch jobs that need to be done. Examples of such processing include billing functions, accounting functions, and the large file sweeps needed by the enterprise to locate exceptions and concerns. The allocation of data to the enterprise server suggested here matches up well with these types of processing concerns.

Summary of Data and Processing Allocation

The following guidelines for data and processing allocations in regard to client/server computing are a good starting point for going-in positions; they are not final solutions. Few designs end up with these exact solutions. At the same time, beginning from a clear starting point uncovers solutions more quickly.

- Changes in the allocation of interactive processing, with significant processing moving toward the workstation.
- Continued use of the enterprise server as the supplier and manager of data needed across the enterprise.
- A newly defined role for a work group server to track and manage the flow of work within the work group.

THE GARTNER GROUP MODEL OF CLIENT/SERVER COMPUTING

There are, of course, other models for looking at client/server computing. One model that has received widespread attention is the Gartner Group's "Five Styles of Client/Server Computing."

The Gartner Group model is based on dividing business processing into three distinct layers: database, application logic, and presentation.

The first layer is the presentation layer. This layer is involved with collecting and returning information from the user. It presents the windows and collects the keystrokes and other events that the business user provides to the application.

The next layer is the application logic of the business process. This is the processing logic needed to meet particular business needs. In the insurance application, for example, the logic to rate the risk of a policy would be an example of application logic.

The data layer is the third layer in the model. For most business processing there is a need to access and store data to support and reflect the processing done by the application logic. The role of the data layer is to access and store information.

Client/server computing involves in part introducing processors and networks over which these layers can be allocated. One way to view client/server is to define possible allocations of presentation, application,

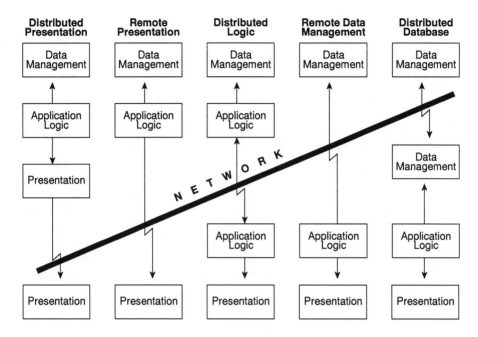

Exhibit I-1-5. Gartner's Five Styles of Client/Server Computing

---

and data on processors across the network. Doing this leads to the Gartner Group's model, graphically represented in Exhibit I-1-5. The solid line labeled "Network" shows which of the five layers are allocated to client and which are allocated to server.

The Gartner Group has given the names shown at the top of the exhibit to the proposed allocations of presentation, application logic, and data. Following is a brief summary of the processing approach implied by the allocation.

Distributed Presentation

In this style of processing, presentation is split between the client and the server. Sometimes this style of computing is referred to as screen scraping. It is found when a traditional 3270 application has its user interface presented on a workstation rather than on the 3270 terminal for which it was implemented. Usually this means that a window is presented to the user and the input is captured and sent to the application on the server. This style is often used to place a new improved terminal and a consistent user interface onto an existing character terminal application. This style of computing alone generally does not justify a move to client/server computing.

Remote Presentation

In this style of client/server computing, presentation logic is placed on the client. The workstation is used primarily to put windows in front of the users and to perform basic input processing.

Examples of such processing might include checking that numeric fields are numeric and that required fields are entered. Application processing remains on the server. The model is not explicit about when the information from presentation is provided to the application logic. However, this style may be adopted to allow for the continued use of legacy systems with a new front-end with extended capability. In this case, it often happens that as a window is filled out, it is provided to the legacy application as a completed screen. In this case, such processing as numeric checks may be done redundantly in the window and the legacy application.

Distributed Logic

In the third style of client/server computing, some of the application processing logic and presentation logic is moved to the client. Some application logic remains on the server. In this style of processing, the workstation takes on a significant portion of the processing load of the application. Data accessing is found only on the server. Experience suggests that this is the most prevalent style of client/server processing.

Remote Data Management

In the next style of client/server computing, the application logic is placed entirely on the workstation. The server has only data management logic.

Distributed Database

In the final style of processing, all application logic, presentation logic, and some data accessing logic are placed on the client. In this case, the client may have local servers that provide information to the client. In addition, data used across multiple clients is placed on a common server.

CONSIDERATIONS REGARDING THE "FIVE STYLES"

The Gartner Group model of client/server computing has had wide exposure in the industry and many organizations have considered the implications of the model for planning and designing client/server solutions. The models have helped frame many issues and concerns. At the same time, experience suggests that organizations must keep in mind a number of things during implementation:

- Any conceptual model must be supplemented with working criteria to help select the appropriate design for implementation. First-time client/server developers need to be aware of the difference between conceptual and physical implementations.
- Remember that data design and allocation is as important a part of client/server design as processing allocation. Designers must begin with what data and information various business users need to do their work.
- Actual implementations are often a mix of the five styles, based on business need. Taking a hybrid approah is vital.

A TECHNICAL ARCHITECTURE FOR CLIENT/SERVER

The discussion thus far has introduced client/server computing in terms of the broad allocation of processing and data across clients and servers. Carrying the discussion to another level of detail requires an examination of the processing components typically found in client/server solutions.

These components, based on repeated experience, are found in one form or another in most client/server implementations. Because they are repeated, there is value in abstracting the components and identifying them. "Architecture" here is an abstraction of components found across multiple applications. When the architecture appears to be usable across a wide net of applications, it is a "technical architecture."

One of the values of such a technical architecture is that it distills numerous experiences over a wide variety of implementations. Thus it can reduce the learning curve of the designer trying to decide what the pieces are and how they fit together. For a site just moving into client/server, a technical architecture can be of real value. Otherwise the site may simply be relearning what others have already learned, thus incurring greater costs and effort.

Another important value of such an architecture is that it provides a standard, consistent approach. With mainframe computing, architectures were often identified too late. Done correctly and consistently, client/server provides the opportunity to get things right the first time because it is an environment most organizations have not worked in before. There are many benefits to this consistency, including the following:

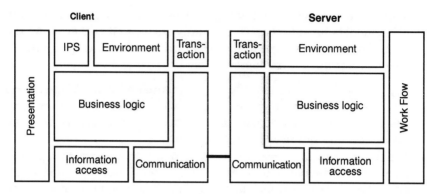

Key:
IPS integrated performance support

Exhibit I-1-6. Execution Architecture for Client/Server

- It provides a development environment.
- It provides a common background for IS personnel.
- It facilitates rapid delivery of solutions.
- It reduces the impact of change.

An architecture, then, is a set of processing components that represents a common approach. Typically these components are presented in a graphical format. The format attempts to portray the major components and their interaction.

Experience suggests that such architectures have three primary manifestations:

- An *execution* architecture, which describes the components required when an application executes.
- A *development* architecture, which describes the components required to create the execution architecture.
- An *operations* architecture, which describes the components required to operate and manage the system.

The critical architecture to understand is the execution architecture. Exhibit I-1-6 illustrates the execution architecture that will be referenced throughout this volume. It has been used widely in a variety of industries and applications over the past several years.

Following is a brief introduction to the graphical notations used to represent the architecture, and an overview of the components and their interrelationships. Subsequent chapters go into detail about each of the components. This introduction provides the basis for much of the following discussion.

Comments on Graphical Representation

Discussions of client/server architectures frequently seem to hit a snag when graphical notations or depictions of the architecture do not make sense. This section attempts to explain what all the graphics mean. To some degree this section is proof that a picture is worth a thousand words.

First, each of the shapes in a graphical depiction of the client/server architecture represents a processing component. The name within the shape provides a notion of what the component is about. The components are described briefly in the paragraphs that follow and then are described in more detail in the following sections. The exhibits are recursive in the sense that one component can and will be broken out into other, lower-level components.

The highest level is systems management. The next level is the client and server and connecting network. It is in turn broken into lower-level components such as presentation and communications services.

In Exhibit I-1-6, the way the components are drawn suggests the degree of interface that exists between components. For example, the business logic component is in close proximity to the information access component. Thus, users can expect the frequent execution of interfaces or application programming interfaces (APIs) between these components. Also, information access services are in close proximity to communications services. This close proximity suggests how information access services request data from a remote server. However, the business logic client component has to interface with other components on the server over the network.

Despite all this, the components are not strictly limited to the interactions implied in the exhibit. For example, the presentation component may have some reason to interact directly with communications components. This is not prohibited by the architecture; it is simply less common. The size of the boxes is unimportant and does not carry any special meaning. The boxes are sized based partly on esthetics and partly on the words that need to fit inside them.

Finally, it is worthwhile to note in the diagram the focus on the separation of components. The intent of an architecture is to separate distinct functions. Doing so benefits the development process by separating development concerns. It also makes it feasible to organize and deliver components as they are needed by teams focused on specific, well-defined pieces of the whole problem.

Client-Side Components

The following discussion presents a first level of detail about what is found in the components on the client side. If the component is repeated in the server side the description found at this level of detail also stands for the server side. When components differ, the section "Server-Side Components" describes the differences.

Business Logic. The core of the diagram is the business logic, the logic that supports the business function. Applications within this component can be differentiated from other components in that they manipulate the data that the business process uses. The business logic tends to represent, over time, where systems builders direct most of their attention. In an insurance application, for example, when it comes time to determine the cost of a new policy, the sums would in all probability be done in an application within the business logic.

Presentation Services. The presentation services component is closely related to the business logic component. Presentation services is responsible for gathering all events and providing them to the business logic component or to whatever component is most appropriate. For example, some window managers in a presentation services component have the ability to do database lookup based on the entry of field. In this case a component within presentation services may go directly to the information access component to look up the field on the database.

Presentation services includes the window manager and the logic that processes the windows. Much of the input that an application receives is through a window on the workstation. The specific mechanism used to obtain data from a window is often referred to as a callback. As an event occurs, the application has a means to tell the window manager if the event is of interest. The window manager alerts the application to the event through a callback using a defined API and allows the business logic component to do the work it needs to do. Because an event may be no more than a click of a mouse or the completion of the entry of a field, this type of invocation can occur literally hundreds of times in a minute on a busy workstation.

Information Access Services. Information access services has responsibility for managing the access of information and data used by other components in the client. This responsibility can include accessing data from a DBMS on the client. It can also include requesting data through communication services from a remote DBMS on some server. Information access services can also include accessing information from traditional file sources such as sequential files, locally or on remote servers.

Once information is accessed, it is common in client/server systems to have the data reside in memory for some time on the workstation to avoid the overhead of moving it over the network to some other server for permanent storage. In this model, information access services will work with services in the operating systems to manage the memory required to hold the data.

Operating systems have various components to manage the movement of data between business logic components that are processing different windows. These mechanisms are often more complex than one might expect. Also, they have a history of changing across releases of the operating system. To shield the complexity and the changes from the business logic components, information access services may have a component that allows for dynamic transfer of data between memory components. Finally, if it becomes necessary to store data temporarily out of memory, information access services may provide this capability.

Communication Services. Communication services address the need to communicate across the network—a capability that is a key aspect of client/server computing. There are an enormous number of ways and reasons to communicate in client/server and approaches evolve rapidly. One of the values of the communication services component is to hide some of this complexity and rapid change.

At a high level, communications needs can be broken down into the following categories: message based, function based, store and forward, and sealed messaging. All these components are found in communications services:

- *Message-based.* processing provides the ability to move data in the form of messages through the network. It is implemented through a wide variety of mechanisms. It also has many refinements such as synchronous messages and asynchronous messages. All these complexities are addressed in the communications services component.
- *Function-based.* communications provides the ability to invoke a function on another server. Once again there are many mechanisms to do this and they would be addressed through the communication services. It should be noted that the need to pass messages to the function may be associated with function-based invocation of services. This need would also be addressed through the function-based component.
- *Store and forward.* provides the ability to send and receive messages, to hold them for periods of time, and then to present them to the

appropriate component or move them to another processor. This work involves messaging, queuing of messages and, very often, directory services.

A key part of communications in a client/server environment is knowing who or what is where. This is referred to as directory services. Systems designers with a noncommunications background tend to feel that directory services is not a very interesting application. As experience grows with client/server solutions, the importance and difficulty of keeping the directory up-to-date gradually emerges as a major concern in the process of building client/server systems. Directory services is a component of communications services.

- *Sealed messaging.* is not an industry standard term, but it is a concept worth understanding. Many components of client/server computing have built-in communications capabilities. Examples include client/server DBMSs and electronic mail (E-mail) systems. Client/server DBMSs have extensive messaging capabilities tuned to the performance and reliability needs of DBMS. E-mail is most often built on the basis of a store-and-forward capability.

These capabilities, although extensive and interesting, are more often than not sealed off from use by other components of the client/server architecture. In this case these components exist, and they need to be placed somewhere in the architecture; because the capabilities most closely relate to communications services they are found here. They will often have built within them some form of directory services. Because these components are also sealed, one of the challenges of client/server computing is to keep all directory services up-to-date and coordinated.

Transaction Services. Client/server applications increasingly focus on the use of multiple computing processes working in parallel to complete a task. To support the business of starting and stopping processes, recovering from failed processes, and communicating the results of parallel processes, we are seeing the increased use of a distributed online transaction processing (D-OLTP). D-OLTP is implemented through transaction monitors. These software components can be rather complex and can have numerous means with which to interact with applications. To shield some of this complexity and facilitate standard approaches for use of transaction monitors, the transaction services component exists within the client/server architecture.

Environment Services. This component deals with the environment that is a part of client/server. In a sense, this component tends to have a mix of capabilities not addressed by other components. One key part is to provide an interface to the operations system services. For example, if an application needs the time of day, this request can be made through an API to environment services.

Security components may be found in environment services. The security components may, in turn, reach components in the operating or system services to support the security needs of the application. Another potential use of environment services is as an interface to the systems management component. In this role, if an application component is encountering unexpected errors from some other component such as the DBMS, it might report the errors through the environment services to the systems management services. Another aspect of systems management services could be the reporting of performance. Thus, as windows are entered, processed, and returned to the business track of elapsed time, they could then be captured and rolled up to some form of a file for subsequent reporting. Such processing could reside in environment services.

Integrated Performance Support Services. Integrated performance support (IPS) is a set of application services designed to support organizational and work force performance. IPS enables application users to do their work better by providing advice, tools, reference, and training on demand and at the point of need. Within the execution architecture, IPS has six distinct components: application help, performance support controller, advisory services, training services, reference services, and job aid services.

Server-Side Components

The server components of the technical architecture are on the whole similar to the client components. One difference is a new component, Work Flow Services, which exists only on the server side. Also, a presentation services component cannot be found on the server because the server does not interact directly with the user.

Work Flow Services. Work flow is the component that has responsibility for moving work through the work group. In this role, this component keeps track of who is working on what work. It also tracks what work is to be done and the conditions that must be fulfilled to submit the work for the next step. When the conditions are met to move to the next stage of work, the work flow services component has responsibility for pulling together required information and conditions for the work to be done and then submitting the work to the next stage of work. As the work is completed and returned to work flow services, this component notes

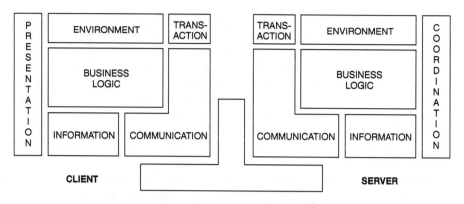

Exhibit I-1-7. Typical Allocation of Processing Functions

the conditions required for the work to be ready for the next step and then begins the ongoing evaluation of criteria for conditions being met.

Extensions to the Client/Server Technical Architecture in a Netcentric Environment

The emerging netcentric computing environment requires a number of additional services that extend the technical architecture introduced here. A full discussion of these additional architectural features, however, is well beyond the scope of this book.

As shown in Exhibit I-1-7, the most obvious extension to the basic client/server architecture is something called the "communications fabric." As communications networks become increasingly complicated and interconnected, the services provided by the network itself have increased as well. Clients and servers are rarely directly connected to one another, but separated by a network of routers, servers, and firewalls providing an ever-increasing number of network services such as address resolution, message routing, security screening, and more.

The communications fabric extends the client/server computing model by placing intelligence into the physical network—acknowledging the network as a kind of standalone system that provides intelligent shared network services. As Exhibit I-1-7 indicates, there is certainly overlap between services typically thought of as part of a client/server architecture and services increasingly being provided by the network itself.

In addition, extensions of the client/server architecture are found within each of the other services. Within presentation services, for example, a netcentric environment requires such additions as browser services, viewer services, and electronic form (E-form) services to account for new user interaction styles. Communication services requires many additional components, such as HTTP Web server services.

Summary of Technical Architecture

Thus far this chapter has presented an overview of a technical architecture for client/server. Subsequent chapters go into detail on what the components are and how to address them in the process of building a client/server-based application.

There are many client/server architectures. Regardless of the architecture to be used, it is vital that the architecture is established and agreed on prior to starting work on the first client/server application. This architecture should be employed by all systems developers as a framework for their design efforts. Further, they should be expected to prove why they cannot work within the confines of the architecture. This process is one of the few ways that one can contain the potential for chaos in going to a new technology such as client/server.

WHAT CLIENT/SERVER COMPUTING IS NOT

Thus far this chapter has addressed what client/server is. In closing, it is important to note what client/server is not—things that are excluded from this text because they are outside or tangential to client/server. Excluding some of these topics does not imply that they do not have value but, simply, that the concerns and issues of succeeding in these areas lie outside the subject of building client/server solutions. The other reasons for noting these topics is that there is so much confusion on the subject of client/server computing that if these are not specifically excluded, the potential for confusion is intensified.

The specific areas excluded from consideration as client/server computing solutions include:

- Downsizing, rightsizing, and rehosting.
- End-user computing.
- Data dipping.

Downsizing, Rightsizing, Rehosting

Some users may object to grouping these together, but they are all closely related. Downsizing and rightsizing appear to be a matter of trying to put a more positive spin on an approach.

Downsizing is moving an application from one hardware base to another, presumably cheaper, hardware base. Implicit in the definition is that there is no change in function in making the change in hardware base. The lack of change in function is a key point in this definition. If users choose to open up the application to functional change, they may well move themselves into a client/server solution. However, this text uses the term "downsizing" when no functional change is made.

The key objective in downsizing, as defined here, is usually a reduction in hardware and software costs. This reduction is achieved by moving to cheaper processors, with often cheaper system software. Such a strategy is essentially a cost-avoidance maneuver, which can be achieved in at least two ways. One is with compilers and translators that are now available. These translators can take certain technology bases such as COBOL/CICS/VSAM and translate them to a C/UNIX environment. With the translations complete, a recompile is needed to bring up the application in the downsized environment.

It is worthwhile to point out that these translators do exist and that they do work as long as one has built reasonably well behaved COBOL/ CICS/VSAM applications. Thus the ability to do the translation exists now and does not present any overwhelming problems. Given the cost differentials on mainframes versus RISC UNIX processors, the real question here might be why everyone is not doing this. In fact, some statistics suggest that a large percentage of shops expect to make such a transition in the next few years.

There are, however, some issues to consider. The apparent savings only occur if the mainframe is eliminated. A mainframe loaded to half of capacity costs no less than one running at 100% capacity. Thus if an organization cannot move everything, it runs the risk of ending up spending more net money by continuing to pay for the mainframe as well as for the additional servers. In some cases a particular division moved an application off the mainframe and achieved lower computer costs. However, the costs to the enterprise as a whole were higher because now two machines were being paid for and two support staffs were being maintained.

Complete transitions to downsized hardware can be difficult. Legacy systems may not be well behaved or may be written with a DBMS for which no porting software is available. Imagine, for example, a high-performance application written in Assembler with IMS. In these cases the system cannot be ported without a rewrite, which will cause the costs of downsizing to escalate.

Applications software packages often present a serious problem when looking at downsizing. The vendor may not be interested in a port, may be out of business, or may have used some poorly behaved technique to support the needs of the application. All this can create problems in trying to downsize. However, an enterprise should not avoid looking at the potential for downsizing but must understand that achieving enterprisewide benefits may be more difficult than is sometimes believed. It takes a careful assessment of the application portfolio to see whether the benefits are there.

Often when downsizing has succeeded, the organization should not have been on a mainframe in the first place or was using it inefficiently. By implication, if a site is using up one or more mainframes and if there is an effective systems management effort in place to optimize use of hardware, downsizing can lead to a case of local optimization and global deoptimization. In any case it can be a long and bumpy road with surprises along the way.

End-User Computing

End user computing refers to a style of computing in which an end user builds a local application. Often the application is built by users for their own use. Many enterprises have moved into client/server computing on the backbone of end-user computing.

There are many end-user applications that are in fact client/server implementations. However, there are many more end-user applications that run entirely within the confines of the workstation. They may be used once or only infrequently, and they do not update data shared across the enterprise. These types of applications can be complex and present many problems for successful development. However, the solutions do not need all the apparatus that is described in this volume for client/server development.

When the end-user application begins to be used in day-to-day business, begins to run across multiple servers, and begins to update the enterprise database, a subtle but very real transition occurs in the demands made on the system building process. In this case much of what is contained in this work is of value in building such systems and should be considered.

Data Dipping

Often, as the end-user computing application matures, it needs access to more and more data. The approach of entering data at the workstation becomes impractical. In this case the user may make the transition to a strategy that obtains data from the enterprise server through some form of an automated bridge. When the data is only accessed and not returned for update through the automated interface, the process is known as data dipping. This use of information, although it also presents many challenges and difficulties, is not viewed as client/server computing in this text. If the data dipping includes updating of the enterprise databases, there is a potential transition to client/server computing as defined here.

CONCLUSION

This chapter began by noting that organizations often spend too much time on formal definitions of client/server computing and not enough time building their first client/server application. The purpose of this chapter has been to map out a range of systems development in which there is real benefit and also real difficulties in building successful systems. As this volume moves along, it builds a case for why an organization wants to do this and then provides a good deal of material on how to build this new age of systems solutions.

I-2
Client/Server Computing and Business Change

This chapter addresses client/server computing and its relationship to such management initiatives as:

- Flattened organizational structures.
- Downsizing.
- Employee empowerment.
- Time compression.
- Business process engineering.

Why should an organization now begin to develop client/server-based applications and client/server solutions? Understanding the right reasons for embracing this new technology is an important step.

As business users work on their first applications, they are most likely to feel as if they are "pushing the envelope"—of knowledge, of experience, of technological presumptions. Acquiring new knowledge is relatively easy in this case; all it takes is an open mind and a willingness to read, listen, and learn. The experience itself is tougher, because it involves trying solutions not tried before. The development effort becomes more difficult, more expensive, and less predictable.

The technological presumptions may be the toughest and most insidious, however, because often people are not even aware of how their view of the world affects their capabilities within that world. The best that can be said here is that in the middle of the client/server revolution, the winners will be those who learned to expect the unexpected. Business users who do not push the envelope risk falling into a career where they face the same challenges and do the same kinds of work over and over.

CLIENT/SERVER AND TODAY'S MANAGEMENT INITIATIVES

Fueled by the normal interest people have for the latest "thing," organizations today seem particularly susceptible to management fads. This susceptibility may be seen, for example, in one company that the *Wall*

Street Journal noted had "converted from total quality management to the learning organization."

Each of those management practices has worth, to be sure, but unless they are implemented in an environment that gives workers the chance really to succeed, they will result in money wasted. As one analyst put it in a *Wall Street Journal* article, "[New management initiatives] may be the right things, but if implemented as the flavor-of-the-month management fad, they create problems."

A number of drivers at work in the business world today, however, are having and will continue to have a major impact on how organizations and their workers perform on a day-to-day basis:

- The "demassification" or "disaggregation" of the modern organization through horizontal management structures, downsizing, and employee empowerment.
- Time compression techniques, especially as they reduce time to market.
- Business process reengineering.

One important point, however, is that client/server computing does not mean throwing a set of workstations, networks, and servers at a business challenge. The ambiguous statistics over the past decade regarding productivity improvements from technology can be traced in part to false beliefs that technology alone can solve every problem. One cannot meet today's business challenges without information technology, but the technology must be part of a larger scheme of vision, leadership, and expertise.

Organizational Disaggregation

Much of the change and churning seen in business organizations today is a reflection of a process that has been described for many years now, using such terms as "demassification" and "disaggregation." In the early 1980s, Alvin Toffler wrote of demassification as one of the key characteristics of "Third Wave" society. The Second Wave was "mass" society, noted for mass media and mass production. Third Wave society, Toffler wrote, will be noted for its demassified groups. These groups will break up the massive technology groups, moving relevant pieces toward particular business actions.

Demassification puts an added burden on the existing information technology structures. The demassification of civilization, Toffler wrote:

> Brings with it an enormous jump in the amount of information we all exchange with one another. And it is this increase that explains why we are becoming an "information society." ... People and organizations continually crave more information and the entire system be-

gins to pulse with higher and higher flows of data. By forcing up the amount of information needed for the social system to cohere, and the speeds at which it must be exchanged, the Third Wave shatters the framework of the obsolete, overloaded Second Wave info-sphere and constructs a new one to take its place.

More recently, James Brian Quinn's book *Intelligent Enterprise* spoke of the implications for the modern organization of what he calls the "disaggregation" or "deverticalization" trends occurring in most industries. Since the 1960s, the average size of industrial firms has decreased. For larger companies, substantial downsizing and decentralization (delayering and elimination of bureaucracies) have been necessary to respond more effectively to customer's demands. Quinn argues that when technology is creatively implemented in service activities, "there appears to be virtually no limit to the potential reporting span—the number of people reporting to one supervisor or center—that a service organization can make effective." Quinn calls these "infinitely flat" organizations.

In essence, demassification or disaggregation is a movement toward the simplification of organizational structures and processes. Traditional hierarchical decision making becomes local decision making based on the situation at hand. The horizontal organization seeks to move as much of the decision making as possible to the people doing the work.

Doing this means, however, that organizations must also place at the command of their knowledge workers the resources they need to perform optimally at all times. These resources cover anything the person needs to get the job done such as money, products, and computing capability. Some specific organizational change phenomena are worth a closer look here as more specific manifestations of the process of demassification.

Horizontal Organizations

Why would organizations want to move toward flatter organizational structures? In his book *Downsizing*, Robert M. Tomasko tells an important story:

> A salesman hears from a customer that the firm's latest bench drill cannot accommodate bits for drilling a recently developed hard plastic. The customer suggests a modified coupling adapter and an additional speed setting. The salesman thinks the suggestion makes sense but has no authority to pursue it directly. Following procedures, the salesman passes the idea on to the sales manager, who ... drafts a memo to the marketing vice president. The marketing vice-president [takes] the idea [to] an executive meeting of all the vice-presidents. The executive committee agrees to modify the drill. The senior product manager then asks the head of the research department to form

a task force to evaluate the product opportunity and to design a new coupling and variable-speed mechanism.

The task force consists of representatives from sales, marketing, accounting, and engineering. ... After months of meetings the research manager presents the group's findings to the executive committee. It approves the new design. Each department then works out a detailed plan for its role in bringing out the new product, and the modified drill goes into production.

If there are no production problems, the customer receives word that he can order a drill for working hard plastics two years after he first discussed it with the salesman. In the meantime, a Japanese, West German, or South Korean firm has already designed, produced, and delivered a hard-plastics drill.

Middle management layers in organizations are on their way out, and seen everywhere is the trend toward horizontal structures that can help organizations operate and make decisions more efficiently. Middle-management layers tended to serve a communications and coordination role. The communications role was both horizontal and vertical. The middle layers of management communicated among themselves what was happening and what needed to be done to keep things moving along. They also communicated upward to more senior management on what was happening in the field in terms of sales, service, and customer needs. Finally, the middle layers of management communicated down to those that reported to them on corporate, product, or policy changes.

With regard to coordination, middle management was expected to watch developments and deploy resources to meet demand wherever it arose. Also, middle managers could serve a role of coordinating across divisions and organizations when the customer's needs went outside the area for which the manager had responsibility.

The tendency today is to remove these layers because they are not adding value. One can well argue that on a day-to-day basis, there is no clear bottom-line impact of communications. Also, it is probably fair to say that, on occasion, middle managers became more concerned with process than with results and lost track of the customers and their needs. Concerns for profitability, a new focus on customer over process, and cost cutting measures came together in the early to mid-1990s to create the horizontal organization. This move has had clear and immediate positive impact on the bottom line in terms of eliminating activities that had no clear direct return on costs. As a result, the flattening of the organization has been viewed, on the whole, as a good thing.

Although flatter structures have been seen as worthwhile and beneficial, the activity of communications and coordination did provide value to the organization. The impact of eliminating this middle management role is slower to emerge but nonetheless can become significant. The impact can be seen in several ways.

Decisions must still be made in situations in which policy and guidelines are not well defined. Because middle management is no longer there in the flattened organization, senior management must become more involved in day-to-day decisions. Senior managers no longer have a middle management to whom they can delegate the decisions. Also, senior management is finding that with middle management eliminated, the flow of information up to management may be cut off. They have no one to assess how things are going in the field, to see where exceptions are occurring, or even to prepare reports.

Personnel who once reported to middle management and looked to them for advice and guidance on how to deal with problems and issues are now finding they have lost access to that information. If there is a need to communicate across the organization, the field personnel must take on this role. If there are new developments, such as a new product or a report on a service problem, field personnel must take the responsibility of finding out about the situation.

Servers—the New Middle Management? This is not to say that flattening the organization is a bad thing. There are valid counterarguments here. For example, senior management benefits from daily contact with the field and with the customer. Field personnel also may be able to get closer to the information they need by getting it themselves. However, the communications and coordination must still be done. Eliminating middle management did not eliminate the need to communicate. These are real problems and, over time, they can be overwhelming in terms of managing a business effectively. It is in meeting the ongoing need for communications and coordination that client/server technology can begin to play a real and very significant role.

The potential benefits of client/server for the flattened, disaggregated organization are that the person in the field, such as a salesperson, can be paired with a workstation. This arrangement makes sense just in terms of allowing the salesperson to do his or her job better by allowing more complete orders to be entered without errors and priced according to corporate guidelines. The workstation provided to the salesperson as a part of a client/server solution allows the salesperson to exchange orders with the home office. The client/server solution has connected the salesperson to the organization as a matter of technical necessity.

This connectivity is key to making the flatter organization work. The first step to communications is connectivity, and that has been achieved through the use of client/server. Many more steps and much effort are necessary to build the processing and data dimension to take advantage of the connectivity, but the first step has been taken.

The intermediate server substitutes for middle-level management. The server does not *become* the middle manager but, rather, when the salespersons are connected via client/server, some of the communications that once occurred through the middle manager can now be flow through the intermediate server. The server can receive the incoming messages, store them, and then forward them to the appropriate person or role in the organization. The message can go upward to higher levels of the organization for guidance on policy or pricing issues, for example. The message can also go across the organization to colleagues seeking information on products or customer background.

Effective communications is an absolute requirement for success in the horizontal or disaggregated organization. Although client/server computing is not by itself the solution, it provides the hardware, network, and intelligence that make those communications happen.

An enterprise still must build the dimensions of processing and data on top of the capability provided by client/server. It might think in terms of such capabilities as E-mail, for example. Much of the commerce of the business is starting to pass through servers as soon as it happens. This provides the opportunity to capture large trends: Products that are selling slowly, for example, or services that are the subject of excessive customer complaint. This can be done at the work group level, and then rolled up to other levels of the organization to monitor the major trends in the business. Suppose, then, that senior management is also connected into the client/server solution. Once again client/server can supply some of the necessary capability to enable management to know what is happening in the business at all levels.

Theoretically, then, client/server can be a tremendous enabler for organizations moving toward more horizontal management structures. The question is whether this theory has ever manifested itself in practice.

In fact, we have now seen the emergence of various groupware or teamware. One of the essential roles of the first generation of these products was to facilitate communications within organizations that had moved toward flatter structures and had to find some means to replace the communication links that had been abruptly lost. Great interest is also growing in what has been termed the "learning organization." Such an organization is able to sustain consistent internal innovation or learning, with the immediate goals of improving quality, enhancing customer or supplier relationships, or more effectively executing business strategy, and the ultimate objective of sustaining profitability. Peter Senge's short definition of the learning organization is one that is continually expanding its capacity to create its future. Such a grand goal cannot easily be achieved without the computing and communications capabilities of client/server.

Downsizing the Organization

Flattening the organization is one way to downsize the organization, in this case by removing middle layers of the organization. As it is most commonly used, however, the term "downsizing" generally means removing people from all levels of the organization. Downsizing has been a major factor in shaping business in the early 1990s, particularly for those organizations looking for quick and dramatic short-term cost reductions.

Downsizing takes the work done by released workers and shifts it to those who remain. It is certain that some of the work that these people were doing was not productive. It is just as certain, however, that some of their work *did* add value to the organization. That important work must now be done by other workers, who probably do not have the time to do it.

We are starting to see evidence of the "downside of downsizing." Unless technology is used to support the performance of those workers who remain in the wake of a downsizing initiative, the organization will be negatively affected. In the US, fewer than half of those companies that have gone through formal downsizing programs since 1988 have improved their profits; only one third of these companies have shown an increase in productivity. Some downsizing cuts have been too severe, and organizations are struggling to fill in the gaps. If the gaps are not filled in, and if cuts continue, inevitably there will come a point at which each cut actually exacerbates costs by causing the business to fail to deliver. Once again, client/server can help this situation.

One of the benefits that a client/server solution can deliver is to allow the individual to do work more quickly. The client/server solution simply allows people to be more effective in doing their work so that they can get more done. Client/server can assist productivity in the obvious way of doing more of the calculations and form filling that is a part of so many business processes. Form-filling metaphors are now used in many graphical user interfaces, ensuring that critical information is always entered correctly, as the business is being transacted.

Indeed, the notion of technology that *supports performance* is now coming to the fore. Old computing and application paradigms were built around the notion of processing transactions. Today, systems can be designed around the paradigm of supporting knowledge workers *as they transact business*.

Client/server can also ensure that the results of transacted business are communicated to others automatically. It can help in terms of making sure that exceptions are put in front of the right people at the right time, so that critical processes are completed when they are needed.

Finally, studies are beginning to show productivity increases from information technology. There are many reasons for these increases. Some analysts believe that only with downsizing efforts did workers actually embrace the technology that had always been there; they embraced it because they no longer had any choice.

Another reason, just as important, is that the client/server computing paradigm has finally begun to penetrate into enough organizations to begin to show an impact. In any event, it is striking that for the first time, computing technology is being seen as making a contribution to the bottom line of the economy.

Employee Empowerment

The final dimension of demassification is employee empowerment. Empowerment can come in two ways: intentionally or unintentionally.

As organizations go through the process of demassification, their workers are going to have greater power, whether they want it or not. Certainly it is better, however, for organizations to, as Steven Covey says in *The Seven Habits of Highly Effective People*, "begin with the end in mind." They must anticipate the needs of their new empowered workers and anticipate how technology can give them the real authority and power they need to work and to make decisions.

Empowered workers find themselves doing things they have never done before and making decisions they have never made before. Because this new environment has probably come about as a downsizing initiative, coworkers they used to seek out for support are not there anymore. And their supervisors are helping somebody else.

Once again, client/server can help this situation. One of the benefits of the workstation is to put in front of knowledge workers the dedicated processing power which, when aligned with the right logic, can make their decisions easier. In these cases the extraordinary dedicated computing power can simply provide the ability to think through complex cases, thus helping workers decide on the best answer or the best course of action to take.

The communications dimension of client/server can also help to empower knowledge workers in today's organization. The communications can put in front of the workers the information that the enterprise thinks they need to perform optimally. This information might be in the form of policies and guidelines on how to conduct the business. It might also be information on the latest prices and delivery dates.

In addition, knowledge workers can use the communications capability to connect to the organization to exchange the knowledge they need with the rest of the organization. One organization uses a knowledge management system called Knowledge Xchange daily to put out requests for information to more than 20,000 consultants. This crucial business support was made possible only because of the capabilities of client/server computing.

Time Compression

Getting products to market is affected by the time required to design and develop products and the time required to create the product that the customer wants. Client/server technology is helping compress time in both these areas.

One of the major factors in reducing the time to design products is the concept of integrated design and manufacturing. Boeing, for example, is using integrated design and manufacturing teams to reduce the typical development time frames for aircraft from four years to three. The bottom-line impact of the annual development costs to deliver a new aircraft is extraordinary.

There are several key challenges to succeeding with this integrated design and manufacturing process. One challenge, though not technical, is perhaps the most difficult: changing the attitudes of design and manufacturing engineers. Historically, in many industries, these groups have not worked sequentially. The design engineer developed the product and the manufacturing engineer determined how to build it. As a consequence, manufacturing was often far more difficult than it would have been had the manufacturing engineers had the opportunity to shape the design as it was being developed.

To achieve an integrated design and manufacturing team these separate groups must be brought together and made to understand the values each brings to the team. If an organization achieves this goal, it must pay attention to the technology needed to support the new interaction among the engineers.

The biggest problem, especially in the case of a company such as Boeing, is that there are literally thousands of engineers who must work together. The results of the design process must be sharable across all the engineers who need the design information. In the case of integrated design and manufacturing, the design is shared with manufacturing engineers as the design engineers develop the product. The manufacturing engineers are evaluating and revising the design to ensure that it can be manufactured. By working together, the two types of engineers are eliminating many of the delays that occurred in the past: when, for example, it was determined in the first assembly process that the product met design specifications but could not actually be assembled for some reason such as the interference or inaccessibility of components.

For these challenges client/server can be part of the solution. First, the task of design is being automated through such software solutions as computer-aided design/computer-aided manufacturing (CAD/CAM). Many CAD/CAM solutions are based on the use of client/server technology for the speed and visualization capabilities that this technology can achieve. Once the results of the design process are captured through the use of CAD/CAM, communications start to fall in place.

The communications capability inherent within client/server can provide the backbone for communicating the results of the design work done by the engineers. However, a great deal of work must still be done to share the information on a timely basis. This includes building into the system the capability to know which engineers need to see what design results and then getting those results to them when needed. The system also needs to ensure that no one else makes changes while the design deliverables are in use or under review. These are not trivial problems, but at least the focus shifts from how to approach the problem to how to deliver the solution.

More broadly, client/server may be able to help in any process that addresses the design and development of products. A product provider can look at automating the process of design and development using the computing capability of client/server. Then the provider can look at sharing the results of the design and development process using the communications capability of client/server. The automation of the integrated process can dramatically reduce time to develop the product for market, and can just as dramatically increase the quality of the first deliverable.

Once the product is developed, it must be sold to customers as they need them. In some cases the sale can be facilitated by client/server just by ensuring that the order is complete and communicated to order fulfillment on a timely basis. If the product is complex, client/server can make a contribution in configuring the order. There are several examples of complex product providers that benefited from the availability of client/server. In such cases, the client side of the solution typically has logic that validates that the proposed product consists of the correct components. Such software solutions are sometimes called configurators.

With complex communication products, this validation can save months of time—time spent, for example, going back to customers to verify one more change because the product is not correct. Doing such validation can represent very complex logic depending on the number of products and the amount of customization a customer may want. It may also get into very sophisticated issues such as evaluating whether a product is restricted from export to certain customers in certain countries.

The immediate impact of this type of capability can be an order of magnitude reduction in the time to develop a product to meet customer needs. It can also mean that when the product is delivered to customers, it is exactly the product they want, configured exactly as they want it. The impression made on the customer—an impression of quality and speed of service—can create a competitive advantage for the manufacturer.

Once again, as the process of creating the order is automated in a client/server-based solution, there is the inherent potential to communicate the order as it is needed throughout the organization. The communications capability can be used to find the quickest source of the product. It can be used to ensure that management located anywhere around the world knows what the customers are interested in. It can also be used to balance manufacturing and inventory levels throughout the organization.

Client/server computing is providing the technology to reduce the time to design and manufacture the product, decreasing the assembly time of products, ensuring that products are completed correctly the first time, and moving information to the parts of the organization where it is needed to deliver the right product on time. All this means that client/server can be a key technology base to speed up time to market, and speed to execution once in the market.

Business Process Reengineering

Reducing the time to market is a specific example of a fundamental shift that is occurring in business today. The shift is called reinventing or reengineering the business process. Although the term has many definitions, this chapter defines reengineering as "fundamental changes in the way of doing business, typically achieved by changing the focus of the business functions."

Typically, reengineering the process represents a shift from a functional focus to a process focus. Exhibit I-2-1 demonstrates. The exhibit provides a conceptual illustration of reengineering the business process for the ordering of plain old telephone service. The vertical columns represent the functional roles that have evolved to provide such a service. These vertical columns are sometimes referred to as functional smokestacks.

At some telephone companies the business process worked somewhat as follows: The first smokestack is customer requirements. In this function, a customer service representative took down such information as what the customer needs and when the service is to be provided. This information was then entered into systems used by the customer requirements function; appropriate forms were filled out by customer requirements and sent through interoffice mail to the provisioning department.

In provisioning, workers considered the availability of equipment and personnel, and the customer's needs were considered to arrive at a date when the service could be provided. This would then be recorded in the systems used by provisioning and some form of requisition would be

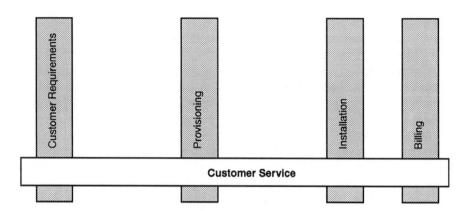

Exhibit I-2-1. Function-to-Process Orientation

moved on to installation. In installation, staff and equipment would be provided for the installation. When that was complete, some form of installation notice would be sent to billing so the customer could be billed for the service.

Nothing is inherently wrong with this individual functional process. The problem is that the customer tends to become lost among all the smokestacks. Many people have had the experience of being bounced and transferred from department to department. When this happens, the customer is lost in the smokestacks.

The fact that customers can become lost is not surprising. Each department in these situations has different goals and different standards by which they are measured. Customer requirements wants to deal with the customer as efficiently and effectively as possible. This department also probably has some product and services sales goals. Provisioning wants to allocate old products and remove them from inventory. This department wants to do optimal loading of personnel so that the minimum number of trips are made. Such objectives may be in direct conflict with a customer who wants phone service tomorrow. Installation has its own problems: sites that are harder to reach and install than expected, products that only a specialist can install, or 10 installs scheduled for a day when only 8 can be done.

This is the downside of a disaggregated business that has not taken the technological steps to reaggregate itself. Each department measures what it considers to be important. Much of the time, these measures have little direct benefit to the customer. One of the results of demassification or disaggregation is a shifting of criteria of success. Prior to demassification, the criteria for success for an organization is often some criteria revolving around making the department run more efficiently. With demassification the focus shifts to what makes the department provide a better product or service to the customer.

Reengineering this process, then, should begin by asking what is to be the fundamental center of the new business process. The new process in this case is going to be the customer and the service provided to the customer. From this new focus, work then proceeds to define how to bridge these many functional smokestacks to build a process that is always focused on the customer. This focus often leads to process flows that can build on what exists already: the legacy systems. But it also ensures that at each step the focus of the process remains on the customers and the service they need. This is not difficult to describe conceptually; even thinking through the new process is not difficult. Reengineering the business, however, is fundamentally difficult to accomplish because it requires a change in the fundamental attitudes of people involved in the new process, who more often than not have many years devoted to the goals and attitudes of the smokestacks.

As an example, consider an individual in provisioning who has spent years balancing work loads and now finds that his focus is supposed to be simply getting the phones to the customers when they need them. This worker must often go through basic changes in thinking about how to do his job and about what constitutes a good job. Reinventing a business is so difficult that very often to succeed there can be no alternative to the change: Desperation is often the mother of reinvention.

If an enterprise recognizes the fundamental need to change and if there is a change management process in place to help business users make the change, the good news is that client/server technology can help in reengineering the business process. First, it can help in the computing dimension. Complex pricing logic and product configuration logic can be placed on the client as described earlier. Furthermore, images, voice, and video can be shown to the business user at the client machine. Sales representatives can make available, for example, the television advertisements currently being shown by the company. This means that the salesperson knows exactly what the customer has seen and is asking for.

Once again, other dimensions of client/server can play into reengineering the business process. For example, as salespersons capture the orders at the beginning of the process, they can use the communications capability to move the orders to the right person or process to do the requisition and then to install. If the order is unusual, they may be able to use the communications capability of client/server to enter into a conversation with all concerned parties in real time to see what can be done to meet customers' needs. Many of the delays—times when pieces of paper are sitting in an inbasket or in a pile on someone's desk—can now be eliminated. Furthermore, if the process is built with the concept of work flow, staff can begin to track where the order is, why it is waiting, and when it is expected to move on.

In addition, they may be able to build these client/server capabilities on a solution with a front-end interface to the legacy systems already running at the site. Some criteria for interfacing with legacy systems are given in Chapter I- 3.

If users can achieve an interface to the legacy systems, the systems, in effect, become functional and data servers to the new generation of systems being built. This interface results in a reduction in build time and, it is hoped, a system that has major components that have been proven over time.

CONCLUSION

It is perhaps in reengineering and reinvention that the full benefits of client/server come to the fore. Computer-intensive capabilities can be combined with the human metaphor and the team metaphor (see Chapter I-3 for more on those concepts) and the backbone of communications to build a new business process. Interface and reuse of legacy all become a part of the potential solution. Perhaps, in a sense, this is not too surprising. The functional smokestacks reflect what could be and was done with the traditional technology of the past 30 years. It may take a fundamental difference in that technology before we can begin to see the potential for change in the business process.

The next chapter looks at some of the implications client/server has for technological change, and at some future developments that will affect client/server solutions.

I-3
Client/Server Computing and Technological Change

How should a business incorporate legacy systems effectively into the overall system? By legacy systems we mean those systems, processes, and procedures that have built up over the last two to three decades of systems building.

For example, several large insurance companies went through an aggressive systems building process in the late 1960s and early 1970s, driven in part by the capabilities of the 360 architecture that was coming into prominence then. The companies continued to build on this technology for the next several years with the advent of online and database management systems (DBMSs). The result is that a remarkable number of sites, not only in insurance but in all other industries, are maintaining applications at the core of the company's operations that were first developed in the early 1970s. To be blunt, these systems are old.

WHY KEEP LEGACY SYSTEMS?

Legacy systems have some remarkable characteristics. First, because they have been around for more than 25 years, they are fairly predictable. When the systems go into production at the start of the day, everyone knows more or less what they are going to do, and an enterprise can base its actions on these expectations.

In being predictable, the systems present little sense of risk. The notion of contained risk is probably the single strongest reason that legacy systems are not replaced. The new system is less predictable and is perceived to be more risky. Legacy systems remain because the enemy we know is often preferable to the one we do not know. Today, there are many predictions about the end of legacy systems, but few of them adequately take into account the staying power of these systems. As Shakespeare put it, it is "a poor thing, but mine own."

Another dimension contributes to the long life of legacy systems.

Legacy systems have often been built by people who then maintained them for most of their careers. Today, these people are reaching retirement age. As they walk out the door, heading for Arizona or Florida, 25 years of knowledge of an application system goes with them. One phenomenon is that retirees are being lured back from the Sun Belt to serve as independent consultants to maintain the application. Someday, however, these independent consultants will have to leave. Many enterprises will then be facing a system containing 25 years of business decisions which few if any people know how to maintain. Going to new systems when no one quite knows the old one is a challenge for many enterprises.

Finally, a lot more than just money is invested in these old systems. The systems represent fundamental knowledge about the company that has built up over the years. Basic business processes are there, as are many other things. There are policies with very complex agreements on adjusting interest rates and returns to the customers. Special fixes are put into processing because of unexpected processing conditions. Understanding all this special, old, or one-time logic is forbidding; deciding how and whether to reimplement is even more of a challenge. Many companies in many industries would prefer to keep the old and evolve from it.

KEEPING THE LEGACY WITH CLIENT/SERVER

At a conceptual level, client/server appears to be an architecture well suited to coping with legacy. In essence, it would be ideal to build the new application logic on the client/server platforms. Then the legacy systems would be used only as servers to provide processing and data needed by the new client/server applications.

Even at an architectural level this scenario plays out well. In essence, communications capabilities can be built on the clients and in the legacy hardware to allow the new application to communicate with the legacy applications. These drivers can be more sophisticated than just passing through the screens from the old systems to the workstations. The data from the screens can be transparently filtered from the incoming screens and used in new processing, often without the legacy application being aware that the changes have happened.

In several cases this strategy has been very successful. In one organization, for example, the source code for the legacy system was lost. The organization was successful in building a new client/server system that displaced the front end of the legacy with new validation underwriting rules and help. This was done without having to change a line of the legacy and while continuing to use it.

So it is feasible to displace the legacy application transparently and to build new logic on the client/server platform. Further, the new application can address all the new developments in business with new logic. It can address new styles of user interaction with the machine through the human metaphor and new styles of interaction with the team through the team metaphor. This is all to the good.

However, the displacement of legacy at the implementation level is not that neat. One of the keys for success in client/server computing is that control of the business process tends to move to the workstation. Often, some of this processing already exists in the legacy systems. Thus one quickly gets into redundant processing and data if the legacy is not altered. Some of the data used to drive the legacy, such as rating data used in insurance underwriting, may need to be stored redundantly in the client/server part of the applications.

Thus, keeping legacy is not necessarily a clean process. It can lead to redundant logic and data that must be maintained as time goes forward.

EVALUATING THE LEGACY SYSTEM

The important question for an organization, then, is whether the continued use of legacy systems is feasible for a specific site. Ultimately, the enterprise needs to carefully evaluate the application portfolio that the site has in place. The evaluation must be based on an understanding that displacing the legacy means redundant logic and data. Although it may seem obvious, it also means that old systems will remain and continue to age. However, continued use does not mean improved use. The evaluation needs to carefully balance the risk of continuing redundant logic and aging systems versus the risk of replacement.

Before doing this detailed evaluation, some major issues can be addressed that may indicate whether the subsequent detailed risk analysis is worth the effort. The first issue to consider is whether the quality of the data on the system is good enough. A new client/server system using legacy data that is incorrect, inconsistent, or obsolete does not improve the situation. Poor data is poor data no matter how pleasant the presentation or how easy it is to share it with others: garbage in, garbage out.

The second issue is whether there is adequate accessibility to the underlying data of the legacy system. For example, if an enterprise is contemplating a highly interactive system and the supporting legacy data is in a sequential file, little can be done about the situation. Even if the data is accessible but only on one key, there may be little hope of building future systems on it. For example, one organization intended to go to a customer focus by building a new front end in client/server. The legacy data was keyed entirely on policy number. The only way to address the problem was to build a customer database with logical pointers to the policy data. Doing so had significant implications in terms of the legacy systems and changes to them.

Finally, an organization needs to look at the underlying computing technology of the legacy system. If, as in one case, the data is maintained through a homegrown DBMS using a now unsupported data access method, continuing with the legacy is a high-risk proposition. Similarly, if the legacy system is based on an online monitor that is no longer available, continued use may only make for bigger problems.

If an enterprise jumps these hurdles, consideration of the continued use of legacy needs to shift to the more detailed risk analysis noted earlier. The decision process is always hard. In most cases there is an almost overwhelming desire to stay with the legacy system rather than making the effort to build a new legacy.

CLIENT/SERVER AND THE NEW COMPUTER USER

With client/server computing comes new computer users: professionals and such knowledge workers as physicians, stock traders, and upper management. These types of business users have not often been seen in business computing environments. Often the clerks in the back office have been entering the results of these professionals' work.

These new business users have some unique characteristics. First, most of them have not used computers much in the past. Second, they tend to be well paid and very often under severe time pressures.

These two characteristics combine to mean that they still do not do computing as computer experts know it. They look at the computer as a source of information and knowledge, and as a means of communication with other professionals. Such users have one final characteristic that must be considered. They are in a position simply to reject a system if it does not meet their needs. The best health care system in the world, for example, utterly breaks down if the doctors decide they do not like it. To provide an effective computing solution for the new business computer user, systems developers must recognize these characteristics in their solutions.

When dealing with such new users, the focus from the beginning needs to be on how the proposed solution can help them in their needs for information, knowledge, and communications. If systems developers meet this need, in time they will be able to address other more traditional data processing concerns (e.g., updating a patient's record).

Second, these new users are under continuous pressure to perform. Any designer who has tried to get an equity trader to sit for three or four hours to define user needs knows what a challenge it is. As a result, designers must work with these new users from the beginning with prototypes and demonstrations of solutions. These users may tolerate some initial prototypes, but fairly quickly systems developers must move to running systems the new user can take into the work environment. In doing this, designers must remember that solutions that *add* work for the worker will fail, even if they are serving a greater good. For example, if a systems solution causes a physician to have to write a patient diagnosis twice—once for the computer and once for the records, that system is likely to fail.

Implications for Systems Developers

The implication here is that these professionals follow a process in their work. The systems designer should begin at the beginning—with what these professionals know and how they work.

The initial automation of this process should address early tasks with breakpoints that make sense from the professional's standpoint. As an example, an early designer's workbench focused on early tasks of systems development such as user requirements and prototyping and then moved through the remainder of the systems development process. From the systems designer's standpoint, early deliverables built a basis for downstream deliverables. This ability to grow the system with the use of the business user over time is one way to use the professional's time without apparent delay.

An implication, however, is that there are often many steps between what the new user does and when some of the traditional information system processing is done today. For example, a physician's first step in a diagnosis may be an interview. There is some distance between this and the delivery of the bill to the patient. Developing systems for these new users means the systems builder must be patient, because the new user is not. For example, as early deliverables are captured, they can be used as a basis for communications with other professionals.

Their drive for information can be another keystone of building systems for these new users. Equity traders spend a great deal of time researching developments in the market. At the same time, much of what they want to know is available through various electronic data services. Often, some straightforward integration can put this information at their fingertips in the morning. For example, one site takes a feed of the *Wall Street Journal* and sends it through various filters to deliver the information to its users. At another site a 24-hour video news feed is provided through the trader workstation using some commercially available video boards.

The new business user's ability to reject a system has several implications for systems developers. Patterning the system on the process to which the professional is accustomed is a key to acceptance. Many of these professionals spent years learning one way to do something, and they are unlikely to change these years of learning for the sake of easier systems building. Second, the system cannot require a long learning curve but must be intuitive from the start or frustration will lead to rejection. Finally, as the system is delivered, the builder must be there with the system, watching the users, listening to their comments, and providing quick changes based on comments.

Making Information Sharing Easier

Given this set of rather severe needs, how can client/server contribute? In many ways, very effectively.

Personal computers have, from their inception, had tools well suited to the needs of rapid prototyping. These tools mean that systems builders can often quickly put in front of the user an initial version of the system with which they can work while it evolves through rapid stages based on feedback from the user. These early versions can also, in a sense, buy time so that an industrial-strength system can be built as user needs begin to stabilize.

At the same time, as the process being automated becomes more complete and there are points where the traditional data processing work can be done, this work can often be triggered with some careful design without direct user interactions. For example, the act of closing a medical case, combined with the history of work done on the case, can be a basis for shipping the correct billing information to the billing system. A well-designed system perpetuates this view.

The need for information, knowledge, and communications is a natural need for client/server to address. As a first step in capturing early deliverables and then proceeding through the entire process, the professional is placed in a position to have the information in a format that can be shared. Then, by taking advantage of the communications dimension, the new user is in a position to share the work with others. For example, a physician may want to do a consultation or a commercial loan officer may want to share a loan portfolio.

In addition, client/server computing means systems designers can think in terms of much richer sets of information to share with the user. For example, a physician might be able to get video of a sonogram done from 1,000 miles away. An engineer may be able to review the visualization of a complex computation of fluid dynamics using client/server. Traders dependent on graphical displays to decide when to move in and out of the market provide another example of how the richness of client/server computing works directly for what they need.

Finally, regarding the potential for rejection, one of the benefits of client/server solutions is that developers can create intuitive interfaces that are natural and easy for the user to learn. Online, context-sensitive help and even online training are becoming an inherent part of client/server solutions under a broad area called integrated performance support (IPS). The IPS approach achieves full power only in a client/server environment.

Thus, depending on perspective, there is either a good deal of opportunity or a lot of problems out there as information technology meets the new business computing user. The fact is, in either case work needs to be done—work different from the work that has been done for the last 30 years. That alone makes it exciting. These are new, quick, and intelligent users. They have a strong sense of quality, and if developers are to meet the challenge of building systems for them, they must be pretty good. In that endeavor, client/server, when applied with intelligence, can provide a winning advantage. Without it, a hard job only gets tougher.

A LOOK AT THE TECHNOLOGICAL FUTURE

Are other computing revolutions on the way? Can we foresee the next real change? If systems developers focus on the broad view that changes in computing technology arise out of changes (1) in the level of interaction and (2) in connectivity, they may be able to anticipate the next technological changes.

Four movements portend to be critical influencers in the field of client/server computing over the next several years:

- The human metaphor.
- Smart systems.
- The universal network.
- The team metaphor.

The following sections look in a general way at each of these critical influencers.

Human Metaphor

The next step in the level of interaction within client/server computing must be *continuous* interaction. Continuous interaction has no discrete starting or stopping point and happens without the user consciously willing the interaction. If this sounds odd, remember that this is the type of interaction that individuals experience with other human beings. For this reason, this type of continuous natural interaction is known as the human metaphor.

The human metaphor describes interaction so natural and unobtrusive that there is no need to learn it or adapt to it. It is so natural that it is invisible. If computing is to meet the demands of the human metaphor, it needs to adapt to all the ways that humans interact with their surroundings. Computing must look to voice, for example, both for recording and for understanding. Indeed, when looking at futurist visions of computing, voice is almost always the primary means of interacting with the machine.

For some applications, physical gesture is the most reasonable and effective means to interact with the machine. Early and rather primitive forms of this style of interaction are found in the mouse. The mouse brings physical gesture to interaction with the machine, but it is not well integrated with the other means of interacting with the computer and as such tends to be as much an interruption as an aid.

A better and more integrated example is the evolving pen computer where the means to record is also the means to note physical gesture. In the future, some of the tools of virtual reality will make their way into interaction with the machine, but only after the devices found in virtual reality technology become much more invisible.

Another aspect of the human metaphor is the ability of technology to integrate multiple forms of information. Humans do this all the time without thinking about it. They read a book, listen to music, watch television, speak to a friend, write a letter, or draw a picture without consciously thinking that they are ending one kind of communication and starting another.

In computing, this capability moves users into the world of multimedia, where image, interactive and recorded video, and all the other ways that individuals acquire and pass on information are essential. These are technologies that have been around for some time, but the tools and facilities to use the technology invisibly are becoming increasingly available. Multimedia is no longer only the concern of expensive specialists, but rather something that everyone can participate in, with remarkably little in the way of special tools.

Smart Systems

The interaction just described is so natural that it becomes invisible. The other requirement of machines so that user interaction can be truly natural is to give the machines the ability to think and react in a humanlike manner. In other words, computers need not only humanlike behavior and actions but humanlike thoughts as well.

Few technologies have had more advances and retreats than applied intelligence, also known as artificial intelligence. The fact remains, however, that we need quality of thought as much as quality of behavior in our computing systems.

Artificial intelligence, or some permutation of that field, must succeed simply because if it fails, business computing will not be able to keep pace with the demands of the future. Such smart systems should lead to systems that are adaptive and flexible.

Universal Network

Changes in the level of interaction, such as those touched on in the section on the human metaphor, are one key dimension of change in information technology. The second key dimension of change is connectivity.

The move from batch processing to online brought with it the wide area network (WAN). Client/server adds the local area network (LAN). The LAN allowed much higher rates of communication and ease of evolving the network in the local office.

Today, client/server is a total communications solution, not just a computing solution. So an essential business requirement is to have the network everywhere and available to everyone at all times. This "anywhere, everywhere" network is known as the universal network.

The sudden emergence of the Internet as a force in the business community reflects the opportunity of the universal network. With the Internet, communications are not only oriented to the needs of the computer user, but they are also available 24 hours a day.

Netcentric computing has brought new technologies to the forefront, especially in the area of external presence and access, ease of distribution, and media capabilities.

The external presence and access enabled by connecting a node to the Internet has opened up a series of opportunities to reach an audience outside a company's traditional internal network users. The Web address is becoming the address through which some pioneering organizations are broadcasting information, collaborating, and even transacting with their clients.

The browser-based application style is offering a new option in distributing functionality to both internal and external users. In traditional client/server computing, distributing an application internally or externally for an enterprise required that the application be recompiled and tested for all specific workstation operating systems. The browser-based application style offers an alternative to this traditional problem.

The use of HTML is providing a method of presenting richer information options for accessing documents as well as traditional data sources. The emergence of plug-ins and some level of standardization of media information formats has made it more possible to support audio and video as appropriate, enabling richer information for Web sites to present. Bandwidth remains an issue, but advances in network technologies and compression continue to make rich, media-enabled applications more feasible on the net.

Although the Internet raises certain concerns, these are matters of implementation and not of need. The need for connectivity is an extraordinary imperative for all systems work over the next ten years. In this context the Internet is a legacy data-oriented communications network. Its universal availability over telephone lines will continue to lead to widespread use. At the same time, its architecture makes it difficult to guarantee delivery, service levels, and unlimited growth. More industry-specific networks and intranets, such as those already used in the automobile and utilities industries, will result.

The growth of the Internet reflects the need for universal networks. At the same time, it is essential to understand that the Internet, as explosive as it is, is actually only a step toward richer and robust universal networks. Much more will follow.

Two other changes in the area of networking are worth noting. One is in easing or overcoming the restriction of always being tethered to the physical network. Most forms of networking now come with this restriction. However, if we are to deal effectively with the next generation of business solutions, it is essential that the network technology be available for the business user when the *user* wants it, not when it is convenient for the network.

The second key change in connectivity is the impact of increasing bandwidth. One can do things on a LAN—moving images, for example—that are not thinkable given the bandwidth found with most WAN technology. Today, we are beginning to see the potential of WAN technology to deliver even greater speeds than LANs. The ability to be connected anyplace, combined with the capability to deliver whatever the business user of the system needs, is something that could provide solutions to problems we do not even recognize we need today.

The Team Metaphor

Much of what has been discussed thus far has dealt with the potential for *technological* change. Just as important, however, is the potential for change in the *business user*.

This does not mean there will be some vital transformation in human nature or human behavior. Human change occurs slowly, often too slowly for the time frames of many business solutions. Nevertheless, there is a change in the type of business user working with computers. Ten years ago stockbrokers did not do computing; today, many trading floors are automated and the brokers know no other way to trade. Executives over the past decade have overcome their initial tendency to view a computer as something that only clerical staff use, and this change has carried over to many professions. Physicians, for example, who once viewed computers as something that only nurses use, are increasingly using computers to research and diagnose cases. Lawyers, too, are now finding computers vital to their work, to verify case histories and research legal precedents. Client/server has expanded the notion of who uses computers. A computer user is now a knowledge worker.

Yet there is another change happening in the business user community. This change is occurring in part because of the computing/communications partnership of the client/server revolution.

One new kind of computer user is not an individual, a single human being, but rather the *team* of individuals that works together to use the solutions that systems developers are providing. The team has emerged in part because client/server technologies and solutions have allowed people to interact over LANs, using the workstation as the basis for input, information sharing, and communications. From this perspective, designers can begin to think of the "team metaphor" as a new computing paradigm. The team paradigm focuses their attention on supporting a wide range of business user needs on the backbone of the client/server solution.

One of the most important needs is for the team to *communicate*. Team communication takes many forms: sharing structured data, sharing business processes, even capturing the most subtle nuances of one person looking to another. The team metaphor means that systems developers will have to deploy all the existing technology and then direct future innovations toward coping with the demands of a team, possibly global, trying to work with tight time and budgets while meeting critical quality goals. It will be a grand problem to solve.

THREE COMMON QUESTIONS FROM MANAGERS

Thus far this chapter has described why users want client/server computing and what it can do to help today's knowledge workers. We have not once stated that client/server computing is easier, quicker, or cheaper. It has not been mentioned because it is not true—or, at least, rarely true. Businesses that undertake client/server solutions for these faulty reasons run the risk of underestimating the effort required.

Is Client/Server Easier?

The user interface for an online monitor has less than 10 types of ways to invoke a program. The majority of programmers never see most of these. A popular graphical user interface (GUI) has more than 500 ways to interact with programs through one application programming interface. Programmers must be able to deal with many of these.

Client/server as described is always a distributed data processing solution. This was hard when it first became popular in the late 1970s. It was so hard then that most developers did it only as a last resort. The languages and tools of client/server are fundamentally different from what developers have known for 25 years. How can it be easier to do something when all the tools and languages one has learned over the past 25 years are obsolete?

Is Client/Server Quicker?

A standard approach for assessing the development effort for traditional systems versus client/server systems is estimating the number of inputs and outputs. The estimating factors associated with screens and windows are essentially the same. The initial conclusion might be that these systems require the same effort. What this method misses is that there tend to be many more windows in a client/server system than screens in a traditional system. Thus the fundamental driver in a client/server system may be two or three times what one finds in a traditional system.

Traditional systems address systems management very completely. Client/server treats systems management in a very fragmentary manner, at least thus far. A guideline for estimating effort is to allow an additional 10% to 40% of the time used for systems development to address system management.

Is Client/Server Cheaper?

When one equates time to money, client/server will not be cheaper in development. Sometimes the point is made that the hardware is much cheaper. Typically, the comparisons are made of price per MIPs. However, the real calculation is price/MIP/person.

If one evaluates this factor for large mainframe servicing, perhaps 1,000 people versus a $10,000 workstation running 100 MIPs, the answer is that the costs of these factors at an engineering level are comparable. Experience in various hardware comparisons, where often the differences were small percentages between price for client/server and mainframe, confirms this point.

If this discussion of price, speed, and ease of development were taken alone, outside the context of this chapter, it would make a convincing argument that client/server is not a good idea. This is clearly not the proper conclusion. Client/server may not always make sense for certain application types, such as batch payroll. In general, however, everyone involved must look past the "easier, quicker, and cheaper" arguments for the real reasons why client/server is a powerful force in business computing.

CONCLUSION

Client/server computing provides many benefits for information system developers, users, and the entire organization:

1. *Increased usability.* GUIs can lead to more usable, intuitive, productive applications.

2. *Improved response times.* Better system response can then lead to more responsive business solutions.

3. *Scalability.* Scalable systems can lead to solutions that expand and contract as business requirements demand.

4. *Improved reliability.* Better reliability can result in reduced downtime and increased system resource availability.

5. *Seamless application integration.* Seamless integration can improve access and usability of all applications required by an end user.

6. *Easier integration of voice, data, and image.* By facilitating the integration of different types of information, system solutions can address the variety of information needs of users.

7. *Simultaneous use of multiple applications.* The ability to use more than one application at a time leads to increased user productivity and reduced business process time.

8. *Increased productivity of professional users.* Better productivity affects both the worker—who feels more satisfied with the job—and the organization, which sees an increase in business processing.

9. *Support for business process reengineering.* Client/server technologies can provide an infrastructure to enable the delivery of applications that support redefined businesses or business processes.

10. *Increased control of, and access to, information.* Client/server solutions improve the information available to end users in support of the business.

11. *Empowerment of end users.* End users who feel more in control of their jobs often participate in developing solutions to their data and processing needs.

12. *More dedicated computing power per user.* Client/server can give users their own, dedicated processing capability.

13. *Exploitation of processor and software strengths and efficiencies.* A business can capitalize on—and share the particular strengths and efficiencies of—different types of processor and software environments (database or print servers, image servers, high-powered number crunching servers).

14. *Support for group or team computing.* Client/server solutions can accommodate and automate applications that support defined work groups working together as a team.

These benefits are being realized today by many organizations around the world. The next chapter relates some of their stories.

I-4
Client/Server Success Stories

This chapter presents success stories of client/server implementation at three international institutions: Deutsche Bank in Germany, YPF SA in Argentina, and the Department of Social Security in the United Kingdom. The technical environments of the three case study companies are outlined so that readers may draw lessons and comparisons for their own organizations from the challenges, solutions, and scenarios described.

FINANCIAL SECTOR CASE STUDY: DEUTSCHE BANK

With 2,400 offices in more than 50 countries, Germany's leading financial institution, Deutsche Bank, ranks as one of the largest and most influential banks in the world. More than 70 offices located throughout Asia and the Pacific Rim—17 countries in all— make it this region's best represented European bank.

One of Deutsche Bank's key businesses in this hub for international trade is the financing of import and export ventures. With work volume reaching 300 transactions processed daily in Singapore alone, the bank knew it needed to streamline its complex documentary credit and collection procedures, the heart of trade finance.

The regional head office in Singapore, responsible for coordinating Deutsche Bank's Asia/Pacific operations, concluded that new information technology would provide efficient alternatives to the paper shuffling and number crunching required by its current methods. As it turned out, automating these manual tasks and integrating data sources using advanced information technology achieved more than streamlined processes. (See Exhibit I-4-1 for a summary of Deutsche Bank's technical environment.)

By gaining more control over information access and processing, Deutsche Bank not only executes transactions faster but also manages risk better and delivers more personalized service. By implementing its solution using a client/server architecture that adapts readily to new

Hardware

Database server:	NCR 3000 Series
File server:	Compaq SystemPro 486/33
Clients:	Compaq 486 PCs

Software

Database server:	NFS UNIX
Clients:	MS-DOS and Microsoft Windows 3.1

Database	ORACLE7
Network	Banyan Vines
Communications	TCP/IP, Oracle SQL*Net
Development Tools	C, Microsoft Development Tool Kit, Oracle applications development software

Exhibit I-4-1. Deutsche Bank's Technical Environment

---

business conditions, Deutsche Bank has secured a long-term return on its technology investment.

The solution created through this partnership between Deutsche Bank and Andersen Consulting, the Trade Finance system, proved so successful it is now being customized for Deutsche Bank's New York, Tokyo, and London offices, and has been packaged for sale to other banks as VISION Trade Finance.

Key Challenges

Around the world, financial services are seeing increased regulations, tighter margins, and more demanding customers. As a result, businesses such as Deutsche Bank are striving to improve work flow, reduce risk, and strengthen client relationships.

Streamline Procedures. At Deutsche Bank, trade finance officers typically process as many as 300 transactions every day. These staff people must review, verify, approve, and finally transmit numerous documents for each transaction: letters of credit, customer and bank correspondence, import and export bills.

Performed manually, these tasks required a great deal of time to complete. To deliver the level of service expected by customers and enforced by regulators such as the International Chamber of Commerce—an organization dictating international trading practices, Deutsche Bank clearly needed faster, more efficient processing methods.

Integrate Work Flow. Finance terms, credit histories, exchange rates: Trade finance transactions involve many kinds of information gathered from many sources, not only internal systems but import and export agents and advising and issuing banks as well. After obtaining the necessary information, staff must process and then verify it against customer checking limits, or have it reviewed by other bank officers.

Collecting and processing all this information made for a complex set of manual procedures and relatively long processing time. Deutsche Bank needed a system that placed all information within easy reach of the user, allowing more timely access for faster service, and ensuring tighter information control for better risk management.

Employ Leading-Edge Technologies Intelligently. In rethinking its strategy for processing trade finance transactions, Deutsche Bank undertook an especially ambitious course. To streamline the flow of documents and improve information access and control, the bank decided to combine organizational changes with one of the first client/server computing solutions ever implemented for trade finance in Asia/Pacific.

A client/server solution made sense. Enterprises such as Deutsche Bank remain competitive in volatile markets partly by creating new products and services. This is also true of technology providers, which continuously advance their products through new releases and upgrades. To accommodate dynamic market forces and the rapid pace of technology evolution, Deutsche Bank required a solution designed for change—one robust enough to meet current challenges, and flexible enough to incorporate future products and assimilate future technologies.

Client/server architectures accommodate change through modularity. That is, work is distributed across different components of the architecture, which can be replaced or upgraded in isolation. Client/server applications are equally modular, allowing elements affected by changes to be modified without affecting the entire system.

Deutsche Bank selected some of the most sophisticated client/server technology available: graphical user interface (GUI)- based workstations, open systems servers, and a relational database management system. However, although these state-of-the-art technologies promised competitive advantage, many products chosen were still in beta-level development when the project began. Moreover, all were dramatically different from the technology the company currently used. So, simply being innovative was not enough. Deutsche Bank required an intelligent, managed plan for implementing its innovative system and rolling it out to users.

Reflect Global Perspective. In the Asia/Pacific region, Deutsche Bank's trade finance transactions span a complex network of national cultures with diverse regulatory requirements. Banking practices in Hong Kong, for example, mean charges and commission are posted in both foreign and local currencies. The Sri Lankan government imposes a business turnover tax on certain types of income, while India follows its own local regulations in handling local bills discounting.

To support a business environment where even business holidays vary widely from country to country, the new system had to reflect the global dimensions of Deutsche Bank's business.

Solution

The Trade Finance system, built on a client/server architecture and employing the latest protocols, tools, and open standards, is a leading-edge solution that enabled Deutsche Bank to bring together trade finance operations and technology to achieve its business strategies.

Advanced Technologies: A Flexible Architecture. Trade Finance was implemented in a client/server environment, powerful enough to support current requirements, and flexible enough to adapt to technological change. The Trade Finance technical architecture includes the following:

- Intelligent client workstations running Windows 3.1 and MS-DOS provide full GUI capabilities.
- A UNIX-based database server running ORACLE7 provides the required data management services.
- A file server houses all of the programs used by Trade Finance applications.
- A Banyan Vines local area network (LAN) connects clients to server systems. Oracle SQL*Net configured with Transmission Control Protocol/Internet Protocol (TCP/IP) communications software enables clients to communicate with the database server.
- A central host banking system contains the logic blocks that update and access other banking databases.

To accommodate the evolution of beta-level technology in the course of building the system, architects isolated capability, structured query language routines, for example, in layered modules that can be modified without affecting the rest of the system. The client/server architecture also provides scalability. The number of additional users and programs the system will support, for example, is limited only by the size and configuration of the servers.

Integrated Work Flow and Data Access. The Trade Finance system supports the full range of functions involved in the life cycle of trade finance transactions, including:

- *Documentary credit.* Letter of credit and export letter of credit.
- *Collections.* Import and export bills collection
- *Guarantees.* Shipping guarantees.
- *Negotiations.* Important bills negotiations and usance import bills.
- *Bills financing.* Trust receipts, export bills negotiable and purchase, packing credit.

Trade Finance users can access all the information and facilities they need to complete these transactions from a single application interface. For example, an online inquiry function retrieves information about products and customers in real time, so that users can create a complete picture of the bank's relationship with a customer.

Trade Finance also comes equipped with the text-processing capabilities often required to complete transactions, letting users format and print the necessary correspondence and create and transmit SWIFT and Telex communications from within the system.

Although designed to function as a standalone solution, the system also supports an online, real-time interface between workstation clients and the Trade Finance central host computer, so users can retrieve information about account balances and customer credit limits, or update account entries on the central host in batch or in real time.

The system also supports an asynchronous interface between the Trade Finance database server and the central host, so that these systems can exchange information about currency exchange rates, for example, or interest rates, general ledger account information and static customer data. Seamless integration with another Deutsche Bank system, Electronic Banking, means the bank's corporate customers access information easily from their own locations.

Automatic Data Processing. The Trade Finance system automatically handles many tasks once done manually, reducing paperwork, preventing processing errors, and eliminating repetitive tasks. Users can even save frequently used phrases and simply insert the stored text rather than retyping it.

For example, Trade Finance automatically computes default charges according to user-defined parameters and automatically validates field-, page-, and transaction-level information before saving or transmitting it. It also performs automatic online, real-time credit checking against customer and drawee limits and country exposure and automatically updates account balances and generates payment orders, customer advises, and other messages.

User-Centric Design and Training. Because the Trade Finance system is so different from the previous environment, its developers took care to design a system that was easy to use as well as effective, so new users can focus on their work while learning the new environment. The windowed interface, for example, displays multiple screens at once, making it easy to perform cross-function procedures. A context- sensitive field prompts display lists of valid entries for users to choose from, another example of simplifying work while reducing error. Online help displays alternative entries when field validation fails.

In addition to instructor-led training, the Trade Finance system also offers a computer-based training program. This program is a self-guided, interactive training tool that participants complete at their own pace. The courses are modular, so participants can select only the training topics they need, and the program allows them to edit sections as they wish.

Benefits

Investment Protection. Designing a client/server architecture using the latest protocols, tools, and standards ensures that Deutsche Bank is positioned for the future. The client/server model is a cost-effective solution for distributed processing that effectively uses the resources and processing power delivered by today's best software and hardware.

The modular system design and architecture also provides flexibility for Deutsche Bank, allowing it to easily integrate the applications and technologies it needs now and those it may adopt in the future. For example, the bank can integrate the Trade Finance system with any centralized host system, and the front-end processing and user interface can remain largely the same regardless of the host technology. This flexibility allows Deutsche Bank to incorporate other platforms within the Trade Finance system according to business requirements with only minimal development effort.

Increased Productivity. In addition to being more flexible, the technology underlying the Trade Finance system delivered a remarkable boost to work output and efficiency. Business volume could increase without needing to increase staff, simply by adapting work flow/handling procedures. The easy-to-use graphical user interface, simplified data entry, and automated procedures contributed to productivity gains exceeding 20% within the first three months at the branches that first implemented the new system.

Improved Customer Service. The same capability that helps make users more productive also means bank customers receive faster, more personalized customer service. The information required for customer transactions is always on hand, easy to process, and highly accurate.

Tighter Control; Better Risk Management. The Trade Finance system also gives Deutsche Bank more control over the accuracy and security of its information resources. One feature ensures that transactions are always reviewed and approved by a second user. Online validation, auditing, and exception reporting are some of the features that aid information management. Other features—online limits controls, automated country exposure checking, drawee limits validation, and realized balance updates—help the bank manage risk by providing it with more accurate statistics on its exposure.

Lessons Learned

Prepare Users for New Technology. The Trade Finance system, with its graphical display and mouse-driven operations, was a major change from the previous character-based applications. To prepare users for this new technology, the engagement team first identified key end users to test the new system and provide feedback. These users were then trained to instruct their colleagues and provide valuable support during the critical period after system rollout. Instructor-led training programs helped to ensure that users understood the new system before they had to use it.

Address System Architecture Early in the Project. Although the client/server-based system provides Deutsche Bank with a competitive edge, it is also more complicated to develop and maintain than conventional systems because of the higher number of components and interactions involved.

At the time of development, many tools and components used by the Trade Finance system were emerging technologies that required extensive testing. To minimize development risks, the project team invested the time required to design a sound system architecture in the beginning. This architecture layers major system elements so that each component is shielded from changes in other components; thus modifications to one component are less likely to affect others.

This architecture also enhances the project team's productivity and system quality by identifying common requirements and approaches, and encouraging consistency among application structure, behavior and interfaces. As a result, the system is easier to build, use and maintain.

GAS AND OIL CASE STUDY: YPF SA

The world's largest initial public stock offering of 1993 involved a Buenos Aires company known as YPF SA, previously the state gas and oil company of Argentina. More than 125 million shares in YPF were traded internationally, raising more than $3 billion.

To position itself for the more competitive private sector, YPF took a good look at critical business functions. A successful initial public offering was critical to the Argentina government, which hoped to use the proceeds to refinance the country's social security system. As a privately held company, YPF would need to comply with more demanding requirements for financial reporting and billing, no easy task considering its farflung production and refinery operations.

YPF decreed major changes to accounting and commercial functions: reorganizing operations, downsizing staff, reengineering systems, and implementing advanced client/server technologies. To execute these strategies, rearchitecting YPF's manual accounting procedures and a billing system based on legacy system technology seemed like obvious tactics. But moving from batch processing to a distributed online architecture raised many issues. How is data integrity maintained? How is data moved through the network? How is the network itself managed?

To help YPF meet its goals, the systems developers mobilized an international team of more than 250 consultants from 11 countries and 22 different offices. The technology integration team consisted of 55 advanced technology experts from its worldwide organization, Technology Integration Services. Working with YPF personnel, this team designed and implemented an advanced solution for distributing YPF's accounting, commercial, and hydrocarbon management applications.

The infrastructure underlying this solution is a technical architecture combining an enterprise network for data transport, communications middleware for data management, and tools and procedures for distributed system management. This architecture was essential to improving the productivity of the accounting function: Monthly financial results are now reported 80% faster. YPF also achieved significant payback in billing efficiency and hydrocarbon inventory control.

Besides assisting YPF's migration to the new environment, the architecture team is now attempting to streamline YPF's development and production operations. (See Exhibit I-4-2 for YPF's technical environment.)

Hardware

Server:	IBM AS/400, RS/6000
Clients:	IBM PCs

Software

Server:	OS/400, Lakeview Mimix, HelpSystems Robot, DCS PM Plus, Silvon Implementor for Migration and Software Distribution
Clients:	MS-DOS and MicroSoft Windows

Networks   X.25, SNA/SAA Wide Area Network (WAN); Scientific Atlanta TDMA, Hughes SCPC VSAT Terminals, Intelsat V Token Ring local area network (LAN) migrating to Ethernet

LAN Internet   Cisco routers, Northern Telecom Passport bandwidth managers, Synoptics Intelligent concentrators

Remote Data Access   Xcellenet NMS Server and Client

Data Management   OS 400 Query Facility and ORACLE7

Systems Management   Candle CT—Automation Center/400, Omegamon, HP OpenView, Peregrine PNMS, Help Systems Robot Scheduler, Save, Monitor

Development Tools   LANSA, RPG, Microsoft Visual Basic

Exhibit I-4-2. YPF SA's Technical Environment

Key Challenges

Automated Production Environment. Because each business division at YPF must collect data from multiple field units, continuing to gather this information manually seemed an unreliable way to satisfy SEC requirements for financial reporting. A more reliable and efficient method appeared to be automating the production batch and data distribution architectures to transfer information automatically between remote units and their business division data centers. To accomplish this, YPF would have to replace its centralized, manual procedures for reporting accounting data with distributed, automated methods.

Synchronize Distributed Data. However, the packaged solution YPF had chosen for its accounting and commercial applications was engineered for centralized operations. Implementing these applications in a distributed environment required a solution for updating and synchronizing remote AS/400 databases automatically, involving a high volume of asynchronous record updates across the network.

Manage Network Operations. In fact, YPF discovered that basing a key business function on distributed technology involved many chal-

lenges. Some challenges were standard. For example, each network location had to continue operating independently in the event of network
failure. Software changes had to be distributed to many remote network
sites.

The newly designed satellite network increased by 32 the number of
backbone satellite links supporting the accounting and commercial applications. YPF required a more comprehensive network and systems
management solution for monitoring faults and managing network-
related problems.

Manage Change. Radically changing a business function as critical
as accounting required a sophisticated change management strategy.
YPF needed a structure, including tools and methods, for making a seamless transition to new processes and technology and long-term training
and support resources to maintain successful operations after the initial
rollout. The cultural shift involved in implementing this degree of change
was a substantial challenge at YPF.

Solution

To satisfy the new requirements for accounting and commercial operations, the systems developers devised a technology infrastructure consist-
ing of the following main elements.

Enterprise Network. The enterprise network is a 32-link VSAT
satellite network combined with microwave backups, running over the
X.25 network protocol. The enterprise network enables YPF to transport
data quickly between remote YPF operating units and their respective
business divisions. The wireless technology, still in its early stages in
Argentina, required sophisticated planning, so the network design process included extensive sizing, risk assessment, and testing.

Communications Middleware. This middleware is system-level
software that synchronizes the information in all databases throughout
the AS/400 network. This information comes from accounting and commercial master files located on the central AS/400 nodes. Master file data
is replicated to remote AS/400 nodes as changes are posted. The middleware implementation for data distribution through this master file replication approach used LakeView Technology's Mimix Hi-Net product.

Operations Management. Managing distributed operations required the implementation of tools and procedures to monitor network
and systems incidents, manage problems, change configurations, and pro-

vide service to end users. This operations management capability was provided through:

- An AS/400–based help desk.
- A software distribution and version control package: Silvon Implementor.
- A utility that monitors network faults and performance and forwards network alert messages across the network. HP OpenView was implemented to monitor network components supporting SNMP agents. Element managers Cisco Works and UB Net Director are used for remote configuration management of routers and hubs.
- A utility that performs automatic backups and tape functions.
- A batch architecture and function for automating production scheduling, using Help Systems Robot job scheduler.
- A function for managing systems and network performance.

Technology Assimilation. A new set of procedures, functions, and organizational structures for managing the distributed processing environment implemented by an international change management effort. This effort also included a postproduction period of system enhancement; the systems developers supported and managed system operations during the early implementation, participating less as YPF personnel gained experience.

Benefits

The new generation of distributed applications also achieved significant performance gains. YPF's efforts to prepare itself for the competitive private sector succeeded in the following ways:

- YPF no longer relies on time-consuming manual procedures, so key accounting and commercial processes now occur in a reduced time frame, significantly reducing the amount of user assistance required. User control has increased with the new systems and technology infrastructure.
- Synchronizing database files means new data is available immediately throughout the enterprise. Data integrity and reliability have improved the speed of decision making. Transferring files automatically ensures that remote data is always available at business center divisions in time for day-end and month-end reporting. As a result, the new accounting system cut the time required to report monthly financial results by 80 percent.

- The new billing system significantly improved the productivity of processes for reconciling accounts and tracking inventory.
- The time taken to determine and valuate current hydrocarbon inventory was reduced from over 18 days to 5 days.
- Techniques for managing software changes throughout the distributed network saved vast amounts of time during the debugging phase of implementation. Changes could be distributed overnight to all 30 network locations. The help desks in the upstream, corporate, and business units connect users to the correct support personnel in a more efficient, structured manner.
- Strategically, the new architecture positions YPF with a foundation to support new business growth. The infrastructure implemented for the accounting and commercial systems is the basis for a more rapid response to changing market forces. The technical architecture has become an "information highway" for future success.

GOVERNMENT CASE STUDY: UK DEPARTMENT OF SOCIAL SECURITY

The Department of Social Security (DSS) in the United Kingdom is the central organization for the country's social security system, providing cradle-to-grave support for millions of British citizens. DSS also collects national insurance contributions via payroll deductions and pays out the associated benefits. Not surprisingly, the operation is huge and complex: 80,000 employees in 500 branches administer more than 35 programs, including retirement pensions, income support, long-term disability benefits, and child benefits.

The Employment Service, with 1,500 offices and 25,000 employees nationwide, pays out unemployment benefits. Thus, in total, the two department have 2,000 offices that work with 10 million pensioners, 5 million people on income support, 2 million unemployed, 285,000 on family credit, and 40 million national insurance contributors.

In the early 1980s, it became clear to DSS that its processes for delivering benefits were coming under increasing strain, thus compromising the quality of service to beneficiaries. Manual methods and aging computer systems were hampering its work. There were no computers in local offices.

In response to these challenges, DSS devised a revolutionary program. It did not simply consider using new information technologies to patch up the problems but went to the heart of the business processes of the two departments, reengineering and automating them, where appropriate, for optimum efficiency and effectiveness. The program, "Operational Strategy," is aligning departmental strategy with its people, technology, and processes. It has improved DSS's delivery process and given

Data Centers	ICL 3980 and SX processors
Operating System	ME (ICL), UNIX, MS/DOS
Languages	COBOL, C, Ingres 4GL, ADS
Network	X.25 WAN and Ethernet LANs running under OSI Transport Layers 3 and 4
Local Office Systems	British Telecom and Bull Terminal System servers and UNIX servers (IBM RS6000, ICL DRS3000, SNI WX 200) connected to dumb terminals and MS/DOC PCs

Exhibit I-4-3. DSS's Technical Environment

---

it a platform for rethinking and restructuring the ways it wants to work into the next decade. (See Exhibit I-4-3 for DSS's technical environment.)

Client/server computing provided the technological vision that made it all work for DSS. The long-term intent of DSS was to focus on the whole person receiving benefits—to move away from older methods of processing claims on a benefit-by-benefit basis. With the help of information technology, DSS wanted to be able to display on one screen a "snapshot" of a person's history of contributions and benefits. DSS also wanted to manage its relationship with the claimant based on the view of the individual as the whole person.

The technological environment at DSS meant that DSS was able to leapfrog the online generation of computer systems. In the late 1960s, DSS had some of the most sophisticated batch systems in the world for administering pensions and maintaining national insurance records. In the 1970s, these systems were extended with some online query facilities but no online updating. Several of the major programs—income support and incapacity benefits, in particular—did not get automated. Moving to client/server, therefore, was a huge step for DSS.

Technical Components

The technical components of the program can be considered as three pieces: the major applications, a technical infrastructure, and the services management center.

Major Applications. Applications systems at DSS include family credit, income support, retirement pensions, unemployment benefits, disabled benefits, and the departmental central index.

The major change in providing income support is that employees no longer rely on paper. This shift has not only changed how they deal with claimants but also what information claimants receive from the department. The information is more complete, and received more quickly. This new system has also changed supervisors' jobs in that they no longer need to spend time rechecking the work of their people. Complex calculations, as well as the status of each case, are now handled by the computer. The system dispatches 74,000 payments a day. The majority of benefits are distributed through 20,000 post offices in booklets of six months' worth of checks that recipients cash each week. Automated bank deposit is also used.

The new retirement pension system enables local office staff to create records online and to make pension awards. Previously, these functions were handled offline at a remote site, so that local office staff faced long delays in getting the information they needed. In addition, the agency has developed a knowledge- based system for forecasting pension entitlements. When these calculations were done by hand, it could take from four to nine months to get an answer because the request was not a high priority. The new system produces a personalized written analysis in 15 minutes, and requestors now receive a reply within eight days. The system handles 99.5% of the cases automatically. It is saving the government $1.6 million a year.

Technical Infrastructure. The "whole person" strategy at DSS depends on significant use of information technology. The Operational Strategy contains four main components in its technical infrastructure: a central index, branch office systems, a countrywide Open Systems Interconnection (OSI) network, and four main data centers.

The Departmental Central Index. To achieve its goal of focusing on the whole person, the department created a central index containing the name, address, and national insurance number of 55 million people, as well as the benefits they receive and the issuing office. This central index is accessible from 40,000 terminals in the 1,700 branches.

The Branch Office Systems. A local server in each branch serves 40 to 50 terminals and workstations on a local area network. The local server in turn acts as a client linking via an X.25 network to all four data centers. In addition to being communication servers, they also store the screen templates and local validation used by the applications to reduce communication volumes over the X.25 network.

The OSI Network. The Strategy Data Network uses those OSI protocols that have been fully defined and implemented by vendors. The network also maintains strategic conformance with the UK government's OSI profile (UK GOSIP). The X.25 wide area network and Ethernet LANs all run under OSI, up to Transport Layer 4. Other important protocols—such as X.400 and TCP/IP—have also been implemented in the networks.

Above Layer 4, DSS wrote its own OSI-like protocol because no OSI terminal service protocol existed at the time of development. This protocol makes efficient use of the network and also supports bulk printing at local offices, message broadcasting, and—security permitting—accessing a variety of services from each terminal.

Data Centers. Together, the department's data centers house 83 mainframes. The Operational Strategy applications were developed and run on these mainframes, rather than on distributed workstations or servers, so that consistency would be maintained across the local offices. Various facilities management firms handle the media and output at the centers. They, in turn, are managed by DSS systems management staff at the services management center, from where mainframe operations and technical support are run.

The Services Management Center. The third piece of the technical structure is technology management. To coordinate the various technical support aspects of the Operational Strategy, the services management center was established. Center staff are also in charge of data center and network management. Management is pushing to create "lights out" data centers—that is, data centers that need very few operators. Programs have been written to monitor and operate the machines remotely in the four centers.

With the department's core business functions now heavily dependent on computing power, providing high-quality service across the networks is critical. Automated systems log each technical problem as it arises and help with speedy resolution. Service levels are reviewed constantly, and automated configuration management tools ensure that all system changes are processed quickly outside of critical working hours.

The DSS services management center represents one of the largest and most comprehensive mainframe, network, and terminal management systems operational in the OSI world today. The center also provides a single point of help for users and has implemented a "customer care" program, which links local offices with the computer centers to guarantee that the centers stay in touch with the needs of the local offices.

Benefits

Ultimately, the chief benefit of the Operational Strategy at DSS is improved service to British citizens. But other more specific benefits have also been realized. For example, DSS can now:

- Assess benefits more accurately.
- Handle cases more quickly.
- Improve communications with citizens.
- Respond to inquiries more quickly.
- Reduce the number of appeals.
- Decrease fraud.
- Reduce staff numbers.
- Decrease double handling of cases.
- Eliminate routine tasks.

CONCLUSION

The organizations discussed here, and countless others like them, succeeded with their client/server implementation projects because they took a systematic, organized, methodical approach. In short, they took an architectural approach. Section II of this book takes readers through the relevant architectures crucial to successful client/server delivery.

Section II
Client/Server Architectures and Technologies

S ection II takes the reader through the major architectural components and technologies—and the related decision points—when implementing client/server computing. Its focus is on the *what*—what the IT manager's options are and what decisions are critical—rather than the how.

The intended audience is chief information officers, chief technology officers, project leaders, or lead architects who must identify the critical architectural components needed for client/server. Specifically, this section covers:

- Components of a technical architecture—including overviews of the development and operations architectures.
- Hardware platform decisions—including processor and operating system options.
- Choices in graphical user interfaces.
- Software programs and their functionality—from integrated performance support services to communications services, information access (including database) services, transaction services, and work flow services.

II-1

An Architectural Framework for Client/Server Computing

Chapter I-3 noted that client/server computing is usually not faster, easier, or cheaper than traditional computing solutions. Justifications for making the move to client/server, therefore, have to focus on the major benefits delivered to users and to the entire business organization. Client/server is the technological enabler for many management initiatives that currently have an impact on the modern organization (e.g., reengineering, flatter reporting structures, downsizing, and worker empowerment).

PRIMARY RISKS OF CLIENT/SERVER COMPUTING

However, client/server development also carries with it certain risks that an organization must anticipate and deal with. Organizations must ensure that their investment in this new technological solution brings an adequate return.

This section identifies the primary risks of client/server computing.

More Complex Development and Maintenance

A number of factors contribute to the complexity of client/server solutions:

- Client/server applications incorporate sophisticated graphical user interfaces (GUIs). GUIs are usually event driven rather than hierarchical. They are interactive and require more complex logic than traditional terminal (e.g., 3270) style interfaces.
- Although numerous fourth-generation language (4GL) development tools exist, at least some portion of most client/server applications must be developed in third-generation (3GL) languages such as CO-

BOL and C. Communications, GUI, and other demands may need to be addressed in these languages.

- Client/server applications have to "cooperate" (i.e., communicate) with other applications. Client/server systems communication code must establish communication connections, ensure that messages are sent and received correctly, manage errors, and handle any required data translation. Such logic is not often in the skill set of typical programmers and designers.
- The skills required for development, installation, and support of client/server systems are hard to find.

More Difficult Operations Support

Operations support for client/server systems is more difficult than for traditional systems. The increased complexity of operations support, including hardware and software configuration management, is directly related to the number and location of distributed nodes. If a system has 100 remote nodes, it is more difficult to ensure that they are at the same software and hardware versions than it is with two local nodes.

In addition, data backup/restore must now occur at multiple locations, and support for hardware, software and communications problems must also be provided locally at multiple sites.

More Complex Data Security

When data is distributed, protecting that data becomes more difficult. Intelligent workstations are inherently less secure than minicomputers and mainframes. The effort required to maintain an equivalent level of data security, therefore, increases.

New Distributed Data Update and Refresh Strategies

Most client/server systems incorporate multiple copies of the same data. This requires logic to ensure that data values in each of those copies are consistent. For example, if a user working off server A wants to change a "balance due" field, how and when will this change be reflected on servers B and C?

Increased Risks Associated with End-User Computing

Because end users in a client/server environment are more likely to develop applications, and because these applications are increasingly more sophisticated, the risks associated with these applications become more important. Because they are not professional developers, end users may produce applications that

- Lack sufficient restore/recovery features.
- Lack required technical and training documentation.
- Do not adhere to standards and are difficult to use and support.
- Are mission critical but not part of a disaster recovery plan.
- Have no resources for ongoing maintenance and support.

Moreover, an increase in the volume of end-user computing may result in the following:

- Duplication of hardware, software, and data.
- Misuse of human resources (e.g., a salesperson may spend more time developing a tracking system than making sales).
- Increased organizational fragmentation.

Increased Susceptibility to Viruses and Malicious Users

Again, this risk is directly proportional to the number of nodes in a distributed system. Each workstation is a potential point of entry for a virus or a malicious hacker.

Higher Communications Loads

Client/server applications must communicate with each other. This is accomplished over communications networks. For a networked system to work well, accurate estimates of the amount of network traffic must be determined. This is often difficult because, as the knowledge and popularity of newly released applications increase, application use (and network traffic) increases. Applications designed with communication speeds in mind may, therefore, end up being "communications bound." In addition, there are not many tools available that model new-age computing communication loads.

High Initial Cost of Hardware and Software

Client/server computing hardware and software costs are often perceived to be higher than they actually are. An initial monetary outlay is often required for client/server solutions. Sometimes, this cost is attributed to the first client/server application to be developed. In reality, it should be divided among all the applications that are developed for that hardware/software platform.

Initial GUI Learning Curve

Because some end users are more familiar with a block-mode, full- screen interface, they need to adapt to a GUI environment. Although this transition is not usually difficult, it must be identified and managed.

Missed Opportunities

Because client/server systems are composed of hardware and software that is continually being improved, it is often difficult to stop waiting for enhancements. Many development teams become "paralyzed," waiting for the next release of some component which promises to facilitate the installation process or enhance the final product.

Lack of Standard Operating Environment

There are many popular operating system and window manager options that can be used to develop workstation applications. Currently it is not clear who will survive and become dominant players and managers. (However, see Chapter IV-1, "Future Architectures and Technologies," for one view.) The risk is in choosing a combination that ends up with little or no support in the long run and requires future migrations of applications and data.

Increased Complexity of User ID and Password Strategies

Because client/server systems require the use of multiple computers, user ID and password strategies become more complex. For example, a security system on one computer may require password changes more frequently than another. Or, maximum and minimum password lengths may conflict on different systems. Even if these issues are not present, the maintenance of security information on multiple platforms is difficult.

THE NEED FOR ARCHITECTURES

The risks outlined in the previous discussion illustrate the need for architectures as crucial aspects of client/server development. An architecture is a proven mechanism and an approach that can be used to isolate and mitigate the risks of delivering client/server applications now and into the future.

According to the Gartner Group, an architecture is "a formal specification of how a computer solution will be organized." Gartner sets forth seven characteristics of a successful architecture:

1. Delimitation of the problem to be addressed.
2. Decomposition of the solution to components with clearly assigned responsibilities.
3. Definition of interfaces, formats, and protocols to be used between the components. These should be sufficiently clear and robust in order to permit asynchronous development and ongoing reimplementation of the components.
4. Adequate documentation to permit compliance by implementers.
5. An auditing mechanism that exercises the specified interfaces to verify that specified inputs to components yield specified results.
6. An extendibility mechanism to enable response to changing requirements and technologies.
7. Policies, practices, and organizational structures that facilitate adoption of the architecture.

THE ENTERPRISE INFORMATION ARCHITECTURE (EIA)

What are the components of an effective architecture? The Enterprise Information Architecture (EIA) framework provides a starting point for understanding what is meant by the various architectures under consideration. The EIA framework contains seven layers (see Exhibit II-1-1):

- The *environment* layer entails those factors that influence the business requirements and technical layers. These factors may be either internal (e.g., profitability) or external (e.g., government regulation and market competition).
- The *business requirements* layer addresses the business needs of the organization. Both the environment layer and the business requirements layer are mainly concerned with business-level processes, strategies, and directions. The layers below are mainly concerned with the information technology to support the business. The business requirements give key input and guidelines on how to define the lower layers. The link from business requirements to the information technology layers is crucial to a successful EIA.
- The *data architecture* layer consists of a high-level data design that describes the structure of an enterprise's data needs in terms of entities and relationships between entities. The structure and relationships of data entities can be used to define the basic relationships of business functions and applications.
- The *applications architecture* layer defines the applications that must exist to support the business functions and their relationships. It also addresses any issues about distributed data processing.

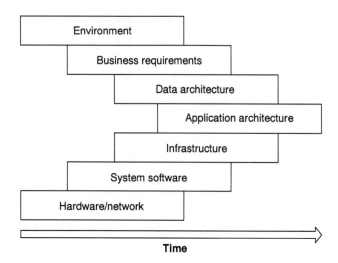

Exhibit II-1-1. Enterprise Information Architecture

- The *infrastructure* layer deals with those components of an architecture that can be used by multiple applications and that are developed and maintained within the enterprise. Usually, these common technical components help support the applications architecture. This layer also includes the infrastructure of the organization that manages the architecture definition and design and its technical components.
- The *systems software* layer encompasses the software and standards obtained from and maintained by outside vendors (e.g., a database management system).
- The *hardware/ network* layer deals with central processing units, local area network, wide area networks, and other hardware and physical network components of the environment.

Redefining the EIA

For purposes of this volume, these components can be grouped into four categories of architecture (see Exhibit II-1-2).

Business Solutions Architecture. Because this chapter does not focus on business specifics, the top three levels can be grouped into a business solutions architecture. It is important to remember, however, that when it comes time to decide what technical architecture to use,

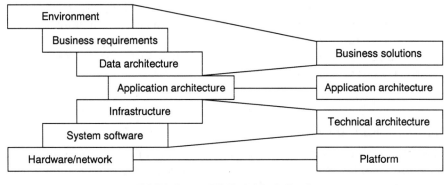

Exhibit II-1-2. EIA Model Redefined

---

many of the answers are found by looking at the business solutions architecture.

Applications Architecture. The applications architecture layer can be defined here as those services that perform business functions on the computer. That is, it is made up of the applications components as they are fit together to make an application.

Technical Architecture. One of the key points of the EIA model is that the only differentiation between the next two levels of the model—the infrastructure layer and the systems software layer—is whether one chooses to build or buy. It will be easier for much of the discussion that follows if, for now, we treat these layers combined as the "technical architecture" layer. This layer is made up of:

- The *infrastructure layer*, which has components that are reusable across multiple applications and which one builds and maintains. When one speaks of architectures or building a development architecture this is the layer that is often being discussed.
- The *systems software architecture layer*, which refers to those components of the architecture that are used across multiple applications and that are purchased from vendors. Compilers, operating systems, databases, and window managers all fit into this category.

Platform Architecture. The final layer in the EIA model is the platform architecture layer. It is often described as "the things you can see." The client/server platform architecture provides a framework for selecting the components of a client/server system: the servers, workstations, operating systems, and networks. This framework represents the overall technology platform for the implementation and deployment of the execution architecture, development architecture, operations architecture, and, of course, the applications. The platform architecture is described in detail in Chapter II-2.

THE TECHNICAL ARCHITECTURE

The technical architecture layer consists of the infrastructure and systems software layer. The differentiation between them is purely a question of make versus buy.

A key decision for organizations intent on "building an architecture" is how much they want to build versus how much they can simply buy from preexisting sources. An organization can choose to build a great deal, thereby making the architecture very close to what it wants. That means that there is a great deal of logic being built by the shop.

Alternatively, the organization can choose to buy most of what it wants. To the extent that business or application demands make it necessary for the tools to be integrated, developers can then do simple assembly, or gluing together, of the pieces. The decision for most organizations depends on balancing demands. On the one hand, the organization has a large front-end commitment to build and an ongoing commitment to maintain an infrastructure architecture; on the other hand, the organization has a tool that is exactly what it wants.

Over the years there has been a tendency to buy rather than make. This is especially the case as the market matures with more technical entrants. It is practical for IS organizations to build technical architecture components only when essential. By purchasing rather than building, they can then more easily apply their strong skills in the applications architecture business.

Components of the Technical Architecture

The technical architecture layer can in turn be broken into three primary components, shown in Exhibit II-1-3. One way to analyze and gain a better understanding of the client/server technical architecture is to consider these three types of information systems architectures: an execution architecture, a development architecture, and an operations architecture.

- An *execution* architecture describes the components required when an application executes.

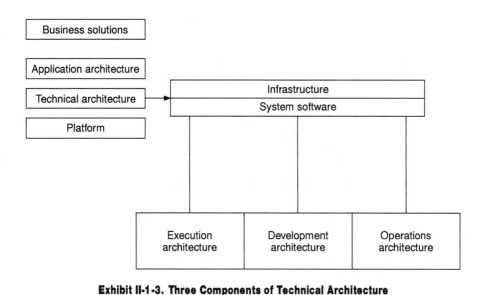

Exhibit II-1-3. Three Components of Technical Architecture

- A *development* architecture describes the components required to create the execution architecture.
- An *operations* architecture describes the components required to operate and manage the system.

These architectures must be flexible enough to accommodate a wide range of technologies, but they must also be structured enough to provide valuable guidelines and to ensure that interoperability is available where it is required.

Each of these architectures should be considered separately because each is equally important and has its own objectives and must satisfy different requirements and users.

Execution Architecture. An execution architecture is a unified collection of run-time services and control structures coupled with an applications infrastructure. The primary users of execution architecture services are applications.

The execution architecture is the processing that runs in the machine supporting the business logic. The client and server elements of an execution architecture reside on production processors. The elements are displayed in Exhibit II-1-4. It is wise for organizations thinking about an architecture to start first by defining the execution architecture. Exhibit

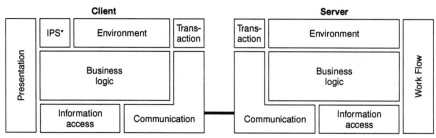

*IPS = Integrated Performance Support

Exhibit II-1-4. Client/Server Execution Architecture Model

II-1-4 portrays the client/server execution architecture model used throughout this volume. (See Chapter I-1 for a more detailed discussion of these components.)

Presentation Services. Presentation services enable an application to manage the human–computer interface: capturing user actions and generating events, presenting information to the user, and assisting in the management of the dialogue flow. Typically, presentation services are only required by client workstations. The major presentation services are a window system, a window interaction manager, a desktop manager, and interaction-style services.

Integrated Performance Support Services. Integrated performance support (IPS) is a set of applications services designed to support organizational and work force performance. IPS enables applications users to do their work better by providing advice, tools, reference, and training on demand and at the point of need. Within the execution architecture, IPS has six distinct components: applications help, performance support controller, advisory services, training services, reference services, and job aid services.

Information Access Services. Information access services enable an application to access and manipulate information stored locally or remotely from files, databases, or external data sources. They minimize an application's dependence on physical storage and location within the network. Information access services may also be used directly by the end user where ad hoc data and information access is integral to the applications work task. Information access services include database services, data sharing services, case management services, file services, codes table services, and transition services.

Communication Services. Communication services enable an application to interact transparently with other applications, regardless of whether they reside on the same computer or on another computer. Communication services include directory services, message management, message services, file transfer services, print services, and terminal emulation services.

Transaction Services. Transaction services provide the transaction integrity mechanism for the application. In small- to moderate-scale environments of less than 150 simultaneous users on a single server, this service may be provided by the database management system (DBMS) software with its restart/recovery and integrity capabilities.

A class of software for larger client/server environments is known as distributed online transaction managers. These transaction managers share server processes across a large community of users and can be more efficient than the DBMS. Transaction services include transaction monitor services, transaction management services, and transaction partitioning services.

Work Flow Services. Work flow services are typically provided on the server because they often coordinate activities between multiple users on multiple computers. Work flow services control and coordinate the tasks that must be completed in order to process a business event.

For example, at XYZ Savings and Loan, to receive a promotion, workers must complete an essay explaining why they should be promoted. This essay and the employee's personnel file must be routed to numerous individuals who must review the material and approve the promotion. Work flow services coordinate the collection and routing of the essay and the personnel file. Work flow services include role management services, route management services, role management services, and queue management services.

Environment Services. Environment services provide miscellaneous applications- and system-level services that do not deal directly with managing the user-interface, communicating, or accessing data. Environment services include batch services, report services, systems services, and applications services.

Business Logic. The execution architecture services are all generalized services designed to support the application's business logic. How applications logic is to be organized is not within the scope of the execution architecture and must be determined based on the characteristics of the applications system to be developed. The business logic component of the client/server architecture addresses the organization of the logic focused directly on the business. This component is implemented by applications developers using the execution architecture services as needed.

Development Architecture. A development architecture is a combination of development tools, methods, standards, and procedures that define a development environment. Usually, at least a one-to-one relationship exists between the execution architecture and the development architecture. That is, there are development tools and standards for each element of the execution architecture.

The development architecture is built by automating the underlying development process. When automating this process, it is important to determine the following:

- Where the designer can gain benefit from automated creation of design deliverables.
- Where the designer can benefit from the sharing of upstream design deliverables with downstream tasks (integration).
- Where the design deliverable can be used to perform various design consistency and completeness checks.

Another major consideration in building a development architecture is to determine how and from where components of the execution architecture can be derived as a part of the development process (execution generation). This later set of decisions is driven in part by the underlying systems software and platform.

Exhibit II-1-5 portrays the model used throughout this book to describe the development architecture. The components of the development architecture model include:

- *Common user interface tools.* These tools provide a common launching place for all the tools in the development environment to make it appear more integrated and consistent.
- *Process management tools.* Such tools provide structure and control over the development process.
- *Repository.* This is the communications backbone of the development environment, making it easy to share and manage information between different processes.
- *Personal productivity tools.* There are many miscellaneous single-user activities commonly encountered on a project: writing memos, preparing presentations, performing simple what-if analyses. These tools are typically oriented toward individuals rather than teams (i.e., no collaboration is required).
- *Quality management tools.* Used to ensure an agreed-on level of

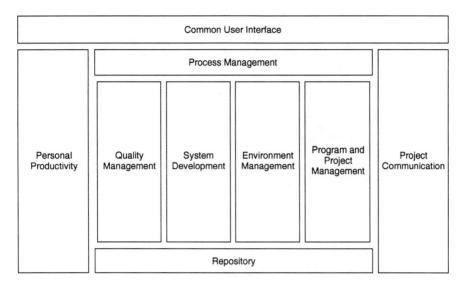

Exhibit II-1-5. Development Architecture

---

quality in the system being developed, such tools provide information and process for improving the quality over time.

- *Systems development tools.* These tools are used by the majority of the development team to capture the systems requirements, the functional design, the detailed design decisions, and the detailed coding and testing and to manage the resulting components.

- *Environment management tools.* By treating the development environment as a production environment (with its users being developers), these tools monitor performance, provide help desk support, manage and distribute changes to the development environment, administer the environment, and track and plan development environment capacity.

- *Program and project management tools.* Such tools aid in the planning and scheduling of a project, along with the tracking and reporting of its progress against the plan.

- *Project communication tools.* Used to facilitate communications across the project team are tools that aid individual communications, such as electronic mail, as well as tools to facilitate communication across a large number or personnel (e.g., groupware and publishing capabilities).

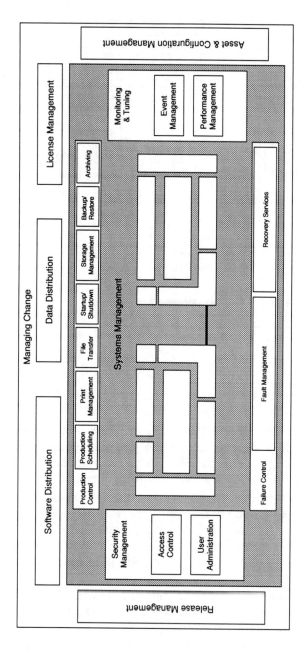

Exhibit II-1 -6. Operations Architecture

Operations Architecture. An operations architecture is a combination of tools, support services, procedures, and controls required to keep a production system up and running well. It differs from an execution architecture in that its primary users are systems administrators and production support personnel. Exhibit II-1-6 portrays a model used throughout this book to illustrate the operations architecture.

Even as recently as three or four years ago, the need for an operations architecture might have been overlooked. Until the advent of client/server computing, an operations architecture was something that happened in the operating system and was addressed by the vendor, with the typical user organization showing little concern. Client/server computing has changed that. The operations architecture has been a subject least talked about by the technology vendor community. Thus companies are being forced to build rather than buy an operations architecture.

The next sections describe the major components of the operations architecture.

Software Distribution. The kind of architectural support needed for the distribution of software is determined mostly by the number of workstations, servers, and locations to be supported. For a relatively small network of workstations in one location, where software changes are not going to be made frequently, a manual approach may be adequate. This involves systems management personnel visiting each machine to load software upgrades on each workstation or server. This approach is, of course, unrealistic for larger environments. Here, automated software distribution tools should be considered for addition to the operations architecture.

Data Distribution. Many of the same factors guiding software distribution apply to data distribution as well. However, some additional operations architecture features may be necessary, depending on the organization's data distribution strategy. Two fundamental approaches are "data replication," for a single master data source from which copies are periodically made and distributed, and "data synchronization," when multiple updatable copies of the same data require updates to be synchronized periodically.

License Management. Because applications software can now be moved around a network as needed, the issue of license management has become increasingly important. Software vendors have experimented with a number of different strategies, and large organizations have struggled with internal management of their software. The market for license management solutions is not yet mature. The absence of standards is one obstacle, though there are several initiatives under way to create a standard. The risk is that major vendors will push out license management solutions on customers, forcing organizations to support multiple, nonintegrated solutions.

Configuration and Asset Management. Successful management of a client/server environment depends on managing assets well and on rigorous change control procedures governing modifications. Information to be tracked includes product licensing information, warranty information, vendor names, such logical and physical device information as total capacity and current utilization, product configuration tracking, software and data version levels, network configuration parameters, physical location, and perhaps accounting information.

Release Management. Release management is made up of several functional areas including rollout management, release control, release testing, and migration control.

Security Management. The two primary components of security management are access control and user administration, placed together because of the close relationship between the access control strategy selected and its associated user administration challenges.

Fault Management and Recovery Services. Failure control is as important in a client/server environment as in a centralized environment. The presence of heterogeneous equipment, however, makes it more difficult to locate the origin of a fault. The fault management services of the operations architecture assist in the diagnosis and correction of system faults. A wide variety of architectural services may be required for fault recovery, ranging from strictly network-oriented components to more systems-level components.

Production Control. Scheduling processes across a distributed environment can be quite complex, requiring significant management effort to ensure that processes happen smoothly. The production control component of the operations architecture assists with such things as print management, file transfer and control, mass storage management, backup and restore, archiving, and system startup and shutdown.

Monitoring and Tuning. Monitoring a client/server system requires more effort because there are more devices, and they are spread across a greater geographic area. Event management is more complex because the number of events generated in the system rises. Performance man-

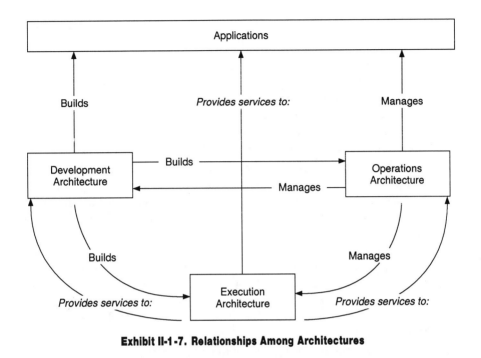

Exhibit II-1-7. Relationships Among Architectures

agement is also more difficult because of the lack of tools to assist with performance in a heterogeneous environment.

Subsequent chapters and sections of this book further decompose and discuss each of these client/server architectures and describe how an organization can begin the process of defining, designing, and implementing them appropriately. Exhibit II-1-7 illustrates the relationships among the execution, development, and operations architectures.

CONCLUSION

This chapter has described a set of complex architectures that can and should be used to support the successful delivery of client/server applications within and across an organization. What are the real benefits of these architectures?

In information processing systems, an architecture can be used to define how a system is structured and how the various components of the system interact. In a client/server computing environment, there are more components and many more interactions that make an architecture even more important.

Organizations that have carefully implemented, delivered, and utilized these architectures have realized some of the following benefits:

1. *Better productivity, and less "reinvention of the wheel."* Architectures can abstract common requirements and approaches from applications and can eliminate having to identify, analyze, and implement them for each application. This improves developer productivity and the quality of the final product.

2. *Consistent, reliable, high-quality applications.* The framework provided by an architecture encourages applications to be built in a consistent fashion or structure, to deliver consistent behavior, and to work with a consistent interface (both to users and other applications), resulting in a system easier to build, easier to use, and easier to maintain.

3. *Rapid delivery of business solutions.* By providing a consistent external interface, an architecture simplifies integration of applications and facilitates rapid delivery of new solutions. This is achieved through the use of standard architecture components, adherence to standards, and the availability of the necessary tools, techniques, and training.

4. *Reduced impact of changes to underlying products and tools.* Because an architecture incorporates "layers" of isolation, new products and tools can be more easily integrated into a system. Changes in one element of the architecture are less likely to affect other architecture elements.

5. *Better integration of business applications within and between organization business units.* By providing consistency of architecture components within and across an organization, the opportunity to build applications that have a higher degree of integration is greater. This should facilitate the exchange of critical information across the company.

6. *Isolation of users and applications developers from the complexities of the underlying technologies.* By having a standard architecture that includes a standard set of tools with a consistent interface, users and developers are not required to know the details of the platform architecture technologies (i.e., the operating system, database, and network). Additional technology components could be added in the future with minimal additional training for the users.

7. *A consistent, standard development framework.* An architecture provides a framework for analyzing the requirements of a system or application. It can help business applications developers by providing a structure from which to work. In a client/server environment, the requirements of a GUI, distributed data, and distributed pro-

cessing contribute to the complexity of the solution. Moreover, these requirements have many interdependencies. Without an architecture to help structure the problem, it is easy for applications developers to become overwhelmed by technical issues and spend insufficient time on the business problems they are there to solve.

8. *A common background for IS personnel.* In addition to providing a common approach for building systems, an architecture provides a common means of describing systems and a common language. As a result, IS personnel are more easily interchanged and cross-trained, providing more flexibility in the management of the organization.

The remainder of the chapters in Section II are devoted to technical architecture and platform, the bottom two layers of the redefined EIA model. (See Exhibit II-1-2.) In many cases, especially in the operations architecture, products are not yet commercially available and standards have not yet been defined. As a result, the services and tools discussed are required or desired but not necessarily available in commercial products.

II-2
Platform Architecture

The client/server platform architecture provides a way to identify and select the major technology components of a client/server system. This framework represents the overall technology platform on which the execution architecture, development architecture, operations architecture, and—most important—the business application is implemented and deployed.

The primary considerations when selecting hardware—dedicated versus multifunction machines, custom development versus packaged solutions, and determining the split of processing and data between the client and the server—are applicable to both the server side and the client side of the selection process.

PRIMARY CONSIDERATIONS

Dedicated Machine vs. Multifunction

If the client workstation is to be dedicated to the application, no other software will run on the machine. Thus, the hardware can be selected purely on the basis of what machine is most suitable for running the application. In contrast, when a client workstation is multifunction, it may be used for office automation and, perhaps, for running some financial applications, spreadsheets, and other custom systems as well.

This distinction is important: It dictates how broad an area the development team needs to look at for requirements. Also, the more multifunctional the machine is, the more likely it is that the organization will have to opt for a "mainstream" (market leading) hardware and systems software configuration to be able to buy application packages and run popular office automation tools.

In contrast, if the client workstation can be a totally dedicated machine, an organization does not have to worry about some of these other issues. It can pick something that is more price competitive; it can also consider more advanced technology, such as an object-oriented environment or something that might be especially appropriate for a particular application.

The same argument applies on the server side of the equation as well.

If a server is going to be used for only one application, the organization can opt once again for the database management system (DBMS), operating system, and hardware best suited to that application. However, if the machine is to be used more as a corporate server, where other applications are going to run—financials, human resources, order processing, and so forth—those systems are also going to add constraints to the selection process and will influence the hardware choice.

Custom Development vs. Package Solution

The second major issue to consider when selecting client/server hardware is whether the strategy will involve a package solution or require custom development. For example, a software package can be purchased from the marketplace for an application for the pharmacy operations of a retail chain. However, the type of package purchased drives what hardware is viable. The applications software vendor largely dictates the operating system, DBMSs, and even the hardware.

In contrast, a custom development environment provides much more control over these decisions. The developer can now look not only at hardware platforms that support a lot of popular applications for pharmacy but at the platform's suitability for building and/or deploying a custom application. Now the important factors to consider are which platforms have the best tools, the best price performance on raw machine horsepower, and high availability.

Client/Server Split

The third broad consideration is deciding what processing and data will be located on the client and what will be located on the server. In client/ server, the application can be split many places across the client/server continuum. Running the majority of the applications on the client drives users toward a higher-powered machine to run the client applications. The other extreme is to run most of the application logic on the server, using the client workstation to handle basically display only. With this choice, a cheaper, less powerful client machine can be used, but a correspondingly more powerful server machine and network is required. This configuration is exemplified by the new "network computer" that runs Java and Internet technologies off of a network.

SECONDARY CONSIDERATIONS

Five additional considerations can be used to further narrow the list of hardware candidates: capacity, growth/scalability, price/performance, vendor viability, and high availability or fault tolerance.

Capacity

When developing very large client/server systems, the capacity limit of a hardware product must be considered much more carefully. Capacity may constrain the field of hardware vendors and products that can be seriously considered for deploying the system.

Growth/Scalability

In some cases a system starts out small but then grows over the course of a few years. This growth may be in terms of transaction volumes, function, or number of users. In such cases, preference should be given to a hardware product line that is easily scalable in small and less expensive increments.

There are different types of scalability. An organization may wish to add workstations and servers or expand the capacity of existing workstations and servers. Scalability also refers to the disks and network of the system.

Price/Performance

Price/performance in a client/server environment should be viewed in terms of the overall business benefits of the application or system. The aggressive cost structures of various vendors may make a component appear very impressive from a cost-per-MIP standpoint. But the true cost should be viewed on a cost-per-seat basis. Cost per seat is determined by totaling all the necessary computing and communications hardware and software costs and dividing by the number of users. The business benefits can then be compared against the system or application cost.

Vendor Viability

If the system is going to be mission critical for the organization and is expected to have a lifetime of 5 or 10 years, it is probably not a good idea to buy unproven hardware even if it is very inexpensive. For critical systems, an enterprise cannot afford to be tied to hardware from a small company that may be out of business in a few years.

High Availability or Fault Tolerance

Fault tolerance is not important to all systems, but some systems may have difficult requirements in terms of high availability. Airline reservations systems or emergency response systems may require no downtime at all, for example. The need for high availability substantially limits the number of viable hardware providers and drives the use of redundancy in configurations.

HARDWARE AND OPERATING SYSTEMS

The three primary criteria and five secondary criteria discussed here shape the ultimate platform for the system. More detailed decisions relate to the specific components of the platform.

This chapter concentrates on the hardware or microprocessor choice and the choice of operating system. Other components of the platform architecture are discussed at relevant points later in the book.

The microprocessor continues to affect the flexibility, shape, and direction of computing platforms and has altered the economics of the computer industry. The evolution has changed the vision of the computing platform as a high-cost, time-sharing vehicle to a range of scalable power that can be applied to specific requirements. The client/server environment has introduced the concepts of dedicated workstation, application server, file server, work group server, database server, and communications server.

Until the 1990s, vendors introduced new operating systems with new hardware platforms. Today, they seek to simplify their operating systems across scalable platforms. This trend has been driven by the success of the original IBM-compatible marketplace, the inability of vendors to support ongoing research and development for proprietary general purpose operating systems, and the move of users to operating systems independent of the hardware vendor.

The Underlying Processor

The primary processor categories in the marketplace are CISC (complex instruction set computing) and RISC (reduced instruction set computing). CISC is based on the historical approach of creating processors that support a variety of instructions at the microcode level. The original CISC approach was based on the slower processor capabilities of that time and the need to move more instructions into the microcode for speed. Examples of CISC machines include IBM System/370, Digital Equipment Corp. VAX, Motorola 68020, and Intel 80X86.

RISC originally established itself as an opposite approach to CISC. RISC keeps the microcode instructions few and simple, making use of increasing processor capabilities to handle more instructions at the software level instead of the microcode level. Examples of RISC machines include the HP PA–RISC Series, the Sun SPARC chips, SGI MIPS R 4000 Series, and the Motorola 88000.

CISC Computers built before the 1970s contained limited instruction sets that were hard-coded directly into the hardware. As the needs of end users grew, however, more complex instructions were added to the central processing unit (CPU). At the same time, high-level languages were developed to address specialized applications. These factors led to the dominance of CISC architectures, which had rich instruction sets and direct support from high-level languages and operating systems.

Through microcoding, more instructions were added to the system's circuitry. However, it now took multiple CPU clock cycles to execute one machine instruction. There were severe drawbacks to CISC systems. They were slow to design, and the reliance on microcode also slowed implementation of design in new technologies.

RISC RISC technology reduces a CPU's overall complexity, emphasizing simplicity and efficiency. Originally, RISCs delivered increased processing power at lower costs than conventional architectures. They were perceived as more reliable, and they had attractive price/performance benefits.

The word "RISC" was first coined during research conducted by David Patterson at the University of California at Berkeley, who advocated "a combination of simple-instruction hardware with superior language compilers that would be adept at expressing what the programs do in sequences of these simple instructions." In the 1980s, the workstation market adopted RISC technology as a foundation for products. As users' demands changed frequently, vendors began to feel CISC processors could not be enhanced at a similar pace, so they began to develop their own cost-effective RISC-based platforms that could be developed and brought to market quickly.

CISC vs. RISC For a time, it appeared that RISC technology would dominate the market. However, over the past several years, CISC development has been catching up. Intel's Pentium chip has effectively eliminated any performance differences between RISC and CISC chips. One analyst reports that the Pentium "has a lot of RISC features in it [such as caching and superscalar units]. RISC products are beginning to add CISC-like features to reduce storage overhead. And once you put an OS on it, who can tell the difference?" In building a platform architecture, therefore, decisions should not be driven by now outdated perceptions about price/performance gaps between RISC and CISC technologies.

Although the CISC versus RISC distinction appears to be narrowing, the major impact continues to be found in how vendors are bringing their products to market.

In today's marketplace, every vendor has transitioned all or part of its product line to a common component, modular approach. At the core of this strategy is a decision to base its products on a proprietary chip, a chip that is cross-licensed to others, or a chip bought in the marketplace.

Multiple Processor Systems

Throughout the last decade, the information needs of most organizations were satisfied by the available system architectures. Processing requirements are now regularly pushed beyond the capabilities of these architectures by information demands generated by increasingly complex applications. Many organizations are looking for systems capable of processing large amounts of data quickly and affordably, so that the business opportunities that lie buried within their enormous databases can be realized.

Although emerging processor technologies are dramatically increasing the speed of processor chips, individual processors still fail to meet many of the demands for greater processing power and may never meet the most strenuous processing demands because of fundamental physical constraints. Because individual processors are unable to meet the processing requirements of some organizations, it has become necessary to consider systems with multiple processors.

Multiple processor architectures are rapidly evolving to the point where they may soon become a powerful alternative to current architectures. The widespread use of multitasking operating systems within the scientific community has paved the way for multiple processor architecture development within the commercial arena. RISC chips and the development of highly integrated open microprocessor architectures have made multiple processor systems practical by reducing their cost and size to reasonable levels. In addition, the developers of hardware, networks, applications and DBMSs are beginning to realize the potential that multiple processor systems possess and are committing themselves to partnerships that are speeding up the overall development process.

Although multiple processor systems promise to provide a number of advantages to commercial users, they do have a few limiting factors. Systems developers have yet to conquer communication bottlenecks and record lockout and recovery problems that need to be eliminated before multiple processor systems can be relied on to perform mission-critical applications. The present lack of off-the-shelf applications, coupled with the inherent difficulties involved with applications development for multiple processor platforms, provides organizations with few uses for the systems. Finally, the present state of flux within the market has left the future of many of the vendors in doubt, and support for a system that is purchased may not be available when it is needed.

The multiple processor market is currently divided into two primary segments: the symmetric multiprocessing (SMP) segment and the massively parallel processing (MPP) segment.

SMP SMP systems typically consist of 2 to 32 processors that have equal access to the operating system. The single copy of the operating system in shared memory ("shared everything") manages the pool of processors over a high-speed bus, distributing tasks to processors from a common task queue as processors become available. SMP systems perform multitasking parallelism, meaning that individual tasks are performed by individual processors but individual tasks are not partitioned across multiple processors.

MPP MPP systems utilize a greater number of processors, ranging into the hundreds and thousands, with no theoretical upper limit as long as an adequate interconnection scheme can be developed. (At this time, the largest systems have incorporated more than 16,000 processors.) MPP systems have distributed memory configurations; processors have their own associated memory and copy of the operating system ("shared nothing"). In addition to being able to perform multitasking parallelism, MPP systems are also able to perform multithreading parallelism, which means that they can take a single task, separate it into multiple components, and then execute these task components simultaneously across multiple processors.

Design Considerations with Multiple Processing Systems Multiple processing systems require a significant degree of design and configuration understanding before they can be purchased and installed. Some major design considerations include the following:

- Instruction stream approaches.
- Memory structure.
- Number of processors.
- Processor design.
- Processor interconnection schemes.
- Operating systems.
- Compilers.

Although system design considerations must be weighted heavily when evaluating systems, systems vendors should also be evaluated with considerable care. It is possible that no vendor offers a system that includes all of the design traits that are desired. It is also possible that the vendors offering systems that meet the established design criteria are unstable, and may not survive to provide the support services that may be required. In either case, potential buyers should be prepared to reassess their priorities continuously and to accept the necessary compromises that may occur between systems vendors and design traits.

Major Challenges with Multiple Processor Systems Although multiple processor systems promise to offer numerous advantages to commercial organizations, at the present time there are still a number of limiting factors that must be considered before a system can be purchased.

The primary factor limiting the success of multiple processor systems within the commercial arena is the overall lack of available software. It can be extremely difficult to write programs for multiple processor systems that use distributed memory architectures. Applications development tools currently available are limited to basics such as compilers. Most advanced languages are also incompatible with multiple processor platforms, which presents additional problems.

Both SMP and MPP architectures pose specific problems that may keep buyers from their potential benefits. Although SMP architectures provide a cost-effective method for improving overall system throughput, these architectures do not speed up individual tasks because they fail to partition tasks across parallel processors. SMP systems are also prone to communication and memory bottlenecks when running demanding applications because of the limitations of the high-speed bus and the shared memory architecture.

MPP systems also have limitations that prospective buyers need to consider carefully. Although there is no theoretical limit to the number of processors that may be used within an MPP system, coordinating processor communications becomes increasingly difficult as the number of processors increases. Unless vendors are able to overcome communication bottleneck problems and record lockout and database recovery problems in MPP systems, they will be unable to perform mission-critical online transaction processing functions. This results in expensive systems, and care must be taken when adding processors so that the gains provided are not offset by the overhead required to synchronize the processors.

In addition to the given software and architectural problems, there are also a number of limiting factors that are applicable to the multiple processor systems market in general. For starters, few people are skilled in MPP, so there are high initial training costs. Also, multiple processor systems are difficult to integrate into existing environments.

Although systems vendors have been more than eager to provide the benchmark results for their systems, these results should be examined closely. No system should be purchased simply on the basis of the reported results of vendor benchmarks, especially from any vendor under the extreme financial pressures that the multiple processor systems market is causing.

If potential multiple processor system buyers see a need for this level of processing power but are reluctant to purchase a system because of the number of unknowns in the present marketplace, a safe option is to choose a product from which it will be simpler to migrate to multiple processor technologies sometime in the future.

Operating Systems

The largest evolutionary change in operating systems with client/server is from proprietary systems specific to particular hardware platforms to systems that can cross many different platforms.

Threads and Processes The key difference among operating systems is the way they handle processing program elements. A primary distinction here is between "threads" and "processes." A "single-threaded" program or process completes one message before processing another. A "multithreaded" process allows more than one path to be followed through the program while executing.

Tasks, too, are handled either singly or in multiples. Single tasking is an environment executing one process to completion before starting another. With multitasking, on the other hand, main tasks and subtasks are executed concurrently.

This section looks at each of the different operating systems currently in the marketplace and discusses some of their strengths and weaknesses, beginning with some of the older systems and moving toward recent offerings such as Windows NT, Windows 95, and IBM OS/2 Warp.

IBM MVS IBM's MVS operating system is the flagship environment for the mainframe product line. MVS continues to go through significant changes as IBM redefines its role from the traditional time-sharing and batch-processing model to that of an enterprise-scale server environment and a leader in netcentric computing. The peer-to-peer communications capabilities provided through LU6.2/APPC and Transmission Control Protocol/Internet Protocol (TCP/IP) extensions enable the MVS platform to be more server accessible, opening up its large transaction and disk handling capabilities to the client/server and netcentric environment.

Although traditionally not as attractive for small- to mid-scale server requirements, MVS remains very much a part of client/server environments because of its installed base which supports the primary legacy transaction databases of large organizations. Evolutions of MVS are also being used in larger data warehousing applications because of its large disk handling capability.

OS/400 The OS/400 (Operating System 400) is IBM's operating system for the AS/400 family of processors. The most distinguishing feature of OS/400 is its high level of systems software integration.

The base OS/400 system offers a built-in relational database, transaction monitor, security, communications support, work management, and development environment. This integrated environment is generally what makes the AS/400s relatively simple to operate and manage. All major systems software components work together seamlessly. In the rare case of a systems software-oriented failure, the only vendor to contact is IBM. OS/400 also incorporates several highly advanced architectural features, such as object orientation, capability-based addressing, and a 64-bit address single-level storage. A single version of OS/400 is offered on all AS/400 models.

IBM released the first AS/400 midrange machine in 1988; since then it has shipped nearly 400,000 machines. The AS/400 designers drew many of the ease-of-use features from the System/38. Because of the architecture similarities between the AS/400 and S/3X machines, it is relatively easy for users to upgrade from a S/3X to an AS/400 (particularly from a S/38).

OS/400 is based on an object-oriented structure. Everything on the system is identified as a certain type of object (programs, data files, print queues, libraries). Invalid actions are not permitted against objects. For example, it is not possible to compile database files; only source code objects permit this operation to be performed. Likewise, only program objects can be called. Objects are identified by a unique name. Then, based on this name, the operating system resolves the address of the object.

Although OS/400 is a very stable operating environment, it is not a fault-tolerant system. High availability configurations are the best that can be achieved. Installations requiring full fault tolerance should consider a different platform.

Being a proprietary architecture, application portability from OS/400 to other environments is marginal. Unless applications are specifically written to be portable, it is not easy to do so. Scalability for the OS/400 is good, with a wide range of AS/400 hardware models available that run the exact copy of OS/400. Applications can easily run on all models of AS/400 machines without modifications.

Although known as a proprietary system, OS/400 does support practical open systems features today, such as TCP/IP. In addition, recent releases contain support for OSF/DCE and a selected implementation of POSIX.

In terms of applications development, the OS/400 development environment is highly productive compared to the base offering of competitive systems. This does not mean that additional tools are unnecessary in OS/400—only that fewer resources must be allocated to the establishment of a productive development environment. OS/400 provides a single set of development tools for multiple languages, and the single integrated DBMS support also helps to keep things simple.

UNIX UNIX is a set of multiuser and multitasking operating systems developed by AT&T, Bell Labs, and the University of California at Berkeley. It was initially developed in 1969 but has been commercially supported only since 1983. UNIX has grown tremendously since that time; a main reason for this success is its perceived ability to run on many hardware platforms.

The UNIX operating system contains three main components:

- *Kernel.* This is the heart of UNIX, and contains the isolations layer and hardware-dependent portions of the operating system. This isolation eases UNIX application portability to other hardware.
- *Utilities.* These are operating system support tools that allow users to accomplish such tasks as backups, sorting, and editing.
- *Shell.* This is a command language interface between UNIX and the user. It interprets commands between the user or application and the kernel or utilities. These commands are translated into actions. There are three main UNIX shells: Korn, Bourne, and C.

UNIX was originally designed as a time-shared and multiuser operating system. UNIX did not originally provide real-time processing capabilities (processing transactions immediately as they are requested). However, many users are pushing for operating systems that can preempt any active process in favor of a process with a higher privilege or priority. Therefore, some vendors have implemented some real-time features.

UNIX uses a hierarchical treelike file system that makes data easier to store, locate, and manage. Users navigate through this structure via a "change-directory" command. However, what makes it different from OS/400 is that the file structure views basic system components (terminals, printers, disk) as files. This allows UNIX to contain "pipes," which allow output from one program to be input into another without needing intermediate files or queues.

The UNIX operating system is written mostly in C and is relatively portable between systems. It can be run on a wide range of hardware from various vendors, ranging from workstations to mainframes. This high level of portability, scalability, and adherence to open standards has been one of its main advantages over other operating systems. Although all UNIX variants are different, most vendors' versions adhere to POSIX and XPG3 branding.

The traditional UNIX interface has been described by many users as cryptic, command driven, and oriented more toward experienced developers than business users. To ex-mainframe developers, a UNIX environment often appears to be unstructured, unmanageable, and difficult to monitor and tune. However, once developers learn the commands, they are able to perform a wide variety of powerful system functions. Implementation of user interfaces has often been left to developers, although third-party products are being developed to address this drawback.

GUI interfaces, such as OSF/Motif and Sun OpenLook, can make the UNIX environment more user-friendly by providing a PC (personal computer) and Windows feel. Desktop support from UNIX servers is available for Windows, MS-DOS, OS/2, and Macintosh workstations.

OpenVMS OpenVMS is Digital Equipment Corp.'s (DEC) general purpose multiuser operating system for both its 32-bit VAX and its 64-bit Alpha AXP architectures. OpenVMS was previously called just VMS, but DEC changed the name after the system achieved XPG3 branding and POSIX compliance. The "Open" portion of the name refers to the new level of openness and portability of a system that was previously proprietary.

A variety of DEC and third-party layered software products are available to run both scientific and business applications including an Internet product suite. The operating system can be used on a wide range of DEC machines, ranging from workstations to mainframe-class hardware. This allows organizations to use OpenVMS to correctly size their critical applications.

OpenVMS comes in two versions:

- OpenVMS for its VAX machines (OpenVMS/VAX 6.0).
- OpenVMS for its Alpha AXP machines (OpenVMS/AXP version 1.5).

One advantage the OpenVMS operating system has over OS/400 and some UNIX versions is its ability to cluster several OpenVMS machines together. Multiple systems can share data and system resources, thus adding incremental processing power and protecting an owner's investment in peripheral devices and CPU. It also enables better failover if one system crashes. Because the clusters are managed as one system, system managers can be more productive and save time. Resources such as data files, disks, printers, and tape drives can be shared by all cluster users.

The OpenVMS operating system is scalable, from the smallest workstations to the largest mainframes within the VAX product line. Applications can be easily ported between any OpenVMS system. OpenVMS supports many industry standards including POSIX 1003.1 (system interfaces) and 1003.2 (shells and utilities), OSF/Motif, and X-Windows. DEC supports a distributed computing environment; this allows for portability of applications to non-OpenVMS environments. In addition, OpenVMS supports OSF/DCE and is C2 security compliant.

Currently a large base of OpenVMS applications exists. OpenVMS contains a wide range of tools to help programmers develop applications, including editors, a linker, a librarian, code manager, file utilities, and a debugger. The OpenVMS Run-Time Library allows string manipulation, input-output (I/O) conversion routines, data and time formatting, and other general-purpose functions. Three DEC-provided text editors are available: LSE, EDIT, and TPU.

IBM OS/2 OS/2 was IBM's and Microsoft's answer to the inadequacies of PC-DOS. DOS brought desktop computing to the marketplace, but as a single-tasking operating system it quickly revealed its limitations. Various products were created that extended the capabilities of DOS (e.g., GEM, DESQview, and 386DOS/Extender), but none of them solved all deficiencies, and these products were often incompatible with each other.

The PC industry needed a vendor whose product solved the DOS deficiencies with a single specification and implementation. In addition, the vendor needed to be strong enough in the marketplace to guarantee that the solution would be accepted as a de facto standard by vendors and developers. IBM's strategy was to create a new operating system called OS/2, which was targeted to replace DOS. In 1984, IBM had pledged to release an advanced operating system that would take advantage of the Intel 80286 (the heart of the then newly released PC AT). Version 1.0's display was text only. Some analysts predicted the end of DOS when OS/2 was released.

OS/2 1.0, a joint effort between IBM and Microsoft, was released in 1987 but did not succeed in penetrating the market. It was complex and somewhat buggy. Version 1.1 was released with a graphical user interface called Presentation Manager in late 1988. Other versions of 1.x were released, but by 1990, OS/2 had sold only 300,000 copies, compared to more than 90 million copies of DOS in circulation. In 1991, Microsoft backed away from OS/2 support to begin developing and promoting Windows. In 1992, OS/2 2.0 was released. It was designed around the 80386, taking advantage of its 32-bit registers, greater capacity, flat memory model, and virtual-86 mode, allowing the operating system to multitask multiple DOS applications. Support for Windows applications was available, but OS/2 did not support Windows' 386 Enhanced Mode.

In October 1994, IBM introduced OS/2 Warp 3.0, which addressed some of the shortcomings of previous OS/2 versions. In September 1996, OS/2 Warp 4.0 was introduced. OS/2 Warp 4.0 contains native support for Java applications, voice recognition technology, and an improved graphical user interface in an attempt to provide more connectivity and ease of use.

With OS/2, a base operating system, or kernel, provides basic functions of multitasking, file services, memory management, keyboard services, and character-mode output. Presentation Manager is an advanced windowing and graphic subsystem. Dialog Manager is a further subsystem that simplifies the writing of PM applications and automatically creates screen dialogs that conform to IBM Common User Access standard. Communications Manager handles communications with PCs, minicomputers, and mainframes.

OS/2 has a number of superior characteristics. It is a technically advanced operating system. It is optimized as a single-user system and has smaller disk and memory requirements than UNIX. However, OS/2 also has a number of limitations because it was designed specifically for Intel-based PCs. It is not portable or scalable. The assembler instructions are tailored to Intel microprocessors only, and the long development cycle for OS/2 means that transition to another hardware architecture is unrealistic.

OS/2 installations continue to be well below expectations, lagging far behind DOS and Microsoft Windows. Acceptance was not helped by the fact that early versions of OS/2 have a limited number of printer and display drivers, which made non-IBM-compatible video and printer equipment difficult to integrate. There is no compatibility between DOS/Windows and OS/2 APIs, forcing developers to choose between DOS/Windows and OS/2. Because OS/2 supports some level of DOS/Windows applications in its WIN-OS/2 box, the package marketplace has focused more on providing applications for the Windows market than for OS/2.

Microsoft Windows Microsoft took a different strategy with regard to the limitations of DOS. By releasing Windows, based on DOS, it extended DOS's capabilities within a strong installed base. Windows provides additional memory, multitasking, and a GUI. Although it is not an operating system in itself, it provides a platform, in combination with DOS, that is comparable to OS/2.

Windows 3.x provided an effective platform for many applications.

Although it lacked OS/2's elegant implementation and some of its sophisticated features, such as priority-based scheduling, Windows offered features that most applications required. It was especially effective in a client/server environment, providing access to DBMSs and host applications. Unlike OS/2, the Windows platform had extensive hardware support, applications support, and tool availability. And developers discovered that applications that may have been targeted for an OS/2 platform could be developed for a Windows platform without dramatically affecting their functionality. Furthermore, it had the commitment from Microsoft and other independent software vendors that regard Windows' market penetration as a measure of its success.

In August 1995, Windows 95, the much anticipated successor to Windows 3.1, was released.

Windows 95 Windows 95 is an Intel-specific solution designed to move the installed base of Windows 3.1 and Windows for Workgroups 3.11 users forward to an improved environment with better technical capabilities. According to Microsoft, the code of Windows 95 is completely new; however, it is not architected for platform compatibility to non-Intel environments. Windows 95 architecture, in its current form, would require substantial rewriting for Microsoft to port the new operating system to RISC chips. Any organization looking to implement Windows-based solutions on non-Intel platforms, such as RISC servers and workstations, must use Windows NT (discussed later).

Windows 95 brings many new features to the Intel-based desktop environment. With minimum platform requirements of a 486/25 MHz-based system with 8MB of memory, it is the first 32-bit, multitasking Microsoft operating system that is practical for the majority of PC users. The redesigned user interface corrects many of the limitations of the Windows Program Manager GUI. The interface is not only more user-friendly but also more powerful. This allows users to accomplish more in a shorter amount of time.

Other features included long filename support, easy Internet access, improved networking capabilities, increased support for mobile users, and plug-and-play compatibility. In addition, there is a large selection of applications, some designed specifically for Windows 95 and some for Windows 95 or Windows NT. These applications range from games to specific business applications.

Windows 95 also provides the best migration path from Windows 3.x and Windows for Workgroups 3.11 to a 32-bit multithreaded, multitasked environment. Windows 95's backward compatibility with previous Windows versions allows developers to develop applications using the new application programming interfaces, creating inroads to new markets while retaining current market penetration.

Windows NT Windows NT (New Technology) is Microsoft's advanced operating system for client/server computing. It is available in a Windows NT "Server" version and a Windows NT "Workstation" version. Windows NT Server contains built-in features for server functionality and Windows NT Workstation is designed with features for workstation operation. Both versions are powerful and flexible operating systems created to meet the needs of both business-critical and high-performance personal computing. The following are among the operating system's strengths:

- 32-bit memory model supporting up to 4 gigabytes of protected virtual memory per application.
- Compatibility with MS-DOS, Windows 3.x, Windows 95, OS/2 1.x (character-based), and POSIX-compliant applications.
- Preemptive multitasking of applications.
- Support for multithreaded applications.
- Symmetric multiprocessing support.
- Networking capabilities integrated directly into the product.
- US Government C2-level security capability integrated directly into the product.
- Support for a variety of hardware platforms, including multiprocessor computers.
- Familiar with Windows 95 GUI in Windows NT 4.0.
- Strong third-party application vendor support.

Microsoft has positioned Windows NT as the upper end of the Windows spectrum of operating systems. Its capabilities comprise all the desktop features and the networking capabilities of Windows 95 and include a rich series of new features such as portability, multithreaded architecture, support for symmetric multiprocessing, and asynchronous disk I/O procedure calls, which make Windows NT suitable to act both as a server platform and as a high-end client platform.

Windows NT can play a role in the following architectures, among others:

- *Windows 95, DOS, or Windows Client, NT Server.* Windows NT would act as a file server for Windows 95, DOS, and Windows clients, providing similar capability to that of a Novell or LAN Manager file server. This design would take advantage of the security and multitasking mechanisms of Windows NT while avoiding additional hardware requirements for the client machines.

- *OS/2 Client, NT Server.* Microsoft is providing the necessary drivers for OS/2 in the Win32 Software Development Kit. In this environment, an existing investment in OS/2 code could be retained on the desktop, and off-the-shelf or new applications could be used on the server side.
- *Windows 95 or Windows for Workgroups (WFW) Client, NT Server.* In this setup, Windows NT would participate as a member of the Windows network. Resources such as printers and files could be shared transparently across both platforms.
- *NT Client, NT Server.* Windows NT could communicate with client machines through workgroup mechanisms (file sharing, print sharing) or through direct interaction via software.
- *NT Client, Other Server.* Windows NT can communicate with a variety of other platforms through layered networking software.

CONCLUSION

This chapter has discussed the important considerations for choosing a platform architecture and provided a brief overview of various processor and operating system options. By proceeding carefully through the primary and secondary considerations discussed in this chapter, making the actual platform decision should be easier.

II-3
Overview of Presentation Services

Presentation services is the component of the client/server execution architecture that controls how users interact with the system. If the user requires a style or form of interaction with an application, the presentation services layer has a function that prescribes how that interaction should be implemented.

Presentation services is vital to effective systems design, in part because it is the most obvious part of the system to the common system user. "You don't get a second chance to make a good first impression" is an adage that applies well to interface design. Indeed, to the new types of business users working in the client/server environment, *the interface is the system.*

THE INTERFACE CONTINUUM

Exhibit II-3-1 illustrates an example of a character-based interface for an airline reservationist making seat assignments. The interface is not pretty, but its main strength is permitting high-quantity use. For so-called heads-down, high-volume or specialized jobs, a character- or code-based interface allows users to work quickly and efficiently—provided they have the time to learn how to use the system, the ability to remember a large set of commands and codes, and do not make mistakes.

Users, however, seldom view this type of system as a source of job satisfaction. From management's point of view, the fatal weakness of systems with character-based interfaces is that great amounts of training are required to use them. Generally, the user has to remember codes even to have basic proficiency, and more sophisticated navigation through the system takes a great deal of experience.

A large number of codes that must be memorized can totally undermine the performance of the workers at the system. One US utility company, for example, recently introduced two new systems for its customer service representatives. Using the old system, representatives only had to remember codes to access about 30 different 3270-type screens. The new

```
Ready?  S
Select Seat?  BU157  2  N  B
12A  12B  BU157  Nonsmoking Business
Print?  Y
Ready?  I
```

Exhibit II-3-1. A Character-Based Interface

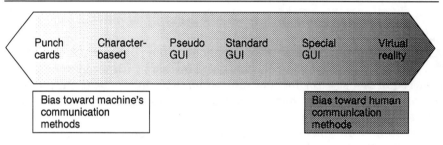

Exhibit II-3-2. Interface Continuum

system required more than 250 screens. Here, a continued reliance on character-based interfaces might pose a real bottom-line threat to the enterprise, because representatives would be hampered in providing high-quality service to customers.

The division of interfaces into "graphic" and "character-based" is arbitrary. It is best to think of different types of user interfaces as a continuum, arranged by the degree of human/machine integration.

Toward one end of the continuum are the early computing machines, where interaction took place on the machine's terms, in the form of punch cards. Toward the other end of the continuum are the interfaces designed in accordance with the so-called human metaphor (discussed in more detail in Chapter IV-2). Here users interact with computers using methods that are natural to them simply because they are human beings (e.g., speech, gestures, writing, and movement). Ultimately, these interfaces move toward virtual reality interfaces where the computer simulates a natural human sensory environment. (See Exhibit II-3-2.)

The interface continuum illustrates character-based interfaces with many of the desirable qualities of graphic interfaces but without some of the costs. Some graphical user interfaces (GUIs), often the result of conversions of legacy systems, are actually character-based interfaces in attractive new wrappings. These interfaces are called pseudo-GUIs, to distinguish them from applications that were originally developed as GUIs.

WHAT IS A GUI?

Today, as users find themselves moving up the continuum toward natural interaction with computers, the state of the market has rapidly become the GUI.

A GUI is an interface that takes advantage of a high-resolution display to present a great amount of meaningful information to the user, grouped and organized graphically. Because of the increased resolution, a graphic interface is able to display more bytes of information at any given time than a character-based interface. The GUI is presented on a bit-mapped display monitor, which enables the software to address each display pixel individually. (A standard bit-mapped display monitor has more than 300,000 pixels; a 3270 screen consists of 1,920 displayable characters.) The GUI has more separately distinguishable parts visible and thus can more easily take advantage of the strengths of the human brain: *to recognize and associate, generalize, and deduce.*

Because of increased processing capacity provided by workstations, it is easy to change the information presented on any part of the screen in response to user actions. The appearance of the GUI responds to actions by users who interact via a mouse, keyboard, touch-sensitive monitors, voice recognition, pen stylus, or any other input device. The sensitivity of the interface to user actions means feedback can be provided quickly and in the most appropriate context.

For example, if a user types in an invalid date, the field could immediately change color to indicate this (compared to the traditional approach of waiting until a PF key is pressed to validate all data). Or, as a user cursors across cells in a spreadsheet, the cell's contents or formula are instantly displayed in an edit field. This type of interface is not possible without the ability to respond to events much smaller than the PF key.

The most important result of GUI flexibility is that the user experiences the system as responsive. When people get immediate feedback from almost any action, they learn more quickly and experience greater satisfaction and a sense of control. Both visually and in terms of responsiveness, GUIs seem to increase rapport or emotional satisfaction and reduce anxiety or alienation. Although these factors are more difficult to quantify, they may still determine the ultimate acceptability of an interface to today's computer user.

More Than Just a Pretty Face

The visual appeal of a GUI is certainly the most obvious facet of today's systems. But the presence of color and effective design is not merely a matter of esthetics. Mere prettiness is not the point; indeed, it is hardly a justification for the cost of such a system. What is the primary *business* benefit of the new GUIs?

To understand this, people need to step back a minute and consider what the introduction of computers did to the manner in which they go about performing their work. Previous forms of office technology—the telephone, the typewriter, the dictation machine—augmented the work they did but did not take it over. They came to their jobs focused on the tasks at hand: x amount of sales in order to make a quota, y number of products to manufacture, z number of customer service inquiries to answer.

For better and for worse, the computer altered that understanding of their work. The computer made those tasks more efficient, but it also put blinders on people: No longer could they look at the whole picture of their work but only that slice of it that a particular system application let them see. Too often, the tasks of workers became oriented around using a system rather than performing work; instead of transacting business, workers were processing transactions. The system was in charge, and that affected the manner in which interfaces were designed.

Over the past few years, systems designers have begun a gradual paradigm shift: from a machine-oriented perspective on design to a user- or human-centered perspective. The shift may have started when people began to suspect that most difficulties they had using a computer system might be the computer's fault, not their fault.

Before GUIs, the notion of designing for usability was somewhat alien to a designer because there was not much the designer could do to make the system usable. The ability to provide clues and quick feedback were limited or impractical. GUIs have given designers new tools and techniques for making systems easier to use. Beyond just looking good, GUIs allow designers to focus on the user as the center of the design process. User-centered design emphasizes the needs of the system user above the needs of the system.

According to Donald A. Norman, in his book *Design of Everyday Things*, there are four important facets of user-centered design:

- Make it easy for the user to know which actions are possible at any moment.
- Make visible to the user such things as the entire conceptual model of the system, the alternative actions, and the results of actions.
- Make it easy to evaluate the current state of the system.
- Make natural to the user the manner in which intentions are linked to required actions, as well as the link between actions and results, and between the visible information and the interpretation of the state of the system.

In short, simply make sure that users can figure out what to do, and that they can also track easily what is going on at any given moment.

To what end should designers operate now on these principles? There are three principal reasons:

1. Training costs for organizations can be drastically reduced if users can reach proficient performance levels quickly. Overall training costs, beyond systems training, can also be reduced eventually as so-called performance support systems become more accepted, delivering training to workers on demand, at their point of need.

2. The success of applications designed for the new computer users—professionals and executives—largely depends on their acceptance and satisfaction with the new system. This in turn demands principles of advanced usability. Minimizing the adverse impacts of technological change is vital for users because they have the influence to reject the system if it does not have a positive impact on their work rather quickly.

3. Organizations are increasingly "hiring the customer" and discovering new ways to move technology beyond the walls of the organization and let the customer control part of the business process. Automated teller machines are the most obvious example, but there are also self-service airline ticketing terminals, shop-at-home services through interactive television, and a wide array of other opportunities for letting customers interact directly with an organization's computer systems. The primary interface of the system must be effective and allow customers to intuitively transact their business via the system.

ICONS

To understand the importance of GUIs, beyond just looking good, a series of exercises, depicted in Exhibits II-3-3 through II-3-5, illustrates how one aspect of GUIs—icons—can affect the usability of a system.

An icon is a small, simplified picture. The experiment in Exhibit II-3-3 depicts the importance of icons in GUI design. It demonstrates how GUI applications can use a human's superior ability to recognize symbols rather than placing demands on the individual's ability to remember.

Exercise 1

The list of codes in Exhibit II-3-3 are order entry codes for a pizza delivery system. They are chosen to be easy to remember and grouped meaningfully to make it easier to learn them. Readers should look at the 14 pizza

LARG	BACO	ONIO	ADDR
SMAL	PEPP	GPEP	NOTE
NUMB	MEAB	OLIV	
	BEEF	MSHR	
		TOMA	

Score_____

Exhibit II-3-3. Exercise 1: Order Entry Codes

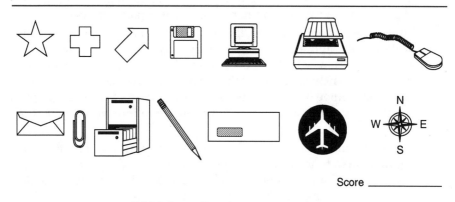

Score _____

Exhibit II-3-4. Exercise 2: Familiar Icons

codes for 30 seconds, close the book and write down as many as they can in any order, and come back and check how many they wrote down correctly.

Exercise 2

Exhibit II-3-4 depicts a set of 14 icons. They are chosen to be familiar and grouped to facilitate memory. Readers should look at the icons for 30 seconds, close the book and write down the names of as many as they can in any order, and come back and check how many they remembered.

Exercise 3

Finally, the 14 icons and their functions depicted in Exhibit II-3-5 are chosen to be natural associations between the real world and common computer functions. Readers should look at them for 30 seconds, then cover up the answers and write as many of the functions as they can in the blanks beside the icons depicted in the bottom of the exhibit.

Most people who have tried this informal test score do best on the exhibit portrayed in exercise 3.

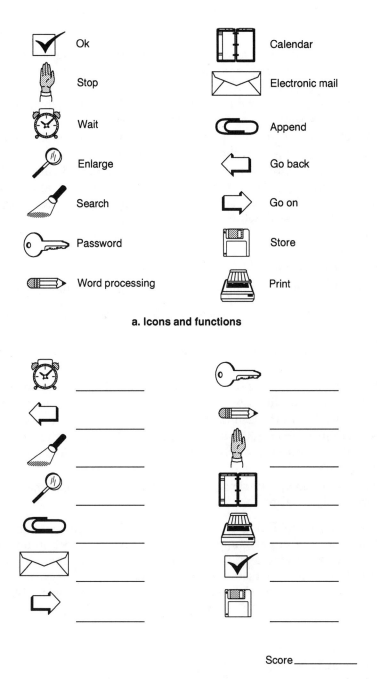

a. Icons and functions

Score _____

b. Fill in the blanks

Exhibit II-3-5. Exercise 3: Icons and Functions

Margins of Error

In exercise 1, the answers have to be exactly right. A code-based system does not usually accept approximations because it is assumed that new codes may be added at any time.

In exercise 2, an individual's personal word for the picture was sufficient. There is some room for personal interpretation in relation to icons. Whether people think "printer" or "printout" when they see this icon, they are still likely to choose it at the right time.

In exercise 3, again, there are more right answers. Some people remember the left and right arrows as previous and next, and some as forward and back. If the concepts are close enough that the icon is chosen at the right times, users will not have difficulty.

The Importance of Icons

Icons and other pictures are often used in GUIs for the following reasons:

- Two icons are easier to distinguish from each other than are two words.
- Icons and pictures can carry more information in less space than words can.
- When the users are partially familiar with an application, icons help them remember functions and select them quickly and correctly. "Partially familiar" is important to remember here. Icons are not usually meant to be 100% self-explanatory. They take their meaning from their context and one's cultural experience. Pictures are less ambiguous.
- In seldom-used applications, icons may be more self-explanatory and more easily recalled.

The exercises in Exhibits II-3-3 through II-3-5 demonstrate a key aspect of GUIs: the use of graphical images to aid recollection and association. The remainder of this chapter discusses two other important aspects of GUIs: metaphors and interaction styles. Both are critical to the successful design of a usable application, and both have been given significantly more flexibility in delivery with the advent of GUIs.

INTERFACE METAPHORS

"Metaphor" has become the word of choice for describing the overall communicative symbolism of the interface. Communication between human beings is filled with metaphorical references.

"The way we think, what we experience, and what we do every day is very much a matter of metaphor," G. Lakoff and M. Johnson, both linguists, write in their book *Metaphors We Live By*. Consider the manner in which people consider arguments to be a kind of war: "Arguments have *sides* that can be *defended* and *attacked*. If a position is *indefensible*, one can *retreat* from it. Arguments can be right on *target;* arguments can be *shot down*." Speech built on metaphors is the rule, not the exception.

As with speech, so it is with the visual world. Metaphors function as common and natural models, which allow people to extend their familiarity with concrete objects and experiences to the level of abstract concepts. The central metaphor of the system interface is the most crucial one for systems designers, one which must be selected with particular attention to the unique needs and work views of the primary user.

In the user interface, metaphors allow people to "talk about" parts of the system as if they were parts of the more familiar physical world. Using a metaphor endows a part of the computer system with a whole set of characteristics belonging to its metaphorical comparison.

Within the more general category of the human metaphor, however, several other types of metaphors are increasingly found in GUIs. Perhaps the most powerful is the workplace metaphor.

Workplace Metaphor. The concept of a workplace metaphor is built on the premise that the worker's electronic work environment should mirror his or her physical environment. This allows applications developers to leverage off what is sometimes called the user's real-world knowledge.

If the person works at a desk, the electronic workplace should resemble a desk. For example, it may contain a calculator, inbox and outbox, assorted filing cabinets, and folders. Workers should be able to manipulate electronic objects, such as files and papers, in the same way they manipulate physical objects. So, instead of physically putting a memo in the outbox, an individual would use the mouse to drag and drop an electronic memo onto an image of the outbox. Because well-designed electronic environments behave similarly to physical environments, users can interact with their electronic tools more naturally.

The physical desk is the most common interface metaphor. It is the default metaphor for the Macintosh, Motif, Presentation Manager, and MS Windows environments. Recently, however, other interface metaphors are becoming available. One of them is the notebook metaphor.

In this case, the user's electronic environment resembles a notebook with tabbed sections. By selecting a tab, the user can flip to that section of the notebook. Because it is appropriate for users who are not deskbound, this metaphor is often implemented in pen-based operating systems. Users can organize and use their portable electronic notebooks just as they would a paper version (though with the added benefit of electronic sorting and searching capabilities).

Workplace metaphors transcend application design. An individual business application is only one of the items users may work with. They may need to work with other business applications, personal productivity tools, or utility applications, such as calculators, or address books. All these applications should conform to the workplace metaphor, whatever it may be.

Another point to note about metaphors is that, technically, they could be separated from the operating system. Many operating systems, however, come bundled with presentation services that already implement a particular metaphor. Microsoft Windows and Macintosh interfaces, for example, present desktop metaphors.

Metaphors create expectations for the user because of their "affordances." All objects have affordances—clues as to what we are supposed to do with them. Most chairs are clearly intended to be sat on; the most prevalent type of light switch is clearly supposed to be moved up or down. But everyone has come across examples of objects with unclear affordances, objects that apparently were designed by someone more interested in esthetics than function. People push on a door that they are supposed to pull, or hit the flight attendant call button instead of the light switch. It is essential that there be a good match between the expectations created by an interface metaphor and the actual functions that the system has to offer.

For example, most people occasionally find that they have tossed an important paper into the wastebasket. In the real world, they simply retrieve—and possibly uncrumple—the paper. When Apple and other manufacturers introduced the wastebasket or bin metaphor for the delete function, there was a potential mismatch. Delete did not necessarily allow undelete. Various implementations of a metaphor for delete have solved this in various ways:

- On the Macintosh, the wastebasket is actually a buffer. Things are not truly deleted until the user gives a command to empty it. This solves the problem by adding both function and complexity. As visual feedback, the wastebasket bulges as it gets full to remind the user to empty it.

- In Lotus Organizer, things placed in the wastebasket are seen to go up in flames. This is not reversible, and it adjusts user expectations in a memorable way.

- In OS/2 2.0, the wastebasket is replaced with the metaphor of a paper shredder. This solution also adjusts user expectations to the fact that a delete is not reversible.

Thus, selecting the appropriate metaphor for a particular application is extremely important.

Following are some tips for systems developers in choosing a metaphor:

1. Select function(s) to be represented by metaphor(s). Which functions are expected to be difficult for users to understand in the abstract? Which functions are essential?
2. Understand the function to be modeled. What does it do, and how?
3. List possible metaphors that have comparable functions. Try to find several.
4. Evaluate the possibilities. Look for the choice that is most concrete, is most familiar to users, and creates the best match between user expectations and function. Look for one that is easy to represent visually.
5. Test the selected metaphor, and possibly an alternative, with the target user community.

Finally, the use of metaphors is not limited only to functions. Applications can have metaphors, too. For instance, a flight planning application might use a graphical map as its metaphor. The map would reflect the charts typically used by pilots for flight planning and would display landmarks, navigational aids, and restricted airspace, for example.

Alternatively, it could use a flight planning form as its metaphor. Which metaphor is most appropriate depends on the user community and is a further example of the need to follow the previous five steps in selecting an appropriate metaphor.

INTERACTION STYLES IN A GUI ENVIRONMENT

Once an appropriate metaphor has been defined for the application being designed, interaction styles must be chosen for performing the various activities and functions within the application. The most common interaction styles in GUI applications are form filling, graphics-based, and direct manipulation. These styles are not mutually exclusive and are often incorporated in the same application and sometimes in the same window.

Form Filling

A windowed form-filling application is similar to its traditional online counterpart. Essentially, users perform their work by completing an electronic form (as opposed to a paper form). Because it is electronic, however, the form has a "behavior."

For example, it may prevent the user from changing protected data,

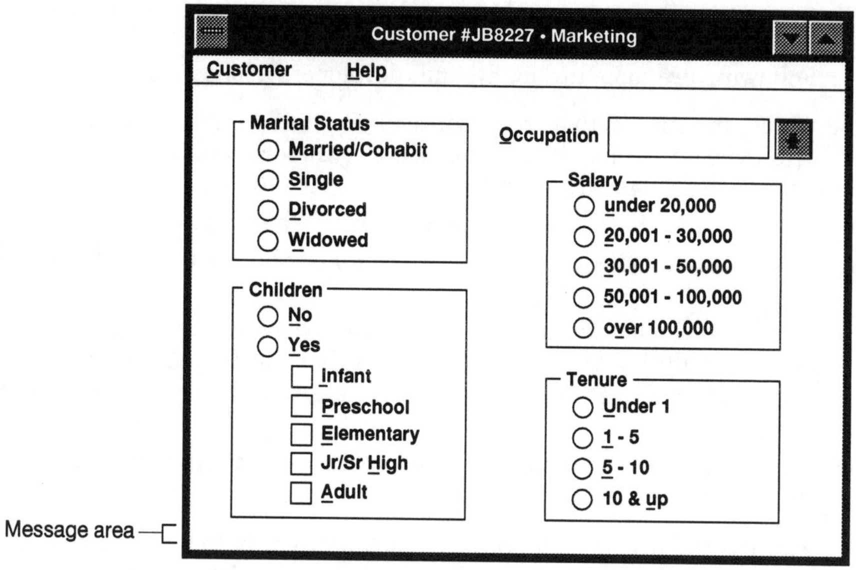

```
┌──────────────────────────────────────────────────────────────┐
│ ▤        Customer #JB8227 • Marketing            ▼ ▲ │
│ Customer      Help                                             │
│                                                                │
│   ┌─ Marital Status ──────┐    Occupation ┌─────────┐  ▣     │
│   │  ○ Married/Cohabit     │              └─────────┘         │
│   │  ○ Single              │   ┌─ Salary ──────────────────┐  │
│   │  ○ Divorced            │   │  ○ under 20,000            │  │
│   │  ○ Widowed             │   │  ○ 20,001 - 30,000         │  │
│   └───────────────────────┘   │  ○ 30,001 - 50,000         │  │
│                               │  ○ 50,001 - 100,000        │  │
│   ┌─ Children ────────────┐   │  ○ over 100,000            │  │
│   │  ○ No                 │   └───────────────────────────┘  │
│   │  ○ Yes                │                                   │
│   │     ☐ Infant          │   ┌─ Tenure ──────────────────┐  │
│   │     ☐ Preschool       │   │  ○ Under 1                 │  │
│   │     ☐ Elementary      │   │  ○ 1 - 5                   │  │
│   │     ☐ Jr/Sr High      │   │  ○ 5 - 10                  │  │
│   │     ☐ Adult           │   │  ○ 10 & up                 │  │
│   └───────────────────────┘   └───────────────────────────┘  │
│                                                                │
│ Message area ─[                                                │
└──────────────────────────────────────────────────────────────┘
```

Exhibit II-3-6. Example of a Form-Filling Window

it may verify that the user enters valid information, it may prompt the user to save changes, and it may dynamically indicate which fields are required. Exhibit II-3-6 depicts a sample form-filling window.

Because many applications maintain large quantities of data, it is often necessary to break up a "form" into multiple windows. In this case, related data should be grouped together and, if applicable, the windows should appear in the order in which they are most frequently used. Another way to accommodate large forms is to employ a "virtual form-based" interaction style. In this style, each window contains one and only one form. If the form is larger than the window, users can scroll vertically and horizontally to view the entry fields in which they are interested.

The form-filling interaction style is primarily text based. The user reads, interprets, and enters information that is primarily textual (although there may be some icons used to supplement the textual information). Form filling is the most common interaction style and almost every GUI application incorporates at least some form-filling windows.

Graphics-Based Interaction

The graphical interaction style uses graphics and images to convey information. These can be in the form of drawings, photographs, charts, and video.

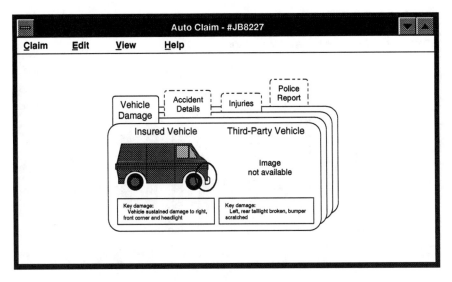

Exhibit II-3-7. Example of a Graphics-Based Window

In its simplest form, the graphics-based style can be used to provide similar functions as the form-filling style. For example, it can allow users to select from a group of related images or can present a list of numbers as a graph. The graphics-based style can also be used to extend form-filling capability to incorporate photographs and full-motion video. For example, in an auto insurance application, it may be beneficial to store a photographic image of a claim form or of a damaged vehicle. It may also be beneficial to store a video record of the crash site. Exhibit II-3-7 depicts a window with a graphics-based interaction style.

Although they are becoming more common, graphics-based interfaces have been slow to gain acceptance because of the complexity of developing them and the high volume of memory and disk space they require for image and video. However, as tools become more powerful, as communication capabilities increase, and as the cost of multimedia-capable hardware continues to decrease, users are going to see more and more graphics-based applications.

Direct Manipulation

Direct manipulation is a style of interaction that allows the user to employ drag-and-drop techniques to manipulate data. Direct manipulation differs from graphics-based and form-filling styles in that it is not typi-

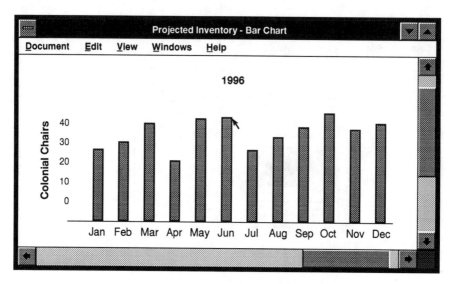

Exhibit II-3-8. Example of a Window that Employs Direct Manipulation

cally independent, and it must be used in conjunction with either a graphics-based or a form-filling interface.

As the name suggests, direct manipulation allows the user to directly manipulate objects on the screen. For example, if the user is viewing a bar chart that indicates projected inventory levels by month, he or she could change the June inventory level by dragging the top of the June bar up or down. (See Exhibit II-3-8.)

Direct manipulation is often used in conjunction with icons. For example, if users want to open a new purchase order for an existing customer, they could drag a customer icon over the purchase order (PO) application icon. This action would open a new PO, which already contains all the customer's header information.

Direct manipulation can also be employed in a form-filling window. For example, if users want to populate a field with an item from a list, they could just drag that item from the list to the field. Or, if they want to delete a line item from a list, they could select that line and drag it to the Trash icon.

Although direct manipulation may provide a more intuitive interface, it is not as prevalent within individual applications because it is more difficult to implement than form filling. (The programmer must sensitize areas of the screen to respond to different types of user input.) As object-oriented programming becomes more popular, however, and as tools and operating systems begin providing support for direct manipulation, direct manipulation should also become more common in system interfaces.

Having introduced the concepts behind the new graphical interfaces, the next chapter looks in more detail at the component parts of GUIs and at what is going on behind the scenes technologically within a GUI environment.

II-4

Graphical User Interface Applications

This chapter provides some context with which to better understand the capabilities and challenges of graphical user interface (GUI) applications, beginning with a simple example of how GUIs work, contrasting GUI systems to traditional, host-based systems, and discussing the most commonly encountered components and terms in a GUI environment. Finally, this chapter focuses on both the key advantages and the primary challenges of GUIs.

Although GUIs have many potential benefits, these benefits do not come cheaply. In general, client/server and GUI solutions are more expensive than traditional solutions. As a result, it is important that the organization is motivated by more than just the desire for a nicer look or a newer technology. The technology must also be a sound business decision.

The list of challenges is intentionally long to help ensure that the subtleties of GUI development are not overlooked when planning and justifying such an effort. By no means are systems developers to be dissuaded from undertaking GUI development. On the contrary, they are more likely to be successful when diving into GUI development if they know where the rocks and shallows are in these new technological waters.

A GUI AT WORK

To provide context, this section discusses the typical layers found in a GUI system and traces an event from its generation by the user, through the layers into the application, and back out to the user in the form of visual feedback. Exhibit II-4-1 depicts the different layers found in most windowed environments.

Operating System and Hardware

The operating system and hardware appear at the lowest level. This level is no different than in a character-based environment except for the

Exhibit II-4-1. Software Layers in a GUI Environment

higher-resolution, graphics-ready display and input that incorporates a mouse or other pointing device.

Window Manager

The next component, the Window Manager, is the core of the windowing system. It is the system software that really delivers the capabilities and characteristics of the GUI, including the display of windows, the interaction with the user and menus, icons, the mouse, and so on. This is where the look and feel of the GUI are implemented.

Windowing Library

The Windowing Library, or "toolkit," sits on top of the Window Manager. This is the interface between the applications programs and the Window Manager. The toolkit provides applications programs with the services necessary to display windows, update the contents of a window, set up menus, display icons, and receive input from the mouse and keyboard.

Behind the Scenes

In a GUI environment, the Window Manager is the software that is able to display images on the screen. This means that while it is executing, a GUI application is continually making "service requests" from the Window Manager. In addition to displaying screen images, the Window Manager also is responsible for routing messages between applications. In some ways, it behaves like a traffic cop; it determines where messages are coming from and routes them to the appropriate application.

The following brief scenario describes what happens when a user interacts with a GUI application, in this case a word processing application. It may be helpful to map the events that occur to their numbered counterparts in Exhibit II-4-2. Also, note that the following typefaces are used to indicate who or what is responsible for invoking actions:

- Plain text indicates actions performed by system, hardware driver, or Window Manager software.

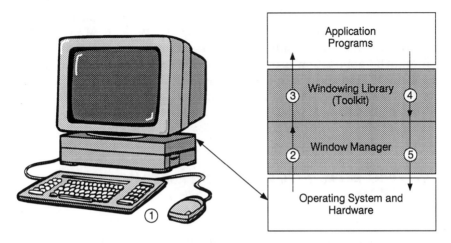

Exhibit II-4-2. Steps in Working With a GUI Application

- Italic text indicates actions performed by business applications software.

Word Processing Scenario

1. Users double-click the mouse over a word they would like to select.
2. The mouse clicks are passed from the hardware and operating system up to the Window Manager so it can interpret the action.
3. The Window Manager determines where on the screen the mouse pointer is and which window that corresponds to. The mouse clicks are translated to mouse "messages" that are sent to the appropriate application window.
4. *The applications program receives the mouse messages and uses the coordinates in the messages to determine where the double-clicks occurred. Because double-clicking is a request for selecting a complete word, the word processor requests the Window Manager to display the text of the word as selected (inverted video). This request is made through the toolkit, which provides applications programming interfaces (APIs) for the functions typically required by applications programs (e.g., create windows and display text/graphics).*
5. The Window Manager determines which pixels on the screen need to change and updates them through the operating system or by directly interacting with the hardware.

This scenario describes only one iteration of a repetitive process that occurs in a hundredth of a second. Every time the user invokes an action with an input device, a message is sent to the Window Manager. The Window Manager then routes this message to the appropriate application and the application usually responds by requesting a service from the Window Manager. Note that because of the granularity of the user-interface events (e.g., mouse movements and keyboard activity), the result can be hundreds of messages per second that the application receives and can act on.

DIFFERENCES BETWEEN GUI APPLICATIONS AND TRADITIONAL ONLINE APPLICATIONS

Program Structure

Traditional online applications are "screen exchange oriented." That is, an application displays a screen and then processes a user's changes against the screen. The user can see and act on only one screen at a time; the application responds to screen-level events—for example, it is not aware of such things as field entry and exit. Exhibit II-4-3 depicts what happens in such an environment.

On the other hand, event-driven programs or "message-based architectures" are structured in an entirely different way. The code may be executed in a nonsequential order and the events can be as small as the movement of the mouse or the pressing of a key.

Exhibit II-4-4 depicts what happens when an event-driven program executes. It takes approximately one to five seconds for the system to process a user's actions in a traditional environment. In a GUI environment, on the other hand, users may expect to see the system respond to their actions in a fraction of a second. (Imagine waiting two seconds for the cursor to change shapes every time the mouse moved.)

Application Responsiveness

GUI applications are much more responsive to user input than traditional systems. For example, on detecting a keystroke (e.g., the letter A or the Tab key), a GUI application can selectively make options available to the user or immediately format data fields.

Application Composition

In most GUI applications, more code is devoted to the user interface than in traditional online applications. When coding to the native windowing toolkit, GUI applications require more code to process the complex message routing that is an integral part of window-based applications. With

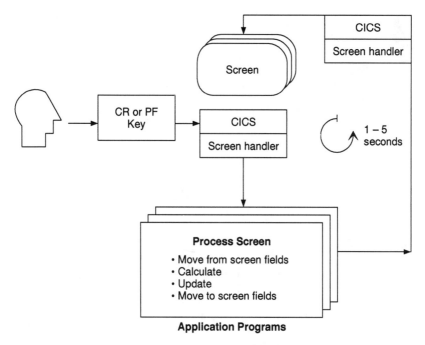

Exhibit II-4-3. Processing Loop in a Traditional Online Application

---

more sophisticated tools or libraries, much of this code is hidden from the applications programmer. However, even in these cases, more code is likely to be required than in a traditional application because of the interactive nature of the GUI and the user expectations of clear and immediate feedback. For example, when a field is invalid, the OK button should be disabled.

GUI COMPONENTS

This section discusses the most commonly encountered GUI components and terminology.

Windows

Windows are the key component of GUIs. A window is normally defined as an area on the display screen used to present a view of an object or to conduct a dialogue with a user. Windows are used to present objects, action options, and messages. Typically, windows have many, if not all, of the components shown in Exhibit II-4-5.

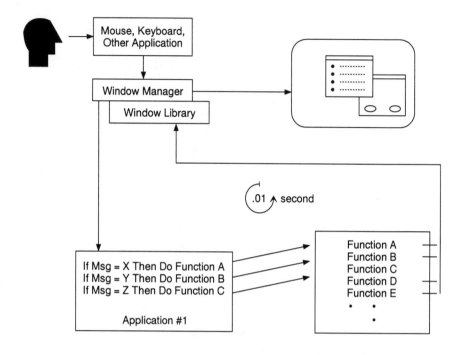

Exhibit II-4-4. Processing Loops in a GUI Application

Border. The border is a rectangular outline denoting the limits of the window. It can often be moved to alter the size and shape of the window.

Title Bar. This is the top bar of the window. It is composed of several different areas: the system menu symbol, the window title, and the window sizing buttons.

- *System menu.* The icon in the upper-left-hand corner of the window contains choices that affect the window and other operating environment specific functions. By selecting this icon, a pull-down menu appears with a list of choices.
- *Window title.* This text area in the title bar identifies the window.
- *Minimize button.* This button contains either a small rectangle or an inverted triangle. When it is selected, it reduces the window to an icon.
- *Maximize/ restore button.* This button contains a large rectangle, a triangle, or two triangles pointing up and down—depending on the

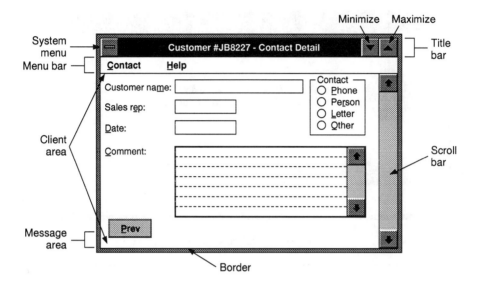

Exhibit II-4-5. A Typical Window

---

state of the window. It is used to restore the window to its previous size or to the size of the work space.

Menu Bar. This area is just below the title bar and contains routing and action choices. When a choice is selected, a pull-down menu is displayed. A menu bar is sometimes called an action bar.

Scroll Bars. This window component informs a user that more information is available than fits in the window's viewable area. If the object being viewed is wider than the client area, a horizontal scroll bar is provided. If the object being viewed is longer than the client area, a vertical scroll bar is provided. Users can manipulate the scroll bars to change the view currently visible in the scrollable area.

Client Area. The client area is where the user works. It is just below the menu bar and inside the scroll bars. This area can contain graphics, text, and controls.

Message Area. Some windows contain a message area. The message area is a rectangular region just above the bottom window border.

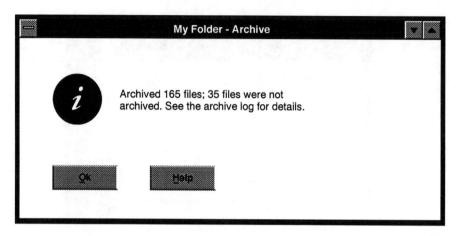

Exhibit II-4-6. An Information Message Box

This area can be used to display nondisruptive messages. Often, these messages relate to the status of objects and actions.

Message Box Windows

Message box windows (or message boxes) indicate that an unexpected event has occurred or that additional action is required by the user. To distinguish between these events, three distinct message boxes are commonly used. An icon is usually placed on the window to indicate the type of message being displayed. When a message box is displayed, the user must act on it before continuing to work on any other window within the application.

Information. An information message appears when some situation occurs that the user can do nothing about. (See Exhibit II-4-6.) Often, this window displays a status message concerning the original request. Users can usually request more information about the situation from the help option.

Warning. A warning message is displayed when the user can continue with the original request but should be made aware of some situation. (See Exhibit II-4-7.) Users can continue the request without modification or can choose to stop processing.

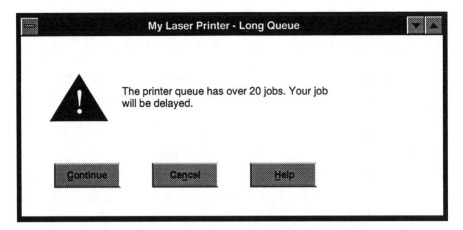

Exhibit II-4-7. A Warning Message Box

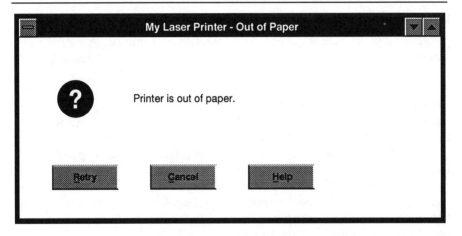

Exhibit II-4-8. An Action Message Box

Action. An action message is displayed when the user must take some action for processing to continue. (See Exhibit II-4-8.) Users can correct the situation or choose to retry the original request.

Parent and Child Windows

Typically, when a window opens another window, the opening window is called a parent and the opened window is called a child. (There are exceptions to this in which a window opens a "peer" window, but this is less common.) A child window can, in turn, have its own child windows. In fact, any number of child windows can be opened, but the depth of nested windows should be limited to minimize the complexity of the program and the user interface.

From a user's perspective, parent/child relationships define how windows behave. Although this behavior is platform dependent, the following is typically true:

- When a parent is iconized, children are iconized.
- When a parent is closed, children are closed.
- When a parent is moved on the display, children are not moved.

In some environments, such as Microsoft Windows, a child window must be drawn within the borders of its parent. If the user attempts to move the child beyond these borders, only the portion of the child that is still visible within the parent window is displayed. This is called clipping.

Modal and Modeless Windows

Windows can be either "modal" or "modeless" (sometimes called non-modal). These terms refer to the manner in which the user interacts with the window.

A modeless window allows the user to activate other windows before closing the current window. Users are free to determine sequence and can work with many windows simultaneously. Modeless windows allow users to take full advantage of the GUI.

A modal window, on the other hand, requires users to respond before working in another window. "System modal" behavior locks all windows in the *system*. "Application modal" behavior locks all windows in an *application*. Because modal windows restrict users to working with only one window at a time, they can be used to implement a sequenced processing in a windowed environment.

Active and Inactive Windows

A window is considered active if it has the input "focus." Several windows may be visible, but if the user types on the keyboard, which window reflects that input? The one with input focus, or the active window. The active window is set apart from other windows with some sort of visual emphasis. The title bar may be highlighted, for example. If a window does not have the input focus, it is considered inactive.

From a user's perspective, only one window may be active at a time. Technically, however, in many modern windowing environments, logic for "inactive" windows may be executing in the background (e.g., spreadsheet recalculation and chart plotting).

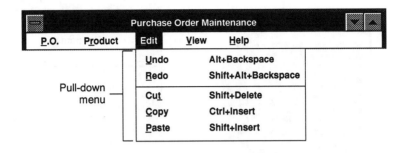

Exhibit II-4-9. A Pull-Down Menu

Menus

Menus are window components that provide users a list of options for making an action, routing, or setting choice. An action choice immediately begins to perform an action, such as Find.

A routing choice displays a menu or window that contains additional choices used to further specify or clarify the routing choice. A setting choice allows a user to change a property of an object. The choices on a menu typically vary depending on the state of the object or application—for instance, charting options only appear when a chart object is selected. Separator lines are used to visually divide groups of choices within a single menu.

There are three menu types that may be combined to meet application requirements.

Pull-Down Menus. Pull-down menus are accessed from the menu bar or the system menu icon. (See Exhibit II-4-9.) These menus typically have action or routing choices that relate to the contents of the window but may also have settings choices.

Cascaded Menus. When a menu choice routes the user to another menu, the resulting menu is called a cascaded menu. These secondary menus usually have settings choices, but may have action or routing choices as well. They are used to reduce the length of a menu.

Pop-Up Menus. Pop-up menus provide choices specific to an object. These menus, often displayed next to an object, are not visible until the user requests that the pop-up be displayed (usually with a specific mouse button).

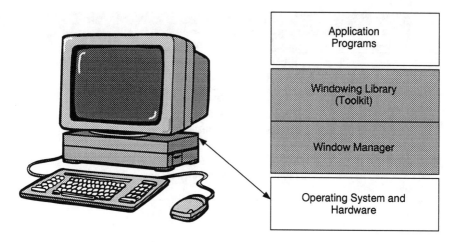

Application Programs
Windowing Library (Toolkit)
Window Manager
Operating System and Hardware

Exhibit II-4-10. Example of a Toolbar

Tool Bars

A tool bar is a graphical area at the top of the window just below the menu bar that contains icons for commonly used functions in the application. (See Exhibit II-4-10.) The action can be invoked by clicking on the toolbar icon instead of pulling down a menu and selecting it from there. Depending on the application, the toolbar may be hard-coded or fully customizable.

Client Area Components

The user works in the client area—the area just below the menu bar but inside the scroll bars. This area can contain graphics, text, and controls. Controls ("widgets" in Motif) are predefined graphical images that allow users to enter or select data elements. Often, a control visibly changes appearance to indicate its state. For example, the label of the control may be gray, not black, indicating that the control is currently inactive.

This section lists many of the common controls.

Pointers and Cursors. A pointer is a symbol, often in the shape of an arrow, that is displayed on the screen and is moved by a pointing device. It is used to point or select choices, or to otherwise interact with objects. (See Exhibit II-4-11.)

The GUI often comes with a set of predefined pointers to convey specific information. For example, an arrow is used to select or move

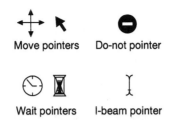

Move pointers   Do-not pointer

Wait pointers   I-beam pointer

Exhibit II-4-11. Examples of Pointers and Cursors

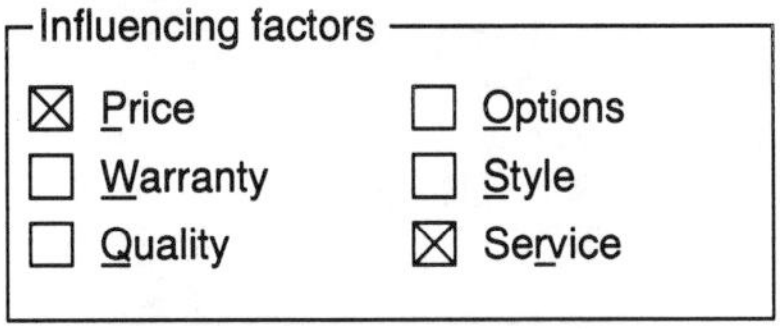

┌─ Influencing factors ─────────────────┐
│ ☒ Price   ☐ Options   │
│ ☐ Warranty   ☐ Style   │
│ ☐ Quality   ☒ Service   │
└───────────────────────────────────────┘

Exhibit II-4- 12. Check Boxes

---

objects. An hourglass or watch is used to indicate that the user must wait while the computer performs some function. An I-beam pointer indicates that the area in which the pointer currently appears is used for text entry.

Check Box. This control is a simple rectangle with two clearly distinguishable states: checked and not checked. It is used to capture and display data of a binary nature (yes/no, on/off). When organized into groups, several of the options can be selected (checked) at once. (See Exhibit II-4-12.)

Radio Buttons. This control is a simple circle with two clearly distinguishable states: on or off. (See Exhibit II-4-13.) Radio buttons derive their name from the radios of older cars. On these radios, only one button could be pressed at a time. With GUIs, radio buttons are always used in a group to provide a set of mutually exclusive choices. Only one button within a group may be on at a time.

List Box. This control displays a list of objects or settings that a user can view and select. (See Exhibit II-4-14.) List boxes can support single or multiple selection of items in the list. In some environments, this control may be editable.

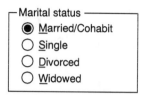

Exhibit II-4-13. Radio Buttons

Magazine titles

List box

Exhibit II-4-14. List Box

Single-Line Entry Field. This control is used for the entry of a single line of text. An entry field can be allowed to scroll horizontally if more information is available than is currently visible.

Multiple-Line Entry Field. This control is used for the entry of more than one line of text. A multiline entry field can be scrolled horizontally or vertically if more information is available than is currently visible.

Drop-Down Combination Box. This control combines the functions of an entry field and a list box. (See Exhibit II-4-15.) The combination box contains a list of objects or settings that a user can scroll through and select. Alternatively, the user can merely type text into the entry field. The entered text need not match the choices provided in the list.

Group Box. This rectangular box is drawn around a group of fields to indicate that the fields are related. (See Exhibit II-4-16.) It has no behavior of its own. Group boxes usually contain labels or titles.

Push Button. This control contains text, graphics, or both, representing an action choice or routing choice (e.g., Cancel, Help, Add, Up-

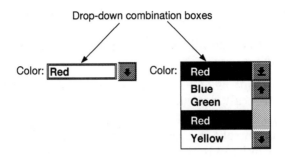

Exhibit II-4-1 5. Drop-Down Combination Box

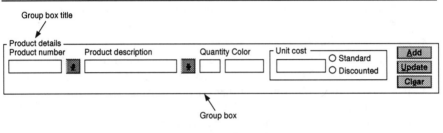

Exhibit II-4-1 6. Group Box

date, Clear) that is activated when a user selects it. Push buttons and menus are generally the only controls used to invoke an action.

Scroll Bar. This control indicates to a user that more information is available than fits in the scrollable area. If the information being viewed is wider than the specified area, a horizontal scroll bar should be provided. If the information being viewed is taller than the area, a vertical scroll bar should be provided. These bars (see Exhibit II-4-5) are often used in conjunction with other controls such as entry fields, combination boxes, and list boxes.

Having discussed the various components of GUIs, the next section takes a frank look at the challenges facing designers in a GUI environment.

ADVANTAGES OF GUIs

Ease of Use and Reduced Training Costs

Although the benefit that comes from ease of system use is difficult to quantify, it is generally agreed that training costs are lower for GUI applications than for traditional online applications. This may be especially important to organizations that have high staff turnover rates and high training costs.

In addition, it is generally agreed that well-designed GUIs are easier and more satisfying to use. There are many reasons for this belief.

1. *Recognition, not recall.* GUI interfaces allow users to recognize, rather than recall, data (i.e., codes).
2. *Faster response.* GUI applications provide a new, lower level of interaction (keystroke, mouse movement), which allows them to respond more quickly to the user. This responsiveness can reduce errors and enhance user satisfaction.
3. *More intuitive.* GUI interfaces can be more intuitive and can provide visual cues to the user as to operations that are valid, available, and expected.
4. *Better help facilities.* The more robust online help available in many GUI applications allows a user to read help text and to simultaneously view the windows he is working in. Moreover, help is often made available through a hypertext mechanism that allows users to select successively more detailed help topics. This gives users faster access to a greater volume of help information.
5. *Support for multiple applications.* Because a windowed environment allows users to view and work on multiple applications simultaneously, it is well suited to professional users who need to switch between applications and tasks more frequently. In addition, GUI applications often make it easy to share text and images between applications and to create new, hybrid documents.

Together, these features make the system easier to learn and use. When designed correctly, a GUI can significantly help the novice or casual user, and, at the same time, not penalize the experienced user.

Integration of Different Data Types

Because GUIs run on graphical displays and utilize a local processor, the platform inherently is suited for the display and manipulation of other types of data types. Video, voice, and many other types of information can be integrated into a GUI application to assist the user in learning about a task, marketing a product or service, or eliminating the handling and routing of information that would otherwise require paper (e.g., a picture of a damaged auto filed with an insurance claim).

Facilitation of Business Process Reengineering

Because GUI applications allow users to do things they were previously unable to do, they can change the type and quality of work produced by their users. For example, GUIs allow auto insurance claims processors to view photographic images of damaged vehicles online; office workers can create professional quality documents and presentations without the help of a graphics department; developers, designers, and customers can view a building's interior before construction actually begins.

In addition, by providing automated support for professionals, it is often possible to reduce or eliminate the need for transcription processes. The insurance agent may now choose to enter information directly into a computer system, eliminating the need for a back office "middle man." Furthermore, with mobile personal computers, the entered information can be used to print a contract instantly in a potential customer's home, thus eliminating wasted time and effort otherwise involved in mailings and corrections.

In these examples, GUI technology changes the business process by allowing unnecessary or non-value-added steps to be eliminated and by providing better information and feedback at the point of need. As a result, GUIs are often key enablers in reengineering the business. In many cases, the costs of a GUI are often justified by the value derived from changing the business process rather than from savings in ease of use.

GUI CHALLENGES

Need for Intelligent Workstation

Because many GUI applications require a substantial amount of local processing, they can run only on intelligent workstations or on X-terminals. (X-terminals are dumb terminals for GUIs.) Although the cost of these workstations continues to fall, it is still higher than the cost of standard dumb terminals. As a result, the costs associated with deploying a GUI to first-time users are typically several thousand dollars per user, above and beyond the cost of the development alone. For a small number of users this is probably nothing to worry about. For large-scale implementations, however, the additional cost can be much more significant.

Demanding Design and Usability Testing

Although an effective GUI design makes an application easy for the user, executing an effective design takes considerable time and energy on the part of the developers.

Efficient GUI designs are typically the result of an effort that involves significant participation from users, systems builders, and usability or human factors experts. Discipline and analysis are required in order to balance the flexibility offered by GUIs with the cost of development and those capabilities that are really useful to users. For example, imagine an airline reservation system for dedicated reservation agents that was based on drag- and-drop GUI techniques. The interface would be wonderful to look at but hardly productive to use eight hours a day every day.

Allowing sufficient time and budget for usability testing is also more critical for GUI applications than for traditional online applications. This is because the GUI interface is more likely to be different from what mainframe applications users are accustomed to.

When users first see a prototype of the system, they are often distracted by the colors and glitz of the new system, and they may not notice any shortcomings in the interface design. It is not until users sit down and actually try to use the system several times to perform an activity that they realize how useful or obstructive the design really is. It is advisable to perform usability tests (using realistic mockups or prototypes) early in the design and construction process so that any significant problems are identified in time to be corrected before release.

Expensive to Develop and Maintain

There are three primary contributors to the high cost associated with GUI applications development. Each of these increases the complexity of the application logic and, correspondingly, the cost of development and maintenance.

GUIs Are Event-Driven. GUIs are continually sending, receiving, and responding to messages. In some cases, while processing one message the application may take an action that causes another message to be generated that gets processed immediately—thus invoking another piece of application code before the current function has completed processing.

Moreover, GUI applications typically manage a great number of messages because it is possible to send messages at very low levels of interaction (for example, when a user presses a character key). This combination of nested messages and the number of possible messages can result in subtle interactions that must be identified and accounted for in the applications design.

Managing Windows and Data Is Complex. Many GUI applications allow users to work in multiple windows simultaneously. Managing these windows and the data they share is complex. For instance, if one window is allowing the user to maintain a customer's address and another window is displaying the shipping address for the same customer, when the customer address is changed and committed to the database, the shipping address window must be updated to reflect this change. Typically, implementing this capability requires custom mechanisms.

There Are More Unit and System Testing Conditions. Development is further complicated by the increased number of unit and system testing conditions that exist in a GUI environment. For example, data validation logic must be tested to ensure that it is invoked when the user exits a field. Similarly, there may be many conditions for enabling and disabling buttons (the OK button, the Add button) that must also be tested. All these conditions must be identified, tested, and verified. Even with automated testing tools, the test planning effort is substantial and should not be overlooked.

APPLICATION STRUCTURE AND SERVICES

Although GUI applications may need to perform the same basic business logic as a traditional application, the way this logic is structured and supported can be substantially different. Some of the biggest differences are discussed next.

Validation

GUI applications usually validate a user's entries at the character or field level. Cross-field dependencies within a window are usually performed on field-exit and must take into account the state of each field involved in the validation (for instance, some fields may still be invalid, in which case the cross-field validation cannot be performed). Field dependencies across windows must take into account whether data has been entered in the other windows.

For instance, totaling an order requires that sales tax be calculated, but if the user has not yet entered customer information (e.g., the state of residence), the tax rate is not available; thus the calculation is meaningless and probably should not be performed.

Window Flow

Although GUI application window flow is determined to a great degree by the user, for some types of applications it is usually necessary to control the user's flow in some way. For example, in an order entry system, it may be desirable to allow a user to specify the customer information first or go directly to the order entry window. However, the order cannot be completed until the order information *and* the customer information are valid. In this case, the order confirmation window could not be opened until the previous conditions were met.

Essentially, the control is indirect; the user is not forced to take actions but is prevented from taking invalid actions. This type of control is enforced through selective enablement of controls and action choices.

Restart and Recovery

Although restart and recovery strategies are desirable in a GUI environment, they are difficult to implement. At the point of failure, an application may have multiple windows open. Moreover, multiple applications may be open. It can be extremely complex to return all these windows and applications to their exact states before failure. The more typical approach is to allow work in process to be saved periodically during lengthy tasks and to rely on the database management system for data recovery and integrity.

CHOOSING A GUI

Although in many ways Microsoft Windows has become the de facto standard GUI, other GUIs are available. The best known are IBM's OS/2 Presentation Manager, Apple's Macintosh, and the Open Software Foundation's Motif for UNIX and the X-Window system. Some of the more common factors to consider when choosing a GUI are discussed next.

Platform and Device Support

The existing hardware or operating system can influence the GUI decision because of an existing installed base, because of plans for future systems, or because of the specific capabilities of a platform. For instance, a shop with a large base of existing Macintosh devices may not be able to justify a move to a different platform. An organization that plans to move to pen-based devices may want to choose the GUI that helps preserve investment in applications development and packaged software. Last, high-powered devices used for complex calculations or visualizations may limit or dictate the GUI choice.

Resource Requirements

The memory/central processing unit/disk requirements of the GUI can affect the cost of the workstation required to effectively run GUI applications (especially if the platform is being rolled out to hundreds or thousands of users). For example, today Windows NT is more expensive to deploy than Windows 3.1 just on the basis of hardware and memory requirements.

Development Tools

The characteristics of some applications in an organization's portfolio may necessitate the use of specific tools that are only available on certain GUI platforms (e.g., special 4GLs targeting a certain type or style of application or such domain-specific tools as scientific math and graphics libraries or data visualization tools).

Applications Software

By far the biggest driver in GUI selection is the availability of third-party applications software. This software may be general-purpose applications software such as electronic mail, word processing, and personal organizers, or it may be special applications programs such as stock ticker monitoring, oil field exploration, and commercial loan risk assessment.

Increasingly, users require and demand access to the GUI desktop and applications, and the availability of various third-party application components is enabling IS personnel to deliver better solutions cheaper and faster by integrating rather than building from scratch. This is by far the biggest factor related to the dominance of Microsoft Windows. It has reached the critical mass of shrinkwrapped applications software to make it highly desirable by users, and it has the installed base to make it worthwhile for software developers to support.

MAKING APPLICATIONS DEVELOPMENT EASIER

Once an organization chooses a GUI platform, a team begins developing and integrating applications for the business users. As noted earlier, a number of challenges face the GUI developer.

Fortunately, in the past few years, the market for development tools has come a long way in terms of providing common capabilities and services required by GUI applications which allow applications developers to focus more on the business problem than on the basic mechanics expected of any effective GUI application.

Painting the Actual GUI

In today's development environment, designers are likely to paint the actual windows and components of the GUI with a GUI tool such as Visual Basic, PowerBuilder, or Borland's Delphi. Following are the primary steps in GUI development:

1. *Lay out the window.* Designers should lay out, or "paint," the window and its various controls (menus, buttons, etc.). Thanks to the

GUI tool, designers can rapidly paint the window by selecting types of controls from the basic graphical palette provided by the development software.

2. *Specify display attributes.* Designers should specify the display attributes of the particular controls chosen. For example, the designer might specify the type of field (numeric? alphanumeric?) and the background and foreground colors for entry fields. He or she might select an icon for a label rather than text. For list boxes, the designer might specify different columns and data that would appear within them.

3. *Specify behaviors.* Designers should begin to specify behaviors—that is, how the controls should respond to user input. For example, when the user clicks on a button that reads OK, what should happen? If the user types a valid entry into a field, how should the cross-field validation be invoked?

4. *Run and test.* Run and test the window. Some tools may require a code generation step here. However, most are ready to run the window after it has been painted. At this point, the designer should run the window to test whether it works correctly and then iterate back to step 1 or 2 for new functions and new windows.

The presentation services model has been extremely useful in the establishment of a productive development environment. The model describes the basic functions and features that an application requires to provide the minimum levels of expected GUI behavior.

Systems designers should purchase tools and libraries that provide as many as possible of the features noted below and then supplement them when necessary to provide a base architecture on which GUI applications can be developed. The model and a description of its various components follows.

PRESENTATION SERVICES MODEL

Tho procontation oorviooo oomponont of tho oliont/oorvor arohitooturo enables an application to manage the human-computer interface. This includes capturing user actions and generating events, presenting data to the user, and assisting in the management of the window flow.

Typically, presentation services are only required by client workstations. The major presentation services components are a window system, a window interaction manager, a desktop manager, and interaction-style services. (See Exhibit II-4-17.)

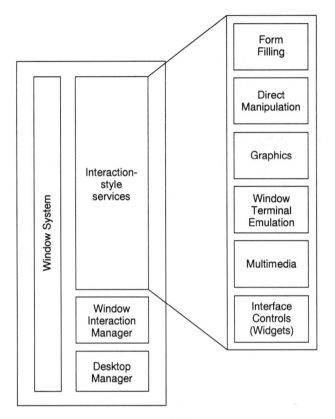

Exhibit II-4-17. Presentation Services Model

Window System

The GUI window system library provides the base capability for detecting user actions, managing windows on the display, and displaying data in windows. Examples of window systems include Presentation Manager for OS/2, Microsoft Windows for DOS, and X- Windows/Motif for UNIX.

Desktop Manager

This element provides services for launching applications and desktop utilities and managing their integration. Most windowing systems contain elementary desktop manager capability (e.g., Microsoft's Program Manager), but often more user-friendly or functional desktop manager services are required.

The most commonly required extension for business applications is the ability to log-in to the application and to customize the desktop based on the user's characteristics, authority level, and preferences. This customization also establishes the necessary context for applications to be able to determine security privileges and database information (e.g., table space to use) without requiring that users log in to each application.

Window Interaction Manager

This element provides an application with services for managing the dependencies between windows within a single application, including services for controlling dialog flow and generating events when a window changes its state (e.g., so that dependent windows can update their display to reflect the change). It can also include services to activate a window that is already displaying data in which the user is interested (e.g., activating the window with Customer X rather than creating another copy).

Interaction-Style Services

The richness of the GUI environment really becomes obvious in regard to interaction services. A GUI application can interact in many different ways with the user, and each interaction style typically has different technical features and correspondingly different services for interacting with the application code.

There are several common interaction styles and capabilities useful in reducing applications development effort.

Form-Filling Services. Form-filling services enable applications to use fields to display and collect data. A field may be a traditional 3270-style field in which a user types data or data is displayed textually, or it may be a more graphical field such as a check box, a radio button, or a list box. Form-filling services provide support for the following:

- *Display, input, validation.* These services support the display and input of different types of data (text, numeric, date) in various formats (e.g., US, European, iconic, custom formatting mask) and perform basic validation such as range or format checks. Often, these capabilities are provided by the controls or widgets (discussed later).
- *Mapping support.* This capability maps window field data to a program variable structure in memory so that applications do not need to issue complex windowing system dependent messages or APIs to view or change values. These services may also automate the merging of application data with predefined electronic form templates. Many 4GLs and object-oriented tools provide this service inherently. Tools that generate

3GL code (e.g., C or COBOL) typically do not provide this service or provide it through additional runtime architecture.

- *Field interaction manager.* A Form-Filling Field Interaction Manager coordinates activity across fields in a window. It manages field interdependencies and invokes application logic based on the state of fields and user actions. For example, the Field Interaction Manager may disable the OK button until all required input fields contain valid data. These services reduce the application logic complexity inherent to an interactive windowed interface.

Graphics Services. Graphics services allow an application to access and manipulate data that is represented to the end user by visual images. Graphics services can be broken down as follows:

- *Display, input, validation.* Graphics services provide support for displaying such simple graphics as lines, boxes, and circles and such business graphics as bar charts and pie charts. More robust graphics services may support three-dimensional graphics, graphics for building complex images (widgets) such as dials and gauges, and interfaces to third-party graphics packages.

  These services enable an application to invoke logic when a user directly modifies the application's images and may enforce predefined validation rules. For example, these services may prevent a user from resizing a bar so that its length corresponds to some number greater than 100%. These capabilities are typically implemented through controls or widgets.

- *Mapping support.* Graphics services map the data associated with the graphics display to a program variable structure in memory so that applications do not need to issue complex messages or APIs to view or change these data values.

- *Windowed terminal emulation.* Windowed terminal emulation services support the display of terminal emulation sessions in windows. They also support the cutting and pasting of terminal emulation data from one window to another. Typically, third-party packages provide these services, allowing users to access host sessions (e.g., 3270 or VT100) from one or more windows on their desktop.

Multimedia Services. Multimedia services enable applications to capture, display, and manipulate image, audio, and video data. These services are divided as follows:

- *Display.* In the case of image and video, these services provide the ability to display an image or playback video within an area of a window. For audio, these services offer the ability to play back audio data. For video and audio, the playback services are typically performed in a multitasking fashion so that the user may interrupt the playback or perform other tasks during playback.

- *Input.* These services allow a user to scan an image or record video/audio. In some cases, users also have the ability to modify or edit this data (e.g., clean up an image or splice out unnecessary portions of audio). In addition, these services frequently offer compression services to reduce the amount of memory required to store the captured data. Mapping support is not usually offered because the data is voluminous and usually is stored in a format not easily manipulated directly by the application.

The display and input services can be provided by controls/widgets (discussed later) or by common functions that can be invoked by the application.

Direct Manipulation Services. Direct manipulation services enable applications to provide a direct manipulation interface (often called drag and drop). A direct manipulation interface allows users to manage multiple "application objects" by manipulating visual representations of those objects. For example, a user may sell stock by dragging stock icons out of a portfolio icon and onto a trading floor icon. Direct manipulation services can be further divided as follows:

- *Display, input, validation.* These services enable applications to represent application objects as icons, to control the display characteristics (color, location) of these icons, and to invoke validation or processing logic when an end user acts on an application object. "Acting on" an object may include single-clicking, double-clicking, dragging, or sizing. These services are slowly emerging from the GUI window managers but are still commonly provided through controls/widgets and common functions.

- *Mapping support.* Mapping support maps the object's display characteristics to a program variable structure in memory. This allows an application's object handler logic to access the object's display data as if it were just data in working storage; the object handler does not need to send messages or invoke APIs. Application logic outside the object handler, however, would have to use a message or an API to access another object's data.

Interface Controls (Widgets). Interface controls, or widgets, provide the lowest-level building blocks for most user interaction. (See the section "Client Area Components" for an introduction to controls.)

The core windowing systems typically provide a basic set of controls—menus, buttons, text fields, and list boxes. Most business applications, however, require capabilities beyond the basics provided by the windowing system. Common requirements include specific validation and formatting for different data types (e.g., numeric, date, and time).

Another common requirement is the ability to display and manipulate lists of columnar data (this is nontrivial with most basic list boxes because of their use of proportional spaced fonts). Many tools either come with or have available control/widget extensions that provide some or all of these additional capabilities. Some tools, such as Visual Basic (and others that support the Visual Basic control protocol), have a large third-party market of controls ranging from 3D buttons, to tables, to voice recording/playback, to facsimile control. Ensuring that the minimum requirements are available is important and determining what other controls are available can help developers deliver better and more interesting applications with minimal additional effort.

Systems must provide hooks to online help for all the styles of interaction. Typically, this help is table driven and can be hooked to fields, display objects, windows, and applications. In many cases, the GUI window manager provides the help display mechanism and offers the ability to link topics with hypertext and to embed graphics in the help text.

National and Multiple Language Support. Some organizations require applications that provide both national language support (NLS) and multiple language support (MLS). Applications that provide NLS display, for example, literals, icon labels, and report headings in the end user's native language. They also accept keyboard entries that correspond to the language's alphabet characters and symbols (e.g., ñ or ö). If an NLS application supported both French and English users, two versions of the application would exist—one in French and one in English.

Conversely, MLS applications can support multiple languages with the same version of code. In these applications, everything (e.g., text strings, messages, and format options) that is language dependent is defined external to the application. The appropriate item to use is controlled by a language or culture parameter specified in a user's profile.

The next chapter looks at a closely related component of the execution architecture, integrated performance support (IPS) services. Presentation services ensure that information is delivered to the client in a powerful fashion whereas IPS ensures that additional forms of support for the use of that information are also provided.

II-5
Integrated Performance Support Services

Integrated performance support (IPS) services are a set of application services designed to support the performance of the user at the point of need. IPS enables application users to do their work better by providing advice, tools, reference, and training on demand. In advanced systems, this support is provided proactively, as well.

One might argue that true *integrated* performance support is a distinctive feature of client/server architectures. Traditionally, information systems have been built to process transactions around specific business functions. Client/server systems are designed and built to transact business across multiple business functions.

IPS allows for the construction of systems that can themselves adapt to meet the needs of the work force, continuously. IPS moves us beyond the conception of the employee as a "system user" to an employee who is a true "knowledge worker."

Client/server allows us to move beyond systems that merely teach and inform to systems that can anticipate performance needs and coach workers through particularly challenging moments. With IPS we move from a "one size fits all" system to a system that provides support that can be tailored to the user's work objectives, background, ability level, preferences, and, indeed, the immediate task at hand. The knowledge worker may never before have encountered his task, but the task must still be supported with knowledge and skill and dispatched with speed and accuracy.

Exhibit II-5-1 shows the components of IPS services within the client/server execution architecture: application help and performance support services, which in turn is made up of advisory services, job aid services, reference services, and training services.

APPLICATION HELP

Application help services enable an application to provide simple context-sensitive help at the field, window, or application level. Once the help

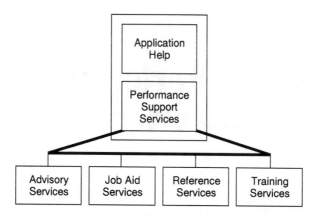

Exhibit II-5-1. Integrated Performance Support Services

system is invoked, it manages navigation through the help text. This is usually done using hypertext links, where selecting "hot spots" in the text invokes the display of more detailed information about that topic.

PERFORMANCE SUPPORT SERVICES

Performance support services comprise four subservices.

Advisory Services

Advisory services acts as the coach or the adviser, providing advice and assistance and suggesting support options to help the worker examine alternatives, make effective decisions, and solve problems. Advisory services can also help a complex organization learn and grow in accordance with management's policies. Support from advisory services includes such things as the following:

- Support in diagnosing problems.
- Case descriptions of how experts and coworkers have resolved similar situations.
- Decision modeling with simulations to help workers make tactical and strategic decisions.
- Guidance to identify the appropriate support services.

Advisory services can provide both minor and major services. It can prompt workers, reminding them of certain rules or procedures that have to be followed. In one system, for example, plant workers shutting down a facility are warned about specific safety procedures that have to be followed for shutdown. The system then walks the workers through these procedures.

But advisory services can also support workers in more complex work such as decision making and problem solving. Some systems can help workers with decision modeling and with pattern recognition—things that machines can sometimes do better than humans. These more complex advisory functions become relevant in situations with one or more of the following:

- Large number of variables.
- Many decision rules.
- High degree of task complexity.
- Inconsistent or conflicting data.
- Unpredictable conditions.

Job Aid Services

Job aid services provide automated tools and techniques to simplify routine and repetitive tasks. Job aid services act as the worker's "personal assistant," automating or simplifying all or some parts of a task. Ideally, the job aid is context sensitive and integrated with the task at hand. Following are some of the functions of this service:

- *Messaging and communication.* Job aid services can route information quickly and efficiently through electronic mail (E-mail), faxing, and other data transmission devices. It also facilitates the distribution of messages to several individuals, both inside and outside the organization. Messages can be enhanced using multiple formats including text, graphics, and video.
- *Computation.* Job aid services can aid in the computation of numerical data. In one system, for example, a lender must price a potential loan to determine how profitable it will be and produce a sample income statement. Job aid services can provide a pricing worksheet, into which all parameters of the loan can be entered, which will produce a sample income statement.
- *Document creation and report generation.* Job aid services can assist with generating documents and reports. Templates can speed the creation of letters and memos. In the system just mentioned, loan documents can be automatically created from variables entered by the lender.
- *Scheduling.* Job aid services can track a knowledge worker's schedule and automatically alert the knowledge worker to upcoming

events. This function becomes increasingly useful for workers with demands on their time.

- *Data representation.* Data representation refers to the ability to quickly change the representation of data based on the preferences or needs of the worker. For example, a tool that shows profit and loss statements may use various types of charting techniques (e.g., graphs and tables) that display numerical data in various formats. Also, the table may allow for quick restructuring depending on the type of work performed.

Many information systems now in operation have some sort of job aid for the user. Word processing software, for example, has spell checking, a thesaurus, grammar checking, and online help. Job aid services, however, deliver *integrated* help.

A job aid connects the current task with the relevant information, and so could be thought of as an "intelligent job aid." It is proactive rather than reactive, active rather than passive, providing the exact job aid that is needed, exactly where and when it is needed. Today's Help Wizards are examples of more integrated help delivery that can assist users in learning or performing a task or in diagnosing a problem.

Reference Services

Reference services serve as the librarian or, perhaps, the historian of the system. They structure and present job-relevant information from an organization's internal knowledge base and from external public- or vendor-supplied databases.

Reference services are particularly powerful in the manner in which they can provide context-sensitive knowledge. That is, when the worker desires, reference services provide information relevant to particular tasks being performed by the worker. Reference services move beyond the mere presentation of random information to the presentation of applicable knowledge.

Reference services provide many different kinds of information, such as:

- Product descriptions.
- Policies.
- Diagrams.
- Pictures.
- Information about the organization.
- Industry-related information.
- Research information.

- Historical information.

Reference services may be used to browse, search and retrieve, and communicate, thus supporting users in special ways. For example:

- *Browse.* Reference services enable knowledge workers to browse through the repository of the organization's knowledge capital by producing information in various formats, including text, graphics, full-motion video, digitized images, and audio. In one system, for example, a commercial lender can use an industry research tool to browse across various industries.

- *Search and retrieve.* Reference services allow knowledge workers to access a topic index (e.g., the Help menu on various software packages) or select context-sensitive support. For example, in one system for the cellular telephone service industry, customer service representatives can quickly access and listen to representative sounds made by telephones that are not working properly. When a customer has a problem, the agent can play the sounds associated with the customer's model of telephone in order to diagnose the problem quickly and to provide a remedy to the customer.

- *Communicate.* Reference services can be used to maintain structured, catalogued, or indexed information that is frequently updated and provided at the point of need. For example, organizations can have a "What's New" knowledge base to communicate the latest revisions to ever-changing policies and procedures. In this way, communication between knowledge workers is facilitated through the knowledge base.

In addition, reference services can be used to facilitate the information exchange between workers. For example, using an E-mail package, a knowledge worker who wants information can post a question regarding a specific process. Workers with expertise on the subject can answer the question, and the new question/answer is catalogued in the knowledge base. Increasingly, support for this type of "conversation" is being seen as an important part of the workplace.

Training Services

Training services play the role of a tutor, a personal instructor. The parallel with tutoring is important here because training within the system is a one-on-one, tailored event, unlike traditional corporate and schoolroom education, and unlike most approaches to computer-based training (CBT). Like a competent tutor, training services provides relevant knowledge, examples, and practice opportunities to help workers gain additional skills.

Training Services Delivers Training in a "Granular" Manner. Traditional corporate training, even CBT, has been structured hierarchically and sequentially according to some overall instructional strategy and approach. For example, many courses consist of a number of modules that are sequenced beginning with orientation and then moving through presentation and exercises on to a final test. The focus of CBT has been directed, for the most part, at providing modular training programs outside of the job context.

The approach to training in IPS services brings training close to the real work at hand, integrating training with current tasks. It is structured in small chunks or "granules" and is provided as an integral part of the work environment. Training can be delivered on the job, where a worker completes training while performing tasks.

Training Services Emphasize "Learning by Doing." Everyone learns best when they can immediately apply their new skills on the job. If individuals do not use learning soon after they acquire it and then reinforce it experientially, it fades from their memories quickly. Training services provide task-specific training on demand, rather than relying on classroom training taking place away from the work site, or relying on a separate "training event."

Training Services Provide Immediate Feedback. Training services present essential information with built-in practice exercises and immediate feedback relevant to the task at hand.

Training Services Support the Adult Learner. Traditional training is instructor- or trainer-controlled. Adult learners in particular must have training tailored to their unique needs, training that they can access in ways that best suit them.

CONCLUSION

The most noticeable aspects of client/server computing for computer users are presentation services and IPS services. This fact has both positive and negative consequences for the developer.

On the positive side, the developer can work with a truly creative set of ideas about usability and human-computer interaction. On the negative side, the developer may get sidetracked into spending too much time with esthetics and not enough time with function. Developers must be sure that their users know that a system is not to be judged entirely on the colors or pretty icons of the primary interface.

II-6
Information Access Services

Today's client/server information is much broader and diverse in nature than traditional data, understood as characters. Client/server information can consist of graphics, image, voice, and full-motion video. This information is extremely complex and difficult to manage, control, and deliver.

The information challenge of the workplace today is twofold, a feast-or-famine syndrome: Workers often cannot find information when they need it, or they may be confronted by too much information at any given time. Information is of no use unless we know where it is and how to get at it. Information access services are where that knowledge of access is achieved.

In a traditional computing environment, an organization's information is usually centralized in a particular location, or it may be fragmented across multiple locations. In a client/server environment, however, information is most often distributed because distribution of processors and data is an inherent part of client/server.

Exhibit II-6-1 presents an example of how information may be distributed in a client/server computing environment. In this example from an airline information system, the reservations are centralized in Dallas. Each region has a server to maintain its own flights and maintenance information (horizontally segmented by region), and each workstation at each region maintains replicated airport and plane data. In general, the following may be said about the information within this system:

- Information that is stable or static is found on all clients.
- Information that is volatile, or specific to particular locations or groups is on the server.
- Information that is accessed and updated throughout the organization is on the central system, or enterprise system.
- Most information (except, perhaps, for some static codes tables) is stored on the server, even though the processing may be distributed across client and server.

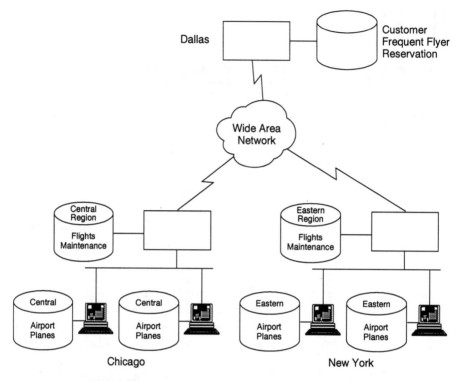

Exhibit II-6-1. Information in a Client/Server Environment

- Putting information on a client may require information replication across clients (usually limited to codes tables), and could lead to synchronization and integrity issues.

CHARACTERISTICS OF INFORMATION IN CLIENT/SERVER COMPUTING

The example illustrates the primary characteristics of information in a client/server environment.

Information Is Distinct From Processes

The most important characteristic of client/server information is that the information itself is kept distinct from the processes that access and use it. The chief function of the client/server architecture is to isolate the business logic from the technology itself. Within the information access services component of the architecture, this isolation is achieved by maintaining two layers, a logical layer and a physical layer.

- From a logical viewpoint, an application issues a request for information, and elements of that information (e.g., location, formats, and management mechanisms) are transparent to the user. A single information request is all that is necessary to retrieve the information, potentially from multiple sources, to support a business function.
- From a physical viewpoint, the information may actually be stored on, and retrieved from, many different sources that are being managed by many different database managers on many different platforms.

Information Is Usually Distributed

Distributed information can be defined formally as "information that is physically separated between locations or platforms." Client/server computing does not imply distributed information, nor does distributed information imply client/server. However, most client/server systems rely on some form of distributed information.

Client/server implies more processing locations (geographic and platform) with local disk storage capabilities. Because information should reside close to the users who need to access that information, information distribution offers important advantages, discussed later.

Information Is Spread Across Multiple Environments

Because of the distributed nature of information in a client/server environment, organizations often have to deal with a multivendor environment. This places demands on the networking and communications aspects of client/server computing, discussed later.

Information Is in Multiple Forms

The graphical environment of today's applications and the ability to send different types of information (e.g., data, graphic, image, voice, or video) directly to the desktop have made the information environment of client/server computing much more complex.

Information May Be Replicated or Duplicated

Because information is generally distributed in a client/server environment, it often means that information must be replicated across multiple locations. The existence of multiple copies of information means that users must be especially concerned with keeping them synchronized and accurate.

Replication of information implies methods to perform the replication, additional disk resources, possible integrity problems because of multiple copies, and information management and ownership issues. These issues are addressed later in this chapter.

Information Is Often Fragmented or Segmented

Because information accessed by an application is heterogeneous and dispersed, it is often fragmented. The information may be recombined in various ways, and so the information access services component of the architecture must have a way of ensuring the integrity of the information in its various combinations.

ISSUES IN THE DISTRIBUTION OF INFORMATION

The ultimate goal of distributed information processing is to give every user transparent access to dispersed, disparate information. With client/server computing, developers seek to isolate applications from knowledge of information location, information access methods, and information management products. At the same time, they seek to ensure that the information is reliable—that it has integrity.

When to Consider a Distributed Database Strategy

When particular business functions have certain characteristics, distributed information and distributed information processing may be considered:

1. *Geographical distribution.* The business functions are spread over several different sites, making it impractical to support some (or all) of the processing requirements from a central site.
2. *Local decision making and independence.* The organizational structure is distributed and the business has several local sites with the authority to make local decisions as to how to process and act upon its information.
3. *Performance.* The response time at the local site becomes unacceptable due to the transfer of data between the central and local sites.
4. *Scalability.* Business growth has caused the volume of data to expand, the volume of processing to increase, or has resulted in expansion to new sites.

Potential Benefits

The potential benefits for a distributed database strategy apply both to true distributed database management systems and to implementations that incorporate distributed data management strategies.

Organization. A distributed system may better reflect an organization's structure, which often is logically distributed (e.g., into divisions, departments, and projects) as well as physically distributed (e.g., into plants, warehouses, and branch offices).

Ease of Growth. Once installed, a distributed system is able to expand more gracefully than a nondistributed system. For example, if significant business growth has caused the volume of information to expand or the volume of processing to increase, it may be easier to expand the system by adding a new site to an existing distributed system than replacing or extending an existing centralized system with a larger one.

Lower Costs. It may be less expensive for organizations to add another server or to extend the server than to add or extend a mainframe.

Local Autonomy. Distributing a system allows individual groups within an organization to exercise control over their own information while still being able to access information at remote locations when necessary.

Increased Availability. A distributed system may offer greater availability than a centralized system in that it can continue to function (though at a reduced level) even if an individual site or communication link has failed. Also, with the support of replicated information, availability is improved in that a replicated information object remains available as long as at least one copy of that object is available.

Increased Efficiency. Response times can be reduced because information in a distributed system can be stored close to its point of use, enabling most information accesses to be local.

Increased Flexibility. Information can be dynamically moved or replicated, existing copies can be deleted, or new information types can be added to accommodate changes in how the information is used.

Simplified User Access. The user can be shielded from the semantics required to locate, access, and query information on heterogeneous systems.

Potential Challenges

Although distribution of information throughout a system has many benefits, it must overcome a number of challenges.

Complex Architectural-Level Communications. In these systems, messages containing information, processing requests, and acknowledgments of previous requests are passed continuously between various remote sites. Coordinating this message flow is complex and can be costly.

Complex Update Control. If two users update the same piece of information, a method must be found to mediate conflicts. One way to ensure information integrity is to employ a locking mechanism. However, the locking strategy becomes more challenging as machines are added and network failure must be accounted for. Added complexity also arises with distributed transactions, where one user updates two data sources simultaneously, and both updates must occur in synch.

Network Dependency. When data is distributed across the network, reliable communications between sites are required or processing may be halted. This increased reliability may require expensive duplication of network resources in order to provide an acceptable amount of system availability for the users.

Complexity of "Location Transparency." In the ideal distributed information environment, the end user or application programmer has access to all required information without having to know where that information is physically located. This feature is known as location transparency and it is supported by only a few of the products currently available. This places a substantial burden on the architecture and its designers to locate the information efficiently and to transport it to the application on request, without excessive processing delays.

Location transparency also complicates user support. A user problem within a single application may originate from any number of remote sites that are transparent to the user, making the problem more difficult to identify and resolve.

Information Synchronization. Maintenance of redundant information over multiple sites and processors increases the complexity of information synchronization routines. Complex time synchronization between separate machines may be required.

Organizations must be aware of what their synchronization requirements are. Timing is one example of a synchronization challenge. When does information need to be synchronized? In real time? Overnight? Several techniques for performing information synchronization efficiently are discussed later.

Changes in Organizational Structure. Changes in the existing organizational structure could invalidate the information design. With distributed information, one must build in flexibility to change as the organization changes.

Security. Managing access to information and preventing unauthorized access are bigger challenges in client/server computing than in a centralized, mainframe environment. Complexity here is a result of the distributed nature of system components (hardware, software, data).

Information Transformation. Because information is on multiple platforms and multiple management environments, the information must be transformed from one format or type to another. Some information types may be supported in one environment, and not in another.

Information Management. Distributed information is more difficult to manage, creating challenges for backup and recovery of information and for overall information integrity.

Heterogeneous Environments. Client/server information may be on multiple databases, file systems, and hardware platforms, connected by multiple network protocols.

Rules for Design

"Location transparency" is a key to successful information design in client/server computing. Database expert C.J. Date puts this principle another way: To a user, a distributed system should look exactly like a nondistributed system. The user or programmer who accesses and manipulates information should be able to do so logically through a single access, as if it were all managed by a single database management system (DBMS) on a single machine.

From this underlying principle, Date sets forth 12 related rules for distributed data design, or distributed information design. Date's guidelines are helpful in designing overall information access in a client/server system, although it is unlikely that any system will conform to all 12 of these rules. Most organizations focus on the need to achieve local autonomy and the need for information independence.

The 12 rules are as follows:

1. *Local autonomy.* All operations at any particular site should be controlled by that site and not dependent on another site to function. Each local site owns and manages its own information, and each site is therefore responsible for the accuracy, security, and integrity of that information.

2. *No reliance on a central site.* A corollary of rule 1, this rule is necessary to prevent bottlenecks and the potential vulnerability of relying on a central site.

3. *Continuous operation.* Planned system shutdowns should never be necessary. Good design means that maintenance, database administration and operations, and upgrades should take place without shutting down the system.

4. *Location independence.* Users and applications should be able to access remote information as if it were local. This simplifies application design and permits information to be moved around without causing changes to existing applications.

5. *Segmentation independence.* If an information relation can be separated into segments for physical storage and access, the distributed database design should support storing the segments at the location where they are used most frequently. Users should be able to access any information logically as if it were not segmented at all.

6. *Replication independence.* Replication of information should be transparent to the users and to the application. Access proceeds logically as if there is only one copy of the information.

7. *Distributed query processing.* Users should be able to make a single query across multiple physical information locations.

8. *Distributed transaction management.* The system should provide a single point of entry for the transaction, even if the transaction involves information from multiple sites to complete the business function.

9. *Hardware independence.* Client/server systems include a variety of machines. The system must be able to present a "single-system image" of the database to the user while allowing different hardware systems to participate as partners in the system.

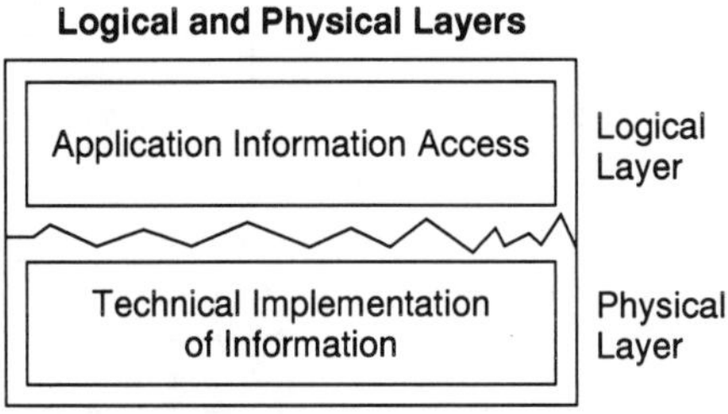

Logical and Physical Layers

Exhibit II-6-2. Logical and Physical Layers

10. *Operating system independence.* Systems with heterogeneous hardware may use more than one operating system. The information should be able to allow all operating systems to participate in the same distributed system.

11. *Network independence.* In a client/server system, multiple communications systems must be able to operate together, transparently to users and application designers.

12. *DBMS independence.* Many system installations have different types of DBMSs. Thus, it is vital that they all support the same interface and that they can interoperate.

Meeting these challenges of distributed information is the function of the information access services framework of client/server architecture.

INFORMATION ACCESS SERVICES FRAMEWORK

A two-layer approach is useful to keep information distinct from the processes that access and use it: a logical layer and a physical layer. Within the client/server architecture, the information access services component maintains this logical/physical distinction. (See Exhibit II-6-2.)

Logical Layer

The logical layer acts to isolate the physical aspects of information (e.g., location, storage format, access language) from applications and applications developers. This layer provides all the detail services associated with information and with access to or from that information.

Physical Layer

The physical layer can be used within a client/server architecture to isolate the detailed technical implementations of information. This layer

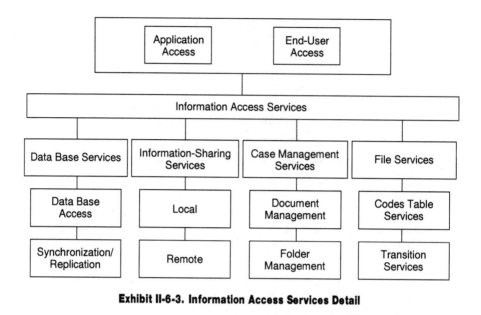

Exhibit II-6-3. Information Access Services Detail

insulates an organization and its applications from the rapid pace of change in information management technology. This layer can also be used to position legacy information sources into the client/server environment, independent from migrating applications and implementing new client/server applications.

Information Access Services

Exhibit II-6-3 depicts all the components of the information access services segment of the client/server architecture. This is a superset of components, so organizations need to understand that they must evaluate their unique requirements to select and deliver the components appropriate for them.

Information access services provide a degree of isolation between applications or end users and the information they access. Information access services are divided between the two main audiences they serve.

Application Access Services. Application access services enable applications to be independent of the underlying physical access and location, which, in turn, allows the application to achieve a level of independence from the underlying information. This separation reduces the impact of physical information design changes and provides applications developers with a single access method for the variety of information media utilized.

End-User Access Services. Similarly, end-user access services provide the same capabilities as application access services directly to the end user. End-user access services include facilities to enable users to intelligently navigate the available information resources in support of their business tasks.

Typical services within information access include the following:

- Retrieve (select) information.
- Update information.
- Add new information.
- Delete information.

Database Access Services

Database access services are responsible for providing access to the physical database for both local and remote data and maintaining database integrity. Database access services support the ability to store information on a single physical platform or in some cases on multiple platforms. These services are typically provided by DBMS vendors and accessed via embedded or call-level structured query language (SQL) variants and supersets. Depending on the underlying storage model, non-SQL access methods may be used instead.

Typical database access services include the following:

- Retrieve (select) data.
- Update data.
- Add data.
- Delete data.

Synchronization/Replication Services

Synchronization services are the facilities that support the database synchronization needs of intermittently connected users or sites. On connection, synchronization services performs the transactions required to make consistent one or more databases, or parts of databases that are intended to mirror each other. This function is especially valuable when implementing applications for users of mobile devices because it allows a working copy of a database to be available locally without a constant network connection. The emergence of teamware-style applications has heightened the need for synchronization services in the execution architecture.

Typical services within synchronization include the following:

- Synchronize data.
- Compare data (check integrity).

Replication services support an environment in which multiple copies of a database or a data subset must be maintained in a real-time manner. For example, ad hoc reporting queries that must occur during online transaction updates might be better served by separate copies of the database for performance reasons. Better availability or recoverability of a distributed application might be possible if information is replicated on alternate servers.

Replication services are sometimes supplied as part of commercial databases or tightly integrated add-on products. Depending on how the information replication scheme is implemented, the execution architecture may be responsible for writing data and replication instructions to multiple databases or transaction logs.

Typical services within replication include the following:

- Copy data.
- Compare data copies.

Local Information-Sharing Services

Information-sharing services facilitate the sharing of information between windows or applications that execute on the same machine and allow applications or windows to register an interest in a piece of information. If this information changes, all processes with a registered interest are notified. In this way, applications do not need to be aware of one another; they only need to be aware of the fact that they may be using information that might be shared by some other application. To help protect information integrity, locking and access control services may also be provided.

Remote Information-Sharing Services

Similar to local information sharing, remote information-sharing services provide a publish/subscribe mechanism to facilitate the sharing of information between machines. Remote information-sharing services are responsible for maintaining the directory of interested workstations or servers and sending notifications when information changes occur.

Typical services within remote information sharing include the following:

- Create shared data.

- Register shared data.
- Notify shared data change.

Document Services

Document services provide access to, and maintain the integrity of, documents stored in both local and remote locations.

A document is defined as a collection of objects of potentially different types with which a business user deals, such as structured data, unstructured text, images, or multimedia. An individual document might consist of a table created using a spreadsheet package such as Microsoft Excel, a report created using a word processing package such as Lotus AmiPro, a chart drawn in Excel, and a more structured form area developed using Lotus Notes or Microsoft Visual Basic controls. Regardless of the software used to create and maintain the component parts, all parts together constitute the document, which is managed as a single entity.

Document services provide functions including the following:

- *Storage and retrieval.* Where large distributed document bases exist, tools and facilities for navigating, storing, and locating information are essential. Technologies such as full text retrieval greatly assist the user or requesting application in locating relevant documents.
- *Check-in/ check-out and versioning.* Particularly in the development of applications centered around documents, control over concurrency and versioning can be critical. These services provide for concurrency control over longer periods than database or file system record-locking facilities. Users or applications may check out documents for extended periods of time (days or weeks).

Folder Management Services

Folder management services enable applications to manage collections of information associated with "large business objects," such as a legal case, a stock portfolio, a patient's medical history, or an insurance claim. An object's information collection may consist of traditional information, image or voice information, or information captured by third-party packages. Folder management services provide a layer of interaction between the application and the required information components. These services also provide the application with the functions required to manipulate and manage this information as a cohesive collection or folder. The application, therefore, does not need to know how to display, for example, the image of a loan application form or a spreadsheet.

Through integration with database, file, and document services, folder management services provide an integrated view and access control mechanism for related case information under the control of these various components.

Typical services include the following:

- Create folder.
- Reader folder.
- Navigate folder.

File Services

File services provide access to, and maintain the integrity of, information stored in both local and remote files (not databases). These services are usually invoked by information access functions, or functions in file access libraries. If a distributed file system is used, remote files or drives may be mapped as "local" to the application.

Typical services here include:

- Open file.
- Read file.
- Write file.
- Close file.

Transition Services

Transition services facilitate integration by providing applications with services for accessing information from legacy systems, packages, or external service providers.

For example, a database bridge product might provide a standard relational database interface (SQL) for a legacy database that is not relational, such as indexed files or a hierarchical database. Or, a packaged application programming interface (API) might provide access to an external information service such as stock price quotations or a multimedia server.

Transition services are often an attractive way to integrate information from multiple sources and platforms, without developing custom interfaces.

Codes Table Services

Codes table services enable applications to utilize externally stored parameters and validation rules. For example, an application may be designed to retrieve the tax rate for the state of Illinois. When the user enters "Illinois" on the screen, the application first validates the user's entry by checking for its existence on the State Tax Table and then retrieves the tax rate for Illinois. Codes tables provide an additional degree of flexibility as well as separation of information and process. If the tax rates change, the information simply needs to be updated; no application logic needs to be modified.

Typical services within codes tables include:

- Create table.
- Populate table.
- Read table.

DDBMS FRAMEWORK

A distributed database management system (DDBMS) promises a number of benefits for organizations, including the ability to expand a system more gracefully in an incremental fashion, local autonomy, increased availability and reliability of information, and increased efficiency and flexibility. Users located in different geographical locations will be able to retrieve and update information from one or more locations in a network, transparently, and with full integrity and security.

CHARACTERISTICS OF DDBMS IN CLIENT/SERVER COMPUTING

Client/server computing allows information to be kept distinct from the processes that use that information. Any DDBMS product used in a client/server environment must be able to maintain this distinction. A number of characteristics of client/server DDBMS products are crucial, and each of these is discussed in turn:

- Stored procedures.
- Triggers.
- Support for referential integrity.
- Two-phase commit.
- Support for nontextual or multimedia information.
- Information replication.
- Information gateways.
- Disk mirroring.

Stored Procedures

A stored procedure is a set of named SQL statements defined within a function, which is compiled within the DDBMS for runtime execution by name. Essentially, it is information access logic coded into the database server for use by all clients.

Stored procedures can be compared to third-generation language (3GL) routines, but they are executed by DDBMS software and contain SQL statements. At runtime, the stored procedure is accessed through a 3GL or 4GL call.

Advantages of Stored Procedures. Stored procedures have a number of important advantages:

- *Information transfer volume is minimized.* Because the stored procedure can execute all SQL statements and information access logic, only required information is returned to the requesting process.
- *Speeds execution.* Stored procedures are usually compiled into the database engine (not the application) for fast execution, which generally improves DDBMS and information access performance.
- *Decreases lines of code.* Applications can have less code, and they do not need to include, within each application, information integrity or reused information access logic.
- *Eases some maintenance activities.* Applications have less data structure information; therefore, it is easier to change table sizes, column names, and so forth.
- *Promotes code reusability.* Stored procedures can be thought of as object processing for information tables; they modularize and encapsulate information operations into a library-like area. Each stored procedure can be reused when accessed by any application that has permission to use it.
- *Enforces distinctions between information and process.* All information access, location, format, and so forth can be addressed within the stored procedure, and therefore removed from the application logic that processes that information.

Potential Drawbacks of Stored Procedures. However, the use of stored procedures has a number of potential drawbacks:

- Each DDBMS vendor's implementation is different. Once an organization chooses a particular DDBMS and uses that vendor's stored procedures, it may be locked in to that vendor. Or, at a minimum, those stored procedures have to be reimplemented.
- Changes in a stored procedure can affect many applications, and the balance of application processing between the application and stored procedure must be understood. Like any library routine, changes require a test of all users.
- System performance may be decreased by the inappropriate use of a stored procedure—for example, a stored procedure that must return multiple information types from multiple sources to respond to a single request.

When to Use Stored Procedures. Stored procedures should be used in the following cases:

- *When a set of SQL calls should be grouped logically for a single business operation.* A logical set of data operations, which perform a single business function and are executed frequently (such as "make reservation"), provide a good base for a stored procedure.
- *When the same set of SQL calls are used in many applications.* As soon as the same SQL statements are used by more than one application, stored procedures are valuable for avoiding problems in updating several applications when changes are made, and for improving the consistency of SQL use within an organization or project.
- *When one wants to decrease information transfer from client to server in complicated information requests.* A stored procedure call often is a smaller information message from a client to a server than a complex SQL statement(s). However, when there is less information transfer, there are more MIPS used on the server.
- *When one wants to maximize processing on a server platform, balancing client processing.* Stored procedures add central processing unit usage on the server, and should be balanced against application processing on the client.

Triggers

Triggers are convenient "start" mechanisms to initiate a stored procedure or SQL command. Triggers can be based on either clock events or data events. A clock-based trigger might be, "At 1:00 a.m. each night, replicate the AIRPORT entity to sites New York, Chicago, and Dulles with the AIRPORT_REP stored procedure." A data-based event might be, "When a new row is inserted into the RESERVATION table, initiate the RESERVATION_ACCOUNTING stored procedure."

Triggers have a number of advantages. They permit applications developers to remove event-based logic from applications or the infrastructure software, and they tie a data-driven event to the actual data that drives the event. However, it is difficult to know what will happen to the database if many triggers cascade on and on. Infinite loops may be possible if designers are not careful and do not conduct thorough testing.

Referential Integrity

Referential integrity is the correctness and consistency of relationships between data tables and the correctness of information content. These are crucial issues in a relational database environment. The most important question with regard to referential integrity is whether it should be handled by the DDBMS or by the applications.

If the DDBMS enforces the integrity rules, integrity is centralized and not maintained in all application programs; integrity can be changed without modifying applications. However, DDBMS integrity enforcement implies a high overhead. Too much integrity checking slows down the system considerably.

In general, application programs should enforce only those integrity rules that can be enforced through application code, based on the amount of processing required to enforce the rules. If the DDBMS enforces the rule, it does just as much work (or more) as the application program would do.

The advantage to using DDBMS-enforced referential integrity is that applications do not have to design and code the logic, and the logic can be centralized in the DDBMS. But applications still have to test it.

DDBMS-enforced referential integrity should not make program structures awkward or less maintainable because programs should not contain the integrity and maintenance of integrity is centralized within the database. However, complex links between tables may force difficult management, loading, and unloading scenarios. For example, if the DDBMS forces a program to process in an awkward fashion, a systems developer would not want to use the DDBMS to enforce referential integrity.

When bulk-loading information into the database, referential integrity constraints should ensure that the database is consistent and accurate after loading. Some DDBMS products have a "backdoor" load that bypasses integrity constraints.

In general, DDBMS- enforced integrity should be used whenever it is justified by business events. However, the DDBMS should not be used to perform application integrity—for example, to validate codes against code tables. These values usually do not change often, and the constant validation is simply unnecessary overhead.

Also, developers should not put more than a manageable number of tables into a single connected referential tree structure that must be maintained by the DDBMS. Developers must understand the characteristics of the specific DDBMS they are working with to determine what that manageable number is.

Two-Phase Commit

Two-phase commit (sometimes abbreviated 2PC) is a protocol used when a logical unit of work updates information in two or more processing locations or "nodes"; 2PC ensures integrity of information between nodes.

In a client/server environment, 2PC is a key component. It can be thought of as an "integrity mechanism" and is especially important when communication between nodes is slow, or when it is not extremely reli-

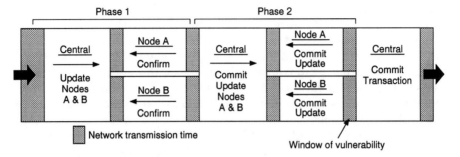

Exhibit II-6-4. Two-Phase Commit

able. Exhibit II-6-4 shows a timeline of activities associated with two-phase commit.

Phase 1. Phase 1, or the prepare phase, queries all the remote sites to verify that they are ready to commit—that is, ready for updating. This phase initiates the clean-up tasks of the memory management facilities at each site.

If a participating site (not the coordinating site) is unable to receive the prepare message (and any subsequent rollback), it checks periodically for unreleased locks (or checks when communication/processing is restored) and queries the coordinator about the status of the transaction. The coordinator responds that the transaction was rolled back because all sites could not participate, and the participating site also rolls back, releasing all locks.

Phase 2. Phase 2, or the commit phase, tells each participating site to write a commit log record. If the commit is successful at all the remote sites involved in the transaction, and the originating site receives a successful acknowledgment from each of the remote sites, the transaction at the originating site is committed. If confirmation is not received from all sites involved, the transaction is rolled back.

Advantages and Disadvantages. Two-phase commits have several advantages. A 2PC approach can ensure that multiple databases remain synchronous. If some other approach is used to guarantee synchronization, it must incorporate similar synchronization logic and could mean building a custom 2PC architecture.

Two-phase commits are DDBMS supported; the DDBMS product can enforce and control the protocol (e.g., sending the messages, waiting for receipt, confirming, committing, and rolling back). Also, 2PCs are application independent: Because they are controlled by the DDBMS, applications do not need to control the execution of the protocol.

However, the 2PC implementation does leave a window of vulnerability: There are gaps in transmission between the central/coordinating site and the nodes involved in the transaction. If the remote site commits but the initiating site does not receive acknowledgment of the commit, the initiating site does not know whether to commit or to roll back. As a result, the initiating site does not know what to do and data integrity may be lost—the whole objective of 2PC. The probability of this occurring increases with the number of sites involved in the transaction. Two-phase commit can also affect overall system and application performance.

Two-phase commit is a complicated strategy— time-consuming and costly. It relies on complex synchronous messaging over the network. Communications failures can have a substantial impact on the practicality of this technique.

In addition, the common approach requires participation and success from all sites involved in the transaction. If one site cannot complete the transaction, the entire transaction fails.

So when is two-phase commit appropriate? Developers should avoid two-phase commits by designing applications so that information updated during a single logical unit of work is located within the same node. If they cannot avoid it, designers should use two-phase commits when they need to have some form of synchronization of information between nodes, although they must remember that inconsistencies in information integrity are still possible and either control the integrity problems with a "data check" program, or with regular off-line downloads or synchronizations.

Multimedia or Nontextual Information Storage

Support for more complex types of information is an important DDBMS capability to evaluate. This information goes by a number of different names: unstructured information, nontextual information, multimedia, and extended information. By whatever name, this information consists of such things as digital images, graphics, video images, voice, word processing documents, and spreadsheets.

The DDBMS has two primary methods by which it can handle these kinds of information: either defined within the database in data types called binary large objects (BLOBs) or defined outside the database structure with a pointer containing the file name where the information is contained within the DDBMS. The decision to use a BLOB or a file should be reviewed to determine application requirements, data administration requirements, and network impact.

BLOB storage has several advantages. The integrity of information is maintained by DDBMS. Also, BLOBs are logically equivalent to other data types, which makes retrieval easier. However, a BLOB is a non-standard SQL data type, so the designer must be careful to ensure that the DDBMS supports it. Current performance levels may be poor as a result of the large size of the BLOBs.

An advantage of storing extended data types outside the database is that the file can be accessed independently of the DDBMS, through operating system services. This may lead to better retrieval performance. Disadvantages to this type of storage include the fact that the integrity of the pointer to the file, and of the information itself, must be maintained by the application. Also, backup and restore operations must use both the DDBMS and file procedures.

Information Replication

Information replication is a critical function of most mission-critical distributed information architectures. Replication is the synchronization of a database or subset of a database from one location to another. Replication can occur regularly or irregularly, automatically or manually. Replication works well for information that does not change frequently, and for data that needs to be synchronized but not in real time. This is the case most of the time.

Replication provides faster access to information and less transfer of information across the network. However, a challenge to replication is keeping multiple copies of information synchronized. If the DDBMS cannot provide automatic synchronization, additional development time is necessary to provide and maintain this synchronization.

Hands-on experience to date suggests that recovery is very complex. In addition, replication can throw unpredictable loads on the network, such that network administration groups are reluctant to allow the feature into the network.

Information Gateways (Middleware)

Information gateways (also referred to as DBMS middleware) are mechanisms that allow applications to access information from a variety of DDBMSs, without extensive platform-specific or DDBMS-specific programming.

An information gateway may be a part of the DDBMS or it may be a separate product. The primary functions of the gateway include transparent routing of SQL calls and translating between various dialects of SQL. Gateways are particularly valuable when there is an existing installed base using a variety of DDBMSs.

An information gateway accepts an SQL statement from the client application and translates it into a format understandable by the target database(s). The gateway then sends the statement to be processed. After processing, the information gateway receives the results, translates them into a form that can be understood by the client, and then returns the information and status to the client.

Gateways allow access to information across multiple data management systems. The applications can use a consistent interface for all information, which saves development time and cost as well as training time for application designers and end users. However, gateways may result in a slower response time to queries because of the time required for formatting, protocol conversion, and other activities of the gateway. Some gateways offer read-only access, so updates must be processed differently. There are also potential information accuracy and integrity issues associated with the use of information gateways.

Disk Mirroring

Disk mirroring is a DDBMS-enforced "hot backup" disk capability within a single platform. It ensures that information is not lost in cases of disk failure. Generally in a disk failure or disk crash, all information inserted since the last tape backup is lost. With disk mirroring, the backup disk is always up-to-date with respect to the primary disk. Disk mirroring also increases the availability of the DDBMS.

With disk mirroring, the DDBMS automatically transfers to the backup disk if the primary disk fails. It then automatically synchronizes the primary disk after the failure is cleared.

Disk mirroring provides obvious advantages to information security; in addition, it is transparent to applications controlled by the DDBMS. However, more disks are required in disk mirroring, and mirroring cannot be done over a LAN. Also, some minor performance decreases may result from mirroring.

MATCHING FUNCTIONS AND FEATURES

In any particular client/server system, some features and functions of DDBMSs may be critical and others may not. When evaluating a DDBMS, it is important to find one appropriate for the specific system and business requirements. A matrix, such as the one in Exhibit II-6-5, is a worksheet for matching functions and features to products under consideration.

	Product A	Product B	Product C
Stored procedures			
Triggers			
Two-phase commit			
Referential integrity			
Multimedia			
Replication			
Gateways			
Mirroring			

Exhibit II-6-5. Matrix of Features (Worksheet)

CONCLUSION

Maximizing the benefits of client/server computing presents some of the greatest challenges to designers and developers. One of the primary business benefits of client/server computing is that knowledge workers have access to more and better types of information, located throughout the enterprise. But that access requires a methodical approach to enabling applications to access and manipulate information, whether it is stored locally or remotely in files or databases. Even the fact that we refer to this part of the client/server architecture as information access (rather than its traditional name, data access) reveals an important part of the information challenge of client/server.

In addition, a key technology in client/server computing is the DDBMS. Although theoretically, a distributed DBMS does not have to be relational, the relational model does provide a simpler and more practical vehicle to support DDBMS functions than hierarchical or network models.

A relational DDBMS also tends to provide better support for the flexible, dynamic information requirements found in many client/server applications. The major DDBMS products in the marketplace today are built on a relational framework, and the success of relational DBMSs has had a direct effect in spurring the development of DDBMS products. More and more, organizations will see distributed DBMS as a practical technology component that is needed to support their growing business needs.

II-7
Communication Services

C lient/server applications drive a variety of communications requirements based on business needs. The communications requirements of the client/server environment can range from the relatively straightforward structured query language (SQL) message-based access across a local area network (LAN) to a relational database management system (DBMS) to a more complex environment that needs more intelligent message formats to access a variety of LAN-based and host-based applications and databases from a single workstation. The requirements of client/server networking are therefore different and far more complex than those of terminal networks.

COMMUNICATIONS REQUIREMENTS OF CLIENT/SERVER SYSTEMS

In traditional terminal-based computing environments, communication is limited to screen interaction. In a traditional screen approach, a formatted screen of data from a host program is sent to a terminal for display. The user then sends the response back to the host program for processing, as needed.

Even in a traditional file transfer approach, an entire file is transferred from one file storage point to a local file storage where the file can then become accessible to another group of users for query and updating. In general, all applications, whether they are business or productivity applications, such as electronic mail (E-mail), are accessible on a single host or a variety of hosts through a common communications architecture supporting the terminal network.

In the distributed computing environment of client/server, applications can have communications requirements that are significantly different from those of traditional applications. Client/server network requirements differ in at least four ways: the potential increased level of interaction driven by the user interface, the potential for access to multiple servers, the types and volumes of information, such as data, image, and video, and the distributed and often heterogeneous communications environment.

Increased Level of Interaction Driven by the User Interface

The nature of the graphical user interface (GUI) means that the interaction with the data server may be on a window or even subwindow level—for example, a control such as a list box (discussed in Chapter II-3). This means that within a single window, the first interaction may retrieve a base set of information, such as the general customer profile, and populate an initial list of orders outstanding. The list of orders may be in a list box; depending on the number of entries, as the user scrolls through the list, a second or third retrieval may be necessary to show all the orders for the customer. This example shows that even if one equates a window to a traditional screen, the level of interaction can be greater than one message per window.

Potential for Access to Multiple Servers

Depending on the business requirements, a client/server environment may require access to multiple types of servers for different functions. One example would be a LAN DBMS server for work group information, a host DBMS for the enterprise customer information file, a local server for E-mail, and possibly a multimedia server providing image, graphics, or video forms of information. This drives the need for a more sophisticated communications network based on a client/server style of interaction.

Distributed, Heterogeneous Communications Environments

The previous example of multiserver access demonstrates how the basic communications environment can become heterogeneous in nature, especially given the need to access legacy host applications and data. For this reason, the client environment often interacts with disparate communications architectures to exchange information across the networks. The need then arises for a consistent communications approach for the application environment to shield it from the details of the varying communications architectures.

LOGICAL CONNECTIONS IN CLIENT/SERVER COMPUTING

Although it has become somewhat of a cliche, the following point nevertheless bears repeating: In client/server computing, the network is the computer.

Because client/server communications occur by means of exchanging messages, a more sophisticated peer-to-peer type of communication is required. Special messaging protocols are needed to support the ability to

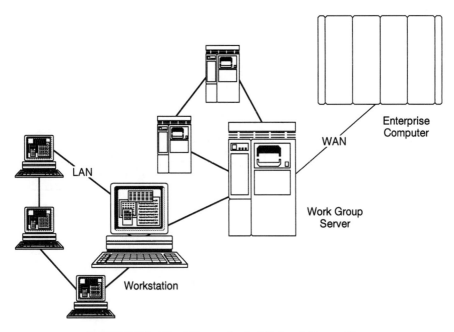

Exhibit II-7-1. Client/Server Logical Network Connections

---

initiate and receive exchanges of information. The purpose of client/
server communications services is to provide the efficient, reliable connections that are required to support the extensive messaging needs of
client/server computing.

Another way of saying that the network is the computer in client/
server computing is that the network is everywhere. Because of the distributed environment, the network is the backbone of the system.

The basic client/server diagram that has appeared throughout this
book (see Exhibit II-7-1) depicts the various kinds of logical connections
within a client/server network. These logical interactions, as dictated by
the business requirements, are what drive the sophistication of the
client/server communications services required.

Six types of logical connections are possible, then:

- Workstation to workstation.
- Workstation to work group server.
- Workstation to enterprise server.
- Work group server to work group server.
- Work group server to enterprise server.
- Enterprise server to enterprise server.

From/To	Workstation	Work Group Server	Enterprise Server
Workstation	File transfer E-mail	Messaging File transfer Remote file access Printing	Messaging File transfer Remote file access Screens Printing
Work group server		Messaging File transfer E-mail Remote file access	Messaging File transfer Remote file access Screens Printing
Enterprise Server			Messaging File transfer E-mail Remote file access Printing

Exhibit II-7-2. Types of Traffic

Types of Traffic in Client/Server Computing

A number of traffic types are possible for each of the logical connections. (Exhibit II-7-2 summarizes each of the traffic types detailed in this section.)

Messaging. Messaging is a type of traffic that allows two or more programs to pass information to each other to complete a business function. It is a typical form of communications in a client/server system.

Messaging can be either consistently driven by the client or driven by either the client or the server. In a client-driven messaging environment (e.g., in typical SQL-access style processing), the client always initiates the requests and receives the reply. In a client- or server-driven messaging environment, either side can initiate and send information, such as a requirement to send broadcast information out to a group of traders on the change in a specific stock from a server monitoring the market feed.

Messaging is typically implemented by means of simple verbs such as "connect," "send," "receive," and "disconnect," which may be accompanied by parameters. Software services interpret the messages between different platforms, allowing developers to take advantage of lower-level communication protocols without knowing the details of how communication needs to be performed. The internal format or business content of the message can range from a simple SQL statement to a more intelligent, predetermined business transaction message.

An example of a more intelligent business transaction message from a logical view would be one such as "Get customer relationship: customer-ID=RYAN," where the message may spawn a series of server data retrievals and merging of information activities to populate the response message to be sent back to the client. This is an example of a more intelligent message because with a single command the client application was able to convey to the server process what it wanted and get its needs filled in a single message.

Under the SQL approach the application would have had to use several messages to get the same information. An intelligent message approach, for complex information needs, allows the server to handle the physical location and merging of the information in the data environment and allows the client application to keep a more logical, business view of the information it needs.

File Transfer. File transfer is the ability to copy a file from one location or machine to another. A client/server system typically has a set of software services that allows for end-to-end distribution, collection, and management of files across heterogeneous platforms and protocols. These tasks are all performed transparently to the user. File transfers can be scheduled (batch) or performed in real time (online). File transfer may create traffic of substantial size, which may occur in irregular bursts. A system that makes heavy use of file transfer should take these characteristics into account when planning the network capacity.

Remote File Access. Remote file access is a type of traffic that allows users to transparently access and use files stored on different platforms across the enterprise as if the files were local. The software may map or mount each individual file structure on each distributed platform to local directories. Thus, the entire file system structure appears as local drives and files to the user.

The major difference between remote file access and file transfer is that with file transfer, the file is physically copied from one platform to the other. With remote file access, files remain on individual platforms but are logically linked. The volume and pattern of network traffic generated by each type of file access are quite different.

Screens. Screens are used to provide access to existing legacy systems, such as a CICS (Customer Information Control System) on an IBM mainframe. Screen access is provided either by dumb terminals or by workstations using terminal emulation. Because screen access is used for existing legacy applications, the traffic patterns and volume generated should be easy to determine.

Printing. Although printing is often not messaging based, a client/server network should provide users with the capability of printing to any printer on the network as if it were local. The impact of printing on the network traffic depends on the answers to such questions as the following: What is being printed? Where is the printer located? What is the type of printing device and type of printing? What is the priority of the printing? What are its security requirements? Printing is similar to file transfer traffic in terms of a potentially heavy and "bursty" traffic pattern.

COMMUNICATION SERVICES IN THE CLIENT/SERVER ARCHITECTURE

The complex communication environment of client/server computing is addressed in the communication services component of the client/server architecture. Communication services enable applications to interact transparently with other applications, regardless of whether they reside on the same computer or on a remote computer.

The primary role of the communication component is to provide a consistent set of services to applications. This section provides an overview of each of the subservices of communication services.

Logical and Physical Views

The logical layer of communication services isolates the physical aspects of communications (differing protocols, differing networks, physical addressing knowledge) from applications and developers. This layer prevents developers from needing to become fluent in each communication protocol to develop client/server applications. The logical layer would be the application programming interfaces (APIs) presented to the developers, such as "send message: parameters" or "transfer file: parameters." (See Exhibit II-7-3.)

The physical layer is used to isolate the detailed technical implementations of communication services and potentially shield against the rapid pace of change in information technology. For example, if the environment must send messages using a less than optimal protocol in today's environment as a result of specific business issues (e.g., a primary legacy vendor's capability), the logical and physical layers can be used together to position the environment for a future change. The applications would be protected from changing their send message: parameters API and the change impact would be isolated to how the physical imple-

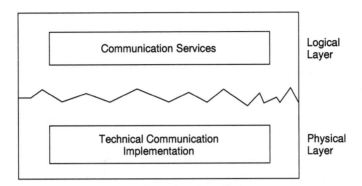

Exhibit II-7-3. Logical and Physical View of Communication Services

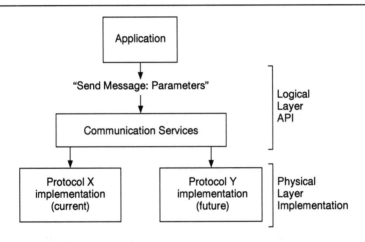

Exhibit II-7-4. Shielding Business Logic from Technological Change

mentation of the API is translated from one protocol to a different protocol. (See Exhibit II-7-4.)

Exhibit II-7-5 provides a more detailed illustration of the logical and physical layers of communication services. The remainder of this section discusses both the logical layer and the physical layer in more detail.

Message Management

A key component in a client/server environment is message management services. Message management services allow the client and server programs to exchange business messages in the style that the application requirements need; the possible styles of message interaction are syn-

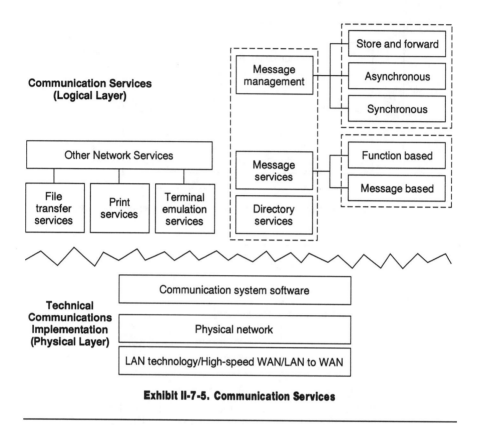

Exhibit II-7-5. Communication Services

chronous, asynchronous and store and forward. An environment may have a need for only one message management service, or possibly a combination of them.

There are a variety of architectural options in a client/server messaging environment. They can be divided into store-and-forward, synchronous, and asynchronous message services.

Store-and-Forward Message Services. Store-and-forward message services provide deferred message service processing. This allows messages to be sent even though the final recipient may not currently be available. A store-and-forward service may utilize an E-mail infrastructure on which to build applications. A common use would be for forms routing in a work flow application.

Synchronous Message Services. Synchronous message services allow or require an application to send a message to another application and wait for a reply before continuing. Synchronous messaging is typically used for update and general inquiry transactions.

Asynchronous Message Services. Asynchronous message services allow an application to send a message to another application and continue processing before a reply is received. Asynchronous messaging is typically used for larger retrieval type-processing, such as retrieval of larger lists of data than can be contained in one message or when application processing does not depend on the results of the message.

Message Services

Two styles of underlying messaging models are typically used to provide these message management services: a function-based approach or a message-based approach.

A function-based service uses the subroutine model of programming. The message interface is built on the calling program passing the appropriate parameters and receiving the returned information. The most common function-based messaging system is the remote procedure call (RPC) implementation. A variety of RPC implementations are on the market.

A message-based approach uses a defined message format to exchange information between processes. Although a portion of the message may be unstructured, a defined header component is generally included.

A message-based approach is not limited to the call/return structure of the function-based model and can be used in a conversational manner. Products providing this type of service may build on such protocols as Transmission Control Protocol/Internet Protocol (TCP/IP) sockets or IBM's LU6.2.

Directory Services

Directory services track the system name/address and physical location of addressable resources in the environment. These resources could range from programs, servers and printers to users and mailboxes.

Directory services provide the logical to physical translation in the environment (e.g., program CUSTSRV3.EXE on server NYSRV04 with Ethernet address xxxxxx can be accessed as "Customer-Service"). Directory services are an emerging area and are becoming more a part of the communication system software environment as the capabilities of the vendors mature.

Other Communication Services

Other services are also useful for a client/server environment:

- *File transfer services.* These services allow programs to send files or other large data streams from one location to another.
- *Print services.* Print services provide printer selection and application or user routing of printing in the environment.
- *Terminal emulation services.* Terminal emulation services capture data streams on an intelligent workstation as if the workstation were a "dumb terminal." These services also receive user input and send data streams back to the host processor. The terminal emulation service may be used to provide the underlying terminal emulation for the windowed terminal display or may be used by front-ending-type software for adding a GUI interface to an existing terminal-based application.

One way in which communications services in a client/server environment tend to be implemented is through the identification and selection of communications middleware products. The next section defines middleware and discusses some particular products.

COMMUNICATIONS MIDDLEWARE

The client/server environment can become extremely complex, depending on the needs of the business. Many of the challenges faced by client/server applications developers center around the integration of business functions and the technical architecture components.

The communication architecture integration represents an extremely complex challenge. Communication protocols specify the rules by which two entities exchange information in an orderly fashion within a data communications network. Examples of commonly used communication protocols include TCP/IP, SNA, OSI, and DECnet.

In some cases, distributed client/server applications are designed and written to interface directly with the underlying communication interface (e.g., an application written with direct TCP socket calls). In those situations, hundreds, if not thousands, of lines of complex communication code are written directly into the business applications to create basic dialogue between two distributed processes.

In addition, because the developed code is usually written to a single, perhaps proprietary, communication protocol, it may only be used in environments in which that communication protocol is available. This results in reduced application portability to other environments which may use different communications protocols. Also, if the communication code is tailored to a specific application, other applications resident on the platform may not take advantage of previously coded communication services. Thus, new communications code may be needed for each new application.

For example, a process of a distributed application was designed and coded to run on a platform that used the TCP/IP communication protocol. If it needed to run on a platform that used a different communication protocol, such as SNA, the process would have to be recoded to support the SNA communications protocol interface. This would be a complex and costly task. This problem would be minimized by isolating the communication architecture code into common libraries which could be used by multiple applications. However, this approach does not remove the need to develop the same communication services in an SNA environment.

As a result of these complexities, some applications developers have avoided developing distributed, client/server applications due to the costs and complexities involved with integrating business applications with multiple communications protocols.

ASSISTANCE IN CREATING DISTRIBUTED APPLICATIONS

Creating distributed client/server applications in today's heterogeneous computing environments usually requires the integration of applications, multiple communication protocols, operating systems, and machine platforms. These factors increase the complexity of coordinating the communications between two or more distributed processes. It also forces developers to spend a significant amount of their development effort on designing, coding, and testing the application interfaces to low-level communication mechanisms.

Given the technical complexities of these activities, specialists usually provide the expertise in interfacing distributed applications across the network. These complexities can increase overall development time and costs. If not performed by a specialist, they can detract from business applications development time.

Recognizing these issues, a new market has developed. The products in this emerging market are specifically designed to assist applications developers in creating distributed applications. Most of the solutions offered by the vendors of these new products are software oriented. The industry has classified this type of software as middleware because it resides below the user application layer and above the communications protocol layers. Exhibit II-7-6 illustrates the relative position of middleware in a generic distributed computing environment.

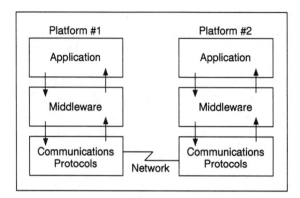

Exhibit II-7-6. Relative Position of Middleware in a Distributed Environment

MIDDLEWARE DEFINED

As discussed earlier, there is a logical and physical view of communication services and of the overall client/server model. Middleware represents the set of system-level software services, either custom developed or vendor provided, that simplify the development of client/server architectures by facilitating information exchange between distributed processes, and by keeping communications distinct from the business processes that need to communicate. More products are now being developed by systems software vendors that shield client/server developers from needing to develop many of the services of the communications area on a custom basis.

As an insulator, middleware acts as the intermediary between business logic and communications resources, thereby allowing applications developers to focus their attentions on solving business problems rather than operating environment or connectivity issues. For these reasons, middleware is viewed as a primary enabler for distributed client/server computing environments.

MIDDLEWARE SERVICES

Middleware software, whether custom developed or vendor provided, provides a base set of services to the application and application developer. Provided benefits and services may include a simplified interface, location transparency, data translation, portability, and other communication services.

Simplified Interface

Middleware reduces the complexity of developing distributed applications by providing application developers with simple and consistent APIs across platforms. APIs present the application programmer with a simple verb set. When called, these APIs invoke communications protocol and operating system commands that perform complex communications tasks transparently on behalf of the application. APIs reduce the development effort by allowing applications developers to use a smaller and less complex set of commands to access middleware services, regardless of the development environment.

Location Transparency

Application processes should not be required to know the exact address of other processes (application location transparency) while communicating with them over the network. Middleware provides the link between distributed processes and ensures that information from one process reaches its intended destination(s) intact, and via the most efficient transport method.

In some cases DBMS middleware provides the applications developer with data location transparency. Applications should be able to access data throughout the enterprise without knowing where the data is stored. Middleware allows programs simply to request the data and leave the low-level addressing tasks to middleware.

Data Translation

Some computer processors represent integer and character data differently. For example, mainframes represent data using the EBCDIC notation standard while UNIX and microcomputers represent data via the ASCII notation standard. Middleware ensures that data is formatted in a fashion compatible with the receiving process.

This concept is especially important when location transparency is provided. If an application identifies its requested service via an alias, it cannot know the data format used on the serving machine. The middleware component must therefore provide the appropriate data format translation automatically. In this case, the middleware would be providing both location and data format transparency.

Portability

Middleware is designed to allow an application operating on one platform (e.g., mainframe) to be used on other platforms (e.g., PC) without major

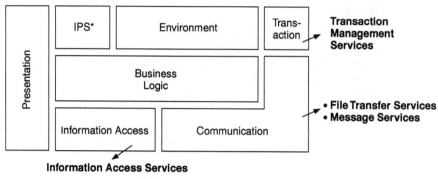

*IPS = Integrated Performance Support

Exhibit II-7-7. Middleware Categories

---

modification. To accomplish this, the middleware software is designed to be modular, allowing lower-level communication protocol interfaces to be interchanged to fit the required architecture environment. Higher-level interfaces—middleware APIs, for example—would remain the same, thus avoiding recoding of the application.

Other Communications Services

To ensure that information is properly delivered, middleware transparently provides many other low level communications services to the application. These functions include security, data segmentation and reassembly, retransmission, error recovery, and flow control.

MIDDLEWARE CATEGORIES

Middleware has five basic categories. Each category is based on the services provided to applications as well as the interface it provides to application developers. These categories are file transfer services, information access services, transaction management services, function-based message services, and message-based message services.

Exhibit II-7-7 indicates where the four communications middleware categories reside in the client/server execution architecture.

Applications developers may use the services of each of the middleware categories to build distributed applications. To provide distributed services, middleware must interface to lower-level communication protocols. To facilitate this interface, each of the middleware categories is built on top of communication systems software.

The communication systems software provides the link between the middleware services and the underlying physical network. Communication systems software services include the sending and receiving of data between distributed platforms. Examples of communications systems software used by middleware include LU6.2/APPC, NetBIOS, Named Pipes, XTI, IPX/SPX, and Sockets.

As vendor-provided middleware software becomes more advanced, the functions these products offer will begin to cross category boundaries and the differences between middleware categories will become less apparent.

In addition to classifications made across middleware categories, differences within a middleware category can also be made. These differences are based on levels of function and services provided by middleware implementations. For example, some middleware implementations provide all the services, whereas others provide only a subset of services. Thus, until the middleware market matures and standards are drafted, middleware categories and services will continue to shift and evolve.

File Transfer Services

File transfer services relate to the distribution, access, and replication of information in both file and database formats in a client/server environment. This category of middleware is most often provided by general utility software or by the distributed DBMS (DDBMS) vendor's solution.

Information Access Services

Within the DDBMS products (discussed in Chapter II-6), vendors often offer middleware solutions to shield developers from networking details. Examples include Oracle and SQLnet.

Transaction Management Services

Transaction management services (often termed "transaction processing monitors" or "online transaction monitors") provide a set of services designed to manage transactions in a distributed computing environment. Chapter II-8 discusses transaction management services in detail.

Message Services Middleware

Message services middleware can be described as a set of services allowing distributed cooperative applications to communicate via the sending

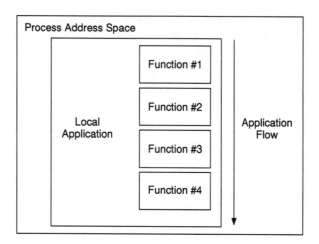

Exhibit II-7-8. Traditional Application Procedural Flow

and receiving of discrete messages. Message services middleware can usually be defined as function based or message based.

Function-Based Message Services. Function-based message services middleware extends the familiar procedure call mechanism across the network. Currently, RPCs are the primary commercially available implementations of function-based message services middleware. Therefore, RPCs are referenced throughout the rest of this section.

Traditional standalone applications are based on sets of functions or procedures that are run together in some coordinated fashion; one program segment calls a function, which returns to the calling segment some information or performs some task and then terminates. The calling program segment can then continue calling other functions/procedures to perform other tasks as required. In addition, both the application and the function/procedure reside on the same machine and within the same memory address space as allocated by the operating system. Exhibit II-7-8 illustrates the traditional view of procedure calls within a standalone (traditional) application.

The RPC approach maintains this structure with one difference: some of the functions of a given application can be distributed to other machines/platforms. To facilitate this distribution, special software routines called stubs are embedded within the application code. These stubs are created when the application is initially compiled.

During the compiling and linking process, the developer specifies how the application will be distributed via an RPC specification. This

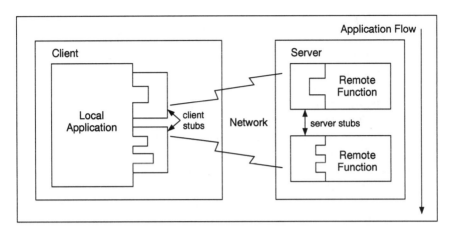

Exhibit II-7-9. Remote Procedures

specification and the original source code are then run through a special RPC compiler that creates the client and server stubs. The client and server stubs are then linked to network interface libraries, which allow them to access and utilize the network protocols present on the platforms on which they execute. The stub code is critical because it facilitates the application's access to a platform's communications services, and provides the link between a local application and the remote procedures it needs to utilize.

The communication services accessed by the stubs include protocol interface link libraries, data dictionaries, state and codes tables, and other necessary system-level code. Exhibit II-7-9 illustrates the remote procedures being called across a network.

RPCs can be used to more fully utilize the hardware and software capabilities of the distributed environment, as well as to increase the efficiency of the application. For example, in an engineering environment, computer-based modeling tools are often required to perform complex mathematical calculations, as well as present the user with an easy to understand interface. RPCs could be used in this case to distribute the modeling application between a PC, which would provide the user interface, and a minicomputer server, which would more efficiently perform the mathematical calculations. The RPCs in this example could leverage each of the platform's strong points, probably increasing performance. Examples of RPC implementations include Sun RPC and HP/Apollo NCS and the OSF Distributed Computing Environment (DCE) RPC.

Message-Based Message Services. Message-based message services middleware allows processes on the same or different platforms to exchange information using discrete control and data messages. Message-based message services provide the applications developer with a set of simple verbs (connect, send, receive, disconnect) which can be used to exchange information with other distributed applications. Through the verb set, message-based middleware lets developers take advantage of the lower-level communication protocols used by a platform without knowing the details of how communication needs to be performed.

For example, to send data to a remote process, the applications developer uses a single SEND verb. This verb, along with the appropriate parameters (this may consist of the data to be sent and the logical or alias process name), is included as part of the application code and is the only communication interface the applications developer needs to know about when creating the distributed application.

Once the verb is executed, the message-based middleware is responsible for managing the interface to the underlying communication architecture via the communication protocol APIs, and ensuring the delivery of that information to the remote process. This interface may require that the message-based middleware perform many complex tasks, including the following:

- Interpreting and validating the supplied parameters (e.g., alias name).
- Translating mnemonic or logical names to operating system readable format.
- Opening a communication session.
- Negotiating the communication parameters for that session.
- Allocating memory space.
- Translating data to the proper format.
- Transferring both data and control messages during the session.
- Recovering any information if errors occur during transmission.
- Passing result information and status to the application.

Exhibit II-7-10 illustrates how the applications developer can take advantage of a simplified verb set and still not give up the capability required in creating distributed application environments. As the exhibit illustrates, the simplified interface of VERB and parameters such as SEND ("hello world," Fred) isolates the developer from having to code all the specific communication programming steps required to carry out the messaging.

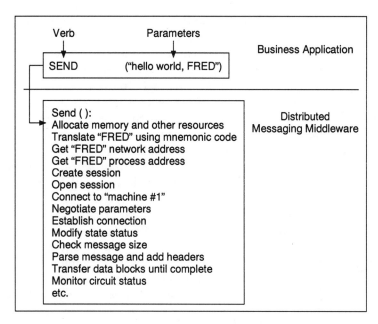

Verb   Parameters

SEND   ("hello world, FRED")   Business Application

Send ( ):
Allocate memory and other resources   Distributed
Translate "FRED" using mnemonic code   Messaging Middleware
Get "FRED" network address
Get "FRED" process address
Create session
Open session
Connect to "machine #1"
Negotiate parameters
Establish connection
Modify state status
Check message size
Parse message and add headers
Transfer data blocks until complete
Monitor circuit status
etc.

Exhibit II-7-10. Message-Based Message Services Architecture

Function Based Versus Message Based

Function-based message services middleware is similar to message-based message services middleware in that communication occurs between application components located on separate machines. The difference between the two, however, is in the way that communication is implemented. The following are some key differences between function-based and message-based message services middleware:

Control. In procedural languages (e.g., C language) some element of control is generally passed from the main logic of a program to a called function, with control returning to the main program once the called function completes its task.

Because RPCs emulate this mechanism across the network, they also tend to pass some element of control from one process to another—for example, from the client to the server. Because the client depends on the response from the server, it is usually prohibited (i.e., blocked) from performing any additional processing until a response is received. This type of data exchange is commonly referred to as synchronous (or blocking) communications.

At the server end, there is a potential problem if many clients wish to access a single server. Although not always the case, RPCs are traditionally blocking at the server, which means that the server code may be used by only one client at a time (the server code is not reentrant). If a client requests a remote procedure currently in use by another client, it is blocked and has to wait until that service is available again before proceeding. Synchronous (blocking) architectures on the client and server can result in performance inefficiencies. There are variations of RPCs emerging that allow asynchronous operation.

With message-based message services middleware, however, the flow of control is quite different from that found in RPC implementations. A process sends a message to another process, frequently with the option of whether or not to halt the calling process until a response is received. Thus, it is possible for the (client) process to continue execution while other (server) processes are servicing requests. This type of data exchange is typically known as asynchronous (or nonblocking) communication. This model of application and communication flow may not be feasible on all operating systems. For example, single-threaded operating systems such as DOS do not easily accommodate one process handling the communication request while the business application continues processing.

Complexity. RPCs tend to be less complex to implement and test than message-based middleware because no state or context information is maintained between multiple RPCs. Thus, each RPC call is completely independent and not connected with any previous or future RPC call.

With message-based middleware, however, applications can be designed to be more conversational. These types of applications retain context-sensitive information as well as maintain certain states of activity throughout the conversation. Context-sensitive conversations increase the complexity of message-based message services middleware.

Flexibility. Message-based middleware allows the decoupling of program elements so that overall, the distributed application is far more flexible. From each program's perspective, the other end is a black box that offers certain services available to anyone who knows the application protocol. With an RPC, the user of the service is inextricably bound to the service provider because the RPC is a specific function, and not a message.

Conversation Initiation. In the RPC model, service requesters start communications with service providers. With messaging, any process can act as a client or server and can therefore initiate or receive service requests (i.e., message-based middleware supports a peer-to-peer model).

BENEFITS OF USING MIDDLEWARE

From a technical architect's viewpoint, middleware can greatly reduce the risk of developing new applications in a distributed environment. This reduction is based on a number of factors.

A Simplified Interface. This simplified interface reduces the complexity of application design and implementation. This provides more time for applications development.

Application Portability. The middleware interfaces (APIs) are always provided in the same way, no matter what platforms or protocols are utilized. Middleware takes care of these details on behalf of the application. Applications are therefore less constrained to a single communication architecture.

Simplified Application Testing Across Platforms. When the middleware architecture has been fully tested, it works the same way regardless of platform or application. Only the portions of the middleware architecture with a direct interface to the platform or protocol are subject to change.

Decreased Development Costs. Using a vendor-supplied product decreases the number of communication experts required on site as well as the technical architecture development time and costs. In many cases functional and technical support can be obtained through the middleware vendor.

Decreased Ongoing Support Costs. Using a vendor-supplied product decreases the level of expertise required by the organization to maintain the infrastructure. This is a key driver behind the preference for vendor-provided middleware over custom middleware. The technical expertise required to build custom middleware must be available for ongoing system maintenance with custom development. This maintenance can be off loaded to vendors with the purchase of packaged solutions.

Standardized Enterprise Communications. The middleware chosen can provide a consistent enterprisewide platform for communications in the corporation.

Support for a Heterogeneous Environment. The middleware chosen can provide support for multiple platforms thus enabling heterogeneous computing capability.

RISKS ASSOCIATED WITH MIDDLEWARE

This section outlines some costs and risks associated with the use of middleware, as well as with distributed computing environments in general.

Middleware Solutions Are Proprietary. Most, if not all, of today's vendor-provided solutions are closed to other middleware vendors' components. Once a middleware product has been selected, the developer can be locked into that solution throughout the architecture and may be dependent upon the middleware vendor for support, upgrades, and so forth. This can pose a risk to the developer if, for example, the developer bases all distributed applications on a middleware product and that vendor either discontinues it or goes out of business.

This issue can be controlled somewhat via the use of project-specific APIs or standards where they exist. Using the project specific API scheme, the project team implements a layer above the middleware package to provide a buffer against vendor lock-in. The project API is mapped to the middleware API. If another middleware product is needed at a later time for any reason, the project specific API must be mapped to the new middleware API.

Middleware Software May Be Costly. Because middleware is generally present on all the machines running distributed applications, development, administration, and management costs tend to be higher than in traditional mainframe-to-terminal communication environments. In addition, the costs of licensing also need to be considered.

This increase in cost, however, is a result of the complexity of the distributed nature of client/server. These increased costs would still be present in some form even if middleware software were not used because of the development and maintenance effort involved with distributed computing software.

It is important to note, however, that some middleware products can reduce this complexity by providing management capability to assist systems administrators in controlling these environments, thus lowering ongoing operations support.

There May Be Performance Trade-offs. Additional software layers between applications and low-level technologies add additional overhead. The trade-offs between performance and middleware benefits (leverage, development time/cost, etc.) must be considered. A reputable middleware vendor builds optimized software that will perform as well or better than a custom middleware solution.

There May Be Too Many Functions. Some middleware products may provide services not required by a target application. When cost/benefit analysis is performed for a middleware component, the ratio of required/total product functions should be considered.

Solutions Are Not as Flexible. In a vendor-supplied solution, if a service does not meet application requirements or needs "tweaking," users may have to lobby the vendor instead of fixing it themselves.

NETWORKING: THE PHYSICAL PERSPECTIVE

Client/server computing requires faster networks (i.e., more bandwidth) for a number of reasons:

- There is much more dialog between clients and servers than among machines in traditional host-to-terminal architectures.
- The distributed processes and/or distributed data inherent within client/server computing can result in large messages and data sets being passed over the network.
- The physical layout of the distributed network can slow traffic.
- Security checking between the client and server can slow transaction time and increase traffic.
- Failed paths in a distributed network can cause the network to be flooded with updates when the path comes back up.
- Backup and recovery can cause large bursts of data to hit the network.

Four key network technologies enable the physical networking components of client/server computing:

1. *Communication system software.* Enabling communications system software and supporting protocols are used to provide program-to-program communications over LAN and wide area network (WAN) facilities.
2. *LAN technology.* LAN data link facilities, such as Ethernet, token ring, and fiber distributed data interface (FDDI), provide higher-speed capabilities in a campus or local setting.
3. *High-speed WAN technology.* WAN facilities, such as private lines,

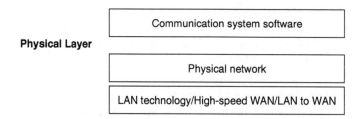

Exhibit II-7-11. Physical Networking Technologies

integrated services digital networks (ISDN), frame relay, and other high-speed communications path options from common communications carriers, allow a network designer to interconnect the LANs of a company and extend the speed and capabilities of the LAN across the wide area, making work groups and hosts accessible at high speeds from all sites, if required.

4. *LAN to WAN interconnectivity.* Bridges, routers, brouters, and gateways are used to join disparate LAN and WAN networks with different degrees of protocol-layer transparency. (See Exhibit II-7-11.)

Communication System Software

Communication system software provides the base on which the rest of the communication services are built. The manner in which these services are provided and invoked is a function of the chosen communication protocols and network hardware. In any case, the communication system software provides the required network session establishment and management capability. It also provides low-level protocol frame recovery and, in some cases, retransmission in the event of a local or remote communications failure.

Depending on the communication system software selected, the software provides any message compression, decompression, or segmentation that may be required to satisfy protocol or other communication constraints.

The communication system software provides the link between the communications services and the underlying physical network. Communication systems software services include the sending and receiving of data between distributed platforms. Examples of communications system software include LU6.2/APPC, NetBIOS, Named Pipes, XTI, IPX/SPX, and TCP/IP Sockets.

LAN Technology

A LAN is a network of personal computers (PCS), workstations, printers, and host computers, usually confined to a building or office area. The LAN provides information at high speeds—typically from 10M to 16M bps, though as high as 100M bps for backbone applications. Speed and connectivity capability make it better suited for client/server computing when connectivity is over acceptable distances. Typically, client workstations and supporting servers are located on the same LAN.

Physical Components of the LAN. The major physical components of the LAN are servers, media, PCS or workstations, and interface cards, each of which is described as follows:

- *Servers.* LAN servers provide a variety of services to attached LAN devices, such as printing, filing, E-mail, communications gateway, and file backup. Servers can provide one type of service or multiple services.
- *Media.* LANs may be implemented over a variety of connection media, including twisted pair, coaxial, fiber optic, and wireless.
- *PCs/workstations.* Because purchasing decisions for PCS and workstations have traditionally been made at the departmental level, an organization typically has many different types of devices. LANs can connect these heterogeneous devices.
- *Interface cards.* Interface cards are the hardware necessary to connect a device to a LAN. They provide the appropriate physical interface to the LAN media.

LAN Topologies. A network's topology is the physical and logical arrangement of its devices in relation to one another. LANs are physically connected in star, ring, or bus topologies. Specifically:

- *Star.* In a star topology, network devices are connected to a central hub.
- *Ring.* In a ring topology, all devices are configured in a ring as shown in Exhibit II-7-12b. Messages are passed from device to device along the ring.
- *Bus.* In a bus topology, network devices are attached to a single length of cable via a drop cable. All attached devices receive all messages but act only on those messages addressed to them. (See Exhibit II-7-12.)

A LAN does not necessarily have the same logical topology as its physical topology. For example, it is common for a LAN that is physically

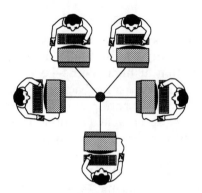

a. Star Topology

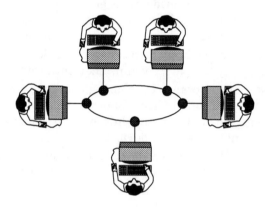

b. Ring Topology

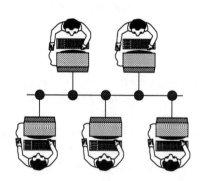

c. Bus Topology

Exhibit II-7-12. LAN Topologies

configured as a star to perform logically as a ring. This is accomplished by the hub, which internally maps each device into the ring topology.

LAN Access Methods. Information from a device is put on and taken off a LAN in two ways, or via two access methods:

- *Contention.* With this access method, each network device "listens" to the LAN before sending. If there is already traffic on the LAN, the device waits until the line is quiet. Contention access methods also allow for the possibility that two devices may send data at the same time. If a "collision" occurs between two sending devices, each device waits a random period of time before it resends its information. Ethernet is a common implementation of a contention access method. Ethernet employs a contention standard known as CSMA/CD (carrier sense multiple access/collision detection). Like token ring, Ethernet can be implemented over a variety of media, including twisted pair, coaxial, fiber optic, and wireless.
- *Token passing.* A token is a series of bytes passed around the ring. When a device has something to send, it must wait for this token. The device takes a free token, modifies it to indicate that the network is busy, sends its data, and then modifies the token when it has finished sending to indicate that the network is free. FDDI and IBM's Token Ring are examples of token passing. Token ring can be implemented over a variety of media, including twisted pair, coaxial, and fiber optic.

RECENT DEVELOPMENTS IN LAN TECHNOLOGY

Three recent developments in LAN technology are important to note, especially as organizations move to a netcentric computing environment:

- High-speed access methods.
- Switching architectures.
- Asynchronous transfer mode (ATM) technology.

High-Speed Access Methods

Currently, network access methods with the largest installed base are Ethernet (10M bps) and Token Ring (4 or 16M bps). Both of these standards are well documented and products are available from a wide variety of vendors.

Because of the need for increased bandwidth, however, vendors have pushed to develop cost-effective, high-speed access methods (i.e., > 100M bps) that allow organizations to upgrade their networks. The two most notable of these are fiber distributed data interface (FDDI) and Fast Ethernet.

FDDI. FDDI is the most mature of the high-speed access methods, with a wide variety of products currently available and commonly implemented. Although FDDI has several beneficial characteristics, it is primarily touted for its significant bandwidth capacity: 100M bps. In addition to the substantial increase in bandwidth, other noted capabilities of FDDI include its deterministic access and its inherent fault tolerance. Deterministic access methods regulate users' access to the network, enabling all users equal access. Therefore, the performance degradation experienced in Ethernet networks (i.e., collisions) are not replicated in FDDI networks. Fault tolerance refers to FDDI's ability to recover automatically from link failures. Referred to as a "self-healing ring," FDDI networks have the capability to wrap around the failed link and still maintain the integrity of the ring. Because of this feature, FDDI is an attractive networking topology for environments requiring high degrees of fault tolerance.

Fast Ethernet. In response to the need for more network bandwidth, a substantial number of internetworking hardware vendors formed the "Fast Ethernet Alliance." The purpose of this alliance was to develop a high-speed networking topology leveraging existing Ethernet technology. This goal was achieved by using portions of the Ethernet standards and combining them with the physical signaling standards used by FDDI.

The new standard (IEEE 802.3u), commonly referred to as "100Base-T," created a new shared media networking technology: 100M-bps Ethernet. Essentially, 100Base-T is the same technology as 10Base-T operating at 10 times the speed. As a result, network managers find 100Base-T to be a relatively easy technology to understand.

Although this technology provides for a substantially increased bandwidth, many of the limitations of current Ethernet technologies, such as collisions, still remain. Additionally, 100Base-T still lacks any deterministic access method or priority queuing capabilities. As a result, 100Base-T is not well suited to support large quantities of delay sensitive data such as voice or video. Because of its increased speed, 100Base-T has some distance limitations, cabling requirements, and repeater configurations that are more stringent than 10Base-T. However, despite the limitations, 100Base-T is designed to run over most existing cabling plants and vendors have announced products with prices significantly lower than other alternatives such as FDDI or ATM.

Switching Architectures

As organizations migrate toward higher-speed access methods, they must upgrade both the network hardware and the network interface cards located at the workstations. In an effort to allow enterprises to improve their LAN network performance without having to upgrade all of the network interface cards, vendors began to develop switching capabilities. Two forms of switching are dominant: port and frame switching.

Port Switching. Port-level switches contain multiple network backplanes (i.e., network segments). Ports are connected to the various backplanes on an individual basis. This dynamic allocation of ports enables network managers to control the distribution of traffic between network segments, thus improving overall performance. To simplify the process of reconfiguring ports, most vendors have developed software solutions that enable network managers to manipulate port mapping from a central location.

Frame Switching

Port switching addresses some concerns about leveraging an organization's installed technology base, but is not usually considered a robust enterprise solution. As a result, vendors have developed frame switching solutions.

Although port switching and frame switching may both be referred to as "switched" solutions, they are significantly different. With port switching, shared media access methods (i.e., Ethernet, Token Ring) are still used. In a shared media environment, the total aggregate bandwidth of the network is shared among all of the connected network nodes. However, with frame switching, the total aggregate bandwidth is determined by the number of switch ports.

As a result of the switched nature of these networks, users are able to realize greater throughput and total aggregate bandwidth than would be possible using a traditional shared media LAN. For example, Ethernet LANs limit the total amount of traffic between network devices to no more that 10M bps. However, when multiple users are connected to an Ethernet switch, the total traffic between network ports can easily exceed 20M bps depending upon the traffic patterns on the network.

Asynchronous Transfer Mode (ATM) Technology

A revolutionary change that has received a great deal of attention is asynchronous transfer mode (ATM). ATM is a technology with the promise of delivering video, voice, and data traffic over a single, high-speed integrated network. The rush of both telecommunications providers and data networking companies to support ATM may eventually blur the distinction between local and wide area networking.

ATM's unprecedented popularity stems from its many technological advantages, its open definition, and its ability to solve problems that the industry has been dealing with for years. By adopting existing standards for physical media transmission, ATM may finally make high-speed network links as common as local area networks are today. By paying careful attention to the needs of all types of data (video, voice, and data), ATM has been designed to provide a single infrastructure capable of supporting multiple data types.

ATM is still, however, a relatively immature technology that represents a significant departure from traditional networking. First, ATM is a connection-based technology. When devices wish to communicate over the network, virtual connections are established. Given the nature of these virtual connections, ATM allows multiple users to share the network resources simultaneously. In addition, depending on the quality of service requested for a virtual link, ATM can guarantee end-to-end timing and a relatively low variation in network access time.

ATM provides many advantages for networking. ATM transports information by setting up multiple virtual connections across a shared physical media. This allows multiple devices to use the network simultaneously, but at a rate that is a subset of the total capacity of the link. In an ATM network there is no real distinction between local area and wide area networking because all network links are assumed to be relatively high capacity.

Other characteristics unique to ATM are the ability to provide feedback to network devices about congestion and the ability to use physical connection rates of 155M bps and higher. All of these advantages allow ATM networks to reduce congestion and intelligently manage network traffic at high speeds.

WAN TECHNOLOGY

A wide area network (WAN) is a communications infrastructure covering geographically dispersed locations. WANs are important building blocks to support corporate network-intensive applications across sites. They can be designed to support various combinations of voice, video, data, and image. There are several different types of WANs, all with varying performance implications. WANs typically have lower bandwidths than LANs.

The physical network options available for implementing a WAN include:

- Analog lines.
- Dataphone Digital Service (DDS).
- Frame relay.
- Integrated Services Digital Networks (ISDN).
- ATM.
- Switched Multimegabit Data Services (SMDS).

ANALOG LINES

Analog lines, which can be dial-up lines or leased lines, are the easiest to install and offer transfer rates up to 56K bps. A dial-up connection creates a temporary circuit between the two points to be connected, whereas leased connections are permanent in nature and offer higher transfer rates. These transfer rates are much less than the transfer rates available on the LAN. Analog lines require the use of modems to convert digital signals to analog signals, and vice versa.

Asynchronous dial-up is most commonly used for remote access and batch applications. From a performance perspective, asynchronous dial-up is most effective in situations where other alternatives are not available. Asynchronous dial-up is an effective means for communications for a traveling user.

DATAPHONE DIGITAL SERVICE (DDS)

As the name implies, DDS is a digital connection that provides higher transfer rates, is less prone to interference, and offers increased reliability. Basic DDS leased lines are available for speeds up to 56K bps. Higher rates are offered through the use of T1 lines. T1 lines are multiple high-speed lines packaged into a single unit aggregating a throughput of 1.544M bps.

The connection is actually composed of 24 64K-bps lines that can be divided for use (referred to as fractional T1s) in an organization that does not have requirements for leasing the entire T1 bandwidth. Even higher bandwidths (up to 45M bps) can be obtained using the T3 class lines. The availability of the bandwidth depends entirely on the service provider. Special devices called Data Service and Channel Service Units (DSU/CSU) are required for connecting the LAN to the WAN.

FRAME RELAY

Frame relay is a packet-switching technology. Rather than providing a user with a dedicated circuit (i.e., circuit switching), frame relay provides many users access to the same circuit, switching each user's individual packets of information over the same connection (i.e., packet switching). As a result, frame relay services are much more efficient in their bandwidth use than is circuit switching.

Most of the time, users have little or no data to send. However, when users do send information, they typically have a large number of packets to send over a short period of time, causing a burst in the network traffic. Because frame relay switches packets, not circuits, anywhere from none of the available bandwidth to all of the available bandwidth can be used. Thus, from a user's perspective, frame relay provides "bandwidth on demand." As a result, frame relay services have become a popular option for providing enterprisewide network connections.

Essentially, frame relay networks represent an evolution from X.25 networks. X.25 networks incorporated a significant amount of overhead relative to fixed packet sizes, extensive error correction, re-transmission facilities, and fixed bandwidth links. Frame relay standards leverage the X.25 packet forwarding architectures while improving overall performance by eliminating some of the error correction and re-transmission capabilities inherent in the network equipment.

These components could be eliminated because today's physical networks are much more reliable than those in place when X.25 was initially developed. With frame relay, error correction and re-transmission is handled at the end nodes by higher-layer networking protocols such as TCP/IP. Additionally, frame relay includes the ability to support varying packet sizes. This eliminates the inefficiencies associated with transmitting short bursty communications over the same network as larger file transfers.

From a market perspective, frame relay has demonstrated tremendous growth over the past several years, as both a wide area networking option allowing companies to link distributed facilities and as a business-to-business option linking multiple companies in a common enterprise. Frame relay presents companies with a cost-effective LAN-to-LAN connectivity option, providing bandwidth availability in the range of 56K bps to 1.54M bps. Bandwidth in this range helps to address some of the wide area bandwidth issues of convergence applications, although frame relay does not address the requirements of time-sensitive applications. Frame relay has also proven to be an effective network option for supporting multiple protocols.

ISDN

Integrated services digital network (ISDN) is a public network service offering based on digital circuit-switched technology that provides the ability to integrate voice, video, and data. Because of the digital nature of the service, ISDN provides highly reliable transmissions. Additionally, ISDN is a scalable service (up to 1.544M bps in the US and 2.048M bps in Europe) that is usually offered in either a basic rate interface (BRI) or primary rate interface (PRI) configuration.

ISDN services have been extremely popular in Europe and Australia and have recently become more popular in the US as well. Much of ISDN's recent success in the US has been due to its ability to provide large amounts of bandwidth on demand. Thus, ISDN has become an attractive service offering to provide dial-up remote access. ISDN capabilities have also been incorporated into networking equipment to provide dial-up backup links to improve reliability. Finally, due to its switched nature, ISDN has also enjoyed significant success as a transport to support videoconferencing.

ATM

ATM can be integrated into an enterprise internetwork in a number of ways. The previous section on LAN architecture focused on the integration of ATM into the user segments and campus backbone. This section focuses on the development of ATM public service offerings by communications providers.

ATM is a connection-oriented service based upon fixed sized cells (53 bytes). The use of fixed sized cells coupled with its connection-oriented nature allows ATM to provide predictable delays and provides quality of service features to support delay-sensitive information. Additionally, ATM is extremely scalable, supporting data speeds from DS-1 (1.544M bps) rates to in excess of OC-48 (2.4G bps) rates.

ATM offers excellent quality of service capabilities, which allow it to support a wide range of applications. Specifically, ATM is capable of supporting constant bit rate (CBR), variable bit rate (VBR), and available bit rate (ABR) traffic. CBR traffic is primarily associated with delay-sensitive material such as voice and video. In these cases, ATM services guarantee applications a predictable delay for a pre-specified data rate. VBR traffic is commonly associated with bursty data traffic similar to that of a local area network.

With VBR traffic, ATM guarantees a specific amount of throughput and then makes a best effort attempt to deliver any data that exceeds the guaranteed rate. ATM also provides ABR services that allow users access to as much bandwidth as is currently available at any given time. However, with ABR services, users are not guaranteed any data rates.

Although ATM encompasses many of the features provided by other service offerings, it is far more complex and expensive. Additionally, most organizations do not yet possess applications that require the sophisticated capabilities of ATM. Therefore, most organizations are still relying on frame relay and SMDS services to support their data traffic and leased lines to support their voice and video traffic. However, as ATM service offerings continue to become more prevalent, and as prices decline, ATM will become a very attractive service offering for many organizations.

SMDS

Switched multimegabit data service (SMDS) is a connectionless cell-relay service developed to support bandwidth-intensive applications such as LAN interconnection services. SMDS uses fixed sized cells (53 bytes) to deliver information and provides bandwidths scaleable from 1.544M bps to 45M bps. The cell-based nature of SMDS is similar to that of ATM, however, SMDS is optimized for connectionless data services, whereas ATM is optimized for connection-oriented services.

Because SMDS is a connectionless technology, it requires minimal connection setup time at the expense of potentially increased latency. Specifically, depending on the network configuration and the current network traffic levels, it may take longer for the data to traverse a connectionless network than a connection-oriented network. As a result, SMDS networks cannot guarantee the timing of data arrivals, making it less suitable for delay-sensitive applications such as those that include voice, audio, and video.

Although SMDS is useful for high-bandwidth applications, it is extremely inefficient for low-bandwidth ones and has minimal burst capability. The underlying reason for this deficiency is the large overhead (374K bps for 1.544M bps) included in the SMDS protocol. Therefore, analysts agree that SMDS cannot carry SNA traffic efficiently.

As of this writing, SMDS is only available in limited geographic areas and is used typically only for niche applications. Although SMDS promises to provide high-speed LAN interconnections, many carriers are opting to provide such services using ATM technologies. SMDS' inability to support delay-sensitive material such as voice and video also hinder its widespread acceptance. However, prior to the full-scale deployment of ATM services, SMDS services offer an attractive alternative when high-speed interconnection services are required.

LAN to WAN Interconnectivity in Client/Server Computing

The distributed environment of client/server computing is expanding the boundaries of the traditional, single-floor LAN. In many cases, departments are located in different buildings. This requires LAN interconnection over a WAN.

The interconnection of identical LAN segments within the same building can be solved by a simple repeater. To isolate traffic or to inter-connect different types of LANs, bridges, routers, brouters, or gateways are required.

Bridges. Bridges are devices used to interconnect LAN segments. Advanced bridges are self-learning and maintain configuration tables that list the devices on their segments. A bridge's configuration table is essentially a matrix that lists LAN devices and the segment to which they are connected. A self-learning bridge automatically updates its own table when a new device is added to one of its segments.

A bridge examines the destination addresses of all messages on its segments. If the destination is on the same segment as the origin, the bridge does nothing. If the destination is on another segment, the bridge passes the message.

Bridges interconnect two LANs that usually have identical protocols at those layers. For example, both LANs might be Ethernet. Because a bridge handles only lower-level communications, the end-user devices and applications must translate the format of the information. Therefore, bridges are most appropriate when communicating devices use identical protocols. To interconnect a LAN across a WAN requires a bridge with remote link capability.

Routers. Routers perform like bridges, with the additional ability to choose among multiple paths. A router connects LANs that are running identical upper protocols. The LANs do not have to be similar in other respects.

For example, a network could be running TCP/IP protocols over Ethernet and coaxial cable and the other could be running TCP/IP pro-tocols over token ring and twisted pair. The key benefit of the router is that it manages traffic congestion through intelligent routing of data packets.

Gateways. Gateways solve the problem of communicating between dissimilar LANs that use different architectures. For example, one par-ticular LAN might be a TCP/IP-compliant LAN, while another might be OSI compliant. Because all the architecture's layers may be different, the gateway is a more complex device than a bridge or a router. A gateway can also serve as a migration path from a company's legacy network, such as SNA, to its LAN.

Brouters. Brouters combine bridge and router capability to allow the network designer to handle multiple connectivity approaches with a single product. Vendors are increasingly putting the functions of bridges, routers, and gateways into devices referred to as multiprotocol routers. Because of this, it is becoming increasingly difficult to distinguish a router from a bridge or a gateway.

Bridges, routers, and gateways solve many issues of LAN interconnection. However, a problem of connecting LANs located in geographically separate locations still remains. The problem is that old WAN technologies move data at slow speeds compared to LAN technologies. Users who access resources across a WAN from a LAN are faced potentially with longer response times as the speed of service is determined by the slowest link in the path. This issue has driven the development of high-speed WAN technologies. It is becoming more common to see LANs connected using high-speed alternatives such as frame relay and asynchronous transfer mode.

The next section looks in detail at "middleware," a new category of communication software.

CONCLUSION

This chapter has addressed the new and more complex networking environment of client/server. To build effective computing solutions in the future, it is essential that the network technology be available for the business user when the user wants it, not when it is convenient for the network. Of all the technological changes currently under way, the impact of the coming universal network is the most profound. The future is bright for those people skilled at designing and implementing networking technology.

II-8
Transaction Services

Today, as companies are becoming more comfortable with client/server computing, and as related technologies continue to stabilize, there has been a concomitant increase in distributed transaction processing. Networks are becoming more stable, operating systems are proving themselves, relational databases have been used successfully, and tools are now being produced to help manage client/server systems. With stabilization and increased confidence in client/server technology, systems building can move from conservative applications (decision support systems, departmental systems) to more mission-critical systems (transaction processing systems, enterprisewide systems).

MISSION-CRITICAL CLIENT/SERVER SYSTEMS

Mission-critical client/server systems can have different requirements than other types of client/server systems. These include:

- Users in many locations share data and resources.
- Complex transactions (sometimes spanning multiple data sources) need to be managed to guarantee completion.
- System availability and reliability become more critical.
- Performance needs to be predictable and controllable as more users and locations are added to systems.

Distributed transaction processing (DTP) is a vital element in managing transactions in mission-critical client/server systems. Many information technology departments today want to increase the price/performance of their systems by moving mainframe applications to smaller operating system platforms, where the processing is distributed among several machines. This distribution of processors is what distributed transaction processing refers to. A transaction is considered distributed if it accesses more than one resource manager, processor, database, file system, printer, or any other shared resource.

WHAT IS A TRANSACTION?

A transaction is a logical unit of work; it consists of the logic and the processing needed to perform an individual, unique business function. When a transaction consists of multiple components and those components occur simultaneously, each component action must be completed successfully before the entire transaction is completed.

A transaction must exhibit what are sometimes referred to as ACID (atomicity, consistency, isolation, and durability) qualities:

- Atomicity guarantees that, in case of error or rollback, no partial transaction data remains to corrupt the database. For example, a transfer of funds consists of two parts: a debit and a credit. Atomicity makes sure that a $20 transfer from savings to checking does not debit a savings account without crediting a checking account.
- Consistency means that the execution of a transaction maintains the interrelationships of all data. Consistency of data is the end result of the other three properties. The work done by a transaction must take resources from one consistent state to another consistent state. Continuing the example, the $20 debited from the savings account must match the $20 credited to the checking account. If a transaction is repeated many times in an identical manner, the results should be identical.
- Isolation means transactions are separated from one another so they can execute concurrently. In other words, the execution of one transaction has no effect on other transactions. In effect, concurrent transactions must behave as if they executed serially.
- Durability reduces the likelihood of a failure and protects the transaction data in case the system does fail. That is, when a transaction succeeds, the effects remain in the database after a system failure.

In a client/server environment, the logical units of work may not be neatly defined and may span multiple processes and resources. Ensuring that these transactions maintain their ACID qualities is the challenge of distributed transaction processing in a client/server environment.

WHAT IS DISTRIBUTED TRANSACTION PROCESSING MANAGEMENT?

In small- to moderate-scale environments of less than 150 simultaneous users on a single server, management of transactions may be provided by the database management system (DBMS) software with its restart/recovery and integrity capabilities. For larger client/server environments, a class of software is starting to appear, referred to as DTP managers.

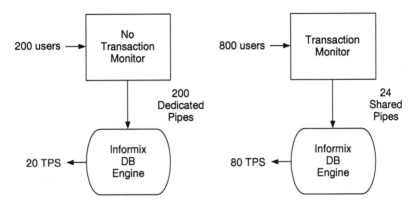

Exhibit II-8-1. Comparison of Performance with and without a TP Monitor

These transaction managers share server processes across a large community of users and can be more efficient and effective than DBMSs. Example products include Tuxedo from BEA Systems (formerly AT&T), Microsoft Transaction Server, and Encina from Transarc.

Performance Improvements

What are the advantages of DTP? One estimate is that the cost of processing a transaction in a distributed environment is about one-fifth what it would be in a mainframe environment.

In a client/server environment, transaction processing (TP) monitors can increase the performance of systems. Exhibit II-8-1 compares a database engine on a server running Tuxedo. The Open/DTP manager increased the transactions-per-second benchmark fourfold.

Not every situation results in this kind of improvement, however. The potential for throughput or performance improvement depends on the nature of both the application and the hardware/systems software being used (e.g., DBMS product). TP monitors can also be used to control and monitor tasks and processes distributed across a network of processors.

Two-Phase Commit in DTP

In a traditional mainframe environment, ensuring the ACID properties was simpler to achieve. If one piece of the transaction failed, the entire transaction failed. In a distributed environment, on the other hand, distributed transactions may be found running on multiple components. The DTP achieves this through the use of two-phase commit. Any component of the system could falter while the remaining pieces continue working to complete a transaction that should have been canceled. Two-phase commit makes sure that a transaction is either committed correctly or aborted in all systems.

In the first phase, the prepare phase, all participants in a transaction (a database or other resource manager, for instance) are polled to see whether they are prepared to commit a transaction. A travel agent trying to make plane, hotel, and rental car reservations at once provides an analogy. The agent does not want to book a flight if a hotel room cannot be reserved, or request a car rental on Tuesday if the passenger cannot get a plane until Wednesday, so the agent finds out whether all the reservations can be made before committing to any of them.

The second phase is called the commit phase. In the same example, if all three participants respond affirmatively, the transaction is committed. If any or all the participants respond negatively, the transaction is rolled back.

TRANSACTION SERVICES IN THE CLIENT/SERVER EXECUTION ARCHITECTURE

TP Monitor Services

TP monitor services are the primary interface through which applications invoke transaction services and receive status and error information. TP monitor services, in conjunction with information access services and communication services, provide for load balancing across processors or machines and location transparency for DTP.

The TP monitor is a critical component of the DTP architecture. TP monitors provide many services, including:

- Providing resource management (e.g., load balancing).
- Scheduling transactions for efficient, high-volume execution.
- Scheduling tasks across heterogeneous resource managers.
- Providing priority-based transactions.
- Providing location transparency of servers.
- Transaction recovery

Two key features separate TP monitors from systems using a database engine without a TP monitor: multithreading and load balancing. Multithreading permits an application to perform more than one function simultaneously, such as collecting multiple files from a database that does not already support multithreading. Because more than one activity is being completed, multithreading typically speeds up transaction throughput.

Load balancing examines which application functions have to be completed and what the work load is on each resource so that needed tasks are shifted to lower-utilized resources. Load balancing can be either equitably based or priority based. With equitably based load balancing, all transactions have the same importance: they are executed in the order received. Priority-based load balancing assigns certain priorities to certain transactions: More important transactions can move in front of those of lesser importance.

Resource Management Services

A resource manager provides for concurrence control and integrity for a single data resource (a database or a file system, for example). Integrity is guaranteed by ensuring that an update is completed correctly and entirely or not at all. Resource management services use locking, commit, and rollback services and are integrated with transaction management services.

Transaction Management Services

Transaction management services coordinate transactions across one or more resource managers either on a single machine or on multiple machines within the network. Transaction management services ensure that all resources for a transaction are updated, or in the case of an update failure on any one resource, all updates are rolled back.

Transaction Partitioning Services

Transaction partitioning services provide architectural support for mapping single logical or business transactions into the required multiple physical transactions. For example, in a package or legacy environment, the single logical transaction of changing a customer address may require the partitioning and coordination of several physical transactions to multiple application systems or databases. Transaction partitioning services provide the application with a simple, single-transaction view.

DTP IN THE X/OPEN MODEL

Another model, the X/Open DTP model, provides a clear comparison. X/Open is an independent consortium that develops standards to promote application portability and interoperability. The X/Open DTP model relates the components of a distributed transaction application, such as resource managers, applications, transaction managers, and communications managers.

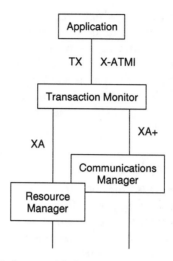

Exhibit II-8-2. Layers of Software in the X/Open DTP Model

The X/Open model is the emerging standard model for DTP. This section discusses the components of the X/Open DTP model, illustrated in Exhibit II-8-2.

In the X/Open DTP model, the application program interacts with only one layer of the architecture, the transaction monitor. The transaction monitor is responsible for commitment and rollback of work, in addition to interacting with the resource manager and the communications manager. The resource manager controls database management and other services. The communication manager controls networking and communication services.

The model also identifies four interfaces: Tx, X-ATMI, XA, and XA+. Tx compliance refers to the transaction-demarcation verbs used between the application and the transaction processing monitor. This tells the application how to begin and end transactions. Tx compliance also has a chained-transaction capability, which allows the completion of one transaction to initiate the next transaction.

X-ATMI compliance refers to the communication verbs used between the application and the transaction monitor. This is a high-level interface that allows clients and servers to communicate in a location-transparent manner. This interface allows programmers the following options:

- Open a connection to a conversational server, a server that performs multiple interactions across client requests.
- Create a new conversational server automatically if a server is not available to handle a conversation request.

- Maintain a global transaction during a conversation.
- Have the conversation span multiple machines.
- Detect and provide notification of connection failures.

The XA interface is for communications between the resource manager and the transaction monitor. This is the mechanism that updates several heterogeneous databases or resource managers with a two-phase commit. The XA, Tx, and ATMI standards are based on Tuxedo application programming interfaces (APIs) developed by UNIX System Laboratories.

The XA+ interface is for communications between the transaction monitor and the communications resource manager. The exact definition of this interface is still evolving.

In this complex environment, determining a DTP architecture and selecting supporting products are challenging tasks. The next sections offer guidance for these tasks.

GUIDELINES FOR DETERMINING A DTP ARCHITECTURE

Determining a distributed transaction processing architecture involves several major considerations:

- When to use a TP monitor.
- How to choose the product best suited for the needs of the organization.
- How to create the DTP components for the particular client/server environment.

The necessary steps for making this determination are as follows.

Step 1. Understand the Basics of DTP A thorough understanding of the concepts involved in distributed transaction processing is a prerequisite for determining whether a TP monitor is necessary for the client/server application the organization is considering deploying. This chapter provided a high-level discussion of these concepts in the previous section.

Step 2. Determine the System Requirements Systems developers must perform a thorough analysis of system needs before deciding on a TP monitor. The following system requirements may affect the need for a TP monitor:

- Number of concurrent users.
- Distributed locations of users and servers.
- Need for heterogeneous platform support or platform independence.

- High transaction volumes.
- Potential future growth of the system (scalability).
- Heightened security needs in a distributed system.
- Nature (type) of applications.

Another "need" concerns the imaging or document management integration. When integrating in either of these technologies, a transaction control mechanism for ensuring both relational database management system (RDBMS) commit and file system write, or image store write, is often necessary.

In many imaging and document management systems, the DBMS cannot support this integration alone. This points to the need for a TP monitor that can provide ACID properties for data stores other than DBMS (e.g., file systems). Any of these requirements either indicates the need for a TP monitor or points to significant benefits that could be achieved with one.

Step 3. Determine Whether a TP Monitor Is Needed A TP monitor is not necessary for all distributed environments. When the system requirements have been identified, developers must complete an evaluation to determine the need for a TP monitor.

Step 4. Create a Product Features Matrix If the need for a monitor is established, developers must choose the most appropriate monitor for the system. (See the section "Choosing Among Monitors," later in this chapter, for a list of questions and a matrix with which to compare the features and usability of the different DTP monitors an organization might consider.)

Step 5. Map System Requirements to Product Features Systems developers should compare the product matrix and the needs of the system to find the best monitor for the project. Functional requirements as well as other business needs (e.g., skill base within the organization) should be mapped to the features provided by each monitor.

Step 6. Determine Target Product and Architecture The next step is to design and develop the DTP monitor and the rest of the execution architecture. Extra effort should be made to ensure that all layers and components of the architecture will work together, and that they will meet the application, system, and organization requirements.

Step 7. Confirm the Architecture by Performing a Benchmark
Developers should conduct a benchmark of the technical architecture to confirm the assumptions made in defining the architecture. The benchmark ensures that various parts of the architecture work together and provides the functions and features required by the system. This benchmark also allows developers to install, configure, learn, and test the selected TP monitor.

STEPS TO DETERMINE WHETHER A TP MONITOR IS NEEDED

Although a TP monitor may be a crucial link in systems projects, a monitor is not necessary or even desirable in every situation. Systems developers must complete a careful evaluation to determine the need for a TP monitor. In this evaluation, developers must consider several questions.

1. *How many users access the system concurrently?* Because TP monitors can be used to manage the system resource requirements of large communities of users, the organization should evaluate the use of a TP monitor in large client/server environments—where there are perhaps hundreds or thousands of users.

Different sources give different answers as to the number of concurrent users that necessitates the use of a TP monitor. The monitor vendors themselves give low values; the database vendors give high values. The middle ground seems to be somewhere around 250 concurrent users. This is by no means definitive, however, and an organization should consider this question in conjunction with each of the other questions before making the choice.

2. *Does the system require high throughput?* Because TP monitors provide load balancing capability and because they may effectively reduce the number of connections that must be made to databases (depending on DBMS product architecture), they will help conserve the resources of the data servers and, as a result, can increase the overall throughput of the system. Systems with high throughput requirements should consider using a TP monitor. As a guideline, systems requiring throughput that is greater than 50 transactions per second are good candidates for a TP monitor.

3. *Does the system require high availability?* Because of their fault tolerance, TP monitors make a valuable addition to systems that require high availability. The automatic restart/recovery feature helps a system recognize when components have failed and attempts to restart them. Also, because of the location transparency capabilities, if an entire node in a system goes down, clients may be able to reach the service they need on another node providing the same service.

4. *Is the system distributed across multiple nodes?* TP monitors provide common administrative facilities to manage groups of distributed servers. These facilities allow a system to be managed from one central location with a common set of commands for each machine within a distributed environment.

5. *Will the system be scaled in the future?* TP monitors offer multiple scalability options. TP monitors can run on machines ranging from workstations to mainframes in a client/server environment. This feature can be used to grow client/server applications as the organization and business volumes grow.

Monitors also scale by allowing new machines to be added dynamically to the system. Adding additional nodes in the production cycle is one TP monitor strength, although some monitors are better at doing this than others. If the organization anticipates that system volumes will increase during the system's lifetime, scalability provides an excellent reason for selecting and using a TP monitor.

6. *Do the online applications need the support of interoperability between autonomous, heterogeneous processors?* Some TP monitors are available across multiple platforms and maintain interoperability (e.g., communication and data translation) between those platforms. For this reason, systems projects that intend to support a heterogeneous hardware environment should consider using a TP monitor.

7. *Is the system mission critical?* TP monitors offer additional capability: two-phase commit, recovery/rollback, naming services, security services, guaranteed processing, and audit trail logging. Therefore, the more mission-critical the system, the more likely it is that the organization should opt for a TP monitor.

8. *Does the system access legacy systems?* TP monitors can access databases and services running in traditional mainframe systems environments. TP monitors frequently include mainframe networking capability and maintain transaction rollback during mainframe accesses. If access to the legacy system is read only, the messaging capabilities of the platforms are probably sufficient. If access is update, however, the messaging and two-phase commit capabilities of the TP monitor would be more dependable and reliable.

9. *Does the system access nonrelational data?* Some TP monitors provide a method of accessing nonrelational data, such as VSAM files or flat files, independently of where the file physically resides. If these data sources require write access, a TP monitor would provide more dependable messaging and two-phase commit capabilities than the platform messaging capabilities alone.

10. *Do the online applications access and update more than one da-*

tabase or more than one type of database? A real strength of TP monitors is their ability to ensure a global two-phase commit over multiple, heterogeneous databases. A system that has this quality is a candidate for a TP monitor. Many client/server database products also provide this capability.

11. *Does the system have complex security requirements?* Many of the TP monitors available today provide security authorization and authentication services. Most of them utilize the Kerberos security approach, developed at the Massachusetts Institute of Technology (MIT).

12. *Is the system not a transaction processing system?* Although TP monitors provide global two-phase commit transaction processing capability, systems that do not need this feature can also benefit by using TP monitors. For example, the load-balancing feature helps increase system performance. Also, the administrative facilities can help simplify system management.

CHOOSING AMONG MONITORS

When an organization decides to use a TP monitor in its client/server environment, the following criteria may be useful to differentiate among TP monitor product offerings:

1. *Is the organization interested in stable technologies or in emerging technologies?* Many of the distributed (client/server) TP monitor products are new to the marketplace; others have been available for years. Systems developers should assess the organization's requirements regarding the stability of both the TP monitor product and the TP monitor vendor.

2. *What is the organization's position on DCE?* Two common TP monitors (Encina and CICS/6000) are built on top of the Open Software Foundation/Distributed Computing Environment (OSF/DCE). DCE is the standard client/server runtime environment adopted by the OSF. Because of DCE's newness to the market, many experts have been skeptical of its acceptance. Also, because of its complexity, additional training is usually required for users of Encina and CICS/6000.

3. *Is the organization installing a new system, or is it rehosting or downsizing an existing mainframe system?* The UniKix, VIS/TP, and CICS/6000 monitors were developed specifically with rehosting of IBM mainframe applications in mind. Other TP monitors are best suited to fresh installations. Developers following this path must be sure to assess carefully the costs and benefits of their TP monitor selection.

4. *Does the organization have existing personnel with mainframe-CICS experience?* CICS/6000 has a programming interface similar to mainframe CICS. The learning curve for mainframe-CICS programmers

to use CICS/6000 is minimal. The learning curve for these same personnel to program using such other TP monitors as Tuxedo and Encina is substantial. On the other hand, because CICS/6000's administrative facilities are not similar to mainframe CICS, administrative personnel face a steep learning curve: They need to learn UNIX, DCE, and Encina, the layers on which CICS/6000 is built.

5. *Does the system use PC-based clients?*   Each TP monitor offers different support for personal computer (PC)-based clients. Most of the primary TP vendors support the Windows platform. However, 32-bit implementations of their products may still not exist.

Tuxedo currently provides support for heterogeneous client environments, offering full support for Mac OS, OS/2, UNIX, Windows 3.1/95, and Windows NT workstations.

6. *Does the organization plan to use Windows NT Server?*   TP monitor support for Windows NT is currently limited to BEA's Tuxedo and Microsoft Transaction Server. As NT gains market share and proves to be a scalable, robust server platform, other vendors should make progress toward supporting the NT platform.

7. *What platforms and operating systems do the servers run on?*
Some TP monitors are capable of running on a wider variety of platforms/operating systems than others. Organizations should be sure that their TP monitor supports the current and planned platform technologies in their client/server environment.

8. *Does the system require mainframe connectivity?*   The leading TP monitors offer varying levels of mainframe connectivity, including 3270, APPC, VTXXX, and Transmission Control Protocol/Internet Protocol (TCP/IP). If mainframe application and data connectivity are required, organizations must ensure that their TP monitor supports the specific protocols.

9. *Does the system need to integrate with Internet/ intranet technologies?*   The leading TP monitors provide varying degrees of Internet/ intranet integration. Some products, such as Microsoft Transaction Server, allow custom business services to be reused by traditional client/server applications, browser-based HTML applications, and Java/ ActiveX applets. Other vendors are simply enabling their communications layer for the Internet by providing support for Internet security technologies, such as proxy servers and firewalls.

Exhibit II-8-3 lists and briefly describes runtime features and configuration features for TP monitors. When evaluating one or more TP monitors,

TP Monitor Features	Description
Nested transactions	Subtransactions within transactions; these can be committed or rolled back independently of the main transaction
Cross-platform data translation	Automatic translation of messages between platforms, independent of the data representation on each machine
Runtime Features	
Synchronous service calls	Service calls from a client to the server that wait for the response
Asynchronous service calls	Service calls from a client to the server that can continue processing without the response
Conversational service calls	Multistep service calls where context is maintained by the server for each step, and all steps are within the same transaction
Embedded service calls:	
• Embedded synchronous calls	Synchronous service calls contained within a service
• Embedded asynchronous calls	Asynchronous service calls contained within a service
• Service forwarding (pipelining)	Service call within a service, where the called service responds directly to the client
Global transactions (two-phase)	Transactions that can span multiple data bases on multiple machines
Reliable queuing	Service that allows transactions to be reliably saved for later processing
Mainframe connectivity:	
• From server to mainframe	Ability to invoke mainframe applications from a server transaction
• From mainframe to server	Ability to invoke server transactions from a mainframe application
Data-dependent routing	Ability to route a request to a particular service based on the content of the message being sent
Unsolicited client notification	Messages sent without client request
Multithreaded transaction processing	Ability to start another task concurrently using threads within an operating environment
Configuration Features	
Load balancing	Ability to spread the transaction load evenly among all available servers
Dynamic load balancing	Automatic startup of multiple copies of a server when the load on a given server increases
Prioritized service calls	Service calls that can be assigned a priority weighting and then be processed in priority order

Exhibit II-8-3   DTP Product Features Matrix

TP Monitor Features	Description
Multiple instances of monitor per machine (regions)	Ability to invoke multiple instances of the monitor on one machine, similar to CICS regions on a mainframe
Automatic recovery/restart	Ability to recognize when services are down, and automatically attempt to restart them
Distributed TP networks	Networks of TP applications in a LAN/WAN environment
Kerberos security	Standard security approach developed at MIT used for authentication services
Other DTP Features	
Software distribution facilities	Utilities that facilitate distribution of applications and system software in a distributed environment
PC connectivity	PC-based client messaging with the TP monitor.

Exhibit II-8-3 (*continued*)

an organization should determine which of these features are required by, or could benefit, its client/server applications.

The features described can be used to evaluate and differentiate among the TP monitor products an organization chooses to consider. It is important to remember that the vendors are constantly adding to and modifying the features of their products. Each product should be carefully reviewed at the time the organization is selecting a TP monitor.

CONCLUSION

This chapter has provided an overview of transaction processing in a client/server environment. As more and more organizations become skilled and comfortable with client/server, the technologies and approaches discussed here will continue to become more prevalent in client/server computing solutions.

II-9
Environment Services

A client/server application runs in an extremely complex environment. This book has described a number of these complexities already, challenges related to managing the user interface, communicating to other programs, or accessing information and data. Other application and system-level services that do not deal directly with user interface, communications, or information access are grouped together within the execution architecture under environment services.

It is important to note at the outset that many of the environment services (e.g., batch) are not unique to client/server computing. Nevertheless, they must be addressed in a distributed environment.

OVERVIEW OF ENVIRONMENT SERVICES

When developing client/server applications it is easy to overlook the core facilities users take for granted in traditional environments. Often companies do not anticipate their batch requirements until shortly before system conversion, which leads to many long hours of intensive work that could have been avoided had the organization anticipated and planned for these needs.

Environment services provide a number of important benefits, including:

- Standardizing approaches for dealing with batch requirements.
- Standardizing approaches for dealing with report requirements.
- Isolating the details and idiosyncrasies of specific operating system implementations and environments.
- Standardizing application error processing.
- Providing consistent application security mechanisms.

ENVIRONMENT SERVICES FRAMEWORK

Exhibit II-9-1 shows the components of environment services.

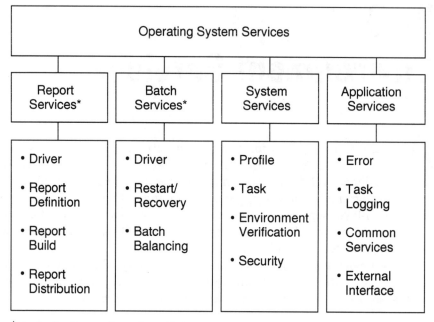

*Typically Server Functions Only

Exhibit II-9-1. Environment Services

Operating System Services

Operating system services are the underlying services typically provided by today's modern operating systems. When necessary, an additional layer or application program interface (API) may be provided to gain either operating system independence or a higher level of abstraction for application programmers. Operating system services include multi-threading, memory allocation, and free memory.

Application Services

Application services are miscellaneous services that applications can use for common functions across multiple applications and systems. The following services need to be considered.

Error Handling. Error Handling Services support the handling of fatal and nonfatal hardware and software errors for an application, providing a consistent mechanism for identifying, evaluating, and reporting application errors.

Examples of error handling services include display error, determine error message, and evaluate and map error.

Logging Services. Logging Services support the logging of informational, error, and warning messages. These messages could be logged to a file, a database, and a workstation.

Examples of logging services include write-to log and read log.

Common Services. These services provide common routines that are required by many application programs but are not specific to the application.

Examples of common services include date/time routines, list handling, common validation routines, and common edit routines.

External Interface Services. External interface services enable custom applications to interface with external software packages and applications. Examples of the types of packages supported include spreadsheets, word processing, knowledge-based systems, electronic mail, and other organization applications.

External interface services enable custom applications to invoke processing or pass data to and receive data from purchased software packages and other organization applications. These services may also notify custom applications when the external applications are terminated.

Examples of external interface services include send data to external application and invoke external application.

System Services

These are services that applications can use to perform system-level functions.

Profile Management Services. Profile management services are used to access and update a system, user, or application profile. These profiles typically contain information that defines the characteristics, preferences, and capabilities of application users. The profiles store information used to control the behavior of the system, such as default language and color preference.

Examples of profile management services include retrieve profile and update profile.

Task Management Services. Task management services allow applications to control individual tasks or processes. They provide options to schedule, start, stop, and restart both client and server tasks.

Examples of task management services include start task, stop task, and abort task.

Environment Verification Services. Environment verification services are usually invoked when an application begins processing. Before continuing, the application can use these services to verify that the correct version of required execution architecture elements, application components, and other applications are available.

Security Services. Security services provide application and application resource-level security (e.g., data) for client/server applications. The basic services include log-on, log-off, authenticate user or requester, and verify user access privileges to data and application resources.

Batch Services

Batch services support the execution of batch application programs within the system. Batch services provide three subservices.

Driver Services. These services provide the control structure and framework for batch programs. Driver services manage the flow of processing within and between modules and utilities (e.g., extracts and sorts) as well as provide integration with checkpointing facilities and context management.

Restart/Recovery Services. These services are used to automatically recover and restart batch programs if they should fail during execution. The services support the restoration of context information and the repositioning of application programs and data sets to the last commitment point prior to the occurrence of a failure.

Without these services, long-running batch programs may need to be completely rerun if they fail, which could jeopardize completion of the batch run within the defined batch window and increase overall system resource requirements and usage.

Batch Balancing Services. These services support the tracking of run-to-run balances and totals for the batch system and help to ensure processing and data integrity. These services can reduce the effort associated with manually checking system control reports.

Report Services

Report services are facilities for simplifying the construction and delivery of reports or generated correspondence. These services help to define reports and to electronically route reports to allow for online review, printing, and archiving. Report services also support the merging of application data with predefined templates to create letters or other printed correspondence. The following subservices need to be considered:

- *Driver services.* These services provide the control structure and framework for the reporting system.
- *Report definition services.* These services receive and identify the report request, perform required validation routines, and format the outputted report(s). After the request is validated, the report build function is initiated.
- *Report build services.* These services are responsible for collecting, processing, formatting, and writing report information (data, graphics, text).
- *Report distribution services.* These services are responsible for printing or otherwise distributing the reports to users.

Because batch and reporting form the heart of environment services, the next two sections look at these components in more detail.

FUNCTIONS AND FEATURES OF A REPORT ARCHITECTURE

The report architecture within environment services supports the generation and delivery of reports. Applications request report services by sending a message to the reporting framework.

The following types of reports are supported by the reporting application framework:

- *Scheduled.* Scheduled reports are generated based on a time or date requirement. These reports typically contain statistical information and are generated periodically (e.g., invoices and bills).
- *On-demand.* Users request some reports with specific parameters. The scheduling of such reports, the formatting, and the data requirements are not known before the request is made, so these factors must be handled at request time.
- *Event-driven.* This report type includes reports whose generation is

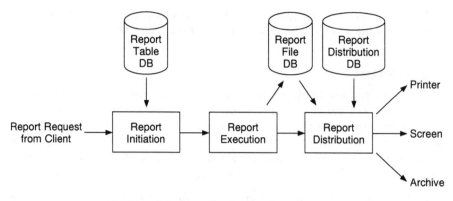

Exhibit II-9-2. Reporting Application Framework

triggered based on a business or system event. A printed trade slip is an example of an event-driven report.

REPORTING APPLICATION FRAMEWORK

Exhibit II-9-2 depicts the three major components of the reporting application framework: report initiation, report execution, and report distribution.

Report Initiation

The report initiation function is the interface for reporting applications into the report architecture. The client initiates a report request to the report architecture by sending a message to the report initiation function.

The responsibility of report initiation is to receive, identify, and validate the request and then trigger the report build process. Reporting initiation has two main components:

- *Receive, identify, and validate a report request.* The identification function determines general information about the request, such as report type, requester, quantity to be printed, and requested time. Based on the report type, a table of reports is examined to gather additional report-specific information and perform required validation routines for the report request.

  After the report identification and validation functions have been successfully completed, the reporting process can continue. If any errors are identified, the report initiation function will return an error message to the requester application.

- *Initiate report execution.* The initiate report execution function processes the report profile and specific distribution requirements and determines the report to be created. It then passes control to the report execution process.

Report Execution

Report execution is the core of the reporting application framework. Report execution has four main components:

- *Format the report.* This function is responsible for formatting the layout of the outputted report, including standard headers, column headings, row headings, and other static report information.
- *Collect the information.* This function is responsible for collecting the information (e.g., data, text, image, and graphics) that is required for the report. This function utilizes the information access services component of the client/server architecture.
- *Format the information.* This function is responsible for formatting the collected information into the appropriate display format based on the report type and the report distribution requirements.
- *Output the report.* This function initiates the report distribution function to distribute the created report to the specified devices (e.g., printers and disks) and individuals.

The process of collecting, processing, formatting, and outputting report data can be accomplished several different ways. For example, one method is to create a program in C for each report format. Here, many aspects of report printing—such as page size, headings, footings, and printer control values—would have to be programmed in function calls to facilitate the report programming process. Information access to files or the database is through information access services.

Another option is to use a third-party report tool, such as the SQR (Structured Query Report Writer) from SQL Solutions. SQR is a robust report generator designed to be used with structured query language (SQL)-based relational databases. SQR insulates the developer from programming in a third-generation language (3GL) by providing a higher-level programming language. SQL queries (information access) are placed directly into the SQR program.

Report Distribution

The final requirement of the reporting application framework is the report distribution function. Once the report has been generated, it must be distributed to the specified targets (devices and users). The report distribution function locates completed report files and routes them to the appropriate devices within the client/server network.

Typically, a report distribution database is used to specify the destinations for each report supported by the report architecture. The report distribution database specifies where, when, how, and to whom to distribute the produced report. Specific destinations can include: printer(s), user(s), user groups, archives (permanent storage), and specific display devices such as workstations and terminals.

Several additional options exist for distributing reports including timed reporting, multiple copy distribution, and report archiving. Also, a user interface function can be built to open and browse report files.

EVALUATION CRITERIA

There are two primary approaches to implementing a reporting architecture: custom and package. Evaluating custom and package solutions involves both functional and technical criteria. Not all the criteria are necessarily required by any particular organization.

Functional Criteria

Following is a list of functional criteria that should be considered during the planning for a report architecture:

1. *Report repository.* The report architecture should work with, and support maintenance of, a report repository on the platforms within the client/server architecture. The report repository contains the detailed definitions of the reports.

2. *Work group report support.* The report architecture should work with and support distribution of reports generated on the work group server.

3. *On-demand reports.* The report architecture must support distribution of reports requested by users on demand. Typically, these reports do not have a set schedule or frequency for distribution. The report architecture must support distribution of these reports without the requirement of manual or user intervention (subsequent to initial set up and conversion).

4. *Scheduled reports.* The report architecture must support distribution of regularly scheduled reports. Typically, these reports have a set schedule and frequency for distribution. The report distribution package must support distribution of these reports without the requirement of manual or user intervention (subsequent to setup and conversion).

5. *Online preview.* The report architecture should allow preview of reports online from a user's intelligent workstation prior to actual

distribution. Ideally, the report architecture itself provides support for online preview of reports through software located on the intelligent workstation.

6. *Graphical user interface.* The architecture should provide users with a graphical user interface.

7. *Bilingual support.* The report architecture for companies that use two or more languages must provide a multinational user interface. (Large report runs targeted for multiple users may require the ability to change languages during the report.)

8. *Basic preview functions.* The report architecture should support basic preview functions. These include:

   • Scrolling up and down.

   • Scrolling left and right.

   • Advancing to end or beginning of report without scrolling through intermediate pages.

9. *Advanced preview functions.* In addition to the basic preview functions, certain advanced preview functions may also be necessary:

   • Page indexing (allows users to jump to specific report pages).

   • Section indexing (allows users to jump to specific report sections).

   • Search capabilities (allows users to search report for occurrence of a specific data stream).

10. *Report-level security.* Occasionally, reports may contain sensitive information. Thus it is important that access to certain reports be restricted to authorized users. The report architecture should provide a mechanism for implementing report level security. This security must be in place on all platforms with the client/server architecture. At the work group level, security may consist of downloading sensitive report files to a secure directory, and having the local area network (LAN) administrator release the report as appropriate.

11. *Section-, page-, and field-level security.* Defining security at the report section, page, or field level provides greater flexibility in determining and implementing report security. This is a desirable, though not mandatory, requirement of the report architecture.

12. *Background processing.* The report architecture should support the processing of reports in the background while the application works in the foreground during online hours. In other words, processing of reports should not negatively affect online response times, or tie up the user's workstation.

13. *Automatic report addressing.* The report architecture should provide a "humanly intelligible" address for all distributed reports.

The address may be used by a print site operator, LAN administrator, or other personnel to manually sort printed output (if required). This criterion can be satisfied by automatic creation of banner pages or other means.

14. *Delivery costing.* A distribution costing function can be useful to provide sufficient information to users so that they avoid accidentally downloading or printing large reports during peak usage hours. This function warns users of reports that would overload the network or a printer. This costing function might provide recipients with a rough estimate of the amount of time that distribution might take. Finally, during the online day, the delivery costing mechanism might disallow transmission of reports that exceed a predetermined cost.

15. *Multiple destinations.* The report architecture should support distribution of a single report to single or multiple destinations.

16. *Destination rationalization.* Some systems might possibly send multiple copies of a report to the same site—to several different users, for example. It is highly desirable to have the report architecture recognize these situations whenever possible and distribute the specified report only once.

17. *Automatic printing.* The report architecture should provide automatic print capabilities. Once a report has been distributed for printing (either through a "push" distribution scheduling mechanism or through a "pull" user request) no further user or operations personnel involvement should be necessary to print the report at the specified location.

18. *Multiple print destinations.* The report architecture should support distribution of reports for printing at centralized, remote, or local print sites without user or operations personnel intervention.

19. *Variable printer types.* Printing on multiple types of printers, including line, impact, and laser printers, should be supported. The user should not have to specify the type of target printer. Ideally, the report architecture would default this information from the user's profile or the default printer defined in the local operating system. This criterion requires that the report architecture support several print mechanisms, such as postscript drivers and host/mainframe protocols (e.g., Advanced Function Printing).

20. *Variable printer destinations.* The report architecture should default the destination printer for a specific report (from the user's profile or operating system parameters). In addition, the architecture should allow the user to change the printer specified. Validation of the print destination also should be included.

21. *Special forms printing.* The report architecture should support distribution of "regular" reports and special forms reports.

22. *Font support.* Some reports may be printed on laser printers and may support electronic forms text (i.e., including the forms text in the report dataset as opposed to printing the report data set on a preprinted form). The architecture should allow multiple fonts to be specified.

23. *Report archival.* The report architecture should provide and facilitate archival or disposition of report data sets. Ideally, the architecture would permit definition of retention periods and disposition requirements.

24. *Report download.* The report architecture should allow distribution of the information contained in a report data set to a user's intelligent workstation. The information should be in a form that can be imported to a local word processing software, decision support software package, or other appropriate application.

25. *Application transparency.* It is desirable for the report architecture to appear to the users as if it were part of the overall application. This does not necessarily mean that the architecture must integrate seamlessly with the application; a message interface between the systems might be acceptable.

26. *Selective printing.* It would be desirable for the report architecture to provide users with the ability to print only selected pages or sections of the report. This should reduce paper usage while still allowing users to obtain a hard copy of the information as required.

27. *Print job restart.* It would be desirable, especially in the case of large reports, if the report architecture allowed a print job to be restarted from the point of failure rather than having to reprint the entire report.

Technical Criteria

Following is a list of technical criteria that should be considered during the planning for a report architecture:

1. *Platform compatibility.* The report architecture must be compatible with the platform architecture. It also should be compatible with local area networks and standalone workstation technology specified in the platform architecture.

2. *Wide area network compatibility.* Most systems will include support for WAN communication, so the report architecture should be compatible with this environment.

3. *Technology standards.* The report architecture should be compliant

with existing formal and de facto standards (e.g., SQL database language, COBOL programming language, C programming language).

4. *External user directory.* The report architecture should make use of an external user directory of preferences and locations.

5. *Data compression in report repository.* To reduce the storage requirements for the report repository, it is also desirable for the report architecture to support data compression in the repository.

6. *Code page compatibility.* Code page compatibility must be considered when translating characters to ASCII (American Standard Code for Information Interchange).

Exhibit II-9-3 summarizes the functional and technical criteria just discussed and provides a framework with which to evaluate particular reporting packages.

CUSTOM REPORTING APPROACHES

If a commercially available reporting product cannot meet an organization's report requirements, the organization may have to consider a custom approach. Exhibit II-9-4 demonstrates how a custom report architecture relates to a workstation platform technical architecture.

This custom report process is responsible for processing all messages requesting generation, manipulation, or distribution of reports. The following services are provided:

- Report generation.
- Report deletion.
- Report printing.
- Report status maintenance.

Report generation is supported by an additional report writer process that contains all application-defined report writer modules. These modules contain the logic to produce each of the report types that may be requested. The report process receives generation requests and ensures that they are forwarded to the report writer process at the current or specified time. All report requests are processed in an asynchronous manner (e.g., service requesters do not wait for completion of report processing).

Exhibit II-9-5 describes the relationships between the major components of the report process and the report writer process.

Design Approach

For the report process in a client/server system, a set of APIs is provided for use within application programs and within the application report

Criteria	Vendor A	Vendor B	Vendor C
Functional Criteria			
1. Mainframe report repository			
2. Work group report support			
3. On-demand reports			
4. Scheduled reports			
5. Online preview			
6. Page-by-page preview			
7. Graphical user interface			
8. Bilingual support			
9. Basic preview functions • Scrolling up and down • Scrolling left and right • Advancing to beginning or end of report			
10. Advanced preview functions • Page indexing • Section indexing • Search capabilities			
11. Report-level security			
12. Section-, page-, field-level security			
13. Background distribution			
14. Automatic report addressing			
15. Delivery costing			
16. Multiple destinations			
17. Destination rationalization			
18. Automatic printing			
19. Multiple print destinations • Centralized mainframe sites • Remote print sites • Work group print sites			

Exhibit II-9-3. Evaluating Reporting Packages (Worksheet)

20. Variable printer types			
21. Variable printer destinations			
22. Special forms printing			
23. Font support			
24. Report archival			
25. Report download			
26. Architecture compatibility			
27. Application transparency			
28. Selective printing			
29. Print job restart			
Technical Criteria			
1. Enterprise/departmental platform compatibility			
2. Wide area network compatibility			
3. Work group compatibility			
4. Technology; standards			
5. External user directory			
6. Data compression during transmission			
7. Data compression in report repository			
8. Code page compatibility			

Exhibit II-9-3. (continued)

writer modules. Each API requests a specific report service (generation, printing, or deletion) which is performed by a report manager module.

The report process maintains an internal database table, a report status table, containing information about each report that has been requested for generation, including:

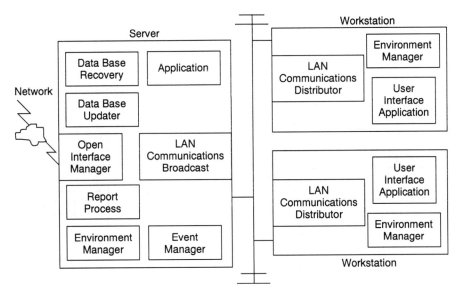

Exhibit II- 9-4. Custom Report Architecture

- Requester ID.
- Report name.
- Date/time requested.
- Status (requested, in process, complete, or error).
- Report-specific parameters.

The requester ID, report name, and date/time are used to uniquely identify the report. These values are passed to APIs, which request report status, print, or delete a previously generated report.

All application-defined report writer modules invoke an API to update the report status table with a status of "completed" after a report has been produced or with "error" if the report cannot be generated. An API is also provided to print the report after the generation if specified in the original request.

Processed report records are removed from the table only after the output reports have been archived. Implementation and frequency of this table cleanup are to be determined in systems management design.

Report Process Flows

Report processing is message driven. Each defined API sends a unique message to the report process. The report process reads the messages from a

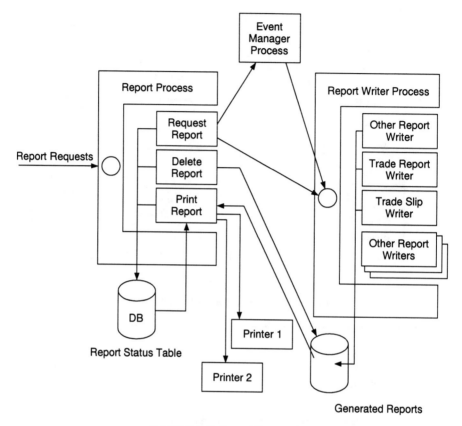

Exhibit II-9-5. Report Processing

queue and invokes the appropriate modules to handle each request. Subsequent process flows differ based on the requested service. In the case of a report generation request, the process flow proceeds as follows:

- A record is added to the report status table.
- A message is sent to the report writer process for immediate generation or to the event manager for generation at a specified time (report scheduling).
- The appropriate application report writer module generates the report, prints it if specified in the original API request, and updates the status in the report status table.

A request to print a report proceeds as follows:

- The report status is retrieved from the report status table.

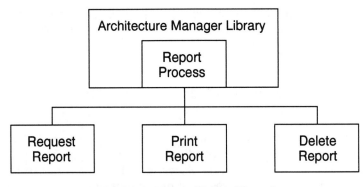

Exhibit II-9-6. Process Module Hierarchy

- The output file is located on disk and sent to the specified or default printer or the request is sent to the event manager for report scheduling.

  Report deletion proceeds as follows:

- The report record is removed from the report status table.
- The report file is removed from disk.

  Status information requests are performed directly from the API using information access services APIs. No interaction with the report process is necessary, which results in improved performance.

Modules

Exhibit II-9-6 shows the module hierarchy for the custom report process. The diagram shows the relationships between modules, not their associated processing flows. It should be used to identify the calling module and the called modules for the process. The report process is supported by the architecture manager library.

The following functions are designed to support this process:

- Generate Report.
- Get Report Status.
- Control Reports.
- Request Report.
- Delete Report.
- Print Report.

Generate Report. This module is called to request report generation and printing (optional). Input data blocks specify the following:

- Report name.
- Report parameters.
- Report generation time (default is immediately).
- Printer name.

The report name must be one of the defined application report types. Valid report parameters vary depending on the report type. Reports may be requested for generation immediately or at a designated future time. All reports are written to a reserved area on disk; however, specification of a printer causes the output to be printed as well as stored on the file system.

Get Report Status. This function retrieves status information about all reports that have been previously requested for generation by the calling process. Returned is a list containing the requested data as well as the number of reports found.

Control Reports. The Control Reports function is responsible for performing various operations on reports. The following services are provided:

- Delete a report request and any associated output
- Print a previously generated report.
- Update report status.

In all cases, the report name is passed through an input data block. For the print service, a printer name is passed. For status update, the new status code is passed.

Request Report. The Request Report function is responsible for processing report request messages written to the report process queue. It creates a new entry in the report status table with a status of "requested" and initiates the report writer process for immediate generation or sends a message to the event manager for future report generation.

Delete Report. The Delete Report function is responsible for removing a report from the Report Status list and deleting the generated output file (if any).

Print Report. The Print Report function sends a generated report output file to a specified or default printer. The report name and requesting process ID is passed to identify the report.

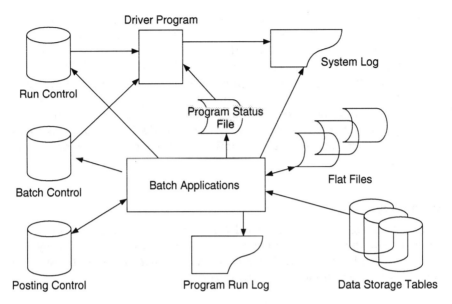

Exhibit II-9-7. Client/Server Batch Architecture

FUNCTIONS AND FEATURES OF BATCH ARCHITECTURE

A type of processing often overlooked in client/server computing is batch processing. It is important to remember that even with today's new technologies, architectures, techniques, and applications, many organizations have—and probably will continue to have—requirements for traditional batch processing. This processing is typically associated with the handling of a batch of many business transactions that have been accumulated over a period of time (an hour, day, week, month, year).

This section presents a sample client/server batch architecture. It is important to note that the third-party product market has recently started to deliver technology and solutions that support batch processing in a client/server architecture.

Exhibit II-9-7 provides an overview of the components of client/server batch architecture.

Driver Program

The driver program is the controlling entity in the batch architecture. This program can control one or more batch applications or other driver programs. Multiple scripts are usually called in succession to form a job flow (e.g., analogous to CL on the AS/400, JCL on mainframes, and DCL on VAX). This program is usually executed asynchronously, and thus does not require an interactive session during execution.

Subprograms invoked within this driver program can be executed in the background, as well. This technique allows a single shell script to control multiple subprograms at once. The driver program remains resident until all previously invoked subordinate programs have completed. Then status files (defined later) are interrogated to ensure successful execution of subordinate programs. Appropriate completion messages are written to the system log (also defined later) and the batch processing is concluded.

System Log

The system log is used to hold all error, warning, and status messages associated with the execution of the batch processing system. The system log becomes a history of all batch activity. This log can be built using the services described under application services.

Flat Files

Flat files are data files, usually containing ASCII or binary data, in the form of fixed or variable-length records. In ASCII form, they can serve as a means for information exchange between the operating environment, batch applications, and other operating components. They may be used as input or output to 3GL, fourth-generation language (4GL), or UNIX driver programs.

Data Storage Tables

Data storage tables are relational database tables defined in one of several database management system (DBMS) environments (e.g., Informix, Sybase, Oracle, and DB2). These tables can interact with 3GL programs using the DBMS embedded SQL language, or with 4GL programs that are designed to support the DBMS. Data storage tables typically contain that information (data) that is processed by the batch applications.

Batch Applications

Batch applications are coded programs designed to operate in a batch mode. The most common programming languages used in a client/server environment are C and COBOL. Specially designed 4GLs, such as Accell, may also be used. When 4GLs are used for batch applications, development times tend to decrease and execution times tend to increase.

Special techniques must be used to ensure data integrity, manage restart processing, and provide execution statistics. Like driver programs coded to run in batch mode, these programs are designed to run in the background—with no interactive processing or user screens required. After the program is executed with the proper input arguments, it processes continuously until successful completion, or until a problem is encountered. Status information and run totals are reported in the form of a flat file, called program run logs (defined later).

Batch application run times may vary from several minutes to several hours, depending on input/output (I/O) requirements and complexity of the application. In general, file system I/O takes significantly less time than DBMS I/O due to DBMS overhead. It is important to plan for batch processing requirements (central processing unit, time, disk) when planning and configuring the client/server environment.

Program Run Log

This log is a flat file that contains various statistics related to a single execution of a batch program. Statistics may include start and stop times and dates, number of records I/O, "hash" totals used to verify data integrity, or error information in case of abnormal program termination.

Program Status File

This file is usually a single byte file containing a 0 or 1, which is used to indicate the successful completion of a batch program. This file may be interrogated by driver programs that execute more than one subprogram to control restart processing and to ensure successful completion of batch applications. Only programs that have completed unsuccessfully for the most recent execution (as indicated by the existence of a 0 or 1 in this file) are reinvoked by the driver programs.

Batch Control

This is a table used to control restart processing and runtime parameters for batch applications. The most significant reason for the existence of this table is to allow for efficient restart processing when a program normally takes several hours to complete execution.

The table is created containing a minimum of two fields: a character field and a numeric field. The character field contains the names of the batch programs designed to use this table. The numeric field indicates the number of records processed by a batch program at various points during its execution.

As the batch program executes, the record corresponding to this program in the table is periodically updated to indicate the number of records processed. If the batch program encounters an unexpected error, or a hardware failure occurs, the numeric field in the database table should still contain the count of records successfully processed before the failure occurred.

When the error is corrected, or the hardware recovers, the batch program is reexecuted (usually by reexecuting the driver programs). The application program's first activity on restart is to interrogate the batch control table by reading its record count contained in the numeric field. If this value is non-0, the program starts processing from the data element or record following the last element or record successfully processed before the error or failure occurred. After successful completion, the record count in the batch control table is reset to 0 so that the next execution begins with the first input data element.

In addition to the record count, it normally is a good idea to store in the batch control table a relatively unique value associated with each input data element. This allows a data integrity check if restart processing is required and helps ensure that no input data elements have been altered or lost.

It is important to note that most DBMS environments allow "transaction logging." This means that during execution, database data inserted or altered by the batch program can be made permanently to the database, or buffered and committed, after several input data elements are processed. Otherwise, disk I/O would be required after each input data element is processed. Transaction logging allows a batch application to restart processing, after an abnormal termination, at the last successful commit.

The batch control updates are only required when data is committed to the database, because the last commit will be undone, or "rolled back," in the case of program or hardware failure. Input data processed since the last commit are reprocessed if restart is required. If transaction logging is not available, the batch control table requires an update after each input data element is successfully processed.

Because a batch program must always interrogate the batch control table on execution to determine which data element to begin processing, "tunable" parameters can reside in the batch control table. These parameters can change characteristics about a batch program each time the program executes. Typical parameters might include the following:

- Number of input data elements to process before committing database inserts, changes, or deletes.
- A value to indicate when to write a status message to the program run log. The message usually includes the number of records pro-

cessed as well as a time stamp. This can be a useful technique to track performance and progress of a batch program which requires several hours to complete.

Posting Control

This is a table used to contain totals of numeric fields on large database tables. As batch modules alter database data, the corresponding totals on this table are also adjusted to reflect adds, changes, and deletes to those numeric fields. This table serves as a reference to ensure that:

- Totals across tables are always equal, or "foot."
- A given database table contains the correct total(s) across all records, and no data has been lost.

Run Control

This is a table used to indicate the status and file size of flat files. Because most operating systems only support basic update locking, this table is used to ensure that a batch program does not attempt to alter a flat file that is being read or altered by another batch program. In addition, the file size is used to ensure that files passed between programs retain their data integrity.

For example, consider a flat file that is output by one batch program and then serves as input to another batch program at some later time. To ensure that the data integrity of the file is preserved, the program to read the file as input should check to ensure that the batch program creating the file is finished writing output, and that the file size has not been altered since file creation.

To accomplish this, the run control table is first updated by the program creating the file, to indicate when output is being written, then to indicate the resultant file size produced.

The program to read the file then interrogates the run control table on start-up. If the "in-use" flag indicates that output is still being written to the file, the program shuts down and indicates a "retry later" error message in the program run log. If the in-use flag indicates that output has been completed, the program to read the file then checks the file size to ensure data integrity has been preserved since flat file creation.

The program first performs an operating system call to determine the current physical size of the file. If this size does not match the file size in the run control table, as indicated by the program that created the file, a "file size" error is written to the program run log, and again the module shuts down. Otherwise, processing continues normally.

OTHER ISSUES IN BATCH PROCESSING

Key factors to consider when defining and implementing batch architecture and applications are:

- To minimize I/O requirements, perform as many operations as possible in internal memory. This ability is most flexible when coding in C.

- Always assume the worst with regard to data integrity. Make sure all batch programs and driver programs contain adequate controls to preserve data integrity, even in the event of hardware failures. Perform as many "sanity" checks as required to ensure that data makes sense. (For example, making sure that a data field that normally ranges from $1 to $5 does not suddenly read $1 million.) A database table containing field name and common minimum/maximum values might be used for this purpose to allow for changes over time to these sanity check values.

- If data aggregation, or summarization, is required for reporting purposes, increment stored totals as often as possible when data is being initially processed, or "posted," to the database. This practice minimizes the need to reprocess the data at a later time to obtain aggregate totals.

- Build common routines, or linked functions, to perform common processing across all batch programs. This might include database I/O, error processing, or restart/recovery routines.

- In batch programs, try to retain as much memory as the environment allows for the duration of the program's execution. Perform memory allocation at module startup, and do not release memory until program completion. This minimizes the need to perform time-consuming reallocation of internal memory many times throughout the execution of the batch program.

- Make sure to plan and test the processing time and resource requirements for all batch applications.

Batch Process Types

Design and construction of application, report, and interface batch processes can start with work unit partitioning. The business events defined during the system design phase are split into client, server, and batch processes. Definition of the work units include defining the operations to be contained within a work unit. A separate batch work unit is defined for each batch program in the application.

Batch procedure diagrams can be used to describe the design from which the code for a batch process will be built. These structure charts are built using the functional specifications defined in the system design phase as input.

In addition, batch process models can be created for the batch process types defined. Designers use these design models as the starting point in design; programmers use programming shells defined for each batch process as the starting point for programming. The following models can be used in a batch design:

- *Database-driven program model.* This model is used for database update and database extract programs that are "driven" by rows or values retrieved from the database. This model opens a database cursor as input, then updates the database, creates error files, or creates temporary files depending on the requirements of the program. Different subprograms are used depending on whether or not the database-driven programs require checkpointing and whether they require the ability to custom define when their checkpointing procedures are called.

- *File-driven program model.* This model is used for batch programs that are driven by records or values retrieved from a file. This model reads a file as input, verifies the input, then updates the database, creates temporary files, or creates error files depending on the requirements of the program. Subprograms are used depending on whether or not file-driven programs require checkpointing.

- *Format report program model.* This model is used for programs that must format data output for standard reports. This model takes an input file (originally created by an extract program) and formats the data as required for the output product. The report is written to an output file. The format report program creates headers and footers, formats the data rows, and defines report control totals.

- *Called module model.* This model is used for procedures that are called from a batch program. Different subprograms are used for called modules that select a single row from the database, select a list of rows from the database, and update the database.

- *Basic program model.* This model is used for programs that do not fall into the other categories.

Design models for each batch process type are defined to support application design and programming.

Batch Process Structure

The structure of batch process models and programming shells should be general enough to accommodate the different types of processing expected in most organizations. Batch processes should contain both shell and application components.

Batch shell components should be developed as procedural copybooks separate from the application code. The shell components required by each batch process type should be included in the models previously described.

Batch Process Content

Following is a sample set of batch application standards, presented as an example only. Designers should define the standards appropriate for their organization, architecture, and applications. For example:

- All batch programs are written in COBOL. Batch program design models and programming shells are used, as described, to simplify and standardize development, and to enhance programmer productivity. These shells also improve the maintainability of programs.
- All I/O routines appear in separate paragraphs within the program. These paragraphs are located at the end of the program (that is, in A6xxx, A7xxx and A8xxx paragraphs) or in separate called modules. I/O routines are isolated from the main code of the program to prevent changes in the underlying data format and storage mechanism from rippling through the program. Further, I/O routines are commonly reused in multiple places through the main program (e.g., priming reads and "end of" loops). Placing code that is frequently used in the same area of the program helps reduce paging.
- All batch programs that interact with the database are SQL standard compliant. Changes in the SQL DBMS with which the program interacts cause only implementation or tuning changes to the program. The programs do not require a complete rewrite.
- Each batch program has an SQL communications area (SQLCA). When an SQL statement is processed, a return code is placed in the SQLSTATE field of the program's SQLCA. This SQLSTATE is examined after each executable SQL statement to determine whether the SQL call was successful.
- DECLARE CURSOR statements are placed in the PROCEDURE DIVISION in the same paragraph as the associated OPEN CURSOR statements. Only one OPEN or CLOSE statement is defined per cursor.
- Each batch program is reviewed by the relevant database expert to ensure that physical I/Os to the database are minimized. In particular, database experts must watch for four common flaws: (1) reading data for every transaction when the data could be read once and kept

in working storage; (2) rereading data for a transaction where the data was read earlier in the same transaction; (3) causing unnecessary table or index scans; and (4) not specifying key values in the WHERE clause of an SQL statement.

CONCLUSION

This chapter has presented an overview of client/server environment services. As designers begin to define the client/server architecture(s) that will be used by their organization, they must remember to define the reporting and batch requirements and determine how to support them within their particular client/server environment.

II-10
Work Flow Services

By putting powerful and easy-to-use computing power in the hands of users, client/server computing has created a new class of computer users. Professionals, like doctors and lawyers as well as other knowledge workers and executives, are increasingly being linked to automated processes. This is a new development.

PRODUCTIVITY AND STREAMLINING THE FLOW OF WORK

Traditionally, these kinds of workers have performed their work parallel to the automated flow of work, relying on clerical assistance to enter their work into the automated process. Doctors, for example, have traditionally used paper-based reporting to record their work with patients. Other parts of the health care process, including processing of insurance claims, then have had to enter this information into the system or have had to include a paper-based step in the flow of work.

In a client/server environment, especially as computing systems have incorporated imaging technologies to eliminate paper-based processes, work flow management has become one of the key applications to enable business reengineering. Work flow-based applications assist the new class of computer users by providing an infrastructure for doing the work and by automating the routine tasks of moving "paperwork" through an organization.

Because of its roots in imaging technology, work flow management has often been driven in the marketplace by imaging vendors. Although work flow management is part of the larger category variously known as teamware, groupware, or document management, it goes further by serving as an automated aid to managing the complex flow of work for a business process.

Such a process may require the participation, and thus the coordination, of many workers before the process is complete. Because many of the individuals involved in a process are the knowledge workers of the organization, work flow management is a key enabling technology to increase productivity by streamlining the flow of information.

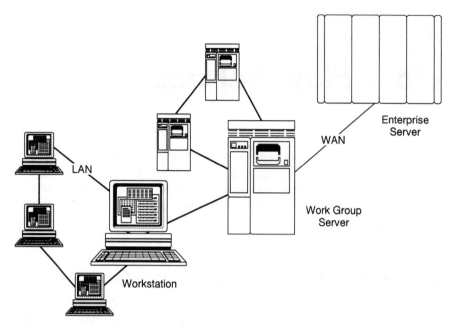

Exhibit II-10-1. Three Levels of Client/Server Computing

CHANGING THE WAY INDIVIDUALS WORK TOGETHER

Exhibit II-10-1, the basic diagram of client/server computing, shows the impact of work flow management on current business processes. Work flow is a concrete application of the left circle representing workstation-to-workstation communication.

Part of the work flow function may include an automated to-do list to track the steps to be completed and the current status of the work. A more active part of work flow is the ability to route the appropriate materials to the individuals in the defined sequence and provide management reports regarding task and process status and completion times. This routing function is enabled and supported by such technologies as electronic mail (E- mail).

Ultimately, work flow changes the ways individuals work together. As a change agent, the rollout of work flow management must be carefully planned.

In some cases, work flow may be used to automate the current process. In those instances, the change can be implemented through user and support personnel training, as it is with any new computer system. In other cases, work flow may introduce new ways of working, new roles, and new organizational structures. This higher level of change, with its

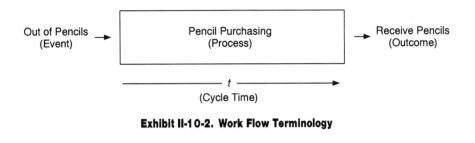

Exhibit II-10-2. Work Flow Terminology

increased potential for benefits, needs much more attention to human resource and organization issues to be successful and needs to be planned and budgeted accordingly.

BASIC ISSUES IN WORK FLOW MANAGEMENT

Concepts and Definitions of Work Flow

Work flow can be defined as the set of all tasks and their relationships required to perform a particular business process. This definition includes people and other resources needed to complete the function. It also includes how these tasks relate to one another.

To describe work flow and its associated systems implications, it is first necessary to introduce additional terminology (see Exhibit II-10-2).

A work flow is a business process (purchasing pencils), initiated by an event (running out of pencils), and resulting in an outcome (receiving pencils). The cycle time for the work flow is measured as the elapsed time from the initiation of the process until the outcome.

Work flow is a process composed of tasks (completing a purchase request, sending a purchase order). Tasks are assigned to roles. For example, the manager role is required for performing the approval task. Tasks are connected by routes and rules which specify the sequence of tasks to be performed.

The reduction of cycle time is often a primary target of work flow and process improvement initiatives. Reducing cycle times can translate into faster product introductions, reduced inventory, or happier customers. Improving quality and decreasing costs are other common targets.

Different Types of Work Flow

There are three types of work flow: recurring, ad hoc, and content dependent.

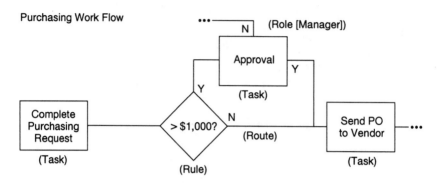

Exhibit II-1 0-3. Purchasing Work Flow (Recurring Process)

Recurring Work Flow. Exhibit II-10-3 illustrates a recurring work flow. A recurring work flow is a process such as order entry, claims processing, or mortgage origination which represents a frequently repeated activity, the handling of which can be described and coded in advance.

Ad Hoc Work Flow. An emerging use of work flow technology is in support of ad hoc processes. An ad hoc process is one that is a one-time event or a unique situation that can still be expressed in terms of tasks, roles, rules, and routes.

The production of a new product brochure for the marketing department is one example. The process may include collecting ideas from the creative department, routing to copy editors for completing text, and finally sending it concurrently to both legal and management for approval. Ad hoc work flows do not occur with enough frequency or consistency of definition for computer work flows to be defined in advance. In this case, the marketing director uses a workstation to define the tasks, roles, rules, and routes for the process.

Content-Dependent Work Flow. Content-dependent work flow adds the notion that the path a process takes is influenced by the content of the work item rather than just the type of work item. For example, in a content- dependent work flow, an order might be routed to a supervisor for approval if the order amount is over $10,000. In contrast, a content-independent work flow may specify that all credit applications progress through the same five steps, regardless of any information that has been captured along the way about the credit applicant.

Content-dependent work flow is more difficult to implement because

- ". . . information flow." (EXP Group)

- ". . . involves electronic way of organizing people, events, paper, and do in a timely manner." (Helix)

- ". . . work flow management is management of work in progress and incl routing . . ." (Gescan Intl.)

- ". . . an automatic, electronic trail of information that would normally be d manually." (NewVision)

- ". . . transfer of information through an organization." (Optical Image Tec

- ". . . marketing hype." (IMAGE Engineering)

- ". . . extension of arm providing basic auto routing to sophisticated rule b . (Optika Systems)

- ". . . movement of information through an enterprise." (PaperClip)

- ". . . active management of the flow of information and the processing of tasks across an enterprise." (Reach Software)

- ". . . sending information." (Summit Software)

Exhibit II-10-4. Different Interpretations of Work Flow

---

it requires that the work flow engine be able to see into (or be told about) the application data, but it is necessary to accurately model all but the most simplistic of business processes.

Different Definitions of Work Flow

As the terms "work flow" and "groupware" became popular in the press, many vendors began to recast their products as "work flow solutions," using a variety of interpretations of what work flow is (see Exhibit II-10-4). Because of their different perspectives, vendors' work flow solutions have different scope and power.

Armed with an understanding of the organization's opportunities and requirements for work flow capabilities, a decision can be made as to which work flow features are needed. Four characteristics of complete work flow solutions more appropriate for enterprisewide critical applications should be kept in mind:

- *Scalable.* A work flow system should scale gracefully as the size of the company changes or as the number of processes being automated increases. The system should be able to support a wide range in numbers of users: from a few users in a single office to a full enterprise system spanning the many locations of the entire company

- *Inclusive.* It is important for the work flow system to be able to include everyone who performs a task in the information flow. Depending on the organization and the processes to be automated, users may have a variety of workstation types and network connectivity.
- *Adaptable.* A work flow system should be easily adaptable as changes in the company's business processes and strategies for delivery evolve.
- *Open.* A work flow system should be able to integrate and interoperate with existing systems.

Some products that have footholds in the work flow solutions market are, in fact, just partial solutions. Although a partial solution may be appropriate for a given use, it is important to be aware of the scope of such products:

- *Groupware.* Groupware (also called teamware) is applications that let users share information or interact as a group. Lotus Notes, for example, can be used as a groupware product. A groupware application can solve parts of a work flow problem, but commonly lacks the sophisticated routing necessary to provide structure to business processes.
- *E-mail products.* An E-mail product is an application that moves information between users on a network. When coupled with the concept of automated "routing slips," E-mail packages are beginning to provide some work flow features. Again, the E-mail product is only part of a work flow solution. These products typically lack the strong data management capabilities to distinguish between and manage different types of messages.

Role of E-Mail Within a Work Flow Environment

In most work flow implementations, E-mail is used mostly to notify users of the arrival of work or to send confirmation notes and reminders. The core work flow activities are handled as transactions against work queues held in database management systems. Users are presented with a to-do list metaphor that provides them a personalized view of the tasks and processes to which they are assigned.

Today, advanced E-mail packages such as Lotus Notes and Beyond Mail are building more work flow and forms-handling capability within the E-mail packages themselves. With the new breed of E-mail systems, users can define routing lists that can express some simple sequential and parallel routing paths. Users participate in work flows simply by responding to E-mail messages and entering information on forms. Although it is tempting to believe this is all that is required, experience shows that a database-centric approach adds the greater security, integrity, and recoverability required of more mission critical applications. This is not to downplay the increasing importance of E-mail integration as a notification and delivery mechanism.

WORK FLOW REDESIGN

A company's success depends on its vision for integrating people, processes, and technology in response to changing marketplace demands. To remain competitive, companies must continually reinvent their business strategy, the processes that support the strategy, and the work flows that make up those processes.

Redesigning work flows can improve a company's processes in a variety of ways, including the following:

- *Increased understanding of a business process.* Many times, the work flow redesign allows the people involved with a particular process to see the role that their process plays in the company's overall operations. In addition, users often better understand how their particular task fits within and affects an overall process.
- *Increased understanding of the inefficiencies.* The work flow redesign often uncovers opportunities to improve process efficiencies. Under examination, the majority of the cycle time for a given process may prove to be attributed to manual filing and retrieving of documents necessary to complete interim tasks along the way. Process redesign concepts may be employed to reorganize people and processes such that filing and retrieving of documents is consolidated within a single task and role. Alternatively, if the process cannot realistically be reorganized, imaging and document management technologies may be introduced in order to speed the task of finding and retrieving information electronically and instantaneously.
- *Awareness of unnecessary tasks.* Sometimes the review reveals that a particular task does not add value to the process. Eliminating unnecessary tasks streamlines the process.
- *Awareness of additional tasks.* It is possible that an additional task added to a business process can make the process run more smoothly or more efficiently. The results of the additional task may also change the way current tasks are performed. For example, adding intelligent character recognition as an additional task may simplify both the data entry and information access portions of a process.

In sum, a well-done work flow redesign effort, tied with solid business reengineering, increases productivity, morale, and the bottom line.

An Example

To see where work flow solutions can have an impact, consider the following actual example of work flow at a major airline (the name of the airline has been changed for privacy).

At "Acme Air," the work flow facilities are named "work group management" to emphasize the routing and control of work to and from various departments, or work groups. The application is Passenger Revenue Accounting, a back office function during which Acme reconciles all airline tickets sold against those that are used.

Much of the application is batch processing performed on the mainframe, but a certain percentage of tickets are "in error" and must be audited or reviewed by Acme Air personnel.

The work flow management facilities utilized by applications at Acme Air include:

- Assignment of work.
- Work processing.
- Review and approval of work.
- Reporting.

Assignment of Work. Batches of airline tickets in error are routed nightly from the mainframe to the work group servers. The work group management subsystem then routes ticket batches to Acme Air users based on user profiles and individual user work loads.

Work Processing. The Acme Air work flow management function also incorporates a user interface (a window listing all outstanding batches of tickets assigned to the user) which automatically invokes the appropriate application for a particular batch of tickets in a given state. A batch of tickets could be in one of several states:

- Unassigned.
- Open.
- Held.
- Suspense.
- Review.
- Complete.

When the user completes processing a ticket or batch of tickets, the batch is marked as completed. Depending on dollar amounts and exception types, the batch is routed to a supervisor for review and approval.

Review and Approval of Work. Built into the routing and control structure of the work flow management at Acme Air is a review and approval step for supervisors who may want, for example, to review tickets at a certain dollar amount or all tickets processed by a new and inexperienced user.

Reporting. Associated with the work flow management system is a series of productivity reports indicating, by work group, the number of batches processed and left outstanding each day as well as other pertinent managerial statistics.

The work flow management features of the Acme Air solution improved coordination, accountability, load balancing, and utilization of employees and enabled routing of like accounting exceptions to specialized users. The use of work flow technology markedly increased overall productivity and control.

WORK FLOW AND REENGINEERING

In many instances, reengineering initiatives focus on reorganizing work around the core processes that deliver value to customers. This represents a change in the structure and flow of work within many organizations that have been traditionally structured around functional skill specializations.

A premise underlying reengineering is that delivering customer value in a timely way requires much smoother coordination of the efforts of employees, as well as the efforts of external partners such as suppliers and customers. Structuring work and people around skill specializations makes it easier to manage the activities of individuals but results in inefficiencies and barriers as work is handed off from one specialization to another (e.g., product design handing off to manufacturing).

As anyone who has lived through a reengineering initiative can attest, one of the great challenges is how to implement, manage, and coordinate the reengineered flow of work, which now crosses former functional boundaries. Client/server computing and work flow in particular are key technologies for crossing these barriers and gaining reengineering benefits more quickly. Client/server provides the mechanism for integrating systems and opening data access across traditional boundaries. Work flow provides the structure and ensures the integrity and completion of business processes.

The work flow system ensures that work moves in a more orderly and efficient manner from task to task, regardless of how many different systems or individuals are involved. A work flow system can also be used to transport information from task to task and person to person. The amount of information transfer through the work flow system depends largely on how integrated the existing legacy computer systems are from an information systems perspective.

Over time, computer systems are often built or bought to automate specific tasks within a business process. One of the common complaints of users today is that the patchwork of systems that have resulted do not integrate well. Data is often manually reentered into systems further downstream, resulting in errors and sometimes conflicting information.

As an example, a mortgage company may have separate systems for prequalifying (assessing a customer's suitability for a loan), closing (more complete analysis, document preparation, and approval), and loan servicing (the ongoing collection of payments). A better solution would be to have a single integrated database which all task-oriented systems would read and write for managing the entire life cycle of the loan—thus reducing redundant data entry and increasing efficiency and control.

With such a system in place, the role of work flow is to provide structure to processes that cross individuals and systems and to ensure that work is assigned and moved through the process as quickly as possible. Unfortunately, for all the companies that have tried to achieve the true single database solution, few have actually succeeded.

For those that cannot quite seem to get to a single database, work flow can provide another approach to the same end. It is possible to construct a work flow system that not only directs traffic but also carries the data required to complete tasks from step to step.

In the example, the work flow system itself could be outfitted with the intelligence to extract the necessary information from the mortgage origination system and provide it in electronic form to the person (or system) responsible for setting up the loan for servicing. In this way, the data flows from task to task as the process progresses, being electronically extracted or entered into the various systems along the way.

Work Flow, Continuous Improvement, and Total Quality Management

The concepts embodied in work flow solutions fit well with the needs and goals of reengineering projects that seek to change the flow of work within an organization.

Continuous improvement initiatives, as the name implies, are characterized not by a one-time reengineering but by a constant attention to improving the process by which work is performed. The features of advanced work flow systems are invaluable to successful continuous improvement and total quality management efforts.

Crucial to continuous improvement and quality initiatives is the increased need for accurate task and process measurements. Work flow applications, structured along task and process boundaries, can provide precisely the necessary measurements and statistics for tracking productivity and cycle times. By monitoring the time each piece of work spends at each task or waiting for action at a particular task, the bottlenecks within a process can be spotted.

Some advanced work flow vendors, such as Action Technologies, also provide the capability to perform what-if analysis on process redesigns. Therefore, the effects of proposed process changes or staffing increases or reassignments can be modeled to show expected improvements. Furthermore, process refinements can be quickly implemented by altering the rules, routes, and roles of the work flow system rather than reorganizing departments and physically moving workers.

Work Flow and Thinning the Management Ranks

Middle-management personnel often feel threatened by the introduction of client/server technology, especially work flow automation. The traditional role of middle management has been twofold:

- To provide a two-way information conduit and filter between the workers and executive team.
- To monitor and coordinate the activities of workers.

Client/server technology promises to give everyone direct access to information. Middle management would then provide little value by collecting and summarizing information. Executive management can now, through client/server technology, directly access and manipulate that information.

Work flow automation technology is starting to erode middle management's other duty, as well—that of coordinating the activities of workers. The rules, routes, and process definitions of a work flow system can provide the structure and coordination mechanism to allow employees to work together without the need for direct intervention and guidance from managers.

Rather than being threatened by the changes these new technologies provide, middle management should be focusing on new ways to contribute to the organization. In a client/server- and work flow-enabled organization, managers need not spend time and effort on repetitive tracking and reporting functions and can instead devote energies to continuously improving the processes for which they are responsible, and to the integration of those processes across the company.

THE ELEMENTS OF WORK FLOW APPLICATIONS

When designing work flow applications it is useful to have a mental model of the key logical components necessary to describe a work flow application. The following seven elements present a useful conceptual framework for this purpose: routes, rules, roles, queues, processes, policies, and practices.

Routes

A "route" is a defined path or sequence of steps along which a business process flows or progresses. A business worker must be able to specify the flow of any type of object (e.g., a document) in a real-world fashion.

One type of route is sequential—that is, one after another. Another route type is a parallel route with a rendezvous point; that is, an object can go off on any number of different sequential routes and then reconcile into a single route at a specified point.

The route can include a broadcast step (the E-mail model, where everyone gets the object at once), or it can be in any ad hoc order as described by the user at the time of processing. Routing needs to take into account more than just the person (or process) to whom the work is routed. It may also need to include which objects—documents, forms, data, applications—are to be routed.

Rules

A business process can be described by routes and by the rules by which various routes are selected and traversed. For example, one process could state that an order amount over $10,000 is to be routed to a supervisor for approval. In addition to navigation, rules can be used to refine which information is necessary for each step in the work flow. Ideally, users without technical knowledge should be able to establish and maintain relatively complex rules.

Roles

A role is a logical designation of who can perform a given task within a business process. A worker routes an object or task to a role, independent of the specific person or process filling that role.

For example, a request is routed to a supervisor or to the purchasing department, rather than to "Mary" or "Tom." If objects are routed to Mary, and Mary leaves the company or is reassigned, a new recipient under a new condition would have to be added to an old event.

Roles are also important when a number of different people have the authority to do the same work, such as claims adjusters. In that case, the request can be assigned to the next available person. In addition, a process or agent can assume a role; it does not need to be a person.

Queues

Inherent in doing business process work across functions and between roles is the need to hold work until the role is ready to perform or until the required information is available. A "queue" is the typical work flow software representation of this concept. Queues may be used anywhere within the process that work can be staged or stored until the appropriate resources become available. The concepts of queues and queue management are therefore essential to understanding and implementing more complex work flow applications.

Routes, rules, roles, and queues can be considered objects that must be defined in a work flow application. But there are people issues involved in work flow as well: processes, policies, and procedures.

Processes

Often, processes are not "designed" but rather defined after the fact. They are described simply as "the way we've always done it." A process is a sequence of activities that together produce some recognizable value to an internal or external customer.

Reengineering existing processes is necessary but painful, particularly as many processes never were engineered in the first place. The importance of eliminating redundancies and identifying bottlenecks is self-evident but can be surprisingly difficult. Most difficult are usually those processes (like those producing external customer outcomes) that cross many functional boundaries within the organization. Redrawing boundaries, or even clearly articulating them, can raise tensions within the organization.

Policies

Policies go beyond just the formal written statements of how certain processes are handled and can define the actual reasons for doing the work at all. Policies define a framework for decision making within the context of the business process.

Practices

Practices are an organization's reflections of its corporate culture and values, including such issues as democratic access to information, responsibility versus authority, and freedom to take risks. When tasks are automated, the people elements—the three Ps—are often overlooked or deliberately ignored. This is a serious error that detracts significantly from the potential value—added aspects of a work flow application. In many cases it threatens the very acceptance of the work flow philosophy.

WORK FLOW SERVICES ARCHITECTURE

Work flow applications have many technical requirements in common, including the ability to move work from one task or person to another and the ability to monitor status. The common features and elements of work flow suggest the need for a common work flow architecture to ensure that capabilities can function across multiple work flow applications.

The following description presents a conceptual framework for developing a work flow architecture. As with other components of the execution architecture, the actual implementation is usually a combination of custom-developed and -purchased components.

Work flow services are typically focused at the server. The server is a logical focal point because work flow applications coordinate activities between multiple users and multiple computers. Work flow information is therefore inherently shared and is best implemented and managed on a shared server machine.

Work flow services control and coordinate the tasks that must be completed in order to process a business event. For example, loan customers at XYZ Savings and Loan must complete an application explaining why they should be given a loan. This document and the customer's account and credit history files must be routed to numerous individuals who must review the material and approve the loan. Work flow services coordinate the collection and routing of the application, account, and credit history. Work flow services can be further defined as necessary.

Role Management Services

A role defines responsibilities that are required in completing a business process. A business worker must be able to route documents and folders to a role, not to a specific named person fulfilling that role.

This requirement can be seen more clearly in the manner in which a government works. The U.S. Constitution, for example, would have been a severely limited document had it referred, for example, only to the actual people who were then president and vice-president. By referring only to titles, the Constitution ensures that the law always remains separate from the individuals charged with upholding that law.

In a work flow application, role management services provide this additional level of indirection. Examples of specific role management services include creating roles, defining roles, and assigning roles to individuals or organizational titles.

Route Management Services

Work flow routing services route "work" to the appropriate work flow queues. When an application completes processing a task, it uses these services to route the work in progress to the next required task and, in some cases, notify interested parties of the resulting work queue changes.

The automatic movement of information and control from one work flow step to another requires work profiles that describe the task and role relationships for completing various business processes. The route information contained within these work profiles may be made available to allow the user to understand the relationship between tasks, or to identify which tasks need to be completed to achieve a particular outcome.

A route manager must be able to provide various styles of processing flow, such as serial, parallel or ad hoc, that map to the business processes being automated. Route management services also support the routing and delivery of necessary information (such as documents, data, forms, and applications) to the next step in the work flow as needed.

Examples of specific role management services include defining routes and branches, and assigning specific activities or tasks to routes.

Rule Management Services

A business process work flow is typically composed of many different roles and routes. Decisions must be made about what is to be routed to which role and when.

Rule management services support the routing of work flow activities by providing the intelligence necessary to determine which routes are appropriate given the state of a particular process and knowledge of the organization's work flow processing rules. Rule management services are typically implemented through easily maintainable tables or rule bases which define the possible flows for a business event.

Queue Management Services

These services provide access to the work flow queues which are used to schedule work. To perform work load analysis or to create to-do lists for users, an application may query these queues based on various criteria (a business event, status, assigned user). In addition, manipulation services allow for queue entries to be modified.

Work flow services allow users and management to monitor and access work flow queue information and to invoke applications directly.

It must be determined early on in a work flow project how much of these concepts are to be built into the applications themselves and how much is to be built into a supporting architecture that is shared by individual work flows.

CONCLUSION

Many businesses have considered reengineering as a viable plan for the foreseeable future. Reengineering may include but is not limited to imaging and multimedia systems, migration from a centralized mainframe environment to a distributed client/server environment, and general business process evaluation and redesign. Businesses are seeking a higher level of control over their information, along with faster access to it. The reengineering trend is causing work flow redesign to emerge as a strong new technology.

Currently, work flow technologies are relatively young. Users with work flow redesign plans represent a small portion of the market right now. Companies that choose to include work flow in their solutions will be leading their industries, in addition to creating an environment enriched by increased productivity, greater flexibility, and lower costs.

Though the advanced work flow solutions market is small right now, the providers of the service are not niche players. The strongest work flow solutions providers are typically ones that have embraced technology leadership in the past.

The use of customizable, off-the-shelf work flow packages will eventually be the norm. Many companies offer integrated imaging and work flow products, with a few providing just work flow. Many of these are prepackaged, customizable applications, with some having open application programming interfaces (APIs). Most large organizations opt for API-based solutions, which allow the most flexibility in customization and integrating the work flow with existing systems and technologies.

II-11
Development Architecture

A s with all types of systems development, successful execution and control of a client/server project require certain basics to be defined and in place—a methodology, organization, tools, and a process.

FOUR COMPONENTS OF SUCCESSFUL DEVELOPMENT

Methodology

Exhibit II-11-1 depicts the four basic components of successful client/server development. A methodology defines the key steps to be performed, the inputs to the steps, and the output deliverables of the steps. It frequently specifies a project organization; it also determines the tools used to support the methodology and organization and provides a framework in which to define detailed processes to support the steps of the methodology. Methodology is a critical component in defining how a project will work and how tools can be used to improve productivity, quality, and execution.

Organization

Organization refers not only to the way a project is organized but also to the types of roles and skills required and the training provided to enable project personnel to be effective. Although the methodology drives organization and the desired skills, the actual skills and the actual roles influence decisions made about the development environment.

Tools

Tools automate the development process and aid in the creation of deliverables to provide leverage in performing a particular activity. This leverage can be in the form of improved productivity, improved quality, and improved satisfaction with the job. The emphasis is on supplement-

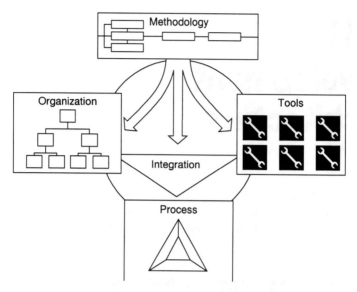

Exhibit II-11-1. Components of Successful Development

ing the work being performed by the project personnel to make them more effective.

Process

Process is a specification for how to perform a particular activity. Although the methodology defines high-level tasks and their input/outputs, many activities within a project must be customized for the culture, environment, and project.

For example, the process for handling bug reports or change requests typically varies from project to project based on the culture of the organization, the philosophy of project management, and the priorities of the project. Some projects track these formally with weekly reports and meetings; other projects may keep a loose-leaf binder with handwritten notes of problems and suggestions. A process documents how these activities should be performed for a specific project. Each process is supported by procedures, standards, and tools. Depending on the process and project, the relative emphasis on and formality of these three differs.

- Procedures specify *how* to perform the task so that the result is in accordance with expectations. Procedures may specify which techniques and tools to use and may offer guidelines.
- Standards specify *what* the result should look like.

- Tools support the tasks of the process. In addition to automated software tools, there are many useful, simple tools such as templates and spreadsheets with precoded formulas and macros.

Integrating the methodology, organization, tools, and process is critical. The tools must be chosen to support a specific organization as it works on specific tasks which form well-defined processes. If one of these is out of sync with the others, the results typically include lost time, lower developer productivity, inconsistent results, ineffective or inefficient communications, and general project management headaches.

Equally important is starting with the methodology in mind, because methodology drives the organization and process and thus the tools that are appropriate. Based on a client/server methodology, the rest of this section describes a development environment that has been successful in supporting this methodology on projects.

For purposes of this discussion, the development environment covers portions of the tools and process components and elaborates on standards, tools, and procedures useful in client/server development. Organization is discussed further in the sections that deal with planning and managing client/server projects.

DEVELOPMENT ARCHITECTURE MODEL

A development architecture is a combination of development tools, methods, standards, and procedures that define a development environment. An architecture model such as the one depicted in Exhibit II-11-2, which places tools into related groups, helps organize the many types of tools, standards, and procedures that may be used on a client/server development project.

As demonstrated throughout this discussion, many of the tools and functions described by this model apply to traditional as well as client/server development. As such, the focus of this chapter is on highlighting those areas that are different for client/server.

In addition, this model represents the set of tools that a project may find useful or important. It is based on what has been successful in implementing client/server applications using large teams (more than 20 people), in tight time frames (6 to 12 months comfortably, 2 to 6 months on the aggressive side), using high levels of automation to maximize productivity and consistency. It does not represent the complete set of tools that every project must have in place.

This model is useful as a "checklist" when establishing the development environment; based on specific projects, only some portions of the model will be appropriate and necessary and should be implemented. Rarely can every capability this model describes be implemented for a

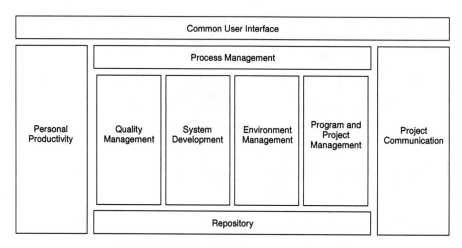

Exhibit II-11-2. Development Architecture Model

first project (though frequently some developers iterate toward more complete implementations of the model). Finally, for readability, "tools" means "tools, standards and procedures" unless otherwise indicated.

At a high level, Exhibit II-11-2 represents the various types of tools required in systems development and management along with common capabilities to integrate these tools. The vertical boxes represent the common development tools and the horizontal boxes represent the capabilities to integrate the tools, to coordinate the definitions being created and maintained by the tools, and to provide a common launching place or look and feel for the various tools.

- Common user interface tools help provide a common launching place for all the tools in the development environment to make it appear more integrated and consistent.
- Process management tools provide structure and control over the development process.
- Repository is the communications backbone of the development environment, making it easy to share and manage information between different processes.
- Personal productivity tools are used for miscellaneous single-user activities commonly encountered on a project: writing memos, preparing presentations, performing simple what-if analyses. These tools are typically oriented toward individuals rather than teams (i.e., no collaboration is required).
- Quality management tools ensure an agreed-on level of quality in the

system being developed and provide information and process for improving the quality over time.

- System development tools are the heart of the development environment. These are the tools used by the majority of the development team to capture the system requirements, the functional design, the detailed design decisions, and the detailed coding and testing and to manage the resulting components.

- Environment management tools are used to treat the development environment as a production environment (with its users being developers). These tools support monitoring performance, providing help desk support, managing and distributing changes to the development environment, administering the environment, and monitoring and planning development environment capacity.

- Program and project management tools aid in the planning and scheduling of a project along with the tracking and reporting of its progress against the plan.

- Project communication tools facilitate communications across the project team. These include individual communications, such as electronic mail (E-mail), as well as tools to facilitate communication across a large number of personnel (e.g., groupware and publishing capabilities).

COMMON USER INTERFACE

The system development tools should be accessible from, and coordinated for, the user (developer, manager, tester) through a single facility. The common user interface provides a graphical user interface (GUI) that allows users to access the development environment tools easily and consistently. The system should be simple to learn and intuitive to use and should assist the developer in navigating through the development environment. The following are recommended capabilities of the common interface:

- *Interactive and graphical interface.* An interactive interface is easy to learn and to use. All tools and resource options should be presented to the developer through graphical icons and windows. This is especially true when the developers themselves are developing a GUI because it helps them better understand the capabilities and standards of such an environment.

- *Shield system-level details.* The developers should concentrate on the purpose of their applications, not the syntax, location, or integration of the tools or data they are using. Developers only need to pick the service by selecting it from a menu or an equivalent action.

They should not be required to have knowledge of, for example, file names, working directories, and configuration files.

- *Support multiple, concurrent activities.* Developers should not be restricted to a single development task. They should be able to execute multiple tools and facilities simultaneously.
- *Completely integrated.* To the extent possible, developers should never be forced to leave the interface to use a service. The interface provides the services, control, and support for a highly productive environment.
- *Security.* The interface should provide access to files, code, and tools, for example, based on privileges defined for each user of the environment. This is especially true on larger projects which may have formal controls for the review and sign-off of deliverables.
- *Standards.* The interface should support the execution architecture standard user interface (Windows, Presentation Manager, Motif).
- *Help.* The system should provide interactive, context-sensitive help to the users.

Menuing systems are frequently used to provide a simple form of this integration, and these capabilities are being built into the desktop managers available with today's common GUIs, as well as into the integrated development tools becoming more common (e.g., Visual Basic, Visual Age C++). As such, the common user interface generally turns out to be a set of guidelines or principles to aid in the selection of tools for the development environment.

PROCESS MANAGEMENT

This category provides structure and control over the development process as a whole (e.g., the methodology, procedures, and supporting processes). As such, it provides for deeper integration than just graphical or desktop integration. It integrates existing and future tools, both package and custom; provides inter-tool communications where appropriate; and integrates tools with the repository.

The process management implementation may vary greatly in complexity. At the simple end is a menu system that presents a single user with the recommended development tasks and can launch the tool appropriate for the selected task. At the high end is a custom, complete work flow implementation that integrates the efforts of different development groups and enforces the project methodology (e.g., it supports the correct sequencing of tasks including reviews and sign-offs).

This latter type of support is starting to appear in some computer-aided software engineering tools but is still fairly uncommon. A more common implementation is software "backplanes" or workbenches that provide a common integration point for the development tools. Examples include SunSoft's ToolTalk, Softbench from Hewlett-Packard (HP), and FUSE (Friendly Unified Software Engineering) from Digital Equipment Corp.

When selecting or implementing process management support, some of the considerations are as follows:

- *Customizability.* This is the ability to tailor the tools to support a specific methodology and process for the organization or project.
- *Platform support.* Because the flow of work across the development process may span multiple developer platforms (Windows, UNIX, OS/2) it is important to choose an implementation that supports the key platforms—both current and planned.
- *Work flow sophistication.* A more advanced implementation allows status information about a task or deliverable to be stored and routing decisions to be based on this information. For example, a design spec could be routed to a reviewer once its status is changed to "complete." After a successful review, its status could be changed to "final" and then marked as frozen in the configuration management system. Finally, sophisticated integration would allow context information (user ID, deliverable being manipulated) to be passed into the selected tool.

REPOSITORY

The development repository is the communication backbone of the development environment, making it easy to share information between people working on different processes. It stores design, construction, and maintenance information such as window layouts, processing specifications, code fragments, and references to source code files. By storing this information in a development repository, several benefits can be realized.

Consistency

By providing a common "template" for the content and format of design information, developers are more likely to create consistent specifications. In addition, by providing a "pool" of common definitions (especially for such low-level objects as data elements, table/record definitions, windows, and reports), a repository can facilitate consistent use and interpretation and, in some cases, reuse.

For example, by providing a common place for element definitions, and including such display information as literals and field size, windows and reports are more likely to integrate with the database definition and more likely to display or interact with the end user in a consistent manner (field validation, the literal to the left of the field, the length of the field). Without this information in a repository, it would be up to individual developers to seek out the "common" information and apply it appropriately while they define their windows and reports.

Impact Analysis

By maintaining relationship information such as window to element, impact analysis can be performed more accurately and easily. Changes are constantly occurring during a project as a result of requirements changes or clarifications and design considerations. Being able to accurately and quickly assess the impact of a change is critical to ensure that appropriate decisions are being made (i.e., that the cost-benefit of a change is being considered properly) and that the change is being implemented correctly and completely.

For example, if the system under construction (or in maintenance) had to convert from five-digit ZIP code to nine-digit ZIP code, the repository information could be used to identify which tables, windows, reports, and common structures used ZIP code and were thus affected. Although the details of the change cannot necessarily be assessed without looking at each individual item affected, an order of magnitude of the change could quickly be determined to arrange for the appropriate prioritization and any necessary resources for making the change.

Traceability

Utilizing the relationship information just discussed, it is possible to link from high-level requirements down through low-level code modules and table definitions. With this information, it becomes practical to trace requirements through to their implementation to ensure that all requirements have been satisfied by logic and data and all requirements (or an agreed-on sufficient set) have been tested. This information can provide a level of comfort on the completeness and quality of the resulting design and implementation.

Reuse

A repository cannot force reuse to occur, but it is a building block on which to start a program of reuse. Because information about low-level (elements) and high-level (functions, subsystems) entities is stored in the repository, it is a logical place to begin looking for reusable building blocks. This reuse commonly happens within a team on a project but can also happen across teams within a project and eventually across projects.

Although a development repository is, in theory, useful for any size project, in practice it is most effective on medium- to large-scale projects (i.e., more than 10 developers or designers). This is because a repository requires a discipline and structure on the part of the development team, a level of tool integration (e.g., database management system definitions, GUI painting tool, source code management, and programming tools), and usually a level of support that may not be cost-effective on small projects (where communications and coordination can still be effective across the team).

PERSONAL PRODUCTIVITY TOOLS

Personal productivity tools are used for miscellaneous, single-user activities commonly encountered on a project (e.g., writing memos, preparing presentations, and performing simple what-if analyses).

These tools are typically oriented toward individuals rather than teams (i.e., no collaboration is required) and consist of the following:

- *Spreadsheets.* Developers should have the ability to access and create spreadsheet data which is used in each phase of the development process. Spreadsheet analysis may be used to analyze reports from the repository, to view test data/results, to perform what-if analyses for impact analysis or estimating, and to assist in modeling such system aspects as performance. Examples include Lotus 1-2-3 and Microsoft Excel.

- *Graphics.* These tools are most commonly used to prepare presentations and supporting graphics for documentation. These may be standalone tools but are much more useful when they can be integrated directly with the repository or at least the spreadsheet package to allow graphical presentation of information (such as productivity information and quality statistics). Examples include Microsoft Powerpoint, Lotus Freelance, and CorelDRAW.

- *Word processors.* A word processing tool should provide basic forms and utilities that can be used (e.g., a form letter or memo template) by developers to document project information. Examples include AmiPro, Word, and WordPerfect.

QUALITY MANAGEMENT TOOLS

Quality management tools are used to ensure that an agreed-on level of quality in the system is reached. They are also used to provide information and process for improving the quality over time.

Although it is easy to agree that a focus on quality must be maintained in all development work, time pressures can weaken the commitment to quality in some cases. To counter this, putting good procedures and tools in place helps reduce this conflict, by making it easier to "do the right thing." Quality management tools provide the plan, the measurement, and the feedback for improvement to meet the quality objectives of a project.

Quality Function Deployment

Quality function deployment is basically the quality plan for the project or the organization. It is the basis for quality management. This plan should specify or reference the following:

- *Quality objectives that are important for a project.* These should be expressed in measurable terms whenever possible. For example, quality objectives may be expressed in terms of reliability (in defects per function point), usability (user training or overall productivity), efficiency (use of systems resources), and maintainability (cost/time to correct problems and provide added functions).
- *Defined input and output (I/O) criteria for each development phase.* This is typically integrated with the development methodology and defines sufficiency criteria for moving from one phase of the project to the next. These criteria are important to ensure that all necessary documentation for a phase has been created and is of the expected quality before beginning a phase. This helps reduce rework due to miscommunications or misunderstandings.
- *Identification and definition of the types of test, verification, and validation activities to be carried out.* This includes a description of the activities, what they apply to (e.g., validate a functional specification), and when they should occur (e.g., before beginning technical design).
- *Specific responsibilities for quality activities.* For example, who is responsible for reviews and tests of the various development components, who has responsibility for configuration management and change control, and who has responsibility for defect control and corrective action? For smaller projects, this responsibility may be spread across the individual developers or teams; on larger projects, responsibility may be assigned to a specific quality team that interacts with the individual development teams.

Quality function deployment tools are used to reveal, document, and prioritize the requirements for the systems under development. Based on these requirements, it is possible to define meaningful goals for product quality along different dimensions (e.g., maintainability, complexity, and performance).

The value of a business system can be measured by business case metrics—demonstrating the benefit of a change brought to the business process. In turn, the business case metrics are supported by product metrics (or quality attributes), such as capability, reliability, usability, efficiency, maintainability, and portability. These characteristics, which have a great deal of influence on architectural design decisions, must be tied directly to the business value they are to enable.

Finally, process metrics support the product metrics by measuring whether the process is likely to result in a system that satisfies the product quality requirements. These metrics typically include productivity and defects.

Measurement and Metrics

Metrics are an important part of quality because they provide operational definitions of quality attributes. An operational definition, according to W. Edwards Deming, is one that is expressed as a method for sampling, testing, and determining whether a work product meets a given criterion.

With operational definitions, different stakeholders can agree that a product objectively meets a requirement, or that a process has been improved by a measurable amount; without operational definitions, stakeholders can only have subjective opinions that may or may not agree.

To fine-tune the development process, it is necessary to be able to measure the important quality attributes. These measurements are still evolving as software engineering matures, but sample metrics could include the following:

- Average number of defects per design packet at the moment construction starts.
- Average number of defects per program at the time of its first migration to system test.
- System availability and causes of downtime.
- Time needed for a new user to learn to use a function of the system.
- User error rate per function.
- Maintainability in terms of time to fix a defect or to add new functions.

To facilitate capture of this kind of information, it is important that the tools used to perform a function provide support for capture of quality statistics. For example, the source code management toolset could allow information to be specified about reasons for a change, and the stage the component had reached (e.g., initial construction, system test, and production). This information could be placed in a quality statistics part of the repository for later reporting.

Quality Process Control

Process control pertains to methodology, work flow, and tools usage. It ensures that quality gets built into the end product from the beginning. Standards and procedures pertaining to quality assurance of the process describe how to use simple tools, such as templates and checklists, and document the mandatory outputs from each work process. Other procedures cover common tasks such as design reviews and code reviews.

Continuous Improvement

These are the tools for capturing feedback on the quality process and taking action to improve it. Such a tool can be as simple as a suggestion mailbox (paper or electronic) or a more proactive approach in which statistical information on productivity and cost of quality is taken into consideration for making improvement suggestions. Once changes are made, the statistics being tracked must reflect the version of the process to which they correspond so that an accurate assessment of the change can be made (improvement, no change, degradation).

SYSTEMS DEVELOPMENT TOOLS

Systems development tools are the heart of the development environment. These are the tools used by the majority of the development team to capture the system requirements, the functional design, the detailed design decisions, and the detailed coding and testing and to manage the resulting (frequently large number) components. Because there are a large number of tools in this category, it is efficient to group them as follows:

- Analysis and design tools.
- Reverse engineering tools.
- Construction tools.
- Testing tools.
- Configuration management tools.

Analysis and Design Tools

Analysis and design tools are used to capture the requirements for the system being developed, to analyze and prioritize them, and to transform them into a functional definition and then into a detailed technical definition suitable for construction. In other words, analysis tools help specify "what" a system needs to do, and design tools help specify "how" a system will implement the "what."

A number of the analysis and design tools are typically part of an I-CASE (integrated computer-aided software engineering) package such as Excelerator, FOUNDATION, IEW, Paradigm Plus, and Software through Pictures. Exceptions to this are noted in the appropriate discussion below. Regardless of whether I-CASE is used, when tools are being integrated across the various analysis and design categories, it is important to take into account the compatibility of the tools and their ability to integrate. For example, can the window painter access element definitions used in the data modeling and database design tools?

There are several types of analysis and design tools.

Data Modeling. These tools provide the capability to graphically depict the logical data requirements for the system. Typically, a tool for data modeling supports diagramming entities, relationships, and attributes of the business being modeled on an entity-relationship diagram (ERD). The key difference from a traditional data modeling tool is the ability to capture information necessary for making data distribution decisions (e.g., ownership of data and frequency of access/manipulation by location).

Process Modeling. These tools provide the capability to depict (preferably graphically) the business functions and processes being supported by a system, including, for example, tools that support documenting process decomposition, data flow, and process dependency information.

As with the data modeling tools, the main difference in these tools for client/server is the ability to capture the information necessary to make process placement decisions—for instance, where the process needs to occur (on a mobile personal computer, at a stationary workstation), the type and volume of data it requires to perform the function, and the type of function (user interaction, reporting, batch processing).

Event Modeling. These tools provide the capability to depict the business events and associated responses of the system. A variety of tools and techniques can be used for event modeling, including word processors to develop simple textual lists of events and diagramming tools to show events and responses. These tools inherently are closely tied to the process modeling tools because events result in a response generally described by a process.

Database Design. These tools provide the capability to capture the database design for the system. They enable the developer to illustrate, for example, the tables and file structures that will be physically implemented from the logical data requirements. The tools also capture the definition of data elements, indexing decisions, foreign keys and referential integrity rules.

Many I-CASE products integrate data modeling, database design, and database construction. Such tools typically generate the first-cut database design from the data model and generate the database definition from the database design.

As with the data modeling tools, the key difference in database design tools for client/server is the ability to capture data distribution decisions and to provide support for creating schemas for multiple database products. For example, the standalone laptop database management system (DBMS) may be different from the work group and enterprise DBMS choices (such as Watcom on the laptop and DB2 at the enterprise level).

Application Logic Design. These tools provide the capability to depict the logic of the application, including application structure, module descriptions, and distribution of function across client/server nodes.

A variety of tools and techniques can be used for application logic design, including structure charts, procedure diagrams (module action diagrams), and graphics packages to illustrate distribution of function across client and server.

Presentation Design and Prototyping. These tools provide the capability to depict the presentation layer of the application, including screens, windows, reports, and dialog flow. Tools in this category include window painters, report painters, and dialog flow diagrammers.

Window painters let the developer design the windows for the application using common GUI window controls (sometimes called widgets) and application variables. The behavior associated with the window can either be captured directly in the window painter tool or using a deliverable known as a CAR (control, action, response) diagram. Frequently specified as a matrix or structure chart, the CAR diagram captures the response to an action taken on a particular widget—for example, what to do when the user exits a field or clicks a button.

Report painters let the developer design the report layout interactively, placing literals and application data on the layout without specifying implementation details such as page breaks. Typical window, screen, and report painters also generate the associated application code or a structure in which remaining code can be placed during construction. In addition, many window painters provide the capability to rapidly prototype the user interface.

Prototyping allows developers to follow a more iterative functional design approach, which is important when dealing with developers and users that may be new to the GUIs typical of client/server systems. In addition, given the responsive nature of a GUI, prototyping becomes an effective way of clearly communicating how the system appears to the user.

Prototyping does not eliminate the need for detailed narrative specifications, but it does improve the users' and other developers' understanding of the system design. The essential feature for prototyping is enabling developers to rapidly build and modify screens and windows. Beyond this basic requirement, some tools may support the specification and prototyping of the dialog flow (e.g., linking windows), simple data interaction such as validation, or more complex data interaction such as the ability to insert, save, and transfer data between screens.

Examples of window painting and prototyping tools include Powersoft's PowerBuilder, Microsoft's Visual Basic, Gupta's SQLWindows, and Visual Edge's UIMX. Examples of report painters include Oracle SQL Report Writer, Sybase's SQR, Crystal Report, and Gupta's Quest.

Communication Design. After the fundamental communication paradigms have been chosen (message passing, remote procedure call, structured query language-based), each exchange must be specified in detail to take into account the detailed design of the sending and receiving modules (clients, services, subroutines, functions) and to lay the basis for more refined performance modeling. These tools allow designers to specify the contents of an exchange and define the "contract" of the exchange in terms of the processing to be performed, the expected preconditions, and the handling of error or unexpected conditions. They can also provide a generation capability for the code or common structures required in construction to send and receive the message.

Performance Modeling. The performance of a system, especially in a client/server architecture, needs to be analyzed as early as possible in the development process. Performance modeling tools support the analysis of the system performance. A simple spreadsheet may be suitable in some well-known and -understood environments, but dedicated performance or simulation modeling tools should be considered on any project with high transaction volumes or complex client/server architectures involving several platforms.

Reverse Engineering Tools

Reverse engineering is a set of techniques to assist in reusing existing system components—either directly (e.g., code/modules) or indirectly (e.g., design rules or algorithms, and record layouts). The activity is well-known on many projects and may be necessary in order to look at certain pieces of code to understand how they work.

Most of the time, this work is done manually: One person sits down and studies thick listings to understand data layouts and processing rules. The person gradually builds a higher-level understanding of how the components work and interact— effectively reverse engineering the system into a conceptual model.

The process can be time-consuming and is notoriously difficult to estimate. Tools to support the effort exist and have been used successfully to streamline the process. Although these tools cannot completely automate the analysis process, they can reduce the amount of manual effort needed, and significantly lessen the amount of non-value-added automatic activities such as "find all the places in a program that affect the value of a given variable." These tools generally fall into four categories.

System Structure Analysis. These tools are used by a developer to identify requirements for a new system from the capability and design of a legacy system. They enable the developer to interactively and graphically navigate through the legacy system, analyzing such system characteristics as system structure, module flow, flow of control within a module, calling patterns, complexity, and data and variable usage.

The tools can also provide cross-reference listings or graphical representations of control or data flows. These tools are most effective when they are used to find and understand the business rules implemented by a system (that may no longer be documented) to provide comparable features in a new system. Examples for the multivendor system environment include VIA Insight, VIA Renaissance, and Compuware PATHVU.

Extraction. An extraction tool, in conjunction with a repository population tool, provides the developer the capability to reuse selected portions of a legacy system. The extraction tool can typically read and extract information from source code, screens, reports, and the database.

The most common information extracted from a legacy system is the data: record or table structure, indexes, and data element definitions. Although it is difficult to extract functions and processes from source code, source code containing complex algorithms is another candidate for extraction. Examples of this type of tool include Adpac's PMSS and Viasoft's Alliance.

Repository Population. The repository population tools are used to load the information from the extraction and structure analysis tools into the development repository. These tools convert the information from the legacy system into the syntax of the repository of the development tools.

Restructuring. Restructuring tools are not analysis tools like the previous categories of reverse engineering tools but rather design and construction tools. They enable the developer to rebuild a legacy system rather than replace it. Examples of this type of process include restructuring spaghetti code into structured code, replacing GOTO's with a PERFORM construct, streamlining the module calling structure, and identifying and eliminating dead code. These are most often encountered on projects that are rehosting one or more applications to a client/server environment and want to upgrade the existing code to make it more maintainable and extend its useful life.

Examples of such a product for COBOL programs is Compuware's PATHVU, Compuware's RETROFIT, Knowledgeware's Inspector, Knowledgeware's Recoder, and IBM's SF.

Construction Tools

Construction tools are used to program, or build, the application: client and server source code, windows or screens, reports, and database. However, there are many different approaches for these tools: traditional procedural languages, fourth-generation languages (4GLs), and visual programming tools. The categories that follow describe tools supporting the manual coding of the application using a 3GL such as C.

However, not only the number of these tools but the fundamental development paradigm in this category has changed in the last few years to include 4GL tools and visual programming tools. These types of tools are listed in the construction tools category because they are alternative ways to provide the capability described in this section.

Client/server 4GL tools are not dissimilar to 4GLs found in other environments but with support added for GUI development and some process or data distribution. These 4GLs provide the capability to develop simple database access systems as well as more complex processing applications. Examples of client/server 4GLs are JYACC's JAM, Information Builders' Focus, and tools from DBMS vendors such as Sybase's APT.

Visual programming tools such as PowerBuilder and Visual Basic support the rapid development of client/server applications. They typically support the client-side of a client/server application and depend on other communication, process, and database products to complete the application.

There are four categories of construction tools.

Source Code Editor. A source code editor is used to enter and edit source code for the application. Traditionally, source code editors have been standalone applications with an optional hook to launch the compiler from within the editor. More recently, they are being integrated into a workbench environment and provide incremental syntax checking, rapid compilation, and the ability to run and test the application without having to leave the editing environment (e.g., C++ development environments from Borland, Microsoft, and IBM).

Generation. These are automated tools that generate some component of the application: source code, common structures, windows, reports, and the database definition. They convert the application design into some form of source code. Some common types of generators include the following:

- *Procedural code generator.* Also known as source code generators, these typically take a pseudo-code specification of a module and generate a module in the appropriate programming language. Alternatively, the procedural code may be specified in the repository using the target programming language (this eliminates an additional language that would have to be learned by a developer). This approach is common in I-CASE products that allow logic to be generated for multiple platforms (such as FOUNDATION and IEF).

- *Shell generation.* When it is not feasible or desirable to specify detailed code within the repository, a shell of a module can be generated with markers for where module specific code should be entered by a programmer. These markers are frequently encountered in window painting tools that can generate the modules required to implement the window with all the housekeeping code already in place. Visual C++ from Microsoft is an example of a tool that offers such a capability—it generates the shell code for windows painted in the environment and allows the programmer to add the business logic at specified drop points.

- *Data design language (DDL) and data manipulation language (DML) generator.* Based on the data and access definitions specified in the repository, these would generate the schema definition for the appropriate DBMS, and the structured query language (SQL) and support code for performing the database I/O. DDL generators are frequently included in some of the I-CASE offerings discussed earlier. DML generators are either custom-developed for a project or may be built on top of general-purpose query tools (such as Q&E or report writers). In the latter case, the query tool is used to build the query and the resulting SQL is copied into the appropriate module.

These types of tools are useful in an integrated development environment as they reuse design information, thereby eliminating errors caused by transcription or redefinition as well as providing additional incentives for keeping the design documentation up-to-date.

Compiler/Linker/Interpreter. A compiler/linker converts source code to executable code and packages it into a runtime module with supporting libraries, such as dynamic link libraries for common code. An interpreter executes the source code directly (or indirectly through a pseudo-compiled intermediate representation).

Interpreters offer the benefit of being able to execute code almost instantaneously (versus having to wait for a compile and link). However, interpreters typically run code slower than compiled code and are thus generally used during development with a compile/link being performed to produce production code. Incremental compiler technology offers the best of both worlds by compiling only the changes in code that allow an application to be run shortly after a change is made. Standalone compilers for C or C++ are offered from vendors like Borland, HP, IBM, and Microsoft. Visual programming environments (such as VisualBasic or PowerBuilder) typically utilize either an interpreter or incremental compiler.

Construction Utilities. Construction utilities are an assortment of tools that facilitate the construction process. These types of tools include the following:

- *MAKE utility.* The MAKE utility automates compilation and linking of numerous modules of an application. It contains information on the dependencies between modules of the system (e.g., FOO.EXE consists of FOO1.OBJ and FOO2.OBJ; FOO1.OBJ is created by compiling FOO1.C; FOO2.OBJ is created by compiling FOO2.C). This allows the MAKE utility to trigger all necessary recompilation and relinking when a module in the system is changed. This utility is useful for streamlining the rebuild process because only those components dependent on the change are recompiled/linked.

  The MAKE file can either be hand-coded or it can be generated based on information in a repository. Generation of the MAKE file tends to eliminate troublesome mistakes, assuming that the repository administrator has done a good job of maintaining the integrity of the repository. MAKE utilities are available either standalone (such as NMAKE from Microsoft or MAKE from Polytron) or built into an integrated workbench environment (e.g., the "project" concept in Microsoft Visual C++ or VisualBasic).

- *Portability checker.* This is a utility that checks compliance with basic portability standards—particularly with programming standards that ensure portability across platforms (ANSI C, POSIX). These utilities are typically used only on the C and C++ programming languages because these are the dominant client/server languages available on numerous platforms and operating systems. Portability checking is sometimes built in to the compiler and can be turned on with a switch or flag specified at compile time or can be performed by separate tools (e.g., the lint utility available under UNIX).

- *Application shells.* Application shells depicting basic application functions for common module types can be used as a starting point (a shell) for design and programming. These shells can be used in detailed design and programming phases of the development life cycle to enable designers and programmers to focus more on the essential business logic and spend less time worrying about structural aspects that can be solved once for everyone (e.g., a structure for dealing with the paging of large lists and an approach for handling data passing between modeless windows). Furthermore, shells are a good mechanism for enforcing standards as they typically embody them and thus the programmers get the standards for free. Because shells are usually project specific, their initial creation is done manually (rather than being generated).

- *Static code or dynamic execution analyzer.* These analyzers can provide the information and metrics needed to monitor and improve code quality and maintainability and make suggestions on how to package the code into modules and libraries for performance optimization.

Testing Tools

Testing is the process of validating that the gathering and transformation of information have been completed correctly and to the expected quality level. Testing is usually considered the process that makes sure there are no bugs in the code. But in a broader sense, testing is about making sure that the system does what it is expected to do (i.e., meets the requirements specifications) at an acceptable quality level (e.g., acceptable numbers of defects per function point, or defects per module).

As automation progresses and an increasing number of business processes are supported by computer systems, testing is changing in nature. First, testing of interfaces to other systems is becoming an ever larger part of the testing effort. Second, testing increasingly applies to a new release of an existing system. Finally, with client/server, the nature of GUIs and the fact that data and process are distributed across platforms and locations increase both the complexity and the importance of testing.

All these factors increase the value of automated testing tools because the work associated with checking that system changes do not have unintended side effects is becoming an ever larger part of testing. Another trend that affects testing is the demand for traceability. Increasingly, users and management wish to know the purpose of a given test condition. This question is answered by tying back to the design and from there to the user requirements.

Testing is a large part of any systems development effort. When requirements are changing, testing can exceed half of the entire development effort. A streamlined environment that enables high productivity is therefore of utmost importance.

There are eight categories of testing tools.

Test Planning. A test plan consists of many pieces: test cycles, test conditions, test scripts, test data, and expected results. Test planning and maintenance tools provide the capability to define and maintain the relationships between the various pieces of the plan. Examples of this type of tool include Mercury Interactive's Test Director and SQA's SQA Manager.

Test Data Management. Test data management tools allow developers to create and maintain input data and expected results associated with a test plan. They include test data and archiving tools which assist in switching between cycles and repeating a cycle based on the original data created for that cycle.

Test Execution. Test execution tools support and automate the conduct of tests. Test execution support includes the tools required to extract input data and expected results from the repository, tools to load this data into appropriate test execution tools, and tools to automate the execution of the test.

The most commonly available test execution tools today are GUI record and playback tools. A typical GUI test execution tool supports test scripting and playback. These tools provide the ability to record execution of a test plan in an online environment, including keystrokes, mouse movements, and button clicks used to navigate through the application. It also captures and replays the data entered into each window related to executing the test scripts. Once the script has been recorded it can be run repeatedly on the same application. Examples of this type of tool include

Mercury's WinRunner and Xrunner, Softbridge's ATF and Segue Software's QA Partner.

Test Result Comparison. Test result comparison tools are typically used to compare expected and actual results. Typically, these tools outline the differences between actual and expected results by comparing files and databases. Most of these tools offer such capability as byte-by-byte comparison of files and the ability to mask certain fields such as date and time. Recently, GUI scripting tools (discussed earlier) have also provided result comparison capabilities, but only for the resulting window display state; database and file changes still need to be compared separately.

Test Coverage Measurement. Test coverage measurement tools are used to document which parts of each program have been executed during the test. It is a test management and quality management tool to ensure that all appropriate components of an application have been tested. Examples of this type of tool include Logicscope's Logicscope, VIA SmartTest and Software Research's STW.

Incident Management. Incident management tools help track each system incident report from detection/documentation through to resolution. In addition to supporting basic entry and status checking, these tools can provide reports of incidents by, for example, age, priority, and module. Mercury's Test Director and SQA's SQA Manager are examples of products that provide incident manager capability.

Source Code Debugger. A source code debugger (sometimes known as a symbolic debugger) is used to step through a program or module at the source code level (as opposed to the machine code level). Although commonly used for debugging programs, source code debuggers are also effective in supporting unit-level testing, because variables can be changed to cause logic to be executed that might otherwise be difficult to simulate using external data (e.g., time-sensitive logic, logic for handling I/O hardware failures). Examples of standalone debuggers include Microsoft Codeview and xdf for UNIX. Debuggers are also typically included in integrated development environments such as Visual C++ and PowerBuilder.

Stubs and Drivers. Stubs and drivers are used to test components of the application or architecture before a complete set of components is available. These are generally custom-coded as part of the component testing effort:

- Stubs emulate subroutines or external functions in a minimal fashion—that is, they basically return with some sample data and the various return code values (e.g., successful and failed). They are useful for testing a module when the modules it calls are not yet ready or available for testing.
- Harnesses and drivers call up a module and emulate the context in which the module will be called in the production environment.

Configuration Management Tools

Configuration management is a broad area that often means different things to different people. In this book the term means the "management of components in an environment to ensure they collectively satisfy given requirements."

"Configuration" designates a set of components in a given environment satisfying certain requirements. The management ensures that consistency is maintained over time, even with changes to the components.

The components are typically hardware, system software, and application components (such as source code, executable modules, load libraries, database DDL, and scripts or job control language), together with their documentation. The development environment also includes test data, test scripts, and other components that must be aligned with a given version of the configuration.

Version control and compatibility of components are key considerations when managing these components. Version control applies to all types of components, not just application components. In case incompatibilities are discovered, it must always be possible to "roll back" to a previous consistent state—that is, to revert to an earlier version of one or more components. To do this, it is necessary to know which versions are compatible. It must be possible to define releases of a configuration—a list of version numbers, one for each component, which together form a consistent configuration.

The environments can be many, and they can have complex relationships. On a large project they may include the following:

- *Design and construction.* This is the most commonly encountered environment, one in which the basic definition, build, and test activities of a project occur.
- *System test.* This is where the different system level tests occur (integration test, user-acceptance test, performance test). Depending on

the organization and the scale of the project, there may be different environments for each of the different system-level tests.

- *Production test.* This is typically the final staging area before a release is turned over to production and the operations group.
- *System software acceptance.* This is where new versions of system software (the operating system, the DBMS, middleware) would be installed and tested before rolling out to the rest of the project.
- *Architecture build and test.* This is where the architecture is developed and maintained. Fixes and enhancements are made here and tested prior to being released to the development teams for their use.
- *Production.* This is the current version of the "live" software.

Migration of consistent configurations from one environment to another is a central part of managing the environments. Examples of migration include the following:

- Migration from design and construction to system test.
- Distribution of software from the architecture team to the designers and programmers on the development project.
- Migration from test to production.

The key to successful migration is the knowledge of what constitutes each environment. Given the number of components commonly encountered on client/server development projects, and given that these components may be spread out geographically and over different platforms, the use of tools to aid in tracking these components becomes more important than in traditional environments.

Based on the previous discussion above, configuration management for the development environment is divided into version control and migration control.

Version Control. Version control tools control access to source code and other development components as they are developed and tested. They typically allow releases to be defined and multiple "snapshots" (i.e., the versions of all the components in the release) to be taken and maintained to facilitate rolling back to earlier releases if necessary. Examples of version control tools include Polytron's Version Control System (PVCS) and the UNIX Source Code Control System (SCCS).

Migration Control. Migration control tools control multiple versions of source code, data, and other items as they are moved across the environments previously discussed. The source code migration control tools manage multiple versions of source code to ensure that changes are applied in the proper environment and that thoroughly tested modules are subsequently migrated to the next environment.

Data migration control tools manage multiple versions of the database and its data to ensure that accurate data and structure are maintained in the environment and that versions of application code and database are deployed consistently. Types of data that would be migrated include base codes data or other reference data (e.g., a state code table or valid order code table) and converted business data.

Other migration control tools manage other types of system objects to ensure that a complete version of all components reside in the production environment (e.g., architecture support files, test definitions, and scripts).

Environment Management Tools

The immediate result of thinking of a development environment as a production environment (for producing a system) is making sure that environment management is planned, organized, executed, and supported to ensure a predictable and productive environment.

Adopting a structured approach to environment management, applying the same principles to development as to production, has several advantages:

- It provides high-quality support for developers.
- It can provide significant experience with the operations management tools in an environment that is generally smaller and carries lower risk than the full production environment.
- It facilitates the tuning of the production support approach before production rollout. The approach is refined from experiences using it to support the development team.

In some respects, the development environment is simpler than the production environment. For example, the development environment is generally smaller in terms of the numbers of hardware components, locations, and users.

In other respects, however, the development environment is more complex. For example, the amount of change in this environment is generally higher than the amount of change in the production environment. In fact, the environment can be so fluid that extreme care must be taken to maintain control.

The greatest need for technical support is generally during detailed design and programming. It is, however, necessary to start building the technical support team and processes (e.g., the help desk for applications developers) before detailed design.

This chapter discusses the components of environment management briefly. Chapter III-13, "Management of Distributed Operations," describes how client/server production environments can be managed. Because the development environment is a form of production environment, that section details each of the following components:

- *Service management.* These are the tools for defining and managing an agreed-on level of service, including service-level agreements, information gathering to check against the service-level agreements, and help desk support for the developer community.

- *System management.* These are the tools for managing the development environment. They provide support for managing security, starting up and shutting down the environment, and performing backups.

- *Managing change.* These are the tools for making, tracking, and distributing changes to the development environment. The most common type of change is upgrading of software (system, architecture, or application), but changes to hardware configurations and network configurations must also be supported.

- *Service planning.* These are the tools for supporting a capacity planning function for the development environment. The environment needs to be monitored and sufficient lead time allowed to support required capacity changes for shared disk space, server size (e.g., central processing unit size, memory, and number of users), network, and workstations (either the number of workstations or the configuration of the workstations).

Program and Project Management Tools

Experience has shown that effective planning and progress tracking are necessary for the success of most client/server projects. Given the more complex nature of client/server systems development and the new types of skills required, good project planning and management are even more critical for a successful outcome.

Although the basics of project management do not change, the estimating factors, the skills required, the learning curve, the level of contingency, and the "management instinct" (i.e., the gut feel developed from lessons learned over multiple projects) are different and must be taken into account by project management. Many of these changes are discussed in more detail in Chapter III-2, "Project Management."

Program and project management tools include the following:

- *Plan.* These tools are tightly linked with the development methodology. They help in estimating the development effort, defining the project tasks and activities, and identifying the type and quantity of resources required (subject matter experts, architects, designers).

- *Schedule.* When estimates and resource requirements have been determined, these tools assist in scheduling the work, identifying dependencies and critical paths, and balancing (level loading) the work across the resources. On an ongoing basis, the scheduling tools also provide administration features that allow tasks to be assigned and reassigned as the project evolves.
- *Track.* These tools provide a mechanism for members of the development team to report time against the project plan. This is typically done on a weekly or biweekly basis.
- *Report.* These tools provide reporting capabilities to reflect the status of the project against the plan. In the simplest form, the reporting consists of budget and schedule information, such as time spent by member, budget variance, schedule variance, estimates to complete, and planned versus actual results. More advanced tools can provide information on productivity and efficiency.

Most project planning and management tools available today provide some capability for each of the above. Examples of these tools include Microsoft Project and ABT Project Manager's Workbench.

Project Communication Tools

When a project team grows beyond 10 to 20 people, communication among project members may deteriorate unless a conscious effort is made to ensure that ideas, decisions, and results are shared in a timely fashion. The problem is more acute if development is distributed across sites. The consequences of communication breakdown can be serious: duplication of work, rework, budget overruns, and declining motivation among project members. On large projects it is therefore crucial to plan how communication will be facilitated throughout the project, and to communicate the decisions to the project team.

The local area network generally provides the basic infrastructure for sharing information. If development is distributed, a wide area network should be in place to connect the different locations.

But networks by themselves are no guarantee that people actually will exchange the kinds of information they should be sharing in a timely manner. At the very least, higher-level tools are needed.

The repository is one such higher-level communication vehicle, but the repositories that are commercially available are generally not sufficiently flexible. For example, most repositories are useful for documenting specific design decisions but not quite as useful for documenting design guidelines and basic design philosophies. They are also not very useful for communicating every kind of information to the project (such as planned server downtime or the scheduled release of a new version of the architecture).

There are several categories of project communication tools.

Mail. An E-mail tool (e.g., cc:Mail, Lotus Notes, or Microsoft Exchange) is valuable for sharing such dynamic information as design documents, meeting schedules, project events, and resource availability. Because these mail tools allow mail to be stored, forwarded, sorted, and filtered dynamically, they improve the quality of communication; they also speed up the flow of information.

E-mail and voice mail are also effective in facilitating communications in environments where people may be difficult to reach at their desks (if, for example, they spend time in meetings, or working with their teams). Rather than play telephone tag or leave notes which can get lost, E-mail and voice mail allow communications to happen asynchronously, reliably, and easily.

Groupware. Groupware (increasingly called teamware) is a relatively new category of tool that allows groups of people to share information easily. These tools typically provide a forum for people with a common interest to share information and ask questions of one another. Depending on the environment, these forums may be called newsgroups, bulletin boards, or databases. What they have in common is the ability to post questions and comments and to search through the existing discussion to see whether the information required is already present. Like E-mail, the posting and reading of information takes on the look of a mail letter. Unlike E-mail, however, the "letters" are openly available to everyone with access to the bulletin board and are saved for an extended period of time.

These databases are similar to the traditional bulletin boards already encountered in offices, except that the type of information is now more specific and the volume of information is much greater than could ever be handled by a traditional, manual bulletin board. Examples of such products include Lotus Notes and SoftArc FirstClass.

Publishing. Large computer systems are among the most complex deliverables produced by humankind. Although repositories go a long way toward organizing the information to make it accessible, there is also a need to publish information on the design and the implementation of the system. Publishing is necessary for the following:

- Information that needs to be communicated externally.

- Users who wish to review the system design but who do not know how to navigate the repository.
- Information that simply cannot effectively be understood when viewed online. Because of old habits and small screens it may still be useful to spread paper documentation across a desk when assimilating complex information.
- Legal or contractual obligations that may require the production and archiving of hard copy documentation.

Publishing tools allow individuals to print anything from single deliverables or specs all the way through the complete set of documentation for the system. Because documentation may be spread over several hardware platforms, and because it may reside in different libraries in different formats and may have to be printed using different tools, it is important to ensure that any chosen publishing tools can interoperate or integrate to allow aspects such as common headers and footers and consecutive page numbering to be handled without overly intensive manual involvement. Examples of publishing tools include Aldus PageMaker, Microsoft Publisher, and Corel Ventura.

CONCLUSION

An effective development architecture can make a complex project manageable and successful. It is important to make sure that the tools support the development process and that there are corresponding standards and procedures when necessary.

The development architecture as described here represents a useful guide. But developers do not need to implement the whole model on every project. Rather, the model is something to aim for during iterations. There will always be enhancements and maintenance for systems, and these should be tied to iterative evolution of the development architecture.

II-12
Operations Architecture

The operations architecture is a combination of tools, support services, procedures, and controls required to keep a production system up and running well. It differs from an execution architecture in that its primary users are systems administrators and production support personnel.

The components of the operations architecture are necessary to keep the production environment available and performing well. The necessary tools and products are often new to most information systems organizations, as are many of the operational issues that must be addressed. The operations architecture is many times the most underestimated architecture cost in deploying client/server applications.

OPERATIONS ARCHITECTURE FRAMEWORK, IN DETAIL

Section I of this volume introduced the operations architecture framework (see Exhibit II-12-1). In this chapter, each component is broken down and described in more detail, including typical requirements, issues, and relevant products or approaches where appropriate.

The framework includes a large number of operations components that are candidates for varying levels of automation. To build state-of-the-art capabilities in each of these areas would be very expensive and time-consuming as well. Which areas to address and what level of investment in support infrastructure should be guided by the requirements of the applications and users.

The key document defining these operational requirements is the service-level agreement (SLA). SLAs should be used to drive out the requirements for the operations architecture and to justify expenditures for tools and infrastructure.

SOFTWARE DISTRIBUTION

Software distribution is the delivery to and installation of applications and systems software on machines throughout a client/server environment. The architectural support required to support software distribu-

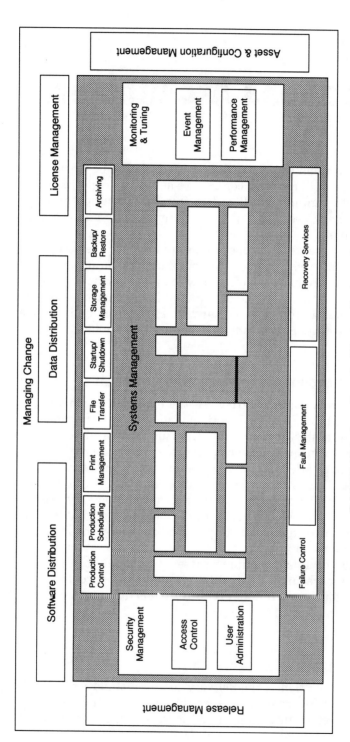

Exhibit II-12-1. Operations Architecture Framework

tion is largely driven by the numbers of workstations, servers, and geographic locations to be served.

For a relatively small network of workstations in a single physical location—where it is not anticipated that software changes will be frequent—a manual approach should not be automatically ruled out. A manual approach involves systems management personnel loading software upgrades on each workstation or server by physically visiting each machine. This approach does not scale well when either large numbers of workstations or servers in a single environment need to be updated or multiple geographic locations are involved.

When it is unrealistic to use a manual approach, an organization should consider adding automated software distribution tools to the operations architecture. Many products from leading vendors such as Microsoft, IBM, and Hewlett-Packard are on the market today that include or specialize in automated software distribution. Systems developers must look for several important features, depending on the specific support requirements.

Creating a Software "Distribution"

The server component of a software distribution solution enables administrators to build distribution packages and control distribution. A distribution is a package of related software files, data, and installation scripts that form an installable unit.

Few significant application installations, systems software installations, or even upgrades can be achieved simply by sending a single file. Configuration files (e.g., config.sys) and system files (e.g., autoexec.bat, .login), as well as multiple software files for a particular application or systems software component, often require changes.

In addition, it is usually desirable to upgrade multiple applications or combinations of systems software and applications in a single distribution rather than performing multiple independent software distributions. Bundling software upgrades together also reduces the amount of release testing required.

A distribution is created by selecting the files and scripts, often through a point-and-click interface. The components are then combined into a single file for transmission. Some software distribution tools provide compression capabilities to reduce the physical size of the distribution. This is particularly important in a wide area network environment where line speeds are an issue.

Scheduling a Distribution: Push vs. Pull

There are multiple approaches to scheduling software distributions. Some solutions use a rigid scheduling mechanism that requires all target machines to be powered on at a specified time when the software distribution is to occur. This mechanism could be characterized as a "push" strategy, where the server machine pushes the software to the client machines at a specified time.

The push strategy may be possible in some smaller situations, but in large organizations it is difficult to ensure that users will leave their machines on, particularly if it is common practice to turn them off at the end of the day.

A more flexible approach is the "pull" strategy, where the workstations check for software updates and pull the software from the designated server or servers at log-in time. Thus, when the user signs on either in the morning or at some point during the day, any pending updates are downloaded to the client machine. When combined with a forced log-off capability, which most networks support, this can effectively mimic the push strategy without the attending problem of some machines being powered off.

Neither the push nor pull scheduling approach is sufficient when large numbers of target workstations are involved. For example, a sales office automation system developed several years ago and used by 1,400 salespeople distributed across scores of locations encountered a problem with these strategies on its first major software upgrade. The sales office used the pull strategy because it was not feasible to have all workstations, locations, and dial-up users connected and powered up at the same time. The distribution was scheduled to be available when the users logged in on Monday morning. This was a substantial functional upgrade to the system, so the software distribution was several megabytes in size.

The problem was obvious: 1,400 machines could not simultaneously download one copy of software off of a server. As a result, most users were unable to retrieve the new software or use the system for several days. The problem was eventually solved by "staging."

Software Distribution Staging

Faced with the problem of scale, two alternatives can be considered. One is simply to acquire more servers with more copies of the software to be distributed. Of course, this is an expensive solution, particularly when these machines are not needed for any other purpose.

An alternative solution that may be better involves the concept of staging. Software distribution staging works by sending a new version of the software in advance of the cut-over date. In effect, the client machines have two versions of the application physically resident simultaneously, but only one is in use.

The existing software is used until the present cut-over date is reached. At that time, the client portion of the software distribution architecture automatically completes the installation and redirects the user to the new version. Using this approach, it is possible to selectively download the software update to subsets of machines well in advance of the cut-over date, thus eliminating the bottleneck.

An enhancement on staging is the ability to cut over to the new version on the receipt of a small command file rather than a preset date. This gives operations more flexibility to alter the cut-over date due to unanticipated events. For example, many adopters fail to anticipate the requirements of having multiple copies of applications stored simultaneously when determining the size of the workstation hard disks required for the users.

Remote Installation

Most software distribution solutions include a client portion as well as a server that resides on the target machine. The client software is responsible for installation of the software distribution onto the target machine's hard disk.

The first step is the unbundling (and uncompressing) of the distribution into the component files, data sets, and scripts (although the better products will first check to see that the required disk space is in fact available). Next, any preinstallation scripts are executed. These scripts may do such various tasks as checking for required components or adding or modifying lines in the target machine configuration or systems files that will be required by the new software (e.g., changing the number of buffers or adding a line to install a necessary driver at startup time). The directories in which the software is to reside are checked or created and then the actual software files are moved into the proper location on the hard disk. At this point a postinstallation script may be invoked that could include rebooting the machine so that the changes to the system and configuration files can take effect.

Cascaded Distribution

In large networks, where tens or even hundreds of servers support individual groups of workstations, a "cascaded" approach may be required. A cascaded software distribution approach allows for a central administrator to schedule the distribution of software updates to designated servers within the network environment. These servers, in turn, distribute the software updates to their associated client workstations.

This approach allows the simple push and pull strategies to be used for larger numbers of workstations without requiring staging. It also better utilizes the servers and communications links in these larger environments. Most products that support a cascaded approach also support staging concepts as well, thus providing much flexibility in how software is to be distributed.

Relationship to Configuration Management

Many of the available software distribution packages offer integrated asset and configuration management capabilities as well. Although not specifically required for software distribution, these functions are naturally related, and integrating these capabilities simplifies the operations architecture.

A useful feature is the ability to check to see whether all the system and application files required by a software distribution, but expected to be already resident on the target machines, are in fact there. For example, when sending a Visual Basic application, this feature checks the target machine to see that the user has not moved or deleted a required file such as VBRUN001.DLL.

A full-function software distribution system needs many of the same capabilities as a configuration management or asset inventory tool. The trend toward combining these functions within the products market will certainly continue.

Error Handling Reporting

When dealing with larger networks of workstations, errors inevitably occur in the software distribution process. There may be insufficient disk space or a required component may be missing. Capability is required both to report errors and to take appropriate actions.

Error reporting normally takes the form of a distribution log file that records success, failure, or errors encountered. In some cases a more active form of error reporting is required, where electronic mail (E-mail) messages may be automatically generated and sent to either the administrator or in some cases the affected user. If a fatal error is detected, the software distribution system should be capable of reversing any changes made to that point and restoring the user's machine to its previous state.

Platform Constraints

The choice of software distribution tools is somewhat limited by the types of workstations, servers, operating systems, and networking software in use. Some products are UNIX based and support only UNIX clients or at least require UNIX servers. Others work well with MS DOS or MS Windows workstations and perhaps IBM mainframes.

In environments where intermittently connected dial-up users need to be provided with software distributions, the existence and unreliability of dial-up connections adds more complexity to the software distribution task. Some products such as Xcellenet's Remoteware provide specific support for dealing with dial-up links. For example, the Remoteware server component is capable of actively dialing client workstations and initiating software transfers—if, that is, the user has left the modem line attached and the power on. In some cases, when requirements are complex or there are unusual combinations of vendor hardware and systems software platforms, there may be no alternative but to custom-develop this component of the operations architecture.

DATA DISTRIBUTION

Much of what has been said about software distribution applies to data distribution as well. However, some additional operations architecture features may be necessary, depending on the organization's data distribution strategy.

Two fundamental approaches to data distribution are data replication and data synchronization (see Chapter II-6). The distinguishing factor is that data replication, in effect, has a single master data source from which copies are periodically made and distributed; data synchronization supplies multiple updatable copies of the same data for which updates need to be synchronized periodically.

The role of the operations architecture and support organization in managing data distribution varies depending on the capabilities built in to the selected data management products. The operations architecture support needed to schedule, extract, send, and update multiple locations can be a substantial undertaking if not provided by the database product.

Data Replication

The data replication scheme is encountered more often, in part because it is less complex and requires less architectural support. Users of this technique frequently take periodic snapshots of a mainframe data source (e.g., a sales database) and replicate the data on a more cost-effective and responsive platform for analysis and modeling—perhaps a lower-cost UNIX, OS/2, or Windows NT platform.

To provide this capability, operations architecture services are required that can periodically extract data from the master source, perform any data conversions necessary for the target platform, transport the data to the target platform (possibly using the same mechanism as used for software distribution), and load the data into the target data management system (e.g., Oracle or Sybase). Products from vendors such as Trinzic, as well as several database vendors, provide varying levels of support for automating these repetitive operations tasks.

Supporting Selective Replication

The operations architecture to support data replication becomes much more complex when selective replication is required. For example, sales force automation systems often need to selectively replicate the customer database records for a given salesperson to that individual's machine. This gives salespeople local access to their customers' data without requiring a machine large enough to store the entire customer database. Selective replication requires additional architectural services to determine assignment of records to target machines and to create and manage the distribution of multiple data replication files—possibly thousands of them.

To further improve the efficiency of a data replication scheme, it may be desirable to have the ability to detect only those records, or portions of records, that have changed since the last replication occurred. This approach would be an improvement over the "brute force" approach of extracting all the data and resending it whether or not it has been altered.

Particularly for larger data sets, transferring updates only can substantially reduce systems and communications requirements. However, few database management systems or file systems can provide the needed information to determine which records have been changed or deleted since some arbitrary date in the past. Developing the generalized operations architecture support to make these determinations can be almost prohibitively complex.

Data Synchronization

Data synchronization shares the complexities of data replication but has the added problem of data integrity. The data replication scheme involves only a single updatable copy of the data; thus, the database management system or file system stops conflicting updates from occurring.

In a data synchronization approach, where more than one copy of the data can be updated simultaneously, the database management system may not, from a cost or technical standpoint, effectively prohibit two users from updating copies of the same record in two different locations at or near the same time. When the periodic or on-demand synchronization is initiated, each location exchanges its updated records. At this time it may be possible to detect that two locations have updated the same record since the last synchronization, but it may not be possible to automatically resolve the update conflict.

As long as distributed data has been a technical possibility, capabilities for data synchronization have been desired. Only recently have solutions come to market that attempt to generically address data replication and synchronization. Lotus Notes and Sybase's System 10 release were two of the early products that made this attempt. Lotus Notes allows for selective data replication and synchronization of semistructured information across multiple servers and locations; Sybase's System 10 release provides similar support for relational data.

The role of the operations architecture is to provide the infrastructure for scheduling, loading and unloading, managing error resolution, and transporting data in support of the data replication or synchronization strategy. Depending on the number of source and target data sources, and the frequency of replication or synchronization, this can be one of the most critical and frequently-used portions of the operations architecture.

LICENSE MANAGEMENT

Since the advent of computer networks that allow applications software to be shipped around the network as required, the issue of license management has become increasingly important. Applications software vendors have been experimenting with various licensing strategies, including unrestricted site licenses, fixed concurrent user licenses, and floating licenses that actually enforce the restriction on concurrent users.

Independent of these actions by software vendors, large organizations have been struggling to keep a handle on exactly what software products they own and how many copies they own. They have also been working to ensure that they are in compliance with software licensing agreements while not paying for more copies of software than they truly need.

The market for license management solutions is immature at this time. The problem is hard to solve without certain standards being in place that applications software vendors can adhere to and rely on.

From an operations perspective, however, the risk is that major applications software vendors will thrust their own license management solutions upon their customers, leaving the operations organization no choice but to support multiple and nonintegrated license management solutions. The problem becomes even more complex as vendors move to more of a usage-based charge, requiring that billing information be extracted from the license management component of the operations architecture.

There are license management products available today such as Key-Server from Sassafrass Software that allow only the licensed number of copies of a particular package to be run simultaneously on the network. If the license limit is reached, additional users trying to run the program are informed that no more copies are available at this time.

In addition to guaranteeing compliance with software licensing agreements, license management provides valuable information about who and how many people are actually using a given software product. If, in fact, usage statistics indicate that the organization has overpurchased, it may be possible to realize some savings by reducing software licensing agreements.

CONFIGURATION AND ASSET MANAGEMENT

To manage a client/server environment successfully, one must have a solid understanding, in basic terms of *what* is *where*, and one must maintain rigor in the change control procedures that govern modifications to the environment. Configuration and asset management information that may need to be tracked includes such details as product licensing information, warranty information, vendor names, logical and physical device information such as total capacity and current utilization, product configuration tracking, software and data version levels, network configuration parameters, physical location, and perhaps accounting information.

For relatively small client/server environments—under 100 workstations, let us say—it may be reasonable to use a manual approach. A manual approach keeps track of information in a personal computer database or in a collection of spreadsheets. For larger environments the manual approach has proven time and again to be an inadequate method, and automated tools are required for collecting asset and configuration information and for periodically auditing the environment.

In larger client/server environments, it is often necessary to have an underlying configuration and asset management database or repository. This database becomes a key information source for those managing, maintaining, and adding to the environment. However, it is only useful if the database is current, reliable, and perceived to be that way. Otherwise, configuration and asset management databases quickly fall into disuse.

Automated Tools

Automatic asset and configuration collection capability is included in many vendor solutions, including OpenView from Hewlett-Packard (HP), IBM's LAN Network Manager, and POLYCENTER Systems Census from Digital Equipment Corp. These products can interrogate the network and discover network and computing devices and collect related information. In addition, these products can perform the needed periodic auditing to detect changes to the environment over time, for example, when a user moves a machine or installs a network game.

Another important and related feature is the ability to restore a machine to a known or initial configuration for problem resolution. The configuration and asset management architecture component both provides facilities for determining the correct initial state for a given machine or network device and initiates any software distribution or configuration changes needed to bring the device back within compliance.

For more dynamic environments, where machine and network configurations are changing frequently, it is even more important to have an active configuration and asset management system. The capability to automatically change configurations of a large number of machines and network components or even to roll back to previous configuration settings for any particular device becomes increasingly important.

Many products that can form the core of the asset and configuration management operations architecture component are bundled with additional related functions for fault and performance management. HP's OpenView is just one example of an integrated suite of operations architecture products that can greatly simplify piecing together an integrated architecture.

Multivendor Problem

When sourcing asset and configuration management products from the marketplace, it is important to consider that they are quite particular in the types of networks and devices they can support. For example, the field of suitable asset and configuration management products becomes quite limited when the client/server components are not in the "mainstream"—such as the Pick operating system or Wang servers—even though management standards such as the Simple Network Management Protocol (SNMP) have increased the coverage of many solutions.

Second, products that specialize in serving smaller market segments, such as Macintosh clients or lesser known network protocols, sometimes do not support as wide a variety of client machines, operating systems, mainframes, and network protocols.

Finally, integrating multiple management platforms is complex, costly, and in many cases impractical.

In sum, the more "out of the business computing mainstream" hardware, systems software, and networking make up the environment, the more difficult it will be to find adequate configuration management solutions from the marketplace. This leaves developers with the daunting challenge of custom development of configuration and asset management capabilities.

Impact Analysis

A well-functioning configuration and asset management component of the operations architecture becomes a vital information source for conducting impact analysis for any requested changes to the environment. The frequency with which unexpected negative side effects are caused by relatively minor configuration changes to the client/server environment has been an embarrassing and frustrating surprise for many adopters of the technology.

Much of the source of these problems relates to the high number of execution architecture components and complex interdependencies between them. Another problem is the reality that most client/server networks involve numerous independent vendors. Changing even the release level of one systems software component may have a ripple effect and may require updates to, or newer versions of, additional software components or applications.

To support this type of impact analysis, dependency information must be maintained. For example, version X of the Oracle database management system requires version Y or greater of the HP-UX operating system and version Z of yet another vendor's Transmission Control Protocol/Internet Protocol product.

It is not uncommon for a user organization to wish to return to a previous operating system release to acquire an application package that does not yet support the latest operating system version. Without an effective configuration and asset management system that maintains relationship information, it is purely guesswork or best recollection if in fact the proposed version change will break any required dependencies. Unfortunately, this is how many organizations approach this problem in the client/server world today—typically with unsatisfactory results.

Appropriate Degree of Standardization

One of the keys to effective configuration and asset management is enforcing the appropriate degree of standardization across environments. For large client/server networks, where thousands of workstations are involved, it is not feasible to effectively manage the environment if each machine has its own unique configuration and combination of software products. On the other hand, it is not typically appropriate to give thousands of users the exact same configuration if the users perform different functions within the organization.

For example, users in such diverse areas as sales, product development, and human resources are likely to require different computing capabilities. The goal is to strike the correct balance between standardization, which simplifies the required operations architecture and tasks, and accommodation to each business area's unique computing needs.

RELEASE MANAGEMENT

Release management is made up of several functional areas including rollout management, release control, release testing, and migration control. In the client/server environment, managing the implementation of new releases or changes to the environment is difficult because of the number of interrelated components that must be simultaneously changed.

The synchronization of changes to such components as applications software, systems software, database format, and content is crucial but typically not specifically addressed by the release management products for client/server that are currently available. Many organizations have addressed the area of release management by instituting strict procedures and checklists to ensure that all necessary steps and tasks are completed successfully and in some cases through the creation of custom operations architecture utilities to automate some of the purely technical tasks.

A key task, often overlooked, is to adequately test the release process. To be confident that an environment change can be effected successfully, it is necessary to test the change process in an environment as close to the production environment as possible. In the client/server environment, this is more difficult and complex than simply setting up a test region on a mainframe processor. Depending on the circumstances, an isolated test client/server environment complete with an independent network of workstations and servers may be necessary.

The costs associated with constructing and maintaining a separate test environment can obviously be substantial; however, many organizations have resorted to this solution due to the frequency with which oversights or "side effects" were experienced when changes were made to the client/server environment or new releases of software were rolled out.

These oversights and side effects are often related to combinations of products and configurations not tested in combination together. In most client/server environments, each department, user type, or maybe even individual user has different combinations of application products and systems software loaded on their machine.

The side effects are often the result of incompatible memory usage between various systems and applications software components or incompatible networking and communications products. It can be challenging and expensive to construct a sufficiently similar test environment that can capture all the possible combinations and permutations found in the various production environments. A release management strategy and architecture must balance these various costs and risks to ensure that the environment can be maintained and evolved to meet the changing business and application requirements.

The marketplace for release management tools and utilities for the client/server environment is immature at this time. Most vendor offerings are limited to what could more accurately be termed "configuration and asset management utilities"; these utilities are capable of producing only the inventory of combinations of hardware, systems software, and applications in use on the network. This information is an important prerequisite to managing change, but is insufficient by itself.

SECURITY MANAGEMENT

The two principle components of security management are access control and user administration. They are defined together because of the strong relationship between the access control strategy selected and its associated user administration burdens.

User Administration

The client/server environment introduces many new challenges to the task of user administration. The majority of these stem once again from the dramatically increased number of system components. Adding a user to the "system" may require adding a user to the network, one or more server operating systems, one or more database systems (so that the user can access data), an E-mail system, and an existing host-based system.

In some cases, the addition of a user required entries to be added to upwards of 15 individual system components. Even determining all the subsystems to which a user must be added can be a frustrating and often unfortunately iterative task with the user.

Deleting a user from the system is even more difficult. Unless careful records are kept, it can be very difficult to determine to which machines, databases, and applications the user had been added originally to delete them. From an administration standpoint this may seem to be only a headache, but from a security standpoint it represents a substantial risk.

Problems related to adding or deleting users from a system are exacerbated by the number of user types and the dissimilarity of their configurations. For example, if mortgage officers, commercial lending officers, and risk management users all have access to different combinations of systems and servers, it can be difficult to determine which components user S. Jones was added to without knowing something about

S. Jones's role within the organization. The problem becomes completely unmanageable as individual users within a department or work group themselves have unique access privileges.

In larger client/server environments with many components and combinations of user capabilities, user administration becomes a significantly more resource-intensive task than in the centralized mainframe environment. In the mainframe world, it was possible to acquire tools such as RACF that could interface with the various systems software components to add, change, and delete user attributes. It was possible to develop these products largely because of the homogeneous and consistent nature of the mainframe environment—typically, all the systems software were sourced from one vendor (such as IBM or Digital Equipment Corp.).

In the more heterogeneous client/server environment, there are few tools that can manage user administration across a broad variety of products. For example, adding a user to the Sybase database product is different from the Informix product or Oracle product, and few user administration solutions cover all the combinations of even a typical client/server environment. The result is often that operations must train personnel in how to do user administration for the various systems software products within the environment and develop custom utilities and tools that are unique to the shop for automating user administration tasks.

Most user administration products on the market today focus on the operating system aspect of the problem (adding user access to the server, setting file permissions, group associations). Although these solutions are certainly helpful, they do not cover many of the more difficult user administration challenges such as database access, E-mail, and networking software. Each of these products often comes with its own administration tools which may simplify the individual administration tasks but do little to help with providing an integrated user administration approach.

Defining a Security Administration Strategy

The complexity and difficulty of managing security administration are linked to some fundamental decisions concerning how secure the system is from unauthorized access, and which mechanisms will be used to implement the chosen level of control. It is not uncommon to deploy simple client/server systems with little more than the network sign-on security provided by networking products such as Novell's Netware or Sun Microsystem's NFS.

In such a minimalist environment, security administration becomes little more than issuing network IDs and passwords. With this level of security, users can access any resource they want once they are in; this is clearly insufficient for mission-critical business systems and information.

Securing the Data

The more common practice is for client/server systems to focus on securing the information resources of the organization, which typically entails storing all corporate information in database products with sufficient security mechanisms for controlling access and update privileges on a per-user or group basis. Database products such as Oracle, Sybase, Informix, and DB/2 have features for implementing robust security policies and having them enforced by the database manager itself. If the data is properly secured, controlling application programs becomes less critical: Even if users can execute an application, they can do little harm if they cannot see or update information based on their security privileges.

However, this approach has several drawbacks, first and foremost in the area of administration. Users, on either an individual or a group basis, must be assigned specific access privileges to tables and databases at a potentially detailed level. (For example, Jane Jones has read privilege on table x and update privileges on tables y and z.) The administrative burden of identifying, entering, and maintaining this information is obvious. In addition, the performance overhead on the database manager can significantly increase resource consumption and response time.

Securing Application Programs with Access Controls

The next level of security sophistication is to control access to specific application programs executable on a user ID or group basis. This capability is provided in both networking software (such as Novell and NFS) and such multiuser operating systems as UNIX.

Both Novell and NFS now provide features that simplify administration in a multiserver environment. In these environments, when the user changes a password, that change is, in effect, propagated to other machines within the environment. However, the same cannot be said for securing data resources. Database products from vendors such as Oracle, Sybase, and Informix employ their own security administration commands and tool sets. Industry initiatives such as OSF's DME and the Kerberos authentication system, and the emergence of digital certificate schemes such as Verisign, hold hope for more unification of security mechanisms, which would simplify the administration task. However, progress in actually shipping products has been very slow to date.

The most common practice in securing client/server systems is to use a combination of all three of these mechanisms: network/server sign- on, securing applications, and securing information. As one would expect, employing all three mechanisms increases the administrative burden.

Single Sign-On

One of the common battlegrounds in trying to strike a balance between burdening the user and securing the system is the issue of single-user sign-on and password for access to all infrastructure and applications that a user needs. In the mainframe environment, security management products existed that could provide this capability. It is much more difficult in the distributed client/server environment.

Only recently have products come on the market with approaches for providing the user simplicity of a single-user ID and password. Some of these products work by intercepting application or systems software requests for user IDs and passwords and by responding with values retained in memory from the user's initial network sign-on. However, these products require substantial customization and integration work to deliver on the single sign-on promise.

Other products such as Verisign employ the concept of a unique digital certificate for each user. Digital certificates use public key encryption to allow the user to sign on and authenticate themselves once and then pass their digital certificate as proof of identification to subsequent applications.

Users to Workstations: One to One, or Any to Any?

Another question that comes up on many client/server implementations is whether users should be able to sit down at any machine in the network and be presented with their own personal user environment as though they were at their own machine. In this way, if an employee's workstation should break down the employee can use any available machine and resume working immediately. Also, this method of user management is appropriate for more mobile professionals who may work in multiple locations during the course of a week or month.

Aside from the security issues of not having a user ID tied to a specific workstation, providing this flexibility raises issues from an operations architecture perspective. Some of the more popular desktop environments such as MS Windows do not natively support the idea of a "virtual" user and are designed with the notion that a user's configuration preferences are stored locally on the user's assigned machine.

With forethought and with the addition of customized log-in scripts it is possible to construct an environment whereby user configuration files (e.g., WIN.INI or SYSTEM.INI) are stored on network drives and downloaded to the user's workstation at log-in time. Other workstation

environments that have for years included support for diskless workstation operation (e.g., the UNIX environment) provide more built-in support for the concept of virtual user machines. This is because diskless
workstations have no hard drive and therefore user information has to be
stored on shared server machines.

In summary, securing and administering heterogeneous client/
server environments is still a very complex and burdensome task. Consequently, the choices made in developing the security strategy must
strike a balance between the integrity and protection of assets from misuse and the burden placed upon both users and administration staff.

FAULT MANAGEMENT AND RECOVERY SERVICES

As with centralized computing technologies, failure control is important
in a client/server environment. The presence of heterogeneous equipment, however, makes it difficult to determine the origins of a fault.
Multiple messages may be generated within the system from a single
fault, making it difficult to separate the fault's cause from its effects.

The fault management services of an operations architecture assist
in the diagnosis and correction of system faults. Faults may include
network-, server-, workstation-, or even application-level faults. Fault
diagnosis may require services for isolation; viewing of host, server, and
workstation error logs; and determining the software and data versions
and configurations of affected machines.

Remote Takeover

To correct faults in a distributed environment, remote fault diagnosis and
correction tools may also be required. It may not be possible to count on
having technical expertise on site, forcing fault management to be
handled from a centralized area. Products that perform these functions
at present, however, provide somewhat limited capabilities in this arena.

In the distributed client/server system where all the machines cannot easily be physically accessed, additional operations architecture facilities are often required for what is sometimes referred to as "remote
control." Remote control, or "takeover," is the ability to remotely access
and take control of a system device such as a server, network component,
or workstation as though one were locally attached. This gives the centralized operations staff the ability to see what the user sees and take
investigative or corrective actions as though they were physically sitting
in front of the machine.

Remote takeover capability is considered essential for performing
accurate fault analysis in a distributed environment where a centralized

operations support approach is being used. Representative products that can provide this capability include Symantec's pcANYWHERE, and CarbonCopy from Microcom Inc.

Managing Networks

Fault management services also encompass network management and diagnostic tools for monitoring and reporting on network traffic and failures. Additional diagnostic tools such as protocol analyzers are required in some cases to determine the true source of the problem.

A wide variety of tools and products for fault management are available on the marketplace. When selecting a tool or vendor, it is important to take into consideration the breadth of client/server networking components to be managed to ensure that the fault management products selected have the necessary breadth of vendor coverage.

Another factor to consider in this selection is the choice between integrated operations environments (typified by HP's OpenView or Sun's NetManager), and point solutions that provide only one function. Although most integrated tool sets today do not adequately address the full breadth of fault management and diagnostic requirements, they can reduce the number of vendors and the complexity of integrating these point solutions.

Once again, multivendor environments increase the complexity and difficulty of providing fault management services. It may be difficult or even impossible to find products that cover the scope of capability required as well as the various hardware and systems software components needing to be managed. In larger client/server installations, some level of centralized fault management is usually employed to leverage specialized skills.

Recovery capabilities are also included in failure control. Recovery capabilities span the range from those required to bring up a device after it has failed to those required in the event of a major disaster. With critical business applications being rolled out on distributed technologies, the recovery of these systems must be easy, quick, and efficient. Loss of the system for even a short period can result in significant financial losses to the business.

A wide variety of architectural services may be required for fault recovery. These range from strictly network-oriented components (for restoring links or reconfiguring components) to more systems-level components (for restarting processes on machines or restoring databases). More involved tasks, such as the distribution of software fixes to workstations or servers, may require the ability to remotely reboot and reinitialize machines, printers, or other network components.

PRODUCTION CONTROL

In distributed environments, processes may be taking place across the entire system on multiple platforms in either a parallel or a serial fashion. Batch dependencies may be required across platforms, and multiple time zones may be involved.

In addition, many non-mainframe-based products do not provide production scheduling capabilities included with the platform. For these reasons, scheduling processes across a distributed environment can be quite complex, requiring significant management effort to ensure that the processes run smoothly. Many other day-to-day activities become more difficult in a distributed environment, including print management, file transfer and control, mass storage management, backup and restore, archiving, and system startup and shutdown.

Print Management Printing is rarely easy in any computing environment. In a distributed environment the sizing and routing of print traffic are more complex. With new systems being installed, only educated guesses about how and when printing will take place can help determine print routing capability. In most cases, some adjustments will be required to the print routing algorithms postrollout to reflect the printing reality.

Although printers are one of the most frequently used devices in a computing environment, management information from printers has yet to be standardized into a common protocol, causing great difficulty in managing print devices. Remote sites have limited capabilities for managing printers, forcing some technical expertise to be located where printers are present.

File Transfers File transfers in a distributed environment are not confined to transfers between hosts. File transfers can take place in a bidirectional fashion among hosts, servers, and workstations. As a result of the geographical disparity and number of devices in these environments, file transfers increase the traffic over the network and require careful scheduling to ensure that the necessary file transfers take place amid the rest of the processing.

Storage Management Mass storage management is more complex in a distributed environment, in part because many more storage options become available. Storage may take place, for example, on disks and tapes, and storage may be centralized or decentralized. The allocation and sharing of storage media is more difficult to plan because users are distributed. Backup and restore processes may now take place centrally, in a distributed fashion, or through a combination of centralized and distributed technologies.

Backup and Restore Processes Backup and restoration processes become more complex in a distributed environment as business-critical information becomes distributed across the system. Backup strategies must coordinate the information across the system and must determine where the backup copy or copies of information will reside.

As with centralized computing environments, restoration processes are directly dependent on how backup was performed. A single restore process no longer suffices. Depending on a particular fault, restoration services may only need to be performed for a portion of the system, while the rest of the system stays up and running.

Some technical expertise may be required on site to perform backups/restores (e.g., on/from server tape drives). In this case, backups and restores may need to take place during the business day, potentially affecting the processing that takes place at the distributed sites. If coordination of the distributed and centralized backup/restore strategies requires participation from someone at the remote locations, scheduling of these tasks becomes more difficult and complex, particularly across time zones.

Archiving The issues surrounding archiving are quite similar to those surrounding backup. Distributed architectures also place limitations on the amount of information that may be archived on a remote system as a result of the space limitations on servers and workstations.

Additional problems are created with archiving in a distributed environment as users have no incentives to perform housekeeping tasks on their devices. Depending on the users' ability to store information on their machines or on the local server, these machines may become cluttered with seldom-used files. Lack of space may affect other processes that need to take place on these devices, such as software and data distribution.

Startup and Shutdown Procedures System startup and shutdown are no longer confined to a centralized site. The "system" is distributed, in effect creating islands of technology that may be started or shut down with the flip of a power switch on a workstation.

Certain processes (e.g., software and data distribution) that rely on the system being up and running may fail if a user has switched his or her machine off before leaving for the evening. Such failures affect the following day's processing capabilities and must be accounted for either by the system or through training. In addition, controlled machine startup may be required to initiate tasks or to perform such activities as configuration checking or virus detection/correction.

It may be necessary, however, to shut down a portion of the system while the rest of the system remains running. In such cases, the design of the operations architecture must account for isolating portions of the system from each other, providing other avenues for processing and computing activities.

MONITORING AND TUNING

The number of devices and the geographic disparity of devices in a distributed client/server environment increase the effort required to monitor the system. The number of events generated in the system rises due to the increased complexity. Devices such as client machines, network components, and servers generate events on startup or failure to periodically report device status.

Event Management

In addition to hardware devices, applications and systems software also generates events. Common event-handling mechanisms are required to provide information to management in a simple, consistent format and to forward important events on for management purposes.

In most environments, events should follow an open format rather than a proprietary one as managed devices are rarely all from a single vendor. Filtering capabilities may also be needed at remote locations to prevent the streaming of events to central/master management consoles.

Performance Management

Performance management is more difficult, due to the lack of tools to assist with performance in heterogeneous environments. Performance is no longer confined to the network or to the central processing unit. Performance needs to be viewed in an end-to-end manner, accounting for all the factors that affect the system's performance relative to a user request.

The creation of a customer order, for instance, may involve multiple server accesses for data and information to be exchanged between the workstation and the host. The performance relative to the entire business event needs to be considered, not simply the performance of a single component involved. To make performance management even more difficult, not all devices provide performance information. It may be necessary to develop surrounding processes that monitor the performance of devices to calculate and provide end-to-end performance information.

CONCLUSION

Client/server computing and distributed technologies and architectures provide a wealth of new capabilities and advantages for those who adopt them. Processes happen more quickly, information is close to those who use it, and the individual is empowered with many new and useful tools. Management of the client/server environment, however, is different and more complex than management of centralized computing technologies. As the power and flexibility of the system has changed and increased, so too has the effort required to manage it.

The software marketplace now sees this opportunity and many competitors have put forth at least partial solutions in the past year or two. The future looks promising, but narrow standards initiatives or products such as POSIX, DME, or Microsoft's Systems Management Server will not completely eliminate the problem any time soon.

The complexity and operations challenge have actually been a hindrance to the adoption of client/server computing despite its demonstrable potential for business benefits. But this does not have to be the case. The client/server environment is manageable, but only with adequate planning and resources, and with an up-front understanding of the issues and inherent risks.

Section III
Client/Server Implementation

Effective business strategy drives client/server implementation. But that strategy, like light, is made up of different "colors," and includes:

- Managing change.
- Effective design and implementation of architectures, applications, and networks.
- Effective rollout.
- Effective management of distributed operations.

These components of implementation are "refracted" through the people and technology of the organization and come together in the reengineered or redesigned processes enabled by client/server technology.

Section III establishes a framework for implementing client/server solutions and then takes the reader through that framework, offering practical suggestions on getting started.

The intended audience is project leaders looking for information about how to structure a project and the critical tasks and steps to be completed for implementation. In addition, the first three chapters of this section may be of value to the business manager in understanding the process to implement client/server.

Project management issues are detailed, from original project organization, through risk management planning, through the effective use of project teams. Challenges of successful site preparation are also detailed, a rarely covered subject.

Architects will find information about how to implement technical platform, execution, and operations architectures. Project team members will find information about how to design highly usable client/server applications and GUIs.

Among the specific design and implementation issues covered are: the mechanics of distributed application design, including update control mechanisms; data and processing allocation; integration with legacy systems; the importance of test activities; and differences in client/server network design.

Finally, the ongoing management of distributed environments is a subject of extreme importance to IS practitioners. The complexity of multivendor distributed operations has, in fact, sometimes been an impediment to the adoption of client/server computing. Ideas for getting the most out of service-level and operational-level agreements, and step-by-step explanations of service management and planning, are described.

III –1
A Framework for Client/Server Implementation

As organizations move to client/server computing, they do not always carefully think through issues associated with successful implementation. Because of the distributed environment, client/server applications are more complex and difficult to implement than traditional applications.

Successful delivery of client/server solutions hinges on the following key areas:

- Project organization.
- Change management.
- Technology architecture decisions and implementation.
- Application design and implementation.
- Network design and delivery.
- Site preparation and installation.
- Systems management.

CLIENT/SERVER PLANNING CHART

Designers can map these considerations onto a comprehensive planning chart for client/server development projects. (See Exhibit III-1-1.) This planning chart has been used successfully on hundreds of such projects around the world. Each box in the planning chart represents a work segment to be done to address one or more client/server implementation issues.

The arrows and lines suggest a sequence as well as an interdependency of the efforts. The completion of a segment usually means that a major work deliverable has been completed.

The diagram is complex because a complex set of interrelated problems must be addressed. At the same time, the exhibit is still at a con-

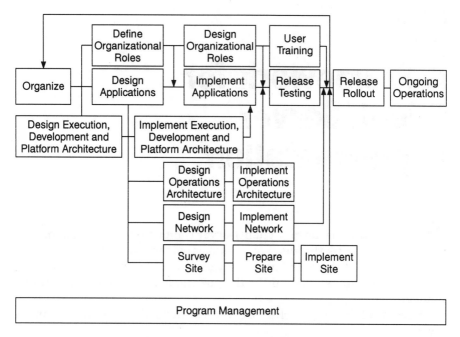

Exhibit III-1-1. Client/Server Planning Chart

ceptual level, because it does not show all the interrelationships or the actual work tasks to be done.

Exhibit III-1-2 maps the implementation issues against the framework, revealing the primary "streams" of client/server development.

This chapter provides an overview of each of the major development streams within the overall planning chart. Subsequent chapters within Part III go into more detail on each item.

PROJECT ORGANIZATION—ROLE OF KEY MANAGERS

Defining organizational structures can be a high-risk undertaking. Such structures often imply a change in who is in charge, a change in goals, and changes in how work is to be done. Put another way, organizational structures strike right where people live. As such, organizational charts tend to be the source of a great deal of concern and, on occasion, angst. However, the fact remains that to undertake the development of a client/server system, organization must be a key concern.

Exhibit III-1-3 presents a generic sample of an organizational chart. It is high level, but it provides a point of departure for a client/server

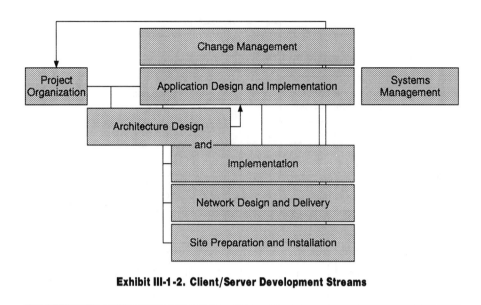

Exhibit III-1-2. Client/Server Development Streams

development effort. Many other factors have to be compared against this sample before an organization can come up with its own usable model. These factors include the skills of personnel involved, their desires, their past histories, and their expectations.

Strategy Manager

The structure shows a single overall leader for the project—here the "strategy manager." There is a great deal of value in having a single individual responsible for, and with authority over, the project as a whole. Such individuals, when they welcome the responsibility, seem to bring to the effort a commitment and concern that is lost when the project is divided among multiple leaders, each with a mix of concerns and constituencies.

Program Management

The project management role appears as an adjunct to the strategy manager. The role of this group is to monitor all the projects that are being pursued to deliver a client/server application. This monitoring function involves more than just tracking overall status. It also includes evaluation of the quality of the deliverables, as well as their cost-effectiveness.

Even when program management itself does not have the direct responsibility for quality review and approval, this function is respon-

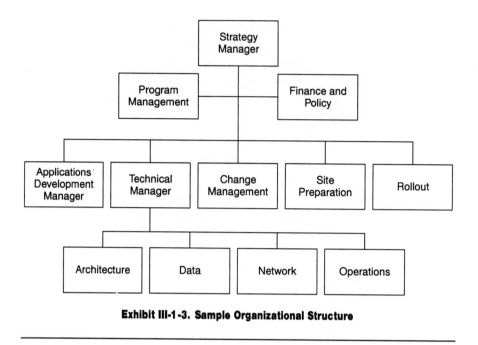

Exhibit III-1-3. Sample Organizational Structure

sible for ensuring that these reviews occur and that they are done by qualified people.

Also, as often happens, if one or more strands of the work start to run late or encounter difficulties, it is program management's responsibility to note the issue, evaluate its impact, and pull together strategies to deal with the situation.

Finance and Policy

The organizational chart also shows the finance and policy group reporting to the strategy manager. This group tracks overall spending on projects and verifies expenditures as time passes. A development project often places new demands on organizations, and new policies to deal with these demands have to be devised.

For example, a client/server engagement may be inherently distributed and require that people be on the road for extended periods of time. The company may have limited policies on reimbursement of expenses and handling of costs that need to be expanded for the project. This expansion would fall to the finance and policy group.

The next level of the chart shows organizations more focused on the actual building and delivery of the applications.

Applications Development Manager

Typically, a client/server development project addresses several business applications such as multiple lines of business and related claims. Each of these applications may have its own project manager. These project managers then report to the applications development manager.

The applications development manager has the overall responsibility to deliver the applications in accordance with time, budget, and quality standards. As such, this manager can make decisions about redeploying resources between applications and also provide a single voice to the business users and to the rest of the project teams about the applications development process.

How Much Span of Control? Should large application projects have direct access to the strategy manager and not report through an applications development manager? The first issue here concerns span of control.

Even with the relatively simple structure in Exhibit III-1-3, the strategy manager has five direct reports, as well as the program management and finance and policy groups. This is often near the limit of effectiveness of the strategy manager. Second, experience suggests that the applications often have a natural set of related concerns which are best resolved by bringing them together under one individual who makes the decisions necessary to get the job done.

Technical Manager

The technical manager is responsible for delivering the technical components of the client/server application. A number of key technological areas report to this manager

Architecture. The architecture function is responsible for the delivery of the overall architecture components, including the development and execution architectures.

Data. Client/server projects often involve difficult decisions about the design and allocation of data across multiple nodes. Often these decisions must be made at the conceptual, logical, and physical levels.

347

There also may be difficult data administration and security demands. Responsibility for addressing these issues falls under the data area.

Network. The logical and physical networks play a dominant role in client/server development. A networking function should also report to the technical manager.

Both the data group and the network group can be used to illustrate some worthwhile points. First, although these groups report to the technical manager their work lies in working with the applications. As a result, most of their time should be spent moving between the applications where they are responsible for the data design and network design for the applications. This responsibility includes ensuring the quality of the design, its timeliness, and its ability to meet current demands and evolve for the future.

The groups report to the technical manager primarily because much of what they decide has a significant impact on the overall technical approach. Changes are best addressed through the technical manager.

Second, because the groups report to the technical manager, they have a person who can resolve conflicting technical issues. For example, if the data design group comes up with a database design that must pump large volumes of information through the network, causing unanticipated impacts on network performance, it may be left to the technical manager to resolve the conflict.

Operations. The operations group has responsibility for implementing the operations architecture. Often, the operations group is also responsible for operating the system in the first few iterations as the system rolls out. Experience shows that an operations group, knowing that it will have to operate what it implements, tends to produce better answers.

Change Management

Change management is responsible for moving the user community through the change process. In this role, change management must interact a great deal with the applications group. However, change management must be viewed by the business community as a conduit to make sure that concerns and issues are being heard and that changes are made based on the trial, evaluation, and ongoing use of the systems.

In some cases the change management group has reported through an entirely different line, often the user community structure. The risk with that reporting structure is that the change management group may become a defender of the status quo rather than an active advocate for change.

Site Preparation

The site preparation group is responsible for preparing the site for the applications. In this role the group addresses the management of the upgrade of each site, and the installation of hardware, applications, and procedures in preparation for taking the site live in the rollout process.

Rollout

The rollout group has responsibility for ensuring that the systems function successfully as each site comes on line, which often means managing conversion of data, completion of go-live checklists, and completion of any miscellaneous tasks that are still outstanding. With early sites this group may be physically present as the site goes live. However, as experience builds, this group can increasingly work from a remote site and still deliver successful installations.

This management structure is a basis from which a project can develop a structure appropriate for its own unique circumstances and needs. The process of defining such a structure can be time-consuming and difficult because of the many concerns that organizational change bring about. However, it is fair to say that without an appropriate organizational structure the question of success in implementation will be left too much to chance.

THE INFORMATION SYSTEMS ROLE IN CHANGE MANAGEMENT

The cost and difficulty of client/server computing can be justified only if the organization is fundamentally changing its business processes. Business process reengineering reflects changes in the roles, responsibilities, and rules that define a business. New processes are essential for any organization attempting the implementation of client/server computing.

To define the reengineered business process, the first thing needed is an understanding of the business, the information technology, and what the technology can do for the business. The organization must analyze the business process and each of its steps, asking why and how they contribute to the business. Only then can a reengineered process emerge.

The most difficult part of business process reengineering is getting the users to accept the new process. Business users must change their behaviors—change the manner in which they perform the process—or reengineering will fail. Successful reengineering and client/server implementation require an extensive change management effort.

The first major segment of work is to define the new business organization. The next work segment is to design the specific work roles in terms of daily tasks and deliverables. Finally, training is defined that ensures that the business user can take on and fulfill the newly defined roles.

Where Does Change Management End and Systems Development Begin?

Change management includes ensuring user awareness and knowledge and conducting trials and evaluation of the reengineered work process. These tasks are some of the most challenging and creative jobs to be found in client/server solution delivery today.

The real difficulty is defining where the responsibilities for change management end and where the role of the systems developers begins. There can be an overlap between what the change management personnel and the systems-building personnel define.

In essence, both groups are making commitments on what the system will do. It is important that these work efforts be coordinated and managed. The key to avoiding the potential overlaps is to have the change management and systems people sit down and determine explicitly what each group will deliver separately, and what deliverables will result from joint efforts.

Change management is just as important for the IS person as it is for the business user. The objective of IS change management is to complete the learning curve in the application of client/server computing. This effort tends to be overlooked or treated in an ad hoc fashion. This is unfortunate because client/server technology can succeed only if systems personnel are well informed, trained, and experienced.

TECHNOLOGY ARCHITECTURE AND PLATFORM DECISIONS

The design architecture work segment refers to making the many decisions about hardware, systems software, and networking. The decisions made in the design architecture work segment form the basis for building the infrastructure of tools, standards, and methodology (the implement architecture segment) that the systems builders need.

Included in the technical architecture are the following:

- Going-in positions on hardware platforms to be allocated by site.
- Associated decisions of operating systems, graphical user interfaces (GUIs), and network strategy.
- Decisions related to the database management system (DBMS) and development tools and languages.
- Positions on the intent to provide support for the developer and user. For example, will the design environment be highly integrated with the implementation environment? Will a repository strategy be

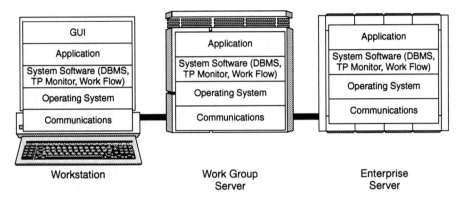

Exhibit III-1-4. Platform Architecture Framework

used? What testing facilities and capabilities are to be provided? What training and help facilities are to be provided?

- The implemented infrastructure that will be used to connect applications to the technologies. This infrastructure is usually packaged as a set of services and application programming interface (APIs) for use by applications developers.

Platform Architecture

One of the most common yet difficult questions organizations have when moving to client/server computing centers on the platform architecture—the technology to select. Exhibit III-1-4 provides a framework with which to evaluate the technology decisions.

This exhibit portrays at a high level the concept of a layered technical architecture. Fundamental technology decisions are needed to define a technology architecture and to address the following:

- Operating system.
- System software, including DBMS, transaction monitor, and work flow.
- Networking.
- GUI.

After these decisions have been made, the next step is a set of decisions on development tools and systems management approaches. These decisions in turn lead to a development architecture and an operations architecture.

These decisions are difficult to make because, in an open systems environment, there are often many options to consider. For example, there may be four to five hardware vendors, an equal number of networking vendors, two to three operating system strategies, four to five DBMS vendors, and two to three GUI vendors from which to choose.

The number of possible combinations of solutions could reach into the thousands. At a minimum, IS should focus on those components that affect the enterprise's ability to interoperate, or share data across departments. If possible, IS should define, at the enterprise level, those components that allow departments to share information.

For example, mixed hardware such as RISC and CISC processors can present ongoing problems with sharing data because of basic dissimilarities in bit patterns. Different networks in different departments present ongoing problems when those departments want to share data. Different DBMSs present basic problems when there is a desire to access one department's information from another department. In each case, a means can be found to circumvent these problems, and systems integrators are widely involved in solving them. However, if IS sets basic guidelines on what constitutes a consistent technical architecture, it does not need to find or pay for workarounds.

Most enterprises, unfortunately, end up with incompatible technical architectures. Many factors contribute to that result, particularly legacy decisions. IS personnel contribute to the problem when they take too long to come to a decision about the technical architecture. When that happens, the end-user community often goes ahead without IS involvement. Therefore, the major reason to focus on interoperability as a criterion for technology decisions is to define a minimal subset of all the decisions so that they can be made more quickly and cohesively.

This ability to have options is both the good news and the bad news of client/server. The good news is that many technologies are available. The bad news is that an organization has to choose from among them. It is also important to note that many IS organizations are structured to make technology choices and decisions. They are accustomed to sole sourcing most, if not all, of their technology from a single vendor.

Operations Architecture

The design operations architecture and implement operations architecture work segments address the steps needed to put the systems management approach in place.

Design operations architecture should begin after the technical architecture decisions have been made and as the functional capabilities and requirements of the application are beginning to be defined. Information on functional capabilities and requirements—as well as technical

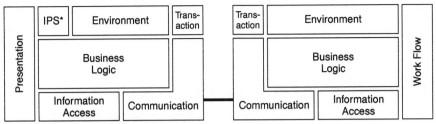

*Integrated Performance Support

Exhibit III-1-5. Client/Server Execution Architecture

requirements such as performance, availability, and reliability—is needed to help determine service-level agreements. The service-level agreement is key to defining and delivering the overall systems management architecture.

When the decisions on the overall systems management architecture have been made, implementation work begins. This is often a matter of purchasing individual tools and integrating them. Included in this effort is the definition of help desk features and the beginning of training and actual implementation of the help desk, along with other support components.

Delivery of Infrastructure

When making decisions on the technical architecture, IS must begin thinking in terms of what reusable components the enterprise must build to make the technical architecture usable by developers and business users. These enterprise-built reusable components are what is called infrastructure.

In a traditional IS shop, guidelines for designers and programmers are often referred to as the development standards. Equivalent guidelines are needed for client/server computing. Indeed, the equivalent may be even more critical because often the designers and programmers do not have the experience in client/server to fill in the gaps.

Some of these standards are addressed by the methodology decision, but many are not. For example, standards for the input/output design of applications using a GUI may be needed. Programming and design standards for workstation environments may be required. Time and effort can be saved if the execution architecture discussed throughout this book is used. (See Exhibit III-1-5.)

Such an architecture must be established, defined, and explained to developers as a consistent framework for all developers to use. After this infrastructure is defined, developers must select or create tools to provide the components, as well as develop designer and programmer guidelines and training in how to use the infrastructure.

APPLICATIONS DESIGN AND IMPLEMENTATION

There are five major activities conducted in the design applications and implement applications work segments:

- User requirements.
- Requirements analysis.
- Applications design.
- Technical design.
- Development planning.

These are, of course, the traditional tasks—the actual work of building the system—found in any systems development. The fact that these are now just one part of a much larger effort points to the additional work required for a client/server project.

In release testing, work is completed to ensure that all components come together as a complete, cohesive, and working system. By definition, client/server systems run in the business environment, perhaps thousands of miles away from the systems developers. Furthermore, if an organization bases a new business process on the system, the business could then become critically dependent on the system. Releasing a system that is not completely tested would be damaging.

Tests are needed to ensure that:

- The application works as a whole.
- The infrastructure and technical architecture to be released are the ones on which applications have been running.
- The installation procedures are usable by someone at the local site.
- All the support mechanisms are in place to keep the applications running smoothly.

Any emergency procedures or error recovery procedures should be tested to determine whether they are understandable and workable by people at the local site. End-to-end performance must be addressed at this time to ensure that the service-level agreements are met. In addition, operations and help desk procedures should be tested to ensure that they perform as expected.

A common way to test all the above is by creating a model office environment. This environment includes an office configured as it would be to run the new systems, a network connected to the model office, and a model operations area that reflects the configuration of hardware and systems software found at both the work group centers and the enterprise level.

Release testing can make a significant contribution to the ongoing reliability and usability of the system. At the same time, it is not a trivial effort—it lasts perhaps as much as two to three months.

NETWORK DELIVERY IN MULTIVENDOR ENVIRONMENTS

The network is the key to making client/server computing happen. Client/server represents the convergence of communications and computing, so there must be as much focus on the network side as on the computing side. The network design and network implementation work segments should begin once the functional capabilities of the application are known.

Client/server computing demands a much tighter integration of network and systems design and building compared with traditional development. Careful attention should be paid to the evolving network design and how extensive an upgrade may be needed from current network capabilities.

The difficulty with network delivery is twofold. First, the typical information processing person is not strong in networking knowledge and design. For many years, the proprietary networks associated with traditional technology were largely the domain of the network specialist or the technology provider. The IS person simply provided the network specialist with requirements, and the specialist did what was required to meet the needs.

At the same time, the network specialist is confronted with a new set of terms and concepts for modern networking technology. In addition, the network has such a profound impact on the capabilities of the client/server solution that network specialists must be brought into the design process much earlier. Often they are the ones to say yes or no to a functional requirement on the basis of the networking capabilities.

The actual delivery of the network usually requires greater lead time to assemble and integrate the required components. With earlier proprietary solutions, the network components usually arrived from the vendor with assurance that the vendor would integrate them after assembly.

In a client/server environment, components from different vendors usually are being integrated to build and support the network, so effort will be required to ensure end-to-end consistency, performance, and fault management. There may also be a need to upgrade the overall network, which can greatly lengthen delivery time frames and costs. Even as the components are assembled and tested, it is common to encounter miscellaneous problems that take extended time to resolve. When the network goes into production, ongoing network problem solving may still be necessary to make the network stable.

SITE PREPARATION AND INSTALLATION

Site preparation and installation work refers to the following:

- The process of reviewing sites and determining what is required to prepare them for installation of the client/server technology.
- The process of readying and installing the sites.
- The process of testing an installed site to ensure that it works as expected.
- The maintenance of an inventory of the site and its status for running an application until systems management can take over the effort.

Some may argue that these efforts are not directly related to client/server computing. In fact, however, most sites involved in the first-time application of client/server technology for business solutions encounter significant and difficult problems at the site preparation stage. If hundreds of sites require upgrades, site installation and upgrade may be the single largest line item in the development budget and may require the longest lead time.

There are many issues in this process of establishing the sites. A first consideration is the state of the current distributed applications. If the enterprise has already installed client/server applications, decisions need to be made on using the installed base of technology for future applications. But for first-time applications, issues need to be resolved regarding the site's suitability to run a client/server application and to support client/server technology. Site readiness issues include power, air conditioning, and possibly the installation of physical wiring.

Some potential problems may be a surprise. For example, at one manufacturing site, a stamping process created a heavy vibration that required additional protection for disk drives. Another site was next to a radio station, which created potentially damaging electromagnetic fields. Such issues as these need to be addressed before they become surprises.

These issues must be recognized and resolved before the purchase and installation of hardware and software. Moreover, revisiting sites to ensure that in the process of building the system, the initial survey/assessment stays up-to-date is an ongoing issue.

There are often issues of arrangements at local sites for local contractors such as carpenters, electricians, and air-conditioning specialists who may need to come to each site to make any necessary changes. Often, there need to be negotiations and ongoing contract management to find parties qualified to do this work. A building contractor may be retained to see the work that is to be done. When many sites are involved, a management challenge arises for which the organization might have little competence. The question of outsourcing versus insourcing this type of work must be addressed with regard to site upgrades.

SYSTEMS MANAGEMENT

Systems management addresses the ongoing operation of the client/server application when it is in production. A central issue in establishing systems management for client/server is the definition of service-level agreements.

These agreements are, effectively, commitments to meet certain levels of overall system performance, reliability, and recovery from problems. Until these agreements are defined, it is difficult to resolve questions on those parts of the systems management environment that specifically contribute to meeting and confirming conformance to service-level agreements. These components are the key deliverables from the systems management efforts.

The typical areas that must be addressed as a part of the systems management in a client/server environment include, but are not limited to, the following:

- Configuration management, which involves managing components found in the application, architecture, and environment, and also managing the status and version of these components.
- Activation and execution of components of the client/server application and architecture. This activity can include bringing up such online and batch components as the DBMS.
- Fault management, which is the determination of fault status, the assessment of reasons for failure, and the initiation of recovery from failure.
- Help desk facilities to answer inquiries from the user and system communities on problems, questions, and steps to recover from problems.
- Determination of performance, reliability, and, potentially, assessment relative to service management contracts.
- Vendor contract management and associated contacts and payments.

Although this list is not complete, it is representative of the range of issues to be addressed when starting with a service-level orientation.

Among client/server solutions, many tools are currently available to the systems builder, but most cover a narrow range of demands. In comparison, traditional computing environments offer highly integrated solutions, often as part of the system software.

The cost of preparing solutions for systems management in a client/server environment is high. Experience suggests that 10% to 40% of the development budget for initial client/server solutions should be devoted to the delivery of the system management facilities.

At the low end of this range, a strong help desk facility can be built. On the high end, organizations can consider building some sophisticated automated support for ongoing operation and problem resolution in a systems management environment. The risk with regard to this investment is that these technologies are evolving very quickly and thus a custom tool assembled today may be rendered obsolete by commercial products in the future.

PROGRAM MANAGEMENT

A key concept in the framework is the just-in-time delivery of components of the parallel work segments. Ideally, people like to do work in a sequential fashion; in today's business environment, this is not practical. Furthermore, it is more efficient to have results shared between the work segments as the work proceeds. As a result, many of the work segments shown in the client/server implementation framework should be performed in parallel.

This just-in-time approach, in which several teams must be kept tied together and working as a whole, is a major challenge. To manage the overall effort, a program management strategy must be used that ensures that individual efforts are proceeding according to an overall plan and that the deliveries from each team meet expectations in terms of quality and timeliness.

Program management establishes an overall plan giving expected deliverables and due dates. This plan includes defining the levels of quality that are expected. It includes evaluating the work being done and providing an ongoing assessment of the status of work against plans. Also, if delays become evident, program management sets up contingencies to address delays.

An Iterative Approach to Client/Server

The return arrow at the top of the client/server planning chart (see Exhibit III-1-1) signifies that the adoption of client/server computing requires an iterative approach. Applications have to be delivered to the users in a timely manner, but technology evolves rapidly. Iterations provide the opportunity to rethink architectures to determine whether previous decisions and approaches have aged or are no longer valid.

Iterations must be done quickly. According to one view, iterations should be done in six months or less; however, it is difficult to get all of these parallel efforts organized and drawn to a conclusion in six months. A more practical approach is a 12- to 18-month cycle for each iteration, considering the number of parallel work efforts involved.

Course of Action

For IS, the course of action depends on where the organization is in the application of client/server technology. The following suggestions apply for organizations just beginning the application of client/server technology:

1. Choose applications that would benefit from the distinct technology features of client/server computing, such as its ability to put processing where it is needed and its inherent communications capability. Publicize that the application is a first delivery of processing capability in a client/server environment. Ensure real and lasting commitment from the business community and management for the application.

2. Build a team with skills in client/server technology. This can be done through the use of training for in-house personnel and by retaining outside expertise. Ensure that users with credibility in the business world are committed to the effort.

3. Organize an effort such that time and resources are dedicated as follows:

   • The change management team defines the reengineered business process and begins the work activities shown in the change management curve (discussed in Chapter II-3).

   • The technical team defines a technical architecture addressing the components of the execution, development, and operations architectures discussed throughout this book.

   • The design of an application to support the reengineered business process is begun and coordinated with the change management effort.

   • As business worker requirements for performance and reliability under the reengineered business process begin to appear, a systems management effort should be initiated to build the systems management capability that can determine whether these needs are being met over time.

- A network design effort is started that brings online the network required to support the effort.
- As required, the site evaluation, installation, and delivery effort should be planned so the sites are ready to run the client/server application as it is implemented.
- A program management effort can be instituted to ensure that all these strands of work deliver the components needed on a timely basis and at a sufficient level of quality to make for an acceptable application.

Managing Parallel Efforts. The execution of a set of parallel efforts as described earlier is inherently a risky process. On occasion, in the rush to meet dates there is a tendency to begin the strands of work with little or no contingency. This is not a good starting position given the risk inherent in client/server implementation.

Thus, each strand should have built into its plan a contingency in schedule that will allow it to deal with surprises and the unexpected while not delaying the overall effort. Contingency is not intended to hide mismanagement. Rather, it should be used on a rational basis to cope with the unexpected. Its use should be one of the watch points in the program management effort.

Client/server computing appears to provide the next level of technology that organizations need to solve the problems of business process reengineering. At the same time, it is a more complex and inherently more difficult technology than traditional computing to implement successfully. It is safe to say that business problems demand that IS address and contain these risks to advance the value of business computing.

CASE EXAMPLE: THE AIRLINE INDUSTRY

The discussion throughout Section III is based on a case example, which allows reader to track one major implementation from start to finish. At relevant points, the chapter presenst an update on the development of the case. Although the case is fictionalized, it is a composite of real experience in implementing client/server development projects around the world.

Overview of UniversalAir

UniversalAir is a large airline with national and international routes; its headquarters is in the United States. The story begins with a merger between UniversalAir and another major airline.

As a result of the merger, UniversalAir's business has doubled almost overnight and it has become a leading national carrier. But its ability to grow is being impeded by a paper-based and labor-intensive system for calculating earned revenue. The process is cumbersome, and the systems do not provide the kind of detailed management information necessary for a major player in the marketplace.

The Paper-Based System

Ticket receipts from UniversalAir flights are stored 7 feet high in an area the size of a basketball court; 1,200 clerical and 45 management personnel handle 5 million documents a month. Staff turnover is extremely high, in part because dealing with the tickets is unappealing at best. Whenever workers need to audit a ticket or research a problem they have to leave their desk, go to the vault room and ask for a ticket number. This takes time, and the employee has to wait while another worker goes through boxes of tickets to find the right one.

Auditors compare audit coupons and computer printouts manually. Handling just one box of coupons can take 2 to 3 days, and finding a missing audit coupon can take anywhere from 10 minutes to 4 hours. On top of everything else, the tickets are messy. Because of the red backing to the ticket receipts, the hands and clothing of the clerical personnel are usually covered with red ink.

When a lifted ticket enters the department, the only fact recorded is that a sale has been made. The passenger's itinerary is not captured, for example, nor is the cost of the fare. UniversalAir samples a small percentage of passenger tickets—about 5%—and uses that sample to extrapolate estimated revenue.

Revenue figures for monthly financial reports are entered and adjusted manually, based on the average fare of the small sample of flight coupons. The accuracy of these figures is checked only twice a year. Although management believes the accuracy to be fairly good, large discrepancies occasionally occur. A bigger problem, however, is the lack of reliable information for analyzing fares and traffic. Sample pricing does not provide the needed detail. Nor does it link commission expense to revenue, to give a true picture of net revenues in each market.

The revenue accounting system is further complicated by the fact that tickets are not always used as sold: Passengers may take a different flight, fly on another airline, or cash in the ticket. In addition, currency transactions, based on exchange rates that vary daily, are a growing part of the business.

In summary, then, many business issues are laying the foundation for a new technological initiative:

- A paper-based system.

- Long learning curves.
- High turnover.
- Possible loss of revenue due to the random sampling method.

The Move to Client/Server

UniversalAir's existing system is a 20-year-old mainframe, predominantly batch, with a cryptic interface requiring mostly coded input. The IS department has been thinking about and working toward a new accounting system for some time, but its original concept was for a traditional mainframe, terminal-based solution. But systems proposals face the problem of handling the paper-based accounting for tickets. Each day, UniversalAir receives data from three sources:

- Electronic files of ticket sales taken from computer reservation systems and consolidated by regional clearinghouses.
- Audit coupons from travel agents and UniversalAir stations.
- Lift coupons collected from passengers as they board a plane.

The first two sources are used in the audit processing step, and the results are combined with the third to calculate earned income.

Thinking about how to deal with those boxes and rooms full of tickets led the head of IS to begin a research project into imaging systems. With imaging, the airline would be able to scan the tickets, store the images electronically, and then make them available to revenue accounting clerks at their desktop. It would be faster and more efficient to retrieve an image of a ticket from an optical platter used in imaging and deliver it to the screen electronically than for the employees to leave their desks and wait at the vault room for a ticket. This would mean a huge improvement in productivity.

An imaging system points the IS department toward client/server technology because it would require bringing an intelligent workstation to the desktop to process and display the image. IS also realized that an intelligent workstation could have a positive effect on the airline's turnover problem with the clerical staff. The GUI of a client/server system would be easier to learn and use. The airline's training director believes that significant savings in training costs could be realized by the airline. New personnel would reach proficient levels of performance more quickly, and their performance could be supported with online help and other support facilities.

Considering its opportunities further, IS soon realized that it has an ideal environment to improve the processing within the revenue accounting function. By using rule-based processing on ticket data, the IS department might be able to subject every ticket to all relevant pricing and auditing rules instead of just the random sampling of tickets it currently does. The team began discussions about a system that would process all ticket images against the rules during the night, flag the exceptions, and then cue those images up for the workers in the morning when they come in.

This ability to track every ticket got the attention of high-level executives at UniversalAir because it represents the opportunity for significant cost savings. Savings in training costs would certainly be realized with the new system. But the possibility of finding big savings through better accounting methods suddenly becomes possible. Client/server looks like the technology that would make this happen for UniversalAir. But now some serious cost/benefit analyses have to take place. And the expertise and experience in client/server have to be found.

CONCLUSION

This chapter has described a set of complex issues, all of which must be addressed to successfully implement a client/server application. The issues are interrelated.

For example, the change management process can have an impact on many other areas. Thus, not only must the various issues be addressed; they must be addressed in an integrated fashion. The answers from one strand of the work have to be made available on a timely manner and at acceptable levels of quality for the other strands.

Timely and high-quality delivery does not happen by accident. The delivery must be planned and managed—a complex challenge best addressed through an activity of program management. Essentially, program management addresses the issue of managing multiple strands of parallel but interdependent work. It provides an ongoing assessment of the status, quality, and cost of the work. In terms of addressing all the above issues in a timely fashion, the implementation of program management may be a key step in succeeding at client/server.

III-2
Project Management

M any, perhaps most, information systems personnel view client/ server development only as a technical process. They see the process of systems development as making technical decisions about how things work and how tasks should be completed. Inherent in this technical view is the perspective that qualified technical employees who work hard can complete any systems job. This view is naive at best.

It has become increasingly clear that any systems job can frustrate even the best technicians working with the best of intentions. Balancing the time, cost, and personnel aspects is at the heart of management control of client/server systems development. The key to successful management control of client/server systems development lies in the often observed management cycle of planning, executing, and evaluating the results of the work and revising the plan based on these results. Although this management cycle is well defined, it is poorly executed more often than not. Most problems with systems development arise from a breakdown in this management cycle.

PLANNING THE WORK— METHODOLOGIES HELP

Even in traditional systems design, many organizations fail to create a systematic plan. Reasons for this vary:

- The project is considered state of the art.
- The method to complete the work is undefined.
- There is no estimating basis to use.
- The deliverables are not defined.
- The scope is unknown.
- The expectations are not understood.

Another reason may be that developers feel they are just too busy doing it and feel they cannot take the time to plan it. These reasons were not valid with mainframe development and they are not valid with client/server development.

With some thought and understanding, IS managers can customize and extend the various well-defined methodologies for almost any client/

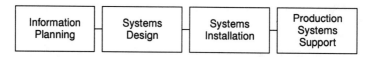

Exhibit III-2-1. An Example of a Systems Management Methodology

---

server development effort. Such methodologies as AC Methods by Andersen Consulting (see Exhibit III-2-1) and Information Engineering by JMA are available from various vendors and consultants.

Regardless of the methodology to be used, client/server still requires an organization to plan its systems, just as must occur in traditional systems development. The organization must:

- Design its systems.
- Code and test its systems.
- Support its systems.

Although there is no generally agreed-on basis for estimating systems development projects, many useful bases for estimating projects are available. Often, a comprehensive project development methodology has an estimating basis.

The key for IS managers is to select one methodology and estimating basis based on previous experience. When estimates are created for a systems project, IS management typically comments that the project cannot possibly take that long. "The estimate has to be wrong—cut it in half." When a project is in progress, however, the most frequently heard comment is, "These estimates are impossible; we'll never make them."

EXECUTING THE PLAN

Many times, a great deal of effort goes into developing a plan that is then ignored. Several underlying reasons cause this problem.

First, IS management has many responsibilities and distractions to address every day. These activities tend to move focus away from developing and executing project plans.

Next, IS management may not know how to use a plan to manage a project. Many systems project managers seem to have trouble connecting the plan to their daily activities. For example, if a plan states that one employee is designing inputs and outputs from April 10 to April 28, the actual project should have a corresponding activity. But, in fact, many systems project managers have trouble committing to their plans, and they lack the self-confidence and discipline to conduct the project based on its plan.

Another reason a plan is ignored is because of a lack of clearly defined deliverables that the project team can create, manage, and understand. One of the first quality assurance points during a plan review is to check that there are clear deliverables defined for all tasks of a project.

Although this may sound pedestrian, one of the obvious signs that problems are on the way is a plan that has such tasks as "Develop understanding of user needs," or "Coordinate liaison activities." Because these tasks have no explicit deliverables associated with them, project management and control become very difficult.

A comprehensive client/server systems development methodology can be valuable in defining deliverables. IS managers must exert management control by insisting on timely and accurate delivery of quality deliverables. A project cannot be controlled solely on good intentions.

EVALUATING THE PROJECT

Nothing reveals basic human nature more than watching a manager confronted with the evaluation task in the management cycle. Essentially, this task requires IS managers to evaluate their project's and staff's performance.

Several common errors occur during this activity. The first is not conducting an evaluation at all. The most common way IS managers can avoid reviewing a systems project's progress and results is to delegate this responsibility. As a result, IS managers may only get status reports on the project; then they must rely on these reports for an accurate account of the project's progress. In some cases, even this formality is absent.

When an IS manager delegates this responsibility and is asked by senior management about the project, a common response is, "Everyone tells me it's going all right." This leaves senior management with no sense of the project's progress.

Although this tactic may result in less anxiety in the short term, managers cannot effectively manage if they are not directly involved with the project. This does not mean or imply that the managers must be actually performing and/or reviewing the work. But they must be involved and must establish a presence with the project team.

IS managers who simply walk around, observing work proceeding on a project, have a more concrete basis with which to make an evaluation. This technique is one way to avoid delegating the responsibility for the evaluation of results.

Managers may occasionally be criticized for being "Big Brother" (e.g., when they are out observing). But project teams quickly learn to recognize when a manager is truly fact finding for the good of the project, and not simply looking for mistakes. Clearly, project managers cannot be expected to examine each member's performance; that is why there is a hierarchy of management. Instead, managers should focus on monitoring and delivering key deliverables.

Quantifying the Work

The other aspect of project evaluation is the more analytical process of collecting counts of deliverables and time, comparing them with the plan, and assessing the project's status from these counts. This is the more quantitative aspect of evaluation work; the previous project review is more qualitative. However, both types are essential.

In the quantitative work, IS managers tend to react to the overall numbers without analyzing them. This causes the managers to focus on the symptoms rather than the underlying problem. The analysis should focus on whether variations arise out of volume, staffing, or estimate variances (e.g., unplanned activities, underestimated activities, shortfalls in staffing, and overestimated activities).

Variance Reporting

Volume variances often indicate that there is more work to be done in terms of units of design. Is the project's scope underestimated in this case? Is the trend a one-time blip or an ongoing problem? If it is an ongoing problem, can it be addressed? (For example, can the scope be trimmed?)

If the variance is due to a shortfall in staffing, it often means that IS management is not meeting its commitment to the project by arranging for adequate staffing. Again, managers have several options. Can temporary workers alleviate the problem? Does the lack of staffing reflect a changing commitment to the project by the organization? Finally, can the old standby of overtime work address the issue? If so, for how long?

Estimate variances present a more difficult problem. If the estimates used are proving unreliable, there is a tendency to say that the project plan as a whole is wrong and should be discarded. This is not desirable. In this case, IS management must be firm. The plan still states what needs to be done; the problem is with the time estimate. The correct reaction for managers is to adjust estimates and evaluate their impact, not to throw out the plan.

REVISING THE PLAN

Revising the plan constitutes a difficult task in the management cycle. Clearly, it is a mistake to change a systems project plan every time a variance arises. But it is also a mistake to cling resolutely to a plan that no longer has any relevance.

The most difficult aspect of revising a plan is finding the initiative to do so. In many cases, even when a project is behind schedule, IS management may have little inclination to act. In these cases, it often seems as if the perceived failure of the plan was a fulfillment of an unspoken wish by management.

The failure of the plan "proved" that there was no point in planning the systems project and that, as a result, there was no point in managing the effort. The downward spiral of planned results, actual results, and expectations seems to leave management in a state of relieved defeat. Or, even worse, it may lead to an effort to hide the actual project results.

This is clearly the path to disaster. The only advice for IS managers is to find the energy and creativity to overcome these problems. The scope of the change, and the amount of time that managers should devote to changing the plan, depend on the situation. Most often, due dates are fixed but budgets have a little more flexibility. Usually, there is also some flexibility in the type of system that is to be delivered to the users.

Staffing

In this context, IS managers dealing with a project that is behind the plan's schedule should first consider additional staffing. *The Mythical Man-Month*, perhaps the best book on the issues of software development (because it is based on the experience of failure), cautions against over-staffing a project. Certainly, employees simply thrown into the project often do not help. They may even push the project further behind. However, employees carefully selected for the project present different possibilities.

A key point in *The Mythical Man-Month* is that the management process of handling additional staff can break down. The solution is, first, to revise the plan to show the impact of additional employees and their roles before adding them to the project team. Then, bring them in and let them begin working on specific tasks according to the revised project plan.

Adding staff is just one technique. Another is to revise the level of the system's capability. Almost all project managers have altered a project's scope to meet scheduled dates. However, a reduction in scope represents a negative rather than a positive management action. The first critical factor controlling the successful management of scope to a date is the active commitment of the system users to the long-term value of the system versus the short-term capability delivered.

If a function is to be delayed, the expectations of the users must be managed. The users must have reason to trust IS management. That trust cannot be built during the last three months of a project, when management suddenly arrives to declare a problem. Trust is built by involving the system users throughout the project and helping them understand what is being done, where problems are coming up, and when the delays might begin to develop.

Most business users deal with changes and delays in their daily work. They can understand that the same types of problems arise daily in systems development. But IS managers must take the time to make the explanation intelligible to nontechnical professionals. Often, IS professionals want to hide problems from the users, and maybe from themselves. But doing so makes their jobs and the users' experience with systems development far more difficult and trying.

MANAGING RISK

The greater complexity of a client/server development project means greater risks, as well. These risks are organized and discussed in terms of the four-part systems management methodology illustrated in Exhibit III-2-1.

The risks are not necessarily unique to client/server development projects. But experience has shown that these risks can lead to failure of the project if they are not properly managed and addressed.

Information Planning Risks

Several risks need to be addressed when planning for the use and implementation of client/server technology.

Failure to Sponsor the Change. A client/server development project affects an organization at all levels. Change ripples through the organization, altering processes and the jobs of the people who perform them. The organization must have a champion or sponsor— beginning at the executive level—to promote the new client/server system and its effects. Without such a sponsor, the organization risks implementing a system and a solution that is resisted and not effectively used by its users.

Typically, this role is a full-time, participative role. Its purpose is to ensure understanding of the system and the solution with all affected individuals and at all appropriate levels of the organization (user, management, and IS). The initial champion, once established, can then be used to develop additional champions, who will be critical during later project phases. This process is sometimes referred to as the cascading sponsorship of change.

Extending Outside the Envelope of Technology. Because specific technologies change rapidly, it is generally best to limit an organization's scope to relatively stable and proven technologies. More important is to make sure that the organization is is driven by actual business needs, not simply technology that sounds innovative. For example, many companies invested in imaging technology but derived no benefit from it because their organizations were not primarily paper driven. A company should choose a technology path and pick the technologies and components that it wants to build on. It should plan for the obsolescence of technology and assume the company will be changing, growing, and upgrading. If it plans for change from the beginning, change is easier when the company has to implement it.

An organizaton must know its vendors and their products and establish relationships with them. In the world of client/server an organization may find itself dealing with many vendors and technology providers, and it is wise to involve them formally in the delivery of the company's solutions. Companies should beware of Beta products, which may be quirky and unreliable and not worth the time and effort. Quite often, it may be more desirable to go with a less capable product if the organization can at least be sure of its strengths and weaknesses.

An organization must understand the client/server technologies and techniques it wants to use. It is not wise to go outside or plan to go outside of what technology can do for the organization. The company must know the technologies it wants to work with and understand its business, its problems, and where it is trying to move the business. An organization must understand the characteristics of the business community to which it is delivering the technological solution. It must weigh and carefully analyze the costs of the technologies against the benefits to be derived from them.

Limited Experience With the Relevant Technologies. Any new technology or technique involves a learning curve for those designing and implementing it. An organization needs to be sure that it has adequately planned for training for all personnel involved with the project. It must beware of overconfidence: Client/server is not easier to learn or apply. Organizations must plan for extensive training programs. If possible, it is wise to use hands-on training to begin to build experience with the new technologies and techniques. To relieve the anxiety associated with learning and building new skills, the company should allow people to experiment and to make mistakes. It should use pilot or prototype projects to build skills early on and it should keep focused on skills.

Inadequate Project Planning. Many systems projects fail because of inadequate upfront planning and then a lack of tracking and revising that plan. New methods, discussed in the section "New Methodology Perspectives," must be used and followed in client/server development.

Even though organizations are striving to develop systems more rapidly and more iteratively, structure and planning are still necessary, as well as increased involvement across the organization, management, users, and the IS departments. New estimating models, metrics, and methodologies exist to help organizations begin their transition to client/server.

Above all, an organization must plan for change, not for stability. It must assume that all its assumptions will change and must constantly monitor and revisit those assumptions.

Systems Design Risks

Several risks need to be addressed during the design phase of client/server development.

Redoing the Old. Organizations will be making large investments in their client/server technologies. They must ensure that they are deriving new and improved business benefits, not merely automating the old ways of doing business. An organization should use external experts to check on its plans and designs to ensure that it is properly utilizing client/server and realizing the benefits it can and should provide. Everyone is susceptible to the problem of doing what worked before rather than doing things different and better.

Designing for the Future. A company must make sure that it is positioned, both from a business and a systems perspective, for the changes that accompany the client/server system. Developers must not just design for today; they must plan immediately for the transitions that their organization will make in the years to come. In short, an organization must strive to "future proof" its system to accommodate changes to both business and technology in the future. Future proofing can result if developers are careful to follow the model, emphasized several times in this book, that separates business function from the technology that supports that function. If a developer designs so that the technology itself becomes the point of the business, technological change may have adverse effects on the entire organization and business change may not be enabled.

Silver Bullet Solutions. There are no silver bullet or "canned" solutions in a client/server environment. Regardless of what the vendor community may advertise and communicate, client/server requires time and effort to implement effectively. An organization must be willing from the beginning to innovate, create, customize, and integrate the technological solution to fit its particular business needs.

A healthy approach is to look at all technology with a kind of skepticism, trying to understand its limits. Such information may be available from reference sites and from outside expertise. If an organization cannot determine where the limits are by information sources, it should plan on testing early to assess the limits.

New Methods, Tools, and Techniques. Client/server methods and tools are new and unfamiliar to many users, designers, and developers. For example, many organizations have trained and built skills around the mainframe environment, COBOL, CICS, DB/2. In the client/server world the language may be C, the database management system (DBMS) Oracle, and the transaction processing monitor Tuxedo. All require new skills and, more important, new methods to use successfully.

Many techniques are theoretically sound, but they may still be unproven in a real business environment, or still be incomplete and incapable of addressing all aspects of delivery. Developers must strive to pick the set of methods, tools, and techniques appropriate to their problem and their organization. In addition, establish design standards and program templates are required that immediately lead to consistency across developers.

Unstable Technology Providers. The definition of a stable technology vendor has changed dramatically in recent years. Indeed, it might be argued that there is no such thing as a stable vendor anymore.

But there are still at least degrees of stability at work in the marketplace, and organizations need to focus on how to make these vendors a part of the design team. They must be sure to execute clear and precise contracts with vendors that specify deliverables, time frames, costs, and quality of what the vendor will provide. They must build in options within the contract to upgrade or change the technology so they do not lock in to today's solutions at the expense of tomorrow's requirements.

Managing the Scope. As discussed previously, one of the risks is going outside the organization's "envelope" of technological competence. Monitoring the scope of the project to guard against overreaching is particularly important in the systems design phase of an organization's client/server development project. Organizations must be sure they can deliver what they promised with their available resources. They must constantly match their business requirements to their technologies and their resources.

An important aspect of managing scope during the design phase of a client/server project is to manage the expectations of management, IS, and the user community. The organization must involve the users at every point by making them a part of the design team. The organization must not make the traditional mistake of contacting the users only at the beginning and at the very end of a project.

Another scope management technique is for the organization to use functional prototyping as an aid to communicate what it is delivering. It must beware, however, of overdesign and overcommitment at the prototype stage. Occasionally, prototypes contain flashier features than the installed system can or will deliver, giving users false expectations of what the system will do. On the other hand, there is also the risk of underdesigning the system, and users will let the organization know about that at the prototype stage also.

Communication Barriers. With client/server, an organization is managing many different types of skills, technologies, and methods. These new aspects of client/server can lead to many problems if the project team is not well organized and communicating on a constant basis.

In traditional systems design, the technical and functional people were generally separated. With client/server, the organization should consider having them work together on teams at all levels, sharing knowledge and experiences. Generally, an organization should look for hands-on people. It wants personnel who will get involved with all aspects of the project, not those who "manage by managing." Also, the organization should look for people who will encourage and support the new team structures necessary to design and deliver a client/server system.

Increasing the skill base of an organization is an effective way not only to improve its ability to deliver but also to ensure that its people are speaking the same language.

Systems Installation Risks

An organization needs to identify and address several risks during the coding and testing of client/server systems.

Lack of Acceptance of the System. The risk at the end of installation is that no one will be there to accept the new system. Here, the fruits of cascading sponsorship should become apparent. Traditionally, change management experts have been called in only at the installation phase of a project, to assist with user training. However, the development of sponsors and champions is a change management effort that must begin early in the project life.

Acceptance of a client/server system depends, naturally, on its usability. Here the integrated performance support aspects of our execution architecture become crucial. Built-in help and navigation aids present a more natural or intuitive system to users, one that blends in well with their overall new job tasks. The system should adapt to its users, how they work and how they want to work. It should not require that the users adapt to it.

Inadequate Integration. With a client/server development project, an organization is often in the integration business, piecing together technologies, vendors, and business organizations into a single, integrated, deliverable solution. Achieving that end, however, is difficult and risky. Vendors and all third parties must be pulled in and made part of the team. An organization should build the infrastructure first (e.g., the architectures) and then build the solutions on top of that. Above all, it should test as early and often as possible.

Missing the Forest for the Trees. During implementation, it is easy to for an organization to become so immersed in details that it loses sight of the more important, overall objectives of the system. The organization must make sure it is doing regular quality assurance checks and bringing in experts from outside the project to check progress, plans, and results. It must ensure that an effective communications program, initiated earlier in the project, is still operating effectively during installation so that everyone understands the what, why, how, and when of the project.

Inadequate Site Preparation. The details of preparing the physical facilities for the new system must be addressed early in the project. Quite often client/server technology is being deployed to sites and locations that have never had to deal with technology before. The organization should use a phased rollout approach and stay close to the users at all times to ensure that they are using the new system correctly and that problems and concerns are identified and addressed as early as possible. (More information about site preparation and rollout is provided in Chapter III-11.)

Production Systems Support Risks

After the organization has converted and delivered new client/server systems, risks still remain that need to be addressed.

Coping With Ongoing Change. Support for the installed system involves reacting both to technology and to business change. The organization must continue to iterate. It must go back to earlier development activities—planning, design, implementation—to meet the new needs of the business or to take advantage of new, proven technology capabilities. Ongoing monitoring of the technology and of the business is vital. Migration and upgrades should be focused on real business benefit, not change for the sake of change.

Losing Touch With Users. User involvement is vital during the entire project. Sometimes, however, organizations neglect to capitalize on user feedback following installation and conversion of the system to assist in iterative development. A form of logging or tracking must be put in place to monitor what is going well and what is not going well from the users' point of view.

NEW METHODOLOGY PERSPECTIVES

The techniques, methodology, and practices required to deliver applications in a client/server environment are in most cases quite different from traditional approaches. The existing methodology for most IS organizations therefore require at least some changes and extensions to practices and deliverables to serve the needs of client/server projects. These changes are driven not by any specific technology platform, but by a change in the approach to developing and packaging applications and the need to apply new technologies to provide optimal solutions.

In general, client/server development efforts should be done in an iterative fashion, meaning that the business/application delivery components should be defined as a series of distinct, yet related functions that can be developed and delivered independently.

For example, the UniversalAir Airlines revenue accounting system (discussed in Chapter III-1 and later throughout several chapters) could be delivered as a set of accounting functions (e.g., basic accounting systems, interairlines receivables and payables, sales commissions, and auditing). This iterative development and delivery approach allows an organization to better manage the project(s), react more quickly to technology change, and, most important, react more quickly to business change.

The remainder of this section provides an overview of the major new and changed development activities in a client/server development environment. The development activities addressed here include the following:

- User involvement.
- Graphical user interface (GUI) development.
- Prototyping.
- Data architecture selection.
- Application architecture.
- Networking.
- Standards testing.
- Rollout.
- Operations support.

User Involvement

Because client/server application development is typically a part of the delivery of new (reengineered) business processes, it becomes increasingly important to involve real business users in the client/server development process.

Program and project management needs to identify and plan for the business users to actively participate in the solution development and delivery process. This participation should focus on having the users actually assigned to tasks and deliverables, while remembering that users are not systems developers. Typical activities for users can include business process design, prototyping, GUI design, testing, and acceptance testing. An added benefit of this user involvement is that typically these users return to their respective business organizations and become the champions for the new applications.

Graphical User Interface

The world of the GUI introduces new challenges to the applications development process. First, GUI programs are "event driven" as opposed to purely procedural. This means that GUI applications must be designed and developed to respond to events related to users, messages, and business changes. A conventional structure chart or flow diagram is insufficient for representing this type of program with these types of events.

Another important GUI issue to be addressed is the level of detail of the design. Because most programmers are unfamiliar with coding in this new environment, more detailed design documents and training are usually required. In order to properly design and deliver a GUI, new deliverables (e.g., control action response diagrams), new tools (e.g., window painters), and new techniques (e.g., prototyping) may be required to ensure successful delivery.

Prototyping

Prototyping becomes far more important in a client/server environment. For example, many users, even at this time have had little exposure to a GUI, so prototyping is a valuable activity early in the design process to gather user feedback on new business processes and new applications.

In addition, an organization might choose to prototype new business application capability (in addition to the user interface to that capability) early in the design process. This functional prototyping can be used to clarify and refine with users and management new business processing activities and the work flow supported by the new client/server applications. Finally, prototypes can also be used to educate and train users and management in the technologies and possibilities of the new world of client/server.

The major risk with prototyping is overselling the user; a prototype often looks and performs better than the actual implemented system does. The organization needs to ensure that the prototype emulates the targeted real-world environment and characteristics as much as possible. Additional time, effort, and complexity are necessary for preparing, installing, and utilizing a prototype within a client/server.

Data

In a client/server world, both the logical and physical aspects of delivering and managing data require changes. During the logical data design activity, time and effort must be allocated to ensure that the logical data deliverables properly reflect and support the new business process design and the data requirements of the system inputs and outputs (e.g., windows, reports). In addition, the logical data design activities should start to identify and address data sources and integration points with existing, installed systems.

Physical database design requires additional tasks and considerations (primarily in the physical DBMS design steps) to address the needs of workstation-based systems. The issues of distributed information and data, data replication, data synchronization, and the appropriate use of workstation and/or mid-tier DBMS products need to be addressed.

An appropriate physical database design and topology is crucial to the performance and integrity of the implemented system. Significant benefits are to be found in using innovative approaches, topologies, and products, but these opportunities are not without risk. There are also many relational database management system (RDBMS) products available with extended features not found in traditional environments.

The final data consideration relates to the objective of keeping data distinct from process. This objective typically leads to designing, coding, and testing data access logic separately from application or business function logic. Time and effort are required to develop the data access components and then to test those components with the related business functions that use the data.

Architecture Selection

Unlike traditional mainframe systems, which have limited and well-known alternatives, the client/server environment presents difficult choices in many hardware and systems software categories, including workstations, work group servers, bridges, routers, gateways, converters, development tools, DBMSs, user interface, and communications.

For example, there are numerous RDBMS vendors to be considered, each with its own strengths and weaknesses. In addition, the user interface software direction can be a major decision effort in itself. It is easy to identify three popular operating systems, three popular DBMSs, three popular network approaches, three hardware providers, and three development tools that might be considered for a client/server architecture. This simple example leads to 243 possible architectures, and the number could be far greater.

To complicate matters further, the pace of technology, competition, and product introductions and upgrades is staggering. A proper choice made today has a significant probability of being "leapfrogged" by its competition tomorrow. The variety of vendors and vendor offerings in the workstation marketplace, coupled with a general lack of experience with these products, combines to increase substantially the amount of time and effort needed to define, implement, and deliver a client/server architecture.

In summary, the good news with client/server is that it provides numerous architectural options. However, the bad news is that with these options, an organization must address the time and effort necessary to make technology decisions and choices. Therefore, activities must be planned early (and sometimes often) to perform architecture (technology) selections.

Application Architecture

In a client/server environment, processing can be divided between the client and the server in a number of ways. At one extreme is the front-end intensive way: The application runs almost entirely on the workstation using the back-end machine as a shared database server. At the other extreme is the back-end intensive way: The application runs almost entirely on the back-end machine, using the workstation as only an input/output presentation device. In between these two extremes is a wide variety of logic/processing allocation strategies.

Experience has shown that no single strategy, regardless of how conceptually pure it may seem, is truly appropriate for all application types. An application architecture framework and logic allocation guidelines must be defined and delivered early in a client/server development effort.

Technical Architecture. Identifying standard application module types in a client/server environment is substantially more difficult because of the wider variety of implementation options and new and unique application requirements. A natural friction exists between trying to identify and standardize on as few module types as possible and fully exploiting the client/server environment for each application. Using personnel without client/server implementation experience in this step can have grave consequences.

The system documentation requirements practice needs to be augmented not only to address the location of processing for a module (in the distributed computing sense) but also to provide guidelines for how, where, and why to break what was previously thought of as a single module across multiple processors.

The process of identifying utilities, functions, and common routines is also expanded in scope. The number of common routines rises significantly for the GUI and interapplication communications. The proper identification, early development, and management of these routines are crucial to installation productivity and application consistency.

An extensive set of common routines reduces application programmer training requirements as well as the amount of application code to be developed and tested. The design standards deliverable should be expanded to include technical architectural considerations in a client/server environment and should be language independent.

Networking

Network design and network management issues and considerations should be resolved early in the design process. With client/server, reliance on networks is greatly increased and, therefore, the importance of getting the network right increases. The following issues should be addressed early and continuously through the development process:

- Reliability.
- Fault processing.

- Rollback fallback (disaster recovery).
- Performance.
- Capacity planning.

Based on the complexity of developing a client/server application, system modeling should be performed before application development and implementation. A new practice and deliverables describing the steps required for distributed system modeling should be defined and executed.

Naming/Programming Standards

Given the pace of change, both technology and business, the need to train and retrain IS personnel, and the wish to standardize efforts, development standards become a key success factor in the delivery of client/server.

For example, the client/server environment supports a directory file structure that allows for flexibility in file, library, job (process), and data set names. Standards and guidelines should be developed or extended to address client/server file system and directory naming.

Activities need to be planned to allow for the creation, delivery, maintenance, and training in the use of appropriate client/server development standards. These standards should be additional practices or extensions to address the following activities:

- GUI design.
- Prototyping.
- Data naming.
- Testing.
- Coding.
- Quality file/directory naming.
- File/directory usage.
- Architecture usage.
- Test job classes (client/server test processes).
- Library naming conventions (library names and location).
- Database naming conventions (support for database-specific conventions).
- Data set naming conventions (client/server data file names and locations).
- Job classes (process and user classes).
- Directory structures (directory file structures for unit test, linkage test, system test, and integration test code; libraries; test data files; etc.).

The C programming language practice should be enhanced to provide a foundation of guidelines for all C programmers to follow. Additional future technologies and techniques such as object-oriented development, team-oriented applications, and multimedia applications (voice, video, image) also have an impact on client/server development methodologies. These subjects are discussed in subsequent chapters of this book.

Testing

Testing takes on an added dimension of complexity because of the distributed nature of client/server applications. Program-to-program communications, distributed data, and GUIs all present new testing requirements that are not well met by existing tools and techniques.

The following discussion describes additions and modifications to testing practices. In general, client/server applications require far more extensive testing than traditional centralized applications to ensure successful delivery and support.

The programming activity from a methodology perspective is largely unchanged. However, the definition of unit test in the client/server environment is somewhat ambiguous. It has proven difficult to unit-test a client/server workstation program that relies heavily on frequent interchange with a host computer (for data, perhaps). The use of stubs involves a substantial amount of extraneous code development because of the frequency of interaction. Extensions should be made to the unit-testing practice to account for client/server considerations. This may affect the following deliverables:

- Common unit-test scenarios.
- Unit-test scripts.
- Unit-test scenarios.
- Unit-test cases and databases.

Developers may note an increase in program bugs discovered at integration or linkage test. These linkage-test tasks typically take much longer to complete for client/server workstation-based systems. The additional time needed is traceable to three factors:

- An increased number of components to integrate (each smaller in size).
- The frequency of interaction among components.
- The complexity of intermachine communications.

In addition, the verification of results for GUI applications has proved to be both time- and resource-consuming. Extensions should be made to the linkage-testing practice to account for client/server considerations. This may affect the following deliverables:

- Linkage-test scripts.
- Linkage-test scenarios.
- Linkage-test cases and databases.

Stress and volume testing become more complex because of the distributed nature of the client/server target applications. Stress and volume testing should be performed on each target environment and across the network. In addition, benchmarking must be performed at various levels—at each workstation, at each server, and across the network.

The following deliverables use the stress and volume testing practice extensions:

- Stress and volume test scripts.
- Stress and volume test scenarios.
- Stress and volume test cases and databases.

Rollout

The final major activity related to the successful delivery of client/server solutions is often rolling out the technology, support structures, training, and applications to the organization. This often is a new concept and activity for most organizations. Many activities and deliverables are associated with site preparation and rollout.

Rollout is the major activity that brings everything else together before going live with the system. Everything includes the technologies (e.g., workstations, servers, networks, and DBMSs), the new business processes and procedures, the new applications, the new support organization, the new support procedures, and the newly trained users. In summary, it is a new business.

Activities and deliverables that address the integration of the aforementioned components and the final verification that all is well with those components prior to declaring a new system live must be planned for within the client/server development and delivery process.

Operations Support

Client/server applications by their very nature tend to be more distributed, the number of intelligent devices in the network increases, and it becomes increasingly more difficult to identify and resolve system discrepancies. As a result of these issues, several aspects of system operations and support become more important and more complex. Areas that need to be addressed through practices and procedures include the following:

- Distributed software and data synchronization.
- Application support.
- System fault identification and resolution.
- Hardware operations and maintenance.
- Ongoing vendor and contract management.
- Network management.
- Release management and coordination.

PLANNING A CLIENT/SERVER PROJECT

Planning and estimating a client/server development project can be particularly challenging. Client/server technology is relatively new. A different planning approach is necessary for such client/server development activities as GUI design and development, data distribution, and process distribution.

The GUI and multiplatform characteristics of client/server architectures tend to result in programming work units that are more modular and more granular than conventional applications. The units also tend to be distributed throughout the network, which in turn creates more complex testing requirements.

In addition, a stable, historical estimating base for client/server may not yet exist, so it is critical that all estimates be sufficiently reviewed by personnel who have experience with similar development efforts and technologies.

The planning dimension of a client/server development project has specific objectives:

- To achieve consensus among the project team, users, and management about the objectives, scope, costs, and approach to the project.
- To develop a common framework against which the project will proceed and be managed.
- To put in place the mechanisms necessary to manage the project and control and monitor its progress.
- To organize, assemble, and enable a skilled project team.
- To obtain management's commitment and approval to begin the core development and infrastructure activities.

Project Organization

Appropriate project organization is fundamental to effective project management and execution. Project organization encompasses the planning,

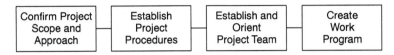

Exhibit III-2-2. Project Organization

structure, and control processes that must be in place for the project to succeed. Project organization can be divided into four phases, as shown in Exhibit III-2-2:

- *Confirm project scope and approach.* This task enables the project team, users, and management to achieve consensus on the goals of the project (e.g., deliverables or schedule). The project manager establishes the project advisory structure to provide direction and sponsorship to the project. This includes confirming the project's scope, objectives, and assumptions. The next step is to develop the project's going-in design assumptions, specifically the conceptual functional design, technical design, and implementation plan. A high-level work plan, organizational structure, and preliminary project timetable are created. It is important to obtain user, IS, and management's commitment to support and participate in the project.

- *Establish project procedures.* This task addresses the implementation of project control standards, procedures, and systems to ensure an effective and efficient approach to completing work. Mechanisms are established for status and time reporting, user review and sign-off, issue resolution, scope control, and project communications. Then the team develops automated (or manual) project control systems to support these procedures and other administrative needs. Also, the team must establish sufficient project work space and facilities.

- *Establish and orient project team.* This task involves identification of project team structure, roles, and skill requirements, and organization of the resources needed to fill the roles. The project team structure must be appropriate for the type of work being performed, the organizational considerations, and the degrees of risk. Project management must finalize the skill and experience requirements and secure the needed personnel. An orientation package should be prepared for the project team to provide the project's background and objectives. It is important to orient team members to both the project and their specific roles and responsibilities.

- *Create work program.* This task involves the finalization of the project plans and the assignment of project team members to specific tasks. Project management must finalize the project's work activities, and define the experience and skill levels needed to perform those activities. The project management function identifies the work packages and workday budgets associated with each activity and then assigns specific individuals to the roles and tasks. Work loads should then be balanced and the due dates finalized for each task. Management's approval and commitment to the final project plans must be obtained.

Project Scope

Confirming and controlling scope are crucial to the success of a client/server project. Given the new tools, techniques, and project organizations, it is easy to continuously add new business functions and/or technical capabilities during design and prototyping activities and then never get to actual implementation. Work performed outside scope may be inconsistent with management and user expectations and can cause schedule delays and budget overruns. Management must approve the defined scope, and the entire team must understand that scope and adhere to it.

A crucial component of managing scope is to put in place the project advisory structure: typically a management advisory committee, a steering committee, and a project sponsor. These groups are responsible for providing overall direction to the project and for championing it throughout the corporate organization. No decisions about the project's scope and approach should be made until these groups are established.

Specifically, the management advisory committee is composed of an organization's senior executives who are going to be impacted by the client/server project. This committee is responsible for understanding the overall scope of the project, the development approach to be undertaken, and the impact of the new system to ensure that the entire organization is committed to success and is ready for the change. The steering committee is composed of management representatives from each department or group affected by the new system. The steering committee is responsible for overseeing the detailed project status, scope, and approach. This committee also assists the project management team with addressing and resolving and project-level issues. Finally, the project sponsor should be the overall champion for the project, responsible for delivering quality and success.

By setting scope, an organization establishes boundaries for what the project is to address. This creates a clear picture not only of the target system but also of the responsibilities and constraints faced by the project team and the entire organization. For this reason, no significant project activities should be undertaken until management has confirmed the scope and approach.

Defining the Scope. Defining scope for a client/server project involves identifying and understanding:

- Business and project objectives.
- Business benefits to be achieved.
- Specific business functions to be implemented.
- Key project success factors and success measures.
- User constituencies and specific user locations involved.
- Activities to be performed by the project team.
- Overall schedule.
- Expected results in terms of work packages and deliverables.
- Extent of personnel involvement from all required organizational units.

The level, depth, and detail of the project scope definition vary depending on the phase of the project:

- During information planning, the scope is very broad, outlining the high-level business areas to be addressed and the project's overall constraints.
- During systems design, the scope defines the project's overall size and the specific functional and technical functions, features, and assumptions.
- During systems installation, the functional and technical scope is fairly well defined, based on the results of the systems design phase. The focus of the scope is more on the project team's responsibilities and on the amount of work required to test and convert the system. In addition, if the implementation represents a subset of a more comprehensive design (a particular release of the system), the scope defines, for example, which functions, locations, and interfaces are to be implemented during this project phase. The initial definition of project scope is subject to revision and may not be finalized until the detailed work effort estimates are complete. As the work plan is developed in more detail, assumptions about project goals and required resources may change. Therefore, the scope should be outlined in as much detail as possible, including all functional, technical, and architectural assumptions. Once the final scope and approach are approved at the conclusion of project organization, subsequent changes to scope should be controlled through mechanisms

such as change request management (change control) and business case management.

Defining the Project Approach. The project approach differs from the scope in that it outlines how the work is to be done rather than what particular work is to be done. The initial approach is stated in broad terms, focusing on items such as the specific methodology and methods to be used, the high-level work segments, the development environment to be used, the work locations, the high-level project organization structure, the project time line, and sign-off procedures.

The approach should also contain a set of assumptions. A scope-and-approach memorandum can document the approach and add further detail as part of the work-planning step during each client/server development phase.

Developing the Work Plan. After confirming the project scope and approach, project managers should develop the work plan, a high-level staffing plan, and the preliminary project timetable. These plans may have been prepared in the previous phase or as part of the project approval process. Nevertheless, they should be reviewed and refined in light of any changes to the current project scope or approach.

The work plan breaks down the confirmed project approach into greater detail. It identifies the segments, tasks, and steps to be performed; the type of work packages, work objects, and deliverables to be produced; the estimated effort; and the key completion dates.

The work plan should be defined at a sufficient level of detail for work to be accurately estimated, scheduled, assigned, managed, and controlled. The work plan's organization should facilitate administration and reporting requirements for both project management and the organization's management. It should highlight major milestones and deliverables that can be precisely defined and easily verified, such as completion of source code or approval of unit-test results. Project management should use these milestones and their associated completion dates as a basis for sequencing tasks and for specifying which tasks occur concurrently or which tasks must occur sequentially. Project management should define a common set of estimating factors and carefully review the estimating assumptions for each activity.

On larger projects, a single project manager may not be able to perform all the work plan development activities. In such cases, project management should develop the overall work plan structure and then give individual team leaders the responsibility to develop detailed work plans for each project area.

Project management must ensure that the structure of these work plans corresponds to that of the overall work plan, and that team leaders use a common set of assumptions and guidelines. It must ensure that the team leaders fully understand each step of the work plan, and that they are prepared to take ownership of their estimates.

The project manager should carefully review the overall project work plan for completeness, appropriateness, and reasonableness.

Simply put, project managers should assume the following jobs: Verify that the work plan properly reflects the defined scope and approach. Ensure that project management, supervisory, support, and user activities are adequately identified and estimated. Recognize that a greater percentage of time is required to support these activities on larger projects, or projects that are complex in terms of technology and/or business functionality, especially when multiple levels of project management are required. Allow enough time to establish and maintain communication between the various management levels and project areas and/or teams. Recognize that additional elapsed time may be required between the identification of a problem and its resolution.

Additional effort may be needed to communicate information to a large project team. A significant amount of time must also be allotted for meetings between the various levels of project management and across the various project areas.

For these reasons, project management should develop the project organizational structure in conjunction with the work plans, identify the various project teams and determine the appropriate levels of supervision and support, and use the organizational structure to confirm that the task budgets are adequately accommodated.

Staffing Plan. The staffing plan describes the high-level organizational structure and identifies the skills, roles, responsibilities, and number of personnel required for the project. Project management should prepare the staffing plan in conjunction with the work plan and project timetable. Project management should propose initial start and end dates for each segment and then determine the skill requirements and number of personnel for each segment. This information should be consolidated to create an overall loading of personnel, by skill classification, over time (by week or month, depending on the overall duration of the phase). Project management should adjust the task and segment durations as necessary to balance the staffing levels, taking into account:

- Dependencies among the activities.
- Reasonable ramp-up, ramp-down and peak staffing levels.
- Effects of learning curve issues and training on staffing rate.
- Effect of any intended piloting on staffing rate.

- Available staffing resources.

The results of the staffing plan activity can be documented in the following forms:

- A preliminary organization chart, identifying the intended project team structure, proposed project team members, and project management levels.
- A bar chart, showing the segment durations and the anticipated staffing levels for the work segments by category, over time.
- A set of skill requirements, defining each skill category and identifying the specific experience levels and skill sets required for each.

Project managers must be sure to consider the requirements for user and support personnel when creating the staffing plans. They should focus the staffing plan on the current phase of work but also prepare a projected staffing plan for subsequent project phases. This is necessary to ensure the continued reasonableness of the overall system delivery plan.

An approximation of the work effort for the subsequent phases should have been prepared as part of the previous phase or as part of the current planning effort. They should prepare a high-level loading of personnel to correspond with these efforts. They must analyze this long-term staffing plan, considering the following:

- Is the ramp-up of personnel from the end of this phase to the beginning of the next phase reasonable?
- Is the peak personnel level of the subsequent phase manageable, in terms of total numbers, ramp-up and ramp-down, available skill base, work space capacity, and technical capacity?

If a long-term staffing plan is not feasible, developers should work with management to address the issue here rather than at the onset of the next phase. They should consider such techniques as the following:

- Accelerating the duration of the current phase to meet the overall target end date.
- Reducing the project scope.
- Adopting a revised approach (e.g., using applications software packages or available technical architectures).
- Implementing the system in multiple releases.

Obtaining User Commitment. The staffing plan should indicate the user staffing and user skill levels required to successfully deliver the system. Project managers should work with the project sponsor and user management to achieve agreement on the project's resource requirements and time frames and obtain their commitment to provide the resources in accordance with those requirements. It is not necessary to identify the individual user participants at this time. As with the IS team members, the final project organization and staffing occur in a subsequent project organization activity.

To facilitate the process of obtaining user commitment, project managers should supplement the staffing plan by representing user skill requirements in terms of level, position, and functional area of expertise. They can further assist the process by specifying what each class of user representatives is expected to do, that is, the tasks in which they will participate and the types of work package they will produce.

Although some of these details do not become finalized until the project work programs are completed, it is important to provide as much detail as possible at the start. This provides a rationale as to why the user resources are required, and it helps user management to understand the necessary qualifications so they can begin identifying specific candidates. This educational process is particularly important in organizations in which the users have not typically been involved in systems development projects. User involvement, commitment, and ownership are key success factors for delivering client/server solutions that enable business change.

Project managers should strive to set proper user expectations. They should forecast total user requirements and set realistic targets as to when the resources will be needed and when the user resource involvement will be concluded. Some users may participate part-time, depending on the work segment; other project team members are typically involved on a full-time basis. In other cases, users may be required on an ad hoc, as-needed basis.

Typically, the largest user involvement is during the systems design phase and during the system test activities in the systems installation phase. Project management should work with the project sponsor and other members of user management to determine the most appropriate method of participation from the standpoint of both the project development team and the supplying user organizations.

Creating a Risk Management Plan. Planning activities associated with project risk management typically expose areas of potential risk to the development effort. (See the section "Managing Risk" for more discussion of risk in a client/server development project.) Each project manager or team leader should prepare a risk memorandum for their area of responsibility, identifying the specific risk areas and proposing risk mitigation and management strategies for each risk. If the project is large enough to require the development of multiple memoranda, they should prepare an overall consolidated risk memorandum for the entire project, and reference the more detailed risk assessments as necessary.

Developers should consider the following key potential risk areas when preparing the risk management plan:

- *Impact.* Will the system being developed affect the company's main business functions? How significantly will it affect the users' daily operations? Are external customers or other public entities affected? Are the scheduled completion dates absolutely fixed, or are they flexible enough to accommodate unforeseen delays or changes?

- *Acceptance.* Has a true business case been made for the system? Are the users, management, and rank-and-file committed to the project and willing to support the resulting changes to their operations? Have the user organizations committed resources to sponsor and support the systems development effort?

- *Project plans.* Are the project plans reasonable, and do they contain adequate cost and schedule contingencies? How significant is the critical path and the overlap among work segments? Has the project been estimated based on historical experience within the current environment? Have the project plans been reviewed by experienced client/server project managers and developers?

- *Organization.* Has the project management team been assembled, and does it possess the right qualifications in terms of experience level and skills? Have the project team skill sets been identified, and can they be obtained? Is there an adequate level of management, supervision and support? Will there be a need to coordinate with a significant number of organizations, both third parties and other corporate departments?

- *Innovation.* Are the following project aspects consistent with the experience of the organization's systems and user personnel: project magnitude, project approach, development time frame, development environment and tools, technical architecture, and the use of proven, stable technologies?

Establishing Project Procedures

The objectives of establishing project procedures are as follows:

- Improve project communication, control, and efficiency.
- Establish a method of evaluating the project's progress.
- Ensure effective and efficient work practices and procedures.
- Promote quality and improve the ability to manage risk.

- Establish a standard framework for managing and executing the project.

Technical standards improve the quality and effectiveness of the design and development process. In the same way, project procedures and administrative and control standards improve project operations and communication, both inside and outside the project team.

To improve communication, operating efficiency and overall control of systems development projects, developers should establish standards and procedures early on. They should develop policies and procedures to address the key project control functions, including:

- Time reporting for all project team members.
- Status reporting at all appropriate levels (individual, team, project).
- Issue management (tracking, monitoring, resolution).
- Scope control and management of scope change management.
- User sign-off.
- Documentation control and management.
- Personnel management.
- Vendor and contract administration.
- Project communications.

Developers should determine the requirements for managing each of these aspects of the project and develop corresponding standards (written, communicated, and understood) describing how the project team should perform these functions and how management should control them. Obtain the consensus of project management on these standards and then include them in the project orientation material and initial project team training to ensure that all team members are aware of and understand the relevant procedures.

The larger the project and the higher the risk it carries, the more critical these standards and procedures are. Projects with tight time frames or multiple physical locations also require increased emphasis in this area. Developers should tailor the detail and formalization of these procedures to the needs and the culture of the project but ensure that each area is adequately addressed.

Establishing and Orienting the Project Team

The objectives of establishing and orienting the project team activity are to do the following:

- Finalize the detailed project organization structure and assemble a skilled team.

393

- Orient the project team to the project organization, objectives, background, scope, approach, expected outputs, and standards.
- Ensure that the project team members understand their roles, responsibilities, and performance expectations.
- Introduce all the project team members to each other.

The primary activity here is to develop a plan for orienting project members to the project's history, purpose, vision, goals, objectives, methodology, scope, organization, standards, business applications, technical environment, and industry background. Team members need general orientation to the project as well as a specific orientation to their team, their role and responsibilities, and their relationship to overall organizational structure. Orientation should excite and enthuse the team members and inspire them to take ownership in the project. A productive orientation process requires structure, commitment, and leadership.

Developers must structure an orientation program that can both launch the project and also accommodate new team members who join the project later in the phase. They can use the orientation package and training as the primary focus and supplement it with any additional material specific to the target audience.

Orientation may also address new techniques, new technologies, approaches, and architectures. Developers should provide project personnel with a sufficient understanding of the basic domain concepts of the project. The domain concepts form the project vocabulary and are indicative of the way the team members may organize and perform their work and communicate results and status. Domain concepts may include technical terms, acronyms, abbreviations, and buzzwords. These concepts may be standard within the industry or specific to the organization.

Depending on the size of the project, and on whether the team members arrive in groups or in a more staggered fashion, orientation sessions may be either formal or ad hoc. In formal sessions, the project manager or a senior project member may address the group to present the project overview and to answer questions. Alternatively, the team members may read through the orientation material in a less structured manner, asking questions of their supervisor as they arise.

Early in the orientation process, team members should be individually briefed on roles and responsibilities by their targeted supervisor. Their duties and deliverables should be placed in the context of the project as a whole. This helps to give them direction and focus throughout the rest of the orientation and their participation on the project.

As part of the overall orientation process, team members should be introduced to the project methodology and development environment. This training occurs as part of the development environment preparation activity. As necessary, developers should provide technical training in specific tools, programming languages, and basic techniques. They should educate the team members about the methodology and work objects that will be used and describe the relevant project, technical, and documentation standards they are be expected to follow. They must recognize that although the orientation process may take only a few days, significant lead time may be necessary to complete the technical training, especially if the project involves significant technical innovation and customized architectures.

After orientation, team members should have an understanding of the project and what is expected of them. Team members must understand their specific responsibilities, whom they will interact with and report to, and how their performances will be monitored and evaluated.

After the initial orientation training, periodic briefing sessions should continue to reinforce training concepts and describe lessons learned, what to expect next, and how the work objects created in earlier stages will be used.

Creating the Work Program

The activity of creating the work program has the following objectives:

- Translating the work plan into a specific assignment of tasks, budgets, and deadlines.
- Confirming the feasibility of the project work plans and address any issues or modifications.
- Balancing the work load sufficiently to maximize the effectiveness of project team members and minimize the project risk.
- Developing a means for adhering to the project scope and objectives and for monitoring and controlling the project's progress
- Receiving management's approval to begin the development activities.

This phase begins by refining the work plan, developed earlier, into a work program by further detailing the tasks and budgets, by assigning specific project personnel to tasks, and by defining specific start and end dates for tasks. The work program can then be used to monitor and control the project's activities throughout the life of the project. It serves as a tool for examining the project's progress and adherence to deadlines, and helps to ensure that the work load is properly balanced and distributed among project personnel. It identifies all tasks to be accomplished during the project, and reveals all work packages, deliverables, due dates, and personnel requirements.

Detailing Tasks and Budgets. The usefulness of the work program depends on the accuracy of the workday estimates. The program should also be detailed enough to allow prompt recognition of deviations from schedule and budget. As necessary, developers can further break down work tasks into steps (lower-level activities) or work packages (groupings of work objects to be produced or acted up).

A general guideline is that no individually scheduled task or work package should take longer than two weeks to complete. Developers should identify intermediate milestones for longer tasks to better monitor and manage their progress. When tasks are broad in scope, such as the programming activity, developers should make assignments at the work package (programming work unit) level.

To the extent possible, developers should consider shifting more time toward the analysis and design activities. Well-thought-out and -documented designs improve the efficiency of the implementation tasks and significantly reduce the amount of rework. It is also more cost- and time-effective to detect and correct errors or misunderstandings in design now than later in the development process.

When finalizing budgets and schedules, developers must consider the effects of the learning curve. Adjusting the duration of a segment due to training and learning curve issues may change the number of team members needed to perform a task.

Because each team member may have a learning curve, the size of the team may dictate how much time is budgeted for learning curve. Carefully consider the one-time learning curve that task supervisors and the project team as a whole may experience (especially when pioneering a new technique or technology), as well as the individual learning curves that may be experienced by each team member performing the task.

The following options may help to control the extent of individual learning curves: using personnel with more skills, teaming unskilled personnel with more skilled personnel, piloting the process first to reduce the impact of the projectwide learning curve, or extending the time frame of the task to reduce the total number of people experiencing learning curve effects.

Contingency in the work program should be included by allocating time and resource capacity explicitly for the unexpected, such as for correcting problems or deficiencies identified during a review. Developers should not assign the contingency to individuals or tasks but, rather, should keep it as a separate item to offset unplanned variances across any and all project activities. If contingency was not previously identified, or if it was not sufficient to cover the risk areas, developers should consider reducing some of the task budgets slightly to create some additional contingency budget.

Developers should not perform a significant amount of detailed planning for tasks more than two to four months into the future as changes over time inevitably cause rework to these long-term plans. Instead, developers should maintain a rolling two- to four-month detailed planning horizon and update the detailed plans.

Balancing the Work Load. As the detailed work program is prepared, it may become evident that the available resources are inadequate or that there is a surplus of certain resources at various stages. Developers should adjust the activity durations, activity relationships, or staffing levels as necessary to create a balanced schedule. They must be sure to inform management of any significant adjustments to the original plan because changes can affect the critical path as well as the requirements for work space and support resources.

Balancing the work load should be driven by the work package-oriented tasks—those tasks that produce the project work objects and deliverables. Once they schedule these tasks, developers should fill in the corresponding elapsed time-oriented support tasks, such as programming supervision, technical support, and project management.

For these tasks, developers should determine the appropriate staffing level to support the related tasks and load their resources accordingly. Then they should check the total resource allocation against the budgets and organizational charts in the original work plans and reconcile deviations by adjusting the durations of the work package-oriented tasks or by adjusting the support levels of the elapsed time-oriented tasks. If the support resources are still insufficient, systems developers must alert management and determine whether adjustments can be made to the overall project plans.

The final balancing of the schedule occurs when the staffing plan is broken down into greater detail, resulting in the staffing schedule. Developers should assign specific individuals to the roles identified in the staffing plan and then compare the staffing schedule to the work program to ensure all staffing requirements are fulfilled and that all tasks are assigned. If specific individuals have not been identified for all positions, especially those that will not be staffed until later in the phase, developers should assign placeholder names (such as Programmer1 and Analyst 2).

Developers should load in specific holidays, vacations, training commitments, and other non-project-related activities for each team member. If this information is not yet known, they should assume a less than 100% availability (typically no more than 85%) to accommodate the inevitable time away from the project. Failure to do this produces an unrealistic staffing plan and is likely to result in excessive overtime or missed deadlines.

For each team on the project, developers should create a revised organizational chart that corresponds to the staffing schedule. Developers should identify reporting relationships and project start and end dates, if applicable. If the organizational charts are likely to change significantly throughout the phase, developers should produce separate charts for each significant activity (e.g., detailed design, programming, and system test).

Finalizing the Schedule. Developers should use the balanced work load and detailed staffing plan to assign specific start and end dates for each task performed by each team member. Developers should consolidate these to produce overall start and end dates for all project segments and tasks. To allow for more efficient management, all start and end dates should be scheduled by week (e.g., all dates should be assigned to either Mondays or Fridays).

Similarly, developers should create a detailed schedule for all project work packages. Often these work packages have been identified as the lowest-level tasks on the work program. If specific work packages are not identified, developers should create a separate schedule to indicate the number and type of work packages expected by person and by week.

Coordinating Multiple Work Programs. If the project consists of multiple applications and project teams, each manager or team leader may develop their own work program. Just as they are being balanced individually, they will also have to be balanced against each other. Developers should Ensure that activity and task schedules are consistent across teams, that the overall critical path and dependencies are maintained, and that the projectwide support tasks, such as technical support and project management, are properly staffed.

Consider the staffing plans for each team, as well as the need to move resources from one activity to another over time. Additional adjustments to individual work programs and staffing schedules may be necessary to smooth the overall consolidated project loadings.

Obtaining Management Review and Approval. Finally, developers must obtain approval of the final work program, project organization, and overall timetable from the steering committee, project sponsor, and other applicable user and IS management. If the detailed work planning process resulted in changes to the project scope, approach, or assumptions, these should be highlighted. If costs have changed significantly, approval by the management advisory committee may also be required.

Developers should update the project scope-and- approach memorandum and any other relevant going-in design objects. These plans and objects now become the baseline for scope management and serve to confirm the agreement between the project team and the system's sponsors.

MANAGING A CLIENT/SERVER PROJECT

The ultimate goal of effective project management is to ensure the delivery of a high-quality system that meets user requirements and is completed on schedule and within the approved budget. This goal contains inherent conflicts, however, which project management must resolve.

Although the guidelines and tasks of project management address techniques to effectively control most projects, each project has unique characteristics that may reduce or enhance the effectiveness of those techniques. The management process must constantly weigh trade-offs between schedule, budget, available resources, capability, user satisfaction, and quality. It is critical that in assigning priorities, project management is guided by the business case and by quality requirements.

Guidelines for Project Management

The degree of project management required is directly related to the size of the project and to the associated risks. For large, high-risk projects, several full-time project management personnel and possibly a separate team may function as support for some of the management activities. On smaller projects, a single project manager may bear these responsibilities or they may be distributed across the project teams. For example, the business systems development team leader might maintain the user relationships while the architecture team leader manages the vendor relationships.

Senior project management personnel and the project's primary team leaders perform the majority of project management activities. However, some work, particularly within the time tracking and issue tracking activities, may be delegated to administrative support personnel.

Project management personnel should have a project management background as opposed to a line management background. They should be driven by goals and products and possess a thorough understanding of the project methodology. Project managers need a mix of functional and technical skills. They do not have to be experts in either area, but they must be able to understand the issues and know where to go to find the necessary detailed information. In addition, they need a clear understanding of the approaches and techniques to be used. The more innovative the project and the higher the risk, the more critical it is to have experienced project management personnel.

A full-time manager can typically manage the activities of six direct reports. On projects of five team members or fewer, the project manager (or team leader) can perform administrative responsibilities as well as some of the core process tasks. When there are more than six members on a project (or team), project management should establish subteams, each with its own supervisor or team leader.

Managing and Reevaluating the Process. The key challenge of project management is to think ahead, anticipating potential problem areas. One way this can be done is to monitor the development process continually for areas of inefficiency, poor productivity, misestimated activities, inappropriately defined requirements, misunderstandings, or insufficient training.

In addition to individual performance indicators, project management must look for trends that might indicate a need to streamline the process. When they identify such a need, supplemental training and the involvement of outside experts or vendor personnel can often improve performance. At other times, it may be necessary to pilot a new process, or to pilot an old process in a new environment. This can help people to understand the process better and to work out any problems in a controlled setting before the majority of the project team embarks on the task, thus streamlining the process, building skills, and reducing the learning curves. Prototyping and early architecture development are important, as are the ongoing reviews of the project standards to ensure that they are, in fact, meeting the overall business and project objectives.

Although it is important to minimize the disruption caused by changing the process or standards midstream, this is sometimes justified if the change avoids more costly problems that would otherwise occur later.

Managing Multilocation Projects. If the project team is in more than one location, project management is more difficult and requires a far greater amount of effort. The problem increases along with the degree of separation. different areas on the same floor, different floors in the same building, different locations in the same city, or multiple geographic locations. The greater the distance, the greater the need for formal communication mechanisms and for additional coordination and management time.

Technology can help with this problem in a variety of ways. Electronic design repositories and electronic mail systems can be connected via local or wide area networks. Facsimile machines can transmit other types of documents instantly. Audioconferences allow people in multiple locations to participate in the same meeting. Videoconferences, which can extend those capabilities to allow face-to-face and image communication, are an effective and cost-effective way of performing long-distance design reviews.

A company can overcome the problems of distance by exploiting technology to the extent possible, but it must recognize that additional time is necessary for a more formal coordination between locations. The organization must recognize, too, that standards and written communications assume a heightened importance because they ensure that team members in all locations are working consistently.

For critical tasks, such as the start of programming or the end of system test, the organization should consider relocating some individuals so that groups that must work together closely are physically coresident. For example, the organization should consider placing on-site technical support personnel with the programming teams and on-site technical support and user personnel with the system test execution teams.

Issue Tracking and Scope Control. Rigorous issue tracking and scope control are keys to successful project management. Formally tracking issues and open points helps to control the analysis and design process by maintaining documentation of all issues and their resolutions.

In addition to tracking, project management must also help to facilitate the resolution process by setting forth a procedure to review, act on, and resolve issues in a timely manner. By circulating issue documentation to all affected parties, management can minimize the risk of misunderstandings being detected later, during detailed design, programming, and systems testing. In addition, the issue documentation serves as an audit trail to justify future design and implementation decisions.

Similarly, formally tracking change requests helps to improve communication between developers and users and to eliminate misunderstandings in later stages of the project. By documenting all potential scope changes and enhancements in the form of change requests, the project team can continue to meet deadlines without the users feeling their requests have been ignored. This process also ensures that management can allow for the prioritization and incorporation of these changes after thorough analysis of the business benefits and of the resulting effects on the project's cost and schedule. It allows for justifiable changes to be made, with less critical requests deferred until future enhancement releases. This approach keeps the project on the course set out by management and ensures users that their requests are are being addressed and not disregarded.

User Sign-Off. User understanding, acceptance, and approval are critical to the success of any systems development project. An organization must be sure to obtain user and management commitment in the early stages and to identify and obtain the participation of key individuals from the affected user departments. The organization should define a formal sign-off process that ensures documented feedback and approval on the system scope, system schedule, system designs, issue resolutions, system test plans and results, and conversion plans.

The organization should educate user participants and management about the importance of their input and stress the importance of timely participation and feedback. It should consider setting up default approval guidelines to ensure that the project does not fall behind due to the inability of users to provide timely review. For instance, the default might stipulate that all designs not receiving feedback within five business days are assumed to be approved.

Specific development techniques, particularly prototyping and joint application design (JAD), can also contribute to effective user approval of the system design. Prototyping allows users to see, touch, and experience the system early in the development process and to review it more naturally than by inferring it from abstract or technical documentation. Similarly, JAD provides a forum designed to build immediate consensus. Concentrating all the key stakeholders on a design or issue at the same time helps to develop a common understanding and approach and to achieve a high-quality, workable solution.

Quality Management. Project managers should ensure that an effective quality management process is in place and is followed. Qualified quality reviewers with experience in similar project management, functional, and technical environments should be identified during project organization and should participate throughout the life of the project. They should schedule and conduct quality reviews on a regular basis. The frequency of the reviews should be commensurate with the duration and risk of the project. Project management should ensure that the project team is prepared for the reviews, that the reviewers document their findings in a timely fashion, and that the project team follows up on any identified review points.

The organization should encourage project managers and team leaders to further benefit from the quality plan by frequently consulting the quality management documentation when planning and executing tasks, as this makes the quality program a more proactive part of the management process.

Design Issues vs. Change Requests. Another management challenge during the systems design phase is to distinguish issues from change requests. Management should address this challenge by defining scope as specifically as possible early in the systems design process.

Project managers should prepare a complete list of the functions, features, and interfaces that the system requires, as well as a list of the assumptions about the technical environment. They should estimate the counts for each key system component (e.g., dialogs, windows, screens, and reports), being as specific as possible (three customer service dialogs, two sales dialogs). The more precisely program managers state the scope, the easier it is to distinguish between design decisions that fall inside, or outside, the approved scope.

An organization should consider budgeting a contingency to cover the inevitable omissions. This will allow the critical change requests to be approved without requiring further project funding authorization.

Scope control becomes particularly important during prototyping tasks, especially when working in a newer environment such as the world of GUIs. During prototyping tasks, project management must guard against overdesigning, overimplementing, and overpromising more than can reasonably or technically be delivered. Project managers must be sure to properly set the expectations of users participating in the prototyping tasks.

Meetings and Communication. The systems design phase of a project tends to require many meetings to interview users, discuss issues, review ideas, and coordinate activities. Although these are critical components of the process, they also are time-consuming. Designers should try to maximize the effectiveness of meetings by:

- Creating an agenda (or interview questionnaire), developing meeting objectives (exit conditions), and preparing participants before actually conducting the meeting.
- Limiting attendance to the required individuals to ensure proper coverage and focus (using minutes, interview notes, issue write-ups, or other forms of documentation to communicate the results of the meeting to others).
- Considering JAD techniques that involve several user constituencies at once, rather than performing a series of individual interviews.
- Recognizing that issues may arise that cannot be immediately resolved, and that they should note these points for later follow-up and assign appropriate due dates to prevent the wrong personnel from dealing with them at the wrong time.

- Using electronic mail to communicate more effectively (including management and users in this process as well).

In conjunction with these techniques, designers should incorporate meeting time into the project plans and track actual versus projected time for all meeting activities. They should monitor this variance to identify and address particular areas of concern as soon as possible.

Iterative Nature of Design. Analysis and design tasks are inherently iterative, especially when significant change is involved—as in the case of client/server GUIs, business process reengineering, or custom architecture development. It may not be possible to perform all tasks sequentially, to complete everything that could be done, or to complete a task without revising it later.

Systems developers should recognize this tendency and adjust project plans accordingly. They can consider holding a percentage of the task budgets and durations for later revision, and they can use the mechanisms of issue, open point, and sign-off aggressively to minimize inefficiencies that are a result of information or untimely feedback.

Developing Detailed Work Schedules

Long-Term vs. Short-Term Scheduling. Although the work planning activities within the project organization activity break down the work into detailed tasks, schedules, and assignments, project planning is nonetheless an ongoing, iterative process. There are several reasons for this:

- It may not be realistic or efficient to plan detailed work assignments for a horizon of longer than three months. Although positions may be identified from the start, specific staff may not be available or identified, so designers should consider waiting to assign the individual work packages until they know the specific range of skills and experience and their availability.
- An initial task may have to be completed before a subsequent task can be planned in detail. For example, if a project is based on an estimate of 50 programming work units, specific programmers will ultimately be assigned to each of those work units and given specific budgets and due dates. However, this may not be feasible until detailed design is well under way and each of the modules and their relative complexities and relationships have been firmly identified.
- Various other circumstances may prevent the project from proceeding exactly as planned, causing reassignment of work and short-term

rescheduling despite efficient planning. These circumstances include underestimating or overestimating a particular task, overruns that result from performance or training problems, or changes in the approved scope. For these reasons, even the most farsighted project managers must be willing to react responsively to events and changes as they occur.

Because detailed scheduling and loading are time-consuming processes, it is more efficient to perform broader, higher-level scheduling at the start of the project, followed by detailed scheduling when preparing for each significant phase of work. This avoids costly revision of schedules and assignments and allows project managers to use the most recent project and system information to more accurately create and refine their schedules and assignments.

Recognizing Different Types of Tasks. In planning detailed work, it is important to recognize that there are different categories of tasks. Some tasks, such as designing windows, designing work units, or coding work units, are driven primarily by the development of work packages. Others, such as requirements analysis, are more decision oriented. Still others, such as managing issues, supervising programmers, or managing the development environment, are based on elapsed time.

The nature of these three categories of tasks affects the way the tasks are scheduled, budgeted and managed. Program managers should:

- *Focus the work package-oriented tasks on the delivery of the work packages.* Budget, assign, manage, and control work by individual work package.
- *Focus the decision- oriented tasks on objectives and goals.* Organize work by logical groupings of responsibility and let the objectives, time frames, and budgets guide the control of the task and level of detail of the work. Define objectives for the timeliness of decision making and issue resolution and monitor task progress against these goals.
- *Make sure the duration of elapsed time-oriented tasks corresponds to the tasks they are supporting.* Therefore, assign sufficient resources to elapsed time-oriented tasks to complement the resource levels of work package-oriented tasks. Recognize the dependencies between the categories and adjust each one accordingly.

In addition, when staffing and managing each type of task, program managers should recognize that the skills and motivational techniques used in each of the three cases may be different.

Managing Day-to-Day Activities

Supervising Personnel. Supervising personnel is a key day-to-day activity of project management. Following is an overview of key techniques to perform the activity more effectively. Program management should:

- Identify tasks that team members can reasonably perform and that are consistent with their level of skill and experience. Try to carve out overall areas of responsibility for each team member, rather than sequentially assigning them random tasks. This promotes task ownership and provides improved motivation. Use personnel resources efficiently, but guard against delegating too much. This can adversely affect work quality, team morale, project schedules, and cost. Clearly communicate project objectives, goals, and quality levels. Instill a set of common values (such as quality) in all team members and recognize achievement in terms of those values. Clearly communicate specific objectives and expectation levels for each task. Make sure team members understand the budget and schedule constraints as well as the nature of the products they must produce and any special techniques they must use. Encourage them to develop their own individual work programs or to-do lists to ensure they understand the activities to be performed. Review these plans to ensure a mutual understanding, and measure progress against them.

- Adjust the degree of supervision and review it periodically during the project to match the complexity of the task as well as the skill and experience level of each team member. Confirm that the work is being done within the proper scope, and that the work produced is of acceptable quality. Ensure that all open points are being addressed and that external review is being sought and utilized when necessary.

- Keep tasks to a manageable size. Identify intermediate deliverables and checkpoints for long-term tasks to ensure that the project is progressing properly. Failure to review work properly and catch problems early have more serious consequences as time goes on.

- Maintain a longer planning horizon than that of the team members. Anticipate problems and develop contingency plans. Strive to balance the work load and make the most efficient use of all team members' time.

- Keep an open line of communication with team members. Encourage them to work independently but also to seek assistance when necessary. Provide direction rather than prescribing what to do, but watch for work that is outside the project scope or for too much time spent investigating superficial items.

Budgets: A Self-Fulfilling Prophecy. Project budgets are often the make-or-break item for a successful or failed client/server development project. Following is an overview of techniques to create more accurate and successful budgets. Project management should:

- Be aggressive when assigning budgets to individual tasks, but should not overlook the impact of learning curves. The first in a series of repetitive tasks (e.g., the first window designed or the first module coded) takes a team member longer, but productivity should subsequently improve as that team member performs similar tasks. If the learning curve is substantial (as in the case of a new programming environment), consider redistributing budgets so that initial items take longer than the later ones. This avoids demoralizing team members at the beginning of a task and encourages productivity improvement as the project progresses. If the learning curve is less significant (e.g., for screen design), use average budgets and expect some slight variances.

- Recognize that budgets can become self-fulfilling prophecies, especially if they are overly generous. Remember to give praise for work completed under budget, in addition to focusing on overruns. Encourage excellence by setting aggressive but reasonable budgets. Allow for minor overruns on initial tasks, and challenge team members to improve their productivity over time. For example, the project manager might target tasks to be completed in 90% of the originally budgeted time and retain the remaining budget as additional contingency. This is generally an effective technique, but it can backfire if the revised budgets are truly unreasonable. Monitor the use of this technique to ensure that team members are not overly pressured, as this can prove even more detrimental.

Resolving Routine Issues. In the course of day-to-day project management, routine issues arise that require the attention of supervisors and managers. These issues may involve an inefficient allocation of resources, an individual performance or training problem, or a need to reschedule a short-term activity. It is important to distinguish these routine items from the project's design, technical, or management issues because these issues typically do not require a high degree of formality. Items that can be resolved within a supervisor's or manager's scope of control, with no impact on the project scope, budget, schedule or quality, should be handled swiftly. Generally, no formal administration is needed. If these items linger, however, or cannot be resolved, project management should escalate them and address them through the formal issue resolution process.

Managing Risk. One of a manager's most important day-to-day responsibilities is managing risk. Management identifies the key potential risk areas during project organization, and also formulates risk mitigation strategies at that time. In addition, they should routinely reevaluate the status of the project against the risk criteria to confirm that additional risk areas have not surfaced. In particular, project managers should revisit the following areas:

- *Organization.* Are the project, user, and management organizations stable, and do they work well together? Is the area of communications adequately and accurately addressed?
- *Innovation.* If there is significant innovation on the project (in terms of business process change, technical environment, or development process), is that work managed properly and progressing as expected? Are the appropriate experts (both inside and outside the organization) being consulted as necessary for review and confirmation?
- *Project scope.* Is the project progressing within the approved scope, and does that scope still support the business case? Is the scope control process effective?
- *Project staffing.* Is the project receiving the required level of qualified staff within the required time frames? Are the skill and experience levels of the project team, management, and user representatives appropriate to the tasks they are asked to perform? Are there any significant performance or learning curve areas that could be addressed by additional training or piloting? Are there any skill areas in which the project is weak or deficient? Should outside experts be consulted? Is the project training meeting the skill needs and requirements?
- *Project progress.* Is the project progressing as expected? Are there particularly troublesome areas that should be addressed by changes in organization, approach, staffing or skill mix?
- *Support.* Are the external and internal support services (clerical support, local area network management, computer resources, legal, purchasing) being provided at an adequate level and quality? In particular, are any areas on the critical path adversely affected by support problems?
- *Quality.* Does the work being produced meet or exceed project quality objectives? Are reviews (both internal and user) generating significant amounts of revision? If so, have the causes been investigated and addressed?

Managing People

Motivation and Team Building. Motivation and satisfaction among team members are critical elements in the success of any project. Team members feel motivated when they see their work as worthwhile or important. The work must challenge their skills, and they must make a noticeable impact on the project. Because team members may not understand the big picture, managers can provide additional motivation by explaining how individual assignments contribute to overall goals. Project managers can take advantage of the orientation process to clarify roles, interdependencies, and management expectations. Also, they use periodic project or team briefings on various aspects of the project to help the entire project team understand broader areas of the work being conducted.

The following techniques can be used to better motivate project teams:

- A leader's management style must promote ownership and personal integrity.
- Project management must make clear that team members may take the initiative but the project managers are accountable for the outcome of team's efforts.
- Project managers should provide feedback on a team member's overall performance, in addition to the results of individual incidents.
- Project managers should further enhance the sense of ownership by structuring teams as a representative cross-section of the work force. For example, a team might contain both user and IS personnel.
- Recognition and reward are keys to establishing and maintaining morale. Rewards may be tangible, such as bonuses or prizes, or intangible, such as positive feedback or team recognition.
- Informal gatherings and team competition are other ways to boost team morale.
- Particular accomplishments, such as completing work units and achieving goals, also help to build team morale. Keep work units to a manageable size— typically two weeks or less—so that progress can be achieved in steps.

The team management approach reward team members with many successes throughout the project and enables them to see the whole team progress. Project management should adapt the team management approach to the characteristics of the team. Specific motivational factors such as praise, advancement, team identification, and competition may not apply to all cultures. Project managers should become acquainted with all the team members to learn what motivational style may be most effective for each of them.

Managers and supervisors should facilitate and monitor the progress and professional development of their team members. They should give informal, constructive feedback frequently and conduct formal progress reviews on a regular, timely basis. They should assign work as appropriate to team member skill and experience levels and identify areas for training or additional skill building. Within the constraints and objectives of the project, managers should strive to satisfy team members' personal career objectives.

Monitoring Progress

Finally, project management entails monitoring the progress of the project. Five key categories of progress measurement are useful for monitoring a project's progress:

- Budget variance.
- Resource variance.
- Schedule variance.
- Work package variance.
- Cost variance.

Although not every project requires that all five categories be monitored or that they all be monitored to the same degree, they are typical of the type of information most projects monitor. Managers should determine at the onset of the project which measures will be monitored and to what degree. Then they should ensure that the work planning and time reporting procedures capture the necessary information. Finally, managers must be sure to address and define the reporting requirements for the project progress measures.

Budget Variance. Budget variance (also known as productivity or efficiency variance) indicates the project progress as measured against the budget. Budget variance provides a sense of how closely the project will meet the estimated number of workdays. An unfavorable budget variance, without any offsetting variances in other areas, generally indicates that the project will finish later than scheduled and at a higher cost.

To determine budget variance, managers should track actual time against the budget. As actual time is incurred, managers should provide a revised estimate to complete that indicates how much effort is required to complete the task. The sum of "actual-to-date" and "estimate-to-complete" yields the projected estimate at completion. The difference between this calculation and the original budget becomes the budget variance.

Resource Variance. Resource variance (also known as staffing, utilization, or expenditure variance) indicates whether anticipated staffing levels have been met. An unfavorable resource variance without any offsetting productivity gains in other areas generally indicates that the project will finish later than scheduled. This, in turn, may contribute to budget and cost variances in other time-driven tasks (as opposed to work package-driven tasks).

To determine resource variance, managers must identify the scheduled hours per week per team member. As actual time is incurred, they must compare the time spent on all productive project tasks with the time originally scheduled. This difference represents the resource variance. Resource variance calculations become even more accurate when projections of future resource availability are combined with the variance experienced by the project to date.

Schedule Variance. Schedule variance indicates whether the project will meet its completion dates. This variance is the combination of the budget and resource variances coupled with any additional impact due to critical path and task dependencies. A simple schedule variance is a straight sum of the budget and resource variances. Budget and resource variances may offset each other (less available time may be compensated by more productive time), but two unfavorable variances have a cumulative effect (less available time is further exacerbated by reduced productivity).

In more complex situations, dependencies between tasks may require more sophisticated extrapolation to determine the full effects on the project's schedule of variances in the schedule of each individual task. Although a schedule variance for a task on the critical path forces a corresponding schedule variance for the project, it may be possible to compensate elsewhere for schedule variances that do not occur on the critical path. Similarly, a schedule variance for a task on the critical path may result in additional budget variances for related, time- driven tasks. For example, delays in extending the schedule for the coding task incur additional programming supervision and technical support time.

Work Package Variance. Work package variance (also known as product, deliverable, or earned value variance) tracks whether work packages are being delivered as scheduled. As with schedule variance, work package variance is a key indicator of whether the project will finish on time.

Work package variance can be used as a reasonability check against budget variances and estimates to complete. For example, if 60% of a task budget (such as design work units in the detailed design segment) has been expended but only 25% of the expected work packages are complete, a problem is indicated. Although some of the variance might be attributable to a learning curve, it is likely that the estimates to complete and the resulting task budget variance have been understated.

Cost Variance. Cost variance translates the budget and schedule variance into dollars. It converts actual days spent and days projected into payroll dollars and then compares them to the original plan. This variance reflects the overall cost-effectiveness of the staffing mix and productivity levels. Cost variances may also reflect planned versus actual levels of outside (nonlabor) expenses.

A cost variance may occur independently of the budget variance or of the resource variance. For example, a task may be over budget by 10%, but the overall cost variance may actually be favorable because the budget variance is due to lower productivity caused by staffing the task with less skilled and less costly resources. Another example of a cost variance occurs when a more expensive resource is used to cover a shortfall in a less expensive resource, increasing the overall project cost. In this example, however, there is no budget or cumulative resource variance because the task takes the same number of workdays.

PROJECT PLANNING AND MANAGEMENT AT UNIVERSALAIR

The project team for the UniversalAir implementation was very large. To ensure successful delivery, the airline decided to adopt a program management strategy for the delivery of the application. This strategy included the following:

- A focus team to develop the application.
- A team to deal with the management of the distributed client/server environment that will be delivered.
- A team to prepare the installation site for the new technology
- A team to deliver the architecture.
- A change management team, deployed to design and develop descriptions of the new jobs that will result from the delivery of the application and to create the training environment to assist system users in making the transition.

The new revenue accounting system represents a complete reinvention of the revenue accounting process in that much of the evaluation of tickets are based on an underlying automated system. Thus, the clerks do not make common decisions or negotiate final amounts for tickets that found to be in error.

This design of the organization is then tied to the initial delivery of the application so that clerks can be trained on the system in preparation for a fairly large-scale deployment. The application initially runs at one site, which has to go through extensive upgrades to accommodate both networking and hardware being introduced because little prior automation existed.

CONCLUSION

One of the most important things to bear in mind when managing a client/server project is something stressed in this volume's opening sections: Client/server is not faster, easier, or cheaper. However, an organization can obtain major business change and benefit with the delivery of client/server-based solutions. Organizations should proceed with caution, always weighing the benefits against the costs of the application of client/server.

The world of client/server applications development and delivery is a new and challenging environment. One of the critical key success factors to prospering in the client/server world is to make sure that development activities are following and adhering to a sound, complete set of methods, procedures, techniques, and deliverables. There is no one right or complete answer to this issue. In fact, numerous interrelated methodologies and techniques (such as object-oriented and information engineering) often must be integrated into a cohesive development approach and methodology. Experience has shown that even the definition and delivery of an iterative approach to client/server is itself an iterative process. Systems designers always need to be assessing what they are currently doing and what they might be doing with a methodology.

This chapter has discussed the major activities, techniques, and issues associated with planning, estimating and managing a project for client/server implementation. Although most of the activities are not inherently unique to client/server development, client/server, like all other systems development approaches, requires sound project management skills and techniques.

III-3
Change Management

For some time, information systems professionals operated under the assumption that the focus of change was on the system *user*. Developers designed and implemented systems, and then trained users—a week or two before conversion— to use the system, believing, "If you build it, they will come."

But the real world of the business user is hardly a field of dreams. One large bank converted to a client/server system that made use of imaging to cut down on the reams of paperwork generated each year. Soon after conversion, the IS department realized that employees were calling up document images and sending them to their printers, so they could have a hard copy anyway.

Or consider the large utility that developed a new customer service system. By every conventional measure, the project was an enormous technological success: on time, on budget, with online performance measured in the low fractions of a second. But the impact on the manner in which employees performed their jobs was huge and not predicted adequately. The utility staffed its customer service center on the presumption that an average telephone episode with a customer would take four minutes. But for the first three months after conversion the average was six and a half minutes. If that customer time could not be reduced, the economics of the entire multimillion-dollar investment would have been undermined.

INTEGRATING CHANGE MANAGEMENT WITH SYSTEMS DEVELOPMENT

There are numerous examples like these: examples not just of making change happen, which is relatively easy, but of making change work, which is very difficult. IS professionals must now expect to initiate a change management program that is integrated with their systems development projects. There are a number of approaches to planning and managing such a change program, and this chapter discusses several.

Change management is a relatively new management dimension and a great deal of innovation has recently come from many different sources. Change management has implications that extend well beyond information technology projects, though that is the primary focus in this chapter.

THE PROJECT TEAM AS A CHANGE AGENT

A client/server development team is a change agent in itself. For the system to bring benefits, the project team must convince its users that the system will make them more effective in performing their jobs and in achieving the organization's business objectives. The project is of no value if the users do not accept and implement the changes implied by the system.

Involving Users

User involvement helps ensure that the system satisfies management expectations. In the long run, the involvement and active participation of qualified, empowered users prevents serious problems, rework, conflicts, and delays. User involvement in the systems development process has the following benefits:

- It facilitates acceptance at an early stage.
- It helps to champion and gain support for the project throughout the organization.
- It maintains a realistic level of expectations.
- It ensures that the true business requirements are being addressed.

Choosing a Project Sponsor

The project sponsor is a key part of the project advisory structure. In the context of change management, the project sponsor plays a crucial leadership role in ensuring the success of the syste m. Effective sponsors can help achieve buy-in from the user community, ensuring that users "own" the change being caused by the new system.

The project sponsor is responsible for demonstrating the organization's overall commitment to a specific systems development project and for ensuring that user and IS organizations remain interested and committed. The sponsor is typically an executive from the user organization who will benefit most from the system and will pay for its development. The sponsor must have a genuine interest in the project and must be able to convey this commitment to both the steering committee and the rest of the enterprise.

If possible, the sponsor should be the steering committee chair and a representative on the management advisory committee. This allows the sponsor to better emphasize the project's importance during meetings and to take appropriate action if progress slows down because of reduced commitment from users or IS personnel.

Despite the heavy involvement of the project sponsor in the system's development, an organization should avoid the tendency to place a senior

IS representative in this role. Such an individual may not be a true representative of stakeholders and their interests. Placing a user representative in the project sponsor role helps to ensure that its users accept the system and integrate it with the business process. The organization should complement the project sponsor by giving an IS representative the lead role in managing day-to-day the project development effort.

Managing User Involvement

The greater the impact of the system on the business organization and its structure, the more complex the challenge to the project team becomes. The change agent role becomes more difficult, and requires more interaction with users, when the project modifies many facets of organizational infrastructure (e.g., numerous organizational units, processes, culture, and reporting relationships). It is critical that users are given the tools and the motivation to change. This is accomplished by involving users in system design and having them help determine the expected benefits.

The development of the system could also require a significant change in IS's skill base and in its investments in network and operations support infrastructure. Involving users early, and demonstrating management's commitment, helps to build the case for significant change in IS. It is also important to ensure that both IS and the user department agree on direction.

Complex client/server applications are more likely to affect white-collar professional positions. Because the related business functions may not have been automated previously, more user involvement may be necessary, especially in the early stages. In addition, this group is likely to have a stronger influence than clerical workers on the look and feel of their system.

Users should play a key role in analysis and design, providing insight into the business, functional, and operational objectives, and details of the target application. Some effective techniques for involving end users in specification and design of systems are joint application design (JAD), focus groups, facilitated meetings, prototyping, usability tests, and participation in issue and business case analysis. During installation, users should participate in detailed design issue resolution, test planning, data purification, test execution, rollout planning, procedure development, and training.

TECHNOLOGICAL CHANGE IN CONTEXT

User involvement is a practical approach to coping with technological change. But technological change must be placed in its larger context. An overall change management program sees human performance—not an information system—as its primary focus. What are the tasks and goals that employees are charged with accomplishing, either individually or as members of a team? How do the information systems of an organization relate to those goals? What kinds of performance support, especially support delivered technologically, do workers need to perform optimally?

This human-centered viewpoint of technological change illustrates technology in its larger context within the organization and works toward the goal of creating an environment in which every worker can perform optimally.

The first issue to consider in empowering workers to attain and sustain optimum performance is: "Can the individual perform the necessary tasks?" This question primarily involves matters of ability: the aptitude, knowledge, and skills of the work force. The second issue, however, relates to motivation as well: "Will the individual perform the necessary tasks?" Here an organization must concentrate on issues of the needs, values, and attitudes of the work force." The third component of the performance model, context (or environment), spans both performance questions. An organization's self-understanding, its technology, and its processes should ensure that adequate support is provided to the worker to ensure optimum performance.

Organizations cannot overestimate the motivational value of that orientation. The employees of a performance-centered enterprise are more satisfied, more fulfilled. Ingvar Petursson, chief information officer of McCaw Cellular Communications, notes that "employees feel frustrated when they do not have supporting resources available to them when they need them. That frustration increases as they get into a more dynamic and fast-changing environment. And frustration leads inevitably to dissatisfaction."

REENGINEERING AND ADVANCED CLIENT/SERVER CONCEPTS

The cost and difficulty of client/server computing can be justified only if the organization is fundamentally changing its business processes. Business process reengineering reflects changes in the roles, responsibilities, and rules that define a business. New processes are essential for any organization attempting to implement client/server computing.

To define the reengineered business process, it is first necessary to understand the business and the information technology, and what the technology can do for the business. The organization must analyze the business process and each of its steps, asking why and how they contribute to the business. Only then can a reengineered process emerge.

But how can people be empowered and supported actually to perform the new process? Traditional computing solutions often unintentionally interfered with natural performance of job tasks by making the system itself the focus of work. One of the dramatic ramifications of client/server computing is that, because of its inherent flexibility and adaptability, information technology can now be designed around the actual performance needs of the business community. Several important facets of advanced client/server computing can, if properly designed and managed, facilitate the management of change:

- Distributed information.
- Graphical user interfaces (GUIs).
- Advanced usability principles.
- Integrated performance support principles.

Distributed Information

The distributed character of information and processing in a client/server environment implicitly empowers employees. Processing power is placed at the workstation, and—within certain well-defined boundaries—workers are given instantaneous access to information for which they previously had to wait hours or days.

With the opening up of an organization's information flow, and with the coming of new kinds of users—from clerical workers to professionals—the "usability gap" drastically increased. It may well be that the well-documented failure of information technology to return on its investment for many organizations over the last decade is traceable to an increase in system complexity accompanied by an enlarged user pool.

To counter this development, systems professionals have increasingly been turning to advanced research in human-computer interaction to increase efficiency and effectiveness of people interacting with systems.

Graphical User Interfaces

GUIs are usually discussed simply in terms of how they enhance system usability. But the importance of GUIs goes beyond usability. A GUI can mimic the work world of an employee; it can represent pictorially the mental model of how a person perceives his or her work. By extension, then, an organization can facilitate change by representing a new work process in a graphical mode for its employees. (Remember, however, that a GUI does not mean a simplistic interface. Some interfaces, such as for factory or refinery applications, can be extremely busy and complex in order to present the work environment just as the users see it. Engineers can then plan, monitor, and control with the aid of the system, which supports their work in a natural way.)

Change, however, can be managed more effectively with an effective GUI. A process change can be reinforced for workers by altering the system interface (and its capability, of course). New kinds of help and performance support, delivered through the system, can then be designed to further facilitate performance of the changed process.

Advanced Usability Principles

Usability of a system goes beyond interface design. Usability is a dynamic quality and relates to every aspect of the interaction between a person and a system. Interaction has many dimensions, but this chapter focuses on three of them: presentation, navigation, and manipulation.

Presentation. A GUI is the most obvious tool with which systems now provide more powerful aid to users. But presentation involves more than the primary interface. Effective presentation in client/server computing means that the user is able to recognize and choose rather than having to remember. The system should not force users to remember things the computer already knows. Technical details should be masked from users—users should not be distracted by or expected to understand technical details.

Navigation. How does a worker discover and then take advantage of all the capabilities, all the functions, of the information system? For example, with what percentage of the full options of their major word processing software packages are users familiar? If the percentage is small, users must ask themselves why. The answer: Because it is difficult to navigate through the application and find everything that a user is able to do.

Options are not dynamically presented in the context of what the user is trying to accomplish, and there is no feedback to let users know they have successfully performed an action. There is little or no advice provided to help users perform, icons and menu options are grouped or labeled in a way that makes it difficult to locate and understand information, and the cost of changing or standardization to a new application package is significant.

The traditional response of organizations to these design problems has been user training. But traditional training is costly, time-consuming, and takes the worker away from the job. Advanced usability principles implemented in client/server systems make navigation through a system more natural and intuitive. Context-sensitive help and advice from the system coach workers through their tasks and point them toward additional system functions that can support their work.

Manipulation. How does a user work with data and information, and move that information around? Until the advent of GUIs, manipulation of data was a labyrinthine process. Consider the amount of effort necessary with older word processing programs to do a simple task: copying a document from the computer's hard drive onto a diskette.

When Apple revolutionized the marketplace with its GUIs, the process became intuitive and obvious: An icon, or symbol, of a piece of paper represented the document; it was located in a file, represented by an icon of a file folder. With the handheld mouse, users pointed at the file, clicked on it, and "dragged" it over to another icon representing the diskette.

Integrated Performance Support Principles

Integrated performance support (IPS) services is one of the components of client/server execution architecture. Generally, IPS represents the future of human-centered systems design. At this time, the vision of IPS—where a system is providing a proactive suite of advice, tools, reference, and training to workers whenever and wherever they need it—is several years ahead of technological reality. However, IPS has begun to make an impact in its most important area: letting system designers know that training can be built into a system rather than administered to users after the system has already been implemented.

ABILITY AND MOTIVATION: AN INCREMENTAL APPROACH TO ACHIEVING USER ACCEPTANCE

In an ideal development world, trained change management professionals are involved from the beginning in an organization's reengineering initiatives, in developing both the business and technology visions prior to systems development, and in helping to design IPS capaability in the system. However, this is not always an ideal world. Indeed, budgets are often tight, and management is still prone to make its first cuts in change management and training line items in the budget. In fact, this point of view places the entire development process at risk. The following discussion presents an approach to change management during systems development that can help your project to succeed.

The traditional mind-set regarding system users focuses only on the "ability" aspect of the change model noted earlier. User training tends to be knowledge based: Put users in a classroom with a collection of reference binders and an instructor and then give them some training at the system. In fact, there is a spectrum of activities needed if system users are truly to be motivated to work in new ways, and enabled to perform optimally.

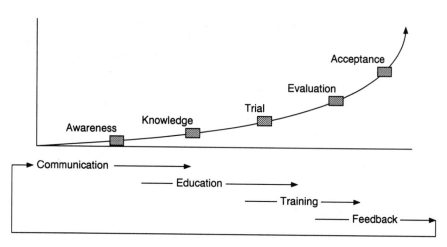

Exhibit III-3-1. A Change Assimilation Curve

Business users move through several stages over time until they attain acceptance of a reengineered business process and a new information system. As the curve in Exhibit III-3-1 indicates, change management begins well in advance of user training.

User Awareness

The first stage is to build awareness of the reengineered business process and any new technologies. This means helping the business user understand what the system is about, why it must be changed, and—at least in a preliminary way—how the reengineered process will work.

Relentless communication is a vital part of this stage: presentations about the new process, prototype demonstrations, and various written and verbal communications. These early communication efforts must be led by a business user who has the respect of the business organization, particularly the users of new systems. Without this, the typical IS person may have a credibility problem in advising business users on the need to do things differently.

User Knowledge

Awareness building is followed by an effort to build real knowledge of the proposed reengineered business process and the new technologies being proposed. This stage involves a more intensive effort to ensure that the user understands how the new process and system behave and how the user will perform with the aid of the system. A model office, including a complete simulation of the proposed work environment, is useful at this stage. The business user can go through significant parts of the workday and deal with specific parts of the new business process.

Trial and Evaluation

Business users need to test the reinvented business process and new system in real time. Do the users have an adequate knowledge of the business? Do the new process and system make the business more effective? It is imperative that the change management and systems building teams listen to the business users' concerns about the new processes, work flows, and new technologies, anticipating potential problems. The teams must carefully consider whether the issues raised by users point to a deficiency in the new process, or whether these issues simply reflect a natural reluctance to change.

If the problem relates to users' reluctance, systems builder must make a greater effort to explain why the new way is the answer for the future. However, if the systems builders determine that there is a need to change the planned reengineered process, the organization must undertake more reengineering work. The business users who wanted the change must review and evaluate it to ensure that it addresses their concerns. This is a way for users to see that they are a part of the systems-building process and can have an impact on results when they have real concerns. This perspective may be invaluable in enhancing the credibility of the systems-building team.

Although strategies vary depending on the size of the user population, the change management effort should attempt to move as many business users as possible through this process. Even if that can be done, however, it is vital to promote champions or change sponsors within the organization. Sponsorship must begin at the highest level within an organization and then ripple or cascade down as successive people become convinced about the importance of the business change and the system that will reflect that change.

The goal, ultimately, is acceptance of the system by those who use it. The larger concept here is increasingly being referred to as ownership of the change. As one executive has been quoted as saying, "Change is a door that can only be opened from the inside. Sponsors or champions are important to push change through an organization, but change has to be pulled from within, as well."

User Training

Once testing, revision, and additional changes to process and system eventually begin to stabilize, the training effort can begin. It is important to remember, however, not to start training too soon. If it is begun too soon, the system may change significantly enough to require retraining—even "untraining" users in aspects of the system that no longer exist.

EFFECTIVE COMMUNICATION

User participation is probably the most effective means of communication with the user community. But an organization should also employ other formal mechanisms. An organization should plan to communicate status formally to user management on a regular basis, as described next.

Project Sponsor

The project manager should hold regular meetings with the project sponsor to report status and resolve issues. The frequency of these meetings (weekly, semimonthly, or monthly) depends on the involvement of the project sponsor, the pace of the project, and the degree of risk. However, these meetings should occur at least as frequently as the steering committee meetings, and probably more often. If possible, the project manager should not combine these status meetings with the (weekly) project status meetings, as it may intimidate the project leaders and prevent them from communicating freely.

If necessary, the project manager should meet with the project sponsor on a regular basis to discuss proposed change requests, either in regular status meetings or separately. The project manager should maintain a close working relationship with the project sponsor. Because they share the responsibilities and the risks associated with the project, they must be able to communicate well and work together effectively.

Steering Committee

Project managers should hold regular meetings (typically monthly) with the steering committee to update members on project progress. Project managers should advise steering committee members of progress as measured by key project milestones and highlight any significant developments. Project managers should discuss major issues—resolved, unresolved, and those requiring the immediate attention of the steering committee. They should review any recommended scope changes (change requests) and obtain steering committee approval.

Project managers should base the frequency of the regular meetings on the degree of project progress and risk. They should convene special sessions of the steering committee when time-critical issues arise and brief the participants prior to the meeting so they will be prepared to resolve issues swiftly. Project managers should consider seeking the counsel of individual steering committee members when specific issues arise that fall within their area of expertise or directly affect their area of responsibility.

Management Advisory Committee

In contrast to the steering committee, which is formed specifically for the project, the management advisory committee (MAC) typically oversees more than one project. For this reason, it has a more limited involvement, usually only at key project milestones.

Project managers should invite the MAC members to the initial steering committee meeting or should consider holding a separate kickoff meeting exclusively for them. Project managers should meet with the MAC near the end of the project when management approval is required to proceed to the next phase. In between, project managers should meet with the MAC either at significant project milestones or on a quarterly basis.

Between scheduled MAC meetings, project managers should keep MAC members informed of project status. Typically, they do this by sending them copies of the steering committee status reporting packages and by encouraging them to attend the steering committees if they wish. Project managers should copy MAC members on all significant correspondence to the steering committee members.

As with the steering committee, project managers should convene special sessions with the MAC when significant issues arise that require MAC members' input or approval.

Other User Management

Project management, in conjunction with the project sponsor, should decide on the mechanism for updating any other user management personnel involved with the project. In some cases it may be appropriate to copy such personnel on the status reports that go to the project sponsor or the steering committee.

At a minimum, any user management personnel involved in the sign-off process should also be involved in the issue-resolution process. Such personnel should regularly receive reports documenting outstanding issues and the resolution of closed issues, as well as reports indicating the disposition of approved and outstanding change requests.

As appropriate, project management should include full-time user project personnel in all project team meetings and communication. This reinforces their status as true members of an integrated project team. Also, project management should consider the need for less formal types of communication or other creative approaches, to garner attention and foster better overall communication.

MANAGING EXPECTATIONS

Managing expectations goes hand in hand with communication. This is especially important for systems development efforts and applies particularly to projects of extended duration. Project management must maintain a delicate balance between users' enthusiasm and realistic expectations.

Overall Management Tasks

First and foremost, project management should manage the expectations of the project sponsor, steering committee, and MAC. These are the project's leading advocates and they must be able to sell the project in realistic terms.

Project managers must make sure they clearly communicate the scope of the project: They must stress the benefits but make sure that everyone understands what is not included because misunderstanding and creative marketing eventually backfire. Project managers must make sure, too, that the project sponsors, steering committee, and MAC understand the development methodology and milestones; only when they know what to expect and when to expect it can they effectively evaluate the project's progress and management's effectiveness.

Project managers must work closely with the project sponsor to determine how to sell the project. They must consider what is necessary to achieve buy-in from the affected user departments, both management and the rank and file. They must consider how the IS department views the development project. Is it an attractive project, for example, in terms of exposure, technical challenges, and pioneering techniques?

Project managers should develop a consistent message about the system's benefits and scope. They must depict the project's time line in a way that makes progress easy to track. As the project progresses, they should provide further detail and examples of the benefits and high-level scope items. This focus on the business case improves users' understanding and encourages them to buy into the new concepts.

When developing client/server systems, an organization should acknowledge the professional status of the users, who tend to be in more powerful positions than the rank-and- file users of conventional systems. Project managers should welcome their feedback; they must avoid condescension, or the appearance that they are telling users how to perform their jobs.

Project managers must work carefully to achieve users' buy-in and enlist their support as advocates throughout the organization. Project managers should exploit users' knowledge by encouraging their participation in areas such as JAD, prototyping (business process, GUI, and application capability), design of new methods or processes (e.g., an improved credit scoring algorithm), change management, and system pilot and rollout.

In client/server environments, project managers must also recognize the inherent complexities of GUIs and message-driven architectures and must set appropriate expectations. They must acknowledge that it may not be possible to test the infinite number of system software interactions and combinations and prepare users for an occasional glitch. They must consider rolling the system out slowly, in a more controlled fashion, to further limit the impact of such complexities.

User Participants

Project managers should be particularly sensitive to the expectations of users directly involved in the project, especially those who are interviewed or who provide review or sign-off. They should orient newcomers by providing the objectives and context of the project, but they should not provide guarantees for any specific capability, especially early on. Project management should solicit as much input as possible during the early stages of requirements gathering but guard against the impression that users and interviewees will have all their wishes satisfied.

Even for items clearly within scope, project managers must make sure that users understand the time frames in which they can expect to realize the benefits. When reviewing designs with users, project managers should be sensitive to their concerns and note their points but avoid scope creep—they should not agree to changes without approval from management within the user department.

Prototyping Is a Double-Edged Sword. Project managers must recognize that prototyping is a double-edged sword. A system may have a no more effective tool to demonstrate its capability and its look and feel, especially in a client/server environment where users may be unfamiliar with GUIs. But there is also no more dangerous tool than a prototype because the more realistic it is, the more likely users are to believe they have a working system.

When reviewing a prototype with users, project managers should stress positively its ability to be representative of the system but also must make sure the users understand the limitations and what it takes to get from here to there. Project managers must recognize the danger of generating tremendous enthusiasm from a prototype's review only to squelch that enthusiasm and do even more damage when users find out how long it will be before the system is actually delivered.

Project managers should emphasize the system's benefits but ensure that users understand that there will be a transition from their current state to the new process, and that they will experience some learning curve before they realize the benefits. Project managers should attempt to minimize the disruption of the conversion through good training and realistic preparation of target users. They can employ change management techniques to plan and achieve this transition.

External Customers

External customers are another class of users whose expectations may need to be managed. This is important for systems that have public or supplier access (such as automated teller machines or voice-response systems), systems that generate output that goes directly to customers (such as billing systems), or systems that closely serve customers (such as customer service applications).

In these cases, project managers should work closely with marketing specialists to determine how to publicize the change and how to prepare customers for the transition. They should not underestimate the lead times needed by marketing for these efforts (3 to 12 months is not unusual). Project managers must be extremely careful not to misrepresent the system to the marketing representatives. They must be sure that they clearly understand the scope and details of the system, and that they do not make any premature claims as to its capabilities or availability. Project managers should involve the project sponsor as the primary liaison in all significant marketing communication.

CHANGE MANAGEMENT AND TRAINING FOR IS PROFESSIONALS

Change management is just as important for the IS person as it is for the business user. The objective of IS change management is to complete the learning curve in the application of client/server computing. This effort tends to be overlooked or treated in an ad hoc fashion. This is unfortunate because client/server technology can succeed only if systems personnel are well informed, trained, and experienced.

Rules, Schools, and Tools Method. One approach to developing training for IS personnel is dubbed the "rules, schools, and tools method." The first step to building new skills for IS personnel is to establish the overall methodology used for development. This methodology defines the tasks, steps, and deliverables within client/server development. It defines the roles of designer, programmer, architect, and project manager. This can be built on a custom basis, but often it is more cost-effective and timely to acquire one from an outside vendor, if necessary.

Once the rules are in place, systems developers can then define the training required for each role. Based on these requirements, developers can then select, purchase, or design the training and deliver it to the IS personnel.

The amount of training depends on the individual's background, the rules and technologies selected, and the architectures in place. It is reasonable to expect programmers to need two to four weeks of training; designers may need one to three weeks and architects one to four weeks. Project managers may need one to two weeks of training.

Following this training, systems developers should count on an additional period of time for the trainee to work with an experienced person doing job-related work. Building real proficiency comes both from classroom training and on-the-job experience. With all these factors considered, training can run from $1,000 to $4,000 per person. When going forward with client/server technology, IS management should plan on one to two weeks of skills upgrading each year for each individual.

With regard to tools, as the rules are established, it becomes more logical to define criteria for selection and opportunities for building the tools to be used as a part of the systems-building effort for future client/server environments. If the rules are not well defined, the selection process can lead to a set of discrete tools that are difficult to integrate and share across the entire development process.

Training Costs

Another issue is how to account for training costs. Companies use several strategies. Many sites simply try to ignore the costs and hope that they go unnoticed. That is not a wise choice. Inevitably, the training either does not happen or is done inadequately, with subsequent loss of effectiveness of the personnel.

A second approach is to have a formal training budget that treats skill upgrades as part of doing business. The advantage to this method is that it allows the IS department to focus on and control the cost of skill upgrades. It allows the organization to implement a program for the IS department, which can ensure a consistent and high-quality training program. Such an effort also creates a sense of the IS department working as a team to meet the shift to a new technology.

The problem with this approach is that when the organization undertakes the large technology shift to client/server, the costs to build skills in the IS department can be so high that they may be questioned and perhaps denied.

Making the Business Case for Learning. A third strategy is to make the cost of learning a part of the business case for the application that is prompting the move to client/server. Because these costs are typically only for the team members committed to the project, they are often smaller and more acceptable as an overall amount. In addition, the costs can be made a part of the business case for the application and thus have a direct payback.

This approach also has its potential drawbacks. It may not be fair to ask one project to absorb all the costs associated with training people when that knowledge can be used across subsequent projects. In addition, the training received may be project specific and may not address the full range of training required for client/server competence. The fact that only team members are trained can also create an "us versus them" situation in which some people seem favored and others do not.

Decisions on how to pay for training depend on the site specifics. A site committed to upgrading the skills of its personnel continuously may value and measure a training budget that shows proof of commitment. A site focused on return on investment for each dollar may insist on the project justifying cost. The key point is that significant training is required for the move to client/server technology. To succeed with this technology, the enterprise must invest in its personnel development.

MANAGING CHANGE AT UNIVERSALAIR

Project managers realized from the beginning that the new system at UniversalAir would cause all involved parties (accounting users, IS personnel, operations personnel, and management) to undergo massive change and restructuring in their jobs, activities, and daily lives. To successfully accommodate and deliver this change, the project team decided to utilize several tools to ensure a smooth transition.

The change management team established project newsletters, user focus group meetings, and open forum presentations to communicate to the organization developments regarding the forthcoming system, business processes, job descriptions, and other components of the new environment. The team developed user interface and functional prototypes to educate the affected parties about the new accounting environment. Also, a demonstration lab was created to allow users and other interested parties to experiment with and evaluate various aspects of the new system, such as the GUI.

To deliver the system successfully, the change management team took a structured and planned approach to training. All users, including operations and IS, were fully trained in their new roles and responsibilities and in use of the new system as a part of this formal training program. The team knew that training must begin early. So training planning and execution started on day 1 of the project.

In addition, the change management team instituted a formal feedback tool and procedures that allow all involved parties to input their concerns, issues, and wishes related to the new accounting environment.

Finally, and perhaps most important, to assist with change management, the entire project team involved (and required) full-time user involvement during the life of the project. This involvement provided several benefits:

- A user's perspective is always available to the project.
- The involved users become the system champions when they return to their departments.
- The project team is able to address the users' requirements and concerns early in the development life cycle.

III-4

Design and Implementation of Client/Server Architecture

C hapter III-1 introduced a framework for client/server development. Four of the activities in this framework revolve around the architectures for the implementation and support of client/server applications. The design and implementation of the platform, development, execution, and operations architectures follow similar approaches. The main difference in approaches is the timing of the efforts, because of different due dates for final results. Exhibit III-4-1 highlights the development activities in the "architecture stream."

This chapter focuses on the activities and considerations involved in this architecture stream.

PHASES OF DEVELOPMENT

In many ways, the process for architecture development is similar to the process for applications development. Developers identify and collect the requirements for the architecture, create a design for the architecture, and then undertake implementation. Architecture implementation shares a number of issues with applications development: Implementation frequently involves a number of "make versus buy" decisions, early piloting and prototyping are common, and designing for performance is important. The two phases described in the framework are "architecture design" and "architecture implementation."

Design

This first phase in architecture development is equivalent to the requirements gathering and initial design done for applications development. The first step of this phase identifies the broad application styles and describes the corresponding architecture requirements. These applica-

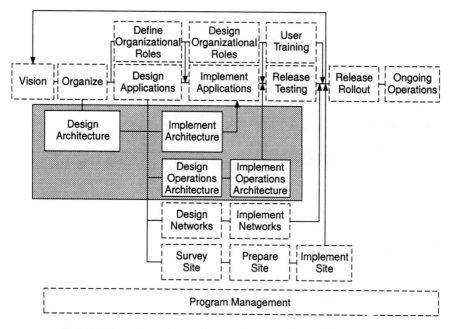

Exhibit III-4-1. Architecture Stream of Client/Server Development

tion styles are driven by the business requirements and the vision of how client/server applications can help meet these requirements.

In addition, developers preliminarily prioritize application styles and architecture capabilities to help sequence the remaining activities. After they prioritize these application styles, the next step in this phase is to define the architecture at a detailed, logical level. Developers create a description of the types of services and features necessary to support the business applications and recommendations for purchase or development of the various components for the physical implementation.

The detailed execution, development, and operations architectures described throughout this volume are examples of logical architectures created in this phase. They describe general classes of capability with specific types of services or tools and they provide a structure for organizing and implementing these capabilities as well as for communicating them to the appropriate audiences.

Implementation

This is the actual implementation, along with the supporting documentation and procedures for the various architectures. In most cases, this consists of purchased and/or custom-developed tools and services combined with any necessary procedures to support the development and operations process.

ARCHITECTURE DESIGN

The first step in the architecture design phase is to collect the key architecture requirements, structure and prioritize them, and create or identify any constraints or assumptions that affect the architecture design and implementation. The output, the conceptual architecture, is typically a high-level deliverable which addresses the layers of a business solution and their interaction and is used in the next step of architecture design.

Three tasks are involved in this step. At a high-level, the process for defining the conceptual architecture consists of the following:

- Identifying architecture requirements.
- Analyzing the requirements and make preliminary decisions.
- Confirming suitability of the architecture decisions.

Identify Architecture Requirements

The objective of this first task is to articulate the key requirements of the architecture based on the business solution needs.

There are four categories of architecture that provide some structure in analyzing the architecture requirements and facilitate focusing on the important decisions and issues. (For a more detailed discussion of the full enterprise information architecture on which this model is based, see Chapter II-1, "An Architectural Framework for Client/Server Computing.") These four architectural layers are:

- *Business solutions.* This category includes the key characteristics of the business solution and the corresponding requirements on the application. This typically encompasses such business decisions and requirements as providing support for field or mobile professionals, using work flow to automate process control, using knowledge-based software to enable less experienced personnel, or extending the system to the customer.
- *Application architecture.* This layer represents the components that provide the automation support for a business function or activity in the business process (but does not include the platform and cross-application architecture). This layer may include applications that interact directly with the user or batch-type functions that perform a function and/or generate a report.
- *Technical architecture.* Technical architecture is the layer of base

software and extensions to system software on which the application is built. It consists of the development architecture, execution architecture, and operations architecture discussed throughout this book.

- *Platform.* Platform includes the core hardware (workstations, servers, printers), systems software (e.g., operating system, data base management system, transaction processing monitors), and network components (the physical network).

As part of the conceptual architecture definition, each of these layers would be broken out into more detail to clearly define their scope and their relationship to the other layers. The emphasis, however, should be placed on the business solutions and application layers because these have the greatest impact on the design of the technical architecture and on the selection of the platform.

The goal is to identify the key requirements, assumptions, and constraints imposed by these two layers and to make sure that the architecture requirements are tied to specific business and user requirements. The result is a set of "guiding principles" for the architecture design and implementation which are key in making feature prioritization and product selection decisions.

Business Solutions and Application Considerations

The business solutions layer is where the following decisions are documented:

- How work flows to achieve a specific outcome.
- The types of processing involved.
- External dependencies (such as customers and suppliers).
- The organization of the involved work groups and departments (distributed or centrally located).
- The types of business personnel involved in performing the work.

These define key characteristics of applications, which in turn define the requirements of the architecture and platform. The most important considerations revolve around decisions that affect the style of processing, the class of user service, and the degree of distribution of data and processing. These along with some of the architectural considerations are discussed next.

Style of Processing. Client/server and the rapid evolution of technology have made new styles of processing possible, each of which may have different architectural demands. Some of the more common application characteristics (or styles) include the following:

- *Online transaction processing.* This is the most common application style. It is characterized by simple, routine business events that translate into a single transaction, completed within seconds or minutes after arriving from the user interface. An example of online transaction processing is order entry. The basic architecture requirements are typically graphical user interface (GUI) interaction, support for local and remote data access, access to enterprise processing and data, and high-performance control of transactions that may span multiple platforms.

- *Batch processing.* This style is characterized by the lack of a user interface and the need to recover from failures in a timely manner. (Rerunning a complete batch of 1 million items is not very desirable.) Processing usually occurs on groups (or batches) of records/transactions according to a schedule, usually by day. The outputs are typically updated data bases, as well as printed reports and documents.

- *Team processing (or work flow management).* These applications support the interaction of teams of personnel to perform business events that are complex and can translate into several transactions which may be processed at different times. The business event involves multiple individuals and may have a long life, typically days or months. Thus the order in which the related transactions occur cannot be determined in advance. The user is usually a knowledge worker who has latitude to make routine decisions and who may need a supervisor to review and authorize exceptional cases. An example of team processing is insurance claims processing. These types of applications typically require an architecture to support GUI interaction, work flow, document management (which may include support for image, voice, and video), and perhaps rule-based processing for advising on business rules and decisions.

- *Management and control reporting.* Management and control reporting provides the information that middle management needs to monitor and direct the organization (e.g., general ledger reports, investment performance reports, and case management work flow analysis).

- *Decision support.* This supports unstructured and unpredictable information retrieval by infrequent computer users. Decision support typically integrates information from multiple operational systems and allows users to view it in many different ways.

- *Mobile operation.* Many traditional applications are delivered to a fixed location, usually on a desktop terminal or workstation. With the advent of lighter, portable computers and improved wireless communications, applications can now be delivered to users who are not consistently located in one place. For instance, it is now possible to provide computing support to sales forces and field workers. The typical architectural requirements are GUI interaction (in some cases with pen support), local or standalone operation, dial-in communications support, and support for store-and-forward type messaging (for transactions and electronic mail).

Many applications combine characteristics of several of the types discussed above. For example, a financial system may have characteristics of transaction processing, batch processing, and work group support applications. Many transaction processing applications and all case processing applications have a strong office component. Thus, the architecture must address the particular mix of application styles that satisfies the user requirements.

Class of User Service. A class of user service defines both a work style and a way for a class of users to interact with a system. If there are several classes of users, there are likely to be multiple architectural traits.

For instance, a patient care system to be used by physicians, nurses, and administrative personnel has several levels of capability. Physicians are mainly interested in reading information; they are typically not interested in spending time being trained on a workstation. Thus, the user interface for physicians must be immediately intuitive and simple. Administrative personnel have more transaction processing to perform; they typically use the application several hours every day and so a training effort can be justified for them. Depending on the hospital's approach to nurses' duties, nurses have requirements somewhere between those of the physicians and administrative personnel. The architecture must thus support several classes of users.

Following are the most common traits that characterize the class of user service:

- Types of users (e.g., mobile vs. stationary, line vs. management).
- Response times required.
- Types of inputs and outputs (for example, forms, images, queries).
- Scheduled system availability and recovery time (in the case of failures).
- Level of security.
- Data integrity and timeliness of data synchronization.
- Process and data volumes.

As with the style of processing activity, an objective of identifying the classes of user service is to ensure important requirements are addressed and to avoid unnecessary architectural features. For instance, an organization should not provide multimedia capability unless the users need it or sophisticated on-the-fly recovery processes if 24-hour recovery is sufficient.

Degree of Distribution. Another key influence on the architecture is the degree of distribution of processing and data. Starting with the requirements of the business, decisions need to be made as to where data will reside and where processing logic will reside. For example, will customer data reside centrally, or be distributed to the local organizations serving a group of customers? Will transaction control occur on a client or server platform? Will reports be generated centrally or on work group servers?

These decisions (especially data distribution) can have significant impact on the architecture. For instance, an organization may choose remote data management instead of distributed logic. This decision affects the data base decision and the need for a middleware package. Similarly, having to support synchronized, distributed data instead of a single copy results in a very different set of architecture requirements.

Dealing With Existing Architectures. In some cases, the organization implementing a system may have one or more existing processing environments that satisfy a need of the new architecture. In such cases, it is important to confirm whether these existing processing environments (and their associated architectural components) satisfy the requirements posed by the new styles of applications and classes of user service. There may be new classes of user service: For example, a traveling sales force must be supported in addition to stationary telephone sales clerks, or the telephone sales clerks require response times not currently supported by existing processing environments. If these new classes of service are present, developers must identify and document any additional requirements during the conceptual architecture phase.

Analyze Requirements

At this point, the developer has identified the key requirements for the architecture. They must now analyze these requirements to make initial decisions on the direction of the architecture and possible approaches for its design and implementation (make versus buy, possible products, and so forth).

A common approach is to start with the deliverables that articulate the following:

- The various platforms (workstation, departmental server, enterprise server).
- The types of processing and data they will host.

- The interactions between these platforms.

Working through each platform in turn, developers identify the key requirements and use them to identify options. On the workstation, for example, the requirement is for delivering a GUI application that integrates with a rules-based engine and can access departmental data and enterprise data.

Using in-house knowledge, outside experts, vendors, and information systems publications, developers identify options for satisfying these requirements. In some cases, many options exist, and the evaluation list may be initially pruned down by high-level criteria such as cost, vendor size, or vendor reputation to keep it manageable. In other cases, few or no products may be available. Thus, developers must consider a custom design and implementation.

In either case, the objective is to identify the options so that the design effort can be estimated and planned. Concurrently, developers should prioritize the architecture features because the effort, cost, and risk for a complete client/server architecture is likely to be too high to be palatable in a single "big bang" approach. The prioritization identifies the work that must be completed initially and then must be followed by iterations to implement the remaining functions (over one or more iterations).

Finally, although the business requirements should drive the architecture, it is important not to ignore the standards and direction of the information systems (IS) organization which play a part in such things as interoperability and maintainability. At this stage of the architecture development, it usually suffices to identify the IS principles and standards that should be taken into account during the architecture design. Examples of these principles and standards could include the following:

- The ability to operate over the standard organizational network (e.g., Transmission Control Protocol/Internet Protocol, or TCP/IP, and X.25).
- Preferred data base management system (DBMS) and access method (e.g., structured query language, or SQL).
- Preference for Intel-based workstations running Microsoft Windows.
- Preferred development language (e.g., Visual Basic or COBOL).

The intent is to provide some considerations that are not directly business related to help make the right decisions during the architecture design.

Confirm Suitability

Once developers have collected and analyzed the architecture requirements, it is important to come back and confirm that the architecture direction supports the business and application requirements with an appropriate level of complexity and effort. That is, it is important that the architecture be neither "overboard" nor "underboard."

It is useful to look at the architecture from a broader perspective to ensure its suitability to the project and the enterprise. Experts can help analyze options and confirm choices. In addition, it is useful to review the analysis and choices with corporate IS, project management, users, and other stakeholders. In preparation for these reviews, it is important to understand the expectations and values of all the stakeholders and objectively assess how the conceptual architecture stacks up against these expectations. Some common questions in preparation for this process include the following:

- Are all the processing environments necessary, or is there a way to consolidate some of them (potentially reducing the number of distinct architecture components to be built and supported)?
- Is the degree of distribution warranted by the application's requirements, keeping in mind the costs and complexity associated with building and supporting distributed data and processes (e.g., issues of data integrity)?
- Does the architecture direction meet unique application requirements (user requirements, quality requirements)?
- Is the direction compatible with existing architectures in the organization and corporate standards?
- Will the direction allow for a proper fit with existing applications?
- Is the direction in step with market directions, and will it provide the required longevity?

Conceptual Architecture Planning Considerations. A typical time frame for the development of a conceptual architecture is up to four months (with a team of 5 to 10 people) depending on the formality of the process and documentation, the scope of the design, and level of innovation. This step utilizes experienced systems personnel along with representatives from the business community. It is important to ensure that sufficient time is allowed for this activity due to the impact on subsequent work. However, it is also important to avoid falling into "analysis paralysis" as a result of the lack of experience or the rate of change of the technology. Experienced technology and architecture personnel must be available.

Detailed Architecture Design. The focus of this step of the architecture design phase is the detailed architecture design. The objective is

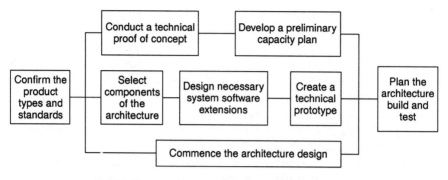

Exhibit III-4-2. Detailed Architecture Design Process

to design a technically feasible, affordable architecture that supports the application's requirements and is consistent with corporate standards and directions. Ideally, architecture development leads the applications development and rollout. However, project schedules do not always accommodate this. In such cases, where application work is occurring concurrently, this phase also identifies the boundary and interaction between the application and the architecture and articulates them so that application design can begin. The design process (see Exhibit III-4-2) consists of the following activities, discussed in more detail throughout the remainder of this chapter:

- Confirm the product types and standards.
- Select components of the architecture.
- Conduct a technical proof of concept (optional).
- Develop a preliminary capacity plan.
- Design necessary system software extensions.
- Create a technical prototype.
- Plan the architecture build and test.
- Communicate the architecture design.

Confirm Product Options and Standards. The conceptual design for the architecture, created earlier in this phase, primarily addresses the following:

- The types of products (e.g., Windows-based workstation, mainframe server, relational DBMS, UNIX operating system).
- Any relevant standards to be used (e.g., SQL in the DBMS domain, TCP/IP for networking).

- Potential products that should be considered during the design.

The first activity of detailed design confirms these going-in positions. For each processing environment, the direction established by the conceptual design is updated, based on several factors.

Architecture Direction. Confirmation of the conceptual architectures may have adjusted the processing environments, system topology, or degree of distribution. Adjust the hardware, system software, and network direction as required.

More Detailed Application Requirements. If applications development is occurring in parallel (as is common), preliminary results may be available from the user requirements or quality requirements-gathering activities. These results should be used to confirm and adjust the architecture direction as required. If the system cannot meet any application requirements, it is important to provide early feedback to the analysts with suggested standards that will conform to the architecture direction.

Technology. If a significant amount of time has passed since the completion of the conceptual design (perhaps six months or more), it is important to account for any market or technology changes (e.g., new vendors or alliances). All relevant areas need to be addressed, including:

- Hardware for workstations and servers.
- Operating system software.
- User interface management software.
- Data management software.
- Network components and connectivity software.
- Programming languages.
- Tools (development and system operations).

Select Components of the Architecture. The objective of this activity is to evaluate and select products for the architecture. The selection process begins by establishing firm requirements and evaluation criteria. Requirements should cover the aspects of hardware, software, training and consulting support, and operations support. Evaluation criteria typically include the following:

- Economic criteria (including rollout costs).
- Technical criteria.
- Business criteria (vendor stability, reputation, reliability).
- Ease of operation.

- Previous experience with the vendor.
- Availability of support for vendor's products.

Section II of this book describes, in detail, considerations for each area of the technical architecture, and these should be utilized as input to this evaluation preparation process.

Depending on the component and volume, a request for proposal (RFP) may be appropriate to communicate requirements and evaluation criteria to prospective vendors. Initially, an RFP gives a vendor the data required to prepare a proposal. Later, it is a framework for checking the completeness of proposals. In today's client/server market, it is often unlikely that a single vendor can respond to a complete RFP. As such, it may be necessary to create separate RFPs for individual components of the architecture.

When an RFP is not necessary or appropriate, communicating the requirements and evaluation criteria to vendors is useful for letting them know of the organization's interest and soliciting their assistance in evaluating their product. The time required to select architecture components varies depending on how new or unfamiliar the components and vendors are, the amount of earlier selection work done, and the degree of innovation and complexity in the environment. If a proven environment is used, this activity requires relatively little time (perhaps six to eight weeks). In a new or innovative environment, significant time (as much as six months) may be required to select and acquire the necessary components because more validation is required.

For projects that are going to use leading-edge and unproven hardware and system software, or when the company is integrating many products from different vendors, it is essential to conduct technical proof of concept tests. These ensure that the resulting architecture will perform as expected before finalizing all the decisions and negotiating final contracts. In addition, when performance is a key issue, it may be necessary to benchmark the winner or leading contenders from the evaluation process to confirm suitability and to provide capacity planning information.

For each product, the organization should finalize choices for specific product models, options, sizes, and releases based on the following:

- The unique requirements of the application.
- The schedule for the project and the system rollout.
- The results of any testing done to date (product testing, technical proof of concept).

Throughout this activity, it is important to manage the process carefully. Project managers should communicate effectively with vendors and upper management and document the whole process rigorously. This helps eliminate mixups and later challenges to their decisions (which can start this process all over).

Technical Proof of Concept. It is generally a good idea to conduct a technical proof of concept when leading-edge hardware and system software are being utilized, or when many products from different vendors are being integrated. The multitude of products being integrated, and the many ways these products can be used (sometimes never intended or envisioned by the vendor) make it difficult for vendors to know whether their product will work with the various other products required to meet the functional requirements.

It is not uncommon with newer products or environments to end up with a product combination that has never been used before. In these situations, project managers should conduct proof-of-concept tests to ensure successful end-to-end connectivity and interaction of components.

Most of the time, this activity is performed prior to finalizing the selections. However, the resulting environment setup is usually maintained and used to allow new versions of products to be installed, integrated, and tested prior to being incorporated into the architecture being used by the rest of the project.

Finally, project management needs to monitor the scope of these proof-of-concept activities closely. It is easy to fall into the trap of perpetual evaluation. This results in an environment that is more of a "play/experiment" environment than one focused on assessing areas of critical risk from a product integration and compatibility standpoint. As such, it is important not to initiate any proof-of-concept activities without specific goals, objectives, a plan, and a schedule. Then it is important to track progress closely to ensure that goals are met on a timely basis.

System Software Extensions. The purpose of this activity is to identify any missing functions in the selected system software environment and to design or select additional software to provide these missing functions. An example of this might be security extensions to the selected GUI tool and desktop to allow applications and fields to be enabled/disabled based on user privileges.

This task may not be necessary if the selected system software provides the required capability, or if an existing set of system software extensions (an existing technical architecture) can be used. This task generally becomes critical when working with new and unfamiliar hardware and system software or with system software that does not provide a full set of basic services.

Technical Prototyping. The purpose of prototyping the technical architecture components is to reduce uncertainty and to identify potential problems before the cost of rework is too great. This is especially important in an environment with new or unfamiliar hardware, system software, or architecture components. The prototyping should be detailed enough to reveal subtle problems and to ensure that requirements can be met using the selected products and approaches. In contrast with the proof of concept performed earlier to confirm the considered products' compatibility, the technical prototype is an evolving product used to test new ideas or risky areas of the architecture.

The benefits of performing a technical prototype include developing skills for the project team and risk (rework) reduction, both of which improve the team's ability to meet the implementation estimates.

Preliminary Capacity Planning. The capacity requirements estimated at this stage are used as input to make preliminary decisions on the specific sizes of hardware and network components. Project management revisits these decisions in the architecture implementation phase and during application construction.

The objective of this initial work on capacity planning is to help define any constraints within which the application must operate. The resulting constraints affect the later implementation of the architecture, the application, and the data bases.

For example, in designing a user interface, it is helpful to know the workstation's available memory capacity and central processing unit (CPU) speed and the network load the system can support. If developers determine that the design will not work within these constraints, they must make a decision whether to change the constraints or change the design.

Although this initial capacity planning is necessarily broad, it is also generally shallow. Sometimes characterized as "back-of-the-envelope" capacity planning, it typically involves paper analysis or electronic spreadsheet models. In this respect, this effort is not intended to be extremely accurate. Rather, it is a means to determine an order of magnitude approximation and to confirm that there are no overwhelming problems. (Discovering the need for a hardware platform 10 times larger than anticipated would be an overwhelming problem.)

If developers use an electronic spreadsheet model, it is important they not get caught up in the implied accuracy of such a model. The model is addressing order of magnitude regardless of how many decimal places the spreadsheet can show.

Developers can take several steps during preliminary capacity planning:

- Describe the typical transaction and message profiles—the composition of the work carried out by the system in response to a transaction or message. Factor in the overhead required by the architecture, for example, to access configuration data or support processes that reside on a remote platform.

- Use the available information on business process volumes to estimate transaction arrival rates and network message rates. Extrapolate from the current system volumes where appropriate (if, for example, the new and the old systems are similar implementations). Factor in growth projections.

- Use volume information from the data design to estimate data base sizes. This affects data base server sizing and, potentially, the number of platforms required to handle the data base size and transaction volume.

- Look at existing network traffic and utilization to assess the kind of capacity available if the network is not being replaced or upgraded.

- Take into account the impact on the GUI tool of large windows or large numbers of windows and what this means to response time and platform requirements. In addition, consider any graphics or other media that will be required to be transferred over the network to the GUI platform (since graphics or images can add several thousand bytes to a message).

- Combine this information with prior experience, published data, or information from reference sites to estimate hardware and network size requirements.

It is important to use information coming from the technical prototype in estimating capacity and performance of the system because these numbers more closely reflect the final system (as opposed to a paper model based on other systems). It is also useful for developers to continue to refine the model as they acquire more knowledge about platforms, users, and applications.

The amount of time spent in capacity planning varies depending on a number of factors:

- The degree of experience with the selected hardware and system software.
- The importance of performance to the success of the project.
- The perceived likelihood that performance requirements can be met.
- The sensitivity of the business case to capacity requirements.

Finally, although the main focus of the capacity planning activity should be the production environment, it is important to consider the development environment and its operation too. In other words, developers must consider the development hardware, system software, and network components that are required by the builders of both the architecture and the application to ensure that the current plans are adequate. Providing insufficient capacity in the development environment can affect developer productivity, which in turn can affect the development effort and time frame negatively.

Communicating the Architecture Design. Applications development activities are generally occurring in parallel with the architecture development efforts. Thus it is important to proactively communicate decisions and status information to personnel outside of the architecture team.

Executive or Management Summary. A high-level summary of the architecture design is recommended to communicate architecture capability to management personnel. It is important to ensure that management understands the importance of the architecture and its progress to date. This summary is also useful for providing an overview of the architecture to the applications development team.

Architecture Designs. Developers should provide design documentation similar to what would be provided for an application design. The primary users of this documentation are the personnel who build and test the architecture components. The level of detail required varies depending on the continuity of personnel between the architecture design and architecture implementation phases. In addition to documenting the components, it is important to document key design issues and the rationale for resolving these issues.

Proof-of-Concept, Technical Prototype, and Capacity Planning Results. The results of these activities should be documented, including the approach taken as well as the conclusions and findings.

Standards. The organization should document the information needed by application designers and developers. This should include the following:

- Functions provided by the technical architecture components.
- Application program interfaces to the execution and operations architecture components.
- Standard dialog flows to be supported.
- Standard program types.
- Program models and templates to be provided.

- Standards on how to use system software components, including things to do as well as things not to do.

Planning the Architecture Implementation Phase. After the technical architecture components have been designed and prototyped, it is important to reassess the approach and effort for building and testing these components. Project managers must prepare a plan that identifies the sequence for proceeding, keeping in mind the dependencies among architecture components and the schedule requirements of the applications developers.

Estimating the effort is generally done "bottom-up." In other words, project managers create estimates for the implementation of each component and roll them up into higher-level units.

For second-time implementations and those based around mature tools, the effort required for the architecture implementation phase is smaller. For first-time implementations or those using new tools, this effort may be substantial and may require additional architecture team skills and resources to meet schedule requirements.

It is important to include sufficient time and budget for architecture testing as well as development and delivery of training for the applications developers. Once project managers produce estimates, they create a schedule for the implementation based on these estimates and a realistic assessment of the available resources (and practical limits on team size).

When scheduling an implementation, especially a first-time implementation, it is essential to address key risk areas prior to the beginning of the application construction phase. The only exception occurs if the chosen platform and architecture have a proven record and experienced personnel have been assigned to the project. In addition, the project team needs to understand the scheduling risks and plan contingencies accordingly.

Considerations for Managing Architecture Risk. Throughout the architecture design and implementation phases, it is important to identify and assess the overall architectural risks. The most common risks involve the following:

- Using a new product or new approach.
- A lack of sufficient vendor support or skills in a product.
- Trying to integrate products from multiple vendors.
- Using products on a different or larger scale than they have been used before.

The project team must recognize these risks and address them throughout the architecture development. There are several ways to address the identified risks, and the various approaches may be used in combination.

Manage Innovation. As much as possible, the project team should use existing architectures or similar experiences to avoid the risks associated with innovation. Projects involving architectural innovation may be subject to high risk and need to have budget and schedule contingency to compensate for the risk. This is not to say that innovation should be avoided at all costs; rather, it must be managed and applied where it makes sense. In addition, project managers need to assign higher-skilled resources to the team to help reduce the risk.

Reference Sites. The team should discuss risks with current users of a product. This may not be relevant if the project is scheduled to be the beta site for the product. However, other beta sites may exist that are further along.

Prototype. The team must develop a working example of the risk-related function or component to evaluate whether the product works as specified, the interfaces are stable and maintainable, and the new features are worth using for the application. The scope of prototyping clearly determines the resources required, but prototyping costs less than substantial redesign work later in the project.

Benchmarking. Benchmarking is an expensive option, usually used to evaluate hardware and system software performance under a unique work load. Benchmarking may be used to help choose among hardware and system software finalists when performance requirements are likely to push the capabilities of the current technology.

The project team may be able to have each vendor benchmark and demonstrate at the vendor's facilities a standard application developed for or by the project team. This procedure lowers the hardware resource costs of the project.

ARCHITECTURE IMPLEMENTATION

Considerations for architecture implementation are similar to those for application implementation: Products must be installed and tested; a collection of modules must be coded, tested, and documented; and training/support must be provided—though now for applications developers and operations personnel instead of end users.

Exhibit III-4-3 highlights aspects of the architecture implementation

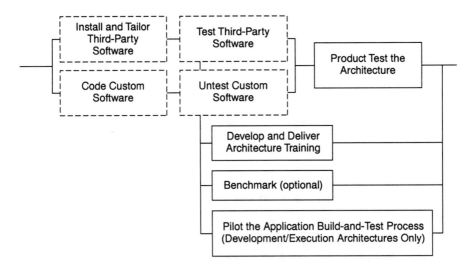

Exhibit III-4-3. Architecture Implementation Process—C/S Highlights

process that are critical to client/server implementations. The implementation of the architecture has the same objectives as do the application programs, and the management, review, and control techniques the application phase uses are also applicable to architecture implementation.

Because installing and testing software or coding and testing software is no different in the case of architecture, this section discusses the following considerations, specific to architecture implementation:

- *Product testing the architecture.* The bulk of the complexity is in the end-to-end integration testing and performance testing.
- *Developing and delivering architecture training.* This is important to ensure the successful and effective utilization of the architecture by the users of the architecture—the applications developers and systems operation personnel.
- *Benchmarking the architecture.* Benchmarking is an optional activity when performance of the system is critical and when performance estimating is either not accurate or shows marginal results.
- *Piloting the application build-and-test process.* This is mostly relevant for the development and execution architectures, and is an important step in "shaking down" the environment the first time through. (The operations architecture is piloted during the application operational readiness testing before rollout.)

Product Testing the Architecture

Product testing the architecture involves the following activities:

- Testing the functions and features to ensure they are behaving as expected.
- Integration testing to ensure all components are working correctly together without unintended, negative side effects.
- Performance or stress testing to ensure the architecture meets its performance criteria.

Throughout all these testing stages, it is important to pay attention to the architecture's ability to meet its objectives, in particular:

- *Performance.* Even if the project team has performed a benchmark, it is important to track performance characteristics and to fix performance problems in a timely fashion.
- *Reliability.* As much as possible, the project team should test boundary conditions to ensure that the architecture components perform reliably and with integrity.
- *Usability.* The team should ensure that developers and operators can use the architecture components and that the components support the usability objectives of the application.
- *Flexibility.* The team must ensure that the architecture isolates the effects of changes; the team should test specific portability and interoperability requirements.

Testing the functions of the architecture is a process similar to performing a function test on an application subsystem. Architecture integration testing is also similar to application integration testing. In fact, both system testing and integration testing follow the same basic process for architectures and applications alike. That process includes preparing a test plan, preparing test cycles, executing the test cycles, verifying the results, making changes, and retesting as necessary.

Differences begin to appear, however, because the architecture is used as a base for building applications. As such, architecture integration testing should test the interaction among components of the technical architecture and between components of the technical architecture and the application.

The goal is not to test applications but to ensure that different components work properly once they are integrated. Several common test cycles are useful for staging the integration test work of architectures.

Development Architecture. As appropriate, project managers should ensure that different tools developed or acquired (perhaps from different vendors) work properly once integrated. They must be sure that any new tools or procedures added to the development architecture are included in the test. The architecture should be easy to use; a designer or programmer should not have to go through many complicated steps to develop a deliverable, such as a module.

Execution Architecture. It is especially important to test the interaction of components that cross platforms. A good example is a test cycle that requires a workstation to request data from a server. All aspects of the execution architecture (in particular, the information access services and communication services) must work together to fulfill such a request.

Operations Architecture. This is an area in which the project is likely to be using new or custom-developed tools. In an innovative environment, the operations architecture may have to address issues that the system has not previously encountered. For example, a traditional mainframe shop may face a new set of issues when moving to client/server applications running on multiple platforms (in particular, configuration management, data integrity and control, and system administration).

Development and Execution Architectures. Components created or generated from the development architecture must function properly with the execution architecture. For example, a generated dialog should run successfully with the execution architecture. Project managers must also ensure that testing tools work properly with the execution architecture.

Development and Operations Architectures. The components of these two architectures may overlap and interact, in particular the configuration management components. Project managers must ensure that these areas work properly when integrated.

Execution and Operations Architectures. The project team must focus on performance and resource monitoring and tuning, batch services, and error handling. For example, the team must test that performance monitoring hooks included in the execution architecture can properly feed the performance reporting components of the operations architecture.

Development, Execution, and Operations Architectures. Project managers must include test cycles that touch all areas of technical architecture, such as data management. They should use the development architecture to define and populate the test data bases and to create data manipulation statements (e.g., SQL). They should use the execution architecture to process the data manipulation request, perhaps crossing platform boundaries. They should use the operations architecture to synchronize multiple copies of data and to test backup/recovery scenarios for the data bases.

Entire Technical Architecture and a Piece of the New Application. Project managers should test the application program interfaces (APIs) between the new application and the technical architecture components. Although these tests could include stub programs, ideally they use actual application code being developed as part of a pilot development effort.

Entire Technical Architecture With Existing Systems. Testing must confirm that new or revised software does not have an unacceptable impact on the performance of existing systems. It is also important to verify that the architectures being developed are compatible with other non-application-related software typically found on a user's workstation, such as word processors, spreadsheets, and electronic mail.

Because the architecture is being developed and tested before applications development, a representative piece of the application may not be available in time for such testing or the piloting process described later. If this is likely to be the case, it is important to allow additional budget for building this test/pilot application to ensure that the budget and resources are available.

Develop and Deliver Architecture Training

Successful delivery of an application requires that users of an architecture understand and utilize the architecture effectively. The applications developers, including designers, programmers, and testers, are the primary users of the development and execution architectures. As such, their training should focus on how these architectures are used to design, construct, and test an application.

Training should address the relevant standards to be followed, appropriate shells and templates available, a description of the services offered by the execution architecture and how they should be used, and the capabilities of the testing tools (such as script capture and playback and test data version management). It is especially useful to have sample design specs and programs to help developers understand what an application looks like using the architecture. Developers can then be walked through the creation process to understand how the tools are used.

Operations personnel, the target users of the operations architecture, require training on the procedures and tools available to them. It is generally useful to structure these around common scenarios that they will encounter on a day- to-day basis (e.g., performing backups, shipping out new versions of software, or adding new users). This helps operations personnel understand the various components of the architecture and their capabilities.

Performance Benchmarking

The purpose of performance benchmarking is to verify that system components can perform adequately with expected volumes of activity and data. This is especially important in an innovative environment where the performance characteristics of new products may be unknown or where existing products are going to be subjected to a new type of work load. On the flip side, there is less need to conduct a performance benchmark if the performance characteristics are predictable (e.g., if an existing technical architecture is being used or the type of work load to be processed is similar to existing applications).

Although some benchmark tests may also have been conducted during the hardware and system software selection process, the prior tests were intended to confirm a selection or to help in selecting from multiple alternatives. If earlier tests were conducted, it makes sense to evaluate whether additional benchmark tests are required.

Benchmark tests usually concentrate on areas of innovation or areas identified as problems by performance analysis. Project managers should conduct benchmarks when the project requires a higher degree of confidence than performance analysis provides.

The activities involved in performing a benchmark test are similar to those involved in integration testing. There are several special considerations for performance benchmarks.

Scope. The benchmarking team should focus on the areas of greatest performance risk and uncertainty. The performance model can help indicate which transactions and processes to benchmark. Team members should document the requirements, goals, and objectives for the benchmark and verify these with the applications development teams, project management, and the operations team. It is important to ensure that there is a clear understanding and agreement as to what the performance goals are and that they are expressed in measurable terms. Only with that understanding can the benchmarking team know if and when those goals are achieved.

For example, a goal of "3 seconds end-to-end response" is concrete and measurable, but "acceptable response time" is subjective and open to misunderstandings. If developers have defined service-level agreements for the application, they should be used as a starting point for the benchmarking goals.

Approach. It is usually not necessary to create a great deal of application code. In general, the runtime required by the application's accesses to the data base and interprogram communication is likely to make up the vast majority of the runtime for the final application.

It may be possible to use application stub programs or to reuse code being created as part of the application pilot. Alternatively, if the user-interface code is being benchmarked, it is necessary to have actual or test windows that represent the situations under review (e.g., windows with 50 or more entry fields). In this case, however, data and network access may not be necessary. If end-to-end performance in worst- case scenarios must be tested, the actual application or equivalent code must be utilized.

Resources. The benchmarking team must ensure that adequate hardware is available (e.g., sufficient secondary storage for production-size data volumes). Also, the team must ensure that the right software is in place to permit executing tests (such as network simulators and scripting tools) and to monitor and measure performance of hardware, system software, network, technical architecture, and application components. Finally, project managers must assign a sufficient number of personnel to the benchmark to ensure it is performed adequately and that it is practical to act on these recommendations.

Benchmark testing typically requires a standalone environment to ensure isolation from other system activity. This could require configuring additional components, using existing components during off-hours, or a combination of both.

Test Cycles. The test cycles may vary in their specificity. Some test cycles are designed to test a particular architecture component, such as the communication link from a workstation to a server. Other cycles involve observing how the system responds when a high-volume transaction work load is pumped through it.

Repeatability. As with any testing, benchmark tests should be repeatable. This means that it should be possible to rerun a test cycle and get the same results. More important, it means that it should be possible to change the configuration of some component, rerun a test cycle, and accurately measure the impact of the change.

Repeatability should be designed into the test cycles. Also, while conducting the benchmark tests, it is important to control changes to the benchmark configuration to ensure repeatability. After the benchmark has been defined and the tests run, team members should compare the benchmark results to the performance requirements of the area being tested. They should identify, test, and recommend alternatives to alleviate potential performance problems or to reduce the need for additional resources. These alternatives might include the following:

- Changing the application design (e.g., changing the program-packaging model, changing the placement of data or processes, or changing the time periods when components run).
- Changing the data base design.
- Changing the technical architecture design.
- Changing the hardware, system software, or network configuration.

Team members should discuss final conclusions with project management and other affected parties, such as applications developers, data base administrators, performance analysts, capacity planning group in corporate IS, and IS operations. The team should publish a benchmark report that documents the approach, results, and recommendations from the benchmark effort.

Finally, based on the benchmark results, project managers should review and confirm previous selections of products and vendors and finalize product options and sizes. Although most selections of hardware and system software vendors and products were made in the architecture design phase, some of these selections may have been deferred to this point, when everyone concerned understands the proposed environment. These changes should now be identified. There should be compelling reasons for changes made at this point because any changes are likely to result in significant rework to the architecture and applications.

Pilot the Application Build and Test

The purpose of this task is to let a group of applications developers use the architecture components, tools, and standards to develop a piece of the new application. This pilot is a beta test for the execution architecture, the development architecture, and the associated development process. If there are any problems, they can be identified and resolved early enough so that their impact is minimized. Successful completion of this activity results in a stable and thoroughly tested architecture and development process.

The pilot is different from a prototype. A prototype is usually thrown away, but the pilot is intended to be the first real application area to be developed. It may have to be significantly refined before it is completed, but it is not intended to be discarded.

Six steps are involved in piloting the application build-and-test process.

Select a Pilot Application. The selected application area should be a representative sample of the rest of the system. In particular, it should represent the types of components that account for the majority of the development time during the installation phase. If possible, the pilot should also include new hardware or software components that the project team has little or no experience in using.

The capability of the pilot should be as simple as possible while still exercising the complete architecture and the development process. A pilot application with complex capability may cause too much time to be spent resolving functional issues. This slows down the pilot and diverts attention from the primary purpose (testing the development process and the architecture). On the other hand, a single window or dialog probably is not representative enough.

Plan the Pilot. Most of the pilot time should be spent on detailed design and programming tasks. Ideally, the pilot can also test out the system test tools and process, but that is a secondary objective.

Depending on the previous experience of the team and the maturity of the environment, the estimating used for the pilot can range from one and a half times the estimates for standard development to 10 or more times the standard estimates. The target should be a small team (two to five developers) working for four to six weeks to ensure a thorough "shakedown" from the pilot.

Staff the Pilot. The team selected to develop the pilot application should possess a blend of business, technical, communication, and interpersonal skills. Their technical skills should be stronger than the average applications developer because the pilot group has to interact frequently with the architecture team. This also allows for faster diagnosis and resolution of architecture problems. Because the developers who work on the pilot are likely to play lead roles during the installation phase, good communication and interpersonal skills are essential.

Develop the Pilot Application. It is important to capture the necessary metrics as the pilot application is being developed. Some metrics assist with planning the application implementation work. These include, for example, metrics on productivity rates for developing different types of application components (e.g., windows versus data access modules versus server programs). Other metrics assist with measuring the effectiveness of the architecture (e.g., the number of problems identified or the time required to resolve problems).

An effective process should be in place for identifying and managing issues. Developers need a mechanism for recording problems they encounter and managers need a way to authorize problem resolution and assign priorities. The attitude going into the pilot should be one of openness and desire to improve (by both the pilot team and the architecture team supporting the effort). The end result should be an environment that the architects are proud of, and an environment that is productive and desired by the applications developer community.

Manage the Pilot. Estimating a pilot is difficult, and the results are often not close to the estimates. As a result, the pilot usually becomes an exercise in scope management and prioritization. It will more than likely be necessary for management to revisit the scope of the pilot periodically because the pilot is a learning opportunity for both management and the developers. Similarly, as lessons are learned, it may be necessary to adjust plans to ensure that the pilot is meeting as many of the planned objectives as possible. Finally, it is important to finish a pilot to ensure that the team has exercised the process and tools from end to end.

Act on the Results of the Pilot. To maximize the benefits of the pilot, the development team should document and communicate the results. Also, they should communicate issues and status continually. At the conclusion of the pilot, the development team should summarize its experiences, interpret metrics, and make recommendations for the application construction phase. The pilot affects the following areas the most:

- *Standards.* The applications development process is largely documented in standards. The team should update them to reflect the results of the pilot.
- *Development and execution architectures.* The team should update components of the development and execution architectures as required. In particular, the pilot may identify the need for additional development tools or new common routines and services to be included in the architecture. The team should update any accompanying project standards when necessary to reflect changes made to the architecture.
- *Application construction planning.* The results of the pilot should be a key input to the application construction estimating and scheduling activities. The pilot provides productivity metrics and helps management understand and plan for dependencies among components.

459

- *Training material.* Training for applications developers should be updated to reflect any changes made to the standards and architecture and should share lessons learned in applying the architecture and development process.

The Importance of Continuous Communication

Throughout the architecture implementation process, and especially as experience with the development and execution architectures grows from testing and piloting, it is important to communicate the capabilities and limitations of the architecture to the development team. Guidelines and standards that are part of the development environment should be updated to provide consistent communications.

Implementation Staffing Considerations

Because the architecture is evolving during the pilot application build activity, this activity typically requires applications developers with better than average technical skills. This activity also requires significant architecture team support to ensure effective understanding by the application build team and to provide timely turnaround on problem reports.

Because of the broad coverage of performance benchmarking, this activity requires deep skills in the chosen hardware, system software, network, and application segments being benchmarked. To supplement available skills with the necessary deep, specific skills, the support team may require vendor personnel or contractors. As with the piloting effort, extensive architecture team support is required to ensure that problems are resolved and that any necessary performance enhancements are made to the architecture on a timely basis.

Although sufficiently skilled personnel are important to the success of the implementation activities, there are also opportunities to leverage the existing skills and begin developing additional skilled resources. For instance, during application piloting or benchmark testing, activities such as performing initial tests and rerunning tests do not require the full-time attention of the more experienced team members. Whenever possible, it is prudent to assign personnel to these activities who can take maximum advantage of the learning opportunity and who will be effective at transferring their knowledge to others during the applications development activities.

OTHER ARCHITECTURE DEVELOPMENT CONSIDERATIONS

Throughout the architecture development process, the enterprise should consider a number of general factors, including:

- Role of the architect.
- The effect of innovation and complexity.
- The compelling need to stay ahead (of the applications development team).
- Communicating the architecture.
- Ongoing architecture support.

The remainder of this chapter discusses these key factors and how they affect the planning and execution of the architecture development activities.

Role of the Architect

Based on experience, an architect is crucial to the success of architecture development and to the entire project. The architect primarily leads the architecture development effort but typically gets involved in various aspects of the applications development effort to ensure that the architecture is appropriate, that it is being utilized properly, and that the overall structure and performance of the applications is within the project quality expectations. An effective architect demonstrates the following attributes:

- *An ability to integrate information from multiple domains and perspectives into an overall system-level view.* Domain knowledge should include:
  - The business organization and its business processes.
  - The system's functional requirements.
  - The selected or comparable hardware and system software.
  - The selected or comparable development tools and the development process.
  - The systems operational requirements and expectations.
- *Experience.* An architect should have extensive systems development experience (both applications development and architecture development). Experience with client/server architecture development is also crucial.
- *An ability to develop abstractions or models creatively.* A good architect should be able to create models that capture the essence of complex problems in a simplified way. This allows broader, more complex systems to be undertaken effectively.
- *Outstanding communication skills.* In addition to creating a feasible vision of how the system will work, the architect must be able to communicate this vision effectively to others.

On most successful projects, one person fills the role of architect. In part, this is because it is often difficult to find more than one person with the proper qualifications. However, it is generally desirable to have only one or two people leading the effort because it reduces the time required to formulate a vision and minimizes the chances of conflicting visions. When a project is too big or complex for one architect to lead effectively, it is possible to supplement the chief architect with a team of one or more specialized architects who possess in-depth knowledge of a single domain (e.g., a technical architect, user interface architect, or application architect). Also, the architect and the project manager roles usually require different skills and therefore are usually different people.

Effect of Innovation and Complexity

Projects involving architecture innovation or extensive customization may be subject to high risk because of new and unfamiliar hardware/software, unstable software, or the challenge of being the first to integrate a set of products from multiple vendors. Using one or more of the following techniques, the enterprise should take these risks into account when planning architecture development:

1. *Allow more lead time for hardware and system software selection.* It may take significant time to identify vendors, solicit bids, visit reference sites, and test products working together.

2. *Allow more time for custom architecture development, because there may be gaps in the coverage of the selected products.* This time may be as long as, or even exceed, the time required to develop the application itself. Also, allow for time to update and review the business case. The business case should reflect the costs of development and ongoing maintenance of the custom architecture.

3. *Allow more time for all forms of testing:*
   - Proof of concept testing.
   - Technical prototyping.
   - Benchmarking.
   - Integration testing.
   - Stress testing.

4. *Acquire outside expertise as required and maintain close relationships with vendors.*

5. *Allow adequate time for skills development by project team members.*

6. *Allow for time and resources to revise corporate standards.* This step also requires commitment from any corporatewide groups to participate in the development and evolution of these standards.

Architecture

	Analyze	Design	Build	Test	Rollout	Support

Application

		Analyze	Design	Build	Test	Rollout	Support

Exhibit III-4-4. Relationship of Architecture and Applications Development Activities

Because architecture innovation often implies building or extending system software, it is important to keep in mind some of the differentiating characteristics of system software development:

- The users of the development and execution architectures are programmers and analysts. They are technically sophisticated and have high expectations and needs.
- The architecture is usually generalized, so it can be used on future applications. Generalized software is much more complex to design, code, test, and support than software that is designed for a specific application.
- Architecture development is often done in a lower-level language than that required for normal applications.

The Compelling Need to Stay Ahead

As discussed earlier, the basic steps required to develop architecture components are similar to those required for developing applications: requirements gathering and analysis, design (high-level and detailed), programming, testing, rollout, and support. However, because the architecture is an application to be used by system developers, it is critical that development of architecture components precede development of the application by one or more life-cycle phases. This allows applications development to continue with clear guidelines on how to proceed and minimizes disruption and rework.

Architecture development and applications development can be thought of as related but separate activities that are staggered and occurring in parallel (see Exhibit III-4-4). Architecture development may be an entirely separate project if multiple application projects need to be executed concurrently while the architecture is being developed.

Communicating the Architecture

Because architectures are frequently abstract, and given that new concepts are likely to be communicated, documentation and training are particularly challenging and important. Some of the more successful techniques are:

- *Creating a sample application that demonstrates the capabilities of the architecture and how to use it.* This approach is very effective because it shows the target applications developers what the end result will look like and how it is built on and around the architecture.

- *Transferring resources from the architecture development team to the application team (or placing applications developers temporarily on the architecture team and then returning them to applications development).* This is especially effective in larger project environments because it helps ensure a consistent interpretation and use of the architecture capabilities and limitations. Because of the relationships established by the time previously spent on the architecture team, this approach also has the benefit of providing very concrete and direct feedback to the architecture team on the strengths and weaknesses of the architecture.

Ongoing Architecture Support

When the architecture is implemented, a team needs to be put into place to handle fixes, enhancements, and help-desk types of support. In many ways, this is similar to putting an application into production and having a support team, but the audience in this case is applications developers instead of business users.

The main point here is to plan for this function to ensure that sufficient budget and staff are available to provide it. It is important to take into account any iterations necessary to expand the architecture's capability based on the original plan or to take into account features that slipped in the current release. This team must also deal with many configuration management issues as more and more application teams begin to use the architectures—because they typically work on different cycles and are likely to need capabilities in a different priority sequence. One team's critical feature may be something another team will not need for another 12 to 18 months.

ARCHITECTURES AT UNIVERSALAIR

Choosing the actual technical architecture was a careful process at UniversalAir. The desire for imaging capabilities had already determined some of the key technologies, but product evaluation and cost/benefit analysis had to take place.

Developers had to carefully evaluate image management hardware and software. They had to find knowledge-based systems development tools. Those evaluating workstations needed to keep in mind two special requirements for workstation processing. First, the workstation has to accommodate large file transfers between the servers because processing will be shared. Developers needed to create a standard way for the CO-BOL applications (on the mainframe) to talk to the C applications (on the workstations).

The second requirement was the need to emulate 3270 terminals on the workstations to access the mainframe-based mail system and the data base.

Data communication was also a challenge to the new, distributed system. Perhaps the biggest communication challenge was to interconnect the IBM host, the workstations, the local area networks (LANs), the image hardware, and the network.

Some product selections proceeded through a fairly traditional sort of evaluation, benchmarking, and selection process. With the imaging systems, for example, extensive discussions with potential vendors took place. Key IS personnel went to the vendors with the airline's requirements to see how the vendors would respond.

Other platform decisions were based not so much on a full-blown evaluation process as on a match between certain products and the airline's requirements in terms of performance capabilities, reliability, and usability.

Still other decisions were based primarily on who the dominant player is in the marketplace. On the desktop, for example, UniversalAir eventually chose Windows because of its widespread acceptance and the availability of development tools.

UniversalAir's justification for the expense of the project was the result of intensive analysis. Discussions during meetings and during equipment testing were extremely detailed. Anyone who wanted to know the workstation cost, for example, could look at multiple-page spreadsheets containing the cost of every piece of software.

Developers evaluated different display monitors to see what size was appropriate and whether they should be color or black and white. Developers soon realized, for example, that resolution had to be excellent and that a GUI was not effective on a 12-inch monitor. They placed different monitors side by side to compare the effects on people who had to stare at a screen for a full workday. Extensive prototyping and testing went on for several weeks. A chief concern became balancing hardware and software capability with cost. Vendor support was also an issue. Which vendors will be responsive and effective partners for this endeavor?

Execution Architecture Components

Presentation Services and Integrated Performance Support Services. At UniversalAir, traditionally, revenue clerks have not stayed on the job for long periods. In fact, the entire department turns over every 14 months or so. Considering the fact that a typical learning curve for the job is anywhere from three to seven months, this means that training is a significant issue and cost for the airline.

The new client/server system promised to have a significant impact on these training costs. The GUI would be more intuitive, making the system easier to learn and to navigate. Performance support and online help mean that users would not have to leave their desks and find someone to assist them. Productivity should increase substantially.

The development team found that learning to think graphically and visually, however, was not as easy as it sounds. Initial screen designs, in fact, were simply redesigned 3270 screens, with spelled-out words such as END or CUSTOMER on the buttons instead of F6 or F2. Some designers even talked about using the windowing tools to carve up the screen so they could put four of the old 3270-type screens on one big monitor.

Gradually, however, the development team began to experiment with designs that would make greater strides in usability. They took some of these screens to users and tested them in "low-fidelity" testing. They placed sketches in front of a user. The user "pressed" on the buttons, and the development team placed the next sketched out windows in front of the user to test how the user would respond to the interface.

Advanced Development. Over time, the team develops expertise, and this aids the development process. The team decided to extend Visual Basic to make it multiapplicational. Team members built a set of common functions to make general windows development easier to do—making it easier to open or close a window and share updates to data between windows. This reduced the development effort by delivering these facilities once for all programmers.

Developers built several additional facilities such as list management, context data management, interwindow messaging, and multicolumn list box support.

They used list management to provide services to applications developers to manage and display lists of information (scrolling of lists larger than a single list box, retrieval of lists, management of lists).

They used context data management to manage and provide information across multiple applications.

Interapplication messaging is a facility that allows different applications and executables to communicate and share information and functions.

The team decided to design help with two components. First is a traditional help component to provide basic guidance for the use of the application and to correct errors. However, to reduce the training required, this facility actually had a related capability to provide extensive application help. This allowed people to identify which revenue accounting rules were used to decide whether ticket settlement was correct.

In addition, performance support was designed so that advisory services and training services within the application could be tailored to the level of experience of the user. Four basic levels of support are provided: novice, basic, intermediate, and advanced.

Information Access Services. Developers began with requirements analysis. They created a process model and then a data or information model for the new system. From there, they moved into the technical design phase, defining how to distribute data and process over the network. They defined message and processing flow and then moved to data base considerations, designing first the logical data base and then the physical data base.

The system interfaces in real time to a new accounting system developed on the mainframe to move the accounting transactions back based on the changed ticket. In addition, the system interfaces to a legacy marketing system on a batch basis to move marketing information back to those systems. This allows the airline to fine-tune its marketing campaigns.

During development, the team used stored procedures to keep data access distinct from process logic; developers separated the data into its own set of logic. They decided, however, not to isolate any further than that.

Developers also decided to go to a division of labor as they proceeded because they realized that it would be impossible to teach everything to every programmer. Some people, for example, just write SQL, developing simple routines for other developers to use. One developer can say, "I need to get this data for a ticket number," and then another person can write the routine and pass the data back. This works well to get the team up and productive quickly.

Communication Services. UniversalAir faced a mix of communication protocols: XNS, SNA, and TCP/IP. The specific image storage and retrieval vendor selected requires XNS. The workstations and servers require TCP/IP using the remote procedure call mechanism. Legacy host file transfer to the servers and messaging, respectively, requires SNA file transfer and LU6.2 messaging.

The various protocols initially caused some problems for the architecture developers. Incompatibility of network protocols led to numerous conversations with vendors about ways to get around the potential problems.

To shield the applications developers from the complexity of multiple communications protocols and multiple location of services they were trying to invoke, two APIs were created. These allowed developers to transparently send and receive messages to the required service without having to know the location of the service.

The two APIs were for the image and data interaction, respectively. The image API allowed the developers to request a specific ticket or set of tickets (e.g., for a flight) by using the ticket number or flight number as a logical level index. The data interaction API allowed the developers to request data information on a logical level. The communication messaging service resolved the issues of locating and retrieving the data, isolating the applications developers from the question of whether TCP/IP or SNA was required.

Transaction Services. The revenue accounting (RA) application at UniversalAir has business processing running across multiple servers and platforms. (Exhibit III-4-5 depicts the set of architectures for the new revenue accounting system at UniversalAir.) To ensure that all business transactions released for processing were successfully completed, a data transaction processing (DTP) monitor was used and incorporated into the technical architecture. After detailing the DTP requirements and evaluating and benchmarking available alternatives, the technical team selected Tuxedo to support the DTP requirements.

Tuxedo helped the team provide transaction management and transaction integrity for the business transactions processed in the UniversalAir client/server environment. In addition, Tuxedo provided resource management and load balancing capabilities, which allowed UniversalAir to better utilize and manage such client/server computing components as servers and DBMSs.

To isolate the complexity of building DTP (Tuxedo) applications, the technical team built and supported a simple API which initiates a transaction for processing. All the detailed begin, commit, end, and rollback, for example, are addressed within the service function and therefore do not have to be designed, coded, or tested by applications developers.

Finally, the technical team worked with the UniversalAir operations group to ensure smooth Tuxedo support for both developers and production applications.

Environment Services. Early in the development process, the project team at UniversalAir realized the importance of the batch and report components of the applications that were being developed. The project team initiated an effort to address the batch and report architecture components.

With regard to the batch architecture, the first steps were to docu-

Mainframe Component:	**IBM ES9000**
Operating System:	MVS/ESA with CICS
Data Base:	IBM DB2
Networking:	IBM SNA and TCP/IP
Language:	COBOL
Client/Server Component:	**HP UNIX and Compaq**
Operating System:	Microsoft NT
Server Data Base:	Sybase
Optical File Servers:	FileNet
Workstations:	Compaq, running Windows 3+
Language:	C++
TP Monitor:	Tuxedo
Knowledge-Based Package:	ART/IM
LAN Networks:	Ethernet
Development Environment:	Miscellaneous upper CASE tools: ERWin, Visual Basic, WinRunner, PVCS
Operations Environment:	
Software Distribution:	Tivoli
Network Management:	HP OpenView
Workstation Management:	Microsoft Systems Management Services

Exhibit III-4-5. Architecture Summary for UniversalAir's Revenue Accounting System

---

ment the batch requirements (e.g., volumes, timings, and restart/recovery) and to look for available off-the-shelf solutions. A quick survey of the marketplace showed that the technology product vendors had not yet started to address the less glamorous batch architecture component. Project managers decided to use the Kron and Script tools in UNIX to create a batch environment on the HP UNIX server.

This environment provides basic services to schedule batch processing, initiate batch processing, restart and recover batch processes, and report on the batch results. The operations support group at UniversalAir now manages and maintains the environment. As the marketplace for batch client/server tools matures, UniversalAir will revisit the implementation approach and, it is hoped, move to a commercial third-party solution.

The report architecture needed to address the report processing requirements at UniversalAir. The architecture team conducted an evaluation of available third-party tools and selected the SQR tool. SQR's support for the Sybase DBMS was a key selection criteria. The SQR tool provided facilities to define and create all the standard reports required by the applications at UniversalAir. In addition, around SQR, the architecture team provided report standards and report templates.

The final environment services component at UniversalAir focused on reducing the operating system complexity in the client/server environment. The team created operating system architecture services and provided them to applications developers. Specific services addressed memory management (allocation and deallocation) and process management (start, stop, and monitor).

Work Flow Services. At UniversalAir, the work flow facilities are named work group management to emphasize the routing and control of work to and from various departments or work groups. Much of the RA application is batch processing performed on the mainframe, but a certain percentage of tickets are "in error" and must be audited or reviewed by UniversalAir personnel.

The work flow management facilities utilized by applications at UniversalAir included the following:

- Assignment of work.
- Work processing.
- Review and approval of work.
- Reporting.

Assignment of Work. Batches of airline tickets in error are routed nightly from the mainframe to the work group servers. The work group management subsystem then routes ticket batches to UniversalAir users based on user profiles and individual user work loads.

Work Processing. The UniversalAir work flow management function also incorporates a user interface (a window listing all outstanding batches of tickets assigned to the user) which automatically invokes the appropriate application for a particular batch of tickets in a given state. A batch of tickets could be in one of several states:

- Unassigned.
- Open.
- Held.
- Suspense.
- Review.
- Complete.

When the user completes processing a ticket or batch of tickets, he or she marks the batch as completed. Depending on dollar amounts and exception types, the user routes the batch to a supervisor for review and approval.

Review and Approval of Work. UniversalAir built a review and approval step into the routing and control structure of the work flow management for supervisors who might want, for example, to review tickets at a certain dollar amount or all tickets processed by a new and inexperienced user.

Reporting. Associated with the work flow management system is a series of productivity reports indicating, by work group, the number of batches processed and left outstanding each day as well as other pertinent managerial statistics.

The work flow management features of the UniversalAir solution improved coordination, accountability, load balancing, and utilization of employees and enable routing of like accounting exceptions to specialized users. The use of work flow technology markedly increased overall productivity and control.

Development Architecture

Given the complexity of the development environment, and given the large number of decisions to be made about products and tools, the UniversalAir team decided not to investigate absolutely every candidate for every possible category in the architecture. Nor did they intend to find products that were clearly the "best of breed" across the board.

Instead, they looked for products with which they had some experience. They also looked for products which, taken as a whole, were adequate to the project, not necessarily the "best." This philosophy saved them valuable time up front. Instead of waiting for exhaustive research findings, the goal was to be moving ahead as quickly as possible.

Some decisions were easily made. The common user interface, for example, was chosen for them because of their desire to have all tools in the environment provide a Windows GUI look and feel.

Similarly, the Microsoft environment led the team to the Microsoft Office Suite for Personal Productivity Tools. Microsoft Word, Powerpoint, and Excel are used for word processing, graphics, and spreadsheets. These tools are also used to create some of the project design deliverables. The team chose Microsoft Project as a project management tool for project planning and tracking functions. It conforms to the common look and feel of the other Microsoft products in the development architecture.

For team productivity tools, the team chose Lotus Notes. This product gives them not only an electronic mail function but also knowledge data bases in which to store and exchange reusable information about the development effort.

Because the development team was not overly large—about 20

people—team members decided that they did not need an integrated CASE (computer-aided software engineering) toolset for system building tools. However, they decide to deploy some point tools for specific functions. For data modeling and data base design, they chose ERWin so they could have a consistent communications model. ERWin is a standalone tool that runs under Windows. As such, some members of the team are familiar with ERWin, making it an effective choice.

Performance modeling for the system is going to be straightforward enough, and team members felt they did not need anything complex. They used some custom spreadsheets to determine order of magnitude response times and loads. The objective was really to do some "back of the envelope" types of performance calculations to see whether they could get reasonable response times and to determine whether the server and network were big enough. They confirmed their findings later with benchmarks and performance tests.

They chose Visual Basic as the window painting, prototyping, and coding tool. There were several reasons for this choice. It is easy to use and it gives the team the ability to design and prototype the GUI rapidly. The team also wanted to take advantage of Visual Basic's large after market for controls so they would not have to build a lot of controls themselves— they required a spreadsheet widget and a widget to incorporate the imaging component of the system. They wanted to leverage that, and Visual Basic gave them a better base to do so.

They used spreadsheets to document the control-action-response (CAR) information for the windows. Not many tools are available today to help with CARs, so spreadsheets are fine for that activity.

The team used a custom generator to implement the templates for Tuxedo services. These templates define the structure of incoming and outgoing messages. They also deal with all the "housekeeping" logic associated with Tuxedo so that designers and programmers can focus on the core business logic for a service.

The team used PVCS as the source management tool because it supports Visual Basic, C, and the Windows and UNIX environments. PVCS is one of the better known tools today and extremely robust. It gives the team the ability to manage multiple developers by keeping version histories and permitting version rollback.

The team chose WinRunner as a scripting tool for testing windows. They created test data using the standard Sybase table maintenance utilities. They documented test cycles, conditions, and expected results using Microsoft Word documents and Excel spreadsheets.

Operations Architecture

As part of its overall RA system installation, UniversalAir established a team under the name "Distributed Systems Management" (DSM). The team's objectives were to implement and build management tools for the online and batch operations of the RA system. The RA system required more than 500 Compaq workstations running Microsoft Windows and 60 NT servers. Specific responsibilities for the team included the following:

- *NT, Windows, and communication hardware installation.* Installation of all workstation, server, disk, and LAN components; installation and testing of all SNA and wide area network communication links and the setup of management tools to perform online management of fault, performance, and configuration data.
- *Volume testing and capacity planning.* Volume testing of the batch schedule of each functional phase cut over, and construction of tools to perform capacity and utilization analysis of the schedule against existing hardware. These tools are used to predict future hardware and software requirements.
- *NT/ Windows environment/ procedures.* Configuration of system, custom, and third-party software for the production batch and online system; development of training materials for long-term client support personnel and formal operation procedures.
- *Distributed operations management tools.* Development of formal standards for documenting operations management procedures; development and implementation of management tools to capture and maintain workstation and server configuration information; development and implementation of change control and trouble ticketing tools for managing the support of a distributed system.

Project Setup. The DSM team was formed as part of the overall project's technical team. Six months after the project began, the DSM team was formed with four primary subteams. The team was composed of 17 people: eight employees, eight consultants, and one third-party contractor. It completed its work in 10 months.

The DSM team's budget was 1,300 man-days of a total technical team budget of 4,500 man-days.

Operations Architecture Solutions and Products. During this project, many of the operations architecture functions were implemented through custom tools and procedures. The operations architecture supports the following functions:

- Production scheduling.
- Print management.
- File transfer.
- System start-up and shutdown.

- Mass storage management.
- Backup/restore management.
- Archiving.
- Event management.
- Performance management.
- Fault management.
- Recovery.
- Security management.
- User administration.
- Asset and configuration management.
- Release management.
- Software and data distribution.

Production Scheduling. This DSM team was responsible for determining the most efficient utilization of hardware and software resources in which to implement the 7x24 RA batch schedule of more than 1,200 programs and 200 daily, weekly, and monthly reports. The team had to balance online user requirements, batch operation time frames, and routine system maintenance (backups, data base checks). Because of the lack of batch scheduling products for the distributed environment, custom facilities were developed for managing the batch work load.

File Transfer/Event, Performance, and Fault Management. The event, fault, and performance management functions were developed around Microsoft's Systems Management Server. Systems Management Server provides the best platform for integrating the client's custom and third-party event and fault management tools into one cohesive system including:

- Hub and bridge/router management through Cabletron, Proteon, and Wellfleet's management systems.
- LAN performance management through the NetMatrix LAN traffic analysis tool.
- Information-gathering capabilities to Sybase through use of the DataPipe product.

In addition, the DSM team developed numerous simple network management protocol agents to alert operators to connectivity or failure fault events within the RA system. The team also developed a custom agent to spot fault events with the IBM mainframe/Compaq workstation file transfer system. Finally, the team developed a multilevel user interface which assists operators and technical support personnel in the management of the RA system.

The DSM team also developed several custom tools as part of the operations architecture to manage system utilization and to assist the capacity planning function. These tools included the following:

- Job performance summary (such as abends, start/stop time, CPU time, and number of transactions).
- Disk utilization and data base growth.
- CPU utilization by job.
- Memory utilization by job.

Print Management, System Start-up and Shutdown, Backup/ Restore Management, Archiving, Security Management. The NT environment and procedures team developed standard procedures for handling all the above systems management functions. Most of these functions were implemented using tools existing in the NT environment and additional architecture building was not required. Two 8mm tape jukebox systems implemented backup, restore, and archiving functions.

Asset and Configuration Management. The DSM architecture team developed custom architecture components to capture workstation and server configuration information. As they installed each workstation or server, team members ran a routine to capture information about the configuration of that machine. They could then run reports to analyze or report configuration information. This information was loaded into Systems Management Server to provide online configuration information for the system.

Release Management. The change control system built by the DSM architecture team manages new releases, migrations, and updates to application software. The change control system also captures any change to system software or hardware. The change control system was built on Remedy's Action Request System and was designed to provide a historical record of all changes and to inform all key support personnel of impending changes.

Updates to existing production software were done within the production system support environment. This environment provides tools to check in and check out production source code and to control the installation of the software back into the production environment.

New releases of application software were tested in the user acceptance (UA) environment before being migrated into production. The UA environment is a reflection of the system software and hardware within the production environment. Change control personnel who use custom-developed migration tools perform migration control of software within the UA environment.

Software and Data Distribution. Microsoft's Systems Management Server product coordinates system software and applications that must be installed on each production workstation. This product performs remote installation of system software and applications eliminating the need for manual intervention at each workstation.

Standardization. The degree of standardization within the environment affects the organizational structure and the skills required by individuals within the organization.

The airline implemented state-of-the-art technology to meet its business objectives. These technologies are not always static. To meet the changing skills challenge, internal human resources are supplemented with design skills and knowledge in key technologies from external vendors and consultants.

The responsibilities for each person in a support role change dramatically. Technology groups (e.g., a network group) no longer exist within the organization. Each person is responsible for completing certain tasks independently from the technologies needed to perform his or her tasks. A person responsible for server data backup, for example, is responsible for defining and scheduling that process across all server platforms. Standardized technologies allow this approach to be used without maintaining deep technical skills.

Operations Architecture Lessons Learned. At a high level, the most important lessons learned from this project about operations architectures are:

- *Most vendors are moving to just-in-time production strategies.* This means that the procurement of equipment must be carefully planned in advance with the vendor to ensure that the necessary quantities of equipment are available on time. This is particularly true in large environments.

- *Vendors do not always provide adequate technical support.* This causes delays in the resolution of incidents and causes frustration for both users and support personnel.

- *Vendor tracking during the incident resolution process is critical.* It is important to know when a vendor was contacted for support to be able to adequately assess the time it takes for a vendor to resolve an incident.

- *Some support personnel require a broad base of technical skills.* This facilitates the coordination and resolution of incidents within the distributed environment.
- *New technologies require new skills.* At this organization, for example, the unfamiliarity with the intricacies of TCP/IP and routing technologies created a number of additional challenges.
- *Select computing technology with operations considerations in mind.* The company had the luxury of having to deal with only a limited set of legacy systems and small installed base. This provided the somewhat unique opportunity to take a holistic cost/benefit approach to technology selection, which fully accounted for operations costs and complexities as part of every vendor and product evaluation. The result was a highly standardized and consistent technology architecture that involves relatively few and stable vendors and products for the client/server environment. Consequently, the operations architecture needed to support this environment is also relatively simple.
- *Focus on service levels.* The operations architecture decisions, as well as the application decisions themselves, were driven by service-level agreements. These agreements with the users helped both business users and information technology staff understand the risks, costs, and benefits of various product and application decisions. The focus on establishing service levels led to pragmatic decision making.
- *The technical architecture and network should be viewed as an investment.* Some resources can easily be identified as attributable to a given business area (e.g., product development or finance). By identifying the owners of these areas, the costs can be justified against specific business benefits and budgets. However, it is difficult to determine ownership for some of the common "infrastructure" services and technologies such as networks and operations architecture investments. The information systems organization must take the lead and champion necessary, though less glamorous, investments in infrastructure.

III-5

Evaluating Client/Server Architectures

A classic Dilbert comic strip describes the challenges and common misconceptions associated with client/server architecture. In this strip, the "boss" character explains that he's taken the initiative to put together a time line for the client/server architecture project. Using the reasoning that anything he does not understand must be easy to do, he concludes that the effort to design a client/server architecture for worldwide operations should take about six minutes. Although this is clearly an extreme position, it does an effective job of summarizing the situation many IT professionals face today: systems work is complex, and client/server just adds to the complexity.

But business problems need to get solved, and they need to get solved quickly. Business unit personnel and management (and sometimes even IT management) do not always appreciate the complexity faced by the systems people because they have their own problems to face. Nor do they want to really get the details of the complexity, they just want a solution. So what is an IT professional to do when the boss comes in and says he or she cannot understand why the client/server architecture cannot be ready for the application development effort that starts next week?

Obviously, complete custom development is not a possibility in such a case. Fortunately, client/server technology has matured in many areas to the point where architectures (or components of the architecture) can now be purchased for some or all of an organization's requirements. This chapter describes an approach for evaluating and selecting client/server architectures.

A SHIFT FROM BUILD TO BUY

Over the past few years, the IT market has shifted from an approach of custom developing a complete client/server architecture to an approach that emphasizes buying major pieces and gluing them together or buying a complete architecture and tailoring it for an organization's needs. The following sections describe the factors driving this shift, from both the supply side and the demand side.

Client/Server Architectures Are Not Cheap. Although simple implementations of a development and execution architecture might require from 500 to 1,000 days, enterprise class architectures covering the spectrum of development through operations typically require at least 3,000 days of effort and can easily grow beyond 5,000 days. Buying key components or a complete architecture should allow a reduction in effort of between 20% and 50% (and in extreme cases, even more).

Time Is of the Essence. Even if IS can fully justify the investment required by a custom built client/server architecture, the development time frame is still 12 to 18 months. That translates into at least a 6 to 12 month precursor to deploying any applications on top of it. (This assumes the architecture is stable enough to build applications on it about two-thirds of the way through architecture development.) That is a long time in today's competitive environment, and business units are looking to IS to find faster ways to deliver necessary capability. Trying to justify a 12 month delay for infrastructure can be quite challenging, 3 to 6 months is generally more palatable.

Client/Server Architectures Can Be Risky. As the demands placed on client/server applications (in terms of scale, volumes, and response time) increase, the chances of problems resulting from a completely new architecture increase dramatically. The result is usually delays in delivery and, in some cases, failure of a project. It is more prudent and much less stressful to identify architectures that have been used for applications with similar characteristics to the one being built rather than hope to account for the subtleties of products and components in a one-off situation.

For example, in the earlier days of client/server computing, it was common for problems to arise with certain GUI products when the size of the application passed a certain threshold. Up to this point, these products worked very well; beyond this point, performance could degrade dramatically. In most cases, workarounds could be identified. Sometimes it was a redesign of the application, other times it was a packaging approach (e.g., what windows were allocated to what executable and library). In either case, rework was required that caused delays and budget overruns.

In most cases, the experiences and solutions were similar. Had an architecture been reused that had already successfully delivered an application of the scale required by the new application, this kind of problem would have been avoided. And although this specific limitation and its workarounds are now well known, there are similar issues waiting to be encountered in other components (either because of similar thresholds or interactions caused by integration with other products). Reusing a proven architecture as a base should greatly reduce such surprises.

Parts of the Traditional Client/Server Market Have "Shaken Out". Although several areas of the client/server market have not yet simplified (e.g., intranets), many have. In the early 1990s, betting on any given component of a client/server architecture was very risky, whether it was the operating system (i.e., OS/2, UNIX, Windows, or Macintosh), database management system (i.e., SQLBase, SQL server, Sybase, Ingres, Oracle, or Informix), or GUI builder (i.e., VisualBasic, PowerBuilder, Neuron Data Open Interface, Smalltalk, SQLWindows, or Easel). Even to reuse an architecture, there were so many permutations, it was nearly impossible to find the one that matched specific needs and combinations of products and platforms.

Client/server architecture is becoming simpler, and although the choices are not down to a single option for any category, they are down to a manageable number. For example, most organizations today are interested in PowerBuilder, VisualBasic, or Visual C++ for their GUI tool. The same is true for operating systems: Windows is the clear favorite (i.e., 3.x, 95, or NT) for client desktops, and UNIX, NT, and MVS are the dominant server OSs. This "shake out" focuses more activity around a smaller set of products and increases the capability and options for buying versus building key pieces of an enterprise architecture. This is what provides the opportunity to obtain architectures for reuse.

ARCHITECTURE EVALUATION AND SELECTION PROCESS

Most organizations feel that their underlying architecture requirements are so unique that to custom build is the only option. In the early 1990s, that was a real problem. There were fewer viable client/server products available from third parties, and if an organization was going to make an investment in architecture, the investment was significant enough that it could justify tailoring it to its specific requirements.

Today, however, more third-party products are available, and the architecture effort has moved up to the integration and extension of these products rather than the development of the underlying products. Discussions of client/server architecture today include the "glue" code required to extend the GUI tool and integrate it with the middleware product used by the organization. Organizations are successfully buying major pieces of their architecture (both from vendors and other organizations) and then tailoring them for their own use. In some cases, they use a complete architecture with some tailoring; in other cases, they purchase just a component (i.e., batch architecture, process server architecture) and integrate it into their architecture. In both cases, the approach is similar. A process for evaluating, selecting, and tailoring an architecture is discussed in the following sections. As Exhibit III-5-1 depicts, there are five major activities to the process:

- *Defining an overall architecture strategy.* In this stage, inputs required for defining architecture requirements are collected and organized and the overall approach for implementing the architecture is defined.

- *Developing detailed architecture requirements.* This activity analyzes application, organization, and user requirements to develop a detailed definition of the desired architecture. This detailed definition serves as the target for assessing and selecting an architecture or components.

- *Screening architecture and component candidates.* This activity involves screening a preliminary list of candidates to identify a short list for more detailed consideration.

- *Selecting architecture and components.* This involves performing a detailed analysis of the short list of architectures and components to ensure a good fit with the requirements of the organization and then selecting the best suited ones.

- *Tailor architecture and components.* Once a final selection is made, any tailoring or extensions required must be planned and rolled into the overall architecture implementation and rollout plan.

When obtaining an architecture, it is important not to limit the initial search for candidates to just commercial software vendors because there may be more suitable architecture code (built on top of industry standard third-party software) available from organizations within or from outside a particular industry.

DEFINING AN OVERALL ARCHITECTURE STRATEGY

To define the architecture strategy, inputs required for defining architecture requirements are collected and organized, and the overall approach for implementing the architecture is defined. A key step in this activity is to identify the broad application styles and describe the corresponding architecture requirements. These application styles are driven by the business requirements and the vision of how client/server applications can help meet these requirements. In addition, a prelimi-

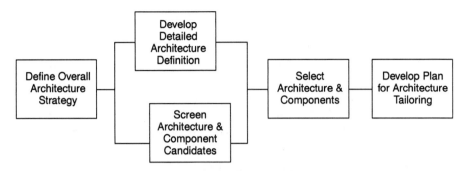

Exhibit III-5-1. Architecture Evaluation, Selection, and Tailoring Process

nary prioritization of application styles and architecture capabilities is usually developed to help with the remaining steps and activities.

In addition to the application styles that drive some of the core technical requirements, a set of guiding principles must be created that address some of the nontechnical, organizational strategy considerations. These guiding principles can be as important as the technical requirements. Some common considerations include:

- *Is there a hardware and software strategy already in place?* If so, what platforms need to be supported?
- Should the architecture be maintained internally or by a vendor?Some organizations prefer to deploy their limited technical resources to address the technical aspects of business problems rather than focus on architecture. Other organizations need more control over the architecture than a vendor could provide.
- *What level of support will be required by the applications and end users?* Does it need to be on site, or will phone support suffice? Is support required globally? Does support need to be available 24 hours a day? These considerations impact decisions on buy-versus-build and also on the vendors selected for pieces that are purchased.
- *Does the company's strategy or industry's direction impact choices?* For example, if a company is reaching out to its customers' systems, it may not be able to dictate the architecture. As a result, this may impact the company's options, such as operating system and platform, desktop environment, and security approach.
- *Does the company predominantly opt for custom or packaged installations?* Packages usually provide their own architecture and specify a set of options for key components (e.g., DBMS supported, network support, operating system, hardware platforms). The organization

may need to integrate multiple architectures or may be best suited by extending a package's architecture rather than creating another architecture that must be integrated.

- *What is the scale of the typical application development effort?* If most projects consist of 5 to 10 developers, then a complex development environment for 500 may not be required. Conversely, implementing an architecture proven for 20 may not be wise if the company consistently uses 200-person teams for application development efforts.

Once the architecture requirements have begun to be documented, it should be possible to begin identifying candidate architectures or components and begin preparing screening questions for use in the screening activity.

Beginning to identify the candidates at this point helps structure the requirements to make the screening and evaluation process more straightforward—for example, by using terminology as used by vendors, by reflecting common packaging of functions and features into products or architecture components (e.g., a GUI tool usually provides a window painter, a widget set, and may provide links to source code management and a repository). Beginning to create the list of candidates now also allows more time for the evolution of the complete list rather than trying to identify all real candidates in a short search. Vendors, technical periodicals, and other contacts in the industry are useful for starting the candidate list.

DEVELOPING A DETAILED ARCHITECTURE DEFINITION

Using the application styles and other requirements defined in the previous activity, the next step is to define the architecture at a detailed, logical level—a description of the types of services and features necessary to support the business applications and recommendations for purchase or development of the various components for the physical implementation.

Rather than start from a blank piece of paper, it is helpful to use proven architecture models as a starting point for this activity. Clearly the final architecture must be tailored to the organization's requirements, but there is usually no benefit in starting a list of components and logical model completely from scratch.

For example, an organization that wants to use an Object Request Broker (ORB) may not immediately recognize that there is a relationship with their groupware requirements. There should be a common set of message delivery and directory services because, at some future point, the objects managed by the ORB will likely overlap with the groupware package (e.g., documents may become objects and objects may be shareable or mailable). This relationship becomes more apparent when one notices that both of these services require directory and transport capabilities.

The basic steps to follow are to walk through the architecture requirements and the components described in the model menu and map them to one another. Working through both lists ensures that no requirements are omitted and no services are overlooked that might not be directly related to a stated requirement.

When working through the lists, it is important to prioritize the components and services, because most architectures cannot be fully built in one iteration within a reasonable time frame. Certain basic components (i.e., common services, presentation services, and data access) tend to be required early on. Other components (e.g., workflow, multimedia support, and document management) may not be required in the first release of the architecture, but must be considered when implementing the core components.

When creating the detailed architecture definition and prioritizing the components and services, work can also begin on the questions and criteria to be used for evaluating candidate architectures and components. The goal is a detailed definition and an evaluation questionnaire upon completion of this activity. An example of a detailed questionnaire is attached as an appendix to this chapter.

SCREENING ARCHITECTURE AND COMPONENT CANDIDATES

This activity screens a longer list of candidates to come up with a short list for more detailed consideration. The idea is similar to a two-stage product selection in which a preliminary screening process eliminates products that do not meet some key criteria and allows a more in depth and thorough analysis to be performed on a handful of finalist products.

The overall goal is to identify and ask key questions that differentiate between candidates and allows the elimination or ranking of them before getting into detailed function and feature comparisons. These differentiating factors may be high-level and driven by the guiding principles—for example, the need to leverage existing COBOL skills by limiting the selection to architectures that use COBOL or COBOL-like languages—or by detailed criteria specific to components (i.e., the TCP/IP dialer must have the ability to be controlled via an API, must not require user intervention, and must support the Winsock standard).

High-level screening questions should be posed concerning the following issues:

- *Scope of the architecture.* What are the key products and components offered by the architecture (e.g., workflow management, integrated performance support)? What is the coverage across the development, execution, and operations architectures? What assumptions or constraints does the architecture make about the overall application architecture? What kinds of applications is this architecture inappropriate for?

- *Support for the knowledge transfer.* What kind of resources are required and available to assist during the evaluation and then during tailoring and rollout? This is especially important when dealing with architecture because the integration of components is generally more complex than an individual product.
- *Information availability.* Is sufficiently detailed documentation available that can be used during the screening and evaluation? Does the documentation accurately describe the architecture, or is it out of date? Does it accurately describe the development process?
- *Site reference information.* Is detailed reference information available from three to five reference sites? The information should include project size (i.e., peak personnel), duration of project, scale of system in production and contact names.

Although there is no "right" answer as to the number of candidates to screen, usually a number between 20 and 40 is a reasonable limit depending on the scope of the architecture, its complexity, and its intended use. If it is an enterprisewide selection, it is better to broaden the search; if the architecture will be used to jump-start a quick project, 10 to 15 candidates may be appropriate. The elapsed time on a screening can be anywhere from one to eight weeks, depending on the number of candidates and the efficiency of the information exchange. A lot of time can be lost waiting for nondisclosure agreements to be approved and signed.

The screening effort should allow between one and two workdays per candidate product for the screening activities and should be spread across a team of between one and three people. The end deliverable of this activity is a finalist list of candidates with preliminary rankings in case time does not permit a full evaluation of all candidates. The goal should be to pare down to a list of three to five candidates for a more detailed analysis and evaluation prior to selection.

SELECTING ARCHITECTURE AND COMPONENTS

There are many ways to make and document an architecture decision. One approach uses a matrix that summarizes the required features along with their priorities and cross-references these to the architecture candidates. The basic idea is to develop a list of selection criteria (i.e., a combination of architecture requirements and other considerations) with weightings that reflect the importance of each to the project or organization. As each candidate is considered, a score is developed for each criteria that is then weighted according to priority. The total score for each candidate is then used to determine an initial ranking of candidates. It is very important not to focus only on a numerical score as the final decision-maker because much subjective information is captured during the evaluation that cannot be fully reflected in a weighting and a score.

The score is useful for providing a common comparison basis and for pointing out areas in which candidates are particularly strong or weak. However, such an important decision cannot easily be reduced to a single number. As a result, once a preliminary ranking is created, additional analysis and discussion is usually performed to drive out a final decision. The matrix and supporting documentation are useful deliverables for communicating the approach and status, facilitating a discussion leading to selection, and then documenting the final decision.

Creating a Matrix for Candidate Comparison

Exhibit III-5-2 shows a pictorial representation of such a matrix. The left-hand column represents the selection criteria that are grouped into application characteristics, technical characteristics, and other considerations. The criteria are explicitly grouped into these categories to ensure that more than just technical considerations are used in the selection.

For example, the most technically adept candidate might not be a good choice if adequate support and knowledge transfer resources are not available to ensure proper skill transfer and training into the target organization within the required time frame. Similarly, if an organization has certain platforms or languages that must be supported, some technical features may need to be sacrificed to fulfill these other requirements. The point here is the importance of looking at all requirements and not focusing only on the technical functions and features of a candidate.

The second column assigns a priority or importance to the criteria. This column is used to differentiate the various line items. Without it, a numerical score would only reflect a sum of the checked items. By assigning a weight to a criteria, candidates that satisfy many unimportant criteria are less likely to be ranked higher than candidates that meet fewer, but very important, criteria. In addition to assisting in the scoring, this column is a useful confirmation with other stakeholders of the priorities placed on the various selection criteria. This way, the head of

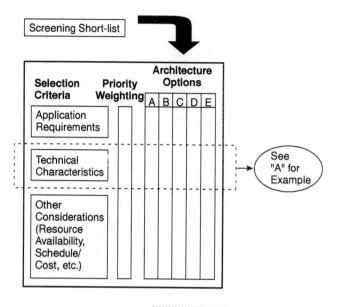

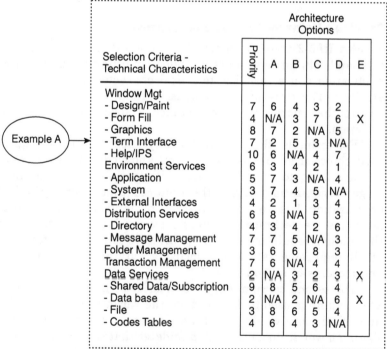

Exhibit III-5-2. Matrix for Comparing Candidates

operations, for example, will be able to verify that his or her requirements have been heard and properly valued in any final decision.

The last set of columns represent the short list of candidates (i.e., one column per candidate). At the intersection of a criteria and a candidate, a score is recorded to reflect how well the candidate satisfies the criteria. A weighted score is calculated for each criteria and a total score summed up for the candidate.

Although the mechanics of the matrix are fairly straightforward, there are some aspects of this activity that are worth noting:

- Constructing the matrix involves performing a detailed analysis of the short list of candidates to ensure a good fit with the requirements of the organization. This is very detailed work that involves a lot of learning and investigation in a very short amount of time. Depending on the level of detail and the scope of the selection, the actual work effort per candidate can range from five to fifteen workdays. This work can usually be split between two or three people, but these need to be personnel that are familiar with the architecture requirements.

- Actively updating the documentation as candidates are evaluated is extremely important because, after a few weeks, the details of each one will begin to blur. By the end of such a selection, it may be difficult to clearly differentiate between the details of each candidate without referring to the evaluation notes.

- Planning the amount of elapsed time per candidate should allow for scheduling visits, getting questionnaires sent and returned, requesting and reviewing candidate documentation, performing an in-depth discussion with the candidate representatives (architects from the vendor or organization that owns the candidate components), checking references, and writing up the results. This process will rarely take less than one week and is usually better planned as three to four weeks.

Along the way, it is important to constantly revisit the priorities of the requirements to balance the desired features against what is available. For example, some features may not be available in any of the candidates (e.g., the link to the source code management system is not quite perfect). In such cases, it is often worth adjusting the requirement or accepting a workaround rather than deciding to implement a custom solution. It is important to keep track of any compromises and workarounds so that they can be reflected in the details and priorities of the architecture definition. The revised definition, along with the details of the selected architecture, represent the scope and approach for the implementation and are key inputs to the next activity.

DEVELOPING PLANS FOR ARCHITECTURE TAILORING

This last activity creates the plans for tailoring and deploying the architecture to the project or organization. The plan should be detailed enough to arrange staffing and set dependent schedules accordingly and to confirm that the scope for the first architecture release is realistic. Preliminary plans for subsequent releases should also be produced, but these are usually at a higher level of detail (i.e., overall number of workdays, total elapsed time, and total number of resources). Once the plans are finalized and any necessary negotiations completed for acquiring the architecture components, the implementation project can be initiated.

SUMMARY

Organizations can significantly reduce their client/server development times by moving from custom development of architectures to an approach based on piecing together ready-made components. The 20-50% reduction in workdays resulting from this approach represents profound cost savings. In addition, the risky domain of client/server development can be lessened considerably by purchasing proven products.

Of course, no reduction in expense and risk will accrue unless companies are careful to evaluate their needs and map them against existing products. In the appendix that follows is a sample of a questionnaire that organizations can use to help develop their detailed architecture definition. Client/server development has reached a point of maturation at which it no longer makes practical sense to begin evaluation from scratch. The logical client/server model that is the basis for this book can be used to more easily map your particular requirements to necessary services.

APPENDIX
SAMPLE ARCHITECTURE QUESTIONNAIRE

INITIAL SCREENING QUESTIONS

Availability of Information

- Can we take documentation with us and use as a reference within our organization?
- Is there documentation that accurately describes the architecture? Does it reflect the current implementation of the architecture?
- Is there documentation that is used to communicate the architecture to developers? Does it reflect the current implementation of the architecture?

Site Reference Information

Site reference information includes:

- Project size (including peak personnel).
- Length of the project (days).
- Current phase of the project.
- Planned production date for the implementation of the architecture (past or future date).

Scope of Architecture

This includes information about the key products in the architecture and key technologies (e.g., workflow management, integrated performance support, migration to client/server). The following questions should be asked to determine the scope of the architecture:

- Is there a clearly defined development, execution, and operations architecture? Or is it more of an application architecture?
- Is at least one application being implemented using the architecture(s) currently or has one already been implemented?
- What is the scope of the development architecture?
- What is the scope of the execution architecture?
- What is the scope of the operations architecture?
- How much of the architecture is package or custom?
- Is the architecture stable and proven?

Support for Knowledge Transfer

Would architecture experts have availability to review requirements and have an on-site discussion over 2 elapsed days?

Preparation Questions

These questions should be sent to the selection team for evaluation:

- What are the work plans for developing architectures?
- What type of documentation is there for the overall structure of the architectures?
- What type of documentation is available for integration points or bridges between components?
- What are the basic methods, standards, and procedures for development?
- What are the layers of isolation for the architecture?

- What does the technical environment include (i.e., hardware, system software, networks, data management, development tools, and operating systems)?
- What is the data location strategy and how was it decided upon?
- What is the process location strategy and how was it decided upon?
- What type of documentation is there for the individual components of the architecture (i.e., security, codes, tables)?

Materials for Vendors to Review Prior to Detailed Discussions

Following are preparation questions for vendors to review before detailed discussions begin:

- What are the development architecture requirements?
- What are the execution architecture requirements?
- What are the operations architecture requirements?

Materials for Vendors to Send to Selection Team for Review Prior to Detailed Discussion

Following are materials that vendors should send to the selection team before discussions begin between them:

- Architectural overview documents.
- Work plans.

Talk to the Experts

Before planning for a new architecture, the following people should be consulted:

- *The technical expert.* This person is responsible for establishing and maintaining the technical environment. The individual should have knowledge of the products, issues, and resolutions of technical issues and integration issues and lessons learned.
- *The development expert.* This person is responsible for establishing the development architecture. The individual should have knowledge about the overall structure, how and why decisions were made regarding the architecture, and lessons learned.
- *The execution expert.* This person is responsible for establishing the execution architecture. The individual should have knowledge about the overall structure, how and why decisions were made regarding the architecture, and lessons learned.
- *The operations expert.* This person is responsible for establishing the

operations architecture. The individual should have knowledge about the overall structure, how and why decisions were made regarding the architecture, and lessons learned.

QUESTIONS FOR DETAILED DISCUSSION

Following are issues that should be addressed during detailed discussions of new systems architecture(s).

Drivers

A summary of the business drivers for the implementation of the architecture should be provided. For example, some of the business drivers for the Universal Airlines architecture are:

- Universal's business applications should offer a consolidated view of business data that allows for mission-critical business information to move in real time ahead of the freight.
- The architecture should dramatically improve the time to market for new and modified Universal business applications.

Overall Architecture Questions

The following questions should be asked before architecture decisions are made:

- Is a manual system being automated or upgraded?
- Did an architecture already exist?
- Was the architecture revamped completely or partially?
- Were there any "stakes in the ground" when the architecture requirements were defined?
- Has the architecture been sold and implemented on other projects? If so, how many times?
- What other architectures were considered and why were they not implemented?

Scale of Architecture Implementation

The evaluation team should establish the scale of implementation that the architecture is suited for by determining the:

- Number of users.
- Transaction rates.

- Database size.
- Number of distributed sites.
- Number of developers supported.
- Technical environment (i.e., hardware, operating system, protocols, database management system).

Estimating the Development Effort in Total Workdays

To estimate the amount of time a development effort should take, the following should be determined:

- The total number of project workdays.
- The number of workdays spent building the architecture.
- The number of days spent training developers (per developer).
- The expected project duration (in months).

Architecture Layers

The following questions should be asked to determine the nature of the architecture layers:

- What APIs or services were developed in the architecture?
- How was the application modularized for isolation and code reuse and portability?
- Where are the processes located? How was this decision made?
- Where is the data located? How was this decision made?
- Does the architecture support application to application interoperability? What if they are on different architectures?
- What was the approach for the location of the SQL? Is the SQL located on the client or server? If it is on the server, is it embedded in services, isolated for reuse, or in stored procedures?
- What methods, standards and procedures were developed? How were they enforced? Is there a table of contents for the standards and procedures? (It is helpful to keep a copy of the table of contents rather than the detail because most architectures have a significant amount of documentation for the standards and procedures.)

Architecture Requirements

To determine architecture requirements, the following questions should be asked:

- Is this an international application with needs for NLS (National Language Support) or MLS (Multiple Language Support)? How is this handled?
- What were the guiding requirements for designing the architecture? What is going to be achieved in the long term (i.e., reuse, isolation, flexibility of product usage, portability)?
- Can the requirements be delineated into the following categories:
  - Overall requirements for the architecture.
  - Requirements for the development environment.
  - Requirements for the execution architecture.
  - Requirements for the operations architecture.
- What style of application is being supported (i.e., the style of interaction, the user service class)?

The following table contains examples of user service classes:

User Service Class	Data Entry	Data Inquiry	ATM
Frequency & Style of HCI	Textual Form Filling	Graphical Interface	User Friendly Interface
Performance	Avg. 3 sec response	Sub second response	Avg. 3 sec response
Resilience	High Resilience	High	High
Security & Access Control	High, restricted to data entry clerks	Low	High
Business Cycles	Daily, monthly cycles	Daily	Daily, monthly cycles
Service Hours	Requires 8 hrs of downtime nightly	24 hr	24 hr
Geographic Location	4 Corporate, 30 Sites	4 Corporate	250 citywide locations
User Numbers	2,000 users	200 users	10,000 users

LESSONS FOR OVERALL ARCHITECTURE

To evaluate the overall development effort, implementers might ask:

- What were the key lessons learned?
- What were the key lessons learned regarding issues and areas of concern?
- When is it appropriate not to use the architecture?

Common Questions for Each Component

Following are questions that can be asked to evaluate the appropriateness of each component of the architecture.

General Questions

- What aspect of the component is used in the architecture?
- What was not implemented and why?
- What was the requirement for using this component?
- Was an isolation layer developed for this component?
- Were services commonly used for reusability?
- What was the complexity of implementing the component based upon the approach (custom versus product)?
- Were services developed for the server to support this component? For the client?

Commercial Product Questions

- Is a commercial product used to meet full functionality of the component? Partial functionality?
- What is the current version of the tool used?
- Is there documentation on why a product was selected?
- Did the criteria used in selecting the product include:
  - Stability of the product.
  - Integration with other architectural components.
  - Vendor relationship.
  - Cost.
  - Features of product.
  - Scalability.
  - Portability.
  - Platform.
  - Vendor support.
  - Skill requirements.
  - Ease of use.
- What were the other product options?
- How were the products chosen? Was an in-depth product evaluation conducted?
- What are the notable features or strengths of the product?
- Does the product have any generic services that are useful?

- What are the weaknesses of the product?
- Are there any problems with product support from the vendor?
- Was vendor relationship a key criterion in selecting a product?
- Is the product used in any other components of the architectures?
- Is the product easy to use? Install? What is the learning curve for using the product?
- Are there particular skills or training that are critical for this product?
- What are the valuable experiences or lessons learned using this product?

Custom Development Questions

- Was any custom development done for this component?
- Was the custom development used to meet full or partial functionality?
- Was the custom development done to extend the functionality of a product?
- Was the customization modularized? Could it be packaged and used by other projects? Would it be useful to other projects or is it very specific to the client business or environment?

Questions Concerning the Interface to Other Architectural Components

- Was the product chosen based on a decision made elsewhere in the architecture?
- Were there any integration issues with products chosen?
- Is there custom development for integration with another architectural component?

Note: The remainder of the questionnaire reflects an example for a particular architecture model. The details would need to be customized for the specific model being used and the components being selected.

SPECIFIC QUESTIONS FOR COMPONENTS

- Does this tool provide the functionality for database design also?
- If not, then is there an interface to allow the output of data modeling to be the input for database design?

- Does the prototype interface accurately reflect the interface that will be used in the application?
- Was the prototype developed using the same tool that will be used in the application development?
- Can the prototype windows be reused in the detailed design of window?
- Can the prototype code be reused in the development of the application?
- Does this tool allow the designer to generate the DDLs to define the database?
- Can these DDLs be used in any database engine (i.e., ORACLE, SYBASE, DB2)?
- Is there an interface to the design repository? Are the data elements defined stored in the repository? If an element changes, is the change reflected in all tables containing the element by regenerating the database from the repository?
- Does the tool allow the definition of common modules? Can these common modules be referenced by multiple components?
- Can application design shells be constructed and used?
- Is there an interface to the design repository?
- Does the presentation design interface accurately reflect the interface which will be used in the application?
- Is there an interface to the design repository? Are the elements used for the windows, reports, screens defined in the design repository? If the element changes in the design repository, is it automatically reflected in the presentation design?
- How are changes to the shells populated to the designs and code using the shells?
- Is there version control for the shells?
- Is there an interface to the design repository? Where are the application design shells stored?

Test Planning

Tooting providoo tho orooo roforonoing of dialogo or oxooutabloo tootod in a cycle to the specific functionality in a design. Following are functions in the testing process:

- Test data management. The test data management interface allows the transfer of test data to be invoked from the test planning tool prior to the execution of a cycle.
- Test execution. This interface relates the actual scripts to test plans to provide automated script playback capability.

- Configuration management. This function provides the cross referencing of dialogs or executables tested in a cycle to the specific functionality in a design.

INTERFACING TO OTHER ARCHITECTURAL COMPONENTS

The evaluation team should determine whether there is an interface to the problem management system to link the test results, expected results, and data comparison results to a problem. Ensuring a smooth interface between architectural components also involves:

- Problem management. The evaluation team should determine whether there is an interface between the components of the new architecture and the design repository.
- Configuration management.
- Version control.
- Commercial product selection. It should be determined whether the application modules can be maintained independently and how many developers can work on a single application.
- Change control.
- Developing an interface to the problem management system. This would link the problem to the change request for changes to the application source code.
- Migration control.
- Selection of information management tools.

Database Requirements

To determine database requirements, the following questions should be asked:

- Is database partitioning implemented? Why? What is the scheme?
- What are the following requirements:
  - Database size and distribution.
  - Estimated number of data entities.
  - Estimated number of data elements.
  - Estimated database size (i.e., in gigabytes).
  - Largest number of rows in a table.
- Is data distributed across multiple DBMS?
- Is the data distributed across multiple locations?
- Is the database access primarily local access? Remote access?

- Is the database access done through ODBC drivers? Natively? Other?
- What is the scheduling of the synchronization—batch or real time or a combination of both?
- What is the frequency of the synchronization—hourly, daily, weekly, or monthly?
- What is the location strategy for the codes tables—local PC, local server, remote server, or enterprise server?
- How are the codes tables replicated and maintained?
- Which of the following criteria are used to determine if a TP monitor is required?
  - Number of users accessing the system.
  - High throughput requirements.
  - High availability requirement.
  - Distribution of systems across multiple nodes.
  - Scalability of system in the future.
  - Interoperability between autonomous and heterogeneous processors.
  - Mission-criticality of the system.
  - Access to legacy systems.
  - Access to nonrelational data.
  - Access and update capabilities to more than one database or more than one type of database.
  - Complex security requirements.
- Which criteria were used to choose between TP monitors?
  - Interest in stable or emerging technologies
  - DCE requirement
  - Type of system (new vs. rehosting/downsizing an existing mainframe system)
  - Existing personnel with mainframe-CICS experiences
  - System uses PC-based clients
  - Plan to use Windows NT
  - Platforms/operating systems that the servers run on
  - Mainframe connectivity requirement

Security

The evaluation team should determine which of the following features will be incorporated into the architecture:

- Security level support.

- User rights definition.
- Security services (i.e., authentication, authorization).
- User login and logout facilities.
- Encryption support.

III-6
The Design of Graphical User Interfaces

The design of client/server applications requires major changes to the traditional approaches of application design in several areas, including the graphical user interface (GUI).

The GUI presents significant new design challenges. Users are demanding easy-to-learn and easy-to-use software. The GUI gives the applications designer the capability to deliver on this demand, but achieving ease of use is more easily said than done.

This chapter begins with an overview of usability concepts and then discusses techniques to make these concepts a reality in application design. The remainder of the chapter outlines a process for designing GUIs to deliver on the goal of usability.

DESIGNING FOR USABILITY

Usability and user-centered design have become essential features of today's application design environment. Client/server computing has opened up information technology to almost every person in the workplace. But this egalitarian and democratic characteristic of computing also puts demands on the design of applications. They must be usable by a wide spectrum of people, from different cultural and educational backgrounds and with differing levels of patience for the intricacies of information technology.

Today's computer "users" do not define themselves in terms of the computer; they demand that the computer systems define themselves in terms of human capabilities. They demand that systems and applications support workers in the manner in which they actually conduct their activities in business.

Today's technologies continue to move us away from rigid interfaces that provide only limited, fixed-terminal access to segmented information. It is becoming more feasible to provide flexible interfaces with seamless, shared, and even mobile computing access to information that crosses traditional boundaries within organizations.

Usability Drivers

The attention being paid today to principles of advanced computing usability is driven by several phenomena:

- *Disappointing preliminary results.* There is a growing sense on the part of users that information technology and the new intuitive interfaces developed to date have not fulfilled their promise that they would increase organizational productivity and effectiveness. Each new application still requires traditional approaches to training. Classes have to be designed and conducted, resulting in direct costs due to lost personnel productivity.

- *Companies are "hiring the customer."* Organizations today are finding new ways to bring customers into processes, allowing them to perform tasks that workers previously did. Automated teller machines, voice response units, web sites, and kiosks, for example, will continue to proliferate. But as the novelty of these devices begins to wear off, customers are rebelling against poorly designed systems. If an organization is to be successful at implementing customer-operated applications, the systems must be designed for maximum intuitiveness and expedience and must require little or no support from a company's service representatives.

- *Shrink-wrapped software packages are "raising the bar" for usability.* Because of successful software in the personal computer (PC) marketplace, users have high expectations for how their business systems should work. Software such as Quicken has set a standard to which business applications are being compared.

- *Capability is exceeding people's ability to use it.* In today's environment, technology can overwhelm users if applied in the wrong way, actually hindering and not enabling their work. For example, in one system, technologists determined that users needed to view images (e.g., a bill). After implementation, however, the organization discovered that retrieving the image took too much user time and effort. The users wanted not the image but a more understandable data representation of the transactions and balances. A key usability concept is spending time with the users, understanding what they need, and then designing a process that matches those needs.

Usability vs. System Acceptability

Usability is one aspect of the overall acceptability of systems. There are at least four interrelated dimensions of system acceptability:

- Social acceptability.
- Practical acceptability.

- Usefulness.
- Usability.

Although the industry at times seems to stress the usability of systems above everything else, it is just as important to address practical acceptability, social acceptability, and usefulness to determine what the users need. In some cases users were unable to use systems efficiently and designers made the mistake of addressing the problem only in terms of usability. Their conclusion: The metaphor and the icons must be wrong. Bring in some graphic designers; try new metaphors; make new toolbars. However, these did not work either because the entire design had flawed social or practical assumptions.

Social acceptability may be a particular problem for customer systems such as automated teller machines. Customers may resent being forced to do work that the company previously did for them. They may also resent the fact that there may be a charge attached to a service that used to be provided for free.

Social acceptability problems also arise in new customer service environments which, for reasons of efficiency, redirect customers away from their local store or branch to a new call center. For example, a local branch or store manager may have waived charges for certain important customers. But when that customer is rerouted, no such relationship exists. In this case, an impersonal call center may actually start driving customers away.

Social acceptability problems also arise when organizations do not take the time to understand their customers. Some companies have introduced 24-hour access voice response systems, only to discover real resistance after implementation. Their customers are hanging up on the voice response system, or pressing 0 for an operator, or even traveling to a local branch to speak with a representative in person. Designers may fail to recognize a variety of factors: Perhaps some customers want more personal interaction, or look upon these calls as partly social experiences, not just business ones. Or perhaps customers are seeking more complex information that cannot be handled efficiently by the voice response system.

Practical usability can surface through flawed practical assumptions. Flawed practical assumptions are usually related to underestimating the cost impacts of a particular technology or architecture.

Take, for example, the decision to use multimedia or imaging as key components of a new system. This decision implies that it is practical to do so—that the benefits justify the necessary and potentially costly new network requirements. But what if the benefits cannot justify it?

Sometimes designers attempt a scaled-down version of the original concept, but this version may end up being unusable simply because it is too slow over the kind of limited network capability that could be set up. The system makes the customer wait too long for a response. The impact of practical acceptability must be assessed early in the planning phase for a new system, especially one demanding major infrastructure or operational upgrades.

Finally, a system must be both useful and usable. "Useful" relates to the utility or actual use of the system or application. If a system or application does not prove useful to a user it does not matter how usable it is. The user has no reason for the application. "Usable" relates to how the system or application is used or operated. If a system or application is difficult to use, acceptance of the system or application becomes an issue for the user and the productivity goals will not be achieved.

Aspects of Usability

Usability has five major dimensions:

- Easy to learn.
- Efficient to use.
- Easy to remember.
- Prone to fewer errors.
- Subjectively pleasing.

Each of these dimensions can be measured quantitatively by task timings, error rates, and user satisfaction ratings.

USABILITY BUILDING BLOCKS

A number of elements must come together to create highly usable software (see Exhibit III-6-1).

Clear Affordances

The first building block of usability is clear "affordances." Affordances are the capabilities and functions of the system—what the system lets the user do.

One way to understand affordances is to look at a chair: From its appearance, its behavior when the user touches it, and from the general experience of living, users can easily figure out what it can do for them—what it "affords" them. The chair's affordances are visible and unmistakable.

With systems, a button on a window is not an affordance in itself; the button affords pushing and the button label describes what will happen

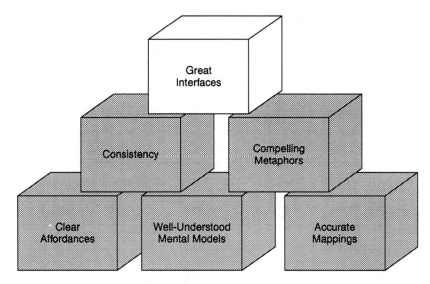

Exhibit III-6-1. Usability Building Blocks

---

when the button is pressed. Affordances are made visible through metaphors that take advantage of the other building blocks.

Well-Understood Mental Models

How do users think of the task? What picture(s) would they draw to describe the different objects and their relationships to each other? For example, a user of personal finance software already knows and understands the concept of a checkbook or check register, so Quicken uses that model in its software.

Compelling Metaphors

Metaphors make affordances visible to the user. Applications can have powerful affordances that are not clear to the user. DOS, for example, has powerful capability and affordances, but they are hidden behind the C:\prompt.

Interface metaphors are usually representations of real-world objects—such as notebooks, trash cans, or buttons—that take advantage of a user's prior knowledge. When users see a button on an interface, they can press on it with a mouse click and have a high degree of confidence that something will happen. If the button is also well labeled, users can also have some confidence about what behavior the button will invoke.

There are many possible mental models from which to choose during design; good metaphors map clearly to the proper mental model of the user. If the user's mental model is well understood, developing appropriate metaphors is simplified.

Accurate Mappings

Designers should seek direct mappings—clear links—between the user's mental model and the system's affordances. The more direct the mapping, the more usable the system is. Users can find features quickly because their mental model is synchronized with the interface. The internal workings of the software may be entirely different from the interface's model. What is important is that the user is never reminded of this difference.

Consistency

The mappings of a user model to system affordances must not only be accurate but consistent as well. Consistency reinforces both the mappings and the user's mental model. Consistency also shields the user from the mechanics of the system.

For example, applications should be consistent about when a user needs to single-click or double-click during any list selection function. Although the PC software world has some strong examples to follow, it may not offer designers the examples they need.

In many cases, designers have struggled to make "File—open, close, print, exit" and "Edit" meaningful for their business applications. What works for the document publishing world may not work for every business. Maybe "Customer—retrieve, search for" is more appropriate. Designers should be consistent but use judgment as well.

These usability building blocks lead to powerful interfaces that are fun and engaging, are invisible (i.e., the user is thinking only of the task, not the mechanics of operating the interface), improve performance of the user, and increase the value delivered to the organization.

USABILITY AND THE DESIGN PROCESS

Advanced usability ultimately is a function of process, not tools. Tools such as style guides and GUI development software (discussed later) provide some low-level consistency: Windows, for example, are laid out consistently and have the same font sizes and color schemes.

But tools cannot help design interfaces with accurate mappings to a user's mental model of a task. These mappings require human experience and knowledge. A tool can provide a methodology, but cannot substitute for direct experience.

In addition, usability is not a science. Unlike conventional system performance, an interface's intuitiveness and learnability cannot be easily predicted with a model or algorithm. It must be tested with real users.

As with performance, usability can and should be measured. Usability objectives, along with other goals related to such things as performance, response time, and business objectives, should be set at the beginning of the development effort. They can be set by examining benchmarks from the current process and systems, if similar ones exist, and competitors' approaches in the same or a similar industry.

Attention to usability concepts moves designers further along toward the ultimate goal of meeting the users' business needs. The challenge of today's technology advancements is not just technical integration but also functional integration. The capability bar is being raised by the ability to process and access more and varying types of information, but usability is the key to fitting into or redesigning the user's work environment.

GUI APPLICATION DESIGN

A graphical user interface can be more intuitive for users, but it forces designers to think of presenting capability in a new and different way. User interface designers should be aware of a set of basic guidelines as well as a documentation technique for capturing and communicating GUI application designs.

Designing the GUI for Usability

GUIs are a driving force behind client/server technology because they are a major factor in delivering systems that are intuitive, efficient, and easy to learn and use. However, designers do not achieve these benefits automatically simply by throwing a graphical front end onto a system.

An inexperienced GUI designer can actually create a graphical interface that is more difficult to learn and use. GUI design gives designers much more freedom, but freedom can easily become anarchy and chaos. The flexibility and multitude of design options that the GUI affords heightens the importance of a more methodical approach to interface design.

This chapter focuses on the tasks related to designing the GUI segment of a client/server application. The planning chart in Exhibit III-6-2 outlines the activities relevant to graphical user interface design within the design application task.

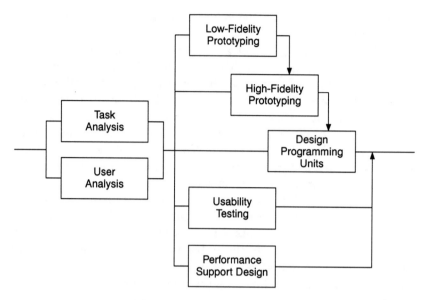

Exhibit III-6-2. Process for GUI Design

Task Analysis. Task analysis defines the activities that users perform or need to perform. If a development project is automating existing tasks, task analysis can be performed through observation. However, the goal often stressed with client/server development projects is not simply to automate existing processes but to use the technology as an accompaniment to a business process reengineering initiative. In that case, task analysis becomes a matter of reinventing processes and user roles.

The goal of task analysis is to identify the steps within the performance of a task or process, as well as the typical and possible orderings in which those steps can occur. In contrast to conventional functional analysis, task analysis is much more user-centered. Whereas functional analysis highlights the need for certain data to be maintained in a system, task analysis describes how users would like to maintain that data. Often, users complain that to complete what they consider to be one task, they must navigate through several windows and software modules. Task analysis helps organize capability according to user needs, thus increasing usability and productivity.

User Analysis. User analysis defines the types of users who will be using the application. When creating any human-computer interface, it is important to understand the "customers" of the system. A system that is appropriate for clerical workers may not be appropriate for executives.

The two most relevant dimensions of user characteristics are their understanding of the task (how much they know about the task is to be performed) and their computer systems usage experience level.

When designing an interface for users with a low understanding of how the task is to be done, the user interface must be much more supportive of the performance of the business process or task, leading users step by step if necessary. Designers must consider how much online help and reference material to make available and how to make that help available within the context of performing a task (e.g., context- sensitive help or online reference materials).

In addition, designers need to take into account the fact that users need much more support the first few times they use an application. If the user will be using the application every day, the user's need for help may be minimal after he or she has become proficient, and so the help facilities should not slow the user's task performance.

Users who already have experience in a graphical windowing environment can be expected to understand such common user interface metaphors as file folders and the desktop. For these users, it is best to try and keep the user interface consistent with GUI applications with which they are already familiar. If, on the other hand, the users are not familiar with computer systems and GUIs, it is worthwhile to look for yet more intuitive metaphors that users can understand without training.

Careful study of the user types can also help in selecting appropriate interface metaphors to which users can relate. For example, if the user population is doctors, a flip chart metaphor that closely resembles the information organization of their current manual system may ease user learning and acceptance.

GUI Design Prototyping. Prototyping is an essential component of the process for designing graphical user interfaces. Prototyping gives designers the chance to test various design concepts on real users.

User interface designers often think they know what the user likes or dislikes, but their track record of accurate predictions has not always been good. Without the appropriate use of prototyping, these wrong assumptions turn up in the final product. When users then object to some aspect of the interface design, they are often told it is too late and too expensive to make a change. The goal of user interface prototyping is to catch design problems in design, when correcting them is usually easier and less expensive.

There are two types of prototyping: low fidelity and high fidelity.

Low-Fidelity Prototyping. A common mistake in user interface prototyping is to invest too much time and money constructing a running prototype of an interface before showing it to the users. The problem with that approach is that few people then want to spend money revising the prototype based on user feedback. Typically, the entire prototyping budget is spent simply creating it. After so much time, effort, and investment of emotional capital, user interface designers are not often receptive to criticisms other than the minor tweaks they expected. If the entire interface metaphor is inappropriate, for example, requiring a total reconstruction of the prototype, it may be too late.

Why not make sure that the basic user interface approach—that is, desktop metaphor versus notebook versus flip chart—is basically on track before making virtually any investment? The key to verifying the basic approach is "low- fidelity" prototyping.

Using computer tools that require programming or scripting look good but require too much investment at this early design stage. An alternative approach that has proven successful is to construct simple, hand-drawn mock-ups of windows on paper. To give the user some sense of navigating through the system, another person plays the role of the "computer"—perhaps placing another paper window on the desk in front of the user as though his or her mouse click caused the window to appear.

This may not seem at first like a professional way to go about systems design. But it can be highly effective in producing a more usable design at a minimum cost. Because it is fast and simple to draw windows on paper and sticky notes, GUI designers can create numerous alternative user interface styles and let the user select the one that is most appealing and effective.

The message is in the medium. Simple low-fidelity pencil-and-paper prototypes also send a message to the user reviewing the mock-up. Because the interface is not computerized or polished, the reviewers of the design are less likely to be intimidated. A pencil-and-paper prototype implicitly tells users that they should be free to speak their minds about the design.

User interface designers are more likely to listen to feedback from users during low-fidelity prototyping. Because designers have not invested a great deal of time in the design, they feel less ownership of the prototype. Thus, they listen to criticisms and changes rather than simply defend the design or only think about how they can do quick fixes. This leads to more iterations of the user interface design before the financial and emotional lock-in on a given design occurs.

Given the low cost of this approach, the scope of the prototypes can be extensive, perhaps covering the entire functional scope of the system to be developed.

High-Fidelity Prototyping. After the basic user interface design has been defined and refined through low-fidelity prototyping, designers can build a more realistic computer-based "high-fidelity" prototype. The goal of a high-fidelity prototype is to present the user with the true look and feel being proposed for the system.

Designers should make the high-fidelity prototype as realistic as possible, including providing a sense of what job performance using the system will be like. Designers should also simulate delays where time-consuming queries or processing are to occur. This gives users more information about performance of the system that will help refine the design.

For example, in the low-fidelity prototype a particular operation may have been instantaneous. In the high-fidelity version the same operation may take 60 seconds. Seeing this, users may suggest that the order of certain operations be switched so they can use that wait time productively.

A high-fidelity prototype can also be a valuable tool for the systems development team. Ideally, the high-fidelity prototype is implemented using the intended tools and technical environment for the end system. Constructing the prototype gives implementers an opportunity to see how easy or difficult it is going to be to code and deliver various aspects of the user interface. The prototype also provides a chance to test some of the technical implementation details on a small scale before committing the project to any unproved technical concepts. Developer feedback should also be included in the refinements to the user interface design to reduce costs, risk, and implementation complexity.

High-fidelity prototype development is not an inexpensive process. To keep the costs of a high-fidelity prototype under control, designers should choose a narrow scope. Implementing one or two functions of the overall system may well be sufficient.

Performance Support Design. There is more to usability than just the design of the GUI. Performance support design activities focus on additional services and support needed to increase user productivity in performing the business task. Areas of opportunity for design improvement can many times be found in items that support the application, including online training or reference materials.

Online Training and Reference Materials. Online training can be used to supplement or possibly even replace instructor-led training. The goal of online training is to speed users through any learning curve the system may require. Online training has the added benefit that it can be delivered at the place and time of need. As a result of logistical difficulties, an enterprise often conducts instructor-led training too far in advance of when the users actually receive the system or begin using it. This time lag reduces training retention and in some cases forces the need for retraining. Furthermore, after the instructor has gone home, the users are often left to their own devices if they have a question or problem about how to use the system later on.

Developing online tutorials has become an increasingly popular way to provide task-specific training on demand. This enables users to learn on the job rather than as a separate "training event" off the job.

Online reference services, which are increasingly being delivered over a corporate intranet, can improve user task performance by presenting job-relevant information from several sources: an organization's internal knowledge base, public databases, and vendor-supplied databases. Online reference material may include policy and procedure manuals that specify how certain situations are to be handled, internal product descriptions and details, or external information sources that can improve the quality of user decision making. The challenge for designers is to understand what information would enhance the performance of the user, and then to make it available online and easily accessible.

Usability Testing. Usability testing ensures that the overall usability of the application is maximized. The most productive usability testing is focused on the achievement of some quantifiable usability goals or targets that are tied to the business case for the system. A usability goal for one application might be that new users achieve 90% proficiency within one week. For another application, the goal might be that users enter one order per minute with less than a 0.1% error rate.

The idea of such goals is to move usability designers beyond soft and vague goals such as user "satisfaction" with the system, which is a subjective and unquantifiable concept. Designers must focus on more specific goals that translate into business benefits. Without such goals, interface designers often stray toward merely creating "pretty" user interfaces. Although users may like to look at them, the mere aesthetics may come at the expense of systems development dollars and end-user productivity.

Usability testing requires a more stringent process compared to conventional user testing. Key differences include the following:

- *Test earlier.* Low-fidelity interface testing should begin early in the design of the system, before coding (even of the high-fidelity prototype) has even begun. The purpose of testing early is to learn more about how users perform tasks so that the interface can be improved and optimized, as opposed to merely confirming that the interface provides at least some way to accomplish the task.

- *Involve more users.* Usability testing sessions should involve enough users to ensure that the views of the test subjects accurately reflect the views of the entire user population.
- *Test more often.* Usability testing must be conducted throughout the development process, beginning with focus groups and ending with formal scripted testing of the software.

Achieving Consistency in GUI Designs

Consistency is often touted as the "holy grail" of user interface design. Consistency is certainly a valid goal, considering the amount of time and money spent on training users to use new software programs. An application designed to present a consistent user interface has great advantages. When the users learn how to use a subset of the software or have learned a similar application, they can expect to learn new functions quickly because menu options and controls behave similarly to windows they have already learned.

Consistency becomes even more powerful if it can be achieved not just within a single application but across a number of user applications. If new applications are designed to present the same or similar operations (e.g., File/Save)in the same way, users do not need to relearn how to perform these basic operations. Cross-application consistency substantially reduces the learning curve for new applications and gives users the confidence to accept and explore new applications and new features.

Designers should consider what other software their users already use or will be using as part of the system under development. The user may already be familiar with a suite of third-party software such as word processors and spreadsheet programs.

Such product suites (e.g., Microsoft Office, Lotus SmartSuite) are designed to provide consistency across common operations. If users are familiar with a such a suite, it is a good idea to adhere to these conventions and the underlying "style guide" on which they are based.

A style guide is a set of basic rules for defining the look and feel of computer applications. A number of style guides have been developed over the past few years, from vendors such as IBM (CUA), Microsoft, OSF (Motif), and Apple. Each guide has converged or standardized an approaches to most user interface issues. Thus a user familiar with applications based on one style guide could learn applications based on the others with little or no formal training. The degree of difference is not unlike the amount of difference between driving a Ford and driving a Chrysler: The brakes are always in the same place, although such things as wiper controls may be in one of several different spots.

User (activity) focused

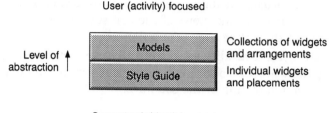

Exhibit III-6-3. GUI Models

Models-Based Design. Style guides provide a base for ensuring that windows have a consistent look. However, they tend to focus on lower-level aspects such as what a button should look like or where standard menu choices should be. They do not generally provide a designer with much guidance on how to consistently implement support for tasks commonly performed by users (e.g., adding an item to a list). Exhibit III-6-3 depicts models useful in supplementing style guides to help designers implement functions consistently.

A model is an example of how a window or section of a window should look and behave for performing a particular user operation, such as maintaining a list of items. The concept of models-based design is founded on the idea of creating a set of models that encompasses the majority of common abstract user activities. User activities include such low-level tasks as the following:

- Selecting an item from a hierarchy.
- Maintaining a list of items, such as adding, changing, or deleting items from a list.
- Entering tabular data, such as inputting a table of parameters.
- Simple parameter entry, such as entering hard-copy printing parameters.

These activities also include more complicated higher-level abstractions. Higher level user interface abstractions include groupings of controls or widgets that allow users to perform more complex tasks than simply pushing a button. Examples include collections of controls for free-form spreadsheets or multicolumn list manipulation.

Models-based design aims to increase interapplication consistency and developer productivity. Models-based design is different from a style guide in that it has a top-down instead of a bottom-up focus. A style guide typically encourages consistency by specifying a set of rules and constraints governing how an individual widget will look, where it will be placed, and how it will function when activated.

Unless some control is placed on design consistency, two designers can too easily implement different combinations of widgets for performing the same abstract user activity. For example, to allow a user to add items to a list box, designer *A* may use a pull-down menu; designer *B* may decide, arbitrarily, to use a button beneath the list box. As long as the button is labeled and placed in accordance with the style guide, both approaches would be consistent with the style guide yet inconsistent from the user's perspective.

As this example shows, the potential problem with style guides is that they address the problem of consistency from the bottom up—how the individual widgets should look, act, and be placed. In contrast, models focus on how widgets are combined to enable users to accomplish common activities, such as adding an item to a list of items.

Across applications, users should be presented with the same user interface (combination and arrangement of widgets) for performing the same user activity. Style guides alone encourage consistency only at lower levels—for example, how buttons are shaped or where menu options are to be found. Models are therefore useful to encourage consistency at higher, more user-oriented levels of abstraction.

However, models do not eliminate the need for a style guide; instead, they are an addition or enhancement to the style guide. The models themselves must be created to be consistent with the underlying style guide rules and constraints.

The total number of models for a given set of applications depends on the variety of distinct abstract user activities. At organizations that have pursued this approach, the number of standard models has ranged from as few as 3 to as many as 50, but a number between 10 and 15 is most common.

Contents of a Model. A model encompasses both the look and the behavior of the interface. It is not enough to create applications that just look similar visually; they must behave similarly and give the user the same feel. To encourage this level of consistency, a model includes the following:

- A picture or diagram of the appearance of the window or group of widgets.
- A high-level description of the abstract activity the model addresses—for example, maintaining a hierarchical list.
- A behavior diagram or similar document that clearly states how both

the user interface and the application respond to the set of possible user actions.

- A data model that shows the relationship of the data entities and attributes included in the model (optional).
- A window flow diagram for models that involve multiple windows and a sequence of windows (optional).
- Shell code or reusable routines that are appropriate for this type of model (optional).
- A guide/discussion for determining where the model should and should not be used.

Benefits of Models-Based Design. Models-based design has three major benefits.

Consistency of Design. A models-based approach can result in greater user interface consistency across applications and across designers when compared with the typical style guide technique of laying down rules and regulations.

Increased Productivity. Models-based design encourages reuse. When a designer begins to design a window, the first step is to review the available approved models and select the one most appropriate to the user task. If no model fits, the designer asks the project member responsible for the user interface design for an exemption or consultation on the development of a new model. Productivity can further be increased by providing "starter packs" for each model which may include reusable code routines or templates customized to the model.

Better Leveraging of User Interface Expertise. For projects with more than just a few application designers, it is helpful to designate one team member as the lead user interface designer. The lead user interface designer is responsible for the definition, design, and approval of the set of models to be used for the project.

If subsequent designers use approved models, there is less need for additional review from the lead user interface designer. This frees the time of the user interface designer to focus on the few windows and user activities for which no standard models have been defined and for which creativity and expertise are required.

The process outlined here, coupled with the right skills, leads to the design of user interfaces that are not just pretty to look at but are affordable to implement and easier to learn and, most important, increase user efficiency in performing business tasks.

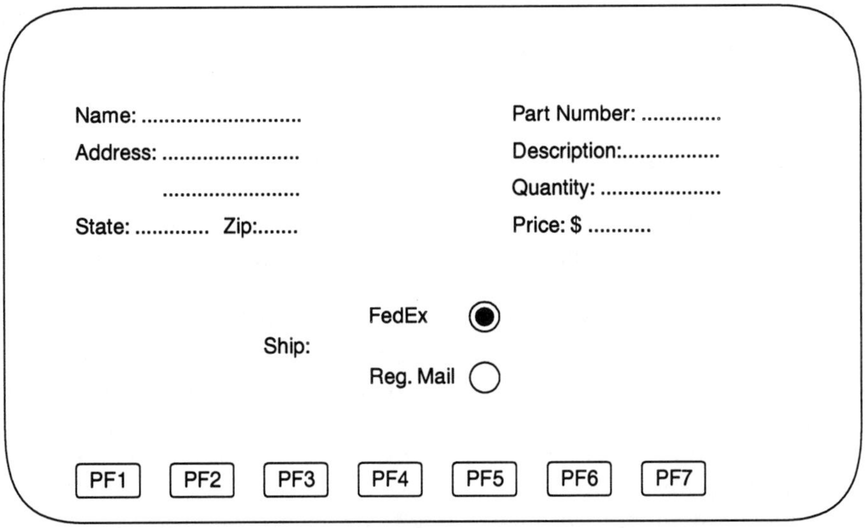

Exhibit III-6-4. The 3270 Paradigm Can Impede Good GUI Design

Basic Guidelines for GUI Design

A set of sample rules helps the GUI designer deliver better end products.

Break the 3270 Habit. If designers have spent time designing traditional, mainframe terminal screens, their ability to design effective GUIs may at first be impeded. GUIs are not an extension of the 3270 paradigm but a new paradigm entirely.

Exhibit III-6-4 is an actual first attempt by a developer of traditional 3270s to design a GUI. The designer has merely substituted entry fields, buttons, and a radio button control for standard 3270 screen elements and PF keys. This kind of result is not unusual; new GUI designers often have a difficult time leaving their tried-and-true 3270 screen layout principles behind.

When GUIs first came along, interface designers often took their 3270 screens and mapped them almost one for one to the GUI: Screens became windows, PF keys became push buttons, and maybe they added a radio button or two to get really fancy. On the second design iteration, interface designers would often say, "Oh how silly, instead of PF1 and PF2 down here at the bottom of the screen, we can use the words that the buttons stand for like Page Up and Page Down."

A fairly large mental shift is involved in truly exploiting the power of the GUI. It may be helpful to immerse new designers in a GUI environment, allowing them to see and use as many examples of good GUIs as possible. This experience will help designers see how to exploit the capabilities of a GUI as well as see a variety of implementations.

Avoid Pop-up Mania. One of the first reactions of some people who are new to GUI design is to fall prey to "pop-up mania": They fall in love with the idea of having many windows pop up. Only later do they realize what a chore it is for users to have to close all those windows once they have popped up. This phenomenon is common in GUI design. Something that is a wonderful idea on day one may be annoying on day seven.

User review of early designs may actually not help this phenomenon. Users who are not accustomed to a GUI can easily be seduced by flashy things. Users often encourage designers to use GUI features that may not ultimately be helpful to them when they have been using an application for many weeks.

Suppose in an application a dialog box pops up and prompts the user to enter a customer name and security type. The user can then request a list of holdings by clicking on a button. Another window pops up with a list of stocks. The user can then choose to buy or sell holdings.

What's the problem with this design? When performing portfolio administration, the user is always going to choose this dialog to buy or sell something. Therefore, there is no need to use two windows. The best thing to do in this case is to avoid all the pop-up windows and create one larger window with all the information immediately accessible (see Exhibit III-6-5).

An initial design tendency for many developers is to use too many small windows. A better design is to consolidate this capability into a larger window. This window allows the user to select the customer name, the security type, the holding, and whether or not to buy or sell, all with one window.

Does this mean it is always better to present more information on a single screen? Not at all, for the designer then may make the screen slightly more complex for the first-time user to understand. Designers must find a balance between ease of learning on the one hand and ease of use or long term productivity on the other hand.

One rule of thumb (acknowledging the inherent limits of "rules of thumb") is that if the user is going to need a particular list or control at least 50% of the time, the designer should use a bigger window, making available all the necessary information all the time. This rule must be tempered by certain constraints, however: screen size, user skill level, and how frequently the user visits the window in question.

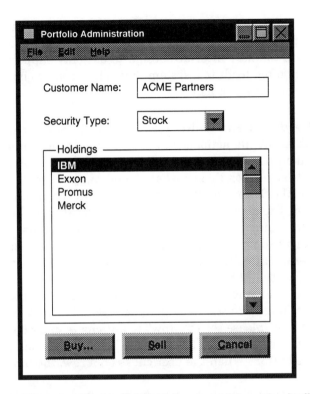

Exhibit III-6-5. One Window Makes All Necessary Information Available

---

Know What Controls the Windowing System Supports. Many popular windowing systems do not support all the kinds of controls that an enterprise would expect or need to build a business-oriented system. Most windowing systems were originally designed to support the development of personal productivity software applications such as spreadsheets and word processors. These types of applications do not require certain kinds of controls that are essential to developing business-oriented applications.

One common example is the multicolumn list box. Most business applications use multiple column lists somewhere—for reports, if for nothing else. However, few windowing systems provide such a control or widget for the programmer. Designers may have to go through extra effort to develop some of these special business controls. In this case, the architecture team may have to create architecture extensions to make these business functions easier to deliver.

An alternative strategy is to understand the set of controls that are natively supported by the windowing system and development tools and then constrain the user interface design to use only supported controls. This approach often leads to a system that is far easier to implement and may get the job done just as well.

User Feedback and Guidance. The user interface should give users feedback about the actions they take and guidance on what actions should be taken. That is, users need to understand what has happened as well as what is now possible or what should happen next.

Exhibit III-6-6a is a multicolumn list box in which no row has yet been selected. The delete button is disabled (indicated to the user by the word "delete" being grayed out). It does not make sense to have the Delete key enabled if nothing has been selected. This is an example of one style of interaction called object-action. The idea is that users need to select an object before they can perform an action.

Consider what would need to happen if the Delete button were enabled and nothing were selected. Designers would have to design a message box reading "please select a row" to anticipate users clicking on the delete button prematurely. This message box can be avoided simply by disabling the button. When the user clicks on a row, the buttons become enabled.

Why even show the button if it cannot be used? It is always better to show users everything potentially available to them in the window. It would be confusing to use the interface if buttons were constantly appearing and disappearing from the window.

Exhibit III-6-6b shows how the user interface changes to reflect the user's action. In addition to highlighting the selected row, the "Delete" and "Change" buttons are now enabled (not gray), indicating that these operations are now available. Enabling the buttons when the user selects a row tells the users that new actions are now available based on what they have just done.

Use Color Appropriately. After being constrained by black and white interfaces for so long, designers often get carried away with color and may make the first-time design error of splashing gratuitous color all over their window designs. As a general guideline, designers should use color only where it conveys meaning. On first impression, users are often dazzled by lots of pretty colors all over the computer display. But like so many other glitzy interface gimmicks, the bright colors become distracting and irritating for users in the long run.

Designers should use color to draw the user's attention to some im-

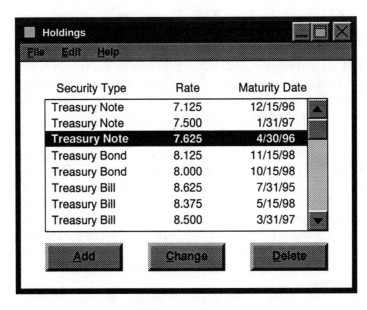

a. Buttons That Cannot Be Selected Are Disabled

b. Buttons Are Enabled

Exhibit III-6-6. Object Action Design

portant item on the screen. If color is overused for decoration it becomes ineffective for that purpose, thus limiting its ultimate effectiveness.

Designers should keep a few things in mind when using colors:

- *Color blindness affects a number of people.* On several occasions when user interfaces relied on color exclusively to convey key information, the interfaces had to be redesigned once it was discovered that one or more key users were color blind.

- *Different countries use various color distinctions.* For instance, mailboxes are blue in the United States, red in the United Kingdom, and yellow in Greece. The Japanese language does not have a clear distinction between the colors green and blue. Culture may also attach different meanings to specific colors. For example, in Japan white is sometimes associated with death.

- *Humans cannot see color in their peripheral vision very well.* Try it. People lose track of colors when they turn away from an object, especially in low-light conditions. This implies that on a large screen, the user may not notice that the color of an icon in the corner of the screen has been changed from gray to blue.

Avoid Making the User Wait. Users should not have to wait, doing nothing, while certain processing functions are occurring. Designers should take advantage of the multitasking features of the operating system that they are building on. If the user can be doing something else on the workstation while a relatively lengthy process is operating, the designer should make that happen. An application can allow this by releasing control to the operating system, or by creating an asynchronous task that can be run on the server rather than tying up the workstation.

Design for Performance as Well as Usability. Designers of GUI applications must often make trade-offs in their designs, choices that may sacrifice a degree of usability in order to improve system performance. Large windows that are rich with information and controls can lead to high user productivity. In some cases, however, the response time penalty of creating and populating the large window may lead the designer to carve the capability into multiple smaller windows, ensuring more rapid response times.

Another performance-vs.-usability choice centers around collecting data in advance of the user opening the window that needs it. Building windows and reading databases in anticipation that the user may need the information can provide users with more immediate response, greater usability, and higher productivity. The performance trade-off is in the excess systems load associated with collecting data that the user may never request.

Design for "Implementability." Designers should evaluate the user interface for "implementability," not just user-friendliness. What does that mean? There is a great deal of value in having cognitive scientists explain what a great user interface would look like because it is important to understand these concepts to come up with more innovative solutions. But once the designer knows what the "ideally usable" design is, they must analyze it for implementability. Can the design be coded cost-effectively? Will performance be adequate?

Various windowing systems and operating systems impose many limitations and constraints on the visual appearance of applications. If the interface is too difficult to implement, design iterations may be required until a happy medium can be found.

Documenting a GUI Design Appearance

When documenting the design of a GUI, it is necessary to capture both the appearance and the behavior of the interface and the application business logic. The appearance of the user interface is simply the basic layout of controls within a window.

Many tools are currently available for painting windows. Window painting tools range from simple prototyping tools to more advanced coomputer-aided software engineering environments that can be used to carry the design documentation forward into construction. As discussed previously, a "low-tech" approach is to document the user interface design through hand-drawn windows on paper or sticky notes.

Behavior. The behavior of the user interface is more challenging to document. The behavior is what happens at runtime in response to user actions. The interface behavior of an application includes the answers to the following questions:

- What happens when I click on this button?
- What if I double click on a row in this list box?
- What happens if I drag this icon onto this other icon?
- What if I choose this menu option?

There can be a fine line between interface behavior and application behavior. Interface behavior is really only what is happening from a visual standpoint: a dialog popping up, rows being inserted in a list box, a button being enabled, rows within a list box being sorted. Application

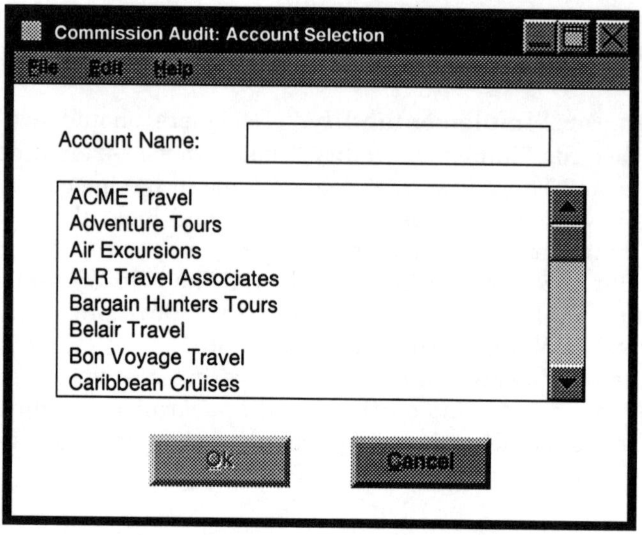

Exhibit III-6-7. Example Appearance Documentation

behavior encompasses more of the traditional data processing activities such as database reads, calculations, and business functions.

When documenting the interface behavior it is important to keep the distinction between the two in mind. Later, this chapter introduces a simple method for documenting user interface behavior with a CAR (control, action, response) diagram.

Finally, the application behavior or logic design should be documented using any conventional programming design method, such as flowcharts or pseudo-code. The point here is that the application logic can be specified in a way independent of the type of user interface being used. Alternatively, the CAR diagramming approach can be used to document both interface and application behavior.

The Role of Prototyping. Why document a graphical user interface design? Why not just create a prototype and give that to the developers? A prototype, by its nature, expresses both the appearance of the windows as well as the behavior of the controls.

Undeniably, a prototype is a key tool in the design of a user interface. The prototype can be used as an iterative design vehicle for gathering user input and feedback on the evolving design. Although a necessary aspect of design, a prototype is not in itself sufficient for capturing the design of a system to the degree necessary for coding to begin.

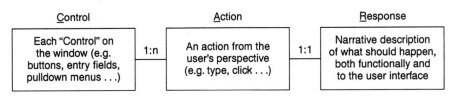

Exhibit III-6-8. CAR Diagramming

Typically, a prototype is not developed for the entire system but rather for some key portions. In addition, a prototype may not cover, or explicitly show, many of the conditional kinds of processing that occur. For example, "If the list box row clicked on is a Treasury Bill, open the Treasury Bill maintenance dialog box."

Behavior Diagramming. Exhibit III-6-7 is an account selection window. The window allows the user to select an account for auditing ticket commissions from a list of existing account names. Users can type in an account name and press enter or select an account directly from the list box. They can also cancel and close the dialog box by clicking on the cancel button. The description of documentation techniques in the following pages refers back to this simple window.

CAR Diagramming. A CAR diagram documents the behavior of the window by detailing the application's response to each user action on each control of the window. The CAR diagramming technique is a simple approach that has proven very useful on numerous client/server development projects. (See Exhibit III-6-8.)

Control. A control is anything that a user can activate, click on, or drag to do something in an application window. Examples of typical controls include the following:

- List boxes, which display a scrollable list of choices.
- Entry fields, which allow for entry of data via the keyboard.
- Push-button, which the user can click on to select an action.

Action. For each control, one or more actions can be performed. For example, with a list box, the user can single-click or double-click on an item. Each of these actions can invoke a different application response.

Response. The response is a common, non-computer-language description of what should happen in the application when this control is

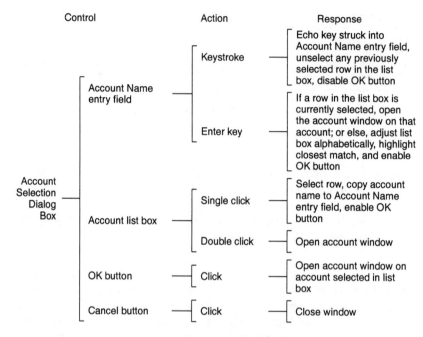

Control   Action   Response

Exhibit III-6-9. Example CAR Diagram

activated. A CAR diagram is meant to be readable by other than just computer programmers—for example, "fill the portfolio list box" or "pop-up the account dialog box window." The response definitions serve as an initial description of the application code that eventually must be written for each control.

Exhibit III-6-9 shows what a CAR diagram might look like for the example account selection dialog box. The window name is the label on the far left of the diagram. The diagram then shows a three-level structure chart approach going from left to right: control, action, response. This can be done with a structure chart editor, as shown, or just as easily with four columns in a spreadsheet.

Exhibit III-6-10 provides a walk-through the CAR diagram. This diagramming technique is independent of any particular window system. The descriptions in the CAR diagram could be documenting a window to be implemented in Microsoft Windows, OSF Motif, Presentation Manager, or the Apple Macintosh.

The benefit of using common non-computer language to describe the interface behavior, besides windowing system independence, is that after the CAR diagram is created it can be used for many purposes:

Control 1:   **Account Name entry field**

Action 1:   The action is to "type a letter."

Response: When a key is struck, the response is to echo the value in the Account Name entry field and disable the OK button. (The OK is disabled, because the user is keying in letters; therefore an account is not currently selected to be opened.)

Control 1:   **Account Name entry field**

Action 2:   The action is to "hit the enter key."

Response: When the ENTER key is pressed, the response is dependent upon whether or not an account name is currently selected in the list box. If an account row is selected, pressing the ENTER key results in the account window (not shown) being launched with the selected account's information. If an account row is not yet selected, the ENTER key causes the list box to be adjusted such that the top entry is in alphabetic order with the string in the entry field. If the user typed "P ENTER," the first name in the list box might adjust to be "Parker Travel" and the row would be selected (highlighted).

Control 2:   **Account list box**

Action 1:   A single click of the left mouse button

Response 1:   Copy the selected name to the Account Name entry field.

Action 2:   A double click of the left mouse button

Response 2:   Open the selected account.

Control 3:   **OK button**

Action: A single click of the left mouse button

Response: Open the account window for the account currently selected in the list box. (Note that this behaves the same as hitting ENTER in the customer name entry field.)

Control 4:   **Cancel button**

Action: A single click of the left mouse button

Response: The window closes and the system returns to its prior state.

Exhibit III-6-1 0. Walk-Through of a CAR Diagram

- The CAR diagram can be used as a high-level systems specification from which detailed designs can be created.
- The testing team can use the CAR diagrams to develop many of the test conditions and scripts that will be used later in the testing phase.
- By virtue of the fact that the CAR diagram is readable by nontechnical people, the diagram can be given to those responsible for developing user procedures. User procedures and help manuals can then be developed concurrently with the actual software.
- Users can gain an understanding of how the system operates by examining both the screen prints and CAR diagrams.

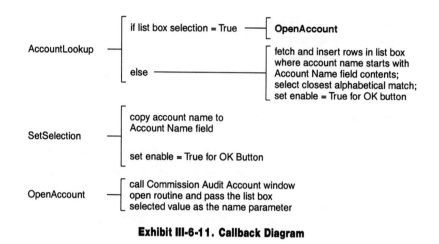

Exhibit III-6-11. Callback Diagram

Detailed Design Specifications. The CAR diagram is useful for capturing and communicating the application design at a high level. However, more detailed design specifications may be required before the application can be coded by programmers. Documenting the next level of design can be accomplished by adding a piece of information to the CAR diagram and creating an additional design document called a callback diagram. (See Exhibit III-6-11.)

The diagram in Exhibit III-6-12 is the same as in Exhibit III-6-11 but in a spreadsheet format. One additional column has been added, "Procedure." (Thus, some call this a CARP diagram.) This new column captures the design name for the callback procedure that is to be invoked.

The callback procedure is the piece of application logic executed when the user performs the specified action on the control. The reason for adding the procedure name is to provide a link to a callback diagram which can further describes the required application logic.

The procedure "OpenAccount" (shown in bold in Exhibit III-6-11) appears twice on the callback diagram, indicating that the same application routine is to be reused and that the user interface provides the user more than one way to invoke this function. An effective user interface often gives the user multiple ways of performing the same function (e.g., keyboard equivalents for pull-down menus).

The callback diagram can specify the design of a callback procedure to a much more detailed level. Whether this additional level of design detail is necessary depends largely on the skills and experience of the programmers who will be coding the system and the complexity of the function. The callback diagram may be considered superfluous for all but

Control	Action	Response	Procedure(s)
Account Name entry field	Keystroke	Echo key struck into Account Name entry field, unselect any previously selected row in the list box, disable OK button	DeSelectListBox()
Account Name entry field	Enter	If a row in the list box is currently selected, open the account window on that account; else, adjust list box alphabetically, highlight closest match, and enable OK button	AccountLookup()
Account list box	Single click	Copy account name to Account Name entry field	SetSelection()
	Double click	Open account window	OpenAccount()
OK button	Click	Open account window on account selected in list box	OpenAccount()
Cancel button	Click	Close window	ExitWindow()

Exhibit III-6-12. Callback Diagram—Spreadsheet Format

the most complex callbacks on projects in which the programmers are already experienced with developing graphical client/server programs.

CONCLUSION

The new design challenges of GUI applications are substantial but manageable with an appropriate design approach. This chapter presented an outline of a design approach and process as well as a few of the key tips and guidelines for producing excellent GUIs.

III-7

Overview of Distributed Systems

C lient/server computing has led many businesses to reevaluate their entire corporate processing strategy. Processing for the existing systems of these businesses may be centralized at corporate headquarters. But that strategy may be inappropriate for the organization's future needs.

Larger organizations making the transition to client/server often face the additional challenge of distributing their corporate processing. Once the organization makes the decision to distribute, a difficult question arises: What should the organization do with the business application processing and data? Should data be located at one central site, at local sites, or in some combination of central and local sites based on usage?

This chapter highlights the benefits and issues associated with distributed systems. The next chapter, III-8, presents a high-level, step-by-step process for making decisions about the data and application placement.

The concepts introduced in this chapter are, in many cases, technical in nature. But application designers should at least be familiar with these terms and techniques to work effectively with the architecture team in defining a data and process distribution strategy. The next chapter builds on these concepts, presenting an approach to deciding where within the network various application and data components should be located.

APPLICATION AND DATA DISTRIBUTION

Consider again the definition of client/server at the heart of this book: "a style of computing involving multiple processors, one of which is typically a workstation, and across which a single business transaction is completed." This definition implies that at least two computers are involved, one a client and the other a server.

Even at this level of complexity, only two computers, the organization has to decide whether data should be on the client or on the server.

Data allocation then becomes exponentially more complicated with large client/server systems, where thousands of workstations and hundreds of servers are spread out across a global network.

Data allocation questions lead to the need for distributed data management. This section begins by defining the concepts and approaches to managing and implementing distributed applications and data in a client/server environment.

Definition of Distributed Data

For the purposes of this volume, distributed data is defined as "data that is physically located separate from the application processing, or that is spread among two or more server computers, which then must be kept coordinated." Distributed data can be spread over multiple sites and/or multiple machines in whatever manner best supports the business application processing requirements.

Discussions of distributed data here use terms specific to relational databases—for example, "rows" instead of "records." This does not mean to imply that these strategies are only relevant to relational databases. Most of these strategies can be applied to data stored in any format. For consistency, and because of the increasing popularity of relational databases, the terms used are primarily relational.

When to Consider Distributed Data

Distributed data and distributed processing may be worth considering if the business process to be supported has one or more of the following characteristics:

- *Geographically distributed.* The business functions are spread over several sites, making it inconvenient or impractical to support some (or all) of the processing requirements from a central site.
- *Local decision making and independence is important.* The organizational structure is distributed and the business has several local sites with the authority to make local decisions as to how to process their data. When centralized processing is used, individual locations are more or less stuck with the level of investment and support decided on by the central site. When locations have more autonomy to make investment decisions (e.g., organizations employing "profit center" management), distributed processing allows for each location to choose whatever level of information systems investment management feels is appropriate. A sales organization could decide to invest in a multidimensional database without the approval, or even awareness, of the centralized information system (IS) function.

- *Special price/performance issues are present.* The response time at the local site becomes unacceptable or the cost of adequate communications bandwidth is excessive as a result of the transfer of significant amounts of data between the central and local sites.

Potential Benefits of Distributed Data

Using distributed data or systems has the following potential benefits:

- *Better reflection of an organization's structure.* An organization's structure is often logically (divisions, departments, projects) as well as physically distributed (plants, factories, warehouses, branch offices). Distribution of data allows the organization unit that uses the data to make the IS decisions and to control the resources. This can lead to better IS-related decision making and resource allocation.
- *Local autonomy.* Distributing a system allows individual groups within an organization to exercise control over their own data while still being able to access data at remote locations when necessary. This makes them less dependent on a remote data processing center, which by definition cannot be as deeply involved in purely local issues.
- *Increased availability.* A distributed system can offer greater resilience than a centralized system in that it can continue to function (though at a reduced level) even if an individual site or communication link fails. To achieve these availability benefits, developers, when designing the strategy, must take care to deemphasize the dependence on real-time access to data stored at other locations. Also, the availability of replicated data is improved in that a replicated data entity remains available as long as at least one copy of that entity is available.
- *Increased efficiency.* Response times and communications costs are likely to be reduced because data in a distributed system can be stored closest to its point of use, enabling most data accesses to be local.

Challenges of Distributed Systems

Although distribution of data throughout a system has many benefits, some serious issues and challenges also must be considered:

- *More complex communications.* Distributed systems continuously pass messages between various remote sites, containing such things as data, processing requests, and acknowledgments of previous requests. Coordinating this message flow is complex and can be costly.

- *Complex update control.* If two users update the same piece of data, a mechanism to mediate conflicts must be in place. One way to ensure data integrity is to employ a locking mechanism. However, distributed locking strategies quickly become complex as the number of machines increases and the organization must be prepared for the possibility of network failure.
- *Network dependency.* When data is distributed across the network, the system requires reliable communication between sites or processing may be halted. This increased reliability can require expensive duplication of network resources to provide an acceptable amount of system availability for the users.
- *Complexity of location transparency implementation.* In the ideal distributed data environment, the end user or application programmer has access to all data without having to know where that data is physically located. This feature is known as location transparency, and it is fully supported by only a few of the database products currently available. This places a substantial burden on the architecture and on architecture designers to locate the data efficiently and to transport it to the application upon request without excessive processing delays. A custom-built location transparency architecture component can support custom applications but not end-user query tools, precluding easy-to-use tools for inquiry on data distributed across multiple platforms. But location transparency also complicates user support. A problem with a single application may originate from any of a number of remote sites that are transparent to the user, making the problem more difficult to identify and resolve.
- *Changes in organizational structure.* If the distributed computing environment is modeled after the organization, changes in the existing organizational structure could invalidate the system design, thus requiring expensive application or technology realignment. When distributing data and processing, the organization needs to consider the flexibility to change the system as the organization changes.

Which Is Right—Distributed or Centralized?

Many organizations today are too quick to settle on a distributed, replicated data solution. Just because the technology exists and the organization can distribute data does not mean it should distribute data. Much of the motivation for distributed data begins with dissatisfaction with the cost or performance of communications lines that link locations. In a world with infinite wide area communications speeds and no costs, few organizations would take on the issues of distributing their data.

With the ever decreasing price of wide area communications, organizations have recently begun to shift back toward centralized data storage. They are providing remote locations with adequate communications bandwidth and reliability to access and update centralized data from remote locations.

The motivation for this trend toward recentralization has been the realization that it is difficult to manage, control, and handle recovery for data that is distributed across many locations. Where is retail customer information? Where is financial information? Where is sales information? As organizations try to make more and more information available to decision makers, hiding the complexities of data location from these users is turning out to be exceedingly difficult.

A small retail store chain with 20 stores spread across the southeastern United States recently faced this decision. Each store had its own data and processing resources locally. When the enterprise undertook a major new systems initiative, it was assumed that the stores' computing systems would be expanded and data would be replicated between the stores and headquarters. Individual store management did not want to give up housing their systems and data locally because they did not want to be dependent on traditionally unreliable communications links and they wanted "control" over their data.

The problem, however, was the investment in upgrading all of these systems and putting in sufficient communications bandwidth to support the substantial data replication load. Also, hiring and training additional computer support personnel at the stores to deal with all this new complexity would have cost far more than holding and managing all of the data at one central location.

By centralizing the data, only one set of systems support personnel was needed, and these personnel could give 24-hour, high-quality support at a fraction of the cost. Second, by not maintaining multiple copies (up to 20 in this case) of some information, the organization substantially reduced total systems investment in database licenses and disk storage.

To preserve the autonomy the store managers had before, 20 servers (one for each store) were actually housed in one location, managed by one operations staff. Each store still had its own server and much of its own data, but the server itself was not physically located in the store. Some of the savings were then used to upgrade the communications infrastructure, adding capacity and redundancy to deliver response times and availability actually better than when the stores managed their machines locally.

THE MECHANICS OF APPLICATION AND DATA DISTRIBUTION

The remainder of this chapter introduces terminology and provides some insights about various techniques for implementing and managing distributed data and applications within a client/server system.

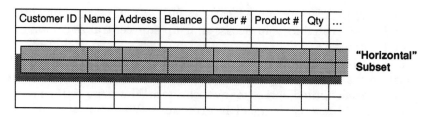

Customer ID	Name	Address	Balance	Order #	Product #	Qty	...

"Horizontal" Subset

Exhibit III-7-1. Horizontal Segmentation

Segmentation Strategy

A data entity can reside at a single processing location or at multiple locations in its entirety (all attributes and all instances copied and held at more than one location), or it can be segmented. Segmentation (sometimes referred to as partitioning or fragmentation) results in reduced storage and transmission costs but adds complexity to the synchronization/replication strategy. Segmentation can be horizontal (Exhibit III-7-1) or vertical (Exhibit III-7-2).

Horizontal Segmentation. Horizontal segmentation refers to splitting the entity by instances (rows/records) according to ownership. Horizontal segmentation results in all of an entity's attributes at a given site, but a subset of the total instances.

Developers should analyze each entity that resides in more than one location to determine whether it should be horizontally segmented (each row resides at a single or few sites) or replicated in its entirety (all rows reside everywhere). For each application, developers must determine what subset of data is needed. This subset is typically related to a user group, not traditional partitioning values such as key ranges.

For example, an order entry application processes orders only for customers in the Midwest sales center. That order entry application may need to look for availability of products in one, all, or selected warehouses, depending on requirements of the business.

Vertical Segmentation. Vertical segmentation refers to splitting an entity by attributes (columns/fields) based on ownership. Vertical segmentation may result in all rows at a given site but a subset of the entity's columns. For example, salary and some other employee attributes are sensitive data belonging to the human resources function. The key to employee data is employee number. Other applications may need other employee data, such as department or job class. This data is also keyed by employee number.

Customer ID	Name	Address	Balance	Order #	Product #	Qty	...

"Vertical" Subset

Exhibit III-7-2. Vertical Segmentation

Exhibit III-7-2 illustrates a single, normalized table that may require vertical segmentation because of application requirements and data sensitivity. Vertical segmentation can be implemented as separate tables, views on a single table, or different logical (and physical) versions of a single table.

Vertical segmentation may also be required for such special data types as binary large objects: hypertext, graphics, word processing documents, spreadsheets, and digital images. Vertical segmentation requires a significant amount of analysis and is typically considered only to resolve performance issues and to limit replication of sensitive data.

UPDATE CONTROL MECHANISMS

Update scenarios describe how data is updated, taking into account where the master data is located, who is authorized to update the data, and where the update will be performed. The location of the update becomes important when multiple copies of the data are distributed throughout the system. If data is placed at only one location, the update task is easier. When the data is duplicated over several locations, the data transfer strategy becomes more complex to distribute the updates throughout the system in a timely way.

Following are common update control mechanisms for distributed data:

- *Single updatable master.* A single updatable master set of data where only the master location can update data. There are three varieties:
  - *Remote online.* A single updatable master where updates can be made from remote locations via online access.
  - *Remote batch.* A single updatable master where updates can be made from remote locations via remotely submitted batch update files.

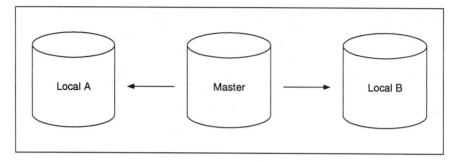

Exhibit III-7-3. Single Updatable Master

- — *Local checkout.* A single updatable master with local sites able to checkout a local copy of the data for updating.
- *Local update—single owner:* Multiple local updatable master data sets with horizontally segmented data ownership by location.
- *Local update— multiple owners:* Multiple local updatable master data sets without unique data ownership by location. Allows for the possibility that the same record could need to be updated in two locations at the same time.

Single Updatable Master

In this scenario, a single master copy of the data is held at a central/ coordinating site with multiple secondary copies distributed across the network to individual local sites (see Exhibit III-7-3). The master database may be updated in several ways.

Central Update. Any updates made to the master data are made at the coordinating/central location and then distributed out to the various local databases (see Exhibit III-7-4). This approach is useful for data maintained by a single or central location but read throughout the organization. An example would be the part numbers or other product information for a company's product line.

Remote Online. The users of the local databases can make changes only to the subset of master data owned by their location using remote log-on to the central/coordinating site. With this strategy (see Exhibit III-7-5), local data is updated only through data replications from the central/coordinating site and not through user or application activities.

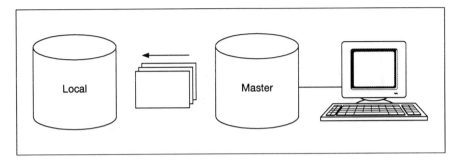

Exhibit III-7-4. Single Updatable Master: Central Update

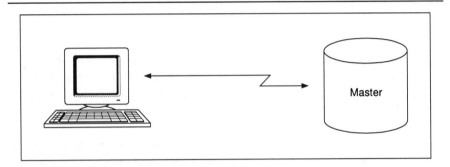

Exhibit III-7-5. Single Updatable Master: Remote Online

This approach requires security controls to regulate the access by local sites to the coordinating/central site and data. The changes made by the local site are then propagated with the next scheduled data replication. This approach allows local control of central data, while still maintaining a centralized master database.

Remote Batch. The local users make changes that are batched locally, then sent to the coordinating/central location for processing (see Exhibit III-7-6). Once again, the changes are reflected in the next update of their local database. This approach also requires adequate security controls to ensure that the local site is updating only its own data.

This is fundamentally the same approach shown in Exhibit III-7-5, but it allows the actual update processing at the coordinating/central location to be scheduled at convenient times.

Batching the updates is useful when local sites will be producing many updates throughout the day—updates that do not need to be made visible to other users immediately. An example is entering customer

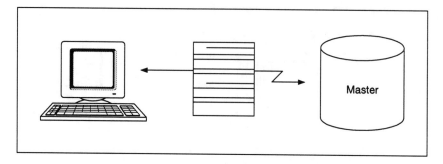

Exhibit III-7-6. Single Updatable Master: Remote Batch

---

contact information that does not require any immediate action. Batching the updates reduces the need for connectivity to the coordinating/central location during the day. The system requires a reliable file transfer mechanism to ensure that the coordinating/central location receives the transaction update files sent.

If this approach is extended to allow multiple sites the ability to update the same data, the central site must have controls in place to resolve update conflicts and to notify the local sites if their transaction has been rejected. An example of one approach to resolving update conflicts is outlined in the section "Local Update—Multiple Owners."

Local Checkout. Local checkout allows the local site to dynamically acquire ownership of any master data and to modify it (see Exhibit III-7-7). In this case, the data is transmitted from the master database (checked out) to the local machine, updated, and then returned after the update.

While the master data is checked out, other accesses are restricted to read-only use. This approach is most effective when many users require the ability to update the same data, but there is no clear owner of the data, and data integrity must be guaranteed.

For example, local checkout can enable sales offices that occasionally service the same customer to check out and update customer information when needed. Implementation of this approach often requires building a custom check-in/checkout locking system, if this feature is not supported by the database management system (DBMS). This strategy requires the data to be transferred on request from the central site to a local site and loaded into the local database. Few database management packages inherently support the required checkout and send feature.

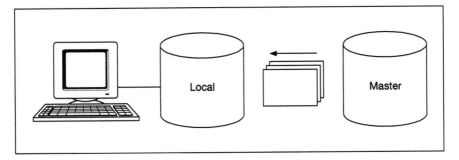

Exhibit III-7-7. Single Updatable Master: Local Checkout

Local Update—Single Owner

In this scenario, updates are made locally by the one local site that owns the data. Each local database contains the data required for local operations and can update data that is locally owned.

For example, a sales office can update the local copy of the territory's customers and then propagate these changes to remote secondary copies throughout the sales organization. In this case, the local copy is functioning as the data master. There is still only one owner for each data instance or row in the system, but the changes are made locally first, then shipped to a central/coordinating site for distribution or distributed directly to other local sites.

Two update scenarios are the candidates for distributing changes in the local database to the other remote databases.

From the Local to a "Coordinator." In this approach, the local site transfers all the changes to the central/coordinating site. The central/coordinating site then propagates the changes to other local sites (see Exhibit III-7-8). The coordinator maintains the information needed to distribute the changes to the local databases. This approach is easier to establish and maintain because the distribution of data to other sites is performed by a single coordinating location. Therefore, a spider web of point-to-point data replication is not required.

From the Local Direct to All Databases. This strategy places the burden of distribution on the local machine because each local site distributes its changes to the other local sites on the system (see Exhibit III-7-9).

Each local site must then be responsible for routing the data to the other sites. If the central site is retained in this scenario and is not

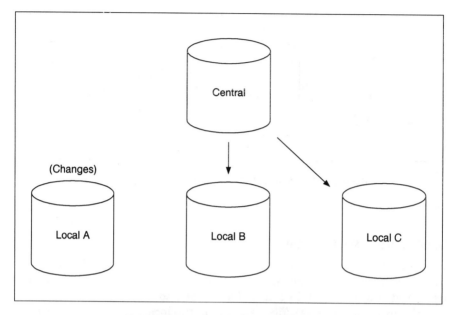

Exhibit III-7-8. From Local to Coordinator

responsible for distribution to the other sites, it may still be utilized for other reasons, including the following:

- *To acquire and maintain an authoritative copy of the data.* If all data is replicated through a central coordinating site, the central location can maintain and preserve a backup copy of all locations' data. This can be useful if data becomes corrupted or lost at the local sites, which may not have the sophistication and discipline to manage vital data.

- *To serve as a source of data for management reports, batch processing, or other enterprisewide needs.* One of the big challenges in distributed data environments is how to produce management reports that require a view of data spread across multiple locations. The requirement to produce such reports alone can drive the need for a central site keeping an aggregated copy of all local site data or at least a summary level.

- *To function as a "hot backup."* In the case of a server or media failure at a local site, if a central location maintains a copy of all site data applications can be "redirected" to access the central copy of the data across the network.

The "local to other databases" scenario is one of the most complex to

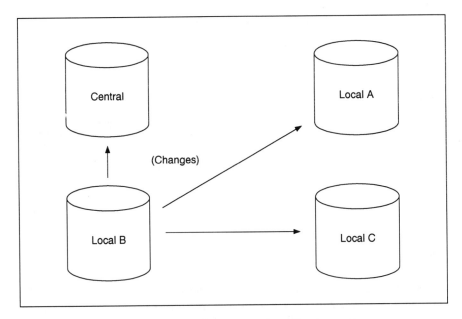

Exhibit III-7-9. From Local to Other Databases

implement successfully. There is a potential for the databases to get out of sync as a result of lost or delayed messages. There are also potential problems of backing out transactions from local copies that are rejected by the central location.

These issues limit the use of this scenario to situations in which strict database synchronization is not a fundamental requirement. It should be avoided whenever possible, and used only when the limitations are fully understood and accepted.

Local Update—Multiple Owners

This scenario introduces the added complexity of giving multiple sites the ability to update the same data. This scenario either removes the ownership from the data or permits multiple owners of the same data. This scenario is the most complex to implement because it gives multiple sites the authority to update the same record.

With this scenario, update conflicts are possible. Because of these conflicts, a means must be developed to detect conflicting updates and either determine which update should be performed or at the very least notify the users or operations of the existence of a conflict. Two major

Master Record, Coordinating Site

Master Update	Local Update	Data
11/29/96 9:30:02		XXX ...

Local Record, Site A

Master Update	Local Update	Data
11/29/96 9:30:02		XXX ...

Local Record, Site B

Master Update	Local Update	Data
11/29/96 9:30:02		ABCD ...

Exhibit III-7-10. Update Conflict

---

ways of implementing this type of update scenario are (1) central site mediator and (2) peer-to-peer databases.

Central Site Mediator. A central/coordinating site, with a master database, can be used as a mediator for a group of autonomous local databases. This scenario allows local sites to update their local data and send the updates to the coordinator. The coordinating site must then be able to mediate conflicting updates to the master database from local sites.

Consider the following example of an update conflict (Exhibit III-7-10) and how it can be detected. The same row is updated by two remote sites and each site sends an update request to the coordinating site. In this scenario, each row in the database contains the data, a time stamp of when it was last updated from the master (master update), and the time stamp of any local update (local update).

Two remote sites now update the same row locally (Exhibit III-7-11). The master site receives the first update and verifies that the master update time stamp from the local update matches the master update time stamp on the master row. The coordinating site changes the master row and updates the master update time stamp with the new local update time stamp.

The second update arrives (Exhibit III-7-12.) The master site compares the master update time stamp on the master row with the same field in the update request. They do not match and therefore the master site rejects the update request. Updates to that row will be effectively rejected until this new master row is distributed to the local databases.

At some point, the master site performs the regular distribution of the master data to the local sites (Exhibit III-7-13). The local sites now have the same master update time stamp on the updated row as in the master database.

Master Record, Coordinating Site

Master Update	Local Update	Data
11/29/96 9:45:37		XXX ...

Local Record, Site A

Master Update	Local Update	Data
11/29/96 9:30:02	11/29/96 9:45:37	XXX ...

Local Record, Site B

Master Update	Local Update	Data
11/29/96 9:30:02		ABCD ...

Exhibit III-7-11. Two Local Sites Update the Same Row Locally

Master Record, Coordinating Site

Master Update	Local Update	Data
11/29/96 9:45:37		XXX ...

Local Record, Site A

Master Update	Local Update	Data
11/29/96 9:30:02	11/29/96 9:45:37	XXX ...

Local Record, Site B

Master Update	Local Update	Data
11/29/96 9:30:02	11/29/96 9:47:19	ABCD ...

Exhibit III-7-12. Second Update from Another Local Site

Master Record, Coordinating Site

Master Update	Local Update	Data
11/29/96 9:45:37		XXX ...

Local Record, Site A

Master Update	Local Update	Data
11/29/96 9:45:37		XXX ...

Local Record, Site B

Master Update	Local Update	Data
11/29/96 9:45:37		ABCD ...

Exhibit III-7-13. Regular Distribution of the Master Data to the Local Sites

This conflict example still requires the addition of error processing. The rejection of the update by the master site must be communicated to the remote site that initiated the update. If that update was made to the local database, that update will be lost when the new master is distributed to the local database.

Error correction procedures such as those needed for this example add to the complexity of a central site mediator scenario. In addition, the complexity increases in magnitude when multiple transactions are added

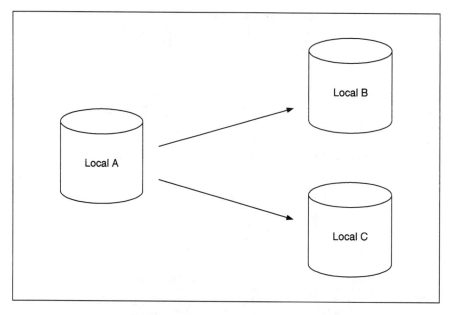

Exhibit III-7-14. Peer-to-Peer Database

to the application that affect multiple rows, in multiple tables, and that comprise a single logical unit of work.

Peer-to-Peer. In this scenario, all databases in the system are equal, so no single site controls the update process (see Exhibit III-7-14). Changes made to data on one database are performed simultaneously on all databases containing duplicates of that data.

This feature is one that many relational database vendors are attempting to integrate into their distributed database management systems (DDBMSs). DDBMSs are discussed later in this chapter, in the section on two-phase commits.

Some of the more sophisticated data distribution strategies require some control mechanism to indicate ownership and use of data. The method chosen may control update capabilities and drive the replication processes. The control mechanism should identify the user group rather than the processing or data location site whenever possible to allow for flexibility in moving user groups and data. This approach requires an additional table or codes file to map user groups to the data placement locations.

The following are some control mechanisms to consider:

- *Database vendor-provided data dictionary.* This method appears to be the emerging trend, but currently few vendors provide it. This method often assumes that all of the organization's data is managed by the vendor's DBMS products.
- *Configuration table.* This method uses a separate configuration table to identify who owns (and/or can access) each row in the database. The configuration table includes the table key and one or more columns indicating owners and users. The configuration table itself may need to be distributed or maintained centrally and updated and accessed for remote transactions.
- *Data columns.* This method adds an extra column(s) to each row for data containing the owner (and users) of the data.

If a configuration table or data columns are used to indicate where the data resides, it is important to consider the impact on application and architecture design to use and maintain the information.

When the data rows of a large table can be used as needed by multiple local sites, some type of subscription or request method can be used, allowing a given location to subscribe to only the exact rows in which it is interested. For example, a benefits claims office subscribes only to those customers for which it is processing a claim, though all customers belong to a central customer file. To support this function, application and support software must be developed. Two possible implementations are worth considering:

- *Subscription.* This allows users to "subscribe" to data on a per-row basis. A subscription (or configuration) table or additional columns on a subscribed-to table can be updated by users at a given location wishing to subscribe to a particular row. It can also be updated by applications that can infer that a location needs to subscribe to a particular row. (For example, in a claims entry application, a customer may call in a claim to an office that has not previously dealt with the customer). The subscription table or columns indicate which components have subscribed to the row and need distribution of future data updates. Initial addition of the row to the local site would be accomplished during normal replication processing. This approach is suitable when the frequency of update is too high and the number of sites too large to reasonably broadcast all updates to all locations.
- *Pull.* This technique may be included in an asynchronous process related to the application that checks for the row locally and asks for it remotely when not found. In this case, no configuration table or additional column is needed. Updates are sent as broadcast messages to all sites and only those that need the update accept it. This ap-

proach is suitable when the frequency of update is low and there are a limited number of sites.

Deciding where to place the data and the applications is the first critical step in designing a distributed processing system. Using the application/data site model described in Chapter III-8 can help visualize the appropriate locations during the placement process. However, locations chosen at this point may change when other issues come into play, such as easy access to the data, data integrity, and how often the data will need to be updated.

DISTRIBUTED DATA MANAGEMENT STRATEGIES

Distributed data management involves the regular transfer of data throughout the system. Distributed data management strategies typically work in the background to support the data needs of the applications and usually do not directly involve applications.

When choosing a distributed data management strategy, there are two main areas of consideration: the data synchronization approach and the data transfer strategies—each of which works as follows:

- The data synchronization approach determines the timing of data movement throughout the system, and the amount of data that must be sent to synchronize databases.
- The data transfer strategies outline the way the data is physically transferred between sites. Data transfer strategies are typically provided through advanced distributed relational DBMS products, custom development, or a combination of the two.

Any system that maintains multiple copies of the same data must determine the need for currency of the data copies. When should the data be updated? How much should be updated? These issues affect when the updates to master data are to be distributed to local databases and how much data will be distributed to ensure that changes are incorporated into all the databases.

Two key aspects of data refresh approaches are frequency of transfer or update and the quantity of data to be transferred.

Frequency

The frequency of data updates determines how often the updates are distributed throughout the system. There are a number of ways to schedule these updates, including the following:

- Periodic (push).

- User initiated (pull).
- Synchronous.
- Asynchronous.

Periodic. Regular updates are made from the master data to the local databases. This update process could be a regular batch job or could be triggered by a scheduler. For example, a scheduler program could be used to run an extract program every (n) minutes. The extract program would then check the master database for updates and distribute them to the local databases.

Periodic updating is useful when immediate distribution of data is not required because it can be delayed to a more convenient time when many updates can be batched and distributed. The delay in propagating updates means that local copies will not have real-time data or even near real-time data. No one would build an airline reservation system using this approach. But if an organization's local sales offices want to look for sales trends over the last few months, odds are that the transactions in the last 15 seconds will not be missed.

User Initiated (Pull). This strategy allows the user of the data on a local database to request an updated copy of the data. The user could be notified when an update has completed and could then begin work using the new data. This strategy works best when the data required is updated often at the master level but rarely requested at the local level.

If the data is requested often at the user level but seldom updated at the master level, there is a high probability that subsequent requests will repeatedly transfer the same data to the local database. The most common use of this tactic is to supply periodic snapshots of data to workstations or remote work groups for end-user computing.

User-initiated refresh is most appropriate when users may not use the data all that often but need the most current information available on those occasions when they do use the data.

Synchronous. With synchronous distributed updating, changes to secondary copy databases are completed as they occur in the master database. The application program initiating updates in the local database does not continue processing until the update has been successfully distributed to all other databases in the system.

The synchronous refresh approach is necessary when changes to all database copies must be made and distributed immediately—for example, to reserve inventory and maintain accurate availability counts at multiple warehouses. These requirements imply the need for a two-phase commit, which is discussed later in this chapter.

Asynchronous. This strategy distributes changes immediately after they are applied to the master, and the initiating process does not have to wait for all updates to complete. Each change is transmitted from the initiating database to the remote databases, typically by means of an asynchronous message containing the update transaction.

Strategies with asynchronous refresh are most appropriate when the changes have to be distributed as soon as possible but the application initiating the change cannot spend the time waiting for the change to be made at all locations. If the customer record being updated is held in 30 replicated copies at sales offices across the globe, waiting for the successful completion of all 30 updates is probably not something users want to do. If even one site is down, all the updates would have to be rolled back.

The asynchronous strategy is not appropriate when the application must know immediately if the change is made at all locations and has to perform additional processing if the change is rejected by some location. In this case, the synchronous, two-phase commit is the only option.

Quantity

The quantity of information that needs to be transferred to keep local sites synchronized is affected by the approach chosen. Full replication versus partial replication dictates how much of the data is transferred from the master database to the local copy during periodic or user initiated updates.

Full Table Replication. Using a full table replication, the entire contents of a table are transferred from the master to the local, regardless of the actual amount of data being updated. This strategy increases the amount of data transferred between sites but reduces the complexity of the processing.

Full replication is appropriate for small tables (country codes or state codes, for example) or for tables in which infrequent mass updating periodically alters the majority of the rows.

The full table replication approach trades network bandwidth for simplicity. Moving the entire contents of a table may consume extra network resources but can be much easier than tracking exactly which rows were changed since the last replication and forwarding and applying just the changes.

Selective Replication. In this approach, only the updated rows are transferred from the master database to the local databases. Using partial refresh reduces the total amount of data transferred but increases the distribution complexity.

In databases or file systems that do not inherently support data replication, this function can be implemented by adding to tables a new column that identifies what action has been performed on the individual rows. This column would be filled out with an "add," "change," or "delete" when the corresponding action is applied to the master copy. An extract program can then detect and transmit these changes to the local databases and clear out the processing codes as well as physically deleting rows marked "delete" on the master database.

Selective replication can also be implemented using time stamps to indicate updates and by using log files containing updates or keys or rows that have been updated.

Selective replication is most appropriate when the changes to a table are relatively small and the table size is relatively large. A strategy that incorporates partial refresh generally increases the processing that must be performed on data, while decreasing the resources required to transfer data across the network.

Full table refresh may be more appropriate when the communication bandwidth is large and underutilized, and the system processing power is overcommitted.

Transferring Data

Regardless of which method or methods are chosen for detecting and batching updates, an approach must be chosen for physically sending and receiving the updates between databases.

Any data transfer strategy must consider the implications of communication failure or data loss and corruption between sites. For example:

- How does the strategy detect the failure of communications to a remote site?
- How is data stored for later transfer while the communications are down? Should it even be retransmitted?
- How is the data retransmitted when communications are reestablished?
- How does the system ensure that the data arrives at the remote site in the correct order?
- How does the system ensure that data arrived without errors?

- How does the system guarantee the delivery of the message and whether there is an acknowledgment?
- How does the system ensure the data is delivered only once?
- What processing should be allowed while the network is down?
- Does the target platform require data translation?

The solutions to these issues define the communication recovery procedures as well as the messaging architecture. These procedures may be automatic, manual, or a combination of the two.

For implementing data transfer in support of data replication, there are two ways to go: use the capabilities of a DDBMS product or devise a custom solution. The advantages and disadvantages of each solution are as follows:

- *DDBMS strategies.* Some advanced relational DBMS products, such as Oracle and Sybase, have recently introduced varying levels of support for keeping distributed database copies in sync with one another. If an organization uses or can use a database product with these capabilities, it is a good idea to try and build its data transport around these capabilities. If, however, the organization uses a mix of older database and file technology or even a mix of newer databases (this is the case with many organizations) this may not be an option because of interoperability constraints and incompatibilities.

- *Custom strategies.* Building a custom data replication system can be a painful and expensive experience. In some cases, however, it is the only option. The good thing about custom development is that the organization has the opportunity to design the data replication system to fit its needs perfectly.

Using a DDBMS

The following strategies transfer data between sites based on the capabilities built into many newer relational database systems. Not all DBMS systems have these capabilities, and these capabilities are not restricted to relational systems. But if these features are part of the DBMS systems, they can significantly simplify the transfer of data between separate databases.

Remote Access. Many DBMSs now offer a function giving the application the ability to access remote databases using standard structured query language (SQL) statements. In these databases, the local database maintains a data dictionary containing information about data stored in remote databases. When the application requests remote data, the database retrieves the data from the remote location and passes it to the application.

The best of these implementations maintains data transparency and the application's logic is no different from that used to retrieve local data. If the implementation does not support full data transparency, it may be necessary to add additional logic, either in the application or in a separate architecture layer, to route the request for data to the correct remote location.

Depending on the vendor's implementation, it may be possible to join multiple tables from multiple sites within a single SELECT statement. Before data administrators attempt an ambitious use of some of the more advanced features offered by a DBMS, they should carefully study the algorithms used by the database when performing these complex operations.

The database should perform a cost analysis of the resources needed to complete the operation to determine the best processing strategy for the request. For example, if two tables at separate locations are to be joined, and one is 10 rows and the other is 10,000 rows, a good cost model does not ship the table with 10,000 rows over the network to the first location.

If the DBMS does not perform cost analysis, or is inadequate for the task, it may be necessary to upgrade the network or processing capacity to perform large joins. It is generally not possible to incorporate a custom or enhanced costing model into an existing database product.

Another concern with remote data access is the lack of detection facilities for a system deadlock, sometimes referred to as a deadly embrace. This can occur if two sites require the same data.

For example, both sites require the same rows in table A and table B. The first site locks the rows in A and then attempts to lock the rows in B; the second site locks the rows in B and attempts to get a lock on the rows in A. At this point each needs the data locked by the other. If the DDBMS is unable to detect this type of problem, processing cannot continue.

The remote access strategy is suitable for the remote retrieval scenario. It allows the application to retrieve data from a remote location with a minimum of effort. The remote access strategy may be suitable for the remote update scenarios if the DBMS supports locks with remote access.

If the database does not lock the record when it is retrieved by the application, there is no way to prevent update conflicts when two applications are attempting to update the same information. Each application would then overwrite the other's data.

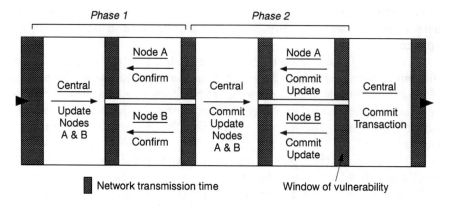

Exhibit III-7-1 5. Two-Phase Commit (2PC)

Two-Phase Commit. Two- phase commit (2PC) is a key component of a true DDBMS. It is the integrity mechanism that attempts to ensure that a transaction is protected and either completed or undone across all sites. This integrity mechanism is divided into a prepare phase and a commit phase. The work done by the DBMS during these two phases may differ depending on the DBMS. Exhibit III-7-15 depicts a common approach. Specifically, the phases work like this:

- *Prepare.* The prepare phase queries all the remote sites to verify that they are ready to commit. The prepare phase initiates the clean-up tasks of the memory management facilities at each site. If a participating site (not the coordinating site) is unable to receive the PRE-PARE message (and any subsequent rollback), it periodically checks for unreleased locks (or checks when communication and processing is restored) and queries the coordinator about the status of the transaction. The coordinator responds that the transaction was rolled back since all sites could not participate and the participating site also rolls back, releasing all locks.

- *Commit.* The commit phase tells each participating local site to write a commit log record. If the commit is successful at all the remote sites involved in the transaction, and the originating site receives a successful acknowledgment from each of the remote sites, the transaction at the originating site is committed.

This 2PC implementation does leave a small margin of vulnerability. If the remote site commits but the initiating site does not receive acknowledgment of the commit, the initiating site does not know whether to commit or roll back. As a result, the initiating site tries to hold on to the locks indefinitely, waiting for the acknowledgment. The probability of this occurring increases with the number of sites involved in the transaction.

Two- phase commit is the best way to ensure that two separate databases remain synchronized. If an organization uses some other approach to guarantee synchronization, it must incorporate similar synchronization logic, which could mean building a custom 2PC architecture.

However, the 2PC is more honored in the breach than in the observance. The strategy is complicated, time-consuming, and costly. It relies on complex synchronous messaging over the network. Communications failures can have a substantial impact on the usability of this system. In addition, the common approach requires participation and success from all sites involved in the transaction. If one site cannot complete the transaction, the entire transaction fails.

Until the organization resolves technical, or if the potential problems are not an issue, 2PC is best used for retrieval and update scenarios in which only one site is being updated although multiple sites may be queried.

In many cases over the years, if the integrity constraints of distributed data were so demanding as to necessitate 2PC, it was worthwhile to reopen the question of the validity of the use of distributed data. Often the absolute need for 2PC indicates that the data under consideration is not suitable for distribution due to some underlying functional issues.

Snapshot. This strategy uses the utilities found in some DBMSs. These utilities allow the regular extraction of data from a database and the transfer of a copy of that data to a remote site. Generally these snapshots are read-only. This strategy can greatly simplify the transfer of data between sites. The database administrator simply configures the DBMS to transfer specific tables at specific times to remote locations; the remainder of the process is automatic.

The snapshot transfer strategy is suitable when a site needs a local read-only copy of nonvolatile data. Any changes to the local snapshot data are overwritten when the next snapshot is transferred from the master location to the local site.

Building Data Distribution Software

When it is not possible to use a distributed database product, it may be necessary for the architecture team to build a custom data distribution approach. The following two approaches, application driven and data driven, have been developed successfully in support of large client/server systems. However, a note of caution is necessary, as implementing the data distribution schemes often proves to be the single most difficult part of such projects.

Application Driven. In the application-driven strategy, the data is modified by an application; the application then transfers the updates out to the remote databases as required. One way to apply the application-driven strategy is for the application to be responsible for both modifying and distributing the data. Or, the application can modify the data and then send a message to another program, which is responsible for distribution of the data.

In both cases, the application must "know" that the updated data should be distributed to other locations. For example, applications programmers must execute some code, no matter how small, after data has been changed. In the first case, the application must also know how to route the data to other locations.

At the initiating or sending site, each application is designed to perform two main functions. First, the application must perform all the processing required to update the database with the new data. Second, the application must decide if the updated data should be distributed to other remote sites, then distribute the updated data or trigger its distribution.

At the receiving site, applications are performing the normal processing for that site, as well as waiting for messages from other sites containing updates to their database. As these messages are received, the applications process them and make the updates to the database.

This application-driven strategy provides for one of the quickest distributions of data as the completion of activity at one site triggers the transfer of the data to other sites.

The application-driven strategy works best in the following situations:

- The routing of the data is static.
- Data is always routed to a remote location.
- No further processing is required after the initial update.

For example, modification of product description information that is always distributed to the same sales offices would be a suitable fit for the application-driven strategy.

If the installation is such that the update to the data requires further processing, and that processing may be local or remote, this strategy may encounter some complications. For example, consider an organization with sales locations and warehouse locations. Some of the sales offices and warehouses are physically located at the same place. If an application (called "take___ order") was creating a sales order, it would have to know which local offices were sales or sales/warehouse operations to determine if and where the order should be distributed.

If an order required distribution, the application would then send that order to the appropriate warehouse where it would be received by another application program (called "fill___order"). Fill___order would finish processing the order, creating a pick list and reserving inventory. If an order can be filled locally, the message is sent internally to the local version of fill___order, which then creates the pick list and reserves inventory.

In this example, the loss of a message anywhere in the process is a serious problem to either of the applications. The take___order application is relying on a message to trigger further processing by fill___order. A means must be found to guarantee the delivery and processing of messages in all situations or there is the risk of incomplete processing. To prevent incomplete processing, programs can be developed to continue processing even after message failure. However, these error correction programs can add considerably to the complexity of the installation.

To reduce the complexity of the applications, the routing of messages between application programs can be incorporated into common distribution modules. For example, a send___message system module can be created to handle the actual routing of the message to the remote site. The application program would call the send___message module, passing it a list of parameters, and allow it to perform the actual routing of the message across the network. The application programmer would be insulated from the detailed steps required to route the message to the remote site, greatly simplifying the application.

The application-driven transfer strategy is very flexible and can be appropriate for many retrieval and update scenarios. It can generally be adapted to the requirements of most installations. The approach was used, for example, by a large government system for processing and sharing benefits information throughout hundreds of sites.

The major weakness of the application-driven transfer strategy is that some form of record locking must be used in conjunction with this strategy to prevent update conflicts. For that reason, an application-driven transfer strategy is usually combined with the central site mediator scenario to handle record locking.

Another drawback is that application programs must be much more aware of which data is held in which locations. Without proper forethought about the structure of applications with regard to data location, this strategy can produce a maintenance nightmare as data locations are moved, split, and combined.

Data Driven. The data-driven strategy requires the initial application to process the data, then set a status flag within the data to signal the completion of a processing step.

With a data-driven strategy, one application does not call the next when complete but rather marks the status in the data itself. Because of that, an event- or time-based mechanism is needed to continue the flow of processing. This can be done in several ways:

- A scheduler initiates application processing every (n) minutes.
- An application program "wakes up" and checks for new transactions it should process every (n) minutes.
- A scheduler monitors a log file of modifications to the database and initiates processing when detecting record changes.
- A database trigger is fired whenever a record is updated that checks to see based on the new status whether an additional application program should now be run. For example, order status has been changed to "shipped," therefore run billing program.
- A user chooses an option on a menu to process all new transactions with a particular status.

In the data-driven strategy, the status of the data drives its processing. Consider what would happen with the addition of multiple sites. A separate group of modules would need to be created to distribute data to other sites. These modules are also triggered by the status of data. If the status changes to an appropriate value, the distribution module will transfer that data to another location. Take the same example given previously in the application-driven strategy. If the take_order program sets the order status to Fill, it can trigger two separate responses:

- If the sales and warehouse are at the same location, the FILL status is discovered by the fill_order program when it automatically checks the database. The fill_order program then creates the pick list and reserves the inventory.
- If the sales and warehouse are at different locations, the Fill status is discovered in the database by the sending distribution modules when they are awakened by the scheduler. The sending distribution modules transfer the order to a warehouse where the receiving distribution modules insert it into the local database. At some point, the fill_order program is awakened by the scheduler and it discovers the Fill status of the order by checking the database. The fill_order program then creates the pick list and reserves the inventory.

The data-driven strategy does not require that the take_order program make the decision whether to fill the order locally or remotely. In fact, the take__order program does not even know of the existence of the fill__order program and does not communicate with it. Each of these programs performs independently of the other. The presence or absence of the distribution modules drives the decision whether or not to fill the order locally or remotely. If the organization has combined functions into the same office, it simply does not install some of the data distribution modules.

In this strategy, the arrival of a message no longer triggers the fill__order application; instead, it is initiated by the scheduler. If the scheduler or application fails, the processing is delayed. Because the application recovery processing is built into the system, it will automatically complete when the problem is corrected.

At the initiating or sending site, applications perform their processing based on the data entered by the user, or based on the status of key fields in the data. When the applications have completed their processing, they set the correct status value in one of the status fields and quit processing. A separate set of system data distribution modules is responsible for transferring the updates to the remote site, based on the status of the data. If local processing is completed, based on the status of the data, the data is extracted and transferred to a remote site by the distribution modules.

At the remote or receiving site, the data distribution modules wait for incoming data from other sites. When new data arrives, the distribution modules insert that data into the database. The receiving site application modules are then able to process this new data the next time they are started, by the scheduler, database trigger, or some user action.

The easiest way to design a database for this strategy is to make the database definition for all sites identical. This allows the developer to place all the application modules anywhere in the system and be assured they will always be able to access the data using the same database calls.

If the database definition is different at each location, different database calls need to be incorporated into the same application depending on where it is located. This can quickly complicate the efforts needed to track system configuration as well as the distribution of later system updates and fixes. Despite the common database definition, there is no need for the database to be completely populated. Each location maintains only the data it requires for its local functions.

The data-driven approach provides excellent decoupling between individual application programs. Rather than applications calling each other, and thus knowing where each one is, applications communicate with each other solely by updating status fields within database records.

The data-driven strategy is suitable for update scenarios. Like the application-driven strategy, it may require additional enhancements if update conflicts are possible and the DBMS does not provide appropriate locking mechanisms. This approach was used, for example, in a global sales and order processing system to enable countries and locations to operate more or less independently and without an undue reliance on communications availability.

Whatever decisions regarding frequency of updating and the quantity of information to be moved, chances are that the decisions will be modified over time as business requirements and other conditions change. This is even more pronounced in a distributed environment than in a nondistributed environment. Distributed environments by their nature are dynamic: the location of data may change, the refresh requirements may change, or the business functions may move from one site to another. It is critical to incorporate flexibility into the implementation of a data refresh strategy so it can easily change with the business.

Processing Distribution

Client/server allows for an application to be divided across two or more computers—typically an end-user workstation or PC and a multiuser server machine. In contrast to traditional centralized mainframe application design, client/server supports dividing a single application across multiple machines.

The nature of the application, the data needed by the application, and the specific benefits of client/server that the project is trying to realize dictate how the application logic is to be divided between client and server. Following are some of the potential benefits of dividing processing in a client/server architecture.

Dedicated Processing Power. In the traditional mainframe configuration, hundreds or even thousands of users share a single mainframe computer. To run mainframes economically, a shop likes to keep processors utilized over 70%. This means that the mainframe is busy at least 70% of the time when a user strikes a key requesting processing; the user must wait in line to be served.

The model suggests that the computer is the important resource and that people should wait in line to use it. Client/server reverses this view by providing each user with a dedicated machine, as well as access to additional shared machines. The desktop computer now has processing power ready and waiting for the user to take some action.

Consider one example of the impact of dedicated, inexpensive processing power. One organization recently implemented a client/server system that replaced an existing mainframe system. The original system supported 800 users with a single 100 MIPS mainframe computer. The new client/server system supported 500 users with 12,000 MIPS of processing power for half the price. The result altered the way the organization thought about the system and about the importance of efficiently using people time rather than computer time. It opened the organization's eyes about new uses of cheap and always available processing power.

Price/Performance Increase. The price of computer cycles on desktop PCs continues to be dramatically less than computer cycles on multiuser mainframe computers. Depending on the configuration, this price differential can be as much as two orders of magnitude. It was this price/performance gap that provided the first spark for moving at least some of the application processing workload off of the mainframe and onto the "cheap" PC.

Enhanced Usability. One direct benefit of the increased availability of cheap dedicated processing power is the ability to devote large amounts of processing resources to produce a better interface for the end user. The most common first step toward ease of use is to provide the user with a graphical user interface. A graphical interface demands large amounts of processing capacity (as anyone can attest who has tried to run Microsoft Windows on a 286 PC). In addition, the processing must be dedicated; making a user wait after clicking on a pull-down menu does not increase usability.

Availability. Availability is an issue in a traditional mainframe environment where all application processing occurs on a centralized mainframe machine. If the machine becomes unavailable for any reason (e.g., for maintenance, backups, or system failure), all hundreds or thousands of users who depend on it will be without any computing access. With client/server, even if the server or servers become unavailable, users still have access to their own workstations.

There is one important caveat about increased availability: developers must carefully think through what data as well as processing resources the user needs access to to continue work. In most client/server configurations, overall availability is not improved by having workstations because all the applications require data (such as inventory statistics) that is stored only on a shared server. If the server goes down, every user is out of luck, just as in the mainframe scenario.

Processing Distribution Approaches

Of the five styles of client/server processing (see Chapter I-1 for a discussion of Gartner's five styles), the three most often implemented are:

1. Remote data management.
2. Distributed logic.
3. Remote presentation.

Remote Data Management. In the remote data management approach, the entire application runs on the client workstation, sending SQL or SQL-like messages to the server, which functions as a shared database machine.

In practice, the server also ends up running the application "batch" load as well. The introduction of client/server computing almost always leads to moving significant portions of application processing out—off the central mainframe and onto the client workstation. The great majority of client/server applications being developed today fit this category. In fact, most popular development tools, such as PowerBuilder and VisualBasic, are largely geared toward building this style of client/server application.

The remote data management distribution approach is excellent for database-centric style applications such as data maintenance or reporting because it offloads application processing from the server platform and is an easy development model to implement.

Distributed Logic. In the distributed logic style the application is split in half, with part running on the workstation and part on the server platform. This configuration allows for the placement of application code on the machine (client or server) that is best suited to the task.

This flexibility can be useful if a particular application routine is processing intensive (such as rules-based or linear optimization) and can be executed on a high-powered server computer instead of the user's desktop PC. In practice, with each increasingly powerful generation of desktop machines, there has been a decrease in the percentage of application situations that can benefit from moving processing to the server (which many users share).

A second benefit of the placement flexibility is the opportunity to reduce network traffic. In the remote data management style, data-intensive application routines that need to scan large volumes of data (but do not need to display that data) can waste network resources because all the data must be transferred from the server to the workstation to perform any required calculations or processing.

With distributed logic, the routine that scans the data can be placed on the server with the database sending only the result back. This eliminates the need to send large volumes of data across the network. This savings can be particularly valuable when the client and server are separated by a relatively expensive wide area network communications link.

The flexibility of distributed logic does not come without a cost, however. Developing distributed logic-style applications is typically more complex and difficult. The chief culprit is the bit of code that allows a client program and a server program to interact. In remote data management, the client-based application talks to the server-based database via SQL and the communications infrastructure is typically supplied by the database.

Remote Presentation. A third client/server style, used less often than the previous two, is to perform all application processing and data manipulation on the server, reserving the workstation for only presentation and user interaction. This has proven to be the least popular client/server form because it fails to use fully the low-cost processing capability of the desktop workstation. Instead, it places almost all the processing load on the shared server machine.

The X Windowing System popular on UNIX-based machines supports implementing client/server applications that fit this model. With the X Windowing System, the entire application and database can be located on a server in the network. The application can "display itself" on the client workstation by sending protocol messages (such as "create window" or "show menu") to the X Windowing System's workstation component. That component then renders the application display messages.

Mix and Match. In reality, few applications of any real size fit nicely into just one of these client/server processing distribution scenarios. Some parts of the application may be well suited to the remote data management approach; others may require the power and flexibility of distributed logic.

A powerful feature of client/server computing is that it supports the mixing and matching of various process and data distribution strategies across applications or even within them. Some people believe, with almost religious conviction, that all client/server applications should be implemented with one or another of these approaches. In fact, all three styles are valid. The trick is to know when to use which.

ADVICE IN CHOOSING A DISTRIBUTED PROCESSING STRATEGY

The ultimate choice of a processing distribution strategy can be hotly contested. Experience has shown that a philosophy of "keeping it simple" offers the best chances of successfully delivering a system.

The simplest approach (not surprising, given its frequent usage), is the remote data management style. Here, the application resides on the workstation and the database resides on the server; all messaging is handled by the DBMS product.

This is a wise going-in position for all applications within the system being developed. Only after it is proved that this approach will not work for a particular function should an organization even consider implementing a more sophisticated approach. Even if it turns out that the development team must implement some function using a message-based, distributed logic messaging architecture, the team should still implement each individual function with the simplest processing distribution approach feasible. Above all, the team must avoid the temptation to overengineer.

III-8
A Strategy for the Allocation of Data and Processing

The previous chapter introduced concepts, approaches, and issues to consider when implementing distributed systems. This chapter describes the analysis process that leads to proper decisions about where to locate data and processing logic throughout the network.

MAKING PLACEMENT DECISIONS

Analysis begins with verifying where business functions are to be performed. Users are then aligned with these locations, and data and application requirements are mapped accordingly. As Exhibit III-8-1 suggests, the decision process is iterative and may require more than one pass to arrive at the best data and processing distribution solution.

Business Function Placement

The first step in defining an overall systems placement design is to identify where the key business functions are to be performed. The business function is what the business user does. Client/server computing gives the business more flexibility and options with regard to placing business activities where they make the most sense, rather than where the computing resources and computer-literate employees reside.

For example, where should salespersons perform their business function? Should they perform validation and pricing back at a sales office where cumbersome traditional mainframe applications are available? It makes more sense for salespersons to enter, validate, and price customer orders on site while with the customer.

In reality, the business function placement decision is often a compromise. The flexibility of new client/server technology may drive the decision, though it is tempered by costs, the inertia of past practices, and the upheaval caused by reorganization and the moving of personnel.

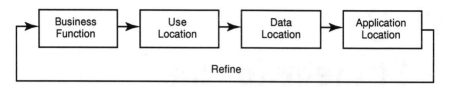

Exhibit III-8-1. The Iterative Process of Data and Processing Allocation

User Group Placement

A "user group" is a homogeneous set of workers who perform the same business function—for example, field sales personnel, order entry clerks, or airline coupon auditors. The members of a user group perform the same business functions with access to the same applications and data types. The location of the various business functions to be performed drives the placement of user groups.

Data Placement

"Data" consists of the information needed by the user to perform the business function. The most obvious strategy here is to link data placement with the user group placement decisions. Data is then placed where the users are located, and thus where the business function is performed.

Although this answer has some intuitive appeal, a good deal of analysis is needed before final data placement decisions can be reached. Technology improvements—particularly in the area of network reliability, cost, and accessibility—have substantially reduced the need to physically locate data near the user. Instead, providing the user access to the data stored elsewhere may be sufficient, and may even be preferable from the perspective of complexity and operations support. Much of this chapter is dedicated to the issues and concerns that surround the data placement decision.

Application Placement

The "application" is the logic implemented to support the user in performing the business function. Application placement depends heavily both on where the user is located and where the necessary data is held. A going-in approach is to place user-intensive application logic (e.g., graphical user interface code or highly user interactive programs) on the user's client workstation.

Application logic that is data intensive (e.g., billing and trend analysis, which require access to large amounts of data) is best co-located with

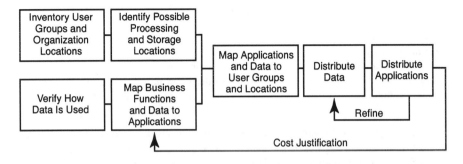

Exhibit III-8-2. Placement Planning Chart

---

the required data. This improves performance by minimizing network time. The goal in application placement is to provide the user with the best performance and availability while still considering the limitations and costs of current networking technology and providing data integrity.

Decisions on placement seem to imply a clear causal sequence of steps. In practice, however, the task of physically placing the elements of a client/server system is an iterative one. Whenever any placement decision or assumption is changed, each of the other components must be revisited to assess the impact of the change. The rest of this chapter provides insights on how to go about refining placement decisions.

PLACEMENT STRATEGY

The task of analyzing placement and distribution requirements begins in the initial systems planning activities and continues on into the early steps of analysis and design. The planning chart in Exhibit III-8-2 highlights the key activities and iteration points in determining and refining a placement strategy for data and applications.

Confirm Inventory of User Groups and Organization Locations

User groups that are supported by the application systems project and the organization location where they reside should be confirmed and documented. A user group is not an individual user but a distinct part of the organization that owns or uses data—for example, a company, division, department, warehouse, or sales office.

A geographical location itself is usually not defined as a user group but rather as an organization location. An organization location is a logical and/or physical grouping of user groups. Some examples of organization locations and resident user groups include:

Organization Locations	User Groups
Regional sales office	Order entry
Distribution center	Distribution
Branch or field office	Order entry and distribution
Central headquarters	Human resources, accounting, and payroll

Some systems development methodologies that do not address client/server or distributed systems design may not include tasks and deliverables for defining user groups. When designing a distributed client/server system, it is essential to understand what kinds of users are in which physical locations and what application functions they need, as well as their related data requirements. This information is necessary for making informed decisions about where to place the application and data assets.

Identify Processing Sites and Data Storage Locations

The next step in the data distribution process is to create an inventory of existing and potential processing sites and data storage locations. Except when a distinction is appropriate, this chapter uses the word "site" to indicate processing sites and data storage locations.

All organization locations should be considered potential processing sites or data storage locations. A site may support one or more organization locations. In creating the inventory, designers must consider both geographic distribution (e.g., multiple data centers) and known processing platform distribution (e.g., mainframes, file servers, database servers, and workstations).

Verify How the Data Is Used

The following documentation generated early in the project is useful to reference when verifying how the data is used. These deliverables are typical of most systems development methodologies:

- *Function/location matrix.* Shows the relationship between business functions and the place of business where they are to be performed.
- *Data/function usage matrix.* Shows the relationship between the business functions performed within the organization and the data used by the organization.
- *Summary of information needs.* Shows major functional areas and specific business functions of the organization, business objectives, or other needs that the information would support. This summary also shows the key data that help management monitor progress toward

business objectives and the conceptual data entity group to which the major data belongs.

- *Corporate data model.* Shows the major data entities used by the organization and the relationships between them.
- *Systems group data model.* Shows the data entities used by the identified systems group and the relationships between the entities. This data model should depict a subset of the entities from the corporate data model, adding more detailed entities and relationships as required.
- *Project data model.* Shows the data entities used by the named project and the relationships between the entities. This data model should be a subset of the systems group data model. It may show more detailed data entities and more specific information about the relationships between the data entities.
- *Entity definition.* Shows information about the entity: description, synonyms, user responsibility, population, growth rates, processing rules, attributes (columns/fields), and related or dependent entities. An entity definition also typically includes information about how the attributes are used within the entity: key usage, occurrence, mandatory/optional indicator, comments.

A thorough review of the project documentation provides the designer with a sound understanding of what information is required and how it is to be used to meet the functional goals of the system.

Map Business Functions and Data Entities to Applications

Once the designer understands how the data is to be used, the next step is to map the business functions and the data entities to the application systems to be developed. The required documents and techniques are not specific to client/server.

Designers must make sure that they have a complete understanding of the business and information needs before attempting to assign physical data and process locations. The two outputs from this task are:

1. *Function/application systems matrix.* Shows how a portfolio of application systems supports the existing or planned business functions.
2. *Data/application systems matrix.* Shows the relationship between the application systems and the data used by the systems.

The placement worksheet in Exhibit III-8-3 is a tool for capturing the relationships among business functions, applications, user groups, and key data entities. It also shows the initial trial decisions about their

Processing Locations		Headquarters			Airport Site	
Business Functions	User Groups / Applications	Fare Auditors	Revenue Clerks	Refunds Clerks	Customer Service Reps	Gate Crew
Fare Audit	Ticket Audit	Ticket Sales, Pricing Rules, Contracts, Agents				
Revenue Adjustment	Ticket Refund			Sales, Ticket, Refund Rules	Sales, Ticket, Refund Rules	
	Interline Reconciliation		Carrier, Ticket, Accounts			
	Sales/Lift Match		Sales, Ticket			
Revenue Data Capture	Coupon Entry					Ticket

Exhibit III-8-3. Sample Placement Worksheet

placement. The left side of the worksheet shows the relationships between applications and the business functions they support. Across the top are the first-cut decisions about which user groups will be placed at each location.

The shading in a cell indicates that the user group needs access to that application. The shaded cells list the data that the application for that user group requires. The contents of a cell represent "need to access" and are not necessarily a recommendation to physically place all applications and data at all points where they need to be accessed. The placement worksheet provides a single place to capture the requirements that the final placement decisions must satisfy.

Map Applications and Data to User Groups and Locations

The inventory of potential and existing processing sites should be documented on the application/data site model (see Exhibit III-8- 4). The field across the top of the model identifies the sites. Peer or like sites should be identified in a generic way—for example, distribution center or field. Processing sites with unique characteristics should be identified individually. For example, the model should identify individually order processing centers that include distribution functions as well as those that do not.

Document User Groups on Application/Data Site Model. User groups should be mapped to one or more sites. This mapping is based on

Processing Locations	Headquarters		Customer Service Center	Airport Site	
User Group Applications					
Ticket Audit					
Ticket Refund					
Interline Reconciliation					
Sales/Lift Match					
Coupon Entry					
Tickets					
Sales					
Contracts					
Agents					
Pricing Rules					
Carriers					
Accounts					
Refund Rules					

Exhibit III-8-4. Application/Data Site Model

---

the organization locations that are supported by the site and the user groups supported by those organization locations. Some illustrations are a human resources department that exists only at the central site and order entry users that exist at sales centers and are supported by a local site. In these examples, some of the users must be documented at a specific level (human resources department) and others at a more generic level (all sales centers).

The model should also note where a user group crosses data storage locations. For example, if a division has individual users in multiple geographic locations, each is considered a separate local site. This information is useful if the organization agrees that data is owned by divisions. Because the division users are at multiple sites, some data replication or remote processing is required.

Define Initial Distribution Strategy. After identifying and documenting processing sites and data classification criteria, the next step is to distribute the data and the applications. In actual practice, design team members most likely implement the decision process concurrently with multiple iterations of the process until they achieve a satisfactory design. It is more important to get the design correct than to follow a strict, step-by-step methodology.

Distribute Data. The data distribution strategy defines how to distribute the data entities. Refining the data distribution strategy involves identifying and resolving data conflicts and defining mechanisms that will assist in the actual distribution of the data.

A "top-down" approach to distributed data design is effective. The designer analyzes the business requirements of the organization first to determine the ideal distribution of data throughout the enterprise. The alternative approach, "bottom- up," is useful when developing a system incorporating a collection of existing systems and databases or mixing existing and new databases.

The end product of the data distribution design process is a data placement scheme. The data placement scheme typically is either documented as an application/data site model or depicted in a logical data model for each storage location.

As distributed database technology matures, it should simplify the mechanics of implementing a distributed data management strategy but not the decision process of defining where data is most appropriately stored.

Review Other Classification Criteria. Several other classification criteria should be considered when determining where to place the data. The classification criteria presented here include frequency of update and access, currency, and security.

"Currency" refers to the freshness of data. User requirements determine whether users require real-time or close-to-real-time data. If the system maintains multiple data copies, user requirements determine how often the data is refreshed and updated. Security is an important criterion because local area network (LAN) environments are usually less secure than a physically secure mainframe environment. As a result, the sensitivity of the data and the corresponding level of security must be taken into account.

Typically, data entities are classified according to some measurement for each criterion. The measurement for each criterion should be specifically defined for the enterprise based on its relative importance and impact on the business. For example, within the currency criterion, the enterprise must establish how current information must be, as measured in seconds, hours, or even days. Exhibit III-8-5 depicts sample criteria with a basic measurement classification for each.

Next, rules or distribution strategies can be established for the enterprise for each measurement class. These rules affect the data placement decisions and also drive the choice of processing strategy. Rules typically encompass several criteria. Some examples are:

Criterion	Measurement Classification

Frequency of Update	• Dynamic: frequently updated (such as daily or weekly)
	• Static: infrequently updated (such as semi-annually).
	  Sometimes called "reference data."
	• Transaction: finite life span and/or distinct statuses
	  through which it moves.

Frequency of Use/ Reference	• Continuous • Frequent (many times per day) • Infrequent (a few times per month)
Required Currency of Data	• Real time • Periodic
Security Restrictions or Sensitivity of Data	• High • Medium • Low

Exhibit III-8-5. Sample Criteria Measurement Classification

- Data that is frequently updated and infrequently read will not be distributed and therefore should be read remotely when needed.
- Data that is frequently updated, frequently read, and requires real-time currency implies that the system needs a centralized solution. Use of two-phase commit instead of a centralized solution requires justification.
- Data that is very sensitive and requires strict security controls should not be placed on a workstation.

Distribute Data Entities. The next step is to distribute the key data entities. Data placement involves determining where in the network of computers to locate specific data items.

Implicit in this task is also the decision of how many copies of a particular data item to maintain around the network. Placement options range from simplicity (centralized—all data in one place) to complexity (placing only the tables and rows of interest at each physical location).

Different placement approaches are appropriate for different types of reference or transaction data tables. Therefore, it is unlikely for a single placement rule to be universally applicable.

Four guidelines are useful for preparing an initial cut at the data distribution approach, but further analysis is required by each site to set the rules that make sense for that site:

1. *Single storage rule.* If an entity is accessed (read or written) at one

Processing Locations	Headquarters		Customer Service Center	Airport Site	
User Group Applications	Fare Auditors	Revenue Clerks	Ratings Clerks	Customer Service Reps	Gate Crew
Ticket Audit					
Ticket Refund					
Interline Reconciliation					
Sales/Lift Match					
Coupon Entry					
Tickets	Master		Read-only copy	Remote access to master	
Sales	Master		Read-only copy		
Contracts	Master				
Agents	Master				
Pricing Rules	Master				
Carriers	Master				
Accounts	Master				
Refund Rules	Master		Read-only copy		

Exhibit III-8-6. A "Going-in" Position for Major Data Entities

location only, designers should assign the data entity to that location.

2. *Replication rule.* If an entity is accessed from one or more locations for read operations only, designers should assign that data entity to each location, replicating from a master location to the other locations.

3. *Segmentation rule.* If an entity is used for write operations from more than one location, and the write operations can be logically segmented horizontally and/or vertically, designers should segment the data entity between locations as appropriate.

4. *Centralization rule.* If an entity is accessed for write operations from more than one location and the write operations cannot be logically segmented horizontally or vertically, designers should centralize the location of the data entity.

During initial distribution, the organization should take other classification criteria—frequency of update/use, currency, and security requirements—into account. The goal at this point is to document a going-in position (as shown in Exhibit III-8-6) for the location of the major data entities. Later steps help refine and adjust this going-in position as required.

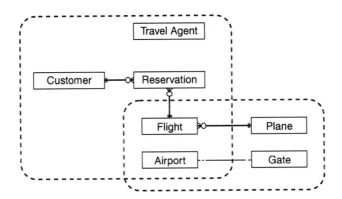

Exhibit III-8-7. Data Model of Data Distribution Strategy

The data distribution strategy may also be depicted on a data model as shown in Exhibit III-8-7. Lines representing processing sites can be drawn around groupings of data entities that will be placed at the processing site.

Distribute Applications

The decision about the placement of the application modules involves several considerations. In general, an objective of a distributed computing application should be to put as much control of the business function as possible on the machine that is dedicated to the user or shared by the least number of users.

However, this is not always desirable or practical. When selecting a processing strategy, a number of considerations must be taken into account to address how application requirements will be met, including the following:

- *Communication capabilities.* The capacity and availability of the communication infrastructure are important when processing is to be split across platforms. The frequency and volume of exchanges between processes and the speed, reliability, and availability of communications have an impact on the performance of an application and must be considered when choosing a processing strategy.

- *Constraints imposed by packaged software.* The use of packaged software to meet specific business functions may necessitate the distribution of logic and data to a specific processing platform. Most application package solutions available on the market today assume a centralized database model with all processing performed either on the server or on the client workstation. These solutions are typically not extensible to accommodate different distribution configurations.

- *Platform interoperability.* Designers must consider the extent to which multiple platforms can work together (interoperate) when defining where specific application processing will occur. In addition, any restrictions must be taken into account, such as only certain data types being supported in translation or only certain protocols.

- *Frequency of change to application code.* If an application is subject to frequent changes or updates, the number and location of target platforms become considerations in terms of the overhead required to distribute updates and to ensure that the system is configured correctly.

- *Reliability and recoverability of the target platform.* The capabilities of a platform must be considered to ensure that it can deliver the required availability and be recovered reliably in the event of a failure.

- *Platform-specific capabilities.* Some applications may require the capabilities of a particular platform. Examples include graphical user interface capabilities, imaging capabilities, high-MIPS capabilities, an attached high- speed printer, or other special environment technology, such as a secured check printer. In addition, there may be a requirement for development tools that are available only on selected platforms.

- *Number of users and resource availability.* The number of users of a particular process and the computing capacities available may influence the choice of platform or the strategy for distributing a process across platforms. For instance, the calculation portion of a numerically intensive application may run better on a user's workstation than on a 95% utilized high-MIPS shared processor.

- *Location of data.* Applications that scan large quantities of data (e.g., trend analysis) are better placed with the required data than near the user to avoid pulling megabytes or even gigabytes of data across the LAN or, worse yet, the wide area network (WAN). The performance degradation from communications often outweighs the benefits of placing the application with the user in these cases.

Having considered these factors, a going-in position on application placement can now be added to the evolving application/data site model (see Exhibit III-8-8).

It is important to remember that in addition to distributing the business applications and the data to support them, designers must also analyze the "infrastructure" or architecture applications and their corre-

Processing Locations	Headquarters		Customer Service Center	Airport Site	
User Group / Applications	Fare Auditors	Revenue Clerks	Ratings Clerks	Customer Service Reps	Gate Crew
Ticket Audit	X				
Ticket Refund			X	X	
Interline Reconciliation	X				
Sales/Lift Match	X				
Coupon Entry					X
Tickets	Master		Read-only copy	Remote access to master	
Sales	Master		Read-only copy		
Contracts	Master				
Agents	Master				
Pricing Rules	Master				
Carriers	Master				
Accounts	Master				
Refund Rules	Master		Read-only copy		

Exhibit III-8-8. A "Going-in" Position on Application Placement

sponding data (e.g., help text, error messages, system parameters) for proper distribution.

Refine Data Distribution Strategy

Once the going-in application/data site model completed, the next step is to refine the strategy. Refining the strategy includes the following:

- Identifying and resolving data conflicts and addressing other data placement issues.
- Identifying the appropriate data distribution control mechanisms.

Identifying and Resolving Data Conflicts. There are two major types of data conflicts: data redundancy conflicts and application processing conflicts.

Data redundancy conflicts occur when a single row of a data entity is placed at multiple locations. Data redundancy may occur for the following reasons:

- No horizontal segmentation has been applied.
- More than one user group has defined the data access requirements.
- A user group spans multiple processing locations.

Application processing conflicts occur when the data entities required by an application are not located at the same processing site as the application. The results can be such things as increased application complexity, higher data transmission costs, and reduced application performance.

The following are required inputs to the process of resolving data conflicts:

- Existing hardware, system software, and network relationships.
- Understanding of hardware, network, and system software.
- Application/data processing site model.
- Required data throughput for each entity by location, in rows or bytes per unit of time.
- Estimation of entity row sizes and number of rows per entity by location.
- Data transfer volume and required network speeds between nodes.

The hardware, system software, and network topology may not be a known input to the data distribution strategy decision but may actually be driven by the data distribution strategy. More often than not, some of the components exist and others need to be upgraded or added to accommodate an appropriate data distribution model.

Additional factors should be considered to resolve data conflicts:

- *Data volume.* The volume of data required for processing by applications affects the strategy for access and location. High data volumes are likely to be accompanied by high costs if multiple copies must be stored. In some cases, it may not be possible to offer local copies due to platform space limitations. Data storage volumes may also preclude storing the data locally.
- *Communications capacity.* Available communications capacity influences the data topology. For example, high-volume data access over slow lines is likely to result in unacceptable performance. The ideal way to build a system is to identify the appropriate data topology and then determine the required communications infrastructure. However, in the real world this is frequently not practical due to cost constraints, schedule constraints, or the need to use existing infrastructure. If a communications infrastructure already exists, however, capacity planning must be completed before the data topology is finalized.
- *Location and type of network.* Distributed computing over a WAN is more costly and less responsive than when implemented using LAN technology. Designers should consider placing data within the LAN environment of its primary users. If this is not possible (e.g., when

primary user groups for data are in two cities), they should consider either data replication or higher-speed, redundant WAN links.

- *Performance of a LAN environment.* In a LAN environment, there may be very little difference in performance when accessing data from the server across the LAN versus the workstation's local hard disk. Locating common data on the server avoids many of the coordination and synchronization issues of replicated data.

- *Response time expectations.* User expectations for quick response times may require that all data required for the application be stored locally. This needs to be weighed against the complexities of data replication and synchronization.

- *Platform interoperability.* Designers must consider the ability (or inability) of two platforms to interoperate when defining the data topology. In addition, any other platform-related restrictions must be taken into account. For instance, only certain data types (e.g., integers but not packed decimal) may be supported in the transformation from one platform to another.

- *Platform capabilities.* Designers must consider the capabilities of a platform to ensure that, given an estimated database size, estimated update volumes, and an approximate number of users, the system can deliver the required availability and performance based on business requirements.

- *Control over integrity.* Designers must consider the risk to data integrity in light of ad hoc user access through non- management information system developed applications (custom application, query tools).

- *Physical database and logical database conversions.* Designers must take into account the number of different physical and logical formats the architecture must support. Each additional format potentially implies another set of conversions that must be written or obtained and maintained and another set of programs that must be executed when data is extracted or copied.

- *Special data types.* Data types with unique characteristics and special storage requirements may dictate that all or part of a data entity be stored in a special data storage location. For instance, video may be stored and managed on specialized video servers.

- *Administration and operation issues.* When data is distributed, some data administration and operating functions may also be distributed. The cost of distributed administration must be measured against the importance of the data to ensure that adequate backup and restore procedures are in place and that a sufficient disaster recovery plan exists. The expertise of the existing local site systems personnel may also be a factor.

- *Data ownership.* Typically, after a first pass at identifying a system's data topology, data resides closest to its primary user groups. Then, performance, capacity, and cost analyses either confirm this approach or suggest that an alternative topology might be more appropriate. Some user groups want particular data on their machines. Others may object to the constant drain on their system's performance because of remote users. Such political issues all too often lead to poor or excessively costly distributed data designs. As much as possible, the organization must focus on the easiest and most cost-effective way to meet system objectives that are tied to overall business objectives.

- *Number, location, and sophistication of data users.* Although owners of the data are likely to be the primary users of the data, other nonprimary users may need access to the data. The number of users, their locations on the network, and the frequency and type of access required (high-volume random or high-volume sequential, for example) must all be taken into account.

- *Referential integrity requirements.* Designers should avoid cross-site referential integrity. Cross-site referential integrity implies crossing processing sites to ensure that referential integrity is not being violated by updates at one site that relate, referentially, to data at another node. This is undesirable both for the network traffic required to validate the integrity and for the complexity and potential for problems it can introduce.

CONCLUSION

Typically, designers must implement several iterations of data and applications placement before they can devise a solution can be devised that meets all the requirements for access, integrity, security, and ownership. But additional, broader iterations may still be required.

Thus far the analysis has not focused on the costs associated with various choices of business function, user group, application, and data placement. At this point in the process, the organization can start to assemble a rough understanding of the deployment and ongoing operations costs of the proposed placement strategy.

With a better understanding of costs, it is now practical to iterate back and look at the all the placement decisions to ensure that such costs are justifiable in terms of business benefits. A sales director, for example, may begin with the conviction that it is "absolutely necessary" that each office have its own data. However, on learning the costs of maintaining perfectly synchronized customer databases at each of 50 sales locations, the director may have second thoughts.

III-9
Integration of Legacy Systems

A major design challenge in client/server development is often the integration of the existing legacy data, application, and technology platforms into the client/server framework. Legacy applications capture an organization's core business functions and data. A successful client/server implementation often requires the incorporation or integrations of aspects of existing systems.

Integration of existing systems continues to be a major challenge because of rapidly changing technology. Traditionally, people thought about integration issues only as they apply to existing mainframe-based systems. In fact, for most environments today, any existing system can represent an integration challenge, even if it is on a nonmainframe platform.

REASONS FOR INTEGRATING NEW AND EXISTING SYSTEMS

Enterprises choose to integrate the existing data, application, and technology platforms for a variety of reasons:

- *No business case support to redevelop.* The core existing applications represent an intensive investment the enterprise has made over time. These systems often serve the core business functions well. It is rare to be able to make a strong business case for completely rebuilding each and every system for client/server.

- *Existing systems hold key data.* The core data stores on which the existing applications have been built often provide the information backbone of the enterprise. The organization's applications may depend, for example, on existing customer and product information. Addressing how to incorporate this information into the new client/server application is often a requirement.

- *Linkage with downstream processing.* The core systems often fulfill the standard, batch-oriented applications of the enterprise, such as invoice/billing generation and ledger posting. Although the potential benefits of client/server may apply to reengineering the upfront order validation and entry, client/server may have little potential to add value in the current batch application functions. Interfacing to and reusing existing batch downstream processes is often required.

- *Schedule.* When the decision is made to redevelop one or more core systems using client/server, the level of effort may determine that an interim transition approach is required. An interim transition approach would use the techniques discussed in this chapter to provide transitional interfaces between new and old systems until the older systems are systematically replaced. To achieve the early business benefits of implementing reengineered processes, the time schedule to fully redevelop the core systems may not be suitable or the development resources may not be available. In practice, it is rarely feasible to rebuild all an organization's systems simultaneously. This means that the development team must take an interim approach.

- *Packaged software.* In most enterprises, a variety of functions can be met by packaged software available in the marketplace. In fact, most enterprises use a hybrid approach of both packaged and custom-developed solutions. Although the platform and operating systems of these packages may remain within the corporate standards of an enterprise, integrating the package's architecture with other applications often presents issues.

- *Existing skills.* In many cases, the organization has functionally and technically skilled personnel supporting the existing systems, and these systems adequately meet the business requirements. The existing system is stable and the organization knows how to support it. In these cases, it makes both economic and operational sense to continue the life of these systems and to integrate them with any new applications needing access to their existing applications, data, or technical platforms.

Warnings About Legacies

None of these reasons for maintaining legacies and integrating them with new systems should be seen as justifying legacies in every case. There are often compelling reasons for keeping legacy applications. But there are also instances when continued use of the legacy can be questionable.

The following questions are key considerations:

1. Does the legacy system have reliable data?
2. Do the data structures support the needs of the business, or do they lack the accessibility and relationship capability that the business requires?

3. Is the core online monitor or data technology underlying the legacy application obsolete, even if the in-house skills to support it exist? For example, is there an application built on a file system or DBMS for which there is no vendor support?

DESIGN TECHNIQUES FOR INTEGRATING WITH EXISTING SYSTEMS

Design techniques for integration with existing systems can be grouped into two broad categories:

- *Front-end access.* Front-end techniques tend to be used for bringing the existing system's functions directly to the users' new desktops in the client/server environment. Front-end access techniques include screen emulation and screen scraping.
- *Back-end access.* Back-end techniques tend to be used when the existing data stores have information that is needed for the client/ server environment but accessing the information through existing screens or functions is not feasible. This technique is often used for direct legacy data store access. Types of back-end interfaces include remote data access, new server logic to access legacy data store, and data replication.

Many client/server applications use a combination of these front-end and back-end techniques.

Front-End Interface Techniques

Screen Emulation. The most direct access to an existing system is to provide a terminal emulation window in the client environment. This provides the user with access to the current capability of the application. It can reuse the existing security infrastructure of sign-on and password if implemented.

The screen emulation approach has limitations, however. Although it may meet the needs of users who were previously familiar with the application, it may present significant training and usability problems to new users, especially if the legacy system had a high learning curve and lacked well-understood procedures.

Screen emulation is sometimes feasible as a bridging technique while the functions it provides are being redeveloped for client/server using one of the other techniques. But it is not suited for longer-term use unless the application is rarely accessed and the cost of restructuring it cannot be justified.

Screen Scraping. Screen scraping attempts to make key functions of a current application blend into the new graphical user interface (GUI) environment. It may be as simple as using a screen-scraping language, such as IBM's 3270-based Extended High Level Language Application Program Interface (EHLLAPI) language. A screen-scraping language provides a facility for intercepting a formatted screen, interpreting the fields of information, and redisplaying them in the appropriate window fields of the new GUI.

This technique works well for legacy applications that can map one screen from the legacy application to one window function in the client/server environment. In these straightforward environments, screen scraping can be an effective approach to adding a GUI to an existing legacy application. Although the capability of the legacy does not increase or change in this situation, accessing it through the GUI allows it to merge more easily with other GUI-based functions in the client/server system.

Screen scraping tends to break down, however, as the mapping of screens to windows moves beyond a one-to-one relationship. Consider the complexity of a window that maps to an existing list detail screen but also uses a list box control that can display more than what a list detail screen occurrence carries.

For example, consider a case in which two traditional list screens, each containing 5 lines of items, are needed to fill an initial 10-line list box in the GUI. Instead of a straight screen-to-window control relationship, the scripting language must be used to scroll forward (i.e., to simulate pressing the 3270 "PF8" key) to get more entries for the list. This introduces two complexities:

1. The scroll forward takes another host interaction. If each screen takes two to three seconds, the end user may wait four to six seconds before the list is completely full. Although the user can be "locked" from selecting from the list until all data is received, techniques can be used in a multitasking environment to allow the user immediate selection capability on the first five entries while the second five entries are being retrieved. This approach can cause confusion for the user, however, as the list box suddenly changes due to the arrival of more information.

2. If the user picks something from the first list detail screen that is no longer in workstation memory, that screen may need to be invoked again to handle the selection. This adds to the complexity of the underlying scripting logic and to the end user response time. Techniques exist to retain key information from all the screens retrieved to the workstation, but all these techniques make the underlying implementation more complex, defeating the potential simplicity of

screen scraping. If these complexities arise, screen scraping may not be the most effective approach.

Screen scraping does not meet new functions well. For example, in a customer relationship system users want an overall snapshot of the customer's relationship. For a financial institution, this may mean all current accounts, current balances, and available credit. If this happens to exist in the current system as a screen then it will map well. If it does not, it can become technically feasible to script but potentially useless in terms of performance.

Imagine the complexity if each product has its own system and no balance is available to be read from the initial product screen. This implies that a specific query screen needs to be executed for each customer to get his or her products. The user then needs to read the screen to find out which product systems to go to. Within each product system an initial screen needs to be invoked to get the detailed balance information.

Again, techniques exist to allow these screens to be executed in parallel, provided there is no dependence on information from one screen to provide keys for the next screen. Scripting can be a powerful tool, but the impact of even minor groupings of transactions can be major in terms of user response time and increasing complexity of the underlying architecture. Using asynchronous techniques can shield the user from some of these performance issues if the data being retrieved is not immediately required for display of the requested window.

One final drawback of screen scraping is maintenance. Even minor changes in the legacy application screens can disrupt the screen-scraped application. Coordinating enhancement and development efforts between the legacy system personnel and the client/server system personnel is required to keep both environments stable and functioning.

Back-End Interface Techniques

Back-end techniques deal with direct access to legacy system databases or files.

Remote Data Access. Remote data access to a legacy-based data store can be accomplished through the use of a database gateway to the legacy platform. A database gateway provides an interface between the client/server environment and the legacy system. The gateway provides an ability to access and manipulate the data in the legacy system.

Database gateways perform one of two functions:

- Allow a client- or server-based program to issue calls in the native data manipulation language format of the target database management system (DBMS).

- Translate the data request call into the format expected by the target legacy system. In essence, this allows programs to perceive that they are accessing the legacy DBMS directly.

Although this solution is very effective, it is subject to the same considerations as any native call to the DBMS would be. If the call would be ineffective from a performance point of view from within the legacy environment, the use of the gateway will be even worse due to the additional overhead of the gateway.

The database gateway approach cannot make up for a structural design deficiency in the legacy's data store which cannot meet a new type of data relationship requirement. Meeting a new complex data relationship requires restructuring the current legacy data store and cannot be done simply through a gateway.

A key indicator of this issue is that a gateway cannot address a data relationship that would not perform or function in the legacy's native data manipulation language. Although that seems obvious, in some applications the versatility of structured query language was thought to be able to overcome the limits of a flat file legacy system.

New Server Logic to Access Legacy Data Store. Another legacy access technique involves coding new server functions directly on the legacy platform. This is useful for more complex data relationship-type transactions because all the data manipulation remains within the host system, providing better performance. Although the new server logic must be developed on the legacy, this approach allows for reuse of the existing data store across both new applications and legacy applications.

This approach has been used when a subset of the user population of that data store is getting a new client/server-based system while the remaining users continue to use traditional screen applications. This approach suffers the same limitations as the gateway: Although its performance may be better, it can still not overcome a mismatch of an existing data model that cannot support a new business requirement without the DBMS being restructured.

Data Replication. A final legacy integration approach is to duplicate key areas of the legacy data store on the new server platform. Replication is appropriate if the design of the existing legacy data store can meet the needs of the new business requirements and if the synchronization considerations are consistent with the overall distribution strategy (see Chapter III-6).

OTHER INTEGRATION CONSIDERATIONS

Reconsider Indexing in the Legacy Data Store

Although there may be a strong match of the legacy data model and the needs of the new system, there may be a mismatch in how the information is accessed. The development team should consider the impact of the new or alternative indexes on the performance of the data store for both the new application and the existing legacy applications.

Data Purification

In many cases, the legacy data store may contain information that was used in the past but is not currently used. In any one field a variety of types of data may be accumulated over the operational history of the data store. This information may legally be required to be maintained, or it may be garbage data that was not cleaned up (such as unique product codes that existed to meet certain promotions or indicators that were used to address a function until the application could be enhanced to actually support it).

The legacy applications may have a variety of validation patches to deal with this information that have been developed over time. New applications must anticipate and handle unexpected data types from the legacy data store, especially if older information may be accessed.

III-10
Testing the New System

C hapters III-5 through III-9, discussing the design and implementation of client/server applications, described the key concepts and tasks associated with building client/server applications. The final step is to test that the resulting applications actually perform as specified, and that they deliver the desired business capability and results.

Much of the testing discussion is applicable to traditional applications development as well. However, client/server applications development makes testing more complex because it increases the number of components and the complexity of their interactions.

Furthermore, failures in client/server production are more costly to the organization and to the information systems department because of the types of applications for which it uses client/server, and because the typical client/server application end user is more often a knowledge worker. The distribution inherent with client/server makes it essential that the systems run properly. Debugging a serious problem from a thousand miles away is extremely difficult. In short, a rigorous and complete testing approach is necessary now more than ever.

THE "V-MODEL" OF TESTING: THE BEST PRACTICE APPROACH

There are several ways to organize the complex effort of testing a system. One model in particular has proven to be a "best practice" in solution development and delivery, resulting in quality solutions that implement the required functional, technical, and quality requirements. The model is called the V- Model of Verification, Validation, and Testing.

The V-Model provides a structured testing framework throughout the development process, emphasizing quality from the initial requirements stage through the final testing stage. All solution components, including application, conversion, and technical architecture programs, can benefit from being subjected to the V-Model testing process.

The V-Model verifies and validates each major deliverable in the development process and tests the implementation of each specification.

Verification checks that the output from a process actually implements the specification that was input to it. In addition, it checks that the output, as well as the process to build the output, conforms to the standards set for it. Verification ensures that the project is doing the "right thing."

Validation checks that the work product contributes to the intended benefits and does not have undesired side effects.

Testing ensures that the specification is properly implemented and assembled and that it performs in accordance with expectations.

Special attention must be paid to the verification and validation performed at hand-off points between teams or individuals within the project. Each inspection, performed at important checkpoints during the development process, must satisfy a set of agreed entry and exit criteria.

The V- Model is depicted in Exhibit III-10-1. This exhibit shows the work flow in the development process, with a series of design activities and systems specifications on the left side (top down) and a series of corresponding testing activities on the right side (bottom up). The specifications listed on the left of the stages are not exhaustive. They are simply examples of specifications developed in each stage.

In concept, the core process stages of analyze, design, and build consist of creating a series of increasingly detailed specifications. Each specification stage refers to the process of producing a design refinement, and each has a corresponding test stage. For example, in the V-Model shown, the business case specification stage is matched with the benefits realization test stage. Work flows between stages in the V-Model when a stage has met all the verification and validation requirements for that stage. When the work product meets these verification and validation criteria, it moves to the next stage.

For example, the program specifications developed in detailed design need to be complete and correct so that the construction stage for the component can begin. Similarly, the testing in one stage must be completed before moving on to the next stage of testing.

In the V-Model, each successive stage of testing ensures that the deliverable of each stage implements the specifications for that stage. For example, component test ensures that the program specifications delivered out of detailed design were properly implemented during construction.

The process of verification and validation is an attempt to catch as many errors as possible, as early as possible, in the development life cycle. Testing ensures that the components of the application are properly constructed and put together correctly and that they implement the functional, technical, and quality requirements. Ideally, testing should only uncover issues made in translating the specifications into product, rather than issues in the specifications themselves.

Stage Containment: Reining in Testing. Experience has shown that as proficiency with verification and validation procedures improves,

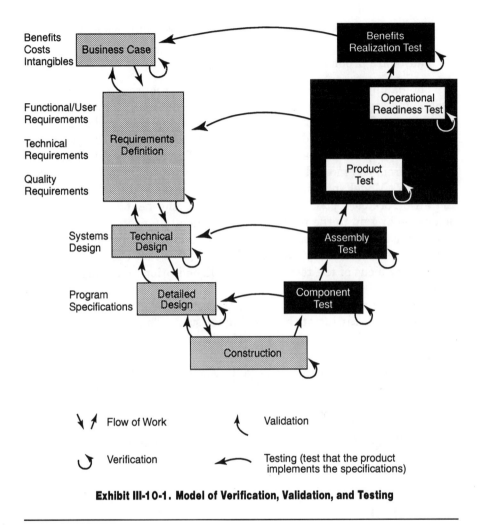

Exhibit III-10-1. Model of Verification, Validation, and Testing

stage containment also improves. Stage containment means identifying and correcting problems in the system development process before they pass to the next stage.

Stage containment can help build and improve quality into computer systems and potentially reduce costs and schedule slips resulting from expensive rework. For the purpose of stage containment, problems are sorted into three categories:

- Errors are defined as problems found in the stage where they were created.

- Defects are problems found in a later stage than when they were created.
- Faults are problems found in production.

For example, if a program specification produced in the detailed design stage included an access to the wrong database table and this is discovered in detailed design, the problem would be classified as an error. If the same problem is detected within the construction stage or any successive stage, it is classified as a defect. The longer a defect remains undiscovered, the more difficult and expensive it tends to be to correct.

The V- Model specifies that testing in one stage must be completed and all errors corrected before moving on to the next stage of testing. Before moving up to the next stage, it is crucial to meet the exit criteria defined for that stage. A part of the exit criteria for each stage is that the test has been successfully executed. This ensures that the test objectives (or primary focus of the test) are accomplished prior to moving on to the next stage.

When the objectives of one test stage are met, there is no need to repeat the same testing at the next higher stage. This is a key concept of the V-Model and one that proves difficult to accept and use in practice.

There is often a desire to retest "just to make sure everything is okay." Doing that, however, inevitably leads to spending too much time on redundant testing. In addition, it usually takes time away from the testing that actually should be performed at the current stage. This leaves little, if any, time for the last stages of testing. Minimizing the gaps and overlaps between the testing stages can increase quality and simultaneously reduce overall testing costs.

TESTING STAGES

Testing is a complex undertaking. To manage the complexity, testing is divided into multiple stages, each with specific objectives and scope. Depending on the environment, some of these stages may be combined, or additional stages of testing may be necessary. The following are the main stages used to test most systems:

- Component test.
- Assembly test.
- Product test.
- Operational readiness test.
- Benefits realization test.

Component Test

Testing at the component level refers to the typical testing that a programmer does to verify that a component behaves as expected. All components are subject to a component test, including application programs, conversion programs, and input/output modules.

The component test verifies that the component specification (detail design) has been properly implemented. When testing components in isolation, upfront planning is required along with the development of generic stub and driver logic that can be used throughout the component testing process.

In the typical case, the programmer executes the required test cases using available tools and captures results from the test. The programmer then reviews and verifies expected results versus actual results. When the test case is completed, the programmer reviews the results with the designer or supervisor. Tests are reviewed and signed off, and the component becomes part of the portfolio of components that are to be promoted to the next level of testing. The test conditions, scripts, and results may be kept in an electronic format where they can be made available for reuse and outside review.

In a client/server environment, the flexible nature of the graphical front end provides numerous navigation paths to perform the same business function. The component tester is responsible for testing each of these paths completely. Therefore, the number of test conditions and test cycles identified is much greater for client/server applications than in traditional systems.

Because a client/server environment is typically distributed, there are additional points of potential failure when all the system components are put together. The network, messaging, and numerous software interfaces are all possible points of failure, which leads to the need for more error and recovery logic testing.

The client/server environment may also allow the production system to support several configuration options. Testing is required for all target system configurations. An approach for testing each of the production configurations is needed before the testing process begins.

Assembly Test

The objective of assembly testing is to test the interaction of related components to ensure that the components function properly after integration. During assembly testing, application designers verify that data is passed correctly between modules and, as required, that messages are passed correctly between a client and a server.

This is essentially a technical test; functional testing is limited to verifying that the flow through the assembled components supports the defined transactions.

Typically, the application designers create the test plan. This plan ensures that all interfaces within the application are exercised. These interfaces could include one program calling another (such as a client program calling a server), data being passed from one program to another, signals or flags being passed from one to another, or transaction files moving between components.

A necessary element of the assembly test plan is a test data model. Although the objective of assembly testing is not complete functional testing, often the most effective way to assembly test is to take the application through parts of the business cycle. In addition, this method of testing exercises exception conditions that cause nonroutine interfaces to be exercised.

The first problems with configuration management usually arise during assembly testing. Client/server systems invariably have more discrete pieces that need to be fitted together. It is important to institute a sound configuration management discipline for tracking which versions of which components are required for each assembly test, and to control the movement of components (such as source code) through the test stages.

Product Test

Product testing focuses on the entire application to ensure that the system has met all functional and quality requirements. Product testing may occur at multiple levels. The first level tests assemblies within an application. The next level tests applications within a system, and a final level tests systems within a solution.

The product test focuses on the actual function of the solution as it supports the user requirements: the various cycles of transactions, the resolution of suspense items, the work flow within organizational units and across these units. The specification against which the product test is run includes all functional and quality requirements. The testing is organized by business function.

The product test determines whether the system is ready to be moved to operational readiness testing and subsequently into rollout. At this stage, the business worker becomes heavily involved in the testing process.

Using a Model Office. A "model office" may be assembled for users to exercise all dimensions of the new system in a realistic setting. This involvement of users is to ensure that the system meets functional expectations. It is the last opportunity for the project team to resolve logic and interface problems in a controlled environment before the system is moved from the development team to those responsible for release management and rollout.

The business process design must be tested to ensure that users will accept the final delivered product. Written approval of the system by user departments should be obtained as a part of completing the product test.

The product test conditions are defined to emphasize testing of the system's business functions rather than testing every processing condition, as this has already been done in component and assembly test. Users, assisted by the development personnel, usually define product test cycles.

Results from all product tests should be captured and retained for use in future regression testing. As it encounters discrepancies between the actual and the expected results, the development team should debug the product or the expected results model. The discrepancies should be documented with some form of incident control or system investigation documents.

Performance Testing. The team should do an overall performance evaluation for the application at this time. It can be helpful to divide performance testing into two separate phases:

1. A low-volume performance test, where, early in the product test, the team tests conversations that were determined to have a potential performance problem due to internal designs and approaches. If the team finds problems, the problems can be addressed while other product testing proceeds.
2. More traditional, performance testing, done later in the testing cycle when the application is stable. Its focus is on the overall system performance that is found when the application is driven at high business volumes.

The development team measures and verifies response time of the product stipulated by the users in the service-level agreement (SLA) during the system design phase. The SLA provides the criteria for success of the performance test. (See Chapter III-13 for a discussion of the SLA.)

Operational Readiness Test

The objective of operational readiness testing is to ensure that the application can be correctly deployed, and that those responsible for systems operations are prepared for rolling out and supporting the applications and associated data in both a normal mode and an emergency mode (e.g., to repair a fault discovered in production).

The increasing focus on distributed solutions such as client/server has caused a dramatic increase in the need for operational readiness testing. Distributed client/server systems typically consist of a relatively large number of discrete components that need to be installed on a number of client and server machines, potentially across a wide geographic area. This is a new and very different problem from rolling out an application on a single centralized mainframe.

In addition, systems sometimes must be installed and operated by personnel at local sites who may have limited knowledge of complex application systems. In these cases, in particular, it is essential that the system be tested as an installable whole prior to being rolled out to the user community.

Operational Readiness. Operational readiness testing has four aspects:

- *Rollout test.* Ensures that the rollout procedures and programs can install the application in the production environment.
- *Operations test.* Ensures that all operational procedures and components are in place and acceptable, and that the personnel responsible for supporting production can operate the production system.
- *Service-level test.* Ensures that when the application is rolled out, it provides the level of service to the users as specified in the service level agreement.
- *Rollout verification.* Ensures that the application has been correctly rolled out at each site. This test, defined by the work cell or team performing operational readiness testing, should be executed during each site installation by the work cell or team in charge of the actual rollout of the application.

Operational readiness testing assumes a completely stable application and architecture in order for it to be successful. Therefore, it relies heavily on the previous testing stages.

Operational readiness testing is the point in the development process when all the applications development, architecture development, and preparation tasks come together. Operational readiness testing brings all these areas together by testing that the application and architecture can be installed and operated to meet the defined SLAs.

Benefits Realization Test

The benefits realization test ensures that the business case for the system will be met. The emphasis here is on measuring the benefits of the new system, such as increased productivity, decreased service times, or lower error rates. If the business case is not testable, the benefits realization test becomes more of a buyer sign-off.

Ideally, benefits realization testing occurs prior to complete deployment of the system and utilizes the same environment that was used for the service-level testing component of the operational readiness test. Tools are put in place to collect data to verify the business case (such as "count customer calls"). A team of people is still needed to monitor the reports from the tools and to prove that the business case is going to be achieved. The size of the team depends on the number of users and the degree to which tools can collect and report the data.

QUALITY FACTORS

When developing a system, the focus is typically on functional and technical requirements. Quality factors are equally important, however, and need to be considered throughout the development of the system. Quality factors include flexibility, performance, reliability, and usability.

Quality requirements should first be specified when defining user requirements for the system and should be validated and verified as part of the specification. These high-level requirements are driven to a lower level of detail as the development effort proceeds. Defining quality attributes and measures early and then refining them throughout the development enables quality requirements to influence decisions at all stages in the systems development life cycle.

For example, a requirement for performance may be a subsecond response time for displaying information on the screen. This requirement will be tested in the performance test cycle of product test. But this requirement may also influence decisions regarding such things as the data distribution approach.

Following is a description of each of the quality factors. The task descriptions contain information on the quality factors that are tested in the corresponding test stage.

Flexibility

Flexibility denotes how easily the application can be adapted to meet changed conditions: new capability, new platforms, failure correction. Flexibility thus addresses maintainability, testability, and portability of the application.

The other dimension of flexibility is the type of change that the system must be able to support. The system must allow for changes to the architecture to allow for introduction of different applications or new technology.

The system must also allow for changes to the application to meet evolving business requirements. Examples of system characteristics that lead to flexibility could include modular design, standards-based, or even fully commenting code to ease maintenance.

"Testability" is the ease with which a system can be tested. Applications can be architected to be self-testing or self-diagnosing to prove that they are functioning correctly. Testing can be greatly facilitated by building into the application such things as self-checking logic, audit trails and logs, balancing and automated reconciliation routines, tracing capabilities, monitoring capabilities, rule verification, and independent calculation routines.

Portability. The last facet of flexibility is "portability," or the ease with which the software can be moved to another hardware and/or system software platform. It is important to test portability throughout the development process. Portability can be enhanced by the following activities:

- Implementing in a language or toolset that can run on many platforms.
- Designing to a common data model.
- Isolating hardware-specific software in routines that can be changed for a new platform without affecting business logic.
- Isolating and modularizing data access routines to ease migrating between database management systems (DBMSs).

In systems development, flexibility has been described as the first and last refuge of the befuddled. In a sense, flexibility could present an unbounded problem. For example, is a general ledger program flexible enough to act as a CAD/CAM program? This may seem absurd, but open-ended statements about the "need for flexibility" can set off endless design and implementation efforts. As one analyst once observed, "We want to end up with a system that is so flexible it's limp."

To avoid overdesigning for flexibility, it is important to define the requirements for flexibility as early in the design process as possible and then to identify test conditions and create cycle(s). If the development team know the specific flexibility requirements, such as the need to port the application to multiple client platforms, the testing criteria are easier to identify. However, if portability is more of a general quality factor for a potential future need, it may be more difficult to craft an appropriate test.

Performance

Performance measures the ability of the system to process all the business events within the targets specified by the SLA, given the number of concurrent users.

The design team should create the SLA early in the project life cycle, no later than the development of user requirements. SLAs should be as specific as possible. An enterprise must avoid nebulous performance criteria such as, "We'll let you know if it's too slow." Criteria defined this way set off an infinite cycle of "not good enough."

Performance should be tested under both average and extreme conditions. Stress testing tests the behavior of the system under extreme conditions such as high transaction volumes and a maximum number of simultaneous users.

Reliability

Reliability measures the system's ability to function correctly under both normal and abnormal operating conditions. Reliability includes error handling, security, recoverability (restart/recovery), and availability (uptime/downtime). Objective and detailed reliability requirements should be documented in the SLA.

Reliability tests ensure that the application fails in a controlled manner and can be recovered from these failures. These tests also make sure that inputs, both correct and incorrect, receive a consistent response. Aspects of reliability can be balanced against each other. For example, if the system is to be able to recover and restart without user or operations staff involvement, there is less of a need for extensive help desk support.

Usability

Usability measures the ease with which users can interact with the system, the ease of learning the system, and ease of its ongoing use. In addition, usability measures whether the system is efficient to use.

Usability testing involves testing the user interface of the application throughout its development stages. The user interface is defined as both the layout and the flow of the application components with which the user interacts (e.g., screens, windows, and reports).

It is important to test the interface before the project is too far into the development process. Usability tests performed after the user interface has been designed yield limited value as any changes identified by those tests are likely to be very costly to implement. For more details on usability testing, see Chapter III-6.

TESTING ACTIVITIES

The V-Model specifies the same basic methodology for all stages of testing. The model specifies that the input to every test stage is a specification package, and that the output of every test stage is an executed test model. Components of the test model include test conditions, test cycles, scripts, input data, expected results, and actual results.

Using this conceptual model, this section provides an overview of the testing activities and then focuses on unique considerations or techniques in the task descriptions for each test stage.

Specifically, the following activities are common to all stages of testing in the application and architecture segments:

- The develop test approach provides the objectives, schedule, environment requirements, and entry and exit criteria for the test stage.
- The plan test includes identification of test conditions and test cycles for the test stage.
- The prepare test defines input data and expected results, scripting the test cycles, and defining stubs and job streams.
- The establish test environment is the process of ensuring that the testing environment is established and tested prior to test execution.
- The execute test involves performing the scripts contained in the test model, comparing the actual results to the expected results, and identifying and resolving discrepancies.
- The manage test stage is the overall monitoring of the test stage, including collection and evaluation of metrics, progress reporting, and continuous improvement.

Exhibit III-10-2 is a schematic illustrating the dependencies between the activities. Further discussion of each of these activities follows.

Although these activities are common to each stage of testing, specific points in the discussion may not be applicable to all stages. For example, component test is highly integrated with construction because the same person (the programmer) is typically responsible for both tasks (construction and component test). This makes certain tasks, such as developing the testing work plan, less complicated for component test than for subsequent stages of testing. The discussion has identified these discrepancies. In addition, any considerations or techniques unique to a particular stage of testing are included in the task description for that testing stage.

Develop Test Approach

When the test strategy for the release is complete, the design team can develop the test approaches for each of the test stages. The test approaches for the individual test stages should further define several components.

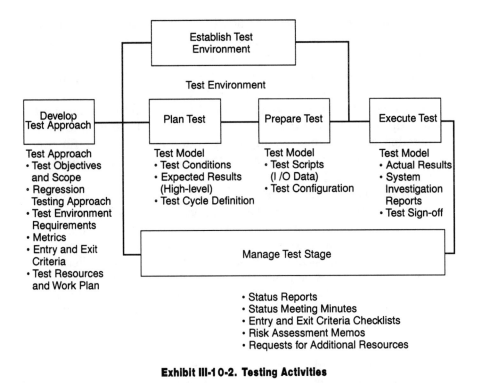

Exhibit III-1 0-2. Testing Activities

Test Objectives and Scope. This component defines the focus or specific purpose of the test stage. It defines what specification (business case, requirements, technical design, or detailed design) is to be tested in this test stage and the scope of the test considering both the specification and the quality factors to be tested. Specifically, the test objectives and scope component defines what will and will not be tested based on the associated risk.

For example, a system that has two configurations may only be product tested using the more complex configuration. If it functions accurately in that configuration, the risk is acceptable that it will function accurately in the less complex configuration.

Test design considerations, such as the structure of the test, should be defined. The test structure is increasingly important in the later stages of testing, when test cycles are more complex.

Examples of test structure approaches that have been successful include the following:

- *Horizontal and vertical testing.* This method defines whether the test is horizontal (a high-level test crossing all functions of the system) or vertical (a detailed test within a single function of the system) or a combination of horizontal and vertical.

- *Three-level test design.* Similar to horizontal and vertical testing, this technique calls for designing the test with three different subsets of scripts. The first level of scripts makes up a high-level horizontal test through all the functions in the solution. The second level is a detailed set of scripts testing each of the conditions or functions within the solution. The third level is made up of independent exception processing scripts.

- *Repeated, fixed execution schedule testing.* This is a structure for product testing primarily of batch applications by designing the test model to run the same cycles on a timed, cycle basis (e.g., every week). An example of this approach would be to run daily batch jobs every Monday night and Tuesday, weekly batch jobs on Wednesday night and Thursday, and monthly batch jobs on Friday. As completed assemblies/functions and corrections to defects become available, they can be scheduled to be tested in the next fixed execution. This is beneficial for systems that have a large number of batch runs and time/date dependencies.

The test team should prepare a preliminary definition of test cycles. A test cycle is a group of logically related test conditions and application functions that can be characterized in one or two sentences based on the test conditions the cycle contains. Even though the conditions have not been defined at this point, it should be possible to outline the cycles based on the testing methodology or functional knowledge.

For example, each component test has at least two cycles: The first tests mainline processing without exception conditions; the second focuses on exception processing.

Regression Testing Approach. Regression testing is the reexecution of previous testing to ensure that bug fixes and corrections have not introduced unexpected errors into the systems. Regression testing is required to ensure that a fix has been implemented properly and has not "broken" anything else. Regression testing is facilitated by planning for multiple test passes; by developing a modular, structured, and repeatable test models; and by automating script execution and results verification.

Test Environment Requirements. It is critical that the test team thoroughly define the test environment early, as part of the test approach for each stage, to ensure that the required hardware and software components are available and that the environment is configured correctly at the onset of test execution. On occasion, a project finds itself waiting for hardware or software components because they are ordered late. Or they may have defined requirements late in the process or inadequately, resulting in the need to reconfigure the test environment. These significant project delays must be avoided.

It may be necessary to work with architecture or technical support personnel to adequately define the test environment requirements. Throughout this activity, risk remains if there are differences between the test and production environments. Ideally, the test environment matches the production environment accurately and as early in the test process as possible. This minimizes the risk of not finding potential production errors during testing as a result of configuration discrepancies. At a minimum, the test team should address several issues during this activity.

External Interfaces. The team should define interfaces with existing systems or other systems under development, as well as the approach to testing those interfaces, to identify any environment influences, such as unexpected data values or bad data being received from other systems. Typically, developers delay the testing of external interfaces until product test. However, testing them as early as assembly test minimizes the risks and costs of problems found late in the process.

Test Data Management. The team should define the approach for the use of common test data. In addition, the team should define any production tapes (typically to support testing interfaces with legacy systems) that will be used during testing.

Source Environment. This section should identify the environment that will be used to create the test environment for this test stage. This is usually the previous test environment.

Automation. This section should address what part of the testing process should be automated and to what level it should be automated. Using testing tools not only simplifies the process but can result in significant cost and schedule savings. Tools should be selected that support the test process methodology and environment being used.

Typically tools are selected to support test planning (capturing business events, test conditions, scripts), issue (error, defect, fault, system investigation request, change request, open point), tracking, configuration management, script recording/playback, data generation and manipulation, mass database changes, multiple user simulation, viewing of the database or files for expected results, automated backup/restore of databases or files, and automated comparison of files. In addition, this section should also describe naming standards and procedures to be followed for using these tools.

System Software Upgrades. The project team should address acceptable timing of introducing upgrades to such things as system software and databases and the impact of these upgrades on testing. In addition, the team should define contingency plans if upgrade attempts are unsuccessful.

Metrics. The project team should also define the metrics that will be collected to measure quality and determine status. The team must address the manner in which these metrics will be collected. Ideally, metrics should be a natural by-product of the process. That is, the process and tools used in the process should provide the data required to calculate the metrics. This makes them meaningful to the team and easy to measure.

Metrics should focus on tangible completions (e.g., test conditions completed in relation to plan or test scripts executed in relation to plan). At a minimum, the project team should capture rework and stage containment metrics to report status and testing effectiveness. Beyond that, the team should also define, collect, and report metrics to prove the effectiveness of a new tool, process, or technique.

Entry and Exit Criteria. It is critical to define entry and exit criteria specifically and to coordinate them with the associated design stage and the adjacent test stages to ensure that the entire test process results in a quality solution and that it runs smoothly.

Entry and exit criteria are a key concept in the V-Model. Each test stage builds on the previous test stage, assuming that the previous test stage was complete and that testing at that level does not need to be repeated. An entry and exit criteria checklist can be useful for recording criteria, inspections performed, and sign-offs.

Test Resources and Work Plan. The test team should develop a detailed work plan showing all planning, preparation, environment, on ecution and management tasks, assigned resources, and budgets. Again, the component test is highly integrated with the construction work plan because the programmer is responsible for both tasks, making development of the work plan somewhat less complicated than for other tasks.

Planning tasks should be estimated based on the existence of a test model and the complexity of any new cycles that need to be planned. Execution tasks should be estimated based on complexity of the cycle and the use of automated testing tools. For example, if the first pass is recorded using an automated scripting tool, subsequent passes typically execute in one-third to one-half the time. Typically, the test team refines the work plan for executing the test to a subcycle level just before execution begins.

When the team develops the test approach for the test stage, the test approach should be reviewed by others including the overall test manager, the architecture team leader, and the development and technical support representatives. This review ensures synchronization regarding sequencing of work, schedules, resources, dependencies, and entry and exit criteria.

The manager of the test stage, with the overall test manager, should obtain resources and work space. The leaders from all stages of testing should develop an orientation package and program that provides training on the testing methodology, application capability, and testing tools. They should establish standards for time and status reporting and roll them out to all test personnel. They should conduct weekly status meetings for each test stage. It is important that these meetings be open to representatives from the other areas to facilitate effective coordination throughout the entire testing effort.

Plan Test

Planning the test includes deriving the test conditions from the specification and design. These activities occur as part of specification development and must be completed to satisfy the exit criteria of the specification stage. This helps to ensure that the specification is testable and is at a sufficient level of detail to proceed with further analysis.

Test conditions are a list of items derived from the specification that must be tested. Ideally, each condition has a corresponding high-level expected result and is cross-referenced back to the specification.

When creating test conditions, the project team must be sure to address the appropriate areas of risk. The team should follow standard testing rules for code-level tests that address typical risk areas (e.g., maximum values, minimum values, and empty files). For higher levels of testing, the team should be sure to thoroughly test areas of business risk (e.g., billing) as well as technical risk (e.g., distributed data).

The project team should then group related conditions into cycles. The team should design test cycles with consideration for repeatability and reuse. When designing test cycles, the team must achieve a balance between completely independent test cycles and sequential cycles that are dependent on each other.

The identification of test conditions and the definition of cycles can happen concurrently with the development of the corresponding specification. For example, the project team should identify product test-level conditions and cycles during requirements definition. The test conditions and test cycles can be validated and verified as part of the specification.

Prepare Test

Preparing the test is the process of (1) defining the input and output data to satisfy the test conditions, (2) scripting, and (3) defining stubs and job streams. These activities happen after the specification and planning activities are complete but prior to test execution.

Scripts should be created by cycle. The project team analyzes test conditions within a cycle to determine the input data that is required to test the condition. Next, the team can define the expected results associated with the input data and conditions. The level to which expected results are defined may vary.

For example, significant time may be required to develop detailed expected results when complex calculations are involved. In this case, using functional or business experts to review the actual results may suffice. The decision should be an upfront decision, not a decision made because there is not enough time left to create detailed expected results before execution. When determining the level of detail for expected results, team leaders must understand the risk, the level of expertise of the personnel executing the test, and the organization's expectations.

Together, the team can combine input and expected results and format them as "test scripts." There are several acceptable formats for scripting: screen prints, a list of step-by-step instructions, or electronic spreadsheets for use by an automated scripting tool. When determining the format of the scripts, team leaders should consider the experience of test execution personnel, the need for a repeatable test model, the need for documentation to support audits, and the ease of maintainability.

The project team should also develop a "test configuration document" for each component or cycle. The test configuration document should define the environment in which the cycle will be executed, including the platforms, architecture, data, source code, job streams, and stub programs. The sequencing of the work should result in minimal use of stubs after component testing to reduce the chance that the actual routines will introduce or uncover errors.

A "cycle control sheet" can be critical to managing the execution schedule. This document lists every cycle that to be executed during the test stage and the associated start and stop dates. If the project team is going to manipulate any system parameters, the document identifies them as well.

Exhibit III-10-3 illustrates the deliverables that comprise a test model and the relationships between the deliverables.

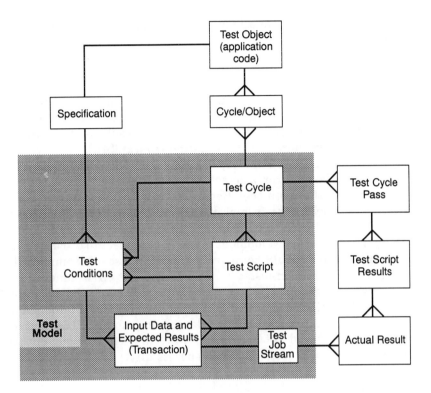

Exhibit III-10-3. Test Model Deliverables

Establish Test Environment

Often, establishing the test environment is not considered until a week or so before the test execution begins. This typically results in delays in starting execution, significant cost overruns, and numerous problems at the onset of execution due to an inadequate or untested environment.

Ideally, the manager of the test stage should ensure that the architecture or technical team is beginning the process of establishing the test environment during test planning so that it is ready to use for testing, especially if scripts are automated. However, situations are rarely ideal. In these cases, the environment must be ready for the initial code migration two to four weeks prior to test execution. Databases and files should also be populated through conversion programs or file load facilities.

To ensure that the environment is correctly set up, a testing resource, in conjunction with a resource involved in setting up the environment, should execute portions of the test. This saves time by reducing the number of problems found that are specifically related to the environment, and it ensures that all testers are productive at the onset of the test execution.

Execute Test

When the test model is complete, executing the test model can begin. The scripts should be executed and the results verified. Each time a discrepancy between the actual results and the expected results is found, the test team should prepare a *system investigation request* (SIR).

Team members should analyze and prioritize each discrepancy. The discrepancy may be an error, a defect, or a problem with the environment or a problem with the test model. Regardless of type, the test team should log the discrepancy in the formal change control system. The problem should be migrated back to be fixed and then regression-tested.

Daily, the test and development teams should meet to discuss defects and which SIR fixes should be migrated into the test environment. The change is then regression-tested in the current test environment. Typically, changes are grouped by test cycle to retest them at the same time. Grouped modifications are easier to control because any interdependencies affected by a change are easier to identify and monitor. The next pass of test execution should not begin until all changes for the current pass have been fixed and regression tested successfully.

Manage Test Stage

The activities required to manage a test stage are largely basic project management activities:

- Monitoring and controlling scope, schedule, budget, resources, and risks.
- Ensuring quality.
- Facilitating communication and coordination.

The most difficult activity within managing a test stage is determining status. As with any part of the life cycle, metrics should be collected to determine status. Analyzing the number of deliverables completed, the number of deliverables in progress, and the number of deliverables not started provides a basis for reporting status. During planning, the test team should monitor the completion of the test conditions and definition of test cycles by specification. During preparation, the team should monitor the number of cycles that have been scripted. During execution, the team should monitor the number of cycles or subcycles executed.

In addition, team members should closely monitor the number and types of defects they encounter throughout the test execution. If they encounter numerous defects in the first few days of execution, it may be the result of unstable code, and the code should be migrated back to the previous environment to be fixed rather than continuing to affect the progress of the current test.

CONCLUSION

Testing has not always been considered an essential part of the systems development effort. Often people seem to feel that testing is a punishment for making mistakes the last time. In fact, testing is vital and the one fixed part of systems development. Languages may change, design approaches come and go, DBMSs are replaced, but testing is forever. This chapter has presented here a more structured and rigorous approach to testing than was typical in traditional development. This approach is necessary because of the difficulty in achieving defect-free client/server solutions.

The need for software quality is even more crucial for an organization's early client/server applications development efforts. If the resulting system is perceived as buggy or unstable, those who resist change will seize upon this as evidence that client/server is not production-ready for mission-critical applications. A strong testing mentality can ensure that the user community gets just the opposite impression. Ultimately, testing is critical to successful implementation of the application.

III-11
Network Design

C lient/server computing is as much a communication solution as it is a computing solution. This chapter addresses the unique challenges of designing and implementing networks for a client/server solution.

FLEXIBILITY OF THE NETWORK

The success of a client/server network is measured differently than a traditional terminal-oriented network. As with traditional terminal networks, a client/server network must be cost-effective and reliable. But in addition, the client/server network must provide higher flexibility. The flexibility is needed to adapt to growth in number of users, to handle varying types of traffic, and to accommodate variations in usage.

Flexibility is achieved by building on the capabilities of local area network (LAN) technology, extended with the capabilities of new backbone wide area network (WAN) techniques to address connecting wide areas. The new network provides end-to-end addressability among all nodes and must be able to accommodate traffic that extends beyond traditional data.

Sizing and designing this network are different processes. The new network must consider the workstations and work groups of the environment and how they interact at all levels instead of just terminals interacting with a processor.

The approach to client/server network design builds on previous network design techniques. But there are two major differences:

1. Instead of taking an application-at-a-time approach, for example, the client/server approach broadens its focus to a community of users. Who needs to interact with whom? What kinds of information do they exchange?

2. The new networks are not designed around average response time for a set of screens but, rather, overall economic service delivery for a variety of potentially diverse applications.

NETWORK DEVELOPMENT LIFE CYCLE

The development of the network in a client/server environment can be summarized in three stages: network planning, network analysis and design, and network installation. This chapter discusses each of these stages in general and then looks at each stage in more detail.

Stage One: Planning

Network planning focuses on understanding the overall environment from both a current and future perspective. In the planning stage, the designer must address all the potential communities of users and how they interact. Understanding the current network environment is important for two reasons:

- To determine and assess the impact on the organization of a new network.
- To determine the costs of either incorporating current networking or migrating from the current network.

Stage Two: Analysis and Design

During network analysis, the project team determines the most appropriate communication architecture component(s) based on functional and technical requirements. Network analysis evaluates architecture options and selects the overall architecture. Network analysis also confirms that a sound business case exists for implementing the communication architecture.

The objective of network design is to refine and finalize the design of each communication architecture component based on requirements, information flows, resources, and projected growth of applications.

Stage Three: Installation

Network installation consists of three parts: network build, network test, and network migrate. Each has its own activities and stages. For example:

- In the network build stage, an organization builds and tests the communication architecture applications and components and prepares for testing with the target application environment.
- The network test stage ensures that the communication architecture components are ready for conversion by comprehensively testing, diagnosing, and resolving any inconsistencies in actually supporting the target application environment, and preparing users for the new system.

- The network migrate stage provides a fully functional, converted communication architecture. It addresses the site-by-site preparation and conversion activities required to implement the new environment.

NETWORK PLANNING IN DETAIL

Understanding the current communication environment is vital to assess the impact of client/server and develop a feasible and economic coexistence or migration approach. An example of a coexistence approach would be a new LAN-based client/server application that supports a 50-person marketing group. The group is located in one site and needs to access the corporate systems network architecture (SNA)-based backbone and legacy databases. A migration example would be the complete move of all the corporate 3270 terminal users to LAN-based client/server applications with no further use of the SNA backbone or legacy databases.

Network planning is actually broken down into four phases:

- Assess communications environment.
- Identify functional and technical requirements.
- Outline communication architecture options.
- Develop implementation plan.

Assess Communication Environment

It is important to begin by acquiring a high-level understanding of the current communication environment. How will the new network interact with the existing environment? Will the existing network be replaced or will the new client/server network require potential interfaces with the existing network? What custom/packaged communication software, if any, is used or being implemented within the environment? What sort of contingency/disaster recovery plan is in place? What is the level of system redundancy and backup?

The following are some key steps to assessing the communication environment:

1. *Understand the current business applications environment.* The project team requires a thorough understanding of the existing applications, traffic, and network connectivity to understand the coexistence or migration issues of the new client/server network on the existing applications.

2. *Review current network, and current service and operation levels.* The team must understand key performance indicators for such things as service requests, trouble tickets, network availability/

utilization, user satisfaction, and response time. Team members should review existing components of the network such as hardware and software platform(s), interfaces, critical components, special features of systems, and contingency/disaster recovery. They must also assess a number of physical network components, such as network topologies, network capacity, physical infrastructure, and bandwidth of circuits. Most important, the project team must assess the current network for internetworking issues concerning existing protocols and systems.

3. *Review network financials.* The project team must identify communications/business unit budgets for equipment, personnel, network services, and any other significant expenditures. The team must understand total communications costs and allocations. This information is in determining the costs of migrating or isolating aspects of the current communication network.

Identify Functional and Technical Requirements

Exhibit III-11-1 shows the logical network connections in a client/server environment that were discussed in Chapter II-7, "Communication Services."

As the exhibit implies, six logical connections are possible:

1. Workstation to workstation.
2. Workstation to work group server.
3. Workstation to enterprise server.
4. Work group server to work group server.
5. Work group server to enterprise server.
6. Enterprise server to enterprise server.

To map out the functional and technical activity that actually occurs along these paths, the analysis must proceed through three steps:

- *Communities.* Step 1 looks at the various communities of users—their location, their usage of communications, and their platform/system characteristics.
- *Location.* Step 2 finds correlations among these communities and groups them by location.
- *Categories of location.* Step 3 groups these locations by category, providing designers with a more manageable understanding of needed requirements.

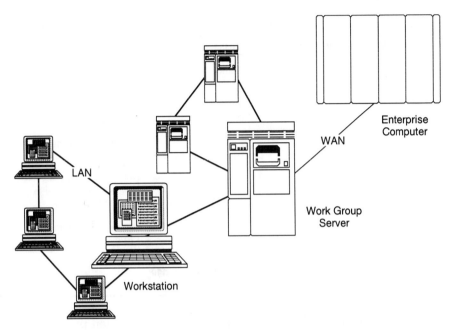

Exhibit III-11-1. Logical Network Connections in Client/Server

Step 1: Determine Communities of Users. Identifying the functional and technical requirements of a client/server network involves looking at communities of users and how they are using the network connections. A community can be very large: The community for an electronic mail application, for example, would be all personnel in the enterprise. Or, the community could be a specific group for one particular application.

Designers should examine each community from three aspects:

- *Location characteristics.* Will the community be dispersed across several locations or concentrated in one or few locations? Will the community be based in the office or is it mobile? When traveling, what connectivity is required? Does the community need to interact with entities external to the company environment—for example, information services, public forums, or aligned companies? Designers must analyze each community in terms of the locations, the population of users at each location, and their connectivity requirements in terms of fixed or mobile access. During this stage the network designer must work with the application architect to understand the approach for placement of data items such as databases, image files, miscellaneous files, and configuration files. Network planners also

From/To	Workstation	Work Group Server	Enterprise Server
Workstation	File Transfer E-mail	Messaging File Transfer Remote File Access Printing	Messaging File Transfer Remote File Access Screens Printing
Work Group Server		Messaging File Transfer E-mail Remote File Access	Messaging File Transfer Remote File Access Screens Printing
Enterprise Server			Messaging File Transfer E-mail Remote File Access Printing

Exhibit III-11-2. Types of Usage

need to understand the distribution of the application process logic and location of the executable files.

- *Usage characteristics.* Will the community have a consistent set of applications or will they differ? Does the community have differing communication needs within the applications? What hours of operation does the community expect? What types of traffic will be exchanged: voice, data, image, and multimedia? What is the nature of the traffic: messaging (real-time, asynchronous, store-and-forward), terminal services, file services (file sharing, file transfer), print services? What volume? Exhibit III-11-2 shows the types of usage based on the six logical network connections in client/server.

- *Platform/system characteristics.* What platforms and systems does each community use? What current communications capabilities exist? What communications options exist for these platforms/systems?

Step 2: Determine Location. After acquiring an understanding of each community's characteristics, the network planner then looks for correlations to begin to understand the complete picture. This means moving from the community level to the location level. The activities of all the communities within each location determine the overall communications requirements of the site. At Level 2, in effect, the planner is moving from the individual community level to the aggregate location category level.

Step 3: **Determine Location Categories.** Finally, the location information can be grouped into location categories. Location categories could be types such as traveling salesperson, sales office, sales/regional management office, distribution center, manufacturing location, and headquarters.

The categories are important for performing the next step of network planning, which requires outlining the communication architecture options. At this level of analysis, working with detailed site location level information is not useful and can become cumbersome. Grouping the locations into categories summarizes the needed requirements at a more manageable level.

One issue network planners must anticipate is large variations within each location category. For instance, sales offices may range from 1 to 50 personnel depending on location. Here, the location categories may be further divided by range of size. Temporary locations may also be necessary. For example, sales locations may be established for certain sales opportunities and then removed. A mortgage sales office might set up temporarily at a new housing development site.

Refining the categories to this level allows the network designer to address similar communications requirements that may have dramatically different economic options. High-speed connectivity may be justified for medium or large sales offices but not for small or temporary offices.

Outline Communication Architecture Options

At this point, designers have worked to understand the communities of users and their functional and technical requirements by determining communities of users, user locations, and categories of location. Now designers move on to outline the communication architecture options.

Working with the location categories, the network designer can outline the physical network and communication systems software options. This section describes the physical network options first, followed by a discussion of communication systems software.

Because the broad topic of network design could merit a book all to itself, this chapter aims only to illustrate some of the options to consider. A designer would use more detailed resources to develop all the appropriate options.

Determine Physical Network Options. Designers need to review each location category its physical network requirements. For mobile locations, designers must consider what method of service would be appropriate:

- Traditional dial-up service, such as 800 number service.

- Dial public data network, such as a public packet network.
- Packet radio network.
- Cellular data capability.

For each of these options, designers must consider whether to use a vendor service or whether a private service is more appropriate. For example, should a private network of 800-type lines be used for dial-up or should the enterprise pursue a contract with a data networking service such as a public packet network? Can the location's requirements be met on a dial-up basis or does the location require constant communications, such as with radio or cellular data networks.

For permanent locations, what LAN requirements exist? Designers need to evaluate the physical network options for these types of location categories in terms of the following:

- *Media.* Does the location require twisted pair, coaxial, fiber, or some other choice?
- *Traffic segmentation and distance issues.* An example could be an office that has applications which are a mix of a basic client/server database application and a second client/server application which uses both data and image information. Because an image application may have an impact on the network response time, there are options such as bridges and routers to segment the LAN into separate services for these applications.
- *Type of network.* This means evaluating the use of Ethernet, Token Ring, or other network implementation. If voice traffic is in the scope of the design, its requirements bring an additional set of networking issues to the location. Some client/server networks integrate voice capability into the workstation, referred to as computer telephony integration (CTI). Here, the interaction between the voice network and the LAN requires planning and a solid understanding of both the voice and data network worlds. Finally, when determining the type of backbone WAN that may be appropriate, options would include public or private network services using digital leased, digital switched, frame relay, or automated teller machine-type services among other options. Again, if voice traffic is in the design scope, its impact on the backbone can be considerable and make a range of higher-speed networking options more economical to consider.

Determine Communications System Software and Middleware Options. While examining the physical network options, the network designer must also consider the communications system software and middleware issues. The base decisions to be addressed are choice of protocols and the services to be provided.

Choice of Protocol. Protocol choices build on and interact with the physical network decisions discussed previously. Protocol considerations address the core reliability mechanism of the network, the management capabilities desired, and the integration options of the processing platforms involved. Dominant choices in this area are usually LAN network operating systems such as Novell, industry standard protocols such as Transmission Control Protocol/Internet Protocol (TCP/IP), and integration interfaces such as IBM 3270 protocol.

Network Service Choices. Network services address file transfer, printing, and messaging middleware. The functions of the messaging middleware address store-and-forward, asynchronous, and real-time messaging services if required. Chapter II-7, "Communication Services," discusses this subject in greater depth.

Determine Cost/Benefits, Resource Requirements, and Key Issues. Network designers then analyze each option in terms of capability to meet the requirements, the costs of implementation, ongoing resource requirements, and risks.

Select Communication Architecture Option. Network designers must compare the options available and select the most appropriate communication architecture based on its capability to the meet needs, economics, and future flexibility requirements and on its ability to move forward into design. At this point, network planners usually prepare the business case for the network as the basis for requesting the network investment.

Develop Implementation Plans

At this stage, designers create detailed work plans for network analysis and design, refine project resource requirements, and develop a migration strategy. They base migration options on location, application function, and business function. For each of these options, the team should outline the required time, resources, support requirements, and conversion preparation.

NETWORK ANALYSIS AND DESIGN IN DETAIL

During network analysis, the design team proceeds to evaluate and select the most appropriate communication architecture component(s) based on functional and technical requirements.

During the network design phase, the team takes the architecture of the prior phase, refines it, and then defines and selects the actual components of the communication architecture. In this stage, it is important initially to stay at the location category level and then to move down to the specific location level. This allows designers to consider practical, not theoretical, capacity limits for throughput for each LAN and internetwork solution. It is important to obtain industry standards on throughput to determine how much of the bandwidth can be used for traffic containing information versus protocol overhead, for example.

Network analysis and design is broken down into several phases:

- Finalize communications software and physical network components.
- Develop network prototype.
- Prepare detailed design of network components.

Another important activity is to develop a preliminary network capacity planning analysis. Estimating assumptions must be defined which include network utilization, expected organizational growth (acquisitions, expansions), average and peak traffic, protocol overhead, and cost. Designers then develop capacity planning scenarios based on significant variances.

Finalize Communications Software and Other Components

As Chapter II-7 discusses, the communication services component of the client/server execution architecture maintains a strict separation between the logical aspect (the communication services) and the physical aspect (the physical components of the network itself). Exhibit III-11-3 summarizes this separation.

The objective at this stage is to identify and then select potential packaged and custom communication options to address the logical communication services to be provided.

A number of considerations are important here. Designers must be careful not to underestimate the customization effort required, even if pursuing a packaged approach. The package may not be oriented to general knowledge developers and may require the addition of a simplified interface to allow client/server developers to be more productive. The interface could also introduce and enforce standardized error handling, security, and logging for the organization, which would require at least some extensions be developed. These issues are discussed in more detail in Chapter II-7.

Certain network applications may require data encryption. Designers must pay special attention to regulatory restrictions governing the transmission of encrypted data within a country or across national borders. Also, they must be sure to consider the impact of industry standards on network applications when identifying network application options

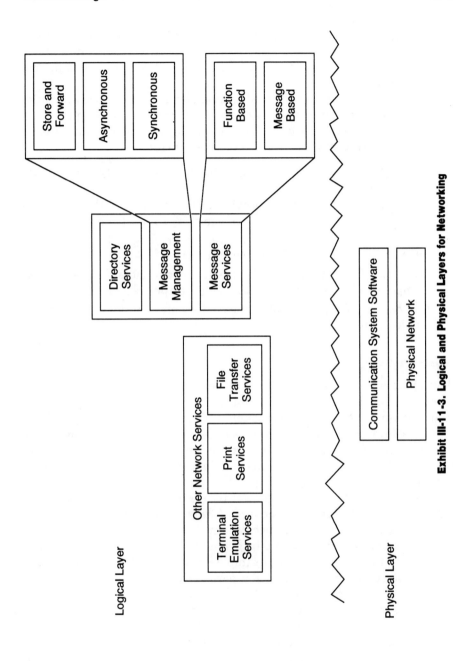

Exhibit III-11-3. Logical and Physical Layers for Networking

and to keep in mind the requirements for the development environment of the new applications. Often the development environment of a major project adds significant additional load to the network for certain location categories.

Designers can take a packaged, custom, or hybrid approach to building the communication network architecture. Factors affecting the decision are similar to those when choosing packaged or custom application software. In both cases the areas to consider include:

- *Functional fit.* Does the package approach reasonably meet the location's needs?
- *Support.* Does the vendor provide solid support? If the designers decide to build a custom solution, can they support the software?
- *Updates.* How will designers address upgrading either a vendor's solution or their own solution over time?
- *Isolation.* Can applications be isolated from the software so that changes can be made without affecting the application environment?
- *Economics.* What is the difference between the options from an economic point of view?

Develop Network Prototype

Developing a prototype is especially important if the communication environment consists of new or unfamiliar hardware, system software, or other network architecture components. The prototype should provide a sufficient level of detail to disclose subtle problems, integration issues, and potential performance bottlenecks, as well as to ensure that requirements can be met. This often represents a significant level of effort and demand from a technology standpoint.

For example, it may be essential to use line monitors to determine what is flowing through the network. Although it is not difficult to use such line monitors, not many people have the skill. In developing such prototypes, consideration should be given to the security and integrity of the existing infrastructure. For example, in some cases personnel testing a new protocol inadvertently used a part of the production network and caused the production network to crash.

Often, the prototyping of a such network components results in the creation of a network testing lab where the testing and integration of components can be done. In practice, design and prototyping may occur simultaneously. Each network architecture component may be individually prototyped to ensure feasibility and effectiveness and may lead to a subsequent design iteration. Critical integration issues between communication architecture components may also need to be included in prototype activities.

A key in succeeding with such a prototype effort is to define prototype objectives early in the process. When network prototyping efforts lack such objectives, they can become a sort of "exploration of interesting ideas in networking." The prototype should also be designed so that pieces of it can be reused during communication design.

Prepare Detailed Design of Network Components

During this stage, designers prepare detailed design specifications for the architecture components they have already evaluated and selected. Each of these components has several important considerations.

Communications Middleware and System Software. Planners must consider middleware issues during the network design, including error handling, restart and recovery, start-up and shutdown, security, data translation, and performance. They must be sure to consider the overall design criteria for middleware:

- Operating system interoperability and protocol interface compatibility.
- Interfaces to business applications and other communication architecture components.
- Minimized number and complexity of customized components that will be included in the middleware solution.

Other characteristics that greatly enhance the quality of the middleware include flexibility, scalability, and manageability.

Local Area Networks. Ensuring compatibility is a crucial aspect of LAN design. Designers must ensure that the protocol drivers are compatible with the network operating system and emulation software and that all physical components of the LAN are compatible. The network interface card must be compatible with the physical cabling and wiring selected.

Internetworks. Internetworking refers to the connections between the locations. It is important to address ownership issues of the internetworking components and services.

The internetwork devices may fall into the management and ownership domain of all interconnected subnets, an individual subnet, or none. These internetworking boundaries are also where service parameters, pricing structures, and security restrictions may differ. To minimize boundary issues, network planners must design internetworks with standard and universally accepted addressing features and network services.

Voice Processing. Designers must ensure that all voice processing components have been considered, including voice network services, PBX/automatic call distributor (ACD) telephone systems, key systems, voice messaging, cabling/wiring, voice response, CTI, predictive dialing, teleservicing software, facsimile response, and workstation-based telephony.

NETWORK INSTALLATION IN DETAIL

During network installation, designers build and test the communication architecture applications and components and prepare for systems integration and stress tests. Extensive testing and documentation during this phase ensure that individual components adequately provide expected functions and features. A typical mistake in this phase is failing to allocate sufficient time for testing. In a client/server environment, testing often exceeds the time needed for coding.

As a project team designs and tests the communication architecture components, team members must bear in mind some important considerations:

- Middleware components should be built and tested before the business and network applications. A solid middleware component provides a stable network environment on which network and business applications can be built and tested, thereby minimizing the overall development effort.

- Business and network applications developers must understand the technical interface specifications required to interact with all communication architecture components. The application teams and the communication architecture team should maintain effective communication channels.

- Developers should communicate often and well with vendors and suppliers. They must ensure that the vendors and suppliers are aware of critical conversion dates because their technical support may be needed.

- Developers must be sure that internetworking components such as bridges, routers, gateways, and switches are compatible with other layers of the communication architecture. They must verify with the vendor that the product supports existing and planned network protocols, network interfaces, emulation software, other network devices, and specific business applications.

- Designers must consider the implications of voice, data, image, and video communications when building the communication architecture.

Network installation has three discrete stages:

- Outline procedures.
- Build and test communication architecture components.
- Update procedures.

Outline Procedures

During this stage, a project team develops procedures for end users, customers, and network personnel for use during installation, conversion, operations, and maintenance. Whenever possible, procedures should be tested on the actual system.

Where do designers begin when developing new procedures? Current procedures manuals are often a good starting point because they embody the end-user culture. However, process reengineering has probably taken place in the overall systems development process. The procedures manuals, therefore, should be seen as a starting point, not to be used unquestioningly. In addition, procedures manuals or other documentation probably is not housed in only one location. Developers must be sure to contact the appropriate people to obtain all existing procedures and documentation.

The new procedures developers create should be intuitive, self-guiding, and easy to reference. They should also be easy to update—periodic modifications should be made to reflect software, hardware, and services changes or enhancements. To ease both the referencing and updating of procedures, developers should always consider online procedures.

Build and Test Communication Architecture Components

During this stage, developers install the components of the communication architecture, build in extensions, and test the components. Each of these components has some important considerations.

Communications Middleware and Systems Software. Testing of middleware components should be scheduled before building and testing the business and network applications. A solid middleware component provides a more stable network environment on which network and business applications can be built and tested. This sequence minimizes the development effort for business and network applications.

Building and testing communications middleware and systems software may require sophisticated programming and debugging tools. It is important to determine workstation requirements associated with these tools ahead of time to prevent delay of software development.

It may be necessary to simulate the communication environment with stub applications programs so that the team can perform unit testing of business and network applications.

Test conditions should contain inputs that test limits of the design requirements' boundary conditions—that is, message sizes larger than the maximum allowed. This ensures stability of the middleware in all scenarios.

LAN Components. Developers should use a universal cabling and wiring scheme to install and document the physical network to support both LAN and PBX requirements where appropriate. They should consider network management software that manages the cabling and wiring element of the network.

A support team must be in place as soon as a new LAN or LAN component is installed to answer end-user questions and fulfill requests. Developers should be sure to involve help desk personnel in the installation of the development environment. Experience gained in the initial installation and testing is invaluable when responding to trouble calls in the production environment.

The network test environment should resemble the production environment as closely as possible. Developers need to document and test differences in these environments prior to conversion.

Internetwork Components. Developers must verify that the internetworking components are compatible with other layers of the communication architecture. They must verify with the vendor the product's support of existing and planned network protocols, network interfaces, emulation software, other network devices, and specific business applications. Hardware testing devices may need to be procured for the internetwork component unit test.

Developers must be sure to factor in adequate budget and lead times for site preparation, hardware and software delivery and installation, and testing. They must find out about, and abide by, international laws and regulations regarding the flow of information.

Voice Processing Components. Project team members responsible for voice processing applications and code should be fully aware of the overall communication architecture requirements, technical interface specifications, and business information flows/work flows.

Project team members must ensure that the voice processing PBX/ACD telephone systems are installed and tested prior to the installation of any other voice processing architecture components. They must ensure that the functions and features of the voice processing architecture components are tested. Applicable contingency/disaster recovery and redundancy/backup methods should also be thoroughly tested.

The project team must ensure that standard interfaces and solutions between voice processing components and communication architecture components are installed whenever possible. Team members must use the recommended vendor's application generator tools and interfaces whenever possible to ensure compatibility and consistency.

Management Services Applications and Components. These components should contain facilities for measuring service levels such as uptime/availability, response time, and time to repair.

Developers should perform extensive testing of the contingency/disaster recovery plan. During testing, they must simulate such things as power failures and line outages.

They must keep up-to-date records of network configuration as part of management services for voice network, LAN, internetwork, cabling, equipment, features, and maintenance.

They must determine the order for system start-up and shutdown on the network and consider installing and maintaining the management services system(s) in a development environment until thoroughly tested.

Update Procedures

In this final stage of network installation, the team compares original procedures for all applications to actual procedures used during testing. Original procedures are modified to reflect more accurately the steps that need to be taken.

Procedures should be distributed to users and support personnel at all relevant locations. Distributing procedures simultaneously ease confusion and improve the end users' confidence in network support personnel. The team must be sure that the procedures represent actual steps to be performed, not simply ideal or theoretical procedures. Situation-based procedures are extremely helpful in this regard. They describe what steps should be taken to correct a user-related problem as opposed to a technical problem.

III -12
Site Preparation and Installation

S ite preparation and installation may not be topics that spring immediately to mind as primary components of client/server computing. But the preparation and installation of the physical sites are, in fact, vital considerations in a client/server environment.

SITE PREPARATION: AN ISSUE NOT TO BE OVERLOOKED, OR UNDERESTIMATED

Consider, for example, one site that was implementing an insurance application. The client/server technology was to be installed in a single large campus that had already been extensively upgraded over time and had terminals spread throughout the campus. Going in, the organization's view was that the technology would only require some renetworking for the specifics of the network protocol; other than that, management believed no additional major effort was required.

During the initial installation of the applications, however, the organization realized that the desks for the business users were not set up for the use of workstations. If the base processor of the workstation was put on the desktop it took up too much room. Those people who put their processors beside their desks found that people were bumping into them. Eventually, new office furniture had to be purchased and the office layout had to be changed to accommodate the machines. This added time and expense to the project.

Perhaps more important, the business users were left with the impression that the systems people had not thought through all the issues of using the system and had not considered the users' needs, when an insensitivity to the user was precisely what the new system was supposed to be overcoming.

At another site, new applications were being developed as part of an enterprisewide reengineering effort. Part of this effort involved moving certain critical customer service activities to a newly built campus.

The developers used a program management effort to manage the overall implementation. It became apparent from the program management effort that the critical path was not applications development. Rather, it was the time needed to build the campus. The lead times for the system construction and for the site were off by several years. In this case, the organization decided to deliver the applications to the existing physical sites and then move to the new campus over time.

In a third case, an organization was preparing to roll out client/ server applications to more than 500 sites. Some of the sites were buildings that were 50 to 100 years old, and that presented some real problems. For example, how does an organization run local area network (LAN) wiring when the walls are made of mud and stones? In this case, upgrading the sites for client/server technology was the single largest-cost line item and was often on the critical path for delivery of the applications.

Although none of these examples illustrates a technology issue, the problems all certainly result from the technology. Perhaps more important, these problems can threaten success as much as an unreliable workstation or a database management system with bugs. This chapter looks at some of the risks associated with client/server implementation and some strategies that can control those risks.

Breaking the Job Down into Three Parts

The previous examples are indicative of the problems an organization can encounter in the rollout of a client/server application. Often computing and communications technology are being introduced into an almost alien environment. Succeeding in such an environment requires planning and structured execution.

Systems management can break down the site preparation and installation effort into three parts:

1. Understanding what is at the sites now.
2. Deciding what needs to be done to upgrade the sites for the installation of the technology and the applications.
3. Implementing the required changes.

If the appropriate technology is already in place and being used, additional effort is minimal. If, on the other hand, there is little or no technology, the site preparation and installation effort can be time-consuming and demanding.

A FRAMEWORK FOR SITE PREPARATION AND INSTALLATION

At the highest level, site preparation and installation consists of three major phases:

- *Site survey.* In the site survey phase, the project team evaluates the site for its readiness to accept and work with the client/server application. The team focuses the evaluation primarily on the readiness of the physical site rather than on the personnel. The change management effort should address personnel readiness, which is discussed in Chapter III-3. Site survey addresses a wide range of concerns from office layout to electricity to air conditioning. From this evaluation comes a plan to make the required changes to the site.
- *Site preparation.* Site preparation is the physical process of preparing the site for the installation of client/server technology. In this phase it is not uncommon to see electricians and carpenters on site making required changes so that the site can be made ready for the implementation.
- *Site implementation.* In the site implementation phase, developers install the required software and deliver the procedures to the site so that it is ready to begin running the application. It is the final activity before going live with the applications in the rollout of the applications.

A set of common considerations apply across all phases of site preparation and installation. These considerations include the following:

- Use of contractors.
- Setting up contracts and plans.
- Use of checklists.

When considering the three phases, it becomes clear that the expertise they require goes well beyond the training and experience of even the best information systems (IS) personnel. It would be rare to find an IS manager who is qualified to review the work of an electrician to determine whether it meets local building regulations and vendor power requirements.

Because of the unique knowledge demands here, it is very common in doing site preparation to use contractors to do much or all of the work. But who decides how much of the work goes to outside contractors and who manages the work these contractors perform so that it meets required levels of quality and timeliness? Different choices are appropriate in different circumstances, but the options must be thought through and resolved early on.

In general, the enterprise should be actively involved in the site survey and then should place more responsibility on outside contractors for site preparation activities. Project personnel may then assume more responsibility for the site implementation.

The discussion that follows presumes that outside contracting is a key component of the site preparation activity. Most designers are not experts in carpentry, architecture, building codes, air conditioning and electricity. Experience shows that most sites choose to use contractors for this work.

Contractors

Coordinating the work of contractors can be a major concern. If an organization is implementing client/server applications at hundreds or thousands of sites, such as occurs with food franchise operations, the sheer problem of managing all that effort may make a general contractor an important part of delivering a quality solution.

If there are multiple sites or sites spread out geographically, the multiple parallel efforts can be coordinated through a general contractor. The organization then has a single point of contact to coordinate, plan the work, evaluate status, react to problems, and ensure that adequate quality is delivered.

But how does the organization ensure that the work being done by outside contractors meets expectations in terms of timeliness, quality, and cost?

Occasionally organizations view these issues only as the contractor's problem. This is a dangerous point of view. Having someone to blame does not fix the problem. At one site an organization found that its fuses would blow any time more than eight workstations were turned on. The users did not see this as a contractor problem; it was a system problem.

Although the contractor may be ultimately responsible, the key to contractor success is oversight of the implementation process by the organization. The most effective procedure is to use contracts with contractors, agreeing beforehand on work to be done, work plans, time lines, checklists, and sign-offs.

Contracts and Plans

The work plans that the contractor submits must be integrated with the overall program plan to implement the systems. In some cases a rollout plan had to be revised based on the ability of various contractors to get the work done. A rollout driven by the speed and skill of carpenters is often not in accord with system objectives. The contractor must be a part of the overall program management team, reporting and coordinating on work done against plan.

Contracts are essential because they define what work is to be done and who is responsible. For example, if carpenters are moving around the site and drop a two-by-four on a customer's foot, the contract should have made it clear who is responsible. The contract should describe the typical things found in building contracts, such as steps in the escalation process. It should identify the basis for payments and the process for settling questions in payments.

The objective of the contract is not to provide an easy way to shift the blame to a contractor. The contract is to define what is expected of each party in terms of specific deliverables, dates, and quality. It is a mechanism to ensure that communication and understanding have been achieved.

If at some point in the difficult process of defining contracts management finds itself thinking that it has slipped something past the contractor, all it has done is bring greater risk to the project. Such practices are inherently questionable.

So that the organization can track work status, some form of deliverables must be provided to note that the work was done and that it meets quality and cost expectations. In one instance, because the work to be done was to install wiring and air conditioning, the organization assumed that it would be apparent when the work had been done simply by looking at it.

That approach might work at a limited installation, but as the number of sites and their distribution increases, the use of "look and see" proves increasingly impractical. Further, if things do not go well and litigation becomes a concern, problems must be documented. The ongoing collection of proof of milestones achieved can be a key aspect of maintaining control of an effort.

Checklists

The proof collected can follow several different formats. One format is the checklist. A checklist defines the steps to be completed and the results of the work for each stage of work at each site.

The contractor is expected to provide the checklists as proof of work steps completed and as a condition for payment. Typically, the checklist has sign-offs both for the contractor and for someone at the site who can verify that the work was done.

Also, if there are documents such as local building inspections to be completed, these are a part of the sign-off package. If the work has met specific quality requirements, such as power supply quality, the sign-off checklist may include an independent evaluation of the work.

The checklists themselves can vary in detail but must be detailed enough to give assurance that the work was done and that it meets expectations. For example, if partitions are to be installed, steps might include the following:

1. A date is set for review of the site to evaluate building impact and the needs to conform to any building code requirements.
2. The review is held and a contractor's report is submitted to describe the work to be done.
3. The work is agreed to and the date for the work to be done is agreed to with the local site and with program management.
4. The work is done and signed off by the local site and, perhaps, by a local civil engineer.

Checklists such as this can vary widely in scope and detail, but at the least they set forth the broad set of steps and provide a means to determine that agreed-to work has been done.

Finally, although the following discussion will treat the site preparation and installation phases as three discrete phases, in reality the phases usually overlap. Site surveys occur at some sites while site preparation and implementation are occurring at others. This overlap is usually unavoidable if the job is to get done on an acceptable time frame.

However, the parallel activities imply a significant additional work load to manage and coordinate the ongoing work. Particularly important is the need to ensure that if one phase is encountering problems that could be addressed by a prior phase, this is captured and used to improve the work being done.

Using the previous discussion as a broad framework, the next sections provide more detail on work to be done within each major phase.

SITE SURVEY

Site survey is the first phase of preparing for site installation. A big part of the survey phase is considering the impact that the implementation has on business users.

The change management process should have been started well in advance of this activity. Ideally, business users should already be aware of and knowledgeable about the system and its impact on their work. (In reality, this kind of advance preparation may not have been done. Users may be simply unprepared or avoiding the changeover.)

The beginning of site survey may be the first time that the user begins to realize that this change really is going to take place. As a result, the initial visits should be handled with some sensitivity to the local business users' concerns. By implication, these initial visits are likely to be more successful if done with participation of personnel from the project team.

The initial visit often involves a presentation of what the system is about and reminds users of what they have seen about the system up to now. Because the business user should have seen this information through the change management effort, much of the focus is on what the site implementation is about.

Generally, the point of these discussions is not to go over function or system concerns (although listening to concerns is always a good idea). The main point is to demonstrate that the systems development effort is proceeding and that, as a result, work needs to start at the local site to get it ready.

Also, the presentation should be honest about the fact that some of the site preparation work may occasionally be disruptive to the daily work of the business and its people. Obviously, the project management should explain that all efforts will be made to minimize disruption. But the fact remains that a carpenter hammering a nail makes a lot of noise and people are going to hear it.

Ongoing communication to business users is vital to ensuring the success of implementation. In some cases organizations have actually tried to disguise development, thinking that would minimize disruption to the business user. At the site survey phase, that strategy always hits the rocks. As workers begin to move through the work space taking measurements, people who were not told about the new system often come to the conclusion that they were considered insignificant parts of the process. That perception makes the already difficult task of site implementation even more difficult.

Unions must also be carefully considered. Unless long-term and on-going involvement with unions is coordinated, misunderstandings and problems can arise.

If the unions are allowed to understand what the system is about and the reasons for going forward, they can be an organizing force to move the effort forward. Without their involvement, problems can arise at site preparation.

A consideration with unions is that they may have cooperative arrangements with other unions; if one goes out on strike others may follow. Given that many of the construction trades are unionized, cooperative actions can shut down the entire implementation effort. Once again, the key point is that relentless and open communication can address the concerns of people and unions. Moreover, such communication must begin well in advance of site preparation.

The Initial Site Visit

The goals of the initial site visit are (1) to understand what is already in place and (2) to define what needs to be done to ready the site for implementation. To this end, the project team should address several issues.

Overall Office Layout and Floor Plan. Usually, offices are selected and laid out to support the work of the current business process. Because client/server goes hand in hand with process reengineering, the office layout must be reconsidered in light of the new business process.

Office Furniture. Client/server introduces technology directly where the worker works. This means that designers should evaluate the type and style of work furniture to see whether it will work with the technology. Anyone who has used a workstation at a desk not designed for typing on a keyboard knows how uncomfortable it can become.

Also, designers should check for lighting in the office, not only electric illumination but also the natural lighting. A computer display in direct sunlight can be unreadable. It is better to anticipate that problem before the first day of conversion. In general, designers must realize that the organization's existing office furniture may or may not work with the new technology. The initial site visit is the time to begin considering this issue.

Hardware Placement. The placement of new hardware such as servers and printers needs to be thought through. This may mean looking at office layout to see where servers and printers might be placed. Work group printers can generate considerable noise and traffic and so should not be placed too close to peoples' desks. The servers may have specific electrical and air-conditioning requirements, so the office needs to be evaluated on that basis. Also, servers can be very expensive and may hold important information. Their physical security needs to be addressed.

Electrical Requirements. Contractors need to address the various questions on this topic. One important question concerns the ability of the office power supply to meet demands of the application. For example, does the area have a history of brownouts in the warm months? The need for uninterrupted power supply should be considered.

If a good deal of new technology is being introduced, the designer may need to extend or increase the number of electric receptacles. Running a bunch of extension plugs from a common receptacle may bring a visit from the fire inspector, if not the fire department.

If the new process requires a new office layout and this is going to be achieved with partitions, how will the electricity be delivered to the partitions? Many partitions allow one to run power wires through the partition but above the floor. Contractors should check that the local authorities do not view such wiring as a fire hazard. It may be worthwhile to determine whether they have preferred partitions.

Air Conditioning. Client/server technology can introduce a good deal of heat into the local office environment. In addition, as processors increase in speed they often run hotter to deliver higher-clocked speeds. Because of this, designers may have to consider more air conditioning to keep the site within acceptable temperature ranges—both for the people and for the hardware. Additional servers may require specific cooling to meet their needs, which may in turn require a separate room and separate air conditioning for the servers.

Air Quality. The air itself is also a consideration. In one case, an organization introduced client/server to a site that made a chemical that was a fine black dust called carbon black; another site was a fast-food restaurant where a good deal of flour dust hung in the air. Both of these situations created problems for the computer disk drives. Keeping the air clean may be an important consideration for some sites, especially those near manufacturing or mining sites, or in parts of the country that are naturally dusty. In any case, it is better to have asked the question than to be surprised.

Communications Technology. Here, designers must evaluate how well the site is prepared for supporting the demands of client/server communications, both LAN and wide area network (WAN).

With regard to the LAN, the designer must decide what the site currently has and what must be done to upgrade the site to meet the new communication needs. If the site already has LAN technology, designers might assume that the current wiring can be used for the new initiative. This assumption can be wrong at the physical level if the wrong type of wiring is in place. It may be wrong at the technical level if the wrong type of software or network servers are used. It may also be wrong if a check on LAN reliability suggests that it will not meet the demands of the application. The main point here is that the designer should not assume that the installed LANs will meet the future needs.

The physical structure of the new site also poses some challenges for new LAN technology. Simply running the wire is a well-known problem, but there may be other concerns. In one case LANs were run near elevators that had large magnets, which caused intermittent interruptions. In another case, the LANs were run near an oven and the heating caused problems. Designers must evaluate the local office for its fitness for the LAN technology.

The previous example noted the case of the nineteenth-century building that was not well suited for LAN technology. The general environment of the office should be considered for activities that could affect the use of LAN technology. High-energy radio frequencies, for example, may cause problems for an inexpensive LAN technology.

Finally, the running of the physical wiring for the LANs may be affected by local building codes. In some situations the LAN technology may be viewed as open wiring and local regulations could alter how the LANs are built.

WAN technology presents it own concerns. First, many requirements may be negotiated once for the project as a whole. But often, there is a need to negotiate by site for specific needs. Looking at the overall planning framework discussed in Chapter III-1, site evaluation begins after the systems design effort has begun.

One reason for this is that the organization should have some clear notion of what is required for WAN communication speeds and reliability. This information should be available to the site evaluation team. The site evaluation team will use it to assess what is in place and to begin discussions with the local telecommunications providers at the site concerning what is needed and when it will be needed.

Lead times for delivery of changing technology vary by region. Lead time can be very short in the United States but may be longer in some European countries. Also, requests for exceptional services, such as a dedicated international line or very high line speeds, can add significantly to delivery lead times. The site evaluation team should consider supplying redundant lines and should review with the local telecommunications provider any special considerations regarding availability. As a part of the discussion, the team should obtain commitments on dates for availability for testing.

When dealing with international telecommunications, legal counsel may be needed to provide guidance about the movement of information across borders or interfacing different telecommunications providers. This should be done prior to site evaluation, and any appropriate documentation should be available for the site visits.

Site Security. A client/server implementation introduces thousands of dollars—if not hundreds of thousands of dollars—of computing equipment. Can the site be secured against physical theft? The machines provide access to the corporate data assets. Can the site be physical and logically secured to restrict access only to those entitled to it in business hours? At one site 50 workstations were installed on a Friday for a Monday application implementation. On Monday morning eight of the workstations had disappeared.

In high-security situations developers may even need to consider the risk of access to information on display screens. Do windows or open partitions risk letting the wrong people see information?

Current Hardware. The hardware currently at the site poses unique challenges. Sometimes information systems (IS) personnel are surprised to find a good deal of computing and network hardware installed at a site. In addition, they often underestimate the level of development found at the site. It is usually not a good idea to assume that whatever is installed at the site can simply be disregarded or thrown away. Often the local user may have invested a good deal of time and money in that hardware.

The hardware and software may also represent a commitment by the local office manager; that manager feels ownership of the installed systems. In this situation the site evaluation team needs to show real interest and concern for what is installed. Inevitably, business users are concerned that the new system will result in a loss of capabilities. The IS people must remember that although the new system may be better, the loss of the old system is still that—a loss—to the users.

Usually, the site survey is not the time to conclude what to do with the installed systems. It is the time to understand what is there and how it is being used. As the site survey team prepares the site installation plans, team members should conclude what is to be done with the installed systems.

General Environment of the Site. It is always worthwhile to stand inside the building and simply look out the window of the site, then walk around the exterior of the site, and then consider the following questions: If large trucks are rolling in and out of nearby buildings, can personnel feel vibrations that might affect the machines to be installed? Is there a manufacturing plant nearby emitting smoke into the air? Air pollution can affect reliability of the machines. Is the neighborhood at risk for theft or vandalism to the hardware investment? What will be the reaction of suppliers when they are asked to make deliveries to the site? If the site has a history of minor earthquakes, what tolerance does the site have for what level of quake?

When wrapping up the initial site visit, it is worthwhile to schedule a closing visit with the local site manager (responsible for physical property). Discussing the results and next steps is part of the communication effort within change management.

Furthermore, developers may want to consider a brief presentation with site personnel to thank them for their help and to let them know about future visits. A brief discussion of major observations can give local site personnel a sense of involvement.

For example, a statement that "clearly something must be done to improve air quality" suggests that the developer has been observant and intends to take action. At the same time, the organization must recognize that specific conclusions about what is to be done may be subject to change.

Site Assessment Report

When returning from such a visit, the developer should immediately prepare an assessment of what needs to be done at that site. The immediate assessment is a pragmatic suggestion. After several site visits, it is easy to forget which office already had open layouts and which did not. Developers should write down everything about the site that they may need any time in the future. Memories fade quickly, especially after many different site visits. From the assessment, designers can develop a site preparation plan giving time frames for when the work needs to be done at the site.

Site Feasibility. A first point to consider is the feasibility of the site. Any of the previous considerations can be a basis for deciding that the site is not viable and a new site must be found.

For example, the application may require an open office layout so that work and communications can flow from one person to another, with verbal communications occurring across the desk. If the local site is an older building with closed offices, tearing out the walls may not be practical from a cost or structural standpoint. In this case the effort may shift to finding a new site for the application. That in turn brings up serious change management considerations for the organization.

If the office is feasible, developers should prepare a detailed definition of the work to be done. What does the office layout look like? Where will servers be put? Are air-conditioning or air purification systems needed? What is needed from a power supply standpoint? What needs to be done to provide physical security?

Site-by-Site Reporting. These and related considerations need to be pulled together on a site-by-site basis, indicating what must be done at each site. In addition, based on application needs, developers need to set the date for final site readiness. From this date, developers can establish a site preparation plan to ensure that the work defined in the site assessment is done on a timely basis.

Tracking Costs and Time Tables. The site preparation plan, by site, should then be registered with the program management team. They, in turn, will begin to track the progress of the site preparation plan in terms of results, quality, cost, and timeliness.

The site assessment and site preparation plan are provided to contractors who will work during the site preparation phase. Prior to this plan, contractual negotiations must take place to make clear what is to be done, at what cost, and in what time frames. Progress through these steps depends on project specifics. If a general contractor is a part of this effort, he or she should be involved in developing the plan.

In some cases, the general contractor agrees to a contract that gives certain standard costs and time frames to upgrade a site. Given that the costs and time estimates were made prior to knowing the specifics of the work to be done, contractors may have misestimated the required effort.

If there has been a significant underestimate, the general contractor should expect to hear about it. (The possibility of overestimating the effort exists, but it is unlikely anyone will hear about that.)

If the general contractor views a cost overrun, as many do, simply as a contractor problem, the general contractor may inadvertently be responsible for lowering the quality of the project, as the contractor is forced to cut costs. At another extreme, the general contractor may only succeed in bankrupting the contractor, which puts the entire project in jeopardy. The point is to listen to the contractor to understand concerns about misestimating the costs and try to work constructively to solve the problems.

If no such prior contract exists, the general contractor will work with contractors at each site going through the assessment and the site preparation plan as a basis to arrange work to be done. The contractors need specifics on what is needed and when. Because, in most cases, they have participated in the initial assessment, they can often provide a reasonable estimate of work to be done and the costs.

If no general contractor has been used, a site preparation team must perform a negotiation process on a site-by-site basis. This process can be time-consuming. Furthermore, success may be a matter of luck if the general contractor does not know the local contractors on a site-by-site basis.

In this approach it is essential that a complete plan be maintained on a site-by-site basis as to what things are to be done and when. As the site preparation proceeds for a large rollout—hundreds of sites, for example—it may be extremely time-consuming to track results in terms of work done, its quality, its timeliness, and its cost. This is not a task to be left to two clerical people who view the job merely as sending out and receiving forms.

As the site preparation team puts together the site assessment and establishes the site preparation plan, it is worthwhile to share this information with local site managers. There are several reasons to do so: (1) so that site managers can see that progress was made based on their cooperation and assistance, (2) to communicate what is planned so that site managers can understand it and also share it with the local personnel, and (3) so that site managers can review the plan to assess its impact and to approve the changes from the standpoint of reasonableness. The site preparation team should ask for some sort of written confirmation of the work.

The site preparation team should also share plans for the installed hardware and software with site managers. This can be a very sensitive issue and may take some care. Team members need to clearly communicate the plans; at the same time, they need to communicate a recognition of the good work done. In addition, they must communicate how the implementation of the new systems and the changes anticipated may affect users.

Keeping Plans and Documents Current. The site assessment, the site preparation plan, and all contracts for doing the work should come under strict configuration management as a part of program management. Changes to the plan should require approval by all concerned parties. At a minimum this includes the site preparation team and the contractors doing the changed work.

In addition, the site preparation team should keep assessment documents current; if something occurs to a local site, this should be reflected in the site assessment and, possibly, in the plan. In one case a site was disrupted due to a riot. The site assessment and implementation plan became moot at that point, as effort turned to the bigger task of selecting a new site.

Communicating Results. As the assessments and plans are pulled together, the information should be communicated back to the local office manager. In addition to its general value as a communication initiative, site preparation teams also want to have local office managers beginning to think about how the local office will work during the implementation phase.

For example, if installing LAN and WAN technology will disrupt phone service, the local office manager needs to begin to think about impact. The manager may reasonably expect some guidance from the site preparation team about what to worry about and how to address it.

Given the amount of work all these issues suggest, an organization might wonder if all offices or sites need to be evaluated. Generally, site management should be forced to prove that an office should not be evaluated. In some cases, such as franchise operations, it may well be that most sites correspond to a limited number of configurations. But there may still be site-specific items that are difficult to be sure of without inspection. For example, proximity to a plant making carbon black is difficult to predict.

One of the values of the site visit is to bring home the idea that the system is going to happen and that people need to begin thinking about it. The visit gives the site personnel a chance to feel a part of the process rather than someone to whom the process is happening.

It also gives system developers the opportunity to see what people on the "other side" of the system are thinking. This can build goodwill that is valuable during the difficult conversion stage. In short, the value of a site visit is so great that skipping it should only occur after great consideration and careful thought.

SITE PREPARATION

The site preparation phase begins as contracts are completed based on the site preparation plan. Contractors are lined up and the sites are to begin upgrades for the applications.

In the site preparation phase, the work to upgrade every site is done. Three items are key to this effort:

- The site preparation plan, defining what is to be done.
- The site preparation contract defining who is to do what, the levels of quality, and the costs.
- The ongoing use of checklists to assess that work has been done at expected levels of quality.

Checklists and Schedules

The three items just noted assume that contractors will do the work. Thus, much of the effort is to ensure that work begins and ends on schedule. Toward that end, checklists are vital.

The dates when the checklists are to be completed and delivered are also key to managing the overall effort. They can ensure that the work to be done is completed as expected in a consistent manner across sites. Although such checklists tend to depend on site specifics, a few general points can be made about what should be included. These include the following:

- *First contact by project team.* Whenever work is to start on a major segment of work—such as redoing electrical supplies or installing new air conditioning—the site preparation team should make the first contact. This contact should occur ahead of when the work is to be done. Often the contact can be made over the phone to explain the work and when it is to start and to identify the contractors who will be doing the work. There are several reasons for this contact. The key reason is that the project team may be sensitive to the impact the project will have on the site when the contractor begins to move desks around. The initial project team contact can show this sensitivity and concern. Also, although the local office manager should be aware of what is going to happen, he or she may not have actually considered the impact of that work on the day-to-day operations of the business. The completion of this contact, and any results or follow-up, should be recorded as a first step in any checklist. This ensures that all ensuing work is done with the full knowledge of the people at the site.

- *Aggressive communications.* During this initial contact, the site preparation team can go over the changes to be made and suggest ways to get ready for the work. Personnel should be advised of the work that is to be done and how work will continue in the office. A briefing package for the local office manager may be helpful to explain the work to be done. Finally, even with the best configuration management, changes slip through and this is the opportunity to identify such changes. In one case the local office manager went out and bought computers and LAN technology and got them running at the site over the weekends. He did so with the best intention—to decrease the effort to get the site ready. Unfortunately, much of the software was not compatible and additional work had to be done to change things at the site.

Setting Up the Checklists

The checklists typically are organized by major work segment and by contractor. Thus there may be a checklist of work to be done for the electrical work and another for the contractor. Most checklists adhere to the following broad outline:

- *Verify with the local site manager the work to be done and when it is to start.* Generally, a contractor should not turn up at a site without having been introduced by the project team.
- *Identify and itemize deliverables from work and the criteria by which the work is to be accepted.* For some construction work this often includes approval by local authorities such as building inspectors. It may also include criteria specific for the project. For example, a building inspector may approve the wiring done by a local contractor. However, the project team may mandate an additional review to ensure that the electrical supply is of adequate quality. Both these checks may be required for approval of the work.

- *Sign-off and verification of work.* The types of approvals noted previously need to be formally signed off by the appropriate authority. The local office manager needs to be involved in the process, and sign-off on the work done is one way to do this. Contractors need to be sensitive and flexible with regard to the local office manager's sign-off. It is not reasonable to expect this person to sign off on things he or she knows little about. For example, the manager cannot be expected to sign off on whether the air conditioning has met the needs of the system. If the office layout was to be reworked, on the other hand, he or she can verify that work was done according to plan. This sign-off responsibility may get the manager thinking about how the office will work with the new layout. Also, the involvement in the sign-off provides the manager with the opportunity to voice any concerns or reservations. For example, if painting has been done as a part of the implementation but looks shabby, the local office manager should have the option to raise concerns and issues.
- *Additional work required.* One may complete a phase of contracted work and find that additional things remain to be done outside the original plan. Local building inspectors may mandate additional work in order to ensure compliance with local building codes. Installed air conditioning may not reach all parts of the building. These types of items need to be inventoried so that they may be subjected to the assessment/planning/contractual process. As a result, the checklist should identify additional work to be done. The site preparation team needs to focus on these items; "small" additional changes can cascade into an avalanche if they are not controlled early in the process.

As the checklists come back, the site preparation team should review each one carefully to ensure that scheduled work was completed. With good contractors and contracts this tends to be the case. However, in a large rollout an organization has to expect problems at some point. These inevitably entail contractor negotiations. Ideally, the negotiations are resolved with discussions. If not, the negotiations can move to some form of arbitration or litigation.

The information services industry on the whole has had remarkably little litigation given the amount of commerce associated with it. As a result, many IS personnel have little or no experience with the sort of verbal legal sparring to which other industries are accustomed. To the uninitiated, threats of litigation are disconcerting. In fact, however, these kinds of threats are a part of this business and IS personnel need to come to grips with them as a part of the negotiations process.

An organization needs to remember to turn to legal counsel if it has no personnel qualified for these kinds of negotiations. If it appears that litigation is a possibility, a lawyer must become involved quickly. The organization must keep all available documentation and continue to document everything.

Another issue to consider as the preparation proceeds is continuous improvement. Site preparation work often proceeds in multiple parallel activities.

On occasion, as site preparation proceeds, team members may encounter problems that could have been avoided by an improved site evaluation activity. Work plans should include a periodic review of site implementation activities; this review communicates what the implementation problems are and whether changes to the site evaluation activity could improve results. Although this may appear to an obvious procedure, the different work groups on the respective phases are often so distributed and on the move so much that these exchanges fail to occur. Scheduling periodic meetings to share results as a part of the planned work can help.

As a part of knowing what is happening, plans should include quality assurance reviews at sites as the site implementation proceeds. These reviews use on-site visits to assess what did and did not work during site implementation.

Part of this assessment can include discussions with local site management and contractors about the work done and about what went well and where rework or additional work is needed. The assessment should include tests that the work completed meets expected goals. For example, can all the hardware be turned on and does it appear to work? Are all items installed, and do the item numbers reflect what is found in the configuration management system?

In general, quality assurance reviews should be fairly intensive in the early site implementation efforts. They can then be performed on a selected basis as the implementation begins to proceed in a fairly procedural manner.

The site installation process by nature tends to disrupt and change local office activities. As a result, it is common to expect local office management to communicate what is happening as the installation proceeds. It is good for the site preparation team to be part of those communications.

To that end, team leaders should plan on periodic communications to describe how the site preparation activity is going. These communications can have many formats: a memo to local office management or part of a program newsletter. (One organization started a newsletter column called "In the Rollout Corner.")

The report should cover what offices have been evaluated and implemented. It should also touch on the experiences of site preparation—what worked well and what did not work well. For example, if the site upgrade involves improvement to the phone service, a comment from a local office manager on how helpful the new phone system is could be useful. If the new office air conditioning makes life more pleasant, even though the office is not yet on the system, it is worth noting that fact. Conversely, if there are problems such as work disruption, the report should communicate that fact, along with steps planned to address the problem.

As local office managers will be communicating the problems, the site implementation team might as well try to provide leadership on the communications. Because the site implementation team is often disrupting work at the sites, this can be a source of interesting or amusing stories (e.g., "interesting things we found when drilling through the wall to run LAN cable"). Humor in these cases never hurts and can provide a more human dimension to the entire process.

SITE IMPLEMENTATION

As site preparation proceeds, those sites that have been prepared move into the site implementation phase. Site implementation consists of the tasks required to install the applications at the site and tests required to be run.

This phase of work is done more by project personnel than by personnel who have not been a part of the project because at this point developers are concerned with the specifics of the application. It may be difficult to find contractors who have the required level of application knowledge to be successful.

There are many viewpoints about when to do site implementation versus site preparation. In rollouts with relatively few sites, the work may be done at the same time, which minimizes disruption to the local office. This strategy may help to find problems in the survey/preparation process. It may also help avoid a last-minute rush to bring over a large set of sites as conversion nears.

On the other hand, the application may not be available and stable for early sites. Also, if the application is changed after a site has been through preparation, it may be necessary to disrupt the local users again. It certainly presents a more difficult configuration management problem.

As a general guideline, if there are a large number of sites (probably greater than 10), preparation must begin long before there is a stable application. In this case, to avoid disruption (as well as to avoid looking somewhat confused), scheduling preparation and implementation as distinct phases is often the answer.

With regard to the physical implementation of the application, the installation should be an automated process driven from the development site. This automation, particularly on a large rollout, may be essential. For example, if the rollout team finds as a part of release testing that many tables must be set or that code must be modified for each site, the team can halt the installation until the automated procedures are completed.

Automated procedures should be in place to install the software and to build local databases and reference files. If, as often happens, personnel, roles, and routes must be described for the application, a starter set of information should be provided so that local personnel can make modifications rather than starting from scratch. For example, if each employee must be identified in a table, the initial version of the table based on who is believed to work at the site should be provided. Then local site personnel should modify the table. Doing so can reduce learning curve and also reduce errors, as long as accurate lists of personnel are kept.

Test Before "Going Live"

The following is subject to some controversy, but experience suggests that it is a workable approach. The issue revolves around how far site preparation proceeds in getting the site ready for "going live."

One useful strategy is to have the site preparation team take the installation to the point where the applications are installed and ready to run for the users when the system goes live. The advantages include the following:

- Users by now know the site preparation team and they will be comfortable having the site preparation team on the ground for the final installation.

- The site preparation team has been responsible for getting the site ready for running the applications. Thus to some degree team members can be expected to take ownership of the site and its readiness to go live.

- The experience of bringing the system up and testing it can provide valuable feedback on the site preparation approach that can improve downstream implementations.

If the site preparation team is to do the implementation, the following applies to them. When the site is installed, it needs to be tested.

The objective here is usually not a full-blown test of all capability; that objective should have been met in release testing. Rather, this test is to ensure that all components of the application that are dependent on local site specifics are working as expected.

The test should also determine that all required applications are in place and complete. It should ensure that all physical components work, including workstations, servers, and LANs. It should test that the expected flow of work between personnel performs as expected and that all routes, roles, and personnel are properly described and work. Because of the need for communications to other sites found in client/server, the communications capability should also be tested. If the communication has restrictions or dependencies based on role or personnel, this should be tested. For example, if only a chief agent at a site can exchange information with a buyer, this should be tested now.

As a result of doing tests, information and data are often built up in files both local and remote. These files must be purged prior to conversion because after that they can cause problems. For example, in one case a site tested that authorized personnel could request printing of checks. Those requests were still in a print spool when the system came up live and began printing them. This test cleanup needs some careful thought because there are usually some subtleties that can cause problems.

The entire process of site installation testing and cleanup should be guided by checklists. In this case, the checklists verify that expected tests were done and that results were as predicted. The checklists should also verify that installation cleanup has been completed.

"Go Live" Checklists

When installation is complete, the site moves toward conversion. In this stage, the site is ready and tested. A final "go live" checklist should be completed that verifies that all needed hardware, software, procedures, and forms, for instance, are in place.

These checklists are completed at each site and rolled up to a supervisory level, such as local office to region management. These levels in turn complete their own checklists and verify that lower levels have done their checklists. Finally, at the program level, the intent is to have a relatively straightforward set of checklists that verify that all levels of checklists are completed and that one is ready to make the go-live decision.

There are several objectives for this process: (1) to verify that things are ready to go at all sites to be converted, (2) to have the local manager participate in the process of deciding to go live, and (3) to ensure that program management has some basis on which to decide that all planned work has been accomplished and that the conversion can go forward.

SITE PREPARATION AND INSTALLATION AT UNIVERSALAIR

Initially, the site preparation and installation of the application at UniversalAir presented fewer problems than is common with some client/server projects. The initial rollout was targeted to a set of sites within the facility where the system was being run. As a result, the rollout did not have to deal with widely geographic sites. In addition, the personnel affected by the system were nearby and it was fairly straightforward to arrange time with them to try out the system and to develop an understanding of the system's capability and its impact on them and their work.

Challenges arose, however, in the upgrade of the physical facilities. New networks had to be laid to support the client/server application. This involved significant building changes and disrupted the work of the business community. Also, the upgrade of the network exposed the site to some risks and affects existing applications.

In addition, the site was not equipped in terms of desk and office layout for the use of client/server. These facilities had to be replaced because of the specifics of client/server. Furniture replacement proved to be expensive. For example, a single chair could cost over $500.

Although every effort was made to minimize the impact on business operations, some building changes and some network outages did affect the overall operations. However, training and change management activities were successful. After site disruption, the system rolled out and received a good reception from the user community.

CONCLUSION

The preparation of sites for client/server computing tends to be an underestimated and understaffed effort. The work can be complex and demanding and can require considerable coordination and planning to execute successfully. Doing the work successfully can result in a set of sites successfully converted and can leave users with a strong sense that the program knows what it is doing and how to do it.

III-13
Management of Distributed Operations

D istributed client/server technologies and architectures provide a wealth of new capabilities and advantages for those enterprises that adopt them. Processes happen more quickly, information is closer to those who use it, and individuals are empowered with many new and useful tools. These systems are increasingly "mission critical." As such, the management of these systems requires careful consideration to provide service to the organization at an affordable cost.

THE MODE FRAMEWORK

Management of a distributed client/server environment is different and more complex than management of centralized computing technologies. As the power and flexibility of the system have changed and increased, so too has the effort required to manage the system.

MODE (Management of Distributed Environments) is a framework for managing the development of client/server systems. In its simplest form, MODE provides a mechanism for understanding what needs to be done, why management tasks need to be performed, and how the management of systems is changed with the introduction of a client/server environment.

The MODE framework has been used to great advantage by a number of organizations during their first implementation of a client/server system. Often, the framework's greatest value is in forcing the deliberate consideration of all aspects of service and systems management early in the process, before problems arise.

MODE: High-Level Diagram

Several models or frameworks for managing in a distributed environment currently exist. Many of these models, however, address only portions of the overall management effort, not the entire management picture. The MODE framework was synthesized from multiple sources and

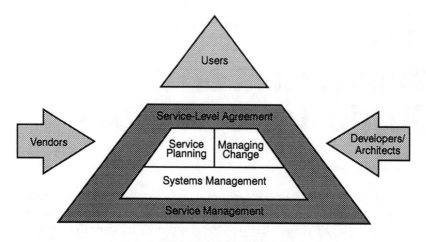

Exhibit III-13-1. MODE Framework

---

represents one view of the distributed computing management picture. Exhibit III-13-1 illustrates a high-level representation of the framework.

The framework focuses on four main areas:

- Service management.
- Systems management.
- Service planning.
- Managing change.

Service Management Service management is the fundamental area within the model. It involves forming liaisons with users, developers/architects, and vendors monitoring the services that are provided and ensuring that the services are meeting standards as defined in service-level agreements (SLAs.)

The key to service management, and to the overall management of distributed client/server systems, is the use of SLAs, which clearly articulate and document the level of service users expect to receive. SLAs should be used to drive out the requirements for the service organization and the operations architecture, as well as to justify expenditures for tools and infrastructure.

Service management is the direct interface to the users of the client/server system. Users are depicted at the top of the diagram to represent the fact that a distributed system is managed to support the users of the system. Systems management organizations must focus on meeting the needs of the users of the system. Ultimately, the users of the system define the service offered to the customer base through SLAs. When the service management concept is implemented correctly, users have a single point of contact for all systems-related problems, suggestions, and planning. It is the service management function which, in turn, navigates and coordinates the needed systems personnel and resources on behalf of the user.

Service management is also the direct interface to the developers/ architects and vendors for the distributed system. Each of these groups has requirements for, and introduce changes to, the distributed environment. Service management controls the overall service to the users and handles the relationships with developers/architects and vendors.

Systems Management Systems management involves all functions required for the day-to-day operation of the distributed system (e.g., event monitoring, failure control, performance monitoring, and tape loading.) Regardless of the changes taking place within the distributed environment, systems management activities must be ongoing.

Managing Change Managing change includes all the functions necessary for effecting changes to the client/server environment in a controlled and orderly way (e.g., software and data distribution and license management.) As a result of the large number of interrelated hardware and software components in a client/server environment, assessing and controlling the "side effects" of system change are crucial to maintaining acceptable system availability.

Service Planning Service planning encompasses all the functions that outline the tactical and strategic planning that needs to take place to manage a distributed environment effectively. Service planning for a distributed client/server environment requires a more integrated approach. Effective planning for any one component such as network capacity cannot be done independently of an understanding of the whole system and how it will be managed. (For example, the chosen software distribution approach may impact the overall network bandwidth required.)

Once a change has been planned, the change is controlled and implemented in detail within either systems management or managing change.

Three-Dimensional View of MODE

Systems management, service planning, and managing change are all represented at the same level to highlight the increased importance of service planning and managing change within the distributed environment. Service planning is emphasized as a result of the degree of integrated planning necessary to meet service requirements. Managing change is emphasized to highlight the risks inherent in making systems changes and the importance of managing those changes.

Effecting changes to the system, such as rolling out new releases of application software/data, is substantially more involved within the distributed environment. Previous centralized management frameworks did not give planning and managing change an equal representation to systems management, if they were represented at all.

Taking the two-dimensional framework and extending it to three dimensions introduces the concept of MODE domains, as represented in Exhibit III-13-2.

MODE domains are represented as "slices" of the framework. Sample domain slices include the following:

- Systemwide domain.
- Host domain.
- Network domain.
- Server domain.
- Workstation domain.

These domain slices indicate that each of the four areas is involved to some degree in managing a particular domain. For instance, some activities from service management, systems management, service planning, and managing change are performed on a systemwide basis. Within specific domains (e.g., network), however, the scope and level of activity associated with each of the components may change.

The domains depicted in the exhibit are merely samples of the domains that a distributed environment could have. Each organization needs to carefully review its distributed environment to determine what its domains are.

For example, a company could define its domains to be UNIX, OS/2, Windows, corporate wide area networks (WANs), and remote local area networks (LANs.) The idea of domains helps decide which functions and activities—and, potentially, software and tools—are required to support their unique environment.

However, users must still be supported by whatever domain management capabilities the organization puts in place. An organization must identify groups of users or user communities and their require-

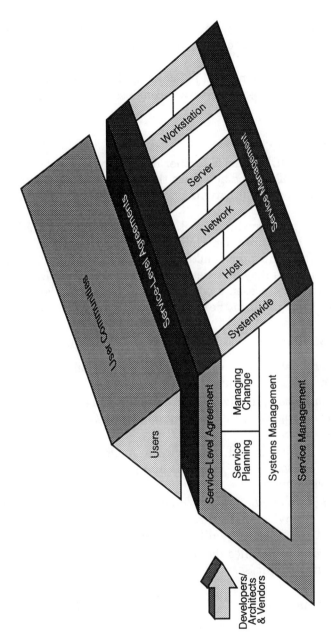

Exhibit III-13-2. Three-Dimensional View of MODE Domains

ments. SLAs maintained with the users by service management reinforce that users receive service from a single organization and not on a domain basis.

As with the two- dimensional framework, developers/architects and vendors have access to the framework through service management only.

MODE Areas and Their Functions

Each of the four MODE areas is further divided into multiple functions. A function is a set of related activities that needs to be performed. This section briefly introduces functions and then discusses them in greater detail.

Functions do not translate directly into how a management organization should be structured. One individual or group within an organization may perform multiple functions. Similarly, the activities to perform a single function may be spread throughout the organization. Once again, the framework presents what needs to be accomplished without addressing who will perform the tasks or how they will be performed.

Service Management Functions within service management are:

- *SLA management.* Involves the creation, managing, reporting, and discussion of SLAs with users.
- *OLA management.* Involves the creation, managing, reporting, and discussion of operational-level agreements (OLAs) with domain suppliers/vendors.
- *Help desk.* Provides end users with a single point of contact and controls the resolution of incidents and problems within the client/ server environment.
- *Quality management.* Ensures quality in the management of the client/server environment through training, as well as through the design and execution of quality improvement plans.
- *Administration.* Handles the financial accounting and legal aspects of managing a client/server environment.

Systems Management The following are functions within systems management:

- *Production control.* Ensures that production activities are performed and controlled as required and as intended.
- *Monitoring.* Verifies that the system is continually functioning in accordance with whatever service levels are defined.
- *Failure control.* Involves the detection and correction of faults

within the system, whether they are minor (a workstation is down) or major (a disaster has occurred.)

- *Security management.* Ensures that the system is accessed only by authorized users and that those users are restricted to authorized resources.

Service Planning The following are functions within service planning:

- *Service management planning.* Defines the financial and training plans for the organization.
- *Systems management planning.* Determines the strategies for day-to-day operation of the system.
- *Managing change planning.* Develops the plans for releasing new sites, services, or updates to existing service.
- *MODE strategic planning.* Formulates the long-term strategy for managing the distributed environment, including people, tools, and processes. It also ensures that the management strategy is in line with the enterprise strategy.

Managing Change Following are the functions within managing change:

- *Controlling.* Monitors change to make sure that change is delivered on time according to established plans, making adjustments to the plan when unforeseen issues or events arise (e.g., rollout management, change control, and asset management.)
- *Testing.* Ensures that changes to the client/server environment achieve the desired result and do not produce unwanted side effects.
- *Implementing.* Executes change within the distributed environment with tested components and techniques according to the appropriate plan(s.) Implementing includes such things as initial installation, software and data distribution, and license management.

Key Functions

The MODE framework presents an ideal way in which to view what is required to manage distributed environments. In reality, because of constraints or the lack of requirements for the capability, subsets of this ideal framework are typically implemented. It is up to each organization to determine what the requirements are and how they can be achieved.

It is important to understand, however, that each of the functions should be carefully considered and a conscious decision should be made as to whether to include or exclude a particular function. Such conscientious effort ensures that excluded functions have been scoped out of the work being performed and have not simply been forgotten. It also ensures that issues can be raised to management and users about the impact of not including particular functions.

SERVICE MANAGEMENT AND PLANNING

Focusing on the End User

The introduction of client/server technology further intensifies the demand that information systems (IS) organizations adopt a more service-oriented approach. As client/server-based applications are given to users higher in the organization, and for increasingly missions-critical purposes, meeting the needs of these users becomes vital to the organization.

This section describes a service management framework that allows systems developers to take a service-oriented approach. The key to the approach is the use of the SLA, which clearly articulates and documents the expectations of service receivers and providers.

Service Management

SLA Management A service-level agreement is an agreement between the users of the system and those managing it which defines the level of service the users expect to receive. SLAs typically address such things as required response time, hours when the system is to be available, and the reliability of the system in terms of unscheduled service outages. They also provide a mechanism through which service managers and users can regularly communicate about the services delivered.

Other topics to be covered in the SLA include the following:

- Guidelines/assumptions on which the service level is based.
- Chargeback costs if necessary.
- Descriptions of how service levels will be measured and reported on.
- Definitions of roles and responsibilities for service provision and the management of service delivery.

In a distributed environment, users of the system should only "see" service. They should not have to understand how service is provided to them because distributed environments are frequently built on a wide variety of complex components. SLAs make this distinction possible, providing the glue between the service seen by the user and the way in which the service is provided.

Ideally, SLAs are defined or enhanced during the functional requirements phase of any systems development activity. The architects and systems developers should have a good understanding of the service levels required by the user before designing and building the system. It is far easier to build the system to reflect service considerations versus retrofitting service on top of a completed system.

In addition, the appropriate personnel should receive requirements in this phase to ensure that the proposed requirements are, in fact, manageable and affordable. Without such review, it can be quite easy to build unmanageable or excessively costly systems.

SLAs are difficult to define in a distributed environment, however, because of the complexities of the technologies and infrastructures. In a graphical user interface environment, no longer can service be simply defined by average screen exchange response time. Instead, service may need to be defined around more granular measures, such as what the response time should be for the "commit order" button. Or they may need to be alternatively defined for higher-level activities, such as the total system time it takes to complete a particular business event (e.g., the system processing/waiting time necessary to complete an entire order instead of the time to move from one screen to the next.)

Multitasking client workstations, which are used for more things than just the application for which the SLA is being defined, present another challenge in SLA definition. If the user is empowered to launch resource consuming office automation or data analysis applications in the background, it may be impossible to guarantee a specific response time for a given application due to contention for the workstation's processor or memory.

SLAs are also difficult to maintain in a distributed environment because the assumptions on which an SLA is based may change frequently. For example, if an SLA is based on a particular architecture which gets changed in some manner (e.g., software or hardware is updated), the SLA may need to change as well. Such changes require close monitoring and consideration to keep SLAs up-to-date and the overall SLA process working effectively.

An organization must also have an accurate way of measuring the service levels achieved. SLAs must not be defined without careful consideration given to how service is to be measured, recorded, and reported. The accurate measurement of an SLA (e.g., the time to create a new customer order) may require "hooks" into an application for isolating "system" time from "user think" time. It is important that this be discussed up front with the user communities to ensure that the information provided is sufficient enough for both sides to agree on the relative quality of service received. It is also important to maintain historical records of service to demonstrate to the users how service has improved (or degraded) over time.

(Because of its importance and central role in the management of a distributed client/server environment, the Appendix provides a sample SLA.)

OLA Management An OLA is an agreement between those responsible for the management of the system and the service providers (either internal or external) who are actually managing the system component(s) or domain(s.)

OLAs are closely related to SLAs in the following way. An SLA cannot be formally set with users until it is clear that the required service levels can be met by one or a combination of service providers through one or more OLAs. To create a customer order, for instance, a user may need to access a database three times, use the WAN twice, and perform some processing on a centralized host. If an SLA is to be based on the time it takes to accomplish those activities, OLAs must be defined (or at least considered) for the level of service delivered from those managing the database, the network, and the host.

As Exhibit III-13-3 illustrates, an SLA can be thought of as the sum of its underlying OLAs. For example, if the SLA dictates an end-to-end user response time of two seconds, the related OLAs will be used to allocate the overall two-second response time across the needed client, network, and server platforms.

Service providers cannot be viewed in isolation. They must work together to achieve their target goals. If the target goals are not achieved, however, the presence of formal agreements with service providers can be an effective means of managing a provider's (either an internal provider or vendor) response to a poor service level.

Often the greatest value of OLAs is their usefulness in cutting through the destructive finger pointing that can occur when an organization experiences service failure. (For example, long response times can lead to network personnel blaming the host or database personnel, and vice versa.)

As with SLAs, OLAs must be redefined as the assumptions on which they have been based change. Because many third-party vendors have OLAs, it is important that the parameters of the OLAs be monitored to prevent vendors from pointing to changed parameters and declaring their contracts null.

The measurement of OLAs is as important as the measurement of SLAs. An OLA should not be agreed on until the organization clearly defines how it will be measured, recorded, and reported on. Historical metrics are also important with OLAs to provide the organization with

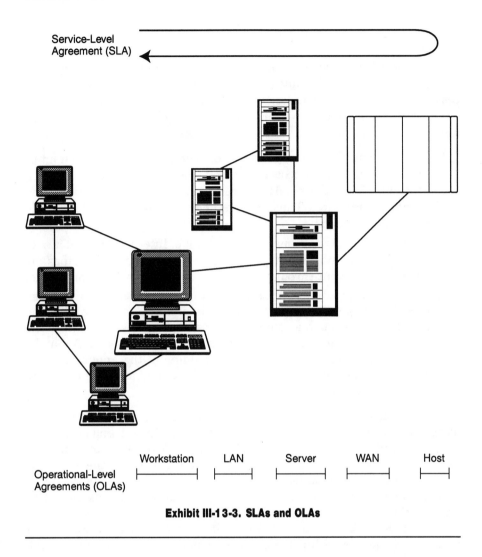

Exhibit III-13-3. SLAs and OLAs

some sense as to how well a particular service provider performs over time.

Help Desk A help desk provides a single point of contact for users within the organization when trouble arises. The help desk sets the users' expectations for incident resolution and assists in managing those expectations during the resolution process.

The help desk may also act as a first level of support for the organization. Users can get answers to simple questions immediately, resulting in a more effective use of high-level and specialized technical support resources.

In traditional environments, the help desk is used to collect and route problems, and it includes at least a minimal problem analysis and resolution role. In a client/server environment, a relatively complete analysis of the problem may be required as the problem occurs. Immediate analysis is needed for at least three reasons:

1. The problem is frequently a result of events on the client computer. The machine has few tools available to capture status and playback of events. Once the client has rebooted, all traces of actions and events are often lost. Thus, the detailed analysis must be done while the situation exists.

2. Client/server applications have a rich set of interactions, and it may be essential to find out at the time the problem occurs what steps the business user went through while they are fresh in the user's mind.

3. A client/server application is probably deeply embedded in the business flow. To get the user working again, it may be essential that the help desk go through a complete assessment and recovery while the user is on the phone seeking assistance. The help desk staff may be required to have a thorough understanding of the application, architecture, and technology, as well as how they are applied in the business process.

In this proactive role, the help desk should be viewed as a problem manager having the authority to contact and prioritize IS and operations personnel and the ability to direct the users' work toward correcting the problem. This approach may raise questions about who has the authority for the direction of personnel. The issue must be resolved in favor of what best supports the business user in need of assistance as well as the entire organization.

The help desk may also be responsible for reducing the number of repetitive incidents within the environment by bringing to closure the process of determining, diagnosing, and correcting the underlying problem(s) causing the incident. Few things decrease user confidence and satisfaction as much as repetitive calls to the help desk to resolve the same incident. Although some problems may require significant rework and effort to fix (and hence longer time scales), notifying users of pending fixes and the provision of workarounds demonstrates an effort to assist the user and provide quality service. An effective and well-run help desk operation can go a long way toward redeeming an otherwise troubled application.

To help users in the ways outlined, a different level of expertise is required than what centralized systems previously needed. Typically, technical support personnel in a client/server environment require far broader and deeper technical knowledge. The interdependencies between the system software, applications, and hardware mean that technical support personnel must have a broader scope of knowledge.

In addition to core business applications, client/server environments typically provide the users with a broad set of office automation and data analysis tools ranging from word processors and spreadsheets to PC databases and ad hoc query tools. A decision must be made as to whether the help desk will provide assistance to users of these general tools as well. The depth to which an individual's knowledge extends varies, but individuals need to understand how they can work together to solve incidents that require varied technical expertise.

High-end solutions include sophisticated software for the detection and isolation of problems. Although only limited software solutions are available at this time, there is reason to believe that more complete solutions will become available from vendors during the next few years. Thus, to avoid investing in systems software solutions that are overtaken by vendor products, IS personnel should focus on the lower end of the scale. Specifically, they should focus on the delivery of a highly effective help desk facility and tools to upgrade the applications and overall configuration.

Quality Management It is often easy to lose sight of how well an organization is or is not doing. A good way to determine how well an organization is managing its distributed environment is to compare its success to the success of other similar organizations. This comparison helps an organization define where it stands within the industry and, potentially, how it can improve service quality.

Training is critical in ensuring the quality of service delivery. Well-trained support personnel are able to keep systems up and running more effectively while providing higher-quality service to the users of the system. Users trained with regard to how they can best utilize the services provided to them also improve the quality and perception of service delivered.

Administration Billing and accounting may be required if chargeback schemes are put in place for users to pay for service usage. To accurately assess costs to users, charges should be allocated and assigned based on predetermined measures. This requires the careful measurement and accurate detailing of services used.

Although cost recovery applications are widely available in a host-based environment, systems that capture necessary statistics from many client/server platforms are either unavailable or rudimentary. Furthermore, tools to initially capture these statistics may be unavailable on many platforms, therefore requiring custom development.

Billing and accounting must also tie into the OLAs or any other arrangements with service providers. Such arrangements can be quite difficult to accomplish as many situations require the reconciliation of bills sent to the organization by service providers against the operational levels actually measured. An organization must give careful consideration to how and when to reconcile these measurements as it defines the OLAs or other arrangements.

Administration also encompasses the legal aspect of managing a distributed environment through contract management. As SLAs and OLAs change, the formal contracts defining these agreements must also change. Contracts must be kept up-to-date at all times, preventing loopholes under which service users or service providers can make unwarranted claims.

Service Planning

Service Management Planning The two main functions within service management planning are service costing and pricing and training planning. Each of these is directly related to how well a service can be delivered in the distributed environment. Each has direct impact on the quality of service delivered.

Costing and Pricing Service costing and pricing involves two major concepts related to an organization's financial planning. The first component concerns understanding the costs associated with providing service. Costs for service provision can be attributed to many things within the distributed environment including people, equipment, physical facilities, and development efforts.

It is essential to first understand what the costs are so that strategies for managing those costs can be developed, implemented, and monitored. Users need to understand the cost implications of the service levels they request, and all costs should be tied back in some way to an SLA with the user community. If a cost cannot be tied back to an SLA, the organization must determine why it is incurring the cost and whether or not there is justification for the cost.

The cost to manage a system must be considered as the system is being developed. Design decisions can directly impact how the system will be managed and the relative costs for managing it. Helping users to understand what service levels will cost the organization helps manage user expectations throughout the systems development process.

Pricing is another way to manage user expectations. Pricing calculates the costs associated with providing a particular service and determines whether users should be charged for use of that service. Performing pricing activities helps an organization understand where the service costs truly lie and with whom. If a chargeback strategy is put into effect, users quickly understand the cost of the services requested and may be more reasonable in their service expectations.

Pricing in a distributed environment has proved difficult. In the host-based environment, simple chargeback schemes divided all systems costs by the number of transactions and disk array storage device (DASD) space consumed. The client/server environment does not easily track and account for system usage. Because of the difficulty in accounting for system usage, many times the majority of systems charges are levied on a per-seat-per-month basis.

Training Training planning also affects how well service will be delivered within the distributed environment. The skill sets required by support personnel change with the introduction of distributed technologies. Support personnel are required to have greater breadth of knowledge. No longer can an individual easily understand the network or the applications. The intertwined nature of a distributed environment forces individuals to understand, at least at a high level, how the system fits together.

In addition to having a wider variety of skills, support personnel need to have some specialized skills. As no single individual can fully understand the detail behind the entire system, teams of specialized support personnel will be required to work together to a greater extent in these environments. This group interaction may require new skill sets not frequently found in traditional support organizations.

Some training may be required for users who assist in the management of the distributed system. This is because local expertise may be required to help rectify faults as well as assist in day-to-day maintenance of the system (e.g., backing up a server to tape.)

To determine a training plan, the organization must assess existing skills and define a forward-thinking training direction. The training plan is likely to emphasize newer technologies and different methods of training with the underlying goal of providing the appropriate level of service as required by the SLAs.

Systems Management Planning To provide consistent day-to-day operational levels, systems management planning must be performed. The operational levels provided by the system should always be tied back to OLAs and ultimately SLAs with the user communities. SLAs should be the driving force for how day-to-day operations are managed.

Several key areas are involved in systems management planning. Among the most important are:

- Security planning.
- Capacity modeling and planning.

With client/server networks, security may no longer be handled through a single, centralized security application. Multiple levels of security access mechanisms can be used to protect applications, data, and networks. Whatever security approach is used must be understandable and manageable by those tasked with security administration and auditing.

Capacity planning and modeling must coordinate the requirements across the system (networks, servers, workstations, central processing units.) Once again, capacity is driven by the need to meet SLAs with the user communities and as part of the planning and modeling process.

Capacity planning in the client/server environment is made more difficult by the variety of system configurations. Unlike a host-based environment, no two client/server shops are the same. The variety of configurations has limited the availability of capacity planning tools and guidelines that can yield specific recommendations.

Most tools concentrate on modeling capacity for a particular component versus the system as a whole. In addition, baseline metrics for these systems are difficult to obtain as historic metrics are not generally available within an organization for client/server systems.

Managing Change Planning One of the greatest differences between centralized and decentralized computing environments is the impact of change. Change in the distributed environment happens much more frequently and affects a greater number of devices and users. Changes must be adequately planned and controlled in a distributed environment to avoid creating faults and adversely impacting system availability.

Rollout Planning Rollout planning handles the greatest period of change in distributed system's management: system rollout and installation. During rollout, every site and every user may be affected by the changes taking place. Rolling out new systems can be particularly challenging when both old and new architecture domains must exist concurrently until the rollout has been completed.

Rollout planning includes the determination of everything from the high-level rollout schedule to the rollout activities that need to take place at each and every site. Successful rollout is likely to involve multiple groups within the organization as well as vendors external to the organization. Schedules and activities must be coordinated and agreed on by all the appropriate parties. Interdependencies within the schedule must be identified prior to rollout to highlight the importance of the schedule and the effort required from each group involved.

Release Planning Release planning coordinates the release of updates (e.g., software, data, and procedures) to the distributed sites. An application, for instance, can no longer be delivered on successful completion of its system test independently but must be tested in the target environment.

Releasing a new application invariably introduces change into the environment, and client/server environments are notorious for adverse side effects of even seemingly insignificant changes. Releases must therefore be planned carefully to ensure that a change does not negatively affect any other component of the system.

MODE Planning For some client/server environments, it may be important to have a plan for future improvements in how the system itself is managed. A MODE planning function is a good idea for organizations establishing their first client/server environment, or that are making substantial changes in the environment or types of applications to be supported. The role of MODE planning is to ensure that the overall service and systems management functions are up to the challenge of supporting future client/server applications.

SERVICE-LEVEL AGREEMENTS

An SLA is a formal agreement for the provision of a stated level of service. The agreement is made between the end users of the application system and the company's organizational unit responsible for computer service and systems management. The SLA document defines, in specific and quantifiable terms, the level of service that is to be delivered to, and expected by, the application's end users.

Conceptually, SLAs are not new. They have been used for a variety of contracting purposes, including the outsourcing of an entire business function to a third party (e.g., payroll), the outsourcing of a data center's operations, or the provision of internal IS support services for a particular business application (e.g., order processing.)

The advent of client/server and distributed computing, however, increases the importance of using SLAs and affects the content of the agreement itself. In the client/server or distributed processing environment, many designs and configuration alternatives are available that affect a given system's response time, availability, development cost, and ongoing operational costs. An SLA clarifies the business objectives and constraints for an application system and forms the basis for both application design and system configuration choices.

In the distributed and client/server environment, it is not uncommon to find requirements in an SLA that can only be supported by being designed into the application or application technical architecture. For example, the response time reporting requirements for a graphical client/server application may not be able to be fulfilled by the primitive application monitoring capabilities of operating environments such as Microsoft Windows and OS/2. In this case, it may be necessary to design into the application the ability to collect and report statistics on end-user response times or productivity.

For this reason, a tentative SLA should be drafted during the systems design phase of an applications development effort as part of documenting the users' complete requirements.

The Appendix at the end of this chapter is a complete example of an SLA for the provision of a particular computer application—in this case, the revenue accounting (RA) application from the UniversalAir Airlines case example.

This SLA demonstrated what a sample SLA could look like for a distributed environment. The example presented is not complete in all details but provides an understanding of the types of information contained in, and requirements addressed by, an SLA in the distributed environment. (Note: Commentary on the importance and type of information to be included in a particular section of the SLA appears in the Appendix as italicized type.)

SYSTEMS MANAGEMENT

Systems management involves all of the activities and procedures required to keep a client/server system up and running on a day-to-day basis. In the mainframe environment, these are the tasks performed by the folks in the machine room who constantly watch, monitor, and react to problems with the host or network.

Keeping a mission-critical client/server application system available and under control and providing a high level of service to the end user are more complex and difficult tasks than they are in a mainframe environment. Yet even this basic realization is somewhat new.

When client/server computing first emerged as an alternative, an organization often chose the UNIX operating system to implement these systems. The early conventional wisdom was that it would be cheaper and easier to manage an all-UNIX client/server system than the existing MVS environment because UNIX was alleged to be easier to administer than MVS and because a single operating system could be used on both workstations and servers.

Early client/server adopters even tried to use these potential savings in operational costs and manpower as justification for client/server downsizing initiatives. In hindsight, few organizations ever realized a reduction in systems management costs, and most saw costs rise and service levels deteriorate.

Why didn't these organizations realize operational cost benefits? In part, because the problem of managing a client/server system is inherently more complex and the marketplace for tools, systems software, and skilled personnel is less mature. The other aspect of this is that people coming from an MVS environment just expected that operations support would be a part of the solution. They did not realize that there was a problem, and so did not think about the cost ahead of time.

When considering setting up a client/server systems management capability, it is vitally important that the effort start with, and be driven by, the definition of SLAs. These agreements represent specific commitments to the user community with regard to overall systems performance, reliability, and availability. These commitments form the primary requirements and justification for expenses associated with creating a systems management capability.

This section provides a sampling of the types of issues, decisions, and complexity drivers that make systems management so challenging in a client/server environment.

Geographic Distribution Impact

Pushing systems software, applications, and data out to client workstations and away from a central control point presents many challenges. These challenges are further compounded when multiple locations, cities, or even countries are added to the management puzzle.

The traditional mainframe environment serviced remote locations relatively easily. The major challenge was monitoring the network links between locations. Prior to client/server, remote locations typically had little more than dumb 3270 terminals, and systems-related changes at remote locations were rare. Remote client/server locations connected by WANs add new problems and requirements for the operations architecture as well as constraints on viable client/server configurations.

WAN communication costs are vastly more expensive and less reliable than the LAN costs used within a single physical location. Therefore, client/server configurations that are network intensive, such as the diskless workstation, are more costly to operate across a WAN environment.

As remote locations become more decentralized and autonomous in capability, they present more difficult challenges for the operations architecture. Thus, another key decision task for the information systems organization is to determine optimal configurations of remote locations, balancing autonomy and capability with operational simplicity and a reliance on central control.

The most centralized approach would be to place only diskless or dataless workstations at remote locations. This minimizes the operational complexity associated with remote locations by reducing or eliminating the need for a software and data distribution architecture. But, the high WAN communications costs and/or the associated performance degradation may limit the attractiveness of this option. Many organizations, however, do use this model for supporting locations with only a few users where the costs of placing and administering server machines on site are not warranted.

Because of the high WAN communications costs, most organizations deploying client/server technology across geographically distributed locations are placing servers as well as client workstations at remote locations. By placing servers at remote locations, an organization can substantially reduce network traffic because program executables, systems software, applications, and data can be stored locally. This also tends to map to the business topography as well. Often, a particular business location has data requirements or local data not needed by others in the organization. It makes sense to store that information locally rather than remotely at a shared central location.

Although placing servers at remote locations has clear benefits, these remote servers introduce a host of operational issues. For example, will a local support staff be needed to maintain these servers and associated LAN configurations, or can they be managed effectively from a central site? This is a key decision that has a substantial impact on the complexity of the operations architecture required.

Multivendor Impact

In the traditional mainframe environment, most of the components including hardware, systems software, and networking were supplied by a limited number of vendors. For example, in the IBM mainframe environment, the hardware, operating system, online monitor, database management system (DBMS), even the networking hardware and software, were typically sourced from one vendor. A key point is that the same single vendor also supplied software and tools needed to manage the environment. By using a standardized environment from one vendor, it was relatively easy for the vendor to supply well-integrated management capabilities because they also supplied most, if not all, of the other system components.

In the client/server world, no single dominant vendor supplies market-leading solutions for all the pieces of a client/server solution. The market is much more fragmented: Vendor A is the leader in workstations, vendor B in workstation operating systems, vendor C in servers, vendor D in database management software, and so on. Therefore, most organizations adopting this technology find themselves thrust into an unfamiliar, multivendor environment. They may buy workstations from one or more vendors and servers from yet another. Many cases today require the integration of technologies and products from 30 or more vendors.

It is usually possible, because of the many actual and de facto standards throughout the industry, to "plug and play" these multivendor solutions together. However, the operations architecture or systems management side of things may be the missing picture puzzle piece. Because of the vast numbers of combinations of different vendor products, it is difficult for vendors of systems management solutions to account for and effectively support more than a few vendor combinations. Products and standards are only recently coming on the market that attempt to simplify this multivendor problem.

Standards are ultimately the answer to the multivendor systems management problem, much as they have been the facilitating factor in enabling multivendor execution architectures. However, the evolution of standards is a slow process. In the interim, support organizations face the difficult challenge of assembling various vendor systems management components into an overall integrated operations architecture.

Complexity and the Role of the Workstation

In a traditional mainframe environment, all computing resources except for terminals and lines typically reside in a single physical location: the glass house. This is a controlled environment to which only authorized and systems knowledgeable personnel have access.

In the glass house are all the organization's computing resources: mainframe processor(s), operating systems, systems software, applications, information. End users have access only to those applications and data that the operations organization has deliberately put into production.

By contrast, client/server application systems move computing capability, applications, and even information away from this centrally controlled point. The more distributed these resources become, the greater the challenge to manage them effectively and, harder yet, to implement a controlled change to the computing environment, such as rolling out a new release of an application system. In fact, the more one can make a client/server system look like the more familiar centralized model, the easier it will be for the system to be managed by a traditional systems management organization.

Because the degree of centralization versus decentralization greatly affects the operational complexity of the system, a key decision for the IS organization is to determine what the role of the client workstation will be. Operational complexity goes up exponentially as the client machines become more full-functioned and autonomous computing resources. Three client workstation variations that trade capability for operational simplicity are diskless, dataless, and full-function workstations.

Diskless Workstations A diskless workstation, as the name implies, is a workstation without a hard disk. The workstation is complete in other aspects and has both a central processing unit and random access memory (RAM.) Because the diskless workstation cannot store anything locally, it relies on a server or servers somewhere on the network (potentially in the existing glass house) from which to load the operating system and application from across the network directly into memory.

The diskless workstation simplifies many operational issues because, in a manner similar to the mainframe model, a single copy of the operating system, systems software, and applications can be maintained in a central controlled place and essentially downloaded at run time to workstations on the network. Because the workstations have no capability to permanently store information, there is no opportunity for multiple versions of systems software and applications to permeate the network of workstations.

An obvious drawback of the diskless workstation alternative is that it becomes absolutely dependent on the availability of the network; these devices also generate a very high amount of network traffic. If the network or a segment should become unavailable, all diskless workstation users are impacted immediately and completely. Because the workstation typically has limited RAM resources, it is constantly paging operating system and application frames across the network. If the network is down, the machines cannot resolve page faults and freeze up. This is typically followed by a spike in activity on the voice/telephone network, as users call to "express their concern" to operations. This degree of network dependence and bandwidth requirement is not appropriate for all client/server applications.

A common variation of the diskless workstation is the X-Terminal. An X-Terminal conceptually fits somewhere between a diskless workstation and a "dumb" terminal. The X-Terminal cannot execute application programs locally but, rather, functions as a windowed display device for programs running on a server. Much of the success of X-Terminals with larger accounts has been because they are easier to manage and administer than a network of more capable and autonomous workstations.

The network computer is a recently introduced computing device with one primary focus: to reduce the cost of computing. Network computers use a "thin client" model usually centered around HTML and Java with no local storage or expansion slots. Network computers download and run applications and systems software from a centrally maintained server, thus simplifying administration of large networks. Although the devices themselves are cheaper than current PCs, the real opportunity for cost savings from network computers comes from lower network administration costs (data maintenance, user authentication, and software upgrades.)

Dataless Workstations In contrast to a diskless workstation, a dataless workstation includes a hard disk drive and, thus, can store information and programs locally. As the name implies, the intent of a dataless workstation is to store only executable code and not more volatile application data.

The dataless workstation reduces the network demands of the diskless workstation by storing a copy of the operating system and, possibly, application programs locally on the workstation's hard drive. Although this form of client machine is more capable, it introduces new operations architecture and administrative challenges—most notably, the issue of software distribution.

For example, when the operating system or some systems software component is to be upgraded, the new executable cannot simply be loaded on one or a few machines inside the glass house. Instead, it must be loaded on to all of the client machines in the network—potentially thousands of machines. The problem is made worse when application programs are also stored locally because application programs tend to have more frequent revision and release cycles than do systems software components.

The dataless workstation configuration is the most commonly seen client/server configuration in most organizations that have built the requisite networking infrastructure.

Full-Function Workstations The distinguishing characteristic of full-function workstations as clients is that they can operate independently of the network for the processing of at least some business functions. This requires that systems software and applications be stored on the local disk but also indicates the capacity to store data locally as well. Whereas the dataless workstation is shut off from data resources while the network is unavailable, the full-function workstation can continue to operate by reading and writing data to and from the local disk drive.

The full-function workstation configuration represents the least centralized or most distributed version of client/server computing and also the most difficult to manage and administer. The problem is that data, unlike systems software or application programs, is usually highly volatile, and the updates need to be shared with other users on the network. This leads to the complex operations architecture issues of data distribution, replication, and synchronization.

Human Resources Impact

An additional factor beyond just the technological issues of client/server systems management is the human resources side of the equation. Developing an operations architecture and managing the ongoing environment requires new and enhanced skill sets to deal with new products, new vendors, and new types of problems.

All this change can be threatening to existing systems management people with years of experience with centralized mainframe operations and systems management tools and techniques. Many existing mainframe systems personnel may fear that their job security is in jeopardy because their years of experience with particular products and technologies have become less important. A younger person fresh out of school may be able to adapt to a client/server environment more readily than a person with years of experience.

Fortunately for the experienced staff, there are few people in the marketplace with skills in client/server systems management and experience. In fact, the lack of skilled people encourages management to invest in the retraining of the current systems management personnel. Their skills, knowledge, and experience are still relevant in the client/server world but need to be developed and adapted to deal with a new problem.

The challenges and investments associated with retraining existing personnel are often underestimated. The skills and the specific product knowledge that have been accumulated over the years must now be relearned in a relatively short period of time—while still managing the existing system as well.

In addition to the new skills, systems management personnel often have to learn to work as a multifunction team. Most traditional support organizations are structured functionally around groupings such as database, networking, and user administration. Because client/server computing cuts across many of the old, well-defined functional boundaries, it requires personnel to work closely together to identify, isolate, and resolve problems. Without this team thinking, staff may waste significant amounts of time denying fault and blaming others, instead of solving problems.

A final possibility is the use of contractors or consultants to assist the organization during the transition period when their own staff are learning new skills and becoming comfortable with the products. This approach can be successful provided it is clear up front that the ultimate objective is to transfer the knowledge from the contractors or consultants to the existing staff. If this is not the case, it can become all too easy to become dependent on the outside help rather than effectively bringing those skills in house.

Most organizations underestimate the impact on systems management of introducing client/server. It is vitally important to understand up front the true costs of client/server computing to judge if it is the appropriate technology for a particular business solution. As is true in systems development, knowing about a problem or issue well in advance increases the solution alternatives and reduces the costs and disruptions.

CONCLUSION

Client/server and distributed technologies and architectures provide a wealth of new capabilities and advantages for those that adopt them. Processes happen more quickly, information is close to those who use it, and the individual is empowered with many new and useful tools. Management of the client/server environment, however, is different and more complex than management of centralized computing technologies. As the power and flexibility of the system has changed and increased, so too has the effort required to manage it.

The software marketplace now sees this opportunity and many competitors have put forth at least partial solutions in the past year or two. The future looks promising, but narrow standards initiatives or products like POSIX, DME, or Microsoft's Systems Management Server will not completely eliminate the problem any time soon.

The complexity and operations challenge have actually been a hindrance to the adoption of client/server computing despite its demonstrable potential for business benefits. But this does not have to be the case. The client/server environment is manageable, but only with adequate planning and resources and with an upfront understanding of the issues and inherent risks. The Appendix that follows this chapter can help readers manage this risk during the creation of service-level agreements.

APPENDIX
SAMPLE SERVICE-LEVEL AGREEMENT

SERVICE-LEVEL AGREEMENT

[Commentary: The title page defines the parties to the SLA. Once it is agreed to, the SLA is signed by the authorized representatives of both organizations. The "effective date" and "expiration date" define the period over which the SLA is in effect. Any reasonable time may be used. A shorter time frame provides both parties the opportunity to renegotiate terms and conditions as experience is gained with the system. A longer time frame reduces the administrative burden of negotiating agreements and enables more meaningful long-range service planning.]

between

Provider: UniversalAir Information Technology Organization (ITO)

..../...../.....
ITO Data Center   Date

Receiver: UniversalAir Finance Organization (UAFO)

..../...../.....
VP-UAFO   Date

For the provision of: Revenue Accounting (RA) application

Effective Date: 9/1/97   Expiration Date: 9/1/99

1. BUSINESS OBJECTIVES AND SCOPE

[Commentary: This section provides a high-level summary of the business objectives the computer system is designed to address and the objectives of the SLA document itself. The scope of service to be provided should include a description of the scope of the application system functions covered as well as the nature of service and systems management tasks to be included. A detailed discussion of included scope is not necessary here because the remainder of the SLA defines the scope of service in much greater detail. Important exclusions from scope may also be listed here.]

The main objective of Revenue Accounting (RA) computer system is to support the processing of some 30,000 tickets per day, including such functions as revenue recognition, refunds, and interairline payables. The variety of product configurations and options required to satisfy our diverse end-user population has necessitated the development of an RA application incorporating advanced intelligent workstations and client/

server computing. In addition, the geographic decentralization of our finance organization requires that application and data components be distributed among multiple locations.

The objectives of this document are to:

- Define a framework for providing efficient high-quality Application Support services to the UniversalAir Finance Organization (FO.)
- Provide a basis and justification for associated ITO hardware and systems software configuration expenditures.

The SLA will achieve this objective by:

- Outlining the formal interface between ITO and FO.
- Describing the service items and service levels agreed between ITO and FO.
- Outlining rules, procedures, and responsibilities for both ITO and FO.
- Defining a reporting structure for reviewing the actual service levels achieved by ITO against specified targets.
- Defining a process that allows changes and continuous improvements to service levels and the overall scope of service to be made in a controlled and structured manner.

The scope of the SLA covers the RA computer application as defined in the RA project definition document. Services to be provided under this agreement include:

- Provision and maintenance of all necessary computer and communications hardware equipment to FO, including intelligent workstations, application and database servers, local and wide area networks, and high- and low-speed printers.
- Provision and maintenance of all necessary systems software, including workstation and server operating systems, windowing systems, relational DBMSs, and communications middleware.
- Ensuring that all necessary components are operational and available during agreed to time schedules as put forth in this document.

Application maintenance is not within the scope of this agreement. The FO is responsible for the design, development, and testing of all maintenance changes and enhancements to the RA system. ITO is responsible for the rollout and installation of fully tested RA versions.

Changes to interfacing applications as a result of the implementation of RA or future RA releases are outside the scope of this agreement, although they must be formally communicated to ITO.

2. POLICIES

[Commentary: This section describes the policies by which the service provider conducts business. Policies are, in effect, applicable to all SLAs entered into by the service provider organization. This section may also include the service provider's standard procedures for handling and escalating incidents or processing requests for configuration changes or application version changes.]

The policies governing the provision of services under this agreement are as follows:

- Services will be delivered based on the service targets documented in this agreement.
- Actual level of service will be monitored, reported, and evaluated against the Service-Level Agreement.
- ITO is only responsible for requests that are logged through the Service Control Center.
- ITO Service Control Center will provide a single point of contact for users.

3. CHANGES TO THIS DOCUMENT

This SLA is jointly owned by the UniversalAir ITO and the UniversalAir Customer Care Organization (FO.) This document may not be altered without the consent of both parties. When agreed upon, changes to the document will be made by ITO.

Review Meetings

Review meetings shall take place the first Monday morning of every month. At least one representative from ITO and one representative from FO shall attend. The objectives of these meetings are to:

- Resolve any outstanding issues and initiate any follow-up actions.
- Update the SLA to reflect any changes in the environment.

Each representative is responsible for communicating the outcome of these meetings to his or her respective group.

4. HARDWARE AND SOFTWARE SUMMARY

[Commentary: Optionally, some service provider organizations will specify the actual hardware and system resources to be used. Specifying the actual inventory of components to be used may clarify the scope of service and reduce misunderstandings.

Other service provider organizations prefer not to disclose specific components, thus allowing for flexibility in configuring the system to meet the customer's requirements at the least cost. In general, the language used in an SLA should be meaningful to the business users rather than characterized by technology jargon and vendor specifics. This helps the user group to focus on actual business requirements rather than dictating technology components.]

Client Workstations: 75
Compaq Pentium PCs
VGA Color
MS Mouse
12 MB RAM
120 MB internal SCSI
MS-DOS 6.0
MS-Windows for Workgroups 3.11

Servers: 3 (dedicated to RA)
HP 887
256 MB RAM
6x1.2 GB DASD
NT Server
Sybase System 10

Mainframe:1 (shared with other departments)
IBM 3090-200
MVS
CICS
DB2

5. SERVICE TYPES

5.1. Scheduled Availability

[Commentary: The SLA must state the hours during which the users need to be at the system. For some applications, this may simply be during the normal working hours of 8:00 A.M. to 5:00 P.M., Monday through Friday. Other applications may be required to be online for a greater portion of the week. Some applications may even be required 7 days a week, 24 hours per day (7 x 24.)

Documenting the scheduled availability times allows the systems management organization to plan system downtime for tasks such as maintenance or system backups, during periods when the users do not need access to the application.

Special operational issues emerge as the scheduled availability approaches the 7×24 level. Many operating systems and DBMS products require some amount of downtime to effect maintenance changes, tuning changes, or upgrades to new release levels. The costs and constraints on suitable products for supporting a 7×24 schedule availability can be considerable. A 6×24 arrangement, or even an eight-hour/week scheduled maintenance window can significantly simplify these issues.

Another issue with high availability is how and when to process batch work loads and backup critical databases. Some operating system and DBMS combinations can accommodate concurrent online and batch processing (though often at degraded performance) or allow database backups to be made while the DBMS remains online while others cannot. These requirements and product constraints must be taken into consideration when determining the scheduled availability window.]

Service Description Availability here is defined to mean that a user can access and execute any online application function from an available intelligent workstation. This definition therefore allows for the failure of the user's primary intelligent workstation providing a "hot" spare is available and accessible.

Availability must be measured on an individual user basis to calculate total RA availability. As a result of measuring difficulties with this approach, unscheduled outages will be approximated by measuring dropped connections to the ticket database on a per-user basis. Additional outage time will be tracked and tabulated via calls to the ITO Service Control Center help desk.

Provider Responsibilities All RA online functions are required to be available during the following periods:
Monday–Saturday 7:30A.M.–8:00 P.M.

Receiver Responsibilities There may be a requirement for the service to support overtime requirements after 8:00 P.M. and during weekends under certain circumstances. An extension to the above hours can be accommodated, if required, provided sufficient notice is given to ITO.

Shared Responsibilities Neither the provider nor the receiver shall remove a working client workstation or server from the network during the availability period outlined above.

5.2 Reliability

[Commentary: Reliability is the percentage of time the application is actually available during the scheduled time period. For example, if an application is scheduled to be available 40 hours per week, a 99.0% per week reliability requirement would mean that total unscheduled system outages cannot exceed 24 minutes in a given week. "Unscheduled system outages" includes downtime as a result of such things as hardware failure, disk failure, operating system failure, network failure, and workstation failure.

In a client/server configuration, it is very important to define in the SLA how reliability will be measured. In a centralized host environment, availability is typically the same for all users: If the host or some component of the host is down, no one has access to the system. These statistics are easily gathered through such facilities as IBM's SMF. The distributed environment complicates the calculation of availability due to the large number of processors and network links. One server failure may affect some, all, or no end users. The failure of a single workstation only affects one user.

The ideal way to track reliability is at the user's workstation. Few workstation operating systems, however, have facilities or tools for gathering and reporting these statistics. Some projects have remedied this shortcoming by building reliability statistics gathering into the application programs themselves.]

Service Description Reliability is calculated as follows:

$$\text{Total Availability} = \frac{\left(\begin{array}{c}\text{scheduled availability}\\ \times\ \#\ \text{of scheduled users}\end{array}\right) - \left(\begin{array}{c}\text{unscheduled outage}\\ \times\ \#\ \text{of affected users}\end{array}\right)}{(\text{scheduled availability} \times \#\ \text{of scheduled users}) \times 100}$$

This formula takes into account that the loss of one client workstation or group of workstations is not as severe as an outage that affects all RA users. Therefore, it penalizes ITO in proportion to the degradation in customer service caused.

Reliability must be measured on an individual user basis to calculate total RA availability. Because of measuring difficulties with this approach, unscheduled outages will be approximated by measuring dropped connections to the ticket database on a per-user basis. Additional outage time will be tracked and tabulated via calls to the ITO Service Control Center help desk.

Provider Responsibilities Because of the critical nature of the RA application, reliability must be at least 99.5% per month for the RA user group as a whole.

Receiver Responsibilities The receiver must contact the ITO Service Control Center help desk as soon it is determined that he or she has lost access to the RA application.

¶ 5.2. RELIABILITY

5.3. Ticket Database Server Failure

Service Description The Ticket Database Server is the server that maintains the local copy of the ticket information. A database server failure is considered to be one in which all RA users at a given distributed location are affected.

Provider Responsibilities Because of the severity of this situation and the unfeasibility of a suitable contingency strategy, a single failure at this level may not exceed 5 minutes as measured from the time the failure is detected by the fault management system until service is restored.

5.4. User Workstation Failure

Service Description A workstation has failed when a user cannot use any of the application capability from that device (e.g., RA or Office Automation applications.)

Provider Responsibilities If the Service Control Center help desk determines that the user's workstation is the point of failure, the user will be informed of the location of the nearest available workstation by the help desk and a replacement workstation will be installed and tested within one hour. If the user elects to use the nearest available workstation, the user must be able to resume work by logging in using the normal log-in procedure.

Receiver Responsibilities It must be appreciated that the 99.5% per month availability/reliability figure can only be effected if all changes to the user environment occur with the consent of ITO. ITO cannot accept liability for user workstation downtime caused by factors outside its control (e.g., users installing personal software.)

684

5.5. Performance

[Commentary: Most SLAs for the host-based environment typically measure performance in terms of "screen exchange" response time. A screen exchange is defined as the time from when the user hits "enter" or a PF key until the next screen is displayed on the terminal. Software is available that accurately measures a terminal's end-to-end response time, thus including both host processing time and network time. A consistent screen exchange response time could be expected even for queries that return "pages" of information, because the user would be sent the data one page at a time.

In the distributed environment, these metrics often do not apply and certainly are more difficult to record and report on. A well-designed graphical user interface (GUI) provides instant feedback to the user, and for many user operations this is feasible and expected. Some operations, however, require requests for services from one or more servers across the local or even wide area network. Given current technology, it is probably unreasonable to expect instantaneous response for these requests. Therefore, in the client/server environment, the response time for the user is highly variable and dependent on the nature of the user's task and where the required resources are located in the distributed environment.

There are several options for overcoming the difficulties of specifying performance targets in a distributed client/server environment, including:

- Set a high threshold. *State that the user will receive response time from the application in less than 10 seconds regardless of the operation. The threshold in this case must be set fairly high to accommodate user actions that may result in complex transactions that will be served by multiple and remote processing and data resources. This approach has the appeal of simplicity but may not work well with the application users because it does not clearly state how long it will take for them to complete a meaningful task (such as finding, updating, and saving an existing customer order.)*

- Structure application to provide consistent response. *Many users of host-based systems find consistent response times reassuring (e.g., screen exchanges always take 2 seconds.) It is possible to structure even a graphical client/server application to behave in this manner, but it will likely result in unnatural breakdowns of application processing (to fit everything into 2-second "chunks") and a less responsive user interface.*

- Lower-level detail in SLA. *Instead of stating that "all user actions will result in subsecond response time," identify meaningful user actions and provide a performance target for each. For example, the SLA may then state that returning product information given a valid product number will take less than 1 second, or returning all customers for a given ZIP (post) code will take less than 15 seconds. This approach, although more difficult to implement, has the benefit of providing more meaningful performance metrics to the end users, the applications developers, and the service/ systems management organization. A useful simplification is to group user operations that consume similar computing resources into performance classes and assign performance targets for each class.*

- Higher-level SLA. *An opposite tack is to disregard individual user action response time and instead focus the SLA at the end-to-end business function being performed by the user. For example, an SLA can be constructed stating that a user will be able to enter a customer phone order in less than 2 minutes, as measured from the time the call is answered until the order confirmation number is returned. This approach simplifies tracking response times, provides more flexibility to the applications developers and systems management personnel, and focuses on what really counts—the timely completion of the business function. However, in this approach the agreement must stipulate how much of the 2 minutes is to be allocated to the user for tasks such as entering information and how much is to be allocated for computer processing. In addition, many business functions are too variable in the amount of "user time" required to complete a transaction to use this approach.*

- Provide performance indication within the application's user interface. *Another variation is to provide indications to the user how long a response to expect for a given user action and tie the SLA to these. For example, a gray button may represent instantaneous response, a green button subsecond, and a red button an operation that will take the computer up to 10 seconds to complete. This approach, only applicable when a GUI is used, helps communicate to users and appropriately set their expectations about response time. The performance targets in the SLA can then be tied directly to the control type (or color.) The application's user interface would have to be designed with this approach in mind.*

Many of these approaches to specifying performance targets require the application program to be able to record and associate system responses with specific user actions. This requires applications or application architectures to be developed with the appropriate hooks or exits.]

Service Description Response times are quoted as both an average and a maximum time within which 95% of transactions should occur. For RA, the online dialogues have been split into four classes:

1. Retrieval of a specific item of information (e.g., a ticket or sales record.)
2. Retrieval of a list of items (e.g., tickets, pricing rules, or refunds.)
3. Saving a new or changed item of reference information (e.g., ticket or sales order.)
4. Saving a new or changed business transaction (e.g., a refund.)

Provider Responsibilities The required application response times for all users averaged over 1 day are:

Log-in through RA main window	≤ 10 sec. average
	≤ 15 sec. 95%
Class 1 dialogues	≤ 2.5 sec. average
Ticket given ticket no.	≤ 1.0 sec.
Account given account no.	≤ 1.0 sec.
Coupon given coupon no.	≤ 1.0 sec.
	≤ 4.0 sec. 95%
Class 2 dialogues (<200 items retrieved)	≤ 2.5 sec. average
	≤ 5.0 sec. 95%
Class 3 dialogues	≤ 1.5 sec. average
	≤ 3.0 sec. 95%
Class 4 dialogues	≤ 3 sec. average
	≤ 5.0 sec. 95%

Subsecond response will be expected for user actions and window manipulations that do not involve saving or requesting information (opening a blank audit window, switching between two windows.)

A target service level is not provided for the RA ad hoc query window. Because of the flexibility of this dialogue and the user's ability to submit requests that may return very large information sets, a performance target cannot be adequately determined at this time.

5.6. Output Handling

[Commentary: This section discusses any requirements and targets for the production of output, including such things as printing, microfiche, and removable magnetic or optical storage. The stringency of the users' output requirements will dictate the location, number, and type of output devices required.]

Service Description Customer service representatives must have access to local letter quality (laser) printers for the printing of correspondence and simple reports.

Provider Responsibilities Less than 1% of user print jobs can result in failure. In the event of a print failure, the user must be able to successfully initiate printing within 15 minutes.

5.7. Security Management

[Commentary: This section defines who is responsible for security administration tasks, how these services are requested, and the responsiveness of the service provider.

It is important to clarify the boundary in responsibility for security management. Typically, the service management organization is responsible only for ensuring that security policy is correctly executed. It is the responsibility of the user organization to ensure that requests for changes in security privileges are timely, necessary, and prudent (such as adding new users or changing authorization limits for users.)

In addition, depending on configuration choices, the application and data security risks may be different from those of a centralized host-based system. For example, data placed on a local workstation hard drive is inherently less secure than data stored on a server or host in the "glass house" where physical security measures are used. It may be important in the SLA to categorize data and application resources depending on their sensitivity. For example, if a stock brokerage client's list is highly confidential, placing this data on the workstation where it could be physically removed is not appropriate. However, reference data like the "country codes table" is likely to require less security precaution and can therefore be placed accordingly within the distributed architecture.

Another security concern within the distributed environment is the LAN itself. LAN protocols such as TCP/ IP and SPX are not high-security implementations and devices can be attached to the network to "read packets." Although it is not a concern to most organizations, some user organizations with highly proprietary or confidential data may require data encryption capabilities. As a result of the extra costs, processing, and network burdens that such security measures often require, the service provision organization needs to be aware of these requirements.]

Service Description The RA application and all associated data assets will be protected in accordance with the UniversalAir corporate security policy with the following exceptions:

- User profile information may be stored on a local medium (PC hard drives.)
- The RA codes table may be stored on a server not under physical security (such as a server in the office environment at remote locations.)

In accordance with the UniversalAir security policy, access to all RA application functions and data assets will be controlled via unique user IDs and passwords.

The ITO security facilities must ensure that only authorized users may access secured resources in an allowable way.

Provider Responsibilities The ITO Service Control Center will be responsible for all user security administration including adding and deleting user accounts, changing user privileges, and changing application and data security options.

Changes will be effected by the start of the next business day for requests received before 3:00 P.M. the day before.

Receiver Responsibilities It is the responsibility of FO management to ensure that authorizations are properly documented and requested. It is imperative that FO management carefully scrutinize all requests for security access for FO employees to ensure that the requested privileges are necessary and prudent. Equally as important, FO management must notify ITO immediately if an employee's security access is to be revoked or changed.

To help control security management requests, only an FO department head or higher may request changes. All requests for security management services must be logged with the help desk in writing.

5.9. Schedule Execution

[Commentary: This section discusses any requirements and targets for the production of output including such things as printing, microfiche, and removable magnetic or optical storage. The stringency of the users' output requirements dictate the location, number, and type of output devices required.]

Service Description Schedule execution refers to the scheduling and executing of the daily, weekly, and monthly batch runs for the RA application.

Provider Responsibilities The scheduling of the various batch runs are as follows:

- All daily batch runs will be completed successfully by 8:00 A.M. of the following business day 95% of the time as measured per month (i.e., 1 exception/month.)
- All weekly batch runs will be completed by 8:00 A.M. of the first

business day of the following week 96% of the time as measured per year (i.e., 50 out of 52 weeks.)

- All monthly batch runs will be completed by 8:00 A.M. of the third business day following the end of the month 90% of the time as measured per year (i.e., 11 out of 12 months.)

5.10. Incident Management

[Commentary: This section describes how problems will be reported, classified, and prioritized. Service levels for responding to incidents are also included. The SLA may include a description of the problem management process and escalation procedures.]

Service Description An incident is any unanticipated or unplanned event that deviates from standard activity or expectations. Incident management refers to the correction of incidents via calls to the ITO Service Control Center help desk.

Provider Responsibilities All incidents are to be reported to the Service Control Center Help Desk where they will be assigned a severity. Each severity has a corresponding initial response time, update time, and target resolution time.

It is anticipated that all calls will be answered within one minute in 95% of cases. On receipt of an incident the help desk will assess its impact and assign a category accordingly:

- A: Entire RA system is down or batch schedule halted.
- B: Major breakdown of part of the system (>100 users affected.)
- C: Significant impact on part of system (~40 users affected.)
- D: Limited impact on part of system (~10 users affected.)
- E: Single user affected.
- F: Minor complaints.
- G: Advice.
- Z: Problem can be cleared at time of logging.

Incidents will be prioritized based on these categories. The following are the target times for responses to the specified categories of incidents raised by users:

Incident Category	Average	Max. (90%)
Category A		
First feedback	5 min.	10 min.

Incident Category	Average	Max. (90%)
Second feedback	20 min.	30 min.
Feedback frequency	30 min.	1 hr.
Category B		
First feedback	20 min.	30 min.
Second feedback	1 hr.	2 hrs.
Feedback frequency	30 min.	1 hr.
Category C, D, E		
First feedback	30 min.	45 min.
Second feedback	1 hr.	2 hrs.
Feedback frequency	1 hr.	2 hrs.
Category F and G		
First feedback	4 hrs.	8 hrs.
Second feedback	1 day	2 days
Feedback frequency	1 day	2 days
Category Z	Not applicable	

The second feedback interval is measured from the time of the first feedback until the second contact has been made.

Receiver Responsibilities The receiver should contact the ITO Service Control Center help desk as soon it is determined that an incident has occurred.

5.11. Contingency/Backup

[Commentary: In a distributed environment, it is important to clarify who will be responsible for backing up and restoring data at "remote" locations. Some organizations require users to perform backups; some staff remote locations with an operations person; still others perform systems management tasks remotely via network connections.

This specification of exactly how these tasks will be accomplished is not necessary within the SLA. The roles and responsibilities of both parties and the expectations of service, however, should be detailed.

It is also important in this section to define the level of the backup being taken. Backups, for instance, can be done on an "image" level or an application data level. Defining this level appropriately ensures that proper data is being backed up in the event of potential failure.]

Service Description Two kinds of archiving will be performed on RA applications and data.

- Daily incremental backups.
- Weekly full system archives, run each Friday.

When it has been determined by the ITO Service Control Center help desk that a restoration of applications and data is necessary, restoration processes will be executed.

Provider Responsibilities ITO is responsible for performing all backup and restoration operations without assistance from any RA personnel. Data stored at remote sites will be backed up or restored via telecommunications links.

The daily incremental backup tapes will be stored in the ITO data center's fireproof safe. The weekly tapes will be transported to and stored in ITO's off-site storage facility. Database logs are written to tape each evening and stored off site as well. These can be used in conjunction with the backup tapes to rebuild the database in the event of any loss.

5.1 2. Business Recovery

[Commentary: The business recovery strategy addresses how quickly service must be restored after a disaster such as flood or fire destroys a data center or user location. In a centralized environment, the definition of a disaster is relatively simple. In the distributed environment, the agreement may be more complex to account for the unlikelihood that all distributed computing resources would be affected by a single disaster.]

Service Description Business recovery involves restoring the RA system for use in the event of a catastrophic loss of the ITO data center (e.g., flood, fire, or tornado.) The recovery plans involve the data center facility itself, as well as the telecommunications links to this facility. Recovery of distributed sites (i.e., those not located physically with the data center) are excluded from the scope of this agreement.

Provider Responsibilities In the unlikely event of a catastrophic loss of the ITO data center, it is imperative that the RA system be operational by 8:00 A.M. on the first business day following such a disaster. All data must be restored and made current to within 24 hours of the disaster. It must be possible at least to manually reenter all orders taken on the actual day of the disaster.

In the unlikely event of a catastrophic loss of any one RA user building (any of the three primary RA user locations), the remaining RA locations must be able to handle orders by 8:00 A.M. on the first business day following such a disaster.

Receiver Responsibilities It is the responsibility of each user location to formulate its own business recovery plans in the event of an on-site catastrophic failure. These plans must include recovery schemes for all hardware and software up to and including the gateway at the user location.

Prior to their finalization, these plans must be agreed to by ITO. Each user location will also be responsible for executing these plans as necessary.

Shared Responsibilities Both the provider and receiver shall work together to achieve business recovery in the event it is necessary. The provider and receiver shall each maintain a current contact list with the names and phone numbers of those individuals responsible for achieving business recovery.

5.13. Reporting Procedures

[Commentary: This section describes how the service provider will report actual service levels versus plan to the end-user organization. Items to be covered include report frequency, contents, and distribution.]

Service Description This section outlines the reporting procedures that are used by the ITO Service Management organization. Daily and weekly reports (contents listed below) are distributed to senior members of ITO and FO user management.

Provider Responsibilities The following reports will be produced as stated and distributed by 8:00 A.M.on the first business day following the reporting period:

- Daily report contents:
  - Planned service availability.
  - Actual service availability.
  - Time of failure.
  - Duration of failure.
  - User Groups affected by failure.
  - Reasons for failure (if available.)
  - Total downtime.
  - Categorized help desk incidents.

- — Categorized help desk incidents closed.
- — Categorized help desk incidents outstanding.
- — Description of major incidents.
- Weekly report contents:
  - — Average service availability (rollup of daily figures.)
  - — Simple mean time between failure (MTBF.)
  - — Details of failures not discussed in daily reports for week.
  - — Performance response-time statistics.
  - — Output handling exceptions, including items missing postal deadline, deviation of batch reconciliation, printer outages, tape difficulties, and reprocess requests.
  - — Problem management exceptions, including items not meeting feedback criteria, planned versus actual first feedback times, and planned versus actual problem resolution times.

Shared Responsibilities Regular monthly meetings are held between designated officers and supervisors and members of the ITO Service Management team.

5.1 4. Application Versions and Major Enhancements

[Commentary: In the distributed environment, rolling out new versions of applications to a large number of workstations may be very complex and labor intensive, as well as destabilizing to the processing environment. For this reason, the service management organization may wish to limit the number of software releases that a user organization can request in a given period. The service management organization also needs to discuss how quickly the major releases or emergency bug fixes will need to be distributed (e.g., in one evening or through a phased approach.)]

Service Description New application versions and enhancements shall be distributed to each of the user locations and updated according to agreed-on schedules.

Provider Responsibilities ITO is responsible for the successful rollout of new RA application releases. Major releases will be phased out to all sites within a one month period. Bug fixes will be phased out to all of the sites within a one-week period.

Receiver Responsibilities Because of the costs and potential for service disruption this entails, FO will be restricted to no more than one major release and no more than three bug fix releases per 6-month period.

Shared Responsibilities Both the Provider and Receiver shall work together to plan the rollout of new RA application releases. Major releases will be planned no later than 6 months in advance. Bug fixes will be planned on an as-needed basis.

5.1 5. Capacity Planning

[Commentary: Capacity planning in the distributed client/ server environment is notoriously difficult. The most important inputs into any capacity plan are accurate and realistic business volume projections. It is unreasonable to expect an organization's information systems department to be able to generate the business volume projections. The user organizations serviced by the information systems department are best positioned to provide these projections. Some companies apply penalties to user departments that provide inaccurate estimates into this process. If such penalties are to be used, the SLA should specify the details.]

Service Description Capacity Planning is performed to ensure that the users of the RA application have optimal use of the system. Capacity in this instance refers to the capacity of the network, servers, and local databases.

Provider Responsibilities The ITO Capacity Planning team performs capacity planning on a quarterly basis, providing capacity projections for the following four quarters. These capacity projections are used to ensure that adequate processing and service resources to fulfill existing service level agreements are available. Because these estimates will be relied on in the making of significant expenditures, ITO expects a 90% confidence interval to be used and will track and report back FO's estimates versus actuals. (A 90% confidence interval is a predicted low and high value within which the actual value will fall 90% of the time.)

Any change in business conduct that may necessitate the installation of a new processing location or a substantial increase in the number of users (>50) at an existing location should be communicated to ITO as soon as it is known but absolutely no later than 6 months in advance.

Receiver Responsibilities The primary input to the capacity planning process is an accurate projection of business volumes for the quarters being studied. It is the responsibility of FO management to provide accurate estimates of business volumes and end user head count projections on a quarterly basis.

III-14
Costs and Frameworks for Managing the Client/Server Environment

C lient/server environments pose three hurdles to success:

- The development for client/server is more complex than for traditional systems, with steep learning curves and often challenging development problems.
- Getting the technology and new business processes introduced into the business environment presents change management and education issues.
- Just when it seems that the build and rollout problems are under control, one more hurdle appears: managing the environment from a systems standpoint.

This chapter expands on the systems management issue discussed in the previous chapter, with the focus here on the cost perspective. Specifically, this chapter gives a framework for understanding what the costs of systems management are in a client/server environment. Within this framework, we give various estimates of what these costs might be.

The chapter will be of value to anyone who wants to understand what the sources of costs are, and especially those people who need to create a cost accounting approach. In addition, the material may be of value when looking at outsourcing systems management of client/server environments. The framework is applied in an outsourcing example to assess coverage of the environment by the vendors' proposals and as a means to compare costs.

MODE REFRESHER

The Management of Distributed Environment (MODE) framework (discussed in detail in Chapter III-13) is the centerpiece of the discussions that follow. MODE is a comprehensive view of the distributed computing management picture. In its simplest form, MODE provides a mechanism for understanding *what* needs to be done, *why* management tasks need to be performed, and *how* the management of systems is changed with the introduction of a client/server environment. The framework focuses on four main areas: service management, systems management, service planning, and change management.

Service Management

Service management involves three functions:

- Forming liaisons with users, developers/architects, and vendors.
- Monitoring the services that are provided.
- Ensuring that the services are meeting standards as defined in service-level agreements.

The service-level agreement (SLA) is used to clearly articulate and document the level of service the users expect to receive. For example, an SLA for an insurance claims environment might identify the number of claims that would be processed in a workday. SLAs should be used to drive out the requirements for the service organization and the operations architecture, as well as to justify expenditures for tools and infrastructure.

Ultimately, the users of the system define the service offered to the customer base through a service-level agreement. When the service management concept is implemented correctly, users have a single point of contact for all systems-related problems, suggestions, and planning. The service management function in turn navigates and coordinates the needed systems personnel and resources on behalf of the user.

Service management is also the direct interface to the developers/architects and vendors for the distributed system. Each of these groups has requirements for, and introduces changes to, the distributed environment. Thus, service management controls the overall service to the users and handles the relationships with developers/architects and vendors.

Functions within service management are:

- *SLA management.* Involves the creation, management, reporting, and discussion of SLAs with users.
- *OLA management.* Involves the creation, managing, reporting, and discussion of OLAs (operational-level agreements) with domain

suppliers/vendors. These agreements represent contractual agreements to achieve agreed levels of performance in terms of information processing targets. An OLA agreement might identify the expected response time for an application.

- *Help desk.* Provides end users with a single point of contact and controls the resolution of incidents and problems within the client/server environment.
- *Quality management.* Ensures quality in the management of the client/server environment through training, as well as through the design and execution of quality improvement plans.
- *Administration.* Handles the financial accounting and legal aspects of managing a client/server environment.

Systems Management

Systems management involves all functions required for the day-to-day operation of the distributed system, such as event monitoring, failure control, performance monitoring, and tape loading. Regardless of the changes taking place within the distributed environment, systems management activities are ongoing. Functions within systems management are:

- *Production control.* Ensures that production activities are performed and controlled as required and as intended.
- *Monitoring.* Verifies that the system is continually functioning in accordance with defined service levels.
- *Failure control.* Involves the detection and correction of faults within the system, whether they are minor (e.g., a workstation is down) or major (e.g., a disaster has occurred).
- *Security management.* Ensures that the system is accessed only by authorized users and that those users are restricted to authorized resources.

Management of Change

Managing change includes all of the functions necessary for affecting changes to the client/server environment (e.g., software and data distribution, and license management) in a controlled and orderly way. Because of the large number of interrelated hardware and software components in a client/server environment, assessing and controlling the "side effects" of system change is crucial to maintaining acceptable system availability. Functions within managing change are:

- *Controlling.* Monitors change to make sure that change is delivered on-time according to established plans, making adjustments to the plan when unforeseen issues or events arise (i.e., rollout management, change control, asset management).

- *Testing.* Ensures that changes to the client/server environment will achieve the desired result and not produce unwanted side effects.
- *Implementing.* Executes change within the distributed environment with tested components and techniques according to the appropriate plan(s). Implementing includes such activities as initial installation, software and data distribution, and license management.

Service Planning

Service planning encompasses all of the tactical and strategic planning functions that must occur when managing a distributed environment effectively. Service planning for a distributed client/server environment requires an integrated approach. Effective planning for any one component, such as network capacity, cannot be done independent of an understanding of the whole system and how it will be managed. (For example, the chosen software distribution approach may impact the overall network bandwidth required.) Once a change has been planned, the change will be controlled and implemented in detail within either systems management or change management.

Functions within service planning are:

- *Service management planning.* Defines the financial and training plans for the organization.
- *Systems management planning.* Determines the strategies for day-to-day operation of the system.
- *Managing change planning.* Develops the plans for releasing new sites, services, or updates to existing service.
- *MODE strategic planning.* Formulates the long-term strategy for managing the distributed environment, including people, tools, and processes. This planning function also ensures that the management strategy is in line with the enterprise strategy.

MODE AS A COST FRAMEWORK

The at-a-glance matrix in Exhibit III-14-1 summarizes the MODE functions; it is essentially a functional outline of what work must be done when managing a distributed environment. There are many ways to work with this matrix.

One way is to think in terms of organization structure: What functions should report to other functions? What processes and procedures

Service Management	Systems Management	Service Planning	Managing Change
SLA Management SLA Definition SLA Reporting SLA Control SLA Review **OLA Management** OLA Definition OLA Reporting OLA Control OLA Review **Help Desk** Incident Management Problem Management Request Management **Quality Management** Quality Management Training **Administration** Billing & Accounting Contract Management	**Production Control** Production Scheduling Print Management File Transfer & Control System Startup & Shutdown Mass Storage Management Backup/Restore Management Archiving **Monitoring** Event Management Performance Management Physical Site Management **Failure Control** Fault Management Recovery Disaster Recovery Hardware Maintenance **Security Management** Security Management	**Service Management Planning** Service Costing & Pricing Training Planning **Systems Management Planning** Physical Site Management Security Planning Capacity Modeling & Planning Contingency Planning Recovery Planning Disaster Recovery Planning Hardware Maintenance Planning **Managing Change Planning** Rollout Planning Release Planning Procurement Planning **MODE Strategic Planning** MODE Strategic Planning	**Controlling** Change Control Asset Management Rollout Management Release Control Migration Control License Management **Testing** Product Validation Release Testing **Implementing** Procurement Initial Installment System Component Configuration Software & Data Distribution User Administration

Exhibit III-14-1. MODE Cost Accounting Framework

are required to support the work to be done and the reporting relation-ships of the organization?

A second option is to take the functions listed in Exhibit III-14-1 and use them as criteria to evaluate tools and automation approaches to support a MODE implementation.

A third way to use this functional framework, and the focus of this chapter, is to use it as a *cost accounting framework* to define the sources of costs and estimate the costs associated with managing a distributed environment. In addition to determining how to actually execute or per-form the functions, it is necessary to determine the cost for each function. As such, the framework can be thought of as a functional breakdown that, in turn, provides a means to define the costs associated with oper-ating a distributed environment.

For example, one function in MODE is to track SLA agreements. Although there are many subfunctions to this activity, at this level an associated cost for performing this function can be assessed. The question then becomes how costs are determined and best used to manage a dis-tributed environment.

Determining the Costs of Managing a Distributed Environment

We have worked with several clients and examined industry sources to define these costs. Following are some key observations that come from these real-world cases; these observations may apply to other distributed computing environments:

- Many times it is possible to define the costs in terms of "costs per workstation per month." Cost per workstation per month is a fairly common measure used in outsourcing arrangements, for example. In such arrangements, the cost per workstation per month is typically agreed to for the length of the contract.

- Using cost per workstation per month as a parameter, and by looking at a variety of cost models and a set of assumptions, we can deter-mine a reasonable cost range and what percentage of total costs the MODE function represents.

- The models that result are fairly comprehensive in their coverage and often point out cases where unexpected costs are significant and could be overlooked without the model.

- The costs are very situation-specific, and it is easy to move a cost well outside of range by changing assumptions.

Underlying Assumptions About Costs. As an example, a cost for site backup can be defined on a workstation-per-month basis. Implicit in these costs is the fact that availability and speed to recovery fall in "typical" ranges, such as 95% availability. If you alter the assumptions to a much more stringent requirement of 7 by 23:50 minutes and one-minute recovery time, then the costs shift dramatically.

When looking at an industry-provided standard or at the numbers discussed throughout this chapter, remember that they must be evaluated in the context of the assumptions behind them. Discrepancies in actual costs versus industry averages can and should be justified as change in assumptions. Unfortunately, often such assumptions are not explicit.

Put another way, the specific costs you will find in this text are of little value without an understanding of the assumptions behind them. Some key assumptions will be explained as the discussion proceeds. The model provided here should be helpful in allowing readers to develop a model of actual costs that they might experience. However, as significant discrepancies are found in others' models and your own, the point is not to reject either but to understand what the different assumptions are that cause the shift in numbers.

Developing Cost Approximations with Activity-Based Costing

The method we employ is an activity-based approach to costing out the work associated with managing a distributed environment. A cost is developed for each major activity that needs to be pursued to accomplish the work. In this case the MODE model can be viewed as an inventory of such costs. The challenge then becomes defining the cost associated with activities found in the MODE model.

How do you determine such costs? If you are currently working in a distributed environment, a first step is to do an assessment of your own costs. In essence, you need to completely understand what each function in the MODE model means. Next, you determine who is contributing to the costs found in the function. In some cases, the cost may be well managed. For example, a help desk with 20 people may be assigned to the Service Management Help Desk.

Example: Personnel-Related Activities and Costs. In doing such an analysis you must decide what costs to account for. For the purposes of our example, the costs under consideration are those associated with people costs. This is partially as a matter of simplification. The other reason is that many of the other costs, such as costs of software and hardware, are often accounted for as indirect or overhead costs and are not always directly transformable to activity-based approaches. For this discussion, we look only at how to develop personnel-related activity costs. Other non-payroll costs will need to be accounted for in other models.

Hidden or Shadow Costs. The determination of costs is not trivial. MODE functions often cut across many organizational functions, and there may be no single place where the costs roll together. In other cases, the cost may not be explicit.

For example, there is frequently an "unofficial" help desk function in many departments where there is a certain individual or individuals who know something about computers and who other people call for help, rather than wait in the queue of calls to the official help desk. This type of unrecognized peer support contributes hidden or shadow IT costs.

For cases such as these, an accounting level of precision may be impractical. An approximation is often adequate. For example, in this case you might estimate that in each department there is a person fulfilling this role and applying approximately two hours per week to the function. The focus should be on identifying sources of costs, and making and documenting reasonable approximations. Inevitably discussions and argument will arise. The discussion process should lead to some revisions and broader acceptance of the proposed costs.

In other cases there may be functions that may not be done. For example, MODE differentiates between service-level agreements and operational-level agreements. In MODE, an SLA is a commitment on business performance. For example, an SLA for an insurance claims department states how many claims the department will be able to process per hour. An OLA, in the MODE context, is a component of the SLA that gives the technology commitments to meet the SLA commitments. To meet the targeted number of claims per hour, an OLA for the department might commit that end-to-end system response time for initial claim collection will be 3 seconds or less at the 95 percentile.

For many information systems organizations there are sufficient challenges in getting OLAs defined and they choose not to define SLAs. While there are many good reasons for using both SLAs and OLAs, the reality is that often it is just not feasible to do all these types of agreements. An organization may choose to forego the development and use of SLAs as defined by MODE and instead treat the OLAs as SLAs. In this case there would be no accounting for SLAs.

In other cases, there may be costs that are not currently available but that can be anticipated to be part of the effort moving forward. For example, if no one is currently doing event management, there will be no way to look to internal costs to determine an activity-based cost. Instead, you need to look at external sources for some views on reasonable costs and then select one of these costs. Particularly in this case, you must understand the assumptions behind the costs. (Sources for such costs are discussed in a subsequent section.)

The act of determining costs is essentially an analytical one with approximations created wherever possible. It is often a cross-department activity, in that costs may need to be collected from many department organizations. Because the costs must come from many departments, support for this effort needs to come from senior management, otherwise individual departments may be reluctant to report internal costs outside the normal lines of reporting. Given the total costs associated, management support should be enlisted to help get the facts.

Normalizing Costs. As these costs are being collected, it is essential to normalize the costs so that there is a basis for comparing costs. Cost estimates for the MODE functions can, in many cases, be normalized according to a *cost/ seat/ month* basis.

The use of this normalizing factor is based on the authors' experiences analyzing services costs for several engagements of Andersen Consulting. By using this normalizing factor, it is possible to compare relative functional costs. There is also a basis for comparing functional costs that come from different sources. This, in turn, provides a basis for comparing annual costs.

Using External Sources for Estimates of Cost

External costs are sometimes needed to fill in some blanks in the cost model. In addition, as the cost model is being developed, there is always value in having additional sources of estimates to confirm your own estimates or to challenge them.

The analysis of external sources of costs that is presented here is not exhaustive, but it does provide some insight and consistency of view of the costs. Remember that the numbers presented are for a given point in time and it is reasonable to expect them to age quickly as we learn better how to manage distributed environments.

Furthermore, remember that the underlying assumptions are key. The factors given can serve as an initial benchmark for understanding potential cost impacts in the area of distributed systems management. They may be of value if you have no cost to go by, but in all cases such costs are best defined based on the actuals at hand.

Some common features that apply across the inputs to the analysis include:

- PC client workstations.
- Local and remote LANs.
- UNIX or NT servers.
- Mixture of TCP/IP and IPX protocols.
- Systems and gateways to host mainframe processing.

None of the cases we analyzed pushed the edge of the envelope in terms of demands for availability, reliability, or recoverability. For example, none of the cases addressed 24x7 (24 hours a day, 7 days a week) or subsecond response time or global processing. Also, although the networks under consideration involved hundreds of workstations, none involved thousands. As a result, costs within a 100-workstation environment may give very little insight to the costs for a 10,000-workstation environment. In larger environments the reality is that the interactions increase geometrically and so, too, may the cost. Furthermore, in the cases presented, where the specifics are known, the costs are associated with US operations.

The cost value also does not include mainframe or wide area network (WAN) support services. For any particular environment, the *cost/ seat/ month* value may be higher if more complex processing requirements are needed, such as the ability to manage more network protocols or platforms. The cost may be lower if the target environment is simpler or there are fewer protocols to manage. Items such as software, hardware, facilities, and premise wiring are not included in the services. Voice support was also not taken into account.

Several sites were used to estimate the costs. Because of confidentiality issues, some specifics cannot be provided. Generally speaking, however, detailed costs were mainly estimated using information from a large systems management engagement client. Costs are based on the following assumptions:

- $100,000 annual salary for manager positions.
- $55,000 annual salary for worker positions.

For many companies, the worker costs may be too low. Estimates were then compared against other estimates to confirm reasonableness.

For the analysis of external sources of costs discussed in this chapter, some of the results are taken from an actual outsourcing arrangement. Some of the other results discussed, such as the Gartner Report numbers, continue to be revised and improved over time and may be updated. So any of the costs discussed should be looked on as examples of how to go about finding external costs, not as final sources for doing your own estimate.

Large Consumer-Products Manufacturer. This site had a $500,000 help desk function. Network management costs were at approximately $400,000 and technical support costs were $700,000. Total annual cost was $1.6 million. There were 450 users at this site, so the monthly per-seat cost was approximately $300.

Gartner Report on Large Enterprise Client/Server Costs. A 1994 strategic analysis report from Gartner Group showed a five-year total cost of $48,400 per user. This comes to $9,680 per year, or $806 per month. When describing cost analysis without end-user labor, the following percentages were given for systems management activities: IS labor for end-user support: 14.6%; IS labor for operations: 15.7%, education and training: 5%, professional services: 2.8%. This totals 38.1%, or an operations per-seat cost of around $307.

Forrester Research Report Vol. 10 No. 4: Client/Server's Price Tag. This February 1993 report showed approximate costs of $1 million over four years, plus an additional $160,000 for training, which totals $1.16 million over four years. There were 140 users in the study, so the per-seat cost comes to $169. However, the report analyzes cost on a per-application basis. Therefore, several applications will probably increase the overall per-seat cost. The report cites an estimate of $475 per user as an average across several applications.

Datamation Report on Client/Server Costs. A *Datamation* article from February 15, 1994 notes that $2.2 million annual costs were spent for support services for a 3,000 user application. This figure included mostly systems management tasks, but not systems administration, the help desk, or training. The annual cost reduced to a per-seat cost is $61/seat just for production and control and some monitoring services. If the entire MODE spectrum of services is taken into account, it would be anticipated that a per-seat cost of $292 would be needed.

This same article referenced a Hyatt Hotels study in which $44.5 million was cited as a five-year cost for its client/server systems, of which 23% represents support costs for a 500-user network. This boils down to $10,235,000 over five years for those costs—$2,047,000 per year; $4,094 per user; and $341 per seat per month.

InformationWeek Report. An *InformationWeek* article (January 3, 1993) described the costs over a five-year period for personnel to support client/server systems. An examination of the PC/LAN and UNIX values shows that the costs are $17,000 per user over five years, or $283 per seat.

Large Communications Vendor Proposal. The proposed cost for help desk services and hardware/software maintenance services for an Andersen Consulting client, a large communications vendor, is approximately $25 per user per month. In addition, four deskside help technicians at approximately $12,000 per year are included. There are 6,500 users at this organization. Therefore, the deskside support adds about $7 per user per month in support costs. This brings the total to $30.50 per user per month for just these services. Utilizing the projected costs for MODE services not covered under this proposal would result in a per-seat charge of around $300.

Dataquest Study. In its 1994 annual edition on software services, Dataquest reported the average dollars spent in 1994 per end user by the study's respondents. It showed a client/server expenditure of $327.54 per user per month.

Cost Breakdown by MODE Functions. In all the previous examples, total costs were established by a roll up from the individual MODE functions. It is the cost at the function level that may be of key value in managing a distributed environment. For example, the cost for the help desk function, as defined in MODE, was estimated at approximately $35 per month per workstation per month across the several cases noted, where it was feasible to determine help desk functions. This was done for each of the MODE functions.

The overall *cost/seat/month* figure for all MODE services appears to cluster around approximately $300. Once again, there is a set of assumptions behind this figure that includes such things as the use of PCs for clients, local and remote LANs, and an average of 100 workstations, but no global processing or 24x7 operations. An estimate of how the $300 cost is broken down by MODE functions is shown in Exhibit III-14-2.

USING THE MODE ESTIMATES

The point of this effort to develop MODE costs is to begin to influence the costs associated with managing a distributed environment.

As a first step, a comparison must be done with external costs to see if internal costs are reasonable. This can and should be done on a MODE function basis.

Recognize that costs are simply approximations at this point. If you determine a total cost of $600 per workstation per month, the approximations may suggest that there is a problem. Similarly, if you find that a MODE function cost (e.g., the cost of the help desk) is at $100 per workstation per month versus perhaps $35 per workstation per month, then there may be an opportunity for improvement. Go back and reexamine the assumptions going into the actual estimate. A discrepancy

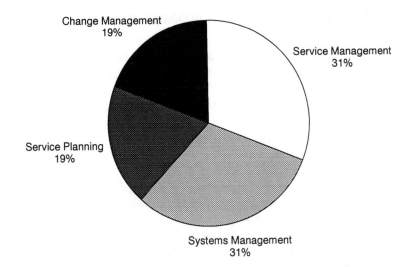

Change Management
19%

Service Management
31%

Service Planning
19%

Systems Management
31%

Exhibit III-14-2. Services Cost Per Seat, Breakdown by Function

may be due to the allocation of costs that are not part of the help desk in the cited estimate.

The estimated costs may approximate actual costs within 25% to 30% for any given set of assumptions. Thus, if costs for a help desk were estimated at $40 per workstation/month, this amount is essentially comparable to the estimated costs of $35. Although there is no major cost discrepancy, the manager should be thinking about what can be done over time to move the costs down. In this case, the $40 becomes the reference and the focus is on improving it over time. The fact is that it is very hard to make such improvements without first having such a reference.

Alternatively, if a cost is significantly lower than industry averages, then it is also worth examining. For example, in the MODE cost models we have developed, the cost for production management (which addresses such functions as network, print, and mass storage management) is estimated to be approximately $80 per workstation per month. If an individual site shows actual costs of $30 per workstation per month, it could perhaps mean that the site is doing a very good job. Conversely, it could mean the service delivered could be greatly improved and the function is in need of further investment and personnel. And, of course, it may again mean that different assumptions apply and the differences can be justified based on the changing assumptions.

MODE COSTS MODELS AND EVALUATION OF OUTSOURCING ALTERNATIVES

The decision to outsource the management of distributed environments is a common one, and the MODE cost model can be applied to outsourcing arrangements.

There are many such reasons to outsource systems management of client/server networks. Often an internal systems management group may have limited skills in operating the technology associated with client/server. Outsourcing can bring a needed skill set to address the problem.

Another reason revolves around the inherently distributed nature of the work. Often the operation of the systems demands that people be on-site to do installations and fix and monitor problems daily. A traditional systems management group may not have the personnel to do this work. Furthermore, an outsourcer may be able to take advantage of economies of scale by being able to place personnel in an area to deal with several local distributed sites.

Other traditional reasons for outsourcing revolve around controlling and perhaps reducing costs. Also, management sometimes turns to outsourcing when it has determined that the skill sets of IS staff do not represent core skill sets of the enterprise.

Leveling the Playing Field with the Outsourcer

If a decision is made to outsource a distributed environment, then the MODE functional framework can be a valuable tool. Outsourcing is essentially a contractual activity. In this process, through negotiation, the enterprise and outsourcer come to an agreement on what services the outsourcer will provide. These agreements are reflected in a formal contract defining services and the associated costs.

In most cases, the contract becomes the centerpiece of any discussions between the enterprise and the outsourcers regarding ongoing services. Frequently an outsourcer will only enter into a discussion with the contract in hand and will provide a service only when it is described by the contract or with an approved change order. Of course, associated with the change order are additional charges. This change-order process then becomes a key determinant in terms of actual versus planned costs. It can also be the source of almost continual discussions between the outsourcer and enterprise.

It is essential, then, that the enterprises enter into the discussion with a solid understanding of what functions it wants provided by the outsourcer. It is safe to assume that a competent outsourcer already knows what it wants to make explicit through the contract and what it would expect to handle through a change-order process. Outsourcers often have an advantage in the negotiations simply because they have more experience in these negotiations than the enterprise looking to outsource.

The MODE functional framework in Exhibit III-14-1 is not exhaustive and it is not at the level of detail needed for contractual negotiations. However, it does give a good starter list of the functions required to manage a distributed environment.

A company that is considering using an outsourcer can, at minimum, use the framework to identify which functions it *does not* want to have included in the outsourcing contract. There have been occasions where an outsourcer believed it was very clear about what it meant by the production control function, but the enterprise assumed this work meant or included the help desk, when it did not. The framework can help to overcome such misunderstandings. It can be used to ask an outsourcer relevant questions, such as who will do service-level agreement reporting and who will handle security management and all the other functions found in MODE.

Examples. In the typical contractual process, the major steps would be:

- Request for information (RFI).
- Request for proposal (RFP).
- Proposal evaluation.
- Contractual negotiations.

The RFI stage starts with the enterprise defining appropriate parts of the problem that it wants the outsourcer to address. If nothing else, this effort allows the enterprise to start off with a common view of its need, but it also provides some advantage to the enterprise if responses from potential vendors are required to be in a format that is consistent with the MODE framework. The evaluation of proposals becomes much more rational if there is a common standard with which to compare them.

By starting with the MODE framework, the user company can also require from the vendors the pricing of the functions. This information is another basis by which to evaluate proposals, comparing costs outlined in each proposal to a common standard to determine which vendor offers the most attractive pricing.

For example, if one vendor bids a help desk function at $10 per month per workstation and another bids it at $40 per month per workstation, there is a really apparent problem. Although the tendency may be to say that the $10 bid is a better deal, the fact is that such a low bid may signal the vendor's lack of understanding of expectations, which may result in many subsequent change orders—this alone should be a source of concern in evaluating proposals.

More generally, it is remarkable how often a company will select a bid that clearly reflects charges that would not cover costs. Sometimes an enterprise will accept a bid with the intent of taking advantage of the vendor. But if the outsourcer is taking on a critical function for the enterprise—such as running the distributed network—and the bid is low, it may be because the vendor does not understand the problem. Does the enterprise really want to entrust this function to them, while they learn the problem?

A vendor that has misunderstood the requirements will not be an effective partner. Worse, if the vendor ends up servicing the deal with subpar personnel and commitment, the enterprise will not be well served. Also, there is always the risk that the outsourcer could simply walk away from the deal or end up in bankruptcy, which will do the enterprise no good.

A "conservation of effort" seems to exist in many of these cases— doing a piece of work adequately is going to take a certain minimum amount of effort and associated costs. There is no magic in this business, so a cost that seems magical should not be believed. Costs truly reflecting this conservation of effort are, at best, going to differ by percentages, not by orders of magnitude. If you find large discrepancies, it is essential to understand why. An outsourcer that is not doing the job expected, or that is losing money every day, is not going to be effective in getting the job done. The MODE model can help with this evaluation, but it cannot guarantee that a vendor grasps the scope of the problem at hand, nor can it provide guidance as to how to proceed with negotiations.

CONCLUSION

The costs associated with management of a distributed environment are a very significant part of the costs of the ongoing use of a client/server environment. Unfortunately, these costs are often not recognized or understood very well.

The MODE framework, detailed in Chapter III-13 and overviewed in this chapter, provides a basis for building an understanding of what the costs are. Then you can implement a program to monitor and improve the costs over time while ensuring that the quality of service remains acceptable—whether functions in the model are being performed in-house or are being considered for outsourcing. MODE can be a basis for not only building the environment for managing distributed operations but also to improving it and reducing costs over time.

Section IV

The Future of Client/Server Computing

The mean time between surprises is very short in the field of information technology, especially in this age of so-called "Internet time," with companies moving ever-faster to introduce new products and new technologies. Section IV examines the various technologies and concepts that are shaping the future of client/server computing.

The intended audience is chief information officers, project leaders, and project team members who need to understand the pivotal technologies related to client/server and their short-term outlooks. The goal here is not to prognosticate about whether client/server computing or any one type of hardware or software will be around in 20 years; the goal is simply to make readers aware of and prepared for some likely scenarios in technology development—developments that will likely affect their choices and their expectations of information technology.

Among the hottest topics worth noting and keeping track of:

- Short-term outlook on workstations and operating systems, processors, DBMS technology, and communications networks.
- Evolution of the user interface and input and output devices that make computing more accessible to more people.
- Technology to support and enable so-called teamnets—giving work groups support for communication and routing, knowledge and process management, collaboration, and group meetings.
- Object-oriented technology—one of the most important enablers of distributed applications.

IV-1
Future Architectures and Technologies

Everyone involved in information technology is constantly sharing opinions about the relative merits of different operating systems, workstations, and processors. People love to try to predict who the winners will be in these intensely competitive markets. This chapter sketches out one picture of the technological future with regard to platform architectures.

TECHNOLOGICAL CATCH-22

The mean time between surprises shortens every month in the field of technology. One quotation seems appropriate here: "If you're foolish enough to predict the future, you lack the judgment to be believed."

This is probably the perfect catch-22 for technology forecasting. It also saves people from having to defend themselves if these predictions do not happen quite the way they predict.

These predictions assume that client/server is the technological baseline, at least over the next 10 years. Some simple statistics from one systems development firm bear this out. Four years ago, 3% of most of the firm's systems integration business was from client/server. The next year it jumped to 17%; then to 37%. Today, client/server accounts for more than half this firm's business.

Another statistic, this one from an IDC study. In a recent survey of about 1,000 companies, 68% of responding companies either already had client/server solutions or foresaw the majority of their future solutions involving client/server. IDC's response was that it had never seen such a jump in a single year. So the presumed base here, at least for the next 10 years, is client/server. Not only is client/server becoming the assumed base, but organizations are now building solutions on top of that which take them off in different directions.

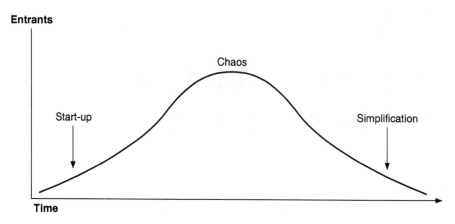

Exhibit IV-1-1. The Chaos Model

A MODEL TO PREDICT THE FUTURE

The fields of systems thinking and "bionomics" lead us to new models for understanding markets. Michael Rothschild has suggested, for example, that a market is its own "ecosystem" : Various competitors are, like organisms in a pond, fighting to survive and become dominant. The first entrepreneur emerges from the pond with a first product. The product s sales in the market and others follow. The next entrants have similar products, but try to differentiate them based on unique features. The number of entrants continues for a period of time and then fallout starts. The entrepreneurs leave. Consolidation starts with companies absorbing other companies and others going out of business. Finally, only a few dominant "species" remain in the pond.

This ecosystem, this movement of technology and products in the marketplace, can be depicted with a bell-shaped curve. A graph with the two axes representing time on the one hand and entrants into the marketplace on the other hand produces a bell-shaped curve almost every time the developer looks at technology. (See Exhibit IV-1-1.)

When a technology starts up there are not many entrants and not many sales. If it looks like the product is going to be commercially practical, the market moves rather quickly toward a period of chaos, where there are more and more entrants. This is followed by a collapse in the marketplace and a final move toward simplification. This is a simple and elegant concept, something found in "nonlinear" or "evolutionary" economics. Now, how does this model work when developers apply it to different aspects of technology?

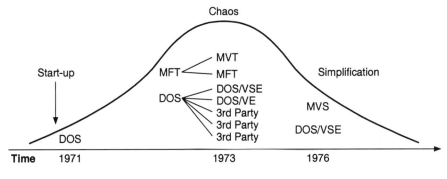

Exhibit IV-1-2. Operating Systems

Operating Systems

In the early 1970s, the market began with an operating system called DOS—a different DOS than we know today—and that was about it. A few years later there was a new entrant, MFT, and then different fragmentations from MFT and DOS. Some people bought third-party operating systems that were arguably better than IBM's. By 1976, that was over. The market had MVS and DOS/VSE and went forward from that simplified base. (See Exhibit IV-1-2.)

There is another crucial point to note about those two competitors left standing after the marketplace battle. Today there are estimates of about 6,000 to 7,000 licenses for MVS. DOS/VSE licenses are estimated to be between 30,000 and 40,000. The implication is that after simplification in the marketplace, two endpoints remain: edge-of-the-envelope in performance on the one hand (i.e., MVS) and high volume in sales on the other hand (i.e., DOS/VSE).

Online Monitors

Online monitors show a similar pattern. In the early 1970s, there was really only one online monitor: CICS. Then came an explosion in available products: IMS/DC, CICS, Environ/1, Shadow, Oplex, and IDMS/DC. There was also the most popular one, the so-called homegrown monitor, the one people wrote themselves because it seemed an interesting thing to do back then. (See Exhibit IV-1-3.)

A few years later, the market simplified, and everything came down to either CICS or IMS/DC. Again, the market ended up with one edge-of-the-envelope product: If an organization wanted to do 1,000 transactions per second, IMS/DC was the answer. But CICS was the high-volume sales product: Estimates ran from 40,000 to 50,000 licenses.

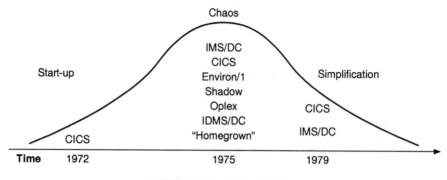

Exhibit IV-1-3. Online Monitors

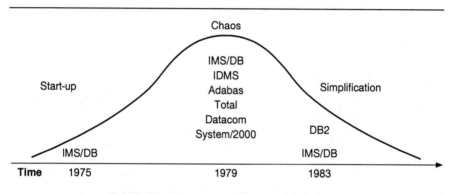

Exhibit IV-1-4. Database Management Systems

Database Management Systems

Currently there are two data points, but look at a third: database management systems (DBMSs). In the early to mid-1970s, IMS/DB got people focused on database issues. A few years later, those people were in chaos, with a large number of options: IDMS, IMS/DB, Adabas, Total, Datacom, and System/2000. A few years after that, simplification arrived: DB2 and IMS/DB. Again, the split was between edge-of-the-envelope performance and high volume sales. DB2 was the big seller. The estimate today is that as much as 98% of all mainframe DBMS sales are DB2. But IMS/DB is the edge-of-the-envelope performer. (See Exhibit IV-1-4.)

TECHNOLOGY ENVELOPE: DECISION-MAKER PERSPECTIVE

What can an organization learn from these curves? First, the technology industry for the past 25 years has been characterized by ongoing chaos. In

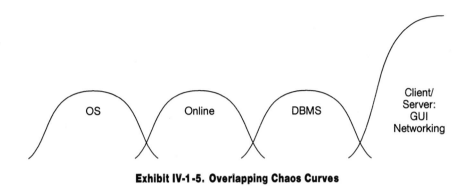

Exhibit IV-1-5. Overlapping Chaos Curves

the mid-1970s, no one had a party to celebrate the fact that the operating system environment was now simplified because people had online monitors to worry about. When those simplified, people had to worry about DBMS. Even as that has calmed down, client/server has entered its own phase of chaos.

Client/server did something else, though, too. No longer were there three organized, separate curves. There were intense discussions about what sorts of operating systems, graphical user interfaces (GUIs), and DBMSs are the best. Now the discussions are about distributed transaction processing monitors. Client/server has all these discussions going at once: The curve now is the sum of a set of different technology curves. This has made for a much more chaotic period as the industry tries to deal with all the changes. (See Exhibit IV-1-5.)

What are the basic time frames? From start-up to chaos appears to be about two or three years. From chaos to simplification is about three to five years. So technologies entering chaos today will see simplification around the turn of the century. Several economists as well have studied this idea of chaos moving to simplification. The economic movement from chaos to simplification recurs throughout history.

The other lesson is that it is impossible to predict accurately, from further back in the curve, who the winners will be at the end. There are just too many different variables.

As for the technology itself—and this is perhaps a disturbing finding—an organization does not need the best technology to be the ultimate winner. It needs an adequate technology. In almost every case with the bell curve model, the best technology in fact was not the sales winner. Installed base becomes very important as an organization proceeds along the curve. The other important component here is regulation.

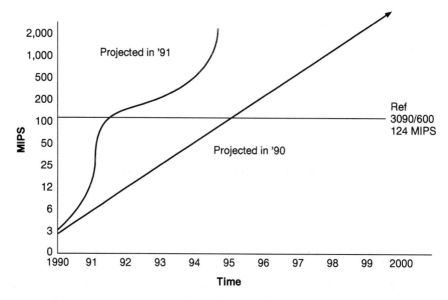

Exhibit IV-1-6. An Explosion in MIPS

The Future of Workstations

There is a crucial point with regard to the future of workstations: A standard projection that has been around some time is that with new technology, an organization can expect to see a doubling in price/ performance every 12 to 18 months. If the organization took hardware that was easily available in 1990, at the end of the decade the organization would be talking about 2,000 MIPS (million instructions per second), running somewhere around $3,500. What actually happened was that the numbers went well above the curve. (See Exhibit IV-1-6.)

At this point developers are faced with an interesting problem. If they get into about a 100 megahertz (MHz) speed on processors, they start running into the limits of how fast electrons can be pushed through the silicon lattice. This is a difficult problem,

The way to beat the problem is to run the chip hotter: by putting more electricity through it. But with silicon technology, developers are running into a physical limit. So how do they continue to show steady MIPS growth? By linking several chips together (i.e., by going to multiple processors). Parallel processing is a definite part of the future.

Some specifics related to workstations: The market is currently in chaos, with a lot of repositioning of current vendors. The market even continues to see new entrants, like the PowerPC chip. But with that chip, both IBM and Apple have run into another technological catch-22. There has to be application software available if the chip is to sell. But if vendors are going to write application software for a chip, they want to make sure that it is selling. This is the technology equivalent of the young job seeker's lament: Every employer wants experience, so how is the young job seeker going to get experience?

The workstation market will begin to simplify over the next couple of years. Intel currently has between 70% and 80% of the installed base. Economists call that technical lock-in.

In terms of its installed base, Intel has just ensured that it will belong to Intel for some time. Intel has all those processors, and if a company wants to take all its software and have it running better and quicker without any recompiles, Intel has a way to do that. So Intel is going to own the workstation market for some time. In particular, the 86 architecture is going to be around for a long, long time.

Another factor here is change in form. There will be an increase in pen computing, for example. One department store has people going through the aisles at its competitors' stores, tracking prices using a pen-based machine. Why? Because the machines are not so noticeable.

The interesting thing here is that the information systems department did not write the application; end users in marketing wrote it!

The market will also see an increase in the workstations as a personal communication device (PCD). Newton is the most famous example here, with well-publicized first- generation issues, but there are others as well.

Client Operating Systems

The operating systems market is also in chaos right now. Current vendors or products include OS/2, Apple, UNIX, Windows 95, Windows NT, and Workplace/OS. It appears that Windows 95 is a success. First, it is a good operating system, one that takes care of 32 bit. Second, Microsoft made sure that both the new and old Windows interfaces could run it.

Using the earlier model showing two eventual winners—one a high-volume seller and the other an edge-of-the-envelope performer, a couple of predictions are possible. For performance that will continue to push the envelope, Windows NT seems to be the one to bet on. At the time of this writing, that is a controversial call, given the number of articles claiming that NT failed. But the truth is, sales of NT in its first year alone matched UNIX sales of another major vendor.

There are also new types of workstations. In the near future, operating systems will appear as object managers, including Taligent and Cairo. Taligent—an IBM-Apple initiative—was going to be a whole new operating system, but it has pulled back on that. It now is being touted as a system with object-oriented frameworks. Cairo from Microsoft has an object- oriented concept called Object Linking and Embedding (OLE), letting users manipulate large such concepts as data and video and tie them all together.

There are also some very interesting systems, such as the ones from General Magic and Apple's Newton operating system. General Magic really is an operating system. The key there is that the system focuses entirely on the problem of how to connect the individual to the rest of the world. It has a component, for example, called Telescript, which is all about how to communicate easily. It strips away the complexity of communications coding and puts it at about the same level as COBOL. It also has an agent concept within it. An organization can send its agent out on the network looking, for example, for the best deal on airline tickets. Whether this concept implemented in products will find appeal in the marketplace remains to be seen.

Finally, the market arrives at the concept of operating systems as all things to all people. Microsoft has a vision of operating systems that goes beyond the way people think about them today.

Whether anyone in the world is smart enough to do that, no one knows. The challenges are formidable. There are now hundreds of versions of Windows out there—Windows on 3 1/2-inch disks, 5 1/4-inch disks, 286, 386, 486, Pentium, color, monochrome— resulting in a huge number of permutations.

User Interaction

User interaction and GUIs again bring the chaos of multiple players: Windows 95, Windows NT, PM, Motif (COSE). This has already simplified somewhat, because Windows appears to be the GUI winner.

In more general terms, pen, gesture, and voice are the areas to watch in terms of new forms of user interaction. Microsoft has had a couple of different offerings in voice recognition, but none are out there today, so there is an opportunity for someone to claim the market. AT&T says it will have a $25 chip soon that users can plug into their personal computer, which will give them 99% voice recognition, in multiple dialects, even taking into account background noise.

Voice recognition in the user interface will become increasingly common. So will virtual reality, though not too many people are taking it seriously enough right now. With the new Boeing 777, to take just one example, more than 30% of the plane was built in virtual reality. The plane could be tested thoroughly before any nuts and bolts were put into place. If there is any physical dimension to the work, virtual reality will increasingly be used.

All these areas—virtual reality, voice, pen, gesture—fall under the area of the "human metaphor," discussed in more detail in Chapter IV-2. That is, the metaphor for interaction with a computer in the future will be natural, human forms of interaction. To the extent that a computer is noticeable, it will be objectionable. By the end of the decade, the computer interface is going to look like another human being.

OLE is another important concept in human interaction. Most people hear of this and think of it as something that will allow them to take their Excel spreadsheet and have it appear in their memo. That is part of it, but not the important part. It is really a whole different development paradigm: the document-centric paradigm. In that context, the main line may well be a word document—and the user simply codes Visual Basic behind it.

Processors

The processor market is a little less clear than some of the ones previously considered. It may become a less important issue in the coming years.

The high-volume sales winner clearly seems to be Intel. Intel owns most of the market already, and the Pentium Pro chip will only solidify its hold. The edge-of-the-envelope performance winner is less clear because the situation is still in chaos.

To understand this outlook on processors, it is necessary to understand the difference between horizontal and vertical markets in computing. For most of its history, information technology was in a world of vertical markets. When users bought a processor it came with an operating system, a DBMS, and an online monitor. That gave the vendor a big advantage. The DBMS people, for example, could see some action they were performing thousands of times and just ask for an upgrade in the microcode to solve the problem.

What comes out of that iterative process is increasingly better performance. With client/server, an organization finds itself in a horizontal market. One company does the processor, another does the operating system, somebody else does the DBMS, and still another does the application. That provides tremendous flexibility to pull things in and out. But the organization loses the ability to tell the chip manufacturer, "Let's put this instruction in so my compiler will run faster."

What we may find happening is that when companies really go after the high-volume performance chip—1,000 to 2,000 transactions per second—one of the vendors may take the lead by reverting to a vertical market approach. Here they would control all levels of software and hardware to achieve edge-of-the- envelope performance.

Massively parallel processing (MPP) is currently getting a lot of play in the press, but it is not really clear what the right model is for it. Thus, in general, the high-performance market is still in chaos. The industry still has many providers, and the key is going to be whether somebody decides to go after the vertical market.

Server Operating Systems

The operating system market on the server side is currently in chaos. OS/2, UNIX, Windows NT, and Workplace/OS are all jockeying for position. In the next three years or so the marketplace will see simplification, with the high-volume sales winner probably ending up to be Windows NT. The high-performer market will be a little more complicated. UNIX will continue to find a niche market at the least. MVS and DOS/VSE will also be players on the server side of the operating system.

The most important development in server operating systems is the whole changing vision of the operating system. Increasingly, organizations are using their operating system as a group object manager, a group communications manager, and a teamware host.

Communication

Communication is a complex part of the client/server environment. From one point of view, it is the most important because communication is what makes the distributed environment really happen.

For wire-based communication, the marketplace has recently simplified. Basic networking services have simplified in terms of the wide area network (WAN) and the local area network (LAN). In WANs, the dedicated options are between T1-based services, public network services—many of which are emerging as economically attractive options for business—or lower-speed digital lines. In LANs, choices are between twisted pair, cable, or fiber for wiring and Ethernet or token ring for an access method. For dial-up access, options are either basic telephone service or integrated services digital network for higher speed.

In the wireless area, however, there is still chaos. In the current voice-oriented cellular market, there are competing methods for handling digital data transmission. PCDs are also competing in this marketplace. It is unclear at this time who the dominant player or players will be.

Database Management Systems

As of this writing, the DBMS market is currently pretty full: Oracle, Sybase, and Informix are currently the major players. Ingres's future is less clear. Other entrants include DB/2/Anywhere and Microsoft. In the next few years, as simplification occurs, Oracle will have a big advantage because of its installed base: Current estimates give Oracle 40% of the market. Sybase may evolve to be the edge-of-the-envelope performer, with Microsoft DBMS as the seller in the NT market.

There are new types of database management systems coming along: object data management systems. These are very interesting but applications are limited at this time.

The other form of object management is the idea of image and video. Particularly when you tie it to the telecommunications point that will become a more common type of solution.

CONCLUSION

The view of future architectures and technologies discussed here leads to the following practical guidelines. When dealing with the chaos of the computing technology market, the focus early on should be on delivering the business solution with the high and fast payback. Later on, the focus should be on delivering the business solution that will run for many years, providing a lower but sustained return on investment.

To build a model on "chaos" might appear unsatisfying at first. However, in light of the overall discussion in this chapter, the satisfaction lies deeper. The drive to make a difference and, in doing so, to receive the reward of wealth is constant and fixed in the market.

There is an excitement in thinking of the market making a thousand decisions a day, each one by itself not conclusive, but the sum rendering a final answer over time. There is an excitement and tension in the fact that those working in the IS field cannot hope any longer to know what is happening in each of those decisions. There is a hope, however, that we can find within the chaos some indicators of where things are going.

By following the signs we begins to see the complexity beyond the chaos. Watching people trying to do the right thing in using the technology is fascinating and even dramatic. We see a cycle driven by people, alternating between problem and opportunity, complexity and simplicity, chaos and order.

IV-2
The Human Metaphor

Humans communicate by means of metaphors. They exchange signs and symbols that represent or stand for other things. Metaphors function as common and natural models, which allow humans to extend their familiarity with concrete objects and experiences to the level of abstract concepts. In client/server computing, systems developers are moving closer to the ultimate metaphor for human-computer interaction: the "human metaphor."

EVOLUTION OF COMPUTING TOWARD THE HUMAN METAPHOR

The idea of the human metaphor grew out of the simple observation that although computers have become pervasive in society, humans are not even aware of their presence most of the time. Families use computers to cook dinner; children use them to adjust the temperature of their rooms; people may use a computer to tell the time of day.

One of the most sophisticated examples of distributed computing involves more than 53 distributed processors and 1,000 meters of electrical wiring. It is a popular automobile. What is most striking about this mass of computing power is that it is completely transparent to the user. Turning on the car's air conditioner with all its associated computing power requires no training, and it certainly never gives a data exception.

Transparent to the User

To be acceptable to people, computing has to be transparent. To the extent a computer is noticeable it is objectionable. But what does "transparency" really mean?

A transparent computer is one that interacts with the human being in an entirely natural fashion. And the most natural way for individuals to interact is as they would with another person. So the model for successful computing is the human, and the metaphor for the shape of computing is human—the human metaphor. The implication of the human metaphor is that to foresee the shape of computing at the end of the decade, people must think about the natural manner in which they interact with another human (e.g., through voice, gesture, and writing).

A strong case can be made that the evolution of computing over the past three decades can be explained in terms of the human metaphor. Consider the batch systems era of the 1960s in the context of human interaction, which had an extremely distant style of interaction. A user submitted a file of transactions to a batch system, went away while the system processed the file, and then returned to get the output. Batch systems were a poor reflection of the human metaphor.

Online systems of 20 years ago allowed users to open up the file of transactions and submit each transaction individually. The level of interaction changed from the file of the batch system to the record for the file in the online system. This change, of course, led to all the benefits usually associated with online systems: better response, fewer errors, better support for the process flow. However, proponents claim that all the changes and benefits that arose from online systems came about because of the change in the level of interaction from file to transaction— that is, by moving closer to the human metaphor.

As the 1980s, the decade of the database management system (DBMS), began something curious happened. DBMSs did not really change the level of interaction with the user, although they allowed users more easily to collect, present, and store data. In retrospect, the benefit from DBMSs—the ability to share information across the enterprise— was not the result of applying technology. It was the result of organizational change that allowed the sharing.

For example, if a user could get different insurance policy lines to share customer information, a DBMS could deliver the benefits of such sharing in shorter time frames. Without organizational willingness to change, there was a widespread view that a DBMS added to the difficulty of work for users, who now had to input more information without much gain.

In this sense, the DBMS concept was more an organizational phenomenon than a technical development. However, in the context of the human metaphor, because the DBMS did not change the nature of the interaction with the computer by moving it closer to the human metaphor, it did not change the shape of computing.

Looking back over three decades of computing, there is evidence that the human metaphor has been at work. When the technology allowed users to move closer to the human metaphor, the technology alone had an impact on the effectiveness of computing. When it did not move closer, the benefits, if they occurred, were outside the technology.

THE HUMAN METAPHOR AND CLIENT/SERVER COMPUTING

Client/server computing and its associated technologies are having a dramatic impact on organizations today because of the manner in which they move closer and closer to natural human interaction. The workstation, for example, has a fundamental architectural difference when compared with earlier generations of computing. This differentiating factor revolves around how the workstation collects input from the user.

In a workstation, each keystroke is made available to processing logic. Similarly, as a user moves a mouse, each detectable movement is passed to a program to determine a response to the input. It can be said that the workstation is event driven; an event can be a keystroke, a mouse movement, the pressing of a button, or a variety of other interactions. This event-level interaction represents a change in the level of interaction with the user when compared with the earlier generations of computing.

Workstation computing changes the level of interaction with the user from the record level of online systems to the keystroke or event level. The computer can respond to the user immediately, making the interaction much more natural and humanlike. So workstations advance computing in terms of the human metaphor.

When allied with the connectivity of client/server systems, workstations fundamentally alter the shape of computing for enterprises that choose to apply the technology to their business. Workstation-based computing can be as different from online systems as online systems were from batch systems. Workstations are leading to a new age of computing that will once again change the way people work and think.

INPUT DEVICES

Associated with workstations and WYSIWYG technology are developments in input technology that move computing closer to the human metaphor. The mouse was an early example of such a development.

In the context of the human metaphor, the dominance of the mouse in computing applications is inevitable. The mouse brought motion to human-computer interaction. Spatial motion is an essential part of human-to-human interaction, and the human metaphor would insist that it become a part of computing. The mouse is an incomplete solution, however, as evidenced by the common complaint one hears about it—that it interrupts work flow.

Graphical User Interfaces

Another widely noted development is the graphical user interface (GUI). A GUI supports the concept of multiple parallel paths of work for the user. For most people who perform parallel tasks (writing a letter, requesting information, contacting customers), the need for multiple parallel paths is essential. The human metaphor says it must be there and, in fact, workstation technology has this capability.

Certainly GUIs take developers closer to the human metaphor, but how close? Given the dominance of Windows and Macintosh interfaces, there is a danger in thinking that GUIs are always the right kind of interface, and a danger in not realizing that GUIs must become more sophisticated than they are now.

Jef Raskin, who created the Macintosh project at Apple, has written that "GUIs have become so pervasive . . . that many computer users can't even think about anything else as a human-computer interface." Raskin argues that there has really been nothing new in interface design since the invention of GUI elements in the 1970s.

Moreover, GUIs as operating systems actually may delay or prevent people from performing their tasks optimally. Raskin describes an ideal system that would overcome this delay:

"When I come to the machine to type a letter, I just sit down and type. If the computer wasn't on, the first keystroke turns it on (and the keystroke isn't lost). The machine doesn't sit there booting for a minute while the thought I wanted to write down evaporates from my mind. I don't have to launch the word processor. I just type; typing is enough of a clue for the interface to do the right thing."

Raskin's point emphasizes the premise of this chapter, that improvements to interfaces must take people closer to the human metaphor. With traditional pen and paper, if an individual wants to sit down and write, he or she just does it. Future systems must approach that capability.

Pen-Based Systems

Pen computing is a means of interacting with a computer through the use of a stylus device, or "pen." Mouse input devices are built on a desktop metaphor; pen computing uses the metaphor of pen and paper. The user "writes" directly on a computer display screen with a pen. The display screen detects the presence of the pen and "inks" the display to create an illusion of actually writing on the surface of the screen.

Personal digital assistants (PDAs) are an example of pen-based systems. PDAs got off to an inauspicious start with the Newton's inconsistent solution to the handwriting recognition problem, but recent versions of Newton software support more consistent recognition of pen strokes. In addition, other PDAs such as the Pilot emphasize desktop connectivity and act as an extension of the desktop, using desktop-based functions for higher volume keystroke entry.

There are three methods of pen interaction: printing, drawing, and gesturing.

Printing. Pen computing eliminates the need for typing skills. The user enters the data by printing directly on the display screen. The printed characters may be translated to computer character codes representing the text, or the "ink" can be retained in its original form. Handwriting recognition can be applied to printed ink immediately or at a later time.

There are two basic categories of printing. Natural-style printing recognizes the true printed characters of a language. Interpretive printing, such as Palm's Graffiti software, recognizes a series of interpreted characters and forces the user to learn to write in its graphical style.

Drawing. Those who draw with a mouse often compare it to drawing with a brick. The pen offers a much more familiar and natural way to draw on a computer. The pen also offers much greater resolution than the mouse—1,000 points per inch (ppi) compared with 400 ppi. The drawing capability of pen computing also permits entry of cursive (script) writing when conversion to text characters is not required.

Gesturing. Printing and drawing notwithstanding, gestures provide the key differentiation to pen computing. Pen gestures—such as circles, arrows, and taps—allow the pen to replace the mouse as a point, select, and command device. More important, gestures allow the simultaneous specification of object and action, thus eliminating the cumbersome object-action paradigm associated with most GUIs.

In the mouse world, for example, the user selects an object—perhaps a word—and then selects an action such as "delete" to apply to the object. In the pen world, the user crosses out the word with an "X" to delete it. Gestures such as the "X" are interpreted in the same way that standard computers respond to mouse actions and function keys.

The importance of gesture goes beyond pen-based systems and into the full dimensions of the human metaphor. There are prototypes available now in such applications as computer-aided design/computer-aided manufacturing, where the design engineer's hand motions are used as directions to move parts of a design. In one application, an engineer's gesture to suggest rotation causes an electric armature to rotate inside an engine casing to check for fit. It seems that the several dimensions of gesture, which are a part of the human metaphor, are a natural part of the solutions beginning to be introduced into computing.

Benefits of Pen Computing. The primary benefits of pen computing are simplicity, portability, and scalability.

Simplicity. Pen computing expands the domain of computer users by making computers easier and more intuitive to use. The pen removes a great deal of the complexity that is normally associated with computers.

Pen computer users do not need typing skills or knowledge of complex and cryptic commands.

Portability. Pen computers are more portable than their notebook predecessors. A notebook computer requires someplace to put it; a pen computer is held in the hand. Social constraints also limit the portability of traditional notebooks. The use of a notebook computer in many business and professional environments would be considered inappropriate because of the distraction generated by the use of a keyboard. The pen computer is quiet and much less obtrusive. Like a paper note pad, it allows the user to record information while continuing to pay attention to the task at hand.

Scalability. The size of the computer keyboard has restricted the degree to which computer size can be reduced. Pen systems can be small, like PDAs, or they can also be large, like white board displays. These large displays are especially helpful as support for team or group work.

Voice Interaction

Voice interaction means both voice recognition and voice synthesis, although recognition has represented the greater challenge for researchers and developers. Algorithms for voice recognition were defined as far back as the mid-1970s. The difficulty with these algorithms is that they were estimated to require 100 to 400 MIPS (million instructions per second) of processing power. Continual advancements in algorithms and lower costs of processors to support them will make voice recognition a common PC-type application method in the near future. Early attempts can already be found in today's home market PCs.

The impact of voice recognition technology can be seen most clearly with the new classes of computer users such as professionals. In one hospital, for example, a dozen doctors share a voice recognition system that transcribes spoken reports on the condition of patients. Doctors previously either wrote reports by hand or dictated them into tape recorders.

In addition to the obvious benefit of reduced turnaround time for producing the reports, the system also has a knowledge base of medical data. Doctors are proactively advised if the system notes medical conditions needing special attention.

OUTPUT DEVICES

Imaging and Multimedia

What are natural forms of output in human interactions with computers? Documents are one such form, and image systems are becoming a common part of computing solutions. The impact of image systems is especially profound when the imaging component is integrated with the application as a whole.

For example, in one auto insurance claims application, if a system supplies all the documents (e.g., doctor's, police, and witness reports) as a part of the claims process, the impact on the speed, accuracy, and service aspect of the claims process can be profound.

Imaging is rapidly evolving into multimedia technology. Multimedia systems address the collection, storage, and presentation of nondigital data—that is, data that cannot be compared by a computer in a meaningful way to other data processed by the computer. Video is a clear example of this type of data. There are various standards to describe how to store video, but a dump of the video data has no logical content in the sense that a computer can compute against it.

This characterization of multimedia also suggests why today's applications comprise less multimedia than one might expect. The multimedia components of systems reduce the importance of the processing aspect of the system to near zero. Because there is no digital content in the data, there is not much processing to do. This is disconcerting to someone who makes a living as a data processor. Multimedia systems essentially have collection, storage, and presentation components.

Furthermore, even the storage process is largely taken on by media management software. So, much of what developers might call the typical data design and implementation issues of digital data are being denied to the information processor when dealing with media data.

Storage and Standards Issues in the Age of Multimedia. However, the challenge and opportunity of handling collection, storage, and presentation of multimedia information should not be discounted. One of the big challenges of image applications, for example, is how to handle the physical documents being imaged. One client had some documents—maps—that were hundreds of years old, some even considered national treasures. Such documents simply cannot be put onto a scanner.

Another collection problem is how to collect and index incoming images so that they can be retrieved and found once stored. This indexing problem is typically one of the major problems of multimedia applications—arising, again, because the data of media has no digital content. As it is stored, there is no natural way to cause indexes and cross-references to be updated to reflect what has been stored, as they can be in a relational database system, for example.

Storage is also fraught with challenges. The first technical problem discovered in a multimedia effort is the impact on network performance when moving video over a typical local area network. Given that 10 seconds of video can require 10 megabytes of storage, imagine the impact on end-to-end performance of moving 10 or 20 minutes of video over a wide area network. Even if it could be moved it, storage problems would quickly develop. Acres of disk packs can be used with this technology. As a result of such concerns, CD-ROM is emerging as the fundamental storage and transport mechanism.

Another important issue in multimedia is the problem of standards. On a simple personal computer it is not difficult to find three or more standard approaches to capture, store, and present voice. There is a similar proliferation of standards for video. In fact, "standards" in multimedia are more like marks in the sand. They will continue to shift, and organizations must address this issue they move toward multimedia.

Multimedia: Land of Opportunity. The larger question with regard to multimedia, however, is where it will take developers. Much exciting work is being done today with virtual reality, but here again, the human metaphor—natural human-computer interaction—will determine winners and losers with virtual reality technology.

There are some computing models coming into view today that may suggest a future of systems. People who start with no baggage about systems design have created some extraordinary games. "Myst" is an excellent example.

The game "Myst" is a journey built on a backbone of multimedia. It has no instructions; the player just starts and makes progress, often without a clear sense of where he or she is going. As the player works through the game, its mysteries presented in images, voice, and video become clear. Is this the shape for systems to be developed tomorrow? Can the business world create systems that are as compelling and intriguing? If not, why not?

IV-3
The Team Metaphor

Until the advent of client/server, the computing revolution often focused on automating individual clerical activities or recording business events after the fact. Although this work was helpful, those tasks were removed from the central business of running complex organizations: coordinating, communicating, collaborating, and negotiating with large groups of employees, customers, and suppliers who are increasingly distributed all over the globe.

"TEAMNETS"

What has not been addressed adequately is the work of teams. Consider an example of settling a claim within an insurance office. In at least one model, this process consists of the subprocess of collection of the claim information, evidence gathering, claim adjudication, and claim settlement.

The team could consist of the claimant, receptionist, the claim taker, claim agent, and the claim settlement specialist. Time and budget constraints are often set by the company based on the desire to deliver a speedy settlement. All these components should be integrated to support the work of the team. To define this solution systems developers need to think of a new class of business user: the team itself. They need to design the applications based on the metaphor of teams.

Partnering and teamwork are being hailed as key enablers for an improved bottom line. "Teamnets" has emerged as a new model for how an organization should view itself: teams of people coming together to achieve a common goal—like joint product development, flexible manufacturing networks, or focused marketing initiatives.

The teamnet approach calls for crossing traditional, often forbidden boundaries, such as the "other" department on the fourth floor, the company's division in Des Moines, suppliers, customers, or even a competitor on the other side of the globe.

The challenge is for teams to change and restructure in concert with changing business conditions. "Virtual corporation," "horizontal corporation," "network corporation" and the like are becoming mainstream notions that challenge traditional organizational approaches.

TEAM METAPHOR VS. GROUPWARE

The team as design metaphor offers a model on which to base future computing solutions. These solutions are known most often as groupware. The business world has moved quickly toward groupware solutions.

At Andersen Consulting, for example, groupware has grown in just two years from a small part of the business at a few key sites to a business that accounts for more than 3% of its $4 billion systems integration work as of 1994. Andersen is convinced that this growth will follow a similar rate that it has seen with client/server computing, work that now makes up more than 50% of its business.

The team metaphor is concerned with the primary activities of the business worker as that worker interacts with others in the team. The computer and the network become an invisible intermediary to the business users, allowing them to work as a part of the team. The real future of client/server computing, founded on the team metaphor, is using computers and communication as a highway over which people interact with people.

The key to a successful team is to have clear goals for the team as well as a commitment to achieving those goals. With a commitment to goals, the computing backbone can add value; without goals, the backbone will not function. Because of this focus on the team, developers have begun to move away from referring to the work as groupware. Groups grope; teams deliver. So they speak more frequently now of the team metaphor.

The team metaphor supports the full richness of human interaction with other humans and captures the entire flow of work including the associated documents. This includes the ability to manage processes across boundaries and harness expertise found both internal and external to the organization. Technology that supports teams also provides for "organic" systems that can easily change and evolve with business need, allowing the end user to incorporate change as a natural part of evolution associated with teams in day-to-day work. This change is inherent in the team metaphor.

THE DIFFERENT FORMS OF THE TEAM METAPHOR

A team can interact in many ways, so the team metaphor takes many forms. A team's approach to work depends on the nature of its tasks, team size, its work processes and the roles of the team members. Among the different forms of interaction styles, and the ways in which team metaphore solutions can help, are:

- Communication and routing.

- Knowledge management.
- Process management.
- Collaboration.
- Meetings.

Communication and Routing. Effective communication among members of a group or organization depends on providing an appropriate channel for choice by the team member. That choice is based on several factors:

- The nature of the information to be communicated.
- The group to be addressed.
- The level of interaction required within that group.
- Keeping the communication timely.

Technology is increasingly being used as a communication vehicle. Electronic mail (E-mail) is a common choice for informal, ad hoc, nonurgent communication.

E-mail is an effective way of requesting information, tracking pending issues, updating colleagues on project status, or requesting a meeting. E-mail systems typically allow users to filter mail, set up group lists and simple distribution lists, and archive messages. Many E-mail systems are often integrated with a larger suite of office capabilities, such as word processing, spreadsheets, graphics, calendaring and scheduling.

In addition, integration of E-mail with other applications through application programming interfaces (APIs) is often supported. Some examples of E-mail products are Lotus cc:Mail, Microsoft Mail, HP Open-Mail, and IBM OfficeVision.

Any E-mail system relies on an accurate, current directory of users to enable the communications between people. In addition to supporting the E-mail messaging architecture, directory services play an integral role in any application that coordinates activities between people. Keeping directories in synch is a challenge in a large, geographically dispersed organization.

In the context of the team metaphor, communications and routing are, essentially, a utility. As such, it is not about defined processes, budget constraints, or quality goals. It is about communications, which is a necessary backbone on which to base the team metaphor.

Knowledge Management. Teams function better when they can draw on an organization's accumulated knowledge and experience. Libraries and filing systems are familiar examples of information repositories in which an organization's collective knowledge is stored: documents, photographs and videos, or engagement histories.

These traditional approaches, however, are no longer adequate. Team members are too much in motion, information and timeliness too critical, and the number of types and volume of information too broad.

Today, groupware products promote information sharing across organizations by providing advanced tools to access information databases and circulate selected information through E-mail. In addition, many groupware products provide users the ability to contribute additional information to the existing base. These learning "knowledge bases" become electronic discussions in which users not only can see the history of dialogue surrounding an issue but can also add to it, thus enhancing the value of the knowledge for the next user.

Lotus Notes is a good example of a product that promotes effective discussion and reference and helps to manage information and knowledge. Other products such as Filenet allow users to store such extended types of knowledge as image, video, and voice.

Process Management. Managing work flow, projects, and schedules in order to meet deadlines and budgets is a major challenge. A fundamental driver in corporate environments today is the shift from a functional to a process orientation. Traditionally, functions such as finance, management, and marketing drove company operations (as well as systems development). This focus typically made one function very efficient (e.g., order processing). However, as developers reinvent the enterprise, there is a need for complete business integration across functions, and developers are gradually beginning to shift their point of view to such cross-functional, coordinated processes as order fulfillment and customer service. Furthermore, these new processes must be done to specified levels of quality while meeting time and budget constraints. It is becoming increasingly clear that such processes drive the business, as shown in Exhibit IV-3-1.

The essence of process management is the completion of cross-function business processes that meet quality goals within constraints of time and budget. Both the process itself and the deliverables from the process must be clearly defined to effectively manage a business process.

Defining "Process." The defined process is perhaps obvious but it needs to be defined in the team metaphor in the context of roles, routes, rules, and queues.

Roles define the responsibilities that must be assigned to specific individuals involved with the process. Routes specify the different paths that the "work-in-process" information can take as it makes its way from

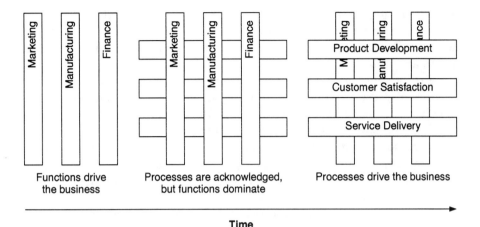

Functions drive
the business

Processes are acknowledged,
but functions dominate

Processes drive the business

Time

Exhibit IV-3-1. Function to Process

person to person and from role to role. Rules determine the specific routing based on information values and other conditions. Queues are those places where work must wait until the next step of the process can be done. (Even with the team metaphor, things still queue.)

Deliverables. The deliverables of a process are less obvious but just as critical. A process that goes on only in people's minds cannot be managed. "Artifacts" from the process are necessary to reflect that the steps of the process are, in fact, happening. These artifacts are the deliverables from the business process. Such deliverables, in the context of the team metaphor, are described as documents.

For the team metaphor, developers must view documents in a very wide context. Integrated image, video and voice, are all forms of "documents" that are required to reflect the full richness of human interaction as defined by the team metaphor.

In this wide context, the business process consists of tasks and steps; from these tasks come a rich mix of documents. These documents reflect the progress of the tasks and, by implication, how the tasks are doing relative to quality, time and budget.

Process management moves the process through tasks from which documents derive. Based on the defined process, developers know the rules for moving the process to the next task. The rules are evaluated based on the existence of certain documents and the specific information derived from these documents. As a task is completed, the associated documents enter one or more queues as folders. Entry to the queue occurs with definition of criteria about when the next task for the folder can, should, and must occur. Process management then enters an ongoing, active evaluation to determine when and if criteria for exit from the queue are met.

Process management embodies business integration. To reap the full benefits of process management, an organization must typically change how it works; it must reevaluate and refine its policies and procedures, and it must establish social contracts and protocols that allow functions to be crossed in completing a business process. When building applications to support business processes, process management for teams provides the structure, consistency, and discipline required by this new generation of applications.

With team metaphore process management, the corporation can decide the focus it wants to place on quality and time and budget and then see that focus reflected in how the team works. Team metaphor process management can span previously monolithic, disparate functions into an integrated flow. This eliminates the traditional "hand-offs" and boundaries found in and between most legacy functional applications.

Collaboration. Collaboration is the act of working jointly to produce a single product or service. It differs from process management in that, for collaboration, the process is not well defined. But the deliverables, the documents, are agreed to.

Individual contributions are a key component of collaborative work. Collaboration asks that individuals do whatever is necessary to get their work done. However, it also asks that the individuals, as members of a team, provide the results of their work in formats and at levels of quality agreed to by the team. The process is assigned to individual members and the agreed-on deliverables are merged to produce the final product.

Collaboration focuses more on support for individual participation and ways for individuals to view and manipulate contributions to the team product. Such systems tend to focus less on time and budget and more on quality.

An example of collaboration is creating an application for a new drug by a pharmaceutical company in the United States. A new drug application to the US Food and Drug Administration consists of a set of documents which, literally, could fill many bookcases. Completing these applications involves dozens of people and can take as long as several years. A document management system helps control the different application sections and subsections, version control, section delegation, annotation, merging, and conflict resolution.

Meetings. Meetings are a setting for teamwork suited to face-to-face interaction. They may include components of group interactions, such as communications, but the main goals of meetings are to make decisions, solve problems, and craft solutions for organizational issues that are not routine.

To make meetings more productive, groups often rely on formal techniques. Sometimes referred to as group decision support systems, these groupware products support domain-specific group problem-solving techniques. They help to structure the discussion of a problem, to provide the framework for brainstorming, to establish criteria for evaluating proposals, and to provide the tools for analyzing the constraints on a business model.

These tools enhance team effectiveness because they support the process the group follows, and because they promote the capture and manipulation of key information—including intermediate results and outcomes—that is difficult to capture with generic software such as spreadsheets or outlines.

To use these tools and the techniques they support, users such as team facilitators must be intimately familiar with the technology, the process, and the group's goals for the meeting. One approach is to train every manager in facilitation skills and techniques and in the technology that supports those techniques.

The direction of technology support for meetings is changing. For example, a great deal of work can be accomplished before a meeting by carrying out preliminary work over a network with other groupware tools. Team members can brainstorm by posting and viewing ideas via discussion databases and then use the face-to-face meeting to clarify and resolve the resulting ideas. Likewise, teams can discuss issues, post opinions, and agree on agenda items.

Future technologies that support meetings will include capabilities for accomplishing work before a meeting and, in many cases, for eliminating the need for meetings. International organizations are interested in using these technologies to eliminate unnecessary travel, avoid delays for important decisions, and provide the flexibility for group members to work on important problems, when they have the time.

Support for Individual Workers

It is clear that there are different types of teams as well as different types of teamwork and human interaction within the team. A given team is likely to find itself engaging in multiple types of groupwork. Furthermore, a given individual may find himself or herself actively involved in more than one team. Thus, it is the objective of the team metaphor to ensure that the full set of capabilities are available for the business

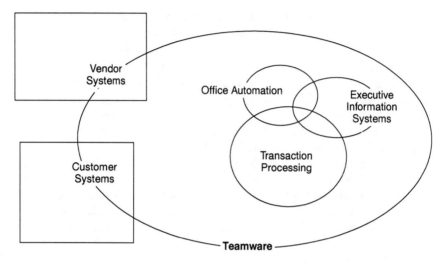

Exhibit IV-3-2. Team Metaphor Application Reach

worker's interaction with teams—from the individual worker's point of view.

Business process analysts should be careful to avoid narrowly defined functional perspectives that base "scope" on criteria that are arbitrary and incomplete to an individual worker. All activities and interactions of the individual user must be considered for successful business process change. No integral subprocess can be left out.

Team metaphor services provide critical links with other business worker applications, as well as legacy transaction applications—both internal to and external to the enterprise. The team metaphor thus touches all applications, as shown in Exhibit IV-3-2.

Different technologies are required for the different types of team interactions described earlier. Many of these technology enablers provide support for more than one interaction style. Because of the complex matrix of user types/team types/interaction types, system architects should have a clear vision of all relevant combinations of team interactions and the requisite combinations of technology enablers into an integrated architecture.

THE IMPACT OF TEAM METAPHOR ON ARCHITECTURE

The desire to support teams affects the client/server architectures discussed throughout this book in a number of ways. This section highlights some of these impacts.

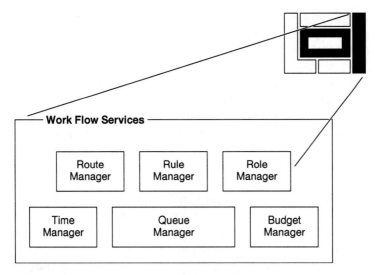

Exhibit IV-3-3. Work Flow Services for Team Metaphor Computing

Execution Architecture

The team metaphor execution architecture is a unified set of runtime services and control structures coupled with an application infrastructure. This execution architecture can be broken down into specific services.

Work Flow Services. Work flow services manages the routes, rules, and roles that make up a business process, within time and budget constraints. It consists of six components. (See Exhibit IV-3-3.)

Role Manager. A role defines responsibilities that are required in completing a business process. A business worker must be able to route documents and folders to a role, independent of the specific person or process filling that role.

For example, a request is routed to a Supervisor role or to Purchasing, rather than to "Mary" or "Tom." If objects are routed to Mary and Mary leaves the company or is reassigned, a new recipient under a new condition would have to be added to an old event. Roles are also important when a number of different people have the authority to do the same work, such as claims adjusters; the request is just assigned to the next available person. In addition, a process or agent can assume a role; it does not need to be a person.

Route Manager. The movement of information from role to role or from person to person automatically requires a routing function. A route manager must be able to capture the flow of any type of object in a real-world fashion—either sequentially (one after another) or in parallel routes with rendezvous points (an object can go off on any number of different sequential routes and then reconcile into a single route at a specified point). Routing needs to take into account more than just the person (or process) to whom the work is routed; it must also include what objects—documents, forms, data, applications, and so forth—are to be routed.

Rule Manager. A business process is typically made up of many different roles and routes. Decisions must be made as to what to route to which role, and when. Also, rules must be exercised to decide when a process must be queued for a period of time. In a manual process, these decision trees are locked away in people's heads, making management of the process difficult. In an automated process, a rule manager must capture the criteria that determine routing and queue activity.

The automated decision process can start out with fairly simple rules that can grow in complexity and robustness over time. Ultimately, the rule manager allows end users to maintain highly complex rules without programming, and even allows for a "learning" capability that adjusts rules on the fly.

Queue Manager. Inherent in doing business process work across functions and between roles is the need to queue work until the role is ready to perform and/or the required information is available. Queue management thus becomes a critical component.

In its simplest form, queue management can be performed by a person in the role of the "pit boss," patrolling the floor where activities are performed and managing hand-offs by direct observation and involvement. However, as business teams are becoming increasingly mobile and geographically dispersed, management of queues of work requires automated support.

Time Manager. To most people, time management means personal calendaring/task management, and scheduling for group meetings. In addition, there are deadlines and time-related influences in most work team processes. The time manager integrates all commitments for an individual—both personal and those relating to the different work team processes that the individual is involved in, thus eliminating the "multiple calendar/to-do list" syndrome.

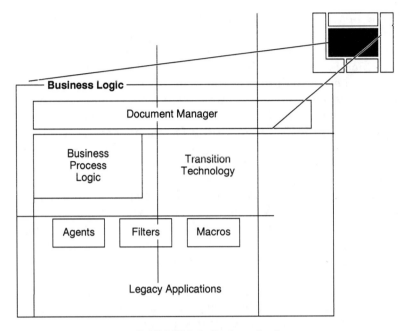

Exhibit IV-3-4. Business Logic

Budget Manager. In addition to elapsed time, budgets must be adhered to. The budget manager controls the amount of resources allocated to specific tasks in the business process.

Business Logic. Business logic consists of three components and several subcomponents. (See Exhibit IV-3-4.)

Document Manager. One trend is that the "document" will become the primary currency of the business worker—with document being defined as a generic container for the different types of objects (structured data, unstructured text, images, multimedia) a business worker deals with. An individual document might consist of a table created using a spreadsheet package such as Microsoft Excel; a report created using a word processing package such as Lotus AmiPro; a chart drawn in Excel; and a more structured form area developed using Lotus Notes or Microsoft Visual Basic controls.

Regardless of the software used to create and maintain the component parts, all parts together constitute the document, which is managed as a single entity. The document manager provides functions such as creating, maintaining, storing, retrieving, and versioning.

Transition Technology. Transition technology can be further broken down into agent, macros, and filters. This set of capabilities enables the business worker to efficiently sift through the enormous wealth of information which is now accessible electronically. These enablers allow the business worker to maintain complex profiles indicating the worker's areas of interest and information timeliness requirements (continuously, hourly, daily, weekly, on request). Then, automated agents perform the actual searches through the relevant information stores, including both internal and external information sources, and notifies the user only of the information that meets his or her criteria.

The searches are performed in accordance with the currentness requirements specified by the user. The underlying information sources are transparent to the user. As new information sources are added (or removed), the user continues as normal, without the need for any programming changes to the system. Likewise, as the user modifies his or her interest profile, the process continues without programming changes.

Legacy Applications. In addition to the new classes of team metaphor applications being created, each individual requires access to legacy applications. This includes not only the legacy transaction applications on the mainframe but also the powerful personal productivity tools that epitomized the 1980s (e.g., word processors, spreadsheets, drawing packages, and project managers).

In addition to use of these legacy applications as they are used today, these applications can become "team- enabled" by the use of APIs in the network messaging infrastructure. For example, the Microsoft MAPI (Mail Application Programming Interface) is already accessible by the Microsoft personal productivity applications such as Word, Excel, and Project, as well as many non-Microsoft applications. Custom-developed applications can also interface with MAPI today.

E-mail and facsimile as separate applications will increasingly disappear as all team metaphor applications will provide these services. However, these communication applications will continue to be used as such for the foreseeable future.

Information Access Services. The team metaphor has a significant impact on the provision of information access services in the execution architecture. (See Exhibit IV-3-5 for a diagram of information access services.) The impact by major component is as follows.

Case Manager. A case is the result of the team's work. The case has all the information relevant to the team's work, including structured data, text and media (image, voice, video). Individuals access and use the case, but the team's deliverable is the case as a whole.

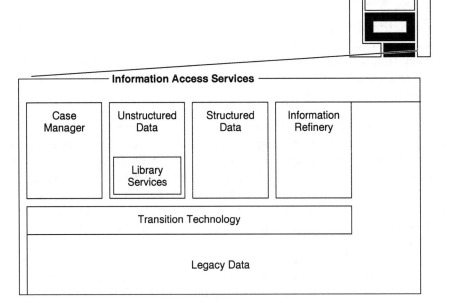

Exhibit IV-3-5. Information Access Services

Many aspects of building the solution focus on how the team works in relation to the case. Questions address such issues as the following: Who on the team has the case? What are they doing as a part of the team? What parts of the case can be worked on while it is in use by the current team member? Further questions address who can and should work on the case as it completes the next stage of work. Where is that person and how can the case be delivered to them? What are the criteria by which one can move the case to the next person? What do we need to know to evaluate progress and effectiveness of the team?

Unstructured Data. Today's business worker manages an enormous amount of unstructured information, in addition to more traditional structured data. This unstructured information is increasingly being referred to as documents that must provide support for the following key functions:

- Storage and manipulation of multiple object types: unstructured text, Rich Text Format, bitmaps, image, and multimedia.
- Object linking.
- Object delegation, merge, compare, and version control.

- Full text retrieval.

Relational database management systems (RDBMSs) alone are typically insufficient to deal effectively and efficiently with unstructured information management, storage and retrieval, although this is beginning to change as binary large objects are supported by the RDBMS vendors.

Library Services. Library services provide the necessary framework and support for effective management of unstructured information. Products such as Saros Mezzanine and Documentum provide a rich set of APIs that serve as the control point for document services such as check-in, check-out, duplicate, mail, and create new version. These APIs provide object-based capabilities to documents by encapsulating the document content and making the content accessible only via the APIs.

Structured Data. The emphasis on unstructured information and document management as described earlier does not eliminate the existence of structured data or diminish the importance of relational technology as part of the total solution.

Information Refinery. "Data warehouse" has become a widely used industry term to describe the information store for large amounts of historical data that are used to drive statistical and trend analysis. Yet traditional relational database principles and approaches are inadequate in this area.

The information refinery defines the properly designed databases and multidimensional database engines required to support the rigorous analysis, slicing, and dicing performed by today's business worker. Decision support systems such as Comshare's Commander provide an integrated support environment for carrying out quantitative analytical work.

Legacy Data. Often, legacy applications are based on relational technology, but this is not necessarily the case. Some legacy applications may be based on IMS or VSAM, for example. Regardless of underlying DBMS technology, legacy systems hold critical data that must be accessible by new team computing solutions. This legacy data must be accessed in its current form so as to not upset the legacy systems.

Transition Technology. Products such as gateways and information transfer agents provide the necessary integration between team solutions information stores and legacy data.

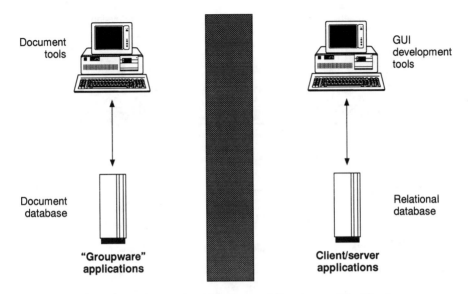

Exhibit IV-3-6. Conventional "Groupware" Development Architecture

DEVELOPMENT CONSIDERATIONS

A variety of different tools are required to properly support team metaphor applications development. Integration between the different tools can be more important than the strengths and weaknesses of a specific tools.

The need to integrate and manage multiple information types is a point of confusion with many of today's groupware products. For example, a product such as Lotus Notes, on the surface, seems to suggest that groupware applications can and should only deal with unstructured document information. Thus, any application requiring structured data (i.e., relational technology) is therefore not a groupware application. A wall exists between these two worlds (see Exhibit IV-3-6).

This view is unrealistic and focuses on the "off-the-shelf" technical implementation of current products rather than business realities. Effective management of business processes requires today's business worker to manage structured, unstructured, and legacy data simultaneously, regardless of the user interface tool used. In addition, behind-the-scenes integration is required between the different information stores, as shown in Exhibit IV-3-7.

In addition, a large number of vendors are trying to protect or establish a beachhead on this new market. Each has an extensive list of different products and product sets, yet these vendors come from widely

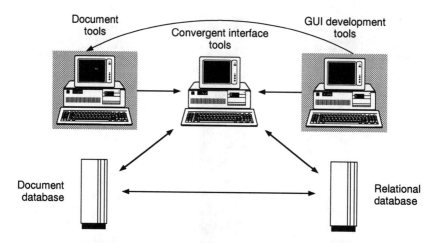

Exhibit IV-3-7. Team Metaphor Development Approach

different perspectives: E-mail, imaging, document management, work flow, integrated office systems.

Most vendors are widening the scope of their products, making the original product classifications and perspectives less meaningful over time. Other vendors seem intent on providing significant work group capability in the operating system itself, which could render many existing products obsolete in the future. Furthermore, the immaturity of the work group computing phenomenon makes vendor product comparisons difficult.

The ability to fulfill the vision of team metaphor computing will be hindered by the sporadic "middleware metamorphosis" within the major relevant application areas (i.e., E-mail, imaging, document management, work flow) over the next few years. Careful product selection will help minimize disruption during this transformation; a comprehensive architecture and strategy will be required to manage this effort.

THE IMPACT OF TEAM METAPHOR ON THE DEVELOPMENT METHODOLOGY

The team metaphor does introduce some significant new issues into the systems development process. This is a result of the complexities of the work group-oriented business processes being supported, as much as—if not more—than the complexities of the individual technologies involved.

First and foremost, new and robust methodologies are required. Traditional methodologies for function-defined applications are insufficient for the new types of teamwork and information integration described above. These new methodologies, in turn, affect the tools and training necessary to effectively build workgroup applications.

The different forms of team metaphor described earlier also affect the development methodology. Building knowledge management applications, for example, calls for different tools and approaches than used for the development of process management applications.

In many instances, the methodology may define the tools used, and vice versa. For example, several vendors offer engines for implementing and tracking work flows that are based on a particular (typically, their own) methodology.

An example of this would be the ActionWorkflow methodology and analysis/build tools from Action Technologies, Inc. The ActionWorkflow methodology provides a rigorous approach for analyzing and defining the commitments made between individuals in a business process. The ActionWorkflow toolset provides an efficient way to document these commitments and generate the resulting work flow application. Use of the Action Technologies toolset without knowledge of the ActionWorkflow methodology would not be feasible. Use of the methodology alone would provide only a limited, partial solution.

Many of the individual technology enablers required to support teams come "preassembled" by vendors and vendor partnerships. These component "packages" provide value-added integration and services but also control the development approach and tools to a certain extent.

An example is WordPerfect Office, which integrates multiple office functions around the WordPerfect word processing package and InForm electronic forms package. Another example is a Microsoft suite of products—Visual Basic Electronic Forms Designer, Windows for Workgroups, and Microsoft Mail/Schedule +. Each vendor's product suite provides value-added integration which disappears when alternative component products are introduced.

CONCLUSION

There are different types of teams and different types of teamwork. A given team is likely to find itself engaging in multiple forms of the team metaphor. Furthermore, given individuals may find themselves actively involved in multiple teams. Thus, it is the objective of team metaphor solutions to ensure that the full set of capabilities are available for the business worker's interaction with others—from the individual worker's perspective.

IV-4
Object-Oriented Systems Development

O bject-oriented development represents a major new theme in systems development. It is significantly different from traditional strategies because it shifts the focus of design toward how the business operates and away from how the machine works.

Object-oriented development encompasses the life cycle of systems development, from requirements analysis to object design to implementation. This chapter presents one position on the use of object technology. It explores the fundamental differences between traditional systems development and the object-oriented approach.

For this discussion, it is important to differentiate between objectives and paths to those objectives. Although object-oriented development does not involve fundamentally new objectives for systems development, the path (methodology, tools, techniques, metrics, design, team structure) to reach those objectives is different.

THE PRIME OBJECTIVES

There are two primary objectives in object-oriented development. The first involves the identification, implementation, and use of reusable components for the solution of business problems. The second involves the delivery of production systems with greater flexibility for adaptation and change. To achieve these objectives, all aspects of implementation attempt to facilitate the delivery of reusable and flexible components.

The goals of flexibility, reduced complexity, and reusability do not represent major deviations from the objectives of traditional systems development. The difference lies in the degree of these objectives.

For example, systems development has pursued flexible code for more than 25 years, but the industry has chosen to place more emphasis on objectives other than flexibility. Both function-driven and data-driven design emphasize that the system must reflect the immediate needs of the business. If flexibility can also be achieved, that is a good by-product;

otherwise the faithfulness of the design to meet immediate business needs is the primary objective.

Although the objectives of object-oriented development differ only slightly from those the industry has known for decades, the implementation process is very different. The analysis and design methodologies no longer focus on functional decomposition. In addition, the tools of implementation are very different with object-oriented development.

FUNDAMENTAL CONCEPTS OF OBJECT-ORIENTED DEVELOPMENT

To achieve its objectives, object-oriented development works from key concepts which it identifies as critical for reusability and flexibility. Object-oriented tools and languages support these concepts in the design and implementation process to ensure that the implementation achieves its objectives. These concepts are as follows:

- Abstraction, classes, and objects.
- Encapsulation.
- Messaging.
- Inheritance.
- Polymorphism.

To understand the impact of object-oriented tools on development, and to interact with those individuals committed to object-oriented development, it is worthwhile to understand these concepts. Although its proponents have chosen to use rather academic and abstract terms, most of the concepts have been associated with this industry for some time.

It is important to note that object-oriented techniques are not new. The first object-oriented programming language was developed before 1970. The first widely available programming language, Smalltalk, emerged by 1980. Finally, by 1990 the popular C++ programming language began to emerge. The first few decades focused on technology and tools, whereas the 1990s have seen the emphasis switch from programming to analysis, design, and full life-cycle methodology.

Abstraction, Classes, and Objects

In object-oriented terms, abstraction is the process of defining things of interest in the real world in a manner convenient for an object-oriented implementation. Once defined, these items are referred to as classes. For example, in the health care industry, items of interest might include patients, visits, labs, bills, or rooms. Consequently, in object-oriented terms, these would correspond to classes. The identification and definition of the patient class is an example of the process of abstraction.

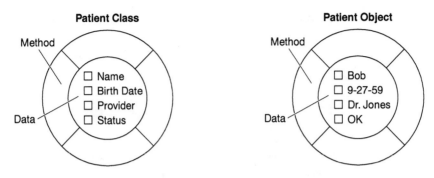

Exhibit IV-4-1. Classes and Objects

A specific instance of a class is an object. Thus, a patient named Bob with an impending appendix operation is an object, or specific instance of the patient class. Identification of a patient class is relatively straightforward, but the abstraction process may not be simple. Many object-oriented implementations require the definition of classes that are not as apparent (e.g., a business transaction class). (See Exhibit IV-4-1.)

From a business perspective, defining classes is not at all abstract. However, from a computer's perspective (i.e., machine processing instructions), the concept of a patient is abstract. Abstraction results in a real description of what the application is to address. The tools for implementation of object-oriented development are required to complete the bridge from the real world to what the computer knows.

This means that tools must make it easy to define the classes users want and, subsequently, to transform those definitions into the solution being implemented. If the tools succeed in this effort, object-oriented development has a fundamental appeal to the practice because it allows developers to move the design focus from technology to business.

In object-oriented terms, a person might speak of a patient going into a lab for a test. Contrast this with the traditional systems development scenario where one thinks and speaks in terms of a conversation. One conversation records the patient moving from the bed; another conversation notes the receipt of the patient at the lab and then updates some underlying database structure to record the events.

Encapsulation

As developers pursue the process of abstraction, they are identifying well-defined items of interest to the business. In this sense, they are defining what things are and what they are not. What things are, if

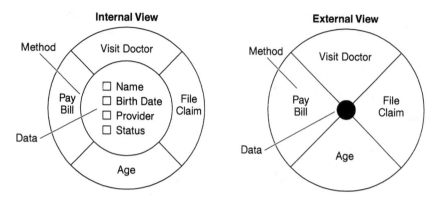

Exhibit IV-4-2. Encapsulation

defined explicitly, allows developers to put limits on them. In object-oriented development, this definition process is called encapsulation. Encapsulation internalizes the behavior and data of classes, thus hiding the internal structure and details of objects from external view.

Exhibit IV-4-2 is a simple example of encapsulation for the Patient class. The data fields (variables) and methods (procedures) of this class are internal to the class (i.e., they are encapsulated). The encapsulation of objects has the effect of forcing modular design on object-oriented implementations. One result of this modular design is that in contrast to traditional techniques, object-oriented methods are typically much smaller than procedural functions or procedures (2 to 20 lines of code per method is normal).

Object-oriented implementation tools encourage, if not enforce, a highly modular implementation, which makes extensive use of encapsulation. The tools do this by imposing a structure on the implementation that only allows units if they are highly modular in nature. These units were previously defined as classes. Ultimately, developers define all the classes necessary for implementing an application, even to a very low level (e.g., a StringConcatenator class). Most important, however, the process of defining classes provides classes at the business level—for example, the Patient class in Exhibit IV-4-2.

Messaging

If classes are well-defined and discrete, there must be some way for them to exchange information and request actions from one another if they are indeed to reflect the flow of business. Object-oriented implementation tools provide a mechanism by which objects can share information. This

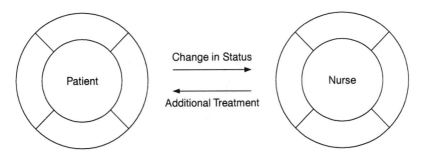

Exhibit IV-4-3. Example of Messaging

mechanism is called messaging. Messaging reinforces the encapsulation of objects because an object cannot, and need not, see what another object does. A given object can only send messages to another object, and the receiving object is expected to process the content of the message, according to the business needs.

For example, suppose an object-oriented application defined two objects: Patient and Nurse. If a patient is not feeling well, a Patient object should have the ability to communicate this fact to a Nurse object. This communication could be accomplished by declaring a message, which might be called ChangeInStatus. This message would be exchanged between the Patient object and the Nurse object whenever a change in status occurred.

This type of interaction between objects, the actions and reactions to messages, is referred to as the behavior of an object. How a Nurse object reacts to the "ChangeInStatus" message defines the Nurse object's behavior. (See Exhibit IV-4-3.)

The bigger challenge for the systems developer is getting accustomed to the fact that if one object wants to request an action from another, it must do so with a message. Objects cannot simply throw data into a common area for use by everyone.

Inheritance

Another fundamental capability of object-oriented design is the ability to extend the capabilities of the system by exception—in other words, basing new capability on existing capability and only specifying what is different. This is accomplished through inheritance.

Inheritance is the ability to have one class receive—that is, "inherit"—capabilities from another class. A class inheriting capabilities from another is referred to as the subclass; the class being inherited from is the superclass. A subclass never physically touches the code defining

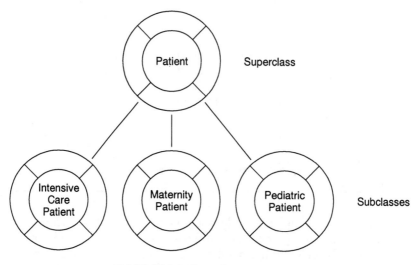

Exhibit IV-4-4. Example of Inheritance

the capabilities and characteristics inherited from a superclass. A subclass may, however, have its own capabilities defined separately from those inherited from the superclass. (See Exhibit IV-4-4.)

As an example, consider the previously discussed superclass called Patient. Systems developers might define a subclass called Intensive Care Patient, which might share many characteristics with the Patient class, such as name, age, social security number, or medical status. By making the correct declarations in the object-oriented tool when the Intensive Care Patient class is defined, the characteristics of Patient would be made available to Intensive Care Patient. Then, for the new Intensive Care Patient class, developers could define additional characteristics specific to this class.

For example, perhaps as a result of the nature of intensive care patients, a great deal more information must be kept on their status than is required for a regular patient (such as EKG diagnostics). In this way, inheritance can contribute significantly to the reusability of both design and implementation.

Once again, inheritance as a concept is not new. Developers can achieve inheritance in traditional environments through the use of standard structures. But as an implementation device, object-oriented tools make inheritance essentially a transparent process; achieving inheritance in a non-object-oriented language would require that a programmer copy and paste the desired code, a nontransparent, arduous process.

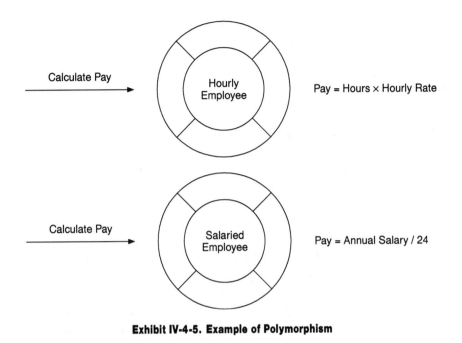

Exhibit IV-4-5. Example of Polymorphism

Thus, as with the other concepts, the difference in object-oriented development is not the basic objectives, but the means for implementation.

Polymorphism

Another object-oriented concept is polymorphism, a mathematical term meaning "to have many forms." Polymorphism describes the ability of a given message to elicit different behaviors from different objects.

A common example of polymorphism involves circle and square objects. If a developer were to send the message "DrawYourself" to both a circle and square object, the developer would get different results; the square would draw a square and the circle would draw a circle. In the hospital analogy, a doctor may instruct a lab to "RunLabTest" without knowing anything about the operations of the receiving lab. Polymorphism allows this single command to evoke a response from either a tissues lab object or a blood lab object.

The key benefit of polymorphism lies in that sending objects do not need to know the details of implementation. In addition, new objects (such as lab tests) can be added without forcing changes in other areas. (See Exhibit IV-4-5.)

Once again, there are parallels in more traditional approaches. To achieve a polymorphic effect in a traditional approach, consider the pass of a parameter through a called interface of the module. The called module behaves differently based on the passed parameter (in C and COBOL, developers use the CASE statement to evaluate the passed parameter).

Following along with this parallel leads to an interesting point: Many developers have had the experience of maintaining a module that has many indicators or switches passed to it. The common experience with such modules is that they can be very difficult to maintain because logic becomes very involved based on the interpretation of the passed parameters. The capabilities provided through polymorphism eliminate the need for case or switch statements and their requisite maintenance.

IMPACT OF OBJECT TECHNOLOGY ON SYSTEMS DEVELOPMENT

The design process in an object-oriented environment revolves around development processes that encourage, if not mandate, encapsulation, inheritance, and messaging. Several design methodologies are available commercially from a variety of authors (e.g., Jacobson, Wirfs-Brock, Schlaer-Mellor, Booch, Coad/Yourdon, and Rumbaugh). In addition, Andersen Consulting has developed an early release of an object-oriented methodology.

As is often the case with a new technology approach, significant effort can be spent explaining the reasons for changing and less time on what to actually do, including steps and deliverables. Although each of the above methodologies differs widely in deliverables, steps, and depth of content, there are some underlying themes.

One common theme involves the extensive front-end effort to define the classes of interest to an application. The detailed tasks may vary for each methodology, but all are intent on creating an initial definition of the classes of interest to the application. These definitions are viewed as "going-in" positions and are further refined by subsequent design steps (object-oriented development is iterative in nature). Thus, in the hospital example, developers might define the class of patient and caregiver early in the process but add more class definitions later.

The need to connect classes to represent the flow of business processes also results in the identification of messages that will be passed among the objects. Thus, in the hospital example, the communications between the caregiver and the patient result in the definition of messages needed to support this interaction, sometimes referred to as collaboration. Once again, as with class definitions, message definitions are refined as the design process proceeds.

As previously stated, object-oriented development encourages a development team to talk about the application in more functional, as opposed to technical, terms. Another benefit from this new focus is that individuals previously excluded from the design process, like those with extensive computer expertise, can now become active design participants. For example, in a health care application recently completed, the lead object modeler was a physician, not a systems analyst.

One of the characteristics of object-oriented development is that until the complete definition is put together, it is hard to get an overall view of the system. For example, suppose as a result of the patient interacting with the nurse, the patient's account is to be billed. All these activities need to be defined for the interaction to happen in the system. Thus, what appears to be a rather simple behavior for the system may actually take a considerable amount of time to develop. Thus, the object-oriented approach typically results in a longer lead time with fewer apparent final deliverables.

As the definition process proceeds, an implementation comes into existence. Experienced object-oriented developers suggest that in most cases there is a point where one "reaches through the eye of the needle and pulls through the objects and one has a system." ("Or one doesn't," as one developer noted.)

In object-oriented development, adding system capability frequently results in changes to existing classes. As a result, as the system is built, classes appear always to be in a state of flux. This delay in visible, stable deliverables is contrary to the culture of having stable deliverables throughout the development process (i.e., "on the shelf"). If the pull-through is successful, the integration of classes into a working system can be expected to go more quickly than in traditional systems. Experience suggests that the deficiency of early deliverables can be mitigated by adopting appropriate tools and progress tracking metrics early in the analysis and design processes.

However, once the system is "pulled through," performance problems may develop. The essence of the problem lies in the abstraction point discussed earlier: The abstraction implicit in defining classes is abstract only from the viewpoint of the hardware and system software.

The concept of a patient is abstract to a machine because all it knows are instructions and data. To make that abstract concept actually "happen," a great many machine instructions (based on a great many messages), across a great many layers of software, and against a great deal of data, must be made to occur. In this "happening" of instructions lies the potential for performance problems.

A typical solution to the performance problem is to examine all the classes on a case-by-case basis and do what systems designers have done previously: apply a detailed knowledge of the underlying architecture.

What the designer is looking at, in this case, is the old-fashioned question of machine path length versus number of executions.

For those persons who have been in the business a while, this is strangely reassuring. Those analysts with extensive design experience know that if there is sufficient understanding into how the machine operates internally, they can always find the performance problems and then, with a suitable execution of skill, eliminate them. This seems to be the essential nature of what is done when addressing performance issues. One by one, the performance problems are identified and eliminated by using all the standard tricks of this trade, including violating object-oriented concepts, use of non-object-oriented languages, and whatever else it takes to fix the problem.

Given the potential for problems and the conceptual differences of object-oriented from traditional development, an organization can recognize the need for skilled personnel. The project team must include personnel skilled in how the machine works if performance issues are to be resolved on a timely basis. The combination of the required business and technical skills suggests that in no sense does object-oriented development represent a deskilling of the staff necessary for success. Indeed, it suggests, and experience confirms, that staff is often much higher in skill. For example, managers may be found designing classes and messages and then writing the code.

As noted, specifics of the design process vary a great deal by methodology. For example, some approaches refine the classes, messages, and methods through the use of prototyping. Other methodologies try to use prototyping to move to an actual implementation through a process called rapid prototyping. Others make the design more of a documentation process, as has been done in more traditional design strategies.

In all cases, the methodologies are still immature when compared with those for traditional development approaches. Also, the published methodologies typically do not call for consistent deliverables as an integral part of the methodology. If a methodology does call for deliverables, those deliverables may depend directly on the tools used for implementation.

OBJECT-ORIENTED IMPLEMENTATION TOOLS

There are several implementation tools available for object-oriented development. It is reasonable to expect more to appear as time passes. As noted, object-oriented development does not represent a new objective in systems development. As a result, it is feasible for developers to use implementation tools they already know, such as COBOL and C (indeed, there are texts available on object-oriented programming with Assembler). One successful object-oriented implementations was based on the language PL/1.

Implementing an object-oriented system without object-oriented development tools can prove to be extremely difficult. To succeed with this type of approach requires an infrastructure that imposes a strict format for design and implementation. Brooklyn Union Gas (discussed later in this chapter in a brief case study) had to provide such an infrastructure.

Implementation tools that are currently available have matured a great deal since their initial introductions. Tools that should be considered include Smalltalk and C++ and, more recently, Java. Each of these tools provides support for the concepts that have been presented in this chapter (e.g., inheritance, polymorphism, and messaging).

Smalltalk Language

Smalltalk is described as a pure object-oriented language because it is built on the concepts of classes, messages, and methods and results in systems built on these principles. Currently, Smalltalk has a reputation for poor performance, but recent experience suggests that the performance has improved significantly. Strengths of the Smalltalk environment include support for rapid prototyping, complex user interfaces, and integration with other tools.

Smalltalk is highly hardware portable for specific vendor code. For example, an application written using vendor *A*'s Smalltalk on an OS/2 machine can be easily ported to vendor *A*'s UNIX implementation. Finally, Smalltalk comes packaged with an extensive class library.

One issue regarding Smalltalk involves its development environment. Although this environment appears highly integrated from a single user's perspective, it has no inherent method for sharing objects and messages among designers, especially on a large team. The implication of this limitation is that if one designer builds a Patient class, it can be difficult to make the Patient definition available to another programmer. This makes the integration of numerous developers more difficult.

This single developer focus has been a problem with Smalltalk since its first use in commercial environments, and only recently has it been addressed. Source code control and configuration management can still present challenges within Smalltalk's development environment and should be considered up front.

C++ Language

The other object-oriented language that has proved popular is C++, an extension to the traditional C programming language. Unlike Smalltalk,

C++ does not enforce the object-oriented paradigm on its programmers. This is both a blessing and a curse.

Although experienced C programmers can adapt to C++ syntax with relative ease, they may fail to capitalize on the object-oriented support provided by C++. As a result, these programmers may miss the paradigm shift necessary for effective C++ implementation. In fact, it is estimated that close to 70% of projects using C++ are not implementing an object-oriented design. Although this is a risk, most experts agree that an evolutionary transition into the world of object-oriented programming is best for traditional programmers. C++ provides a good platform for that transition.

Experience indicates, however, that an approach involving total immersion can work effectively when experts are available for design and supervision. Unfortunately, there are few experts currently available to act as tutors.

Strengths of C++ include good performance, C-likeness, vendor support, and flexibility. C++ is flexible in that it provides access to procedural languages when needed. Weaknesses of C++ include a steep learning curve for non-C programmers, complex infrastructure development, and poor support for rapid prototyping.

Java

Java is the programming language developed by Sun that has taken the industry by storm because of its use in Internet development. Java offers platform-independent applications that are specifically targeted at the Internet (though not limited to it).

Java is based on the C++ language and as such has many of the same characteristics of C++ (both good and bad). The major differences from C++ are: no explicit memory pointers and stronger platform-independence.

The lack of memory pointers is the result of the need to be secure in a network-centric environment such as the Internet. A by-product of this is also simplified memory management and a dramatic reduction in coding problems typically encountered by C and C++ programmers.

The stronger platform-independence comes from the need to be able to run Java applets—small applications downloaded over the Internet—on any platform, regardless of operating system and underlying hardware. As such, there are platform-independent class libraries (e.g., the Advanced Windowing Toolkit) that allow Java applications to interact with the user through a GUI, but through a platform-independent manner. Thus, the AWT offers services for creating windows, interacting with the user, displaying fields, listboxes, and so forth, independent of whether the applet is running on a Windows 95 machine, a Macintosh, or an OS/2 machine.

To do this, Java code is typically compiled down to bytecodes rather than native assembler, in order to allow the single run-time applet to be deployed to any CPU or operating system. The bytecodes are either interpreted by a Java virtual machine running on the native platform or compiled down to native CPU instructions by a just-in-time compiler (invoked when the Java application is first loaded).

Although Java is receiving much attention around the Internet, it is also suitable for applications development as an alternative to C++. Examples of how Java is being used beyond the Internet include developing new GUI applications that do not require organizations to deploy them to all of their PCs. This model is sometimes called a "thin client." In other words, applications are downloaded temporarily only when they are needed, rather than having them permanently reside on users' hard drives. Thus, when a new version is released, the next time any user accesses the application, they receive the latest, greatest version rather than the one they got the last time the LAN team updated their hard disk.

An additional benefit of such a strategy is the ease with which an organization can later extend the use of these applications to their customers, suppliers, or other business partners (as a result of the platform independence).

Another use of Java is as a better C/C++ (for GUI or server programs). The elimination of pointers greatly simplifies a programmer's job and also eliminates the most common cause of problems in C/C++ programs: stray pointers that allow an application to corrupt itself, or, in some cases, other applications. Such problems are often extremely difficult to capture, and many slip through testing into production. With Java, testing efforts have decreased significantly with regard to these types of problems. The normal effort is still required to test if a module/program does what it was intended to.

Due to its relative newness, Java tends to lack the sheer number of class libraries and development tools currently available for C++. This, however, is changing very rapidly due to the momentum and interest in Java. The implication for a company today would be the need to work with less mature tools and perhaps take a temporary step back in richness of function from their tools and libraries.

In addition, integrating Java with other parts of a corporate architecture (database access, middleware/communications, and so forth) may offer challenges to a client. Most of the time, these can be overcome, but extra effort and some compromises will result.

Java may also not be suitable for mobile users. Applets for business applications can get very large very quickly (200K and more), and downloading one over a 28K bps modem can take a relatively long time. Although faster modems are making this less of an issue, they do not address the needs of users who may not have the option or ability to connect. In such a case, some of the benefits of the "thin client" approach are eliminated due to the need to store Java applications on a laptop's hard drive.

OO-COBOL

As object technology has become more mainstream, the industry has begun to develop an object-oriented version of the COBOL programming language. This effort has been driven primarily by the major COBOL vendors working together through a standards body (American National Standards Institute Committee X3J4). Although the final standard is not expected to be released before 1997, early versions of OO-COBOL are available on a variety of platforms today.

As object-oriented programming languages become increasingly popular, OO-COBOL could well represent a migration path for the vast number of COBOL programmers still available in today's information systems shops. However, it is still not clear whether OO-COBOL will become an important development language.

First, because object-oriented development represents a significant change in analysis and design of systems, without first undergoing such a change in thinking, COBOL programmers may not see the need for or make use of the features provided by OO-COBOL. In addition, where COBOL programmers do embrace the object-oriented approach, the switch to a different language (i.e., Smalltalk or C++) may well represent the easier learning curve. Finally, like C++, OO-COBOL has the disadvantage of being a hybrid language which does not enforce an object-oriented approach.

The real wild card with OO-COBOL is that it may become the first language to offer object-oriented support on all platforms, from the workstation up through the enterprise machine (e.g., the mainframe). In this case, it would become more practical to deliver a full end-to-end solution that is object oriented rather than one that is object oriented for online but not for batch. This would enable an organization to fully benefit from object-oriented system flexibility.

Distributed Objects

When object technology is mixed with client/server, an inevitable question arises about how to create object-oriented applications that can communicate transparently with one another. The goal is to allow objects in one program to communicate with objects in another program the same as they would if they were contained within the same program. In addition, the two objects might reside in programs on separate machines connected through a network.

Distributed objects are an emerging technology with a few dominant evolving solutions. One solution approach is represented by the Object Management Group, which defines a Common Object Request Broker Architecture. This architecture specifies a system software component referred to as an Object Request Broker (ORB) to perform the translation of messages between programs and devices. Other current initiatives to provide similar capability include IBM's Distributed System Object Model and Microsoft's Object-Linking and Embedding technology.

As larger client/server systems are developed using object technology, the distributed object model becomes increasingly important. Therefore, this area represents one of object technology's greatest challenges for the immediate future.

Synthesis

Smalltalk is a powerful tool for front-end prototyping. The number of large live implementations however, is few. C++, on the other hand, has been used more for large implementations which need to be hardened for ongoing use. Both tools are witnessing the emergence of commercially available class libraries. These libraries are, in effect, extensions to the languages. They consist of prebuilt and pretested classes written in the particular programming language. Purchasing these classes means that the development team will not have to write and test them.

For example, developers can buy class libraries to allow Smalltalk to interact with a relational database management system. Developers could also write these classes, but purchasing a class library saves time and effort. As class libraries with more of a business flavor are developed, software will become even more reusable. Because class libraries can significantly reduce the development time frame, any object-oriented project team should carefully consider using them.

Also, the availability of a wide set of class libraries may indicate the commercial interest of the tools. Because the object-oriented market is changing rapidly, evaluation of class make/buy, as well as tool selection, is a necessary part of the decision process.

Both Smalltalk and C++ still have significant shortfalls in terms of development. One problem is keeping track of the classes and methods and assessing their potential for reuse. As the number of classes and methods grows to hundreds and then thousands, neither development tool provides facilities to assist the analysts in determining whether a class has the characteristics it needs.

This factor alone could undo the effectiveness of any object-oriented development approach. Currently, developers are addressing this problem through careful documentation and good memories. Products are being built to assist with this issue, and some project teams have developed custom solutions.

Finally, these tools lack features to help assess a machine's processing capabilities, however, in C++, developers have access to all operating system utilities. Because few tools are available to assist with performance evaluation, and because most development is being done in new machine environments (which themselves provide few utilities to analyze machine performance), significant efforts may be required to overcome performance bottlenecks.

All these shortfalls are problems developers have seen before. As with previously maturing technologies, it means they must build tools and infrastructures necessary to overcome these shortfalls. Developers should consider these issues prior to undertaking such efforts.

Other Tools

The object-oriented development language (OODL) of the object management architecture typically supports message handling and inheritance but may also include additional dynamic object handling techniques, such as the following:

- *Scripting.* The execution architecture runs a fourth-generation language (4GL)-like procedural control flow.
- *Generic function calls.* The execution architecture implements polymorphism using function calls.
- *Daemons.* The execution architecture automatically executes a process when a given pattern occurs in the data or a given event occurs.
- *Backward chaining.* The execution architecture automatically executes processes that are prerequisites of a goal object.

In addition, these OODLs are attempting to correct some of the development environment deficiencies encountered when using native Smalltalk and C++. They are providing code editors, design repositories, testing tools, and other development aids. Some are even claiming to deliver object-oriented lower CASE development environments.

Market perception of OODLs currently runs the gamut from violent detractors to avid proponents. The detractors believe that OODLs are a last-ditch attempt to revive such "failed" technologies as CASE, artificial intelligence (AI), and 4GLs by jumping on the object-oriented bandwagon. The proponents see OODLs as a natural evolution of object orientation, CASE, AI, and 4GLs.

Developers should approach OODLs with a combination of healthy skepticism and an open mind. By assimilating the best of object orientation into an easier to use tool, OODLs could provide the means by which object-oriented technology is assimilated into the systems development culture.

However, the jury is still out as OODLs are immature, and their rich feature set can be a disadvantage in the hands of novice users. In addition, they suffer from some of the same multiple developer and system performance issues as the traditional object-oriented tools.

CASE STUDIES

It is valuable to consider the lessons learned from a couple of ground-breaking object-oriented development projects.

Brooklyn Union Gas—CRIS II System

Systems developers worked with Brooklyn Union Gas to build a new customer information system (involving a 70G byte DB2 database, CICS, and PL/1). The new system was based on a custom object-oriented architecture developed using PL/1. The environment has been described by leading object-oriented expert, Alan Kay, as one of the most sophisticated object-oriented environments ever implemented. The application is currently in production and being evolved by the client.

Developers learned a number of important lessons from this project:

- Although much of the discussion in this chapter has implied the uniqueness of object-oriented development tools, in fact, designers can develop object-oriented implementations in traditional languages such as COBOL, PL/1, and even Assembler. However, the reality is that if this must be done, as it was at Brooklyn Union Gas, a great deal of infrastructure must be created to support the development and run time environments needed for such an effort.
- This system was developed in approximately the same amount of time as one using a standard development approach. However, any time that may have been gained during development was lost as the engagement moved to system test. The project team unfortunately encountered severe performance problems. To combat those problems, each object had to be reviewed on a case-by-case basis, while also considering the performance impact of each implementation approach. This review process resulted in changes in performance levels of 10 transactions/sec., with even subsecond response times being achieved. Overhead of the object-oriented architecture has been measured at about 5%.

- The application code is now more efficient. The 1.5 million lines of code in the original system have been reduced to 900,000 lines. In addition, the support staff has been cut from 25 to 12.

A Large Health Care Application

For this project, developers implemented a health care application system (incorporating physician's workbench and clinical lab components) using an object-oriented approach. The system was implemented on a Sun/Sybase platform using a Motif-like graphical user interface and C++. The project was done with a team of 50 developers.

Object-oriented development was used for this project to shield the complex set of data relationships that were needed in this environment. In addition, the system runs over the hospital's local area network, and the client wanted to shield the impact of change in underlying telecommunications technology from business applications. Finally, the organization felt that object-oriented development would add greater flexibility and easier tailoring when installing at different sites having different underlying technologies.

This project team experienced an unusual situation at one point when one team developing the communications gateway used C++ in a "near C"-like manner. Simultaneously, another team developing the workstation component used a stronger object-oriented approach. In comparison, both teams developed roughly the same amount of logic.

In this situation, the team using the traditional approach began to see results sooner, with less initial slippage. However, their experience in integration testing was typical of what is found in traditional applications in that it was both difficult and time-consuming. On the other hand, the team using the object-oriented approach had significant initial slippage and appeared to be headed toward significant delays in final delivery. However, the integration test was significantly smoother for the object-oriented team. The object-oriented team was finished in essentially the same time as the team using more traditional approaches.

The following are some important lessons learned from this project:

- Once again, the object-oriented development approach did not provide significant productivity gains for this first-time development. Furthermore, there were less measurable results than are found in a more traditional development, and this appeared as slippage in project reporting. However, as noted, when the system was pulled together, it integrated much more quickly than the traditional approach.
- This project team also encountered significant performance problems in the testing phase, and once again a detailed review of classes

and methods was required to eliminate performance problems. It was also difficult to predict the success of a designer/programmer in the object-oriented environment. In several cases, a highly skilled analyst who had been expected to succeed actually had difficulty in adapting to the object-oriented environment.

Summary of Lessons Learned

When considering the lessons learned and their impact on development, the following repeated experiences occur:

- Object-oriented development does not provide a silver bullet. It is a tool for enabling developers, but it still requires good design and implementation skills.
- Because object-oriented development has a significant impact on all aspects of development including design, development, and project management, it is critical that a core group of personnel with object-oriented systems experience be involved in the project from the very beginning (i.e., before any technical architecture or functional design has begun). Any attempt to "switch" to an object-oriented approach later on in the project can seriously affect previous work performed.
- An organization should plan on a considerable skills upgrade for personnel new to object-oriented development. Time to become productive varies from 6 to 18 months. Further, there is considerable evidence that some experienced analysts have difficulty understanding object-oriented design.
- There is no consistent evidence to suggest that object-oriented development reduces the overall development time frame of initial applications. However, time frames for future application development should, theoretically, be reduced.
- There is considerable evidence that first-time use of an object-oriented approach may actually increase development time because of the learning curve and infrastructure development. Therefore, it can be a serious mistake to make a switch to an object-oriented approach and assume that project estimates and schedules will not need to be modified.
- An object-oriented approach does not reduce overall development time frames on initial projects. It does, however, increase the ratio of design time to programming time. During development, little of the traditional "deliverables on the shelf" are visible.
- As is still the case today with client/server, performance characteristics are difficult to predict in advance. To avoid serious performance problems, it is critical that performance requirements be

identified as part of the design process and carried on through implementation. At the same time, performance prototypes of both the technical and application architecture can identify potential performance problems well in advance of system test.

- The term "object oriented" means different things to different people. It is essential that all stakeholders begin with a clear understanding of what they mean by object oriented: merely the use of $C++$? object-oriented design and programming? the use of object-oriented databases? the use of a distributed objects architecture?

- Experience suggests that the use of an object-oriented approach makes the processes of change impact analysis, configuration management, and testing more difficult. Developers should plan on considerably expanding the roles of these tasks. This is primarily for two reasons: (1) an object-oriented development approach creates a larger number of smaller software components each requiring its own testing and version control, and (2) it encourages the reuse of software components throughout the system, causing a change in one object to potentially have an impact in many places.

- Although development time is not reduced, there is evidence to suggest that ongoing maintenance is reduced by the use of object-oriented techniques.

- Much of the early experiences with object-oriented development were with completely new systems which did not have to integrate with existing legacy systems (such as mainframe or traditional client/server). The reality is that many business systems cannot afford this luxury, thus complicating efforts at object-oriented development.

CONCLUSION

The subject of object-oriented systems development raises a number of issues that this chapter has attempted to address. Following are a number of questions and answers that sum up the discussion of object orientation.

1. *Does object orientation represent the future in systems development?* The first question to be addressed is whether object-oriented development represents a fundamental change for the better in technology. Object-oriented development pursues the objectives of highly modular and reusable design, leading to an implementation which is done in an effective and flexible manner, and which can be maintained through its life cycle with a reduced commitment of staff. Object-oriented development tries to achieve these objectives with the concepts of encapsulation,

classes, messages, methods, inheritance, and polymorphism. The tools are different and enforce these concepts. Success of these tools is a key issue for the success of object-oriented development.

2. *Does the use of object-oriented tools require the large scale replacement of the installed base of legacy applications?* The general view is that object-oriented tools can coexist with existing applications. In fact, some recent object-oriented tools promote the idea of placing the legacy systems in objects, which then allows them to be used with newer object-oriented systems.

3. *Will the object-oriented tools have a significant impact on current hardware and software capital investments?* Object orientation is typically found in client/server applications. Motivation for the use of such hardware solutions lies in application needs; thus the cost of the hardware is an issue for the application. Although the compilers and runtime components for object-oriented technology do represent an extra expense, the incremental difference is negligible, given the total cost of building a new application.

4. *Will the object-oriented tools have a significant impact on the computing culture?* Herein lies the problem for object-oriented languages. Object-oriented languages do present a significant learning curve for programmers of two to six months and longer for analysts. Furthermore, the eventual success of an experienced programmer at object-oriented techniques is not at all assured.

Today, the reality is that a large base of programmers within IS departments know COBOL. Extensive experience suggests that this base is on the whole very reluctant to move to new languages, even when the languages have some clear advantages such as PL/1 in the 1970s, some 4GLs, and C for workstations. Given that these languages should have made the job easier for the programmer, the fact that object-oriented technology is initially more challenging suggests that in fact the acceptance of object-oriented tools will be very slow.

Furthermore, if acceptance is mandated by management, reports can be expected to appear from unwilling programmers that the languages are difficult, unreliable, and less productive than traditional approaches. Management will then find itself in the awkward position of defending tools it does not understand against programmers who will be able to show cases where the tools are causing problems. This may be mitigated as new graduates arrive in IS departments; however it will remain a significant change management issue for the current installed base of programmers.

The latter point suggests that object orientation has a significant hurdle to overcome in countering the current culture of programming. If it is to do so, it must provide some benefits that are dramatically beyond what is seen today. If it can do this, management will have a reason to override programmer objections.

5. *Is there any reason to believe that object-oriented development provides such an order of magnitude advantage in some aspect of the corporate computing environment?* With regard to development time frames, no evidence supports the contention that an object-oriented approach reduces development time for initial systems. Thus, organizations cannot look for savings here (however, they should consider the longer-term benefits of development savings).

Finally, data points suggest that an object-oriented approach reduces ongoing maintenance by 50%. Given that more than 80% of a system's cost lies in ongoing maintenance, this can be a reason for considering it. The key issue, in this case, is that management must be asked to "suspend disbelief" for the time required to build the system.

6. *Why should anyone consider object-oriented technology?* Recent press coverage of object orientation has been unfavorable. Though somewhat biased, this coverage probably points to organizational frustrations with the learning curve for object orientation. Without proper management, solid design, and sufficient tools, experienced programmers may have difficulty making the transition. Given this, and the significance of the paradigm shift to object orientation, it is reasonable to expect that the acceptance process of object-oriented development will be slow. Furthermore, the developers can probably expect a series of articles in a few years talking about what went wrong with initial object-oriented development and efforts.

Nevertheless, object-oriented technology is a technology most organizations should consider. One reason is qualitative but real. The process of object-oriented development shifts the design to a more business focused effort. This can result in a system closer to business needs. Once developed, these systems work closer to what the user expects from the very first days of implementation.

A second, more quantitative, reason to consider the technology is evidence that such technology could reduce ongoing maintenance costs by 50%, thus enabling systems to accommodate the remarkable change in technology the industry is currently witnessing.

To succeed with this new technology, developers need to understand a significant number of issues. These issues range from numerous tool decisions, to changes in development process, both in steps and personnel involved, to the hard issues of change management in introducing what experience says is a significant and real change to how to deliver systems.

About the Authors

H ugh Ryan is a partner with Andersen Consulting and the current Managing Director of a group within Technology Integration Services-Worldwide devoted to Large Complex Systems. In his 25 year career with Andersen Consulting he has worked on leading-edge applications of information technology, from the earliest online systems and DBMSs in the 1970s through today's emerging client/server applications built on the convergence of computing, communications, and knowledge. He has written more than 30 articles on various aspects of computing and contributes a regular column on systems development to the journal *Information Systems Management*. He has been a featured speaker at more than 50 conferences on the impact of computing on business solutions.

Scott Sargent is a partner in the Technology Integration Services-Americas organization of Andersen Consulting. He leads the Innovative Computing group, which supports Andersen's worldwide consulting organization in the planning, design, and implementation of advanced client/server systems that integrate existing data processing and office systems with emerging technologies. He has extensive experience with open systems, client/server systems, professional workstation systems, image systems, and data communications. He specializes in the telecommunications, transportation, insurance, financial services, aerospace, and manufacturing industries.

Timothy Boudreau, a partner with Andersen Consulting's Technology Integration Services-Worldwide organization, is responsible for the Solutions Architecture group, which specializes in using innovative delivery channels to address solutions for user interface technologies; component system building techniques; data, text, and multimedia information management; netcentric architectures; client/server architectures; and mobile computing. He has worked with private and government organizations throughout North America and Europe and is a frequent presenter at seminars and industry gatherings addressing Internet, netcentric, and architecture issues. He has provided his services to the financial, insurance, transportation, health care, and telecommunications industries.

Yannis Arvanitis is an associate partner with Andersen Consulting's Technology Integration Services-Worldwide organization. He is a member of the Architectures group, which supports Andersen's worldwide consulting organization in planning, designing, and implementing systems using new and emerging technologies. He has extensive project experience with client/server architectures and applications, GUI design and development, object-oriented development, and Internet technologies, including HTML and Java. He is also an inventor on a patent held by Andersen Consulting for client/server architecture and tools.

Stanton Taylor has more than 12 years' experience working with large US and European corporations in applying emerging information technology for competitive advantage. He is currently an associate partner with Andersen Consulting's Technology Integration Services-Worldwide organization. He has extensive experience in the planning, design, and implementation of client/server workstation-based solutions using state-of-the-market technologies and products, and has helped more than a dozen organizations in the conceptualization and implementation of enterprisewide technology strategies. He has worked with a broad range of companies in the financial services, transportation, retailing, pharmaceutical, and oil and gas industries.

Craig Mindrum teaches at DePaul University in Chicago and has more than 15 years of experience as a consultant and writer in the areas of organizational ethics and the effects of information technology on workforce performance and purpose. He is a regular conference speaker on issues related to human performance within organizations. He served as primary researcher and editor for *FutureWork: Putting Knowledge to Work in the Knowledge Economy* (New York: The Free Press, 1994). He received his doctorate from the University of Chicago, following previous studies at Indiana University and Yale University. His current research involves a forthcoming book on the subject of dignity in organizations.

Index

S

X